Family Maps
of
Jackson County, Florida
Deluxe Edition

With Homesteads, Roads, Waterways, Towns, Cemeteries, Railroads, and More

Family Maps
of
Jackson County, Florida
Deluxe Edition

With Homesteads, Roads, Waterways, Towns, Cemeteries, Railroads, and More

by Gregory A. Boyd, J.D.

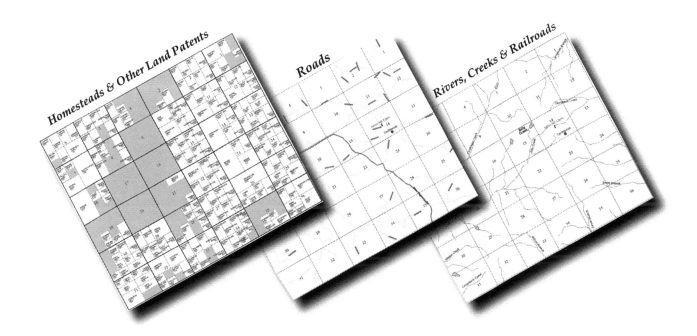

Featuring 3 *Maps Per Township...*

Arphax Publishing Co.
www.arphax.com

Family Maps of Jackson County, Florida, Deluxe Edition: With Homesteads, Roads, Waterways, Towns, Cemeteries, Railroads, and More.
by Gregory A. Boyd, J.D.

ISBN 1-4203-1476-9

Published by Arphax Publishing Co., 2210 Research Park Blvd., Norman, Oklahoma, USA 73069
www.arphax.com

First Edition

—LEGAL—

This book is dedicated to my wonderful family:

Vicki, Jordan, & Amy Boyd

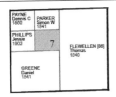

Contents

- Part I -

The Big Picture

- Part II -

Township Map Groups

(each Map Group contains a Patent Index, Patent Map, Road Map, & Historical Map)

Appendices

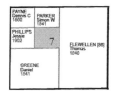

Preface

The quest for the discovery of my ancestors' origins, migrations, beliefs, and life-ways has brought me rewards that I could never have imagined. The *Family Maps* series of books is my first effort to share with historical and genealogical researchers, some of the tools that I have developed to achieve my research goals. I firmly believe that this effort will allow many people to reap the same sorts of treasures that I have.

Our Federal government's General Land Office of the Bureau of Land Management (the "GLO") has given genealogists and historians an incredible gift by virtue of its enormous database housed on its web-site at glorecords.blm.gov. Here, you can search for and find millions of parcels of land purchased by our ancestors in about thirty states.

This GLO web-site is one of the best FREE on-line tools available to family researchers. But, it is not for the faint of heart, nor is it for those unwilling or unable to to sift through and analyze the thousands of records that exist for most counties.

My immediate goal with this series is to spare you the hundreds of hours of work that it would take you to map the Land Patents for this county. Every Jackson County homestead or land patent that I have gleaned from public GLO databases is mapped here. Consequently, I can usually show you in an instant, where your ancestor's land is located, as well as the names of nearby land-owners.

Originally, that was my primary goal. But after speaking to other genealogists, it became clear that there was much more that they wanted. Taking their advice set me back almost a full year, but I think you will agree it was worth the wait. Because now, you can learn so much more.

Now, this book answers these sorts of questions:

- Are there any variant spellings for surnames that I have missed in searching GLO records?
- Where is my family's traditional home-place?
- What cemeteries are near Grandma's house?
- My Granddad used to swim in such-and-such-Creek—where is that?
- How close is this little community to that one?
- Are there any other people with the same surname who bought land in the county?
- How about cousins and in-laws—did they buy land in the area?

And these are just for starters!

The rules for using the *Family Maps* books are simple, but the strategies for success are many. Some techniques are apparent on first use, but many are gained with time and experience. Please take the time to notice the roads, cemeteries, creek-names, family names, and unique first-names throughout the whole county. You cannot imagine what YOU might be the first to discover.

I hope to learn that many of you have answered age-old research questions within these pages or that you have discovered relationships previously not even considered. When these sorts of things happen to you, will you please let me hear about it? I would like nothing better. My contact information can always be found at www.arphax.com.

One more thing: please read the "How To Use This Book" chapter; it starts on the next page. This will give you the very best chance to find the treasures that lie within these pages.

My family and I wish you the very best of luck, both in life, and in your research.   Greg Boyd

How to Use This Book - A Graphical Summary

Part I
"The Big Picture"

Map A ▸ *Counties in the State*
Map B ▸ *Surrounding Counties*
Map C ▸ *Congressional Townships (Map Groups) in the County*
Map D ▸ *Cities & Towns in the County*
Map E ▸ *Cemeteries in the County*
Surnames in the County ▸ *Number of Land-Parcels for Each Surname*
Surname/Township Index ▸ *Directs you to Township Map Groups in Part II*

The Surname/Township Index can direct you to any number of **Township Map Groups**

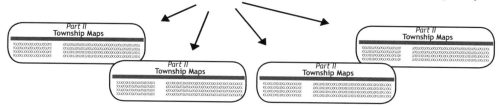

Part II
Township Map Groups
(1 for each Township in the County)

Each Township Map Group contains all four of of the following tools . . .

Land Patent Index ▸ *Every-name Index of Patents Mapped in this Township*
Land Patent Map ▸ *Map of Patents as listed in above Index*
Road Map ▸ *Map of Roads, City-centers, and Cemeteries in the Township*
Historical Map ▸ *Map of Railroads, Lakes, Rivers, Creeks, City-Centers, and Cemeteries*

Appendices

Appendix A ▸ *Congressional Authority enabling Patents within our Maps*
Appendix B ▸ *Section-Parts / Aliquot Parts (a comprehensive list)*
Appendix C ▸ *Multi-patentee Groups (Individuals within Buying Groups)*

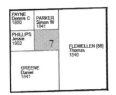

How to Use This Book

The two "Parts" of this *Family Maps* volume seek to answer two different types of questions. Part I deals with broad questions like: what counties surround Jackson County, are there any ASHCRAFTs in Jackson County, and if so, in which Townships or Maps can I find them? Ultimately, though, Part I should point you to a particular Township Map Group in Part II.

Part II concerns itself with details like: where exactly is this family's land, who else bought land in the area, and what roads and streams run through the land, or are located nearby. The Chart on the opposite page, and the remainder of this chapter attempt to convey to you the particulars of these two "parts", as well as how best to use them to achieve your research goals.

Part I
"The Big Picture"

Within Part I, you will find five "Big Picture" maps and two county-wide surname tools.

These include:

• Map A - Where Jackson County lies within the state
• Map B - Counties that surround Jackson County
• Map C - Congressional Townships of Jackson County (+ Map Group Numbers)
• Map D - Cities & Towns of Jackson County (with Index)
• Map E - Cemeteries of Jackson County (with Index)
• Surnames in Jackson County Patents (with Parcel-counts for each surname)
• Surname/Township Index (with Parcel-counts for each surname by Township)

The five "Big-Picture" Maps are fairly self-explanatory, yet should not be overlooked. This is particularly true of Maps "C", "D", and "E", all of which show Jackson County and its Congressional Townships (and their assigned Map Group Numbers).

Let me briefly explain this concept of Map Group Numbers. These are a device completely of our own invention. They were created to help you quickly locate maps without having to remember the full legal name of the various Congressional Townships. It is simply easier to remember "Map Group 1" than a legal name like: "Township 9-North Range 6-West, 5th Principal Meridian." But the fact is that the TRUE legal name for these Townships IS terribly important. These are the designations that others will be familiar with and you will need to accurately record them in your notes. This is why both Map Group numbers AND legal descriptions of Townships are almost always displayed together.

Map "C" will be your first intoduction to "Map Group Numbers", and that is all it contains: legal Township descriptions and their assigned Map Group Numbers. Once you get further into your research, and more immersed in the details, you will likely want to refer back to Map "C" from time to time, in order to regain your bearings on just where in the county you are researching.

Remember, township boundaries are a completely artificial device, created to standardize land descriptions. But do not let them become a boundary in your mind when choosing which townships to research. Your relative's in-laws, children, cousins, siblings, and mamas and papas, might just as easily have lived in the township next to the one your grandfather lived in—rather than in the one where he actually lived. So Map "C" can be your guide to which other Townships/ Map Groups you likewise ought to analyze.

Of course, the same holds true for County lines; this is the purpose behind Map "B". It shows you surrounding counties that you may want to consider for further reserarch.

Map "D", the Cities and Towns map, is the first map with an index. Map "E" is the second (Cemeteries). Both, Maps "D" and "E" give you broad views of City (or Cemetery) locations in the County. But they go much further by pointing you toward pertinent Township Map Groups so you can locate the patents, roads, and waterways located near a particular city or cemetery.

Once you are familiar with these *Family Maps* volumes and the county you are researching, the "Surnames In Jackson County" chapter (or its sister chapter in other volumes) is where you'll likely start your future research sessions. Here, you can quickly scan its few pages and see if anyone in the county possesses the surnames you are researching. The "Surnames in Jackson County" list shows only two things: surnames and the number of parcels of land we have located for that surname in Jackson County. But whether or not you immediately locate the surnames you are researching, please do not go any further without taking a few moments to scan ALL the surnames in these very few pages.

You cannot imagine how many lost ancestors are waiting to be found by someone willing to take just a little longer to scan the "Surnames In Jackson County" list. Misspellings and typographical errors abound in most any index of this sort. Don't miss out on finding your Kinard that was written Rynard or Cox that was written Lox. If it looks funny or wrong, it very often is. And one of those little errors may well be your relative.

Now, armed with a surname and the knowledge that it has one or more entries in this book, you are ready for the "Surname/Township Index." Unlike the "Surnames In Jackson County", which has only one line per Surname, the "Surname/Township Index" contains one line-item for each Township Map Group in which each surname is found. In other words, each line represents a different Township Map Group that you will need to review.

Specifically, each line of the Surname/Township

Index contains the following four columns of information:

1. Surname
2. Township Map Group Number (these Map Groups are found in Part II)
3. Parcels of Land (number of them with the given Surname within the Township)
4. Meridian/Township/Range (the legal description for this Township Map Group)

The key column here is that of the Township Map Group Number. While you should definitely record the Meridian, Township, and Range, you can do that later. Right now, you need to dig a little deeper. That Map Group Number tells you where in Part II that you need to start digging.

But before you leave the "Surname/Township Index", do the same thing that you did with the "Surnames in Jackson County" list: take a moment to scan the pages of the Index and see if there are similarly spelled or misspelled surnames that deserve your attention. Here again, is an easy opportunity to discover grossly misspelled family names with very little effort. Now you are ready to turn to . . .

Part II
"Township Map Groups"

You will normally arrive here in Part II after being directed to do so by one or more "Map Group Numbers" in the Surname/Township Index of Part I.

Each Map Group represents a set of four tools dedicated to a single Congressional Township that is either wholly or partially within the county. If you are trying to learn all that you can about a particular family or their land, then these tools should usually be viewed in the order they are presented.

These four tools include:

1. a Land Patent Index
2. a Land Patent Map
3. a Road Map, and
4. an Historical Map

As I mentioned earlier, each grouping of this sort is assigned a Map Group Number. So, let's now move on to a discussion of the four tools that make up one of these Township Map Groups.

Land Patent Index

Each Township Map Group's Index begins with a title, something along these lines:

MAP GROUP 1: Index to Land Patents
Township 16-North Range 5-West (2ⁿᵈ PM)

The Index contains seven (7) columns. They are:

1. ID (a unique ID number for this Individual and a corresponding Parcel of land in this Township)
2. Individual in Patent (name)
3. Sec. (Section), and
4. Sec. Part (Section Part, or Aliquot Part)
5. Date Issued (Patent)
6. Other Counties (often means multiple counties were mentioned in GLO records, or the section lies within multiple counties).
7. For More Info . . . (points to other places within this index or elsewhere in the book where you can find more information)

While most of the seven columns are self-explanatory, I will take a few moments to explain the "Sec. Part." and "For More Info" columns.

The "Sec. Part" column refers to what surveryors and other land professionals refer to as an Aliquot Part. The origins and use of such a term mean little to a non-surveyor, and I have chosen to simply call these sub-sections of land what they are: a "Section Part". No matter what we call them, what we are referring to are things like a quarter-section or half-section or quarter-quarter-section. See Appendix "B" for most of the "Section Parts" you will come across (and many you will not) and what size land-parcel they represent.

The "For More Info" column of the Index may seem like a small appendage to each line, but please

recognize quickly that this is not so. And to understand the various items you might find here, you need to become familiar with the Legend that appears at the top of each Land Patent Index.

Here is a sample of the Legend . . .

LEGEND

"For More Info . . . " column

A = Authority (Legislative Act, See Appendix "A")
B = Block or Lot (location in Section unknown)
C = Cancelled Patent
F = Fractional Section
G = Group (Multi-Patentee Patent, see Appendix "C")
V = Overlaps another Parcel
R = Re-Issued (Parcel patented more than once)

Most parcels of land will have only one or two of these items in their "For More Info" columns, but when that is not the case, there is often some valuable information to be gained from further investigation. Below, I will explain what each of these items means to you you as a researcher.

A = Authority
(Legislative Act, See Appendix "A")

All Federal Land Patents were issued because some branch of our government (usually the U.S. Congress) passed a law making such a transfer of title possible. And therefore every patent within these pages will have an "A" item next to it in the index. The number after the "A" indicates which item in Appendix "A" holds the citation to the particular law which authorized the transfer of land to the public. As it stands, most of the Public Land data compiled and released by our government, and which serves as the basis for the patents mapped here, concerns itself with "Cash Sale" homesteads. So in some Counties, the law which authorized cash sales will be the primary, if not the only, entry in the Appendix.

B = Block or Lot (location in Section unknown)
A "B" designation in the Index is a tip-off that the EXACT location of the patent within the map is not apparent from the legal description. This Patent will nonetheless be noted within the proper

Section along with any other Lots purchased in the Section. Given the scope of this project (many states and many Counties are being mapped), trying to locate all relevant plats for Lots (if they even exist) and accurately mapping them would have taken one person several lifetimes. But since our primary goal from the onset has been to establish relationships between neighbors and families, very little is lost to this goal since we can still observe who all lived in which Section.

C = Cancelled Patent

A Cancelled Patent is just that: cancelled. Whether the original Patentee forfeited his or her patent due to fraud, a technicality, non-payment, or whatever, the fact remains that it is significant to know who received patents for what parcels and when. A cancellation may be evidence that the Patentee never physically re-located to the land, but does not in itself prove that point. Further evidence would be required to prove that. *See also*, Re-issued Patents, *below*.

F = Fractional Section

A Fractional Section is one that contains less than 640 acres, almost always because of a body of water. The exact size and shape of land-parcels contained in such sections may not be ascertainable, but we map them nonetheless. Just keep in mind that we are not mapping an actual parcel to scale in such instances. Another point to consider is that we have located some fractional sections that are not so designated by the Bureau of Land Management in their data. This means that not all fractional sections have been so identified in our indexes.

G = Group
(Multi-Patentee Patent, see Appendix "C")

A "G" designation means that the Patent was issued to a GROUP of people (Multi-patentees). The "G" will always be followed by a number. Some such groups were quite large and it was impractical if not impossible to display each individual in our maps without unduly affecting readability. EACH person in the group is named in the Index, but they won't all be found on the Map. You will find the name of the first person in such a Group

on the map with the Group number next to it, enclosed in [square brackets].

To find all the members of the Group you can either scan the Index for all people with the same Group Number or you can simply refer to Appendix "C" where all members of the Group are listed next to their number.

O = Overlaps another Parcel

An Overlap is one where PART of a parcel of land gets issued on more than one patent. For genealogical purposes, both transfers of title are important and both Patentees are mapped. If the ENTIRE parcel of land is re-issued, that is what we call it, a Re-Issued Patent (*see below*). The number after the "O" indicates the ID for the overlapping Patent(s) contained within the same Index. Like Re-Issued and Cancelled Patents, Overlaps may cause a map-reader to be confused at first, but for genealogical purposes, all of these parties' relationships to the underlying land is important, and therefore, we map them.

R = Re-Issued (Parcel patented more than once)

The label, "Re-issued Patent" describes Patents which were issued more than once for land with the EXACT SAME LEGAL DESCRIPTION. Whether the original patent was cancelled or not, there were a good many parcels which were patented more than once. The number after the "R" indicates the ID for the other Patent contained within the same Index that was for the same land. A quick glance at the map itself within the relevant Section will be the quickest way to find the other Patentee to whom the Parcel was transferred. They should both be mapped in the same general area.

I have gone to some length describing all sorts of anomalies either in the underlying data or in their representation on the maps and indexes in this book. Most of this will bore the most ardent reseracher, but I do this with all due respect to those researchers who will inevitably (and rightfully) ask: *"Why isn't so-and-so's name on the exact spot that the index says it should be?"*

In most cases it will be due to the existence of a Multi-Patentee Patent, a Re-issued Patent, a Cancelled Patent, or Overlapping Parcels named in separate Patents. I don't pretend that this discussion will answer every question along these lines, but I hope it will at least convince you of the complexity of the subject.

Not to despair, this book's companion web-site will offer a way to further explain "odd-ball" or errant data. Each book (County) will have its own web-page or pages to discuss such situations. You can go to www.arphax.com to find the relevant web-page for Jackson County.

Land Patent Map

On the first two-page spread following each Township's Index to Land Patents, you'll find the corresponding Land Patent Map. And here lies the real heart of our work. For the first time anywhere, researchers will be able to observe and analyze, on a grand scale, most of the original land-owners for an area AND see them mapped in proximity to each one another.

We encourage you to make vigorous use of the accompanying Index described above, but then later, to abandon it, and just stare at these maps for a while. This is a great way to catch misspellings or to find collateral kin you'd not known were in the area.

Each Land Patent Map represents one Congressional Township containing approximately 36-square miles. Each of these square miles is labeled by an accompanying Section Number (1 through 36, in most cases). Keep in mind, that this book concerns itself solely with Jackson County's patents. Townships which creep into one or more other counties will not be shown in their entirety in any one book. You will need to consult other books, as they become available, in order to view other countys' patents, cities, cemeteries, etc.

But getting back to Jackson County: each Land Patent Map contains a Statistical Chart that looks like the following:

Township Statistics

Parcels Mapped	:	173
Number of Patents	:	163
Number of Individuals	:	152
Patentees Identified	:	151
Number of Surnames	:	137
Multi-Patentee Parcels	:	4
Oldest Patent Date	:	11/27/1820
Most Recent Patent	:	9/28/1917
Block/Lot Parcels	:	0
Parcels Re-Issued	:	3
Parcels that Overlap	:	8
Cities and Towns	:	6
Cemeteries	:	6

This information may be of more use to a social statistician or historian than a genealogist, but I think all three will find it interesting.

Most of the statistics are self-explanatory, and what is not, was described in the above discussion of the Index's Legend, but I do want to mention a few of them that may affect your understanding of the Land Patent Maps.

First of all, Patents often contain more than one Parcel of land, so it is common for there to be more Parcels than Patents. Also, the Number of Individuals will more often than not, not match the number of Patentees. A Patentee is literally the person or PERSONS named in a patent. So, a Patent may have a multi-person Patentee or a single-person patentee. Nonetheless, we account for all these individuals in our indexes.

On the lower-righthand side of the Patent Map is a Legend which describes various features in the map, including Section Boundaries, Patent (land) Boundaries, Lots (numbered), and Multi-Patentee Group Numbers. You'll also find a "Helpful Hints" Box that will assist you.

One important note: though the vast majority of Patents mapped in this series will prove to be reasonably accurate representations of their actual locations, we cannot claim this for patents lying along state and county lines, or waterways, or that have been platted (lots).

Shifting boundaries and sparse legal descriptions in the GLO data make this a reality that we have nonetheless tried to overcome by estimating these patents' locations the best that we can.

Road Map

On the two-page spread following each Patent Map you will find a Road Map covering the exact same area (the same Congressional Township).

For me, fully exploring the past means that every once in a while I must leave the library and travel to the actual locations where my ancestors once walked and worked the land. Our Township Road Maps are a great place to begin such a quest.

Keep in mind that the scaling and proportion of these maps was chosen in order to squeeze hundreds of people-names, road-names, and place-names into tinier spaces than you would traditionally see. These are not professional road-maps, and like any secondary genealogical source, should be looked upon as an entry-way to original sources—in this case, original patents and applications, professionally produced maps and surveys, etc.

Both our Road Maps and Historical Maps contain cemeteries and city-centers, along with a listing of these on the left-hand side of the map. I should note that I am showing you city center-points, rather than city-limit boundaries, because in many instances, this will represent a place where settlement began. This may be a good time to mention that many cemeteries are located on private property, Always check with a local historical or genealogical society to see if a particular cemetery is publicly accessible (if it is not obviously so). As a final point, look for your surnames among the road-names. You will often be surprised by what you find.

Historical Map

The third and final map in each Map Group is our attempt to display what each Township might have looked like before the advent of modern roads. In frontier times, people were usually more determined to settle near rivers and creeks than they were near roads, which were often few and far between. As was the case with the Road Map, we've included the same cemeteries and city-centers. We've also included railroads, many of which came along before most roads.

While some may claim "Historical Map" to be a bit of a misnomer for this tool, we settled for this label simply because it was almost as accurate as saying "Railroads, Lakes, Rivers, Cities, and Cemeteries," and it is much easier to remember.

In Closing . . .

By way of example, here is *A Really Good Way to Use a Township Map Group*. First, find the person you are researching in the Township's Index to Land Patents, which will direct you to the proper Section and parcel on the Patent Map. But before leaving the Index, scan all the patents within it, looking for other names of interest. Now, turn to the Patent Map and locate your parcels of land. Pay special attention to the names of patent-holders who own land surrounding your person of interest. Next, turn the page and look at the same Section(s) on the Road Map. Note which roads are closest to your parcels and also the names of nearby towns and cemeteries. Using other resources, you may be able to learn of kin who have been buried here, plus, you may choose to visit these cemeteries the next time you are in the area.

Finally, turn to the Historical Map. Look once more at the same Sections where you found your research subject's land. Note the nearby streams, creeks, and other geographical features. You may be surprised to find family names were used to name them, or you may see a name you haven't heard mentioned in years and years—and a new research possibility is born.

Many more techniques for using these *Family Maps* volumes will no doubt be discovered. If from time to time, you will navigate to Jackson County's web-page at www.arphax.com (use the "Research" link), you can learn new tricks as they become known (or you can share ones you have employed). But for now, you are ready to get started. So, go, and good luck.

– Part I –

The Big Picture

Map A - Where Jackson County, Florida Lies Within the State

--- Legend ---

— **State Boundary**

— County Boundaries

▨ Jackson County, Florida

--- Helpful Hints ---

1 We start with Map "A" which simply shows us where within the State this county lies.

2 Map "B" zooms in further to help us more easily identify surrounding Counties.

3 Map "C" zooms in even further to reveal the Congressional Townships that either lie within or intersect Jackson County.

Map B - Jackson County, Florida and Surrounding Counties

——— Legend ———

——— State Boundaries (when applicable)

——— County Boundary

—— Helpful Hints ——

1 Many Patent-holders and their families settled across county lines. It is always a good idea to check nearby counties for your families.

2 Refer to Map "A" to see a broader view of where this County lies within the State, and Map "C" to see which Congressional Townships lie within Jackson County.

Map C - Congressional Townships of Jackson County, Florida

Map Group 1
Township 7-N
Range 13-W

Map Group 2
Township 7-N Range 12-W

Map Group 3
Township 7-N Range 11-W

Map Group 4
Township 7-N Range 10-W

Map Group 5
Township 7-N Range 9-W

Map Group 6
Township 7-N
Range 8-W

Map Group 7
Township 6-N
Range 14-W

Map Group 8
Township 6-N Range 13-W

Map Group 9
Township 6-N Range 12-W

Map Group 10
Township 6-N Range 11-W

Map Group 11
Township 6-N Range 10-W

Map Group 12
Township 6-N Range 9-W

Map Group 13
Township 6-N Range 8-W

Map Group 14
Township 6-N
Range 7-W

Map Group 15
Township 5-N
Range 14-W

Map Group 16
Township 5-N Range 13-W

Map Group 17
Township 5-N Range 12-W

Map Group 18
Township 5-N Range 11-W

Map Group 19
Township 5-N Range 10-W

Map Group 20
Township 5-N Range 9-W

Map Group 21
Township 5-N Range 8-W

Map Group 22
Township 5-N
Range 7-W

Map Group 23
Township 4-N
Range 12-W

Map Group 24
Township 4-N Range 11-W

Map Group 25
Township 4-N Range 10-W

Map Group 26
Township 4-N Range 9-W

Map Group 27
Township 4-N Range 8-W

Map Group 28
Township 4-N Range 7-W

Map Group 29
Township 4-N
Range 6-W

Map Group 30
Township 3-N
Range 12-W

Map Group 31
Township 3-N
Range 11-W

Map Group 32
Township 3-N
Range 10-W

Map Group 33
Township 3-N Range 9-W

Map Group 34
Township 3-N Range 8-W

Map Group 35
Township 3-N
Range 7-W

Map Group 36
Township 3-N
Range 6-W

Map Group 37
Township 2-N
Range 12-W

Map Group 38
Township 2-N Range 11-W

Map Group 39
Township 2-N Range 10-W

Map Group 40
Township 2-N
Range 9-W

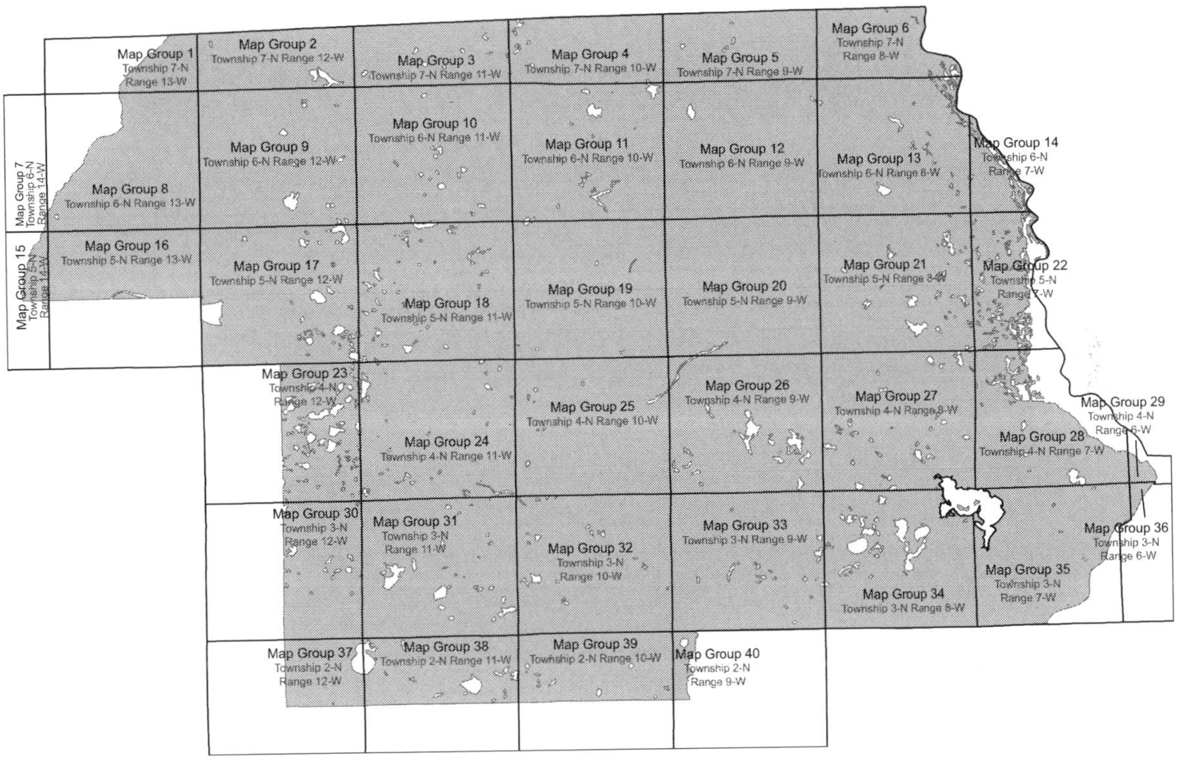

—— Legend ——

Jackson County, Florida

Congressional Townships

—— Helpful Hints ——

1 Many Patent-holders and their families settled across county lines. It is always a good idea to check nearby counties for your families (See Map "B").

2 Refer to Map "A" to see a broader view of where this county lies within the State, and Map "B" for a view of the counties surrounding Jackson County.

Map D Index: Cities & Towns of Jackson County, Florida

The following represents the Cities and Towns of Jackson County, along with the corresponding Map Group in which each is found. Cities and Towns are displayed in both the Road and Historical maps in the Group.

City/Town	Map Group No.
Alford	30
Alliance	33
Bascom	12
Browntown	2
Buena Vista	13
Butler (historical)	22
Campbellton	9
Chipola Terrace	20
Collins Mill	1
Compass Lake	37
Cottondale	18
Cypress	27
Dellwood	21
Ellaville	3
Ellis	11
Ellis Church	4
Glass	17
Graceville	8
Grand Ridge	27
Greenwood	12
Haynes	14
Hornsville	13
Hyhappo (historical)	34
Inwood	28
Jacobs	9
Kent Mill	30
Kynesville	24
Lovedale	13
Mallory Heights	25
Malone	5
Marianna	25
Oakdale	25
Ocheesee Gardens	35
Oktahatko (historical)	11
Osochi (historical)	35
Parramore	13
Rambo	2
Richter Crossroads	16
Rock Creek	33
Round Lake	30
Shady Grove	34
Sills	10
Simsville	33
Sinai	35
Sink Creek	33
Sneads	28
Star	26
Steele City	23
Tamathli (historical)	28
Tocktoethla (historical)	22
Two Egg	21
Waddells Mill	18
Yamassee (historical)	35

Map D - Cities & Towns of Jackson County, Florida

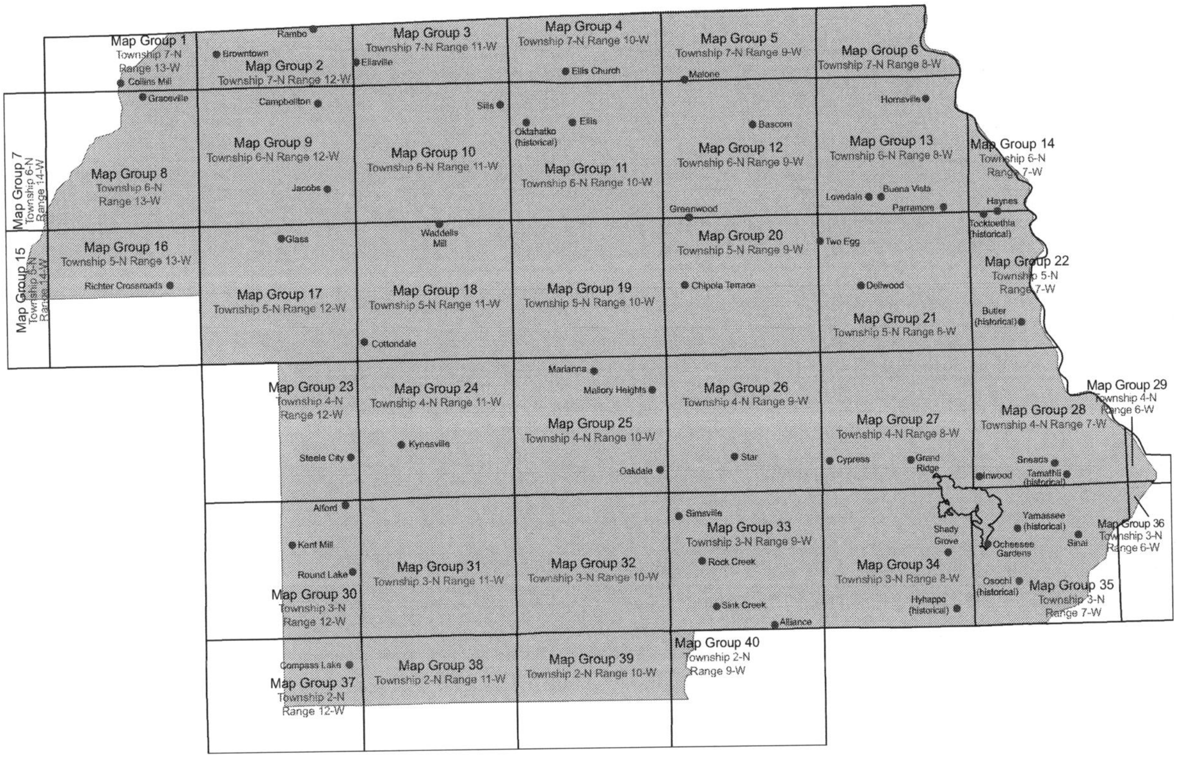

Legend

Jackson County, Florida

Congressional Townships

Helpful Hints

1 Cities and towns are marked only at their center-points as published by the USGS and/or NationalAtlas.gov. This often enables us to more closely approximate where these might have existed when first settled.

2 To see more specifically where these Cities & Towns are located within the county, refer to both the Road and Historical maps in the Map-Group referred to above. See also, the Map "D" Index on the opposite page.

Map E Index: Cemeteries of Jackson County, Florida

The following represents many of the Cemeteries of Jackson County, along with the corresponding Township Map Group in which each is found. Cemeteries are displayed in both the Road and Historical maps in the Map Groups referred to below.

Cemetery	Map Group No.
Bazzell Cem.	13
Braxton Cem.	25
Carpenter Cem.	27
Coonrod Cem.	5
Cow Pen Cem.	21
Damascus Cem.	8
Dyke Cem.	25
Dykes Cem.	28
Elder Cem.	32
Evergreen Cem.	33
Friendship Cem.	10
Fulgum Cem.	27
Grant Cem.	25
Hays Cem.	11
Hill Cem.	26
Hinson Cem.	2
Jerusalem Cem.	32
Lipford Cem.	32
Little Rocky Cem.	33
Logan Cem.	33
Maddox Cem.	32
McCormick Cem.	31
McNeally Cem.	11
Mount Zion Cem.	16
Nubbin Ridge Cem.	12
Orange Hill Cem.	25
Pelt Cem.	25
Pinecrest Memorial Gardens	19
Pledger Cem.	32
Pope Cem.	28
Poplar Spring Cem.	26
Riverside Cem.	25
Robinson Cem.	22
Roulhac Cem.	25
Sand Ridge Cem.	21
Simpsons Cem.	27
Sims Cem.	25
Sinai Cem.	35
Stephens Cem.	27
Victory Cem.	31
Walters Cem.	34
Wester Cem.	27
Whiddon Cem.	22
Yon Cem.	35

Map E - Cemeteries of Jackson County, Florida

Map Group 1 — Township 7-N Range 13-W
Map Group 2 — Township 7-N Range 12-W
Map Group 3 — Township 7-N Range 11-W
Map Group 4 — Township 7-N Range 10-W
Map Group 5 — Township 7-N Range 9-W
Map Group 6 — Township 7-N Range 8-W
Map Group 7 — Township 6-N Range 14-W
Map Group 8 — Township 6-N Range 13-W
Map Group 9 — Township 6-N Range 12-W
Map Group 10 — Township 6-N Range 11-W
Map Group 11 — Township 6-N Range 10-W
Map Group 12 — Township 6-N Range 9-W
Map Group 13 — Township 6-N Range 8-W
Map Group 14 — Township 5-N Range 7-W
Map Group 15 — Township 5-N Range 14-W
Map Group 16 — Township 5-N Range 13-W
Map Group 17 — Township 5-N Range 12-W
Map Group 18 — Township 5-N Range 11-W
Map Group 19 — Township 5-N Range 10-W
Map Group 20 — Township 5-N Range 9-W
Map Group 21 — Township 5-N Range 8-W
Map Group 22 — Township 5-N Range 7-W
Map Group 23 — Township 4-N Range 12-W
Map Group 24 — Township 4-N Range 11-W
Map Group 25 — Township 4-N Range 10-W
Map Group 26 — Township 4-N Range 9-W
Map Group 27 — Township 4-N Range 8-W
Map Group 28 — Township 4-N Range 7-W
Map Group 29 — Township 4-N Range 6-W
Map Group 30 — Township 3-N Range 12-W
Map Group 31 — Township 3-N Range 11-W
Map Group 32 — Township 3-N Range 10-W
Map Group 33 — Township 3-N Range 9-W
Map Group 34 — Township 3-N Range 8-W
Map Group 35 — Township 3-N Range 7-W
Map Group 36 — Township 3-N Range 6-W
Map Group 37 — Township 2-N Range 12-W
Map Group 38 — Township 2-N Range 11-W
Map Group 39 — Township 2-N Range 10-W
Map Group 40 — Township 2-N Range 9-W

Cemeteries shown: Coonrod, Hinson, Friendship, Damascus, Hays, McNeally, Nubbin Ridge, Bazzell, Mount Zion, Pinecrest Memorial Gardens, Sand Ridge, Whiddon, Cow Pen, Robinson, Fulgum, Orange Hill, Riverside, Roulhac, Dyke, Poplar Spring, Simpsons, Dykes, Braxton, Pelt, Stephens, Wester, Hill, Carpenter, Popio, Grant, Sims, Jerusalem, Little Rocky, Logan, Victory, Lipford, Evergreen, Sinai, Lyon, Pledger, Elder, Walters, McCormick, Maddox

— Legend —

Jackson County, Florida

Congressional Townships

— Helpful Hints —

1 Cemeteries are marked at locations as published by the USGS and/or NationalAtlas.gov.

2 To see more specifically where these Cemeteries are located, refer to the Road & Historical maps in the Map-Group referred to above. See also, the Map "E" Index on the opposite page to make sure you don't miss any of the Cemeteries located within this Congressional township.

Surnames in Jackson County, Florida Patents

The following list represents the surnames that we have located in Jackson County, Florida Patents and the number of parcels that we have mapped for each one. Here is a quick way to determine the existence (or not) of Patents to be found in the subsequent indexes and maps of this volume.

Surname	# of Land Parcels	Surname	# of Land Parcels	Surname	# of Land Parcels	Surname	# of Land Parcels
AARONS	3	BLACK	1	CANELEY	2	CREAMER	2
ABERCROMBIE	1	BLACKMAN	1	CARAWAY	2	CREMER	1
ACOCK	6	BLACKMON	2	CARLISLE	4	CROUCH	1
ADAMS	16	BLACKSHEAR	9	CARMICHAEL	1	CROWELL	1
ADKINS	10	BLACKWELL	6	CARPENTER	8	CRUTCHFIELD	10
ALDERMAN	7	BLOOD	3	CARROLL	6	CULPEPPER	1
ALFORD	3	BLOUNT	8	CARTER	18	CULVER	3
ALLEN	42	BOGGS	3	CARTWRIGHT	3	CUNNINGAME	1
ALMAROAD	6	BOIT	1	CHAIRES	30	CURRY	2
ALSOBROOK	5	BOLTON	1	CHAMBLESS	1	CUSHING	1
ANDERSON	16	BONTIUE	2	CHAMBLISS	1	CUTCHIN	3
ANDREWS	8	BOON	6	CHANCE	2	DABBADGE	1
ARMISTEAD	9	BOONE	1	CHAPMAN	23	DALTON	1
ARMSTRONG	6	BOROUM	11	CHASON	14	DANFORD	3
ARNOLD	6	BOUTWELL	2	CHASTINE	1	DANIEL	21
ASKINS	2	BOWEN	1	CHERRY	1	DANIELS	1
ATTAWAY	2	BOWER	2	CHESTER	2	DARDEN	1
AUSTIN	2	BOYKIN	1	CHRISMAS	1	DAUGHERTY	1
AUSTON	1	BOZEMAN	1	CHRISTIE	1	DAUGHTRY	2
AVERY	6	BRADBERY	6	CHRISTMAS	1	DAVIDSON	4
BAGGETT	6	BRADLEY	6	CHRISTOFF	1	DAVIS	25
BAIRD	3	BRADSHAW	2	CHUMNEY	1	DAWSON	3
BAKER	13	BRANAN	1	CLARK	17	DAY	3
BALDWIN	1	BRANNON	1	CLAY	2	DEKLE	13
BALL	5	BRANON	3	CLEMENTS	23	DELOACH	1
BALTZELL	6	BRANTLEY	1	CLEMMONS	1	DEMONT	2
BAMBURG	1	BRANTLY	1	CLOUD	12	DENHAM	3
BANKS	7	BRAXTON	2	CO	9	DICKENS	5
BAREFOOT	5	BRETT	3	COBB	6	DICKERSON	2
BARFIELD	6	BRIDGEMAN	1	COE	8	DICKEY	2
BARKLEY	15	BRINSON	1	COGBURN	4	DICKINSON	3
BARNACASCEL	3	BRITT	2	COKER	3	DICKSON	27
BARNACASTLE	11	BROCK	7	COLBERT	2	DILLMORE	4
BARNES	5	BROGDEN	3	COLEMAN	2	DIVINE	1
BARNETT	1	BROGDON	3	COLLINS	25	DOLTON	3
BASFORD	8	BROOKS	8	COMERFORD	10	DONALD	7
BASS	2	BROOM	3	COMPTON	5	DORSON	3
BATES	2	BROWN	44	CONELLY	3	DOUGHTERY	1
BATIE	2	BROXTON	3	CONELY	1	DOUGHTRY	2
BATTLE	13	BRUNER	11	CONNELL	1	DOWLING	1
BAXLEY	2	BRUNSON	1	CONNER	7	DOZIER	1
BAXTER	53	BRUTON	2	CONRAD	2	DRAKE	8
BAYLES	2	BRYAN	57	CONROD	2	DUBOSE	1
BAZZEL	6	BRYANT	5	COOK	31	DUDLEY	7
BAZZELL	8	BUCHANAN	1	COOLEY	2	DUKES	2
BAZZLE	3	BUIE	1	COONROD	10	DUNCAN	8
BEASLY	1	BULLOCK	3	COOPER	2	DUNHAM	1
BEAUCHAMP	6	BURKETT	3	CORBIN	4	DUNLAP	5
BEESLEY	3	BURNES	4	CORBITT	1	DURDEN	5
BELCHER	1	BURNHAM	1	CORLEY	1	DURHAM	11
BELL	11	BURNS	2	CORNISH	1	DYKES	12
BELLAMY	17	BUSH	49	CORTNEY	2	EAGLE	1
BELSON	1	BUTLER	5	COTTON	1	EDENFIELD	9
BENEFIELD	3	BYRD	9	COULLIETTE	2	EDWARDS	15
BEST	3	CADWELL	1	COULTER	1	ELDRIDGE	4
BEVERIDGE	5	CAIN	3	COURTNEY	1	ELLIS	4
BEVILL	3	CALHOUN	6	COWAN	1	ELMORE	5
BEVIS	1	CALL	17	COWARD	1	EMANUEL	1
BIBB	9	CALLAWAY	6	COWART	1	EMBREY	2
BIRD	15	CALLOWAY	6	COX	18	ERWIN	4
BIRGESS	2	CAMP	1	COXWELL	1	EVERITT	3
BISHOP	1	CAMPBELL	4	CRAWFORD	1	FAIRCLOTH	3

Surname	# of Land Parcels	Surname	# of Land Parcels	Surname	# of Land Parcels	Surname	# of Land Parcels
FAISON	1	GRANGER	6	HORN	1	LEWIS	20
FARMER	1	GRANT	10	HORNE	2	LIPFORD	4
FARR	2	GRANTHAM	3	HORT	1	LISTER	1
FAUST	1	GRANTLAND	10	HOUGH	3	LITTLETON	6
FENNEL	2	GRAVES	1	HOVEY	2	LOCKART	2
FERGUSON	4	GRAY	5	HOWARD	18	LOCKHART	6
FILLMAN	1	GREEN	3	HOWEL	1	LOFTIN	6
FINCH	1	GRICE	1	HOWELL	3	LOGAN	4
FINLAYSON	1	GRIFFIN	14	HUBBARD	2	LOGATHREE	1
FINLEY	3	GRIMESLEY	3	HUDSON	1	LONG	30
FLETCHER	1	GRIMSLEY	4	HUFF	3	LOOPER	1
FLORIDA	4	GRISSETT	4	HUGHES	5	LOTT	10
FLOYD	7	GRUBB	2	HULL	2	LOVE	5
FOLSOM	11	GRUBBS	2	HUNTER	2	LOVVITT	2
FOLSOME	1	GUATIER	1	HURST	4	LOWRY	22
FORAN	2	GUNDERSON	2	HUTSON	1	LYNCH	2
FORD	1	HADDOCK	1	HYATT	1	LYNN	4
FOREHAND	8	HAGAN	3	INGRAM	2	MACK	1
FOREST	1	HAIR	5	IRVIN	1	MADDOX	24
FORT	5	HAIRE	2	IRWIN	18	MADDUX	2
FORTUNE	14	HALEY	2	JACKSON	17	MALONEY	3
FOSCUE	12	HALL	12	JARDAN	1	MALTSBY	2
FOSTER	3	HAM	2	JARRATT	2	MANDELL	2
FOULK	5	HAMILTON	27	JEMISON	7	MARCHANT	4
FOUNTAIN	1	HAND	5	JENKINS	4	MARSHAL	2
FOWLE	1	HANSFORD	6	JETER	5	MARSHALL	5
FOWLER	6	HARDEN	8	JOHNSON	37	MARTIN	19
FOXWORTH	1	HARDIN	14	JOHNSTON	4	MASHBURN	3
FRANCIS	2	HARE	2	JOINER	1	MATHEWS	12
FRANKLIN	5	HARGROVE	1	JONES	36	MATHIS	4
FREEMAN	8	HARPER	17	JORDAN	2	MATTHEWS	14
FULGHAM	7	HARRELL	6	JOWERS	1	MAULDIN	5
FULLERTON	4	HART	6	JUSTICE	4	MAWHINNEY	1
GABLE	7	HARTSFIELD	2	JUSTISS	1	MAY	2
GAFF	1	HARVEY	13	KEEL	1	MAYO	20
GAINER	4	HATCHER	4	KEISER	2	MAYS	2
GAKRINS	3	HATHAWAY	4	KEITH	18	MAZLEY	1
GALLAWAY	1	HATTON	2	KELLEY	1	MCANULTY	10
GAMBLE	6	HAWKINS	1	KELLY	2	MCBAIN	2
GARBETT	2	HAYES	3	KEMP	2	MCCARTY	2
GARDNER	1	HAYNES	4	KENT	24	MCCLELAN	1
GARNER	3	HAYS	6	KETTLEBAND	3	MCCLELLAN	4
GARRETT	3	HAYWOOD	9	KIDD	3	MCCORMACK	2
GAUTIER	8	HEARIN	2	KILBEE	16	MCCORMICK	7
GAY	22	HEARN	8	KILCREASE	3	MCCORQUODALE	2
GEE	4	HEATH	1	KIMBELL	3	MCCOY	1
GILBERT	8	HEISLER	2	KING	8	MCCRARY	8
GILCHRIST	17	HELMES	1	KINGRY	1	MCCREARY	1
GILES	8	HENDRIX	3	KINGSLEY	1	MCCROAN	1
GILLIS	1	HENRY	1	KIRKLAND	7	MCCULLOH	1
GILLSTROP	1	HERNDON	1	KNAPP	4	MCDANIEL	36
GILMER	10	HERRING	4	KNIGHT	2	MCDONALD	5
GILSTRAP	1	HEWETT	8	KNOWLES	2	MCFARLAND	2
GLADDEN	6	HICKMAN	1	KOONCE	1	MCGEE	3
GLASS	4	HICKS	5	LAMB	1	MCGUIRE	4
GLISSON	7	HILL	16	LAMBERT	1	MCINTOSH	1
GLOVER	2	HINSON	19	LANCASTER	2	MCKAY	8
GODFREY	1	HODGES	5	LAND	5	MCKEOWN	2
GODWIN	16	HODGSON	17	LANE	2	MCKINNE	10
GOFF	5	HOGG	7	LANGSTON	1	MCLAIN	1
GOLDEN	7	HOLDEN	3	LANIER	1	MCLANE	1
GOLDING	1	HOLDER	3	LARAMORE	2	MCLELLAN	1
GOODWIN	3	HOLLAND	2	LASHLEY	7	MCLENDON	3
GORDY	1	HOLLEY	1	LAWRENCE	4	MCLEOD	3
GORMAN	3	HOLLIDAY	1	LAWSON	4	MCLEROY	2
GOTAIR	1	HOLLIMAN	1	LEADBETTER	3	MCLEVY	1
GOTIER	1	HOLLINGSWORTH	1	LEE	7	MCMILLAN	10
GRACE	5	HOLMES	9	LEONARD	7	MCMULLEN	4
GRAINGER	4	HOOTEN	1	LEVEY	1	MCMULLIAN	1
GRANBERRY	2	HOPSON	1	LEVY	2	MCNEALEY	1

Surname	# of Land Parcels	Surname	# of Land Parcels	Surname	# of Land Parcels	Surname	# of Land Parcels
MCNEALLY	3	PADGET	3	RICHTER	4	SLOAN	3
MCNEALY	21	PADGETT	18	RICKS	4	SLOANE	1
MCNEELY	2	PADJETT	8	RIDDICK	2	SMITH	34
MCNEILLY	1	PAGE	1	RILEY	2	SNEAD	2
MCPARLAND	1	PARISH	2	RIVERS	3	SNELL	12
MCQUAGE	1	PARKER	11	RIVES	1	SNELLING	6
MCQUAGGE	7	PARRAMORE	2	RIVIERE	2	SNIPES	4
MCQUAIG	1	PARRISH	3	RIVIRE	1	SNOW	5
MCQUEEN	1	PARROT	1	ROACH	7	SOREY	6
MCRAE	2	PATRICK	3	ROBBIRDS	1	SOUTER	1
MEARS	12	PATTERSON	20	ROBERSON	7	SPEAR	3
MEDLOACK	1	PATTON	2	ROBERTS	33	SPEARS	13
MEDLOCK	3	PAULK	1	ROBINSON	38	SPEIGHT	2
MELVIN	6	PAYTON	1	RODGERS	4	SPEIGHTS	1
MENDHEIM	1	PEACOCK	22	ROGERS	3	SPEIR	3
MERCER	19	PEEBLES	4	ROSE	1	SPIER	1
MERRETT	1	PELT	10	ROSS	1	SPIERS	4
MERRITT	10	PENDER	12	ROULHAC	9	SPIVEY	2
MESSER	1	PENNINGTON	5	ROWE	3	SPOONER	10
MICH	1	PERKINS	3	ROYAL	2	STALEY	9
MICHAUX	4	PERRITT	3	ROYALS	1	STAPLETON	4
MILES	7	PERRY	11	RUCKER	2	STELL	2
MILLAR	1	PETERS	2	RUSK	14	STEPHENS	49
MILLER	14	PETERSON	1	RUSS	9	STEWART	8
MILLS	6	PEYTON	6	SADLER	7	STILL	4
MILTON	17	PHILIPS	4	SANBURN	2	STINSON	1
MINCHIN	3	PHILLIPS	3	SANDERS	1	STOCKTON	2
MING	10	PIGG	1	SAPP	2	STONE	14
MITCHELL	7	PILCHER	1	SAXON	1	STOWERS	2
MONEY	3	PINKHAM	1	SCAMMELL	1	STREETMAN	1
MONEYHAM	2	PIOUS	1	SCARLOCK	1	STRICKLAND	9
MONIN	1	PIPPEN	2	SCHURLOCK	1	SUGGS	3
MONK	2	PITTMAN	29	SCOTT	22	SULIVAN	4
MONTFORD	1	PITTS	2	SCURLOCK	14	SULLIVAN	15
MONTFORT	1	PLAYER	7	SEARCY	2	SUMMERLIN	7
MOON	1	PLEDGER	13	SEAY	3	SUMMERS	1
MOORE	5	POLK	1	SELLERS	10	SUTTON	8
MOORING	4	POLLOCK	1	SEWELL	3	SWAILS	5
MORGAN	11	POOSER	12	SEXTON	6	SWANSON	1
MORRIS	12	POPE	20	SHACKELFORD	4	SWEARINGEN	1
MORRISON	2	PORTER	40	SHARON	3	SWEARINGIN	1
MOSES	2	POWELL	12	SHARP	2	SWEET	6
MOSS	1	POWERS	1	SHARPE	1	SYFRETT	11
MOTT	1	PRATHER	10	SHELFER	3	SYPETT	1
MOWHINNEY	1	PRESTON	2	SHERMAN	1	SYPHRETT	2
MULKEY	1	PREVATT	1	SHINHOLSTER	2	TANNER	2
MURDOCK	1	PRIM	4	SHIPE	3	TATUM	4
MURPHY	3	PROCTOR	2	SHIPES	3	TAWN	1
MUSGROVE	2	PUMPHRAY	3	SHIVER	4	TAYLOR	25
MYRICK	6	PUMPHREY	7	SHORES	12	TEMPLE	1
NALL	2	PURSER	1	SHOUPE	1	THARP	12
NASH	1	PURVIS	5	SHOUPPE	3	THIGPEN	1
NEAL	1	PYKE	1	SHUTES	2	THIRBY	1
NEEL	33	RABOURN	2	SIKES	1	THOMAS	25
NEELY	1	RAINS	2	SILLIVENT	3	THOMPSON	12
NELSON	7	RAMSAY	1	SILLS	1	THORNTON	1
NEWSOME	1	RAMSEY	2	SIMMES	1	TIDWELL	4
NICKELS	6	RANEY	1	SIMMONS	3	TILLINGHAST	4
NIX	2	RASK	1	SIMMS	9	TIPTON	1
NOBLES	3	RATHIEL	1	SIMONS	3	TONEY	8
NOLL	2	RAWLS	2	SIMPSON	5	TOOLE	16
NOOGIN	1	RAY	1	SIMS	49	TOUCHSTONE	1
NORRIS	2	REDDICK	2	SIMSON	1	TOWERS	1
OBRIEN	1	REDDING	2	SINGHTON	1	TOWLE	1
OLIVE	2	REGISTER	11	SKETO	10	TRAMMEL	7
ONEAL	4	REISSER	2	SKINNER	8	TRAMMELL	6
ONEIL	2	REVERE	1	SKIPPER	1	TRAYLOR	5
OSWALD	6	REYNOLDS	9	SKRINE	1	TREVATHON	1
OVERTON	2	RHODES	8	SLATER	7	TRIPP	1
OWENS	15	RICHARDSON	2	SLATON	4	TRIPPE	5

Surname	# of Land Parcels	Surname	# of Land Parcels
TRUSSELL	1	YORK	5
TUCKER	2	YOUNG	29
TURNER	10		
TYUS	1		
UNDERWOOD	9		
VAN PELT	1		
VANCE	1		
VAUGHN	4		
VICK	1		
VICKERS	5		
VICKERY	7		
WACASER	4		
WACHOB	3		
WADDELL	1		
WADKINS	3		
WALKER	3		
WALSH	2		
WARD	5		
WARDLOW	1		
WATERS	1		
WATFORD	22		
WATSON	9		
WATTS	5		
WEBB	5		
WEEKS	7		
WELCH	2		
WEST	1		
WESTER	11		
WESTON	4		
WETHINGTON	3		
WHICHARD	2		
WHIDDON	2		
WHITAKER	4		
WHITE	15		
WHITEFIELD	3		
WHITEHEAD	7		
WHITEHURST	15		
WHITFIELD	5		
WHITTINGTON	1		
WILCOX	7		
WILEY	2		
WILLEFORD	6		
WILLIAMS	72		
WILLIAMSON	134		
WILLIFORD	1		
WILLIS	2		
WILLSON	3		
WILSON	28		
WILTON	1		
WIMBERLEY	2		
WIMBERLY	5		
WIRT	3		
WITCHARD	1		
WITHERINGTON	1		
WOMBLE	2		
WOOD	6		
WOODALL	1		
WOODARD	2		
WOOLDRIDGE	3		
WOOTEN	1		
WORLEY	3		
WRIGHT	2		
WYATT	1		
WYNN	3		
WYNNS	2		
YARBOROUGH	12		
YARBROUGH	4		
YAWN	1		
YON	5		
YONGE	1		

Surname/Township Index

This Index allows you to determine which *Township Map Group(s)* contain individuals with the following surnames. Each *Map Group* has a corresponding full-name index of all individuals who obtained patents for land within its Congressional township's borders. After each index you will find the Patent Map to which it refers, and just thereafter, you can view the township's Road Map and Historical Map, with the latter map displaying streams, railroads, and more.

So, once you find your Surname here, proceed to the Index at the beginning of the **Map Group** indicated below.

Surname	Map Group	Parcels of Land	Meridian/Township/Range		
AARONS	**31**	3	Tallahassee	3-N	11-W
ABERCROMBIE	**3**	1	Tallahassee	7-N	11-W
ACOCK	**11**	2	Tallahassee	6-N	10-W
" "	**4**	2	Tallahassee	7-N	10-W
" "	**19**	1	Tallahassee	5-N	10-W
" "	**20**	1	Tallahassee	5-N	9-W
ADAMS	**16**	8	Tallahassee	5-N	13-W
" "	**14**	4	Tallahassee	6-N	7-W
" "	**9**	2	Tallahassee	6-N	12-W
" "	**17**	1	Tallahassee	5-N	12-W
" "	**8**	1	Tallahassee	6-N	13-W
ADKINS	**39**	5	Tallahassee	2-N	10-W
" "	**32**	3	Tallahassee	3-N	10-W
" "	**31**	1	Tallahassee	3-N	11-W
" "	**35**	1	Tallahassee	3-N	7-W
ALDERMAN	**37**	4	Tallahassee	2-N	12-W
" "	**38**	3	Tallahassee	2-N	11-W
ALFORD	**34**	2	Tallahassee	3-N	8-W
" "	**13**	1	Tallahassee	6-N	8-W
ALLEN	**10**	14	Tallahassee	6-N	11-W
" "	**14**	8	Tallahassee	6-N	7-W
" "	**28**	5	Tallahassee	4-N	7-W
" "	**21**	3	Tallahassee	5-N	8-W
" "	**20**	3	Tallahassee	5-N	9-W
" "	**8**	3	Tallahassee	6-N	13-W
" "	**29**	2	Tallahassee	4-N	6-W
" "	**25**	1	Tallahassee	4-N	10-W
" "	**24**	1	Tallahassee	4-N	11-W
" "	**19**	1	Tallahassee	5-N	10-W
" "	**22**	1	Tallahassee	5-N	7-W
ALMAROAD	**6**	4	Tallahassee	7-N	8-W
" "	**13**	1	Tallahassee	6-N	8-W
" "	**12**	1	Tallahassee	6-N	9-W
ALSOBROOK	**12**	5	Tallahassee	6-N	9-W
ANDERSON	**1**	7	Tallahassee	7-N	13-W
" "	**4**	4	Tallahassee	7-N	10-W
" "	**13**	2	Tallahassee	6-N	8-W
" "	**2**	2	Tallahassee	7-N	12-W
" "	**28**	1	Tallahassee	4-N	7-W
ANDREWS	**10**	8	Tallahassee	6-N	11-W
ARMISTEAD	**35**	9	Tallahassee	3-N	7-W
ARMSTRONG	**3**	6	Tallahassee	7-N	11-W
ARNOLD	**21**	5	Tallahassee	5-N	8-W
" "	**30**	1	Tallahassee	3-N	12-W

Surname	Map Group	Parcels of Land	Meridian/Township/Range		
ASKINS	**9**	2	Tallahassee	6-N	12-W
ATTAWAY	**25**	1	Tallahassee	4-N	10-W
" "	**24**	1	Tallahassee	4-N	11-W
AUSTIN	**37**	1	Tallahassee	2-N	12-W
" "	**4**	1	Tallahassee	7-N	10-W
AUSTON	**15**	1	Tallahassee	5-N	14-W
AVERY	**13**	5	Tallahassee	6-N	8-W
" "	**12**	1	Tallahassee	6-N	9-W
BAGGETT	**9**	3	Tallahassee	6-N	12-W
" "	**33**	2	Tallahassee	3-N	9-W
" "	**8**	1	Tallahassee	6-N	13-W
BAIRD	**21**	3	Tallahassee	5-N	8-W
BAKER	**27**	2	Tallahassee	4-N	8-W
" "	**19**	2	Tallahassee	5-N	10-W
" "	**9**	2	Tallahassee	6-N	12-W
" "	**14**	2	Tallahassee	6-N	7-W
" "	**13**	2	Tallahassee	6-N	8-W
" "	**2**	2	Tallahassee	7-N	12-W
" "	**11**	1	Tallahassee	6-N	10-W
BALDWIN	**31**	1	Tallahassee	3-N	11-W
BALL	**8**	2	Tallahassee	6-N	13-W
" "	**1**	2	Tallahassee	7-N	13-W
" "	**9**	1	Tallahassee	6-N	12-W
BALTZELL	**22**	5	Tallahassee	5-N	7-W
" "	**14**	1	Tallahassee	6-N	7-W
BAMBURG	**34**	1	Tallahassee	3-N	8-W
BANKS	**25**	4	Tallahassee	4-N	10-W
" "	**32**	2	Tallahassee	3-N	10-W
" "	**33**	1	Tallahassee	3-N	9-W
BAREFOOT	**31**	2	Tallahassee	3-N	11-W
" "	**25**	2	Tallahassee	4-N	10-W
" "	**8**	1	Tallahassee	6-N	13-W
BARFIELD	**24**	6	Tallahassee	4-N	11-W
BARKLEY	**33**	11	Tallahassee	3-N	9-W
" "	**12**	4	Tallahassee	6-N	9-W
BARNACASCEL	**12**	2	Tallahassee	6-N	9-W
" "	**13**	1	Tallahassee	6-N	8-W
BARNACASTLE	**13**	10	Tallahassee	6-N	8-W
" "	**12**	1	Tallahassee	6-N	9-W
BARNES	**23**	3	Tallahassee	4-N	12-W
" "	**30**	1	Tallahassee	3-N	12-W
" "	**20**	1	Tallahassee	5-N	9-W
BARNETT	**33**	1	Tallahassee	3-N	9-W
BASFORD	**21**	8	Tallahassee	5-N	8-W
BASS	**17**	2	Tallahassee	5-N	12-W
BATES	**12**	2	Tallahassee	6-N	9-W
BATIE	**32**	2	Tallahassee	3-N	10-W
BATTLE	**25**	6	Tallahassee	4-N	10-W
" "	**26**	6	Tallahassee	4-N	9-W
" "	**11**	1	Tallahassee	6-N	10-W
BAXLEY	**1**	2	Tallahassee	7-N	13-W
BAXTER	**11**	28	Tallahassee	6-N	10-W
" "	**12**	17	Tallahassee	6-N	9-W
" "	**4**	8	Tallahassee	7-N	10-W
BAYLES	**35**	2	Tallahassee	3-N	7-W
BAZZEL	**13**	6	Tallahassee	6-N	8-W
BAZZELL	**13**	5	Tallahassee	6-N	8-W
" "	**21**	3	Tallahassee	5-N	8-W
BAZZLE	**13**	3	Tallahassee	6-N	8-W
BEASLY	**3**	1	Tallahassee	7-N	11-W

Surname	Map Group	Parcels of Land	Meridian/Township/Range		
BEAUCHAMP	**33**	3	Tallahassee	3-N	9-W
" "	**2**	2	Tallahassee	7-N	12-W
" "	**3**	1	Tallahassee	7-N	11-W
BEESLEY	**3**	3	Tallahassee	7-N	11-W
BELCHER	**20**	1	Tallahassee	5-N	9-W
BELL	**4**	7	Tallahassee	7-N	10-W
" "	**20**	2	Tallahassee	5-N	9-W
" "	**32**	1	Tallahassee	3-N	10-W
" "	**26**	1	Tallahassee	4-N	9-W
BELLAMY	**11**	7	Tallahassee	6-N	10-W
" "	**25**	3	Tallahassee	4-N	10-W
" "	**19**	3	Tallahassee	5-N	10-W
" "	**24**	2	Tallahassee	4-N	11-W
" "	**10**	2	Tallahassee	6-N	11-W
BELSON	**13**	1	Tallahassee	6-N	8-W
BENEFIELD	**37**	3	Tallahassee	2-N	12-W
BEST	**8**	3	Tallahassee	6-N	13-W
BEVERIDGE	**25**	4	Tallahassee	4-N	10-W
" "	**9**	1	Tallahassee	6-N	12-W
BEVILL	**35**	3	Tallahassee	3-N	7-W
BEVIS	**27**	1	Tallahassee	4-N	8-W
BIBB	**17**	9	Tallahassee	5-N	12-W
BIRD	**35**	9	Tallahassee	3-N	7-W
" "	**22**	6	Tallahassee	5-N	7-W
BIRGESS	**34**	2	Tallahassee	3-N	8-W
BISHOP	**24**	1	Tallahassee	4-N	11-W
BLACK	**26**	1	Tallahassee	4-N	9-W
BLACKMAN	**21**	1	Tallahassee	5-N	8-W
BLACKMON	**27**	1	Tallahassee	4-N	8-W
" "	**20**	1	Tallahassee	5-N	9-W
BLACKSHEAR	**20**	7	Tallahassee	5-N	9-W
" "	**25**	2	Tallahassee	4-N	10-W
BLACKWELL	**11**	3	Tallahassee	6-N	10-W
" "	**10**	2	Tallahassee	6-N	11-W
" "	**3**	1	Tallahassee	7-N	11-W
BLOOD	**27**	3	Tallahassee	4-N	8-W
BLOUNT	**33**	3	Tallahassee	3-N	9-W
" "	**9**	3	Tallahassee	6-N	12-W
" "	**24**	1	Tallahassee	4-N	11-W
" "	**17**	1	Tallahassee	5-N	12-W
BOGGS	**39**	3	Tallahassee	2-N	10-W
BOIT	**13**	1	Tallahassee	6-N	8-W
BOLTON	**13**	1	Tallahassee	6-N	8-W
BONTIUE	**17**	2	Tallahassee	5-N	12-W
BOON	**6**	6	Tallahassee	7-N	8-W
BOONE	**34**	1	Tallahassee	3-N	8-W
BOROUM	**21**	10	Tallahassee	5-N	8-W
" "	**14**	1	Tallahassee	6-N	7-W
BOUTWELL	**31**	2	Tallahassee	3-N	11-W
BOWEN	**17**	1	Tallahassee	5-N	12-W
BOWER	**18**	1	Tallahassee	5-N	11-W
" "	**14**	1	Tallahassee	6-N	7-W
BOYKIN	**28**	1	Tallahassee	4-N	7-W
BOZEMAN	**3**	1	Tallahassee	7-N	11-W
BRADBERY	**3**	6	Tallahassee	7-N	11-W
BRADLEY	**34**	4	Tallahassee	3-N	8-W
" "	**27**	1	Tallahassee	4-N	8-W
" "	**9**	1	Tallahassee	6-N	12-W
BRADSHAW	**2**	2	Tallahassee	7-N	12-W
BRANAN	**31**	1	Tallahassee	3-N	11-W

Surname	Map Group	Parcels of Land	Meridian/Township/Range		
BRANNON	**31**	1	Tallahassee	3-N	11-W
BRANON	**24**	3	Tallahassee	4-N	11-W
BRANTLEY	**18**	1	Tallahassee	5-N	11-W
BRANTLY	**2**	1	Tallahassee	7-N	12-W
BRAXTON	**25**	1	Tallahassee	4-N	10-W
" "	**17**	1	Tallahassee	5-N	12-W
BRETT	**3**	2	Tallahassee	7-N	11-W
" "	**2**	1	Tallahassee	7-N	12-W
BRIDGEMAN	**10**	1	Tallahassee	6-N	11-W
BRINSON	**13**	1	Tallahassee	6-N	8-W
BRITT	**10**	2	Tallahassee	6-N	11-W
BROCK	**23**	4	Tallahassee	4-N	12-W
" "	**24**	3	Tallahassee	4-N	11-W
BROGDEN	**13**	2	Tallahassee	6-N	8-W
" "	**21**	1	Tallahassee	5-N	8-W
BROGDON	**13**	3	Tallahassee	6-N	8-W
BROOKS	**31**	5	Tallahassee	3-N	11-W
" "	**6**	2	Tallahassee	7-N	8-W
" "	**24**	1	Tallahassee	4-N	11-W
BROOM	**8**	3	Tallahassee	6-N	13-W
BROWN	**2**	9	Tallahassee	7-N	12-W
" "	**13**	8	Tallahassee	6-N	8-W
" "	**24**	5	Tallahassee	4-N	11-W
" "	**8**	5	Tallahassee	6-N	13-W
" "	**22**	3	Tallahassee	5-N	7-W
" "	**11**	3	Tallahassee	6-N	10-W
" "	**1**	3	Tallahassee	7-N	13-W
" "	**35**	2	Tallahassee	3-N	7-W
" "	**28**	2	Tallahassee	4-N	7-W
" "	**4**	2	Tallahassee	7-N	10-W
" "	**40**	1	Tallahassee	2-N	9-W
" "	**9**	1	Tallahassee	6-N	12-W
BROXTON	**17**	2	Tallahassee	5-N	12-W
" "	**1**	1	Tallahassee	7-N	13-W
BRUNER	**17**	4	Tallahassee	5-N	12-W
" "	**3**	4	Tallahassee	7-N	11-W
" "	**16**	2	Tallahassee	5-N	13-W
" "	**31**	1	Tallahassee	3-N	11-W
BRUNSON	**12**	1	Tallahassee	6-N	9-W
BRUTON	**22**	2	Tallahassee	5-N	7-W
BRYAN	**20**	35	Tallahassee	5-N	9-W
" "	**25**	7	Tallahassee	4-N	10-W
" "	**13**	6	Tallahassee	6-N	8-W
" "	**19**	4	Tallahassee	5-N	10-W
" "	**21**	4	Tallahassee	5-N	8-W
" "	**33**	1	Tallahassee	3-N	9-W
BRYANT	**27**	5	Tallahassee	4-N	8-W
BUCHANAN	**24**	1	Tallahassee	4-N	11-W
BUIE	**16**	1	Tallahassee	5-N	13-W
BULLOCK	**33**	3	Tallahassee	3-N	9-W
BURKETT	**9**	3	Tallahassee	6-N	12-W
BURNES	**21**	4	Tallahassee	5-N	8-W
BURNHAM	**26**	1	Tallahassee	4-N	9-W
BURNS	**21**	2	Tallahassee	5-N	8-W
BUSH	**10**	21	Tallahassee	6-N	11-W
" "	**32**	5	Tallahassee	3-N	10-W
" "	**23**	5	Tallahassee	4-N	12-W
" "	**2**	5	Tallahassee	7-N	12-W
" "	**3**	4	Tallahassee	7-N	11-W
" "	**24**	3	Tallahassee	4-N	11-W

Surname	Map Group	Parcels of Land	Meridian/Township/Range
BUSH (Cont'd)	**25**	2	Tallahassee 4-N 10-W
" "	**11**	2	Tallahassee 6-N 10-W
" "	**9**	1	Tallahassee 6-N 12-W
" "	**4**	1	Tallahassee 7-N 10-W
BUTLER	**30**	2	Tallahassee 3-N 12-W
" "	**32**	1	Tallahassee 3-N 10-W
" "	**17**	1	Tallahassee 5-N 12-W
" "	**11**	1	Tallahassee 6-N 10-W
BYRD	**26**	5	Tallahassee 4-N 9-W
" "	**40**	3	Tallahassee 2-N 9-W
" "	**27**	1	Tallahassee 4-N 8-W
CADWELL	**2**	1	Tallahassee 7-N 12-W
CAIN	**21**	2	Tallahassee 5-N 8-W
" "	**8**	1	Tallahassee 6-N 13-W
CALHOUN	**17**	4	Tallahassee 5-N 12-W
" "	**20**	2	Tallahassee 5-N 9-W
CALL	**28**	8	Tallahassee 4-N 7-W
" "	**25**	7	Tallahassee 4-N 10-W
" "	**29**	1	Tallahassee 4-N 6-W
" "	**6**	1	Tallahassee 7-N 8-W
CALLAWAY	**10**	6	Tallahassee 6-N 11-W
CALLOWAY	**10**	4	Tallahassee 6-N 11-W
" "	**3**	2	Tallahassee 7-N 11-W
CAMP	**10**	1	Tallahassee 6-N 11-W
CAMPBELL	**24**	3	Tallahassee 4-N 11-W
" "	**32**	1	Tallahassee 3-N 10-W
CANELEY	**20**	2	Tallahassee 5-N 9-W
CARAWAY	**34**	1	Tallahassee 3-N 8-W
" "	**25**	1	Tallahassee 4-N 10-W
CARLISLE	**5**	3	Tallahassee 7-N 9-W
" "	**31**	1	Tallahassee 3-N 11-W
CARMICHAEL	**8**	1	Tallahassee 6-N 13-W
CARPENTER	**27**	6	Tallahassee 4-N 8-W
" "	**40**	1	Tallahassee 2-N 9-W
" "	**34**	1	Tallahassee 3-N 8-W
CARROLL	**26**	4	Tallahassee 4-N 9-W
" "	**30**	1	Tallahassee 3-N 12-W
" "	**34**	1	Tallahassee 3-N 8-W
CARTER	**2**	4	Tallahassee 7-N 12-W
" "	**11**	3	Tallahassee 6-N 10-W
" "	**6**	3	Tallahassee 7-N 8-W
" "	**17**	2	Tallahassee 5-N 12-W
" "	**35**	1	Tallahassee 3-N 7-W
" "	**25**	1	Tallahassee 4-N 10-W
" "	**20**	1	Tallahassee 5-N 9-W
" "	**10**	1	Tallahassee 6-N 11-W
" "	**9**	1	Tallahassee 6-N 12-W
" "	**8**	1	Tallahassee 6-N 13-W
CARTWRIGHT	**27**	3	Tallahassee 4-N 8-W
CHAIRES	**19**	9	Tallahassee 5-N 10-W
" "	**28**	7	Tallahassee 4-N 7-W
" "	**25**	6	Tallahassee 4-N 10-W
" "	**32**	4	Tallahassee 3-N 10-W
" "	**33**	3	Tallahassee 3-N 9-W
" "	**31**	1	Tallahassee 3-N 11-W
CHAMBLESS	**20**	1	Tallahassee 5-N 9-W
CHAMBLISS	**9**	1	Tallahassee 6-N 12-W
CHANCE	**39**	2	Tallahassee 2-N 10-W
CHAPMAN	**32**	10	Tallahassee 3-N 10-W
" "	**25**	9	Tallahassee 4-N 10-W

Surname	Map Group	Parcels of Land	Meridian/Township/Range		
CHAPMAN (Cont'd)	**40**	2	Tallahassee	2-N	9-W
" "	**33**	2	Tallahassee	3-N	9-W
CHASON	**39**	12	Tallahassee	2-N	10-W
" "	**32**	1	Tallahassee	3-N	10-W
" "	**9**	1	Tallahassee	6-N	12-W
CHASTINE	**32**	1	Tallahassee	3-N	10-W
CHERRY	**28**	1	Tallahassee	4-N	7-W
CHESTER	**34**	2	Tallahassee	3-N	8-W
CHRISMAS	**1**	1	Tallahassee	7-N	13-W
CHRISTIE	**8**	1	Tallahassee	6-N	13-W
CHRISTMAS	**3**	1	Tallahassee	7-N	11-W
CHRISTOFF	**19**	1	Tallahassee	5-N	10-W
CHUMNEY	**11**	1	Tallahassee	6-N	10-W
CLARK	**18**	9	Tallahassee	5-N	11-W
" "	**26**	7	Tallahassee	4-N	9-W
" "	**12**	1	Tallahassee	6-N	9-W
CLAY	**26**	2	Tallahassee	4-N	9-W
CLEMENTS	**3**	5	Tallahassee	7-N	11-W
" "	**24**	4	Tallahassee	4-N	11-W
" "	**2**	4	Tallahassee	7-N	12-W
" "	**10**	3	Tallahassee	6-N	11-W
" "	**26**	2	Tallahassee	4-N	9-W
" "	**19**	2	Tallahassee	5-N	10-W
" "	**20**	1	Tallahassee	5-N	9-W
" "	**11**	1	Tallahassee	6-N	10-W
" "	**9**	1	Tallahassee	6-N	12-W
CLEMMONS	**25**	1	Tallahassee	4-N	10-W
CLOUD	**21**	8	Tallahassee	5-N	8-W
" "	**27**	3	Tallahassee	4-N	8-W
" "	**13**	1	Tallahassee	6-N	8-W
CO	**19**	4	Tallahassee	5-N	10-W
" "	**18**	2	Tallahassee	5-N	11-W
" "	**17**	1	Tallahassee	5-N	12-W
" "	**10**	1	Tallahassee	6-N	11-W
" "	**9**	1	Tallahassee	6-N	12-W
COBB	**21**	5	Tallahassee	5-N	8-W
" "	**20**	1	Tallahassee	5-N	9-W
COE	**11**	4	Tallahassee	6-N	10-W
" "	**35**	3	Tallahassee	3-N	7-W
" "	**36**	1	Tallahassee	3-N	6-W
COGBURN	**30**	3	Tallahassee	3-N	12-W
" "	**24**	1	Tallahassee	4-N	11-W
COKER	**13**	2	Tallahassee	6-N	8-W
" "	**25**	1	Tallahassee	4-N	10-W
COLBERT	**24**	2	Tallahassee	4-N	11-W
COLEMAN	**25**	1	Tallahassee	4-N	10-W
" "	**6**	1	Tallahassee	7-N	8-W
COLLINS	**5**	12	Tallahassee	7-N	9-W
" "	**27**	4	Tallahassee	4-N	8-W
" "	**4**	3	Tallahassee	7-N	10-W
" "	**24**	2	Tallahassee	4-N	11-W
" "	**15**	2	Tallahassee	5-N	14-W
" "	**8**	2	Tallahassee	6-N	13-W
COMERFORD	**26**	6	Tallahassee	4-N	9-W
" "	**34**	3	Tallahassee	3-N	8-W
" "	**2**	1	Tallahassee	7-N	12-W
COMPTON	**22**	5	Tallahassee	5-N	7-W
CONELLY	**20**	3	Tallahassee	5-N	9-W
CONELY	**20**	1	Tallahassee	5-N	9-W
CONNELL	**25**	1	Tallahassee	4-N	10-W

Surname	Map Group	Parcels of Land	Meridian/Township/Range		
CONNER	**24**	6	Tallahassee	4-N	11-W
" "	**9**	1	Tallahassee	6-N	12-W
CONRAD	**5**	2	Tallahassee	7-N	9-W
CONROD	**5**	2	Tallahassee	7-N	9-W
COOK	**12**	11	Tallahassee	6-N	9-W
" "	**33**	6	Tallahassee	3-N	9-W
" "	**34**	5	Tallahassee	3-N	8-W
" "	**26**	3	Tallahassee	4-N	9-W
" "	**39**	2	Tallahassee	2-N	10-W
" "	**25**	1	Tallahassee	4-N	10-W
" "	**19**	1	Tallahassee	5-N	10-W
" "	**21**	1	Tallahassee	5-N	8-W
" "	**13**	1	Tallahassee	6-N	8-W
COOLEY	**25**	1	Tallahassee	4-N	10-W
" "	**16**	1	Tallahassee	5-N	13-W
COONROD	**5**	10	Tallahassee	7-N	9-W
COOPER	**11**	2	Tallahassee	6-N	10-W
CORBIN	**23**	4	Tallahassee	4-N	12-W
CORBITT	**14**	1	Tallahassee	6-N	7-W
CORLEY	**11**	1	Tallahassee	6-N	10-W
CORNISH	**9**	1	Tallahassee	6-N	12-W
CORTNEY	**23**	2	Tallahassee	4-N	12-W
COTTON	**24**	1	Tallahassee	4-N	11-W
COULLIETTE	**33**	2	Tallahassee	3-N	9-W
COULTER	**21**	1	Tallahassee	5-N	8-W
COURTNEY	**8**	1	Tallahassee	6-N	13-W
COWAN	**35**	1	Tallahassee	3-N	7-W
COWARD	**25**	1	Tallahassee	4-N	10-W
COWART	**10**	1	Tallahassee	6-N	11-W
COX	**35**	8	Tallahassee	3-N	7-W
" "	**13**	5	Tallahassee	6-N	8-W
" "	**28**	4	Tallahassee	4-N	7-W
" "	**17**	1	Tallahassee	5-N	12-W
COXWELL	**34**	1	Tallahassee	3-N	8-W
CRAWFORD	**9**	1	Tallahassee	6-N	12-W
CREAMER	**23**	2	Tallahassee	4-N	12-W
CREMER	**23**	1	Tallahassee	4-N	12-W
CROUCH	**34**	1	Tallahassee	3-N	8-W
CROWELL	**27**	1	Tallahassee	4-N	8-W
CRUTCHFIELD	**8**	10	Tallahassee	6-N	13-W
CULPEPPER	**35**	1	Tallahassee	3-N	7-W
CULVER	**13**	3	Tallahassee	6-N	8-W
CUNNINGAME	**34**	1	Tallahassee	3-N	8-W
CURRY	**31**	2	Tallahassee	3-N	11-W
CUSHING	**8**	1	Tallahassee	6-N	13-W
CUTCHIN	**23**	2	Tallahassee	4-N	12-W
" "	**26**	1	Tallahassee	4-N	9-W
DABBADGE	**11**	1	Tallahassee	6-N	10-W
DALTON	**28**	1	Tallahassee	4-N	7-W
DANFORD	**8**	3	Tallahassee	6-N	13-W
DANIEL	**10**	6	Tallahassee	6-N	11-W
" "	**37**	5	Tallahassee	2-N	12-W
" "	**38**	3	Tallahassee	2-N	11-W
" "	**27**	2	Tallahassee	4-N	8-W
" "	**13**	2	Tallahassee	6-N	8-W
" "	**3**	2	Tallahassee	7-N	11-W
" "	**2**	1	Tallahassee	7-N	12-W
DANIELS	**31**	1	Tallahassee	3-N	11-W
DARDEN	**31**	1	Tallahassee	3-N	11-W
DAUGHERTY	**27**	1	Tallahassee	4-N	8-W

Surname	Map Group	Parcels of Land	Meridian/Township/Range		
DAUGHTRY	**27**	2	Tallahassee	4-N	8-W
DAVIDSON	**34**	2	Tallahassee	3-N	8-W
" "	**24**	1	Tallahassee	4-N	11-W
" "	**18**	1	Tallahassee	5-N	11-W
DAVIS	**6**	8	Tallahassee	7-N	8-W
" "	**34**	3	Tallahassee	3-N	8-W
" "	**25**	3	Tallahassee	4-N	10-W
" "	**1**	3	Tallahassee	7-N	13-W
" "	**23**	2	Tallahassee	4-N	12-W
" "	**26**	2	Tallahassee	4-N	9-W
" "	**33**	1	Tallahassee	3-N	9-W
" "	**16**	1	Tallahassee	5-N	13-W
" "	**21**	1	Tallahassee	5-N	8-W
" "	**8**	1	Tallahassee	6-N	13-W
DAWSON	**10**	2	Tallahassee	6-N	11-W
" "	**33**	1	Tallahassee	3-N	9-W
DAY	**13**	2	Tallahassee	6-N	8-W
" "	**26**	1	Tallahassee	4-N	9-W
DEKLE	**37**	4	Tallahassee	2-N	12-W
" "	**38**	3	Tallahassee	2-N	11-W
" "	**11**	3	Tallahassee	6-N	10-W
" "	**4**	2	Tallahassee	7-N	10-W
" "	**17**	1	Tallahassee	5-N	12-W
DELOACH	**1**	1	Tallahassee	7-N	13-W
DEMONT	**35**	2	Tallahassee	3-N	7-W
DENHAM	**9**	2	Tallahassee	6-N	12-W
" "	**17**	1	Tallahassee	5-N	12-W
DICKENS	**24**	2	Tallahassee	4-N	11-W
" "	**26**	2	Tallahassee	4-N	9-W
" "	**25**	1	Tallahassee	4-N	10-W
DICKERSON	**31**	1	Tallahassee	3-N	11-W
" "	**20**	1	Tallahassee	5-N	9-W
DICKEY	**25**	2	Tallahassee	4-N	10-W
DICKINSON	**13**	2	Tallahassee	6-N	8-W
" "	**20**	1	Tallahassee	5-N	9-W
DICKSON	**20**	8	Tallahassee	5-N	9-W
" "	**13**	6	Tallahassee	6-N	8-W
" "	**12**	4	Tallahassee	6-N	9-W
" "	**33**	3	Tallahassee	3-N	9-W
" "	**28**	3	Tallahassee	4-N	7-W
" "	**34**	1	Tallahassee	3-N	8-W
" "	**25**	1	Tallahassee	4-N	10-W
" "	**18**	1	Tallahassee	5-N	11-W
DILLMORE	**23**	4	Tallahassee	4-N	12-W
DIVINE	**10**	1	Tallahassee	6-N	11-W
DOLTON	**27**	2	Tallahassee	4-N	8-W
" "	**28**	1	Tallahassee	4-N	7-W
DONALD	**9**	5	Tallahassee	6-N	12-W
" "	**2**	2	Tallahassee	7-N	12-W
DORSON	**5**	3	Tallahassee	7-N	9-W
DOUGHTERY	**1**	1	Tallahassee	7-N	13-W
DOUGHTRY	**35**	2	Tallahassee	3-N	7-W
DOWLING	**24**	1	Tallahassee	4-N	11-W
DOZIER	**12**	1	Tallahassee	6-N	9-W
DRAKE	**17**	4	Tallahassee	5-N	12-W
" "	**19**	2	Tallahassee	5-N	10-W
" "	**25**	1	Tallahassee	4-N	10-W
" "	**10**	1	Tallahassee	6-N	11-W
DUBOSE	**18**	1	Tallahassee	5-N	11-W
DUDLEY	**34**	4	Tallahassee	3-N	8-W

Surname	Map Group	Parcels of Land	Meridian/Township/Range		
DUDLEY (Cont'd)	**19**	1	Tallahassee	5-N	10-W
" "	**14**	1	Tallahassee	6-N	7-W
" "	**13**	1	Tallahassee	6-N	8-W
DUKES	**35**	2	Tallahassee	3-N	7-W
DUNCAN	**9**	3	Tallahassee	6-N	12-W
" "	**8**	3	Tallahassee	6-N	13-W
" "	**31**	2	Tallahassee	3-N	11-W
DUNHAM	**32**	1	Tallahassee	3-N	10-W
DUNLAP	**28**	5	Tallahassee	4-N	7-W
DURDEN	**34**	4	Tallahassee	3-N	8-W
" "	**33**	1	Tallahassee	3-N	9-W
DURHAM	**33**	5	Tallahassee	3-N	9-W
" "	**25**	5	Tallahassee	4-N	10-W
" "	**20**	1	Tallahassee	5-N	9-W
DYKES	**34**	5	Tallahassee	3-N	8-W
" "	**27**	3	Tallahassee	4-N	8-W
" "	**25**	2	Tallahassee	4-N	10-W
" "	**35**	1	Tallahassee	3-N	7-W
" "	**26**	1	Tallahassee	4-N	9-W
EAGLE	**32**	1	Tallahassee	3-N	10-W
EDENFIELD	**34**	6	Tallahassee	3-N	8-W
" "	**27**	3	Tallahassee	4-N	8-W
EDWARDS	**20**	12	Tallahassee	5-N	9-W
" "	**26**	2	Tallahassee	4-N	9-W
" "	**27**	1	Tallahassee	4-N	8-W
ELDRIDGE	**23**	3	Tallahassee	4-N	12-W
" "	**17**	1	Tallahassee	5-N	12-W
ELLIS	**31**	3	Tallahassee	3-N	11-W
" "	**35**	1	Tallahassee	3-N	7-W
ELMORE	**9**	2	Tallahassee	6-N	12-W
" "	**8**	2	Tallahassee	6-N	13-W
" "	**15**	1	Tallahassee	5-N	14-W
EMANUEL	**26**	1	Tallahassee	4-N	9-W
EMBREY	**21**	1	Tallahassee	5-N	8-W
" "	**20**	1	Tallahassee	5-N	9-W
ERWIN	**13**	4	Tallahassee	6-N	8-W
EVERITT	**1**	2	Tallahassee	7-N	13-W
" "	**24**	1	Tallahassee	4-N	11-W
FAIRCLOTH	**28**	3	Tallahassee	4-N	7-W
FAISON	**32**	1	Tallahassee	3-N	10-W
FARMER	**38**	1	Tallahassee	2-N	11-W
FARR	**25**	1	Tallahassee	4-N	10-W
" "	**19**	1	Tallahassee	5-N	10-W
FAUST	**36**	1	Tallahassee	3-N	6-W
FENNEL	**31**	1	Tallahassee	3-N	11-W
" "	**30**	1	Tallahassee	3-N	12-W
FERGUSON	**5**	3	Tallahassee	7-N	9-W
" "	**11**	1	Tallahassee	6-N	10-W
FILLMAN	**23**	1	Tallahassee	4-N	12-W
FINCH	**37**	1	Tallahassee	2-N	12-W
FINLAYSON	**19**	1	Tallahassee	5-N	10-W
FINLEY	**32**	3	Tallahassee	3-N	10-W
FLETCHER	**19**	1	Tallahassee	5-N	10-W
FLORIDA	**11**	2	Tallahassee	6-N	10-W
" "	**37**	1	Tallahassee	2-N	12-W
" "	**23**	1	Tallahassee	4-N	12-W
FLOYD	**11**	6	Tallahassee	6-N	10-W
" "	**34**	1	Tallahassee	3-N	8-W
FOLSOM	**33**	6	Tallahassee	3-N	9-W
" "	**25**	5	Tallahassee	4-N	10-W

Surname	Map Group	Parcels of Land	Meridian/Township/Range		
FOLSOME	**33**	1	Tallahassee	3-N	9-W
FORAN	**31**	2	Tallahassee	3-N	11-W
FORD	**13**	1	Tallahassee	6-N	8-W
FOREHAND	**8**	8	Tallahassee	6-N	13-W
FOREST	**4**	1	Tallahassee	7-N	10-W
FORT	**19**	4	Tallahassee	5-N	10-W
" "	**2**	1	Tallahassee	7-N	12-W
FORTUNE	**19**	13	Tallahassee	5-N	10-W
" "	**25**	1	Tallahassee	4-N	10-W
FOSCUE	**10**	7	Tallahassee	6-N	11-W
" "	**34**	2	Tallahassee	3-N	8-W
" "	**17**	2	Tallahassee	5-N	12-W
" "	**9**	1	Tallahassee	6-N	12-W
FOSTER	**9**	3	Tallahassee	6-N	12-W
FOULK	**13**	5	Tallahassee	6-N	8-W
FOUNTAIN	**1**	1	Tallahassee	7-N	13-W
FOWLE	**25**	1	Tallahassee	4-N	10-W
FOWLER	**15**	5	Tallahassee	5-N	14-W
" "	**2**	1	Tallahassee	7-N	12-W
FOXWORTH	**31**	1	Tallahassee	3-N	11-W
FRANCIS	**35**	1	Tallahassee	3-N	7-W
" "	**34**	1	Tallahassee	3-N	8-W
FRANKLIN	**8**	3	Tallahassee	6-N	13-W
" "	**13**	2	Tallahassee	6-N	8-W
FREEMAN	**38**	3	Tallahassee	2-N	11-W
" "	**34**	3	Tallahassee	3-N	8-W
" "	**31**	1	Tallahassee	3-N	11-W
" "	**28**	1	Tallahassee	4-N	7-W
FULGHAM	**27**	5	Tallahassee	4-N	8-W
" "	**21**	2	Tallahassee	5-N	8-W
FULLERTON	**12**	4	Tallahassee	6-N	9-W
GABLE	**33**	4	Tallahassee	3-N	9-W
" "	**34**	3	Tallahassee	3-N	8-W
GAFF	**24**	1	Tallahassee	4-N	11-W
GAINER	**1**	2	Tallahassee	7-N	13-W
" "	**31**	1	Tallahassee	3-N	11-W
" "	**2**	1	Tallahassee	7-N	12-W
GAKRINS	**24**	3	Tallahassee	4-N	11-W
GALLAWAY	**10**	1	Tallahassee	6-N	11-W
GAMBLE	**10**	6	Tallahassee	6-N	11-W
GARBETT	**13**	2	Tallahassee	6-N	8-W
GARDNER	**13**	1	Tallahassee	6-N	8-W
GARNER	**27**	3	Tallahassee	4-N	8-W
GARRETT	**29**	2	Tallahassee	4-N	6-W
" "	**11**	1	Tallahassee	6-N	10-W
GAUTIER	**25**	4	Tallahassee	4-N	10-W
" "	**19**	4	Tallahassee	5-N	10-W
GAY	**24**	8	Tallahassee	4-N	11-W
" "	**30**	4	Tallahassee	3-N	12-W
" "	**39**	3	Tallahassee	2-N	10-W
" "	**33**	3	Tallahassee	3-N	9-W
" "	**32**	2	Tallahassee	3-N	10-W
" "	**23**	2	Tallahassee	4-N	12-W
GEE	**36**	4	Tallahassee	3-N	6-W
GILBERT	**23**	4	Tallahassee	4-N	12-W
" "	**17**	2	Tallahassee	5-N	12-W
" "	**25**	1	Tallahassee	4-N	10-W
" "	**24**	1	Tallahassee	4-N	11-W
GILCHRIST	**33**	3	Tallahassee	3-N	9-W
" "	**6**	3	Tallahassee	7-N	8-W

Surname	Map Group	Parcels of Land	Meridian/Township/Range		
GILCHRIST (Cont'd)	**32**	2	Tallahassee	3-N	10-W
" "	**25**	2	Tallahassee	4-N	10-W
" "	**24**	2	Tallahassee	4-N	11-W
" "	**19**	2	Tallahassee	5-N	10-W
" "	**17**	1	Tallahassee	5-N	12-W
" "	**10**	1	Tallahassee	6-N	11-W
" "	**9**	1	Tallahassee	6-N	12-W
GILES	**12**	8	Tallahassee	6-N	9-W
GILLIS	**39**	1	Tallahassee	2-N	10-W
GILLSTROP	**9**	1	Tallahassee	6-N	12-W
GILMER	**17**	10	Tallahassee	5-N	12-W
GILSTRAP	**9**	1	Tallahassee	6-N	12-W
GLADDEN	**5**	4	Tallahassee	7-N	9-W
" "	**12**	2	Tallahassee	6-N	9-W
GLASS	**30**	2	Tallahassee	3-N	12-W
" "	**9**	2	Tallahassee	6-N	12-W
GLISSON	**13**	7	Tallahassee	6-N	8-W
GLOVER	**12**	2	Tallahassee	6-N	9-W
GODFREY	**25**	1	Tallahassee	4-N	10-W
GODWIN	**13**	8	Tallahassee	6-N	8-W
" "	**12**	4	Tallahassee	6-N	9-W
" "	**17**	2	Tallahassee	5-N	12-W
" "	**27**	1	Tallahassee	4-N	8-W
" "	**1**	1	Tallahassee	7-N	13-W
GOFF	**24**	2	Tallahassee	4-N	11-W
" "	**26**	1	Tallahassee	4-N	9-W
" "	**18**	1	Tallahassee	5-N	11-W
" "	**13**	1	Tallahassee	6-N	8-W
GOLDEN	**8**	7	Tallahassee	6-N	13-W
GOLDING	**8**	1	Tallahassee	6-N	13-W
GOODWIN	**24**	2	Tallahassee	4-N	11-W
" "	**9**	1	Tallahassee	6-N	12-W
GORDY	**34**	1	Tallahassee	3-N	8-W
GORMAN	**28**	3	Tallahassee	4-N	7-W
GOTAIR	**31**	1	Tallahassee	3-N	11-W
GOTIER	**19**	1	Tallahassee	5-N	10-W
GRACE	**1**	4	Tallahassee	7-N	13-W
" "	**22**	1	Tallahassee	5-N	7-W
GRAINGER	**4**	3	Tallahassee	7-N	10-W
" "	**10**	1	Tallahassee	6-N	11-W
GRANBERRY	**20**	1	Tallahassee	5-N	9-W
" "	**12**	1	Tallahassee	6-N	9-W
GRANGER	**4**	3	Tallahassee	7-N	10-W
" "	**3**	2	Tallahassee	7-N	11-W
" "	**22**	1	Tallahassee	5-N	7-W
GRANT	**8**	5	Tallahassee	6-N	13-W
" "	**21**	3	Tallahassee	5-N	8-W
" "	**26**	2	Tallahassee	4-N	9-W
GRANTHAM	**38**	1	Tallahassee	2-N	11-W
" "	**26**	1	Tallahassee	4-N	9-W
" "	**5**	1	Tallahassee	7-N	9-W
GRANTLAND	**35**	8	Tallahassee	3-N	7-W
" "	**25**	1	Tallahassee	4-N	10-W
" "	**6**	1	Tallahassee	7-N	8-W
GRAVES	**20**	1	Tallahassee	5-N	9-W
GRAY	**21**	2	Tallahassee	5-N	8-W
" "	**12**	2	Tallahassee	6-N	9-W
" "	**28**	1	Tallahassee	4-N	7-W
GREEN	**9**	2	Tallahassee	6-N	12-W
" "	**21**	1	Tallahassee	5-N	8-W

Surname	Map Group	Parcels of Land	Meridian/Township/Range		
GRICE	**5**	1	Tallahassee	7-N	9-W
GRIFFIN	**13**	5	Tallahassee	6-N	8-W
" "	**35**	4	Tallahassee	3-N	7-W
" "	**24**	2	Tallahassee	4-N	11-W
" "	**6**	2	Tallahassee	7-N	8-W
" "	**11**	1	Tallahassee	6-N	10-W
GRIMESLEY	**13**	3	Tallahassee	6-N	8-W
GRIMSLEY	**28**	4	Tallahassee	4-N	7-W
GRISSETT	**30**	3	Tallahassee	3-N	12-W
" "	**27**	1	Tallahassee	4-N	8-W
GRUBB	**27**	2	Tallahassee	4-N	8-W
GRUBBS	**27**	1	Tallahassee	4-N	8-W
" "	**26**	1	Tallahassee	4-N	9-W
GUATIER	**19**	1	Tallahassee	5-N	10-W
GUNDERSON	**26**	2	Tallahassee	4-N	9-W
HADDOCK	**30**	1	Tallahassee	3-N	12-W
HAGAN	**33**	3	Tallahassee	3-N	9-W
HAIR	**34**	2	Tallahassee	3-N	8-W
" "	**28**	2	Tallahassee	4-N	7-W
" "	**22**	1	Tallahassee	5-N	7-W
HAIRE	**27**	2	Tallahassee	4-N	8-W
HALEY	**9**	2	Tallahassee	6-N	12-W
HALL	**4**	8	Tallahassee	7-N	10-W
" "	**34**	2	Tallahassee	3-N	8-W
" "	**24**	1	Tallahassee	4-N	11-W
" "	**9**	1	Tallahassee	6-N	12-W
HAM	**35**	2	Tallahassee	3-N	7-W
HAMILTON	**27**	11	Tallahassee	4-N	8-W
" "	**21**	7	Tallahassee	5-N	8-W
" "	**22**	3	Tallahassee	5-N	7-W
" "	**11**	3	Tallahassee	6-N	10-W
" "	**2**	2	Tallahassee	7-N	12-W
" "	**10**	1	Tallahassee	6-N	11-W
HAND	**5**	3	Tallahassee	7-N	9-W
" "	**39**	1	Tallahassee	2-N	10-W
" "	**13**	1	Tallahassee	6-N	8-W
HANSFORD	**34**	5	Tallahassee	3-N	8-W
" "	**33**	1	Tallahassee	3-N	9-W
HARDEN	**8**	4	Tallahassee	6-N	13-W
" "	**5**	4	Tallahassee	7-N	9-W
HARDIN	**19**	8	Tallahassee	5-N	10-W
" "	**5**	6	Tallahassee	7-N	9-W
HARE	**22**	2	Tallahassee	5-N	7-W
HARGROVE	**13**	1	Tallahassee	6-N	8-W
HARPER	**3**	4	Tallahassee	7-N	11-W
" "	**24**	3	Tallahassee	4-N	11-W
" "	**27**	3	Tallahassee	4-N	8-W
" "	**8**	3	Tallahassee	6-N	13-W
" "	**4**	2	Tallahassee	7-N	10-W
" "	**28**	1	Tallahassee	4-N	7-W
" "	**21**	1	Tallahassee	5-N	8-W
HARRELL	**8**	5	Tallahassee	6-N	13-W
" "	**17**	1	Tallahassee	5-N	12-W
HART	**4**	3	Tallahassee	7-N	10-W
" "	**5**	3	Tallahassee	7-N	9-W
HARTSFIELD	**20**	2	Tallahassee	5-N	9-W
HARVEY	**13**	6	Tallahassee	6-N	8-W
" "	**20**	4	Tallahassee	5-N	9-W
" "	**19**	2	Tallahassee	5-N	10-W
" "	**25**	1	Tallahassee	4-N	10-W

Surname	Map Group	Parcels of Land	Meridian/Township/Range		
HATCHER	**28**	3	Tallahassee	4-N	7-W
" "	**21**	1	Tallahassee	5-N	8-W
HATHAWAY	**26**	4	Tallahassee	4-N	9-W
HATTON	**11**	2	Tallahassee	6-N	10-W
HAWKINS	**25**	1	Tallahassee	4-N	10-W
HAYES	**17**	3	Tallahassee	5-N	12-W
HAYNES	**25**	3	Tallahassee	4-N	10-W
" "	**32**	1	Tallahassee	3-N	10-W
HAYS	**11**	2	Tallahassee	6-N	10-W
" "	**9**	2	Tallahassee	6-N	12-W
" "	**2**	2	Tallahassee	7-N	12-W
HAYWOOD	**22**	8	Tallahassee	5-N	7-W
" "	**9**	1	Tallahassee	6-N	12-W
HEARIN	**2**	2	Tallahassee	7-N	12-W
HEARN	**12**	7	Tallahassee	6-N	9-W
" "	**20**	1	Tallahassee	5-N	9-W
HEATH	**34**	1	Tallahassee	3-N	8-W
HEISLER	**8**	2	Tallahassee	6-N	13-W
HELMES	**6**	1	Tallahassee	7-N	8-W
HENDRIX	**9**	3	Tallahassee	6-N	12-W
HENRY	**28**	1	Tallahassee	4-N	7-W
HERNDON	**34**	1	Tallahassee	3-N	8-W
HERRING	**2**	3	Tallahassee	7-N	12-W
" "	**33**	1	Tallahassee	3-N	9-W
HEWETT	**21**	3	Tallahassee	5-N	8-W
" "	**35**	2	Tallahassee	3-N	7-W
" "	**28**	2	Tallahassee	4-N	7-W
" "	**27**	1	Tallahassee	4-N	8-W
HICKMAN	**34**	1	Tallahassee	3-N	8-W
HICKS	**16**	3	Tallahassee	5-N	13-W
" "	**8**	2	Tallahassee	6-N	13-W
HILL	**27**	6	Tallahassee	4-N	8-W
" "	**26**	4	Tallahassee	4-N	9-W
" "	**31**	2	Tallahassee	3-N	11-W
" "	**8**	2	Tallahassee	6-N	13-W
" "	**24**	1	Tallahassee	4-N	11-W
" "	**11**	1	Tallahassee	6-N	10-W
HINSON	**22**	12	Tallahassee	5-N	7-W
" "	**27**	3	Tallahassee	4-N	8-W
" "	**21**	2	Tallahassee	5-N	8-W
" "	**2**	2	Tallahassee	7-N	12-W
HODGES	**26**	4	Tallahassee	4-N	9-W
" "	**17**	1	Tallahassee	5-N	12-W
HODGSON	**28**	14	Tallahassee	4-N	7-W
" "	**27**	2	Tallahassee	4-N	8-W
" "	**20**	1	Tallahassee	5-N	9-W
HOGG	**9**	4	Tallahassee	6-N	12-W
" "	**17**	2	Tallahassee	5-N	12-W
" "	**18**	1	Tallahassee	5-N	11-W
HOLDEN	**8**	3	Tallahassee	6-N	13-W
HOLDER	**20**	2	Tallahassee	5-N	9-W
" "	**12**	1	Tallahassee	6-N	9-W
HOLLAND	**10**	2	Tallahassee	6-N	11-W
HOLLEY	**23**	1	Tallahassee	4-N	12-W
HOLLIDAY	**38**	1	Tallahassee	2-N	11-W
HOLLIMAN	**39**	1	Tallahassee	2-N	10-W
HOLLINGSWORTH	**12**	1	Tallahassee	6-N	9-W
HOLMES	**31**	3	Tallahassee	3-N	11-W
" "	**34**	2	Tallahassee	3-N	8-W
" "	**35**	1	Tallahassee	3-N	7-W

Surname	Map Group	Parcels of Land	Meridian/Township/Range		
HOLMES (Cont'd)	**24**	1	Tallahassee	4-N	11-W
" "	**9**	1	Tallahassee	6-N	12-W
" "	**13**	1	Tallahassee	6-N	8-W
HOOTEN	**2**	1	Tallahassee	7-N	12-W
HOPSON	**19**	1	Tallahassee	5-N	10-W
HORN	**26**	1	Tallahassee	4-N	9-W
HORNE	**19**	2	Tallahassee	5-N	10-W
HORT	**19**	1	Tallahassee	5-N	10-W
HOUGH	**16**	3	Tallahassee	5-N	13-W
HOVEY	**30**	2	Tallahassee	3-N	12-W
HOWARD	**3**	5	Tallahassee	7-N	11-W
" "	**31**	3	Tallahassee	3-N	11-W
" "	**32**	2	Tallahassee	3-N	10-W
" "	**33**	2	Tallahassee	3-N	9-W
" "	**25**	2	Tallahassee	4-N	10-W
" "	**24**	2	Tallahassee	4-N	11-W
" "	**2**	1	Tallahassee	7-N	12-W
" "	**5**	1	Tallahassee	7-N	9-W
HOWEL	**10**	1	Tallahassee	6-N	11-W
HOWELL	**31**	1	Tallahassee	3-N	11-W
" "	**25**	1	Tallahassee	4-N	10-W
" "	**28**	1	Tallahassee	4-N	7-W
HUBBARD	**28**	2	Tallahassee	4-N	7-W
HUDSON	**2**	1	Tallahassee	7-N	12-W
HUFF	**16**	3	Tallahassee	5-N	13-W
HUGHES	**33**	3	Tallahassee	3-N	9-W
" "	**16**	1	Tallahassee	5-N	13-W
" "	**8**	1	Tallahassee	6-N	13-W
HULL	**18**	2	Tallahassee	5-N	11-W
HUNTER	**25**	1	Tallahassee	4-N	10-W
" "	**19**	1	Tallahassee	5-N	10-W
HURST	**11**	3	Tallahassee	6-N	10-W
" "	**25**	1	Tallahassee	4-N	10-W
HUTSON	**9**	1	Tallahassee	6-N	12-W
HYATT	**12**	1	Tallahassee	6-N	9-W
INGRAM	**26**	1	Tallahassee	4-N	9-W
" "	**3**	1	Tallahassee	7-N	11-W
IRVIN	**6**	1	Tallahassee	7-N	8-W
IRWIN	**6**	13	Tallahassee	7-N	8-W
" "	**5**	3	Tallahassee	7-N	9-W
" "	**34**	2	Tallahassee	3-N	8-W
JACKSON	**21**	5	Tallahassee	5-N	8-W
" "	**18**	3	Tallahassee	5-N	11-W
" "	**1**	3	Tallahassee	7-N	13-W
" "	**31**	2	Tallahassee	3-N	11-W
" "	**8**	2	Tallahassee	6-N	13-W
" "	**34**	1	Tallahassee	3-N	8-W
" "	**33**	1	Tallahassee	3-N	9-W
JARDAN	**13**	1	Tallahassee	6-N	8-W
JARRATT	**10**	2	Tallahassee	6-N	11-W
JEMISON	**24**	2	Tallahassee	4-N	11-W
" "	**17**	2	Tallahassee	5-N	12-W
" "	**10**	2	Tallahassee	6-N	11-W
" "	**26**	1	Tallahassee	4-N	9-W
JENKINS	**24**	2	Tallahassee	4-N	11-W
" "	**3**	2	Tallahassee	7-N	11-W
JETER	**27**	5	Tallahassee	4-N	8-W
JOHNSON	**34**	12	Tallahassee	3-N	8-W
" "	**39**	5	Tallahassee	2-N	10-W
" "	**5**	4	Tallahassee	7-N	9-W

Surname	Map Group	Parcels of Land	Meridian/Township/Range		
JOHNSON (Cont'd)	24	3	Tallahassee	4-N	11-W
" "	17	3	Tallahassee	5-N	12-W
" "	6	3	Tallahassee	7-N	8-W
" "	9	2	Tallahassee	6-N	12-W
" "	8	2	Tallahassee	6-N	13-W
" "	35	1	Tallahassee	3-N	7-W
" "	23	1	Tallahassee	4-N	12-W
" "	27	1	Tallahassee	4-N	8-W
JOHNSTON	17	3	Tallahassee	5-N	12-W
" "	9	1	Tallahassee	6-N	12-W
JOINER	25	1	Tallahassee	4-N	10-W
JONES	3	10	Tallahassee	7-N	11-W
" "	26	4	Tallahassee	4-N	9-W
" "	35	3	Tallahassee	3-N	7-W
" "	32	2	Tallahassee	3-N	10-W
" "	24	2	Tallahassee	4-N	11-W
" "	27	2	Tallahassee	4-N	8-W
" "	17	2	Tallahassee	5-N	12-W
" "	9	2	Tallahassee	6-N	12-W
" "	13	2	Tallahassee	6-N	8-W
" "	2	2	Tallahassee	7-N	12-W
" "	31	1	Tallahassee	3-N	11-W
" "	25	1	Tallahassee	4-N	10-W
" "	28	1	Tallahassee	4-N	7-W
" "	21	1	Tallahassee	5-N	8-W
" "	10	1	Tallahassee	6-N	11-W
JORDAN	27	1	Tallahassee	4-N	8-W
" "	8	1	Tallahassee	6-N	13-W
JOWERS	17	1	Tallahassee	5-N	12-W
JUSTICE	9	3	Tallahassee	6-N	12-W
" "	17	1	Tallahassee	5-N	12-W
JUSTISS	21	1	Tallahassee	5-N	8-W
KEEL	33	1	Tallahassee	3-N	9-W
KEISER	17	2	Tallahassee	5-N	12-W
KEITH	19	14	Tallahassee	5-N	10-W
" "	10	3	Tallahassee	6-N	11-W
" "	2	1	Tallahassee	7-N	12-W
KELLEY	13	1	Tallahassee	6-N	8-W
KELLY	13	2	Tallahassee	6-N	8-W
KEMP	28	2	Tallahassee	4-N	7-W
KENT	30	9	Tallahassee	3-N	12-W
" "	34	4	Tallahassee	3-N	8-W
" "	19	3	Tallahassee	5-N	10-W
" "	35	2	Tallahassee	3-N	7-W
" "	24	2	Tallahassee	4-N	11-W
" "	37	1	Tallahassee	2-N	12-W
" "	31	1	Tallahassee	3-N	11-W
" "	23	1	Tallahassee	4-N	12-W
" "	10	1	Tallahassee	6-N	11-W
KETTLEBAND	34	3	Tallahassee	3-N	8-W
KIDD	11	2	Tallahassee	6-N	10-W
" "	13	1	Tallahassee	6-N	8-W
KILBEE	32	5	Tallahassee	3-N	10-W
" "	19	4	Tallahassee	5-N	10-W
" "	25	3	Tallahassee	4-N	10-W
" "	6	2	Tallahassee	7-N	8-W
" "	20	1	Tallahassee	5-N	9-W
" "	11	1	Tallahassee	6-N	10-W
KILCREASE	35	2	Tallahassee	3-N	7-W
" "	21	1	Tallahassee	5-N	8-W

Surname	Map Group	Parcels of Land	Meridian/Township/Range		
KIMBELL	**12**	3	Tallahassee	6-N	9-W
KING	**17**	3	Tallahassee	5-N	12-W
" "	**22**	2	Tallahassee	5-N	7-W
" "	**25**	1	Tallahassee	4-N	10-W
" "	**24**	1	Tallahassee	4-N	11-W
" "	**27**	1	Tallahassee	4-N	8-W
KINGRY	**4**	1	Tallahassee	7-N	10-W
KINGSLEY	**33**	1	Tallahassee	3-N	9-W
KIRKLAND	**8**	3	Tallahassee	6-N	13-W
" "	**1**	2	Tallahassee	7-N	13-W
" "	**27**	1	Tallahassee	4-N	8-W
" "	**17**	1	Tallahassee	5-N	12-W
KNAPP	**11**	4	Tallahassee	6-N	10-W
KNIGHT	**39**	1	Tallahassee	2-N	10-W
" "	**24**	1	Tallahassee	4-N	11-W
KNOWLES	**21**	2	Tallahassee	5-N	8-W
KOONCE	**22**	1	Tallahassee	5-N	7-W
LAMB	**24**	1	Tallahassee	4-N	11-W
LAMBERT	**17**	1	Tallahassee	5-N	12-W
LANCASTER	**12**	2	Tallahassee	6-N	9-W
LAND	**31**	2	Tallahassee	3-N	11-W
" "	**24**	2	Tallahassee	4-N	11-W
" "	**17**	1	Tallahassee	5-N	12-W
LANE	**34**	2	Tallahassee	3-N	8-W
LANGSTON	**18**	1	Tallahassee	5-N	11-W
LANIER	**35**	1	Tallahassee	3-N	7-W
LARAMORE	**32**	2	Tallahassee	3-N	10-W
LASHLEY	**32**	3	Tallahassee	3-N	10-W
" "	**39**	2	Tallahassee	2-N	10-W
" "	**13**	2	Tallahassee	6-N	8-W
LAWRENCE	**24**	4	Tallahassee	4-N	11-W
LAWSON	**13**	4	Tallahassee	6-N	8-W
LEADBETTER	**16**	2	Tallahassee	5-N	13-W
" "	**35**	1	Tallahassee	3-N	7-W
LEE	**31**	3	Tallahassee	3-N	11-W
" "	**13**	2	Tallahassee	6-N	8-W
" "	**33**	1	Tallahassee	3-N	9-W
" "	**9**	1	Tallahassee	6-N	12-W
LEONARD	**21**	6	Tallahassee	5-N	8-W
" "	**24**	1	Tallahassee	4-N	11-W
LEVEY	**24**	1	Tallahassee	4-N	11-W
LEVY	**17**	2	Tallahassee	5-N	12-W
LEWIS	**29**	6	Tallahassee	4-N	6-W
" "	**21**	5	Tallahassee	5-N	8-W
" "	**24**	2	Tallahassee	4-N	11-W
" "	**19**	2	Tallahassee	5-N	10-W
" "	**31**	1	Tallahassee	3-N	11-W
" "	**18**	1	Tallahassee	5-N	11-W
" "	**20**	1	Tallahassee	5-N	9-W
" "	**11**	1	Tallahassee	6-N	10-W
" "	**9**	1	Tallahassee	6-N	12-W
LIPFORD	**39**	2	Tallahassee	2-N	10-W
" "	**32**	1	Tallahassee	3-N	10-W
" "	**31**	1	Tallahassee	3-N	11-W
LISTER	**10**	1	Tallahassee	6-N	11-W
LITTLETON	**14**	5	Tallahassee	6-N	7-W
" "	**29**	1	Tallahassee	4-N	6-W
LOCKART	**4**	1	Tallahassee	7-N	10-W
" "	**6**	1	Tallahassee	7-N	8-W
LOCKHART	**6**	5	Tallahassee	7-N	8-W

Surname	Map Group	Parcels of Land	Meridian/Township/Range		
LOCKHART (Cont'd)	**4**	1	Tallahassee	7-N	10-W
LOFTIN	**35**	5	Tallahassee	3-N	7-W
" "	**25**	1	Tallahassee	4-N	10-W
LOGAN	**33**	4	Tallahassee	3-N	9-W
LOGATHREE	**11**	1	Tallahassee	6-N	10-W
LONG	**19**	17	Tallahassee	5-N	10-W
" "	**20**	5	Tallahassee	5-N	9-W
" "	**31**	3	Tallahassee	3-N	11-W
" "	**38**	2	Tallahassee	2-N	11-W
" "	**24**	1	Tallahassee	4-N	11-W
" "	**11**	1	Tallahassee	6-N	10-W
" "	**9**	1	Tallahassee	6-N	12-W
LOOPER	**13**	1	Tallahassee	6-N	8-W
LOTT	**11**	8	Tallahassee	6-N	10-W
" "	**25**	1	Tallahassee	4-N	10-W
" "	**19**	1	Tallahassee	5-N	10-W
LOVE	**30**	3	Tallahassee	3-N	12-W
" "	**31**	1	Tallahassee	3-N	11-W
" "	**19**	1	Tallahassee	5-N	10-W
LOVVITT	**13**	2	Tallahassee	6-N	8-W
LOWRY	**4**	21	Tallahassee	7-N	10-W
" "	**11**	1	Tallahassee	6-N	10-W
LYNCH	**9**	2	Tallahassee	6-N	12-W
LYNN	**34**	4	Tallahassee	3-N	8-W
MACK	**35**	1	Tallahassee	3-N	7-W
MADDOX	**32**	9	Tallahassee	3-N	10-W
" "	**39**	8	Tallahassee	2-N	10-W
" "	**20**	5	Tallahassee	5-N	9-W
" "	**25**	1	Tallahassee	4-N	10-W
" "	**3**	1	Tallahassee	7-N	11-W
MADDUX	**20**	2	Tallahassee	5-N	9-W
MALONEY	**22**	3	Tallahassee	5-N	7-W
MALTSBY	**25**	2	Tallahassee	4-N	10-W
MANDELL	**25**	1	Tallahassee	4-N	10-W
" "	**19**	1	Tallahassee	5-N	10-W
MARCHANT	**30**	4	Tallahassee	3-N	12-W
MARSHAL	**2**	2	Tallahassee	7-N	12-W
MARSHALL	**11**	2	Tallahassee	6-N	10-W
" "	**37**	1	Tallahassee	2-N	12-W
" "	**25**	1	Tallahassee	4-N	10-W
" "	**2**	1	Tallahassee	7-N	12-W
MARTIN	**20**	7	Tallahassee	5-N	9-W
" "	**5**	7	Tallahassee	7-N	9-W
" "	**32**	1	Tallahassee	3-N	10-W
" "	**19**	1	Tallahassee	5-N	10-W
" "	**9**	1	Tallahassee	6-N	12-W
" "	**12**	1	Tallahassee	6-N	9-W
" "	**2**	1	Tallahassee	7-N	12-W
MASHBURN	**24**	2	Tallahassee	4-N	11-W
" "	**31**	1	Tallahassee	3-N	11-W
MATHEWS	**4**	4	Tallahassee	7-N	10-W
" "	**35**	2	Tallahassee	3-N	7-W
" "	**9**	2	Tallahassee	6-N	12-W
" "	**12**	2	Tallahassee	6-N	9-W
" "	**20**	1	Tallahassee	5-N	9-W
" "	**8**	1	Tallahassee	6-N	13-W
MATHIS	**27**	2	Tallahassee	4-N	8-W
" "	**35**	1	Tallahassee	3-N	7-W
" "	**17**	1	Tallahassee	5-N	12-W
MATTHEWS	**19**	9	Tallahassee	5-N	10-W

Surname	Map Group	Parcels of Land	Meridian/Township/Range		
MATTHEWS (Cont'd)	**38**	2	Tallahassee	2-N	11-W
" "	**20**	2	Tallahassee	5-N	9-W
" "	**25**	1	Tallahassee	4-N	10-W
MAULDIN	**19**	5	Tallahassee	5-N	10-W
MAWHINNEY	**27**	1	Tallahassee	4-N	8-W
MAY	**33**	2	Tallahassee	3-N	9-W
MAYO	**31**	7	Tallahassee	3-N	11-W
" "	**32**	5	Tallahassee	3-N	10-W
" "	**23**	3	Tallahassee	4-N	12-W
" "	**30**	2	Tallahassee	3-N	12-W
" "	**39**	1	Tallahassee	2-N	10-W
" "	**37**	1	Tallahassee	2-N	12-W
" "	**33**	1	Tallahassee	3-N	9-W
MAYS	**31**	2	Tallahassee	3-N	11-W
MAZLEY	**11**	1	Tallahassee	6-N	10-W
MCANULTY	**5**	10	Tallahassee	7-N	9-W
MCBAIN	**2**	2	Tallahassee	7-N	12-W
MCCARTY	**34**	2	Tallahassee	3-N	8-W
MCCLELAN	**33**	1	Tallahassee	3-N	9-W
MCCLELLAN	**25**	4	Tallahassee	4-N	10-W
MCCORMACK	**31**	2	Tallahassee	3-N	11-W
MCCORMICK	**26**	3	Tallahassee	4-N	9-W
" "	**32**	2	Tallahassee	3-N	10-W
" "	**35**	2	Tallahassee	3-N	7-W
MCCORQUODALE	**35**	2	Tallahassee	3-N	7-W
MCCOY	**34**	1	Tallahassee	3-N	8-W
MCCRARY	**16**	4	Tallahassee	5-N	13-W
" "	**9**	3	Tallahassee	6-N	12-W
" "	**28**	1	Tallahassee	4-N	7-W
MCCREARY	**8**	1	Tallahassee	6-N	13-W
MCCROAN	**26**	1	Tallahassee	4-N	9-W
MCCULLOH	**29**	1	Tallahassee	4-N	6-W
MCDANIEL	**9**	15	Tallahassee	6-N	12-W
" "	**11**	13	Tallahassee	6-N	10-W
" "	**17**	6	Tallahassee	5-N	12-W
" "	**4**	2	Tallahassee	7-N	10-W
MCDONALD	**35**	3	Tallahassee	3-N	7-W
" "	**21**	1	Tallahassee	5-N	8-W
" "	**6**	1	Tallahassee	7-N	8-W
MCFARLAND	**27**	2	Tallahassee	4-N	8-W
MCGEE	**13**	2	Tallahassee	6-N	8-W
" "	**6**	1	Tallahassee	7-N	8-W
MCGUIRE	**24**	4	Tallahassee	4-N	11-W
MCINTOSH	**8**	1	Tallahassee	6-N	13-W
MCKAY	**5**	6	Tallahassee	7-N	9-W
" "	**9**	2	Tallahassee	6-N	12-W
MCKEOWN	**28**	2	Tallahassee	4-N	7-W
MCKINNE	**37**	4	Tallahassee	2-N	12-W
" "	**38**	3	Tallahassee	2-N	11-W
" "	**8**	2	Tallahassee	6-N	13-W
" "	**18**	1	Tallahassee	5-N	11-W
MCLAIN	**30**	1	Tallahassee	3-N	12-W
MCLANE	**27**	1	Tallahassee	4-N	8-W
MCLELLAN	**33**	1	Tallahassee	3-N	9-W
MCLENDON	**1**	2	Tallahassee	7-N	13-W
" "	**31**	1	Tallahassee	3-N	11-W
MCLEOD	**27**	3	Tallahassee	4-N	8-W
MCLEROY	**20**	2	Tallahassee	5-N	9-W
MCLEVY	**24**	1	Tallahassee	4-N	11-W
MCMILLAN	**4**	7	Tallahassee	7-N	10-W

Surname	Map Group	Parcels of Land	Meridian/Township/Range		
MCMILLAN (Cont'd)	**34**	1	Tallahassee	3-N	8-W
" "	**28**	1	Tallahassee	4-N	7-W
" "	**27**	1	Tallahassee	4-N	8-W
MCMULLEN	**27**	3	Tallahassee	4-N	8-W
" "	**25**	1	Tallahassee	4-N	10-W
MCMULLIAN	**27**	1	Tallahassee	4-N	8-W
MCNEALEY	**11**	1	Tallahassee	6-N	10-W
MCNEALLY	**11**	3	Tallahassee	6-N	10-W
MCNEALY	**11**	19	Tallahassee	6-N	10-W
" "	**32**	1	Tallahassee	3-N	10-W
" "	**26**	1	Tallahassee	4-N	9-W
MCNEELY	**11**	2	Tallahassee	6-N	10-W
MCNEILLY	**11**	1	Tallahassee	6-N	10-W
MCPARLAND	**26**	1	Tallahassee	4-N	9-W
MCQUAGE	**25**	1	Tallahassee	4-N	10-W
MCQUAGGE	**25**	5	Tallahassee	4-N	10-W
" "	**17**	2	Tallahassee	5-N	12-W
MCQUAIG	**25**	1	Tallahassee	4-N	10-W
MCQUEEN	**38**	1	Tallahassee	2-N	11-W
MCRAE	**38**	2	Tallahassee	2-N	11-W
MEARS	**33**	7	Tallahassee	3-N	9-W
" "	**34**	5	Tallahassee	3-N	8-W
MEDLOACK	**32**	1	Tallahassee	3-N	10-W
MEDLOCK	**38**	3	Tallahassee	2-N	11-W
MELVIN	**23**	4	Tallahassee	4-N	12-W
" "	**30**	2	Tallahassee	3-N	12-W
MENDHEIM	**7**	1	Tallahassee	6-N	14-W
MERCER	**12**	11	Tallahassee	6-N	9-W
" "	**26**	3	Tallahassee	4-N	9-W
" "	**20**	2	Tallahassee	5-N	9-W
" "	**34**	1	Tallahassee	3-N	8-W
" "	**25**	1	Tallahassee	4-N	10-W
" "	**27**	1	Tallahassee	4-N	8-W
MERRETT	**33**	1	Tallahassee	3-N	9-W
MERRITT	**25**	6	Tallahassee	4-N	10-W
" "	**9**	3	Tallahassee	6-N	12-W
" "	**26**	1	Tallahassee	4-N	9-W
MESSER	**21**	1	Tallahassee	5-N	8-W
MICH	**30**	1	Tallahassee	3-N	12-W
MICHAUX	**20**	4	Tallahassee	5-N	9-W
MILES	**9**	5	Tallahassee	6-N	12-W
" "	**17**	1	Tallahassee	5-N	12-W
" "	**8**	1	Tallahassee	6-N	13-W
MILLAR	**9**	1	Tallahassee	6-N	12-W
MILLER	**8**	11	Tallahassee	6-N	13-W
" "	**26**	1	Tallahassee	4-N	9-W
" "	**10**	1	Tallahassee	6-N	11-W
" "	**1**	1	Tallahassee	7-N	13-W
MILLS	**13**	3	Tallahassee	6-N	8-W
" "	**20**	2	Tallahassee	5-N	9-W
" "	**35**	1	Tallahassee	3-N	7-W
MILTON	**26**	8	Tallahassee	4-N	9-W
" "	**20**	8	Tallahassee	5-N	9-W
" "	**40**	1	Tallahassee	2-N	9-W
MINCHIN	**12**	2	Tallahassee	6-N	9-W
" "	**5**	1	Tallahassee	7-N	9-W
MING	**26**	9	Tallahassee	4-N	9-W
" "	**25**	1	Tallahassee	4-N	10-W
MITCHELL	**21**	4	Tallahassee	5-N	8-W
" "	**28**	3	Tallahassee	4-N	7-W

Surname	Map Group	Parcels of Land	Meridian/Township/Range		
MONEY	**34**	3	Tallahassee	3-N	8-W
MONEYHAM	**28**	1	Tallahassee	4-N	7-W
`\\` `//`	**21**	1	Tallahassee	5-N	8-W
MONIN	**35**	1	Tallahassee	3-N	7-W
MONK	**31**	2	Tallahassee	3-N	11-W
MONTFORD	**10**	1	Tallahassee	6-N	11-W
MONTFORT	**18**	1	Tallahassee	5-N	11-W
MOON	**16**	1	Tallahassee	5-N	13-W
MOORE	**28**	3	Tallahassee	4-N	7-W
`\\` `//`	**32**	1	Tallahassee	3-N	10-W
`\\` `//`	**2**	1	Tallahassee	7-N	12-W
MOORING	**10**	4	Tallahassee	6-N	11-W
MORGAN	**11**	10	Tallahassee	6-N	10-W
`\\` `//`	**27**	1	Tallahassee	4-N	8-W
MORRIS	**30**	8	Tallahassee	3-N	12-W
`\\` `//`	**23**	2	Tallahassee	4-N	12-W
`\\` `//`	**25**	1	Tallahassee	4-N	10-W
`\\` `//`	**24**	1	Tallahassee	4-N	11-W
MORRISON	**39**	2	Tallahassee	2-N	10-W
MOSES	**2**	2	Tallahassee	7-N	12-W
MOSS	**4**	1	Tallahassee	7-N	10-W
MOTT	**13**	1	Tallahassee	6-N	8-W
MOWHINNEY	**27**	1	Tallahassee	4-N	8-W
MULKEY	**33**	1	Tallahassee	3-N	9-W
MURDOCK	**8**	1	Tallahassee	6-N	13-W
MURPHY	**20**	2	Tallahassee	5-N	9-W
`\\` `//`	**26**	1	Tallahassee	4-N	9-W
MUSGROVE	**33**	2	Tallahassee	3-N	9-W
MYRICK	**25**	4	Tallahassee	4-N	10-W
`\\` `//`	**11**	2	Tallahassee	6-N	10-W
NALL	**34**	2	Tallahassee	3-N	8-W
NASH	**22**	1	Tallahassee	5-N	7-W
NEAL	**2**	1	Tallahassee	7-N	12-W
NEEL	**13**	10	Tallahassee	6-N	8-W
`\\` `//`	**6**	10	Tallahassee	7-N	8-W
`\\` `//`	**21**	8	Tallahassee	5-N	8-W
`\\` `//`	**27**	4	Tallahassee	4-N	8-W
`\\` `//`	**28**	1	Tallahassee	4-N	7-W
NEELY	**9**	1	Tallahassee	6-N	12-W
NELSON	**23**	3	Tallahassee	4-N	12-W
`\\` `//`	**38**	2	Tallahassee	2-N	11-W
`\\` `//`	**37**	1	Tallahassee	2-N	12-W
`\\` `//`	**33**	1	Tallahassee	3-N	9-W
NEWSOME	**31**	1	Tallahassee	3-N	11-W
NICKELS	**21**	5	Tallahassee	5-N	8-W
`\\` `//`	**13**	1	Tallahassee	6-N	8-W
NIX	**39**	2	Tallahassee	2-N	10-W
NOBLES	**13**	3	Tallahassee	6-N	8-W
NOLL	**19**	2	Tallahassee	5-N	10-W
NOOGIN	**18**	1	Tallahassee	5-N	11-W
NORRIS	**13**	2	Tallahassee	6-N	8-W
OBRIEN	**16**	1	Tallahassee	5-N	13-W
OLIVE	**24**	2	Tallahassee	4-N	11-W
ONEAL	**2**	4	Tallahassee	7-N	12-W
ONEIL	**13**	2	Tallahassee	6-N	8-W
OSWALD	**6**	5	Tallahassee	7-N	8-W
`\\` `//`	**5**	1	Tallahassee	7-N	9-W
OVERTON	**10**	2	Tallahassee	6-N	11-W
OWENS	**38**	5	Tallahassee	2-N	11-W
`\\` `//`	**13**	5	Tallahassee	6-N	8-W

Surname	Map Group	Parcels of Land	Meridian/Township/Range		
OWENS (Cont'd)	**27**	2	Tallahassee	4-N	8-W
" "	**21**	1	Tallahassee	5-N	8-W
" "	**14**	1	Tallahassee	6-N	7-W
" "	**6**	1	Tallahassee	7-N	8-W
PADGET	**25**	2	Tallahassee	4-N	10-W
" "	**32**	1	Tallahassee	3-N	10-W
PADGETT	**32**	6	Tallahassee	3-N	10-W
" "	**25**	6	Tallahassee	4-N	10-W
" "	**24**	3	Tallahassee	4-N	11-W
" "	**33**	2	Tallahassee	3-N	9-W
" "	**18**	1	Tallahassee	5-N	11-W
PADJETT	**32**	4	Tallahassee	3-N	10-W
" "	**25**	4	Tallahassee	4-N	10-W
PAGE	**32**	1	Tallahassee	3-N	10-W
PARISH	**17**	2	Tallahassee	5-N	12-W
PARKER	**8**	8	Tallahassee	6-N	13-W
" "	**21**	1	Tallahassee	5-N	8-W
" "	**10**	1	Tallahassee	6-N	11-W
" "	**9**	1	Tallahassee	6-N	12-W
PARRAMORE	**13**	2	Tallahassee	6-N	8-W
PARRISH	**9**	3	Tallahassee	6-N	12-W
PARROT	**2**	1	Tallahassee	7-N	12-W
PATRICK	**13**	1	Tallahassee	6-N	8-W
" "	**6**	1	Tallahassee	7-N	8-W
" "	**5**	1	Tallahassee	7-N	9-W
PATTERSON	**34**	6	Tallahassee	3-N	8-W
" "	**6**	5	Tallahassee	7-N	8-W
" "	**11**	4	Tallahassee	6-N	10-W
" "	**35**	3	Tallahassee	3-N	7-W
" "	**28**	1	Tallahassee	4-N	7-W
" "	**19**	1	Tallahassee	5-N	10-W
PATTON	**32**	2	Tallahassee	3-N	10-W
PAULK	**4**	1	Tallahassee	7-N	10-W
PAYTON	**20**	1	Tallahassee	5-N	9-W
PEACOCK	**27**	6	Tallahassee	4-N	8-W
" "	**3**	6	Tallahassee	7-N	11-W
" "	**33**	4	Tallahassee	3-N	9-W
" "	**4**	4	Tallahassee	7-N	10-W
" "	**34**	1	Tallahassee	3-N	8-W
" "	**28**	1	Tallahassee	4-N	7-W
PEEBLES	**10**	2	Tallahassee	6-N	11-W
" "	**32**	1	Tallahassee	3-N	10-W
" "	**34**	1	Tallahassee	3-N	8-W
PELT	**25**	5	Tallahassee	4-N	10-W
" "	**11**	2	Tallahassee	6-N	10-W
" "	**9**	2	Tallahassee	6-N	12-W
" "	**10**	1	Tallahassee	6-N	11-W
PENDER	**12**	12	Tallahassee	6-N	9-W
PENNINGTON	**9**	5	Tallahassee	6-N	12-W
PERKINS	**21**	2	Tallahassee	5-N	8-W
" "	**13**	1	Tallahassee	6-N	8-W
PERRITT	**23**	3	Tallahassee	4-N	12-W
PERRY	**35**	11	Tallahassee	3-N	7-W
PETERS	**34**	2	Tallahassee	3-N	8-W
PETERSON	**24**	1	Tallahassee	4-N	11-W
PEYTON	**19**	5	Tallahassee	5-N	10-W
" "	**25**	1	Tallahassee	4-N	10-W
PHILIPS	**8**	4	Tallahassee	6-N	13-W
PHILLIPS	**8**	2	Tallahassee	6-N	13-W
" "	**2**	1	Tallahassee	7-N	12-W

Surname	Map Group	Parcels of Land	Meridian/Township/Range		
PIGG	**33**	1	Tallahassee	3-N	9-W
PILCHER	**17**	1	Tallahassee	5-N	12-W
PINKHAM	**2**	1	Tallahassee	7-N	12-W
PIOUS	**28**	1	Tallahassee	4-N	7-W
PIPPEN	**17**	2	Tallahassee	5-N	12-W
PITTMAN	**3**	7	Tallahassee	7-N	11-W
" "	**32**	4	Tallahassee	3-N	10-W
" "	**25**	4	Tallahassee	4-N	10-W
" "	**24**	3	Tallahassee	4-N	11-W
" "	**26**	3	Tallahassee	4-N	9-W
" "	**9**	3	Tallahassee	6-N	12-W
" "	**4**	3	Tallahassee	7-N	10-W
" "	**33**	2	Tallahassee	3-N	9-W
PITTS	**26**	2	Tallahassee	4-N	9-W
PLAYER	**35**	2	Tallahassee	3-N	7-W
" "	**28**	2	Tallahassee	4-N	7-W
" "	**27**	2	Tallahassee	4-N	8-W
" "	**13**	1	Tallahassee	6-N	8-W
PLEDGER	**32**	13	Tallahassee	3-N	10-W
POLK	**4**	1	Tallahassee	7-N	10-W
POLLOCK	**6**	1	Tallahassee	7-N	8-W
POOSER	**26**	11	Tallahassee	4-N	9-W
" "	**33**	1	Tallahassee	3-N	9-W
POPE	**28**	7	Tallahassee	4-N	7-W
" "	**24**	3	Tallahassee	4-N	11-W
" "	**29**	3	Tallahassee	4-N	6-W
" "	**25**	2	Tallahassee	4-N	10-W
" "	**18**	2	Tallahassee	5-N	11-W
" "	**14**	2	Tallahassee	6-N	7-W
" "	**13**	1	Tallahassee	6-N	8-W
PORTER	**32**	23	Tallahassee	3-N	10-W
" "	**38**	8	Tallahassee	2-N	11-W
" "	**31**	2	Tallahassee	3-N	11-W
" "	**19**	2	Tallahassee	5-N	10-W
" "	**2**	2	Tallahassee	7-N	12-W
" "	**25**	1	Tallahassee	4-N	10-W
" "	**24**	1	Tallahassee	4-N	11-W
" "	**27**	1	Tallahassee	4-N	8-W
POWELL	**39**	3	Tallahassee	2-N	10-W
" "	**17**	3	Tallahassee	5-N	12-W
" "	**8**	3	Tallahassee	6-N	13-W
" "	**24**	1	Tallahassee	4-N	11-W
" "	**20**	1	Tallahassee	5-N	9-W
" "	**10**	1	Tallahassee	6-N	11-W
POWERS	**25**	1	Tallahassee	4-N	10-W
PRATHER	**11**	10	Tallahassee	6-N	10-W
PRESTON	**27**	2	Tallahassee	4-N	8-W
PREVATT	**6**	1	Tallahassee	7-N	8-W
PRIM	**16**	4	Tallahassee	5-N	13-W
PROCTOR	**27**	2	Tallahassee	4-N	8-W
PUMPHRAY	**32**	3	Tallahassee	3-N	10-W
PUMPHREY	**32**	5	Tallahassee	3-N	10-W
" "	**39**	1	Tallahassee	2-N	10-W
" "	**38**	1	Tallahassee	2-N	11-W
PURSER	**4**	1	Tallahassee	7-N	10-W
PURVIS	**21**	5	Tallahassee	5-N	8-W
PYKE	**13**	1	Tallahassee	6-N	8-W
RABOURN	**21**	2	Tallahassee	5-N	8-W
RAINS	**22**	2	Tallahassee	5-N	7-W
RAMSAY	**3**	1	Tallahassee	7-N	11-W

Surname	Map Group	Parcels of Land	Meridian/Township/Range		
RAMSEY	**24**	2	Tallahassee	4-N	11-W
RANEY	**32**	1	Tallahassee	3-N	10-W
RASK	**22**	1	Tallahassee	5-N	7-W
RATHIEL	**9**	1	Tallahassee	6-N	12-W
RAWLS	**24**	1	Tallahassee	4-N	11-W
" "	**20**	1	Tallahassee	5-N	9-W
RAY	**13**	1	Tallahassee	6-N	8-W
REDDICK	**8**	2	Tallahassee	6-N	13-W
REDDING	**4**	2	Tallahassee	7-N	10-W
REGISTER	**9**	4	Tallahassee	6-N	12-W
" "	**8**	4	Tallahassee	6-N	13-W
" "	**1**	2	Tallahassee	7-N	13-W
" "	**32**	1	Tallahassee	3-N	10-W
REISSER	**27**	2	Tallahassee	4-N	8-W
REVERE	**24**	1	Tallahassee	4-N	11-W
REYNOLDS	**10**	7	Tallahassee	6-N	11-W
" "	**38**	2	Tallahassee	2-N	11-W
RHODES	**16**	5	Tallahassee	5-N	13-W
" "	**7**	2	Tallahassee	6-N	14-W
" "	**8**	1	Tallahassee	6-N	13-W
RICHARDSON	**38**	2	Tallahassee	2-N	11-W
RICHTER	**16**	4	Tallahassee	5-N	13-W
RICKS	**8**	3	Tallahassee	6-N	13-W
" "	**13**	1	Tallahassee	6-N	8-W
RIDDICK	**17**	2	Tallahassee	5-N	12-W
RILEY	**31**	2	Tallahassee	3-N	11-W
RIVERS	**11**	2	Tallahassee	6-N	10-W
" "	**4**	1	Tallahassee	7-N	10-W
RIVES	**9**	1	Tallahassee	6-N	12-W
RIVIERE	**18**	2	Tallahassee	5-N	11-W
RIVIRE	**24**	1	Tallahassee	4-N	11-W
ROACH	**13**	3	Tallahassee	6-N	8-W
" "	**2**	2	Tallahassee	7-N	12-W
" "	**27**	1	Tallahassee	4-N	8-W
" "	**6**	1	Tallahassee	7-N	8-W
ROBBIRDS	**34**	1	Tallahassee	3-N	8-W
ROBERSON	**12**	6	Tallahassee	6-N	9-W
" "	**11**	1	Tallahassee	6-N	10-W
ROBERTS	**11**	14	Tallahassee	6-N	10-W
" "	**19**	7	Tallahassee	5-N	10-W
" "	**12**	6	Tallahassee	6-N	9-W
" "	**6**	2	Tallahassee	7-N	8-W
" "	**33**	1	Tallahassee	3-N	9-W
" "	**27**	1	Tallahassee	4-N	8-W
" "	**21**	1	Tallahassee	5-N	8-W
" "	**13**	1	Tallahassee	6-N	8-W
ROBINSON	**19**	13	Tallahassee	5-N	10-W
" "	**26**	9	Tallahassee	4-N	9-W
" "	**13**	5	Tallahassee	6-N	8-W
" "	**20**	4	Tallahassee	5-N	9-W
" "	**22**	2	Tallahassee	5-N	7-W
" "	**21**	2	Tallahassee	5-N	8-W
" "	**31**	1	Tallahassee	3-N	11-W
" "	**27**	1	Tallahassee	4-N	8-W
" "	**11**	1	Tallahassee	6-N	10-W
RODGERS	**8**	2	Tallahassee	6-N	13-W
" "	**6**	2	Tallahassee	7-N	8-W
ROGERS	**12**	3	Tallahassee	6-N	9-W
ROSE	**9**	1	Tallahassee	6-N	12-W
ROSS	**5**	1	Tallahassee	7-N	9-W

Surname	Map Group	Parcels of Land	Meridian/Township/Range		
ROULHAC	**11**	6	Tallahassee	6-N	10-W
" "	**27**	2	Tallahassee	4-N	8-W
" "	**25**	1	Tallahassee	4-N	10-W
ROWE	**35**	3	Tallahassee	3-N	7-W
ROYAL	**22**	1	Tallahassee	5-N	7-W
" "	**6**	1	Tallahassee	7-N	8-W
ROYALS	**6**	1	Tallahassee	7-N	8-W
RUCKER	**32**	2	Tallahassee	3-N	10-W
RUSK	**22**	9	Tallahassee	5-N	7-W
" "	**21**	5	Tallahassee	5-N	8-W
RUSS	**18**	6	Tallahassee	5-N	11-W
" "	**24**	1	Tallahassee	4-N	11-W
" "	**27**	1	Tallahassee	4-N	8-W
" "	**19**	1	Tallahassee	5-N	10-W
SADLER	**27**	5	Tallahassee	4-N	8-W
" "	**28**	2	Tallahassee	4-N	7-W
SANBURN	**22**	1	Tallahassee	5-N	7-W
" "	**13**	1	Tallahassee	6-N	8-W
SANDERS	**9**	1	Tallahassee	6-N	12-W
SAPP	**23**	1	Tallahassee	4-N	12-W
" "	**17**	1	Tallahassee	5-N	12-W
SAXON	**22**	1	Tallahassee	5-N	7-W
SCAMMELL	**5**	1	Tallahassee	7-N	9-W
SCARLOCK	**28**	1	Tallahassee	4-N	7-W
SCHURLOCK	**28**	1	Tallahassee	4-N	7-W
SCOTT	**26**	5	Tallahassee	4-N	9-W
" "	**31**	3	Tallahassee	3-N	11-W
" "	**34**	3	Tallahassee	3-N	8-W
" "	**27**	3	Tallahassee	4-N	8-W
" "	**35**	2	Tallahassee	3-N	7-W
" "	**21**	2	Tallahassee	5-N	8-W
" "	**3**	2	Tallahassee	7-N	11-W
" "	**24**	1	Tallahassee	4-N	11-W
" "	**4**	1	Tallahassee	7-N	10-W
SCURLOCK	**17**	6	Tallahassee	5-N	12-W
" "	**28**	4	Tallahassee	4-N	7-W
" "	**18**	2	Tallahassee	5-N	11-W
" "	**10**	1	Tallahassee	6-N	11-W
" "	**9**	1	Tallahassee	6-N	12-W
SEARCY	**36**	1	Tallahassee	3-N	6-W
" "	**35**	1	Tallahassee	3-N	7-W
SEAY	**23**	3	Tallahassee	4-N	12-W
SELLERS	**21**	9	Tallahassee	5-N	8-W
" "	**34**	1	Tallahassee	3-N	8-W
SEWELL	**37**	2	Tallahassee	2-N	12-W
" "	**30**	1	Tallahassee	3-N	12-W
SEXTON	**31**	3	Tallahassee	3-N	11-W
" "	**38**	2	Tallahassee	2-N	11-W
" "	**25**	1	Tallahassee	4-N	10-W
SHACKELFORD	**21**	3	Tallahassee	5-N	8-W
" "	**25**	1	Tallahassee	4-N	10-W
SHARON	**8**	3	Tallahassee	6-N	13-W
SHARP	**21**	2	Tallahassee	5-N	8-W
SHARPE	**32**	1	Tallahassee	3-N	10-W
SHELFER	**27**	3	Tallahassee	4-N	8-W
SHERMAN	**22**	1	Tallahassee	5-N	7-W
SHINHOLSTER	**4**	2	Tallahassee	7-N	10-W
SHIPE	**16**	3	Tallahassee	5-N	13-W
SHIPES	**8**	3	Tallahassee	6-N	13-W
SHIVER	**9**	4	Tallahassee	6-N	12-W

Surname	Map Group	Parcels of Land	Meridian/Township/Range		
SHORES	**23**	6	Tallahassee	4-N	12-W
" "	**37**	3	Tallahassee	2-N	12-W
" "	**30**	2	Tallahassee	3-N	12-W
" "	**31**	1	Tallahassee	3-N	11-W
SHOUPE	**17**	1	Tallahassee	5-N	12-W
SHOUPPE	**17**	3	Tallahassee	5-N	12-W
SHUTES	**38**	2	Tallahassee	2-N	11-W
SIKES	**1**	1	Tallahassee	7-N	13-W
SILLIVENT	**17**	3	Tallahassee	5-N	12-W
SILLS	**20**	1	Tallahassee	5-N	9-W
SIMMES	**25**	1	Tallahassee	4-N	10-W
SIMMONS	**25**	2	Tallahassee	4-N	10-W
" "	**21**	1	Tallahassee	5-N	8-W
SIMMS	**26**	4	Tallahassee	4-N	9-W
" "	**20**	4	Tallahassee	5-N	9-W
" "	**19**	1	Tallahassee	5-N	10-W
SIMONS	**11**	2	Tallahassee	6-N	10-W
" "	**19**	1	Tallahassee	5-N	10-W
SIMPSON	**34**	3	Tallahassee	3-N	8-W
" "	**27**	1	Tallahassee	4-N	8-W
" "	**10**	1	Tallahassee	6-N	11-W
SIMS	**25**	18	Tallahassee	4-N	10-W
" "	**26**	10	Tallahassee	4-N	9-W
" "	**33**	7	Tallahassee	3-N	9-W
" "	**34**	6	Tallahassee	3-N	8-W
" "	**16**	3	Tallahassee	5-N	13-W
" "	**32**	2	Tallahassee	3-N	10-W
" "	**27**	2	Tallahassee	4-N	8-W
" "	**31**	1	Tallahassee	3-N	11-W
SIMSON	**27**	1	Tallahassee	4-N	8-W
SINGHTON	**9**	1	Tallahassee	6-N	12-W
SKETO	**31**	7	Tallahassee	3-N	11-W
" "	**39**	2	Tallahassee	2-N	10-W
" "	**32**	1	Tallahassee	3-N	10-W
SKINNER	**24**	5	Tallahassee	4-N	11-W
" "	**38**	3	Tallahassee	2-N	11-W
SKIPPER	**6**	1	Tallahassee	7-N	8-W
SKRINE	**35**	1	Tallahassee	3-N	7-W
SLATER	**9**	7	Tallahassee	6-N	12-W
SLATON	**10**	2	Tallahassee	6-N	11-W
" "	**9**	2	Tallahassee	6-N	12-W
SLOAN	**19**	2	Tallahassee	5-N	10-W
" "	**8**	1	Tallahassee	6-N	13-W
SLOANE	**8**	1	Tallahassee	6-N	13-W
SMITH	**2**	9	Tallahassee	7-N	12-W
" "	**1**	5	Tallahassee	7-N	13-W
" "	**9**	4	Tallahassee	6-N	12-W
" "	**35**	3	Tallahassee	3-N	7-W
" "	**12**	3	Tallahassee	6-N	9-W
" "	**31**	2	Tallahassee	3-N	11-W
" "	**16**	2	Tallahassee	5-N	13-W
" "	**24**	1	Tallahassee	4-N	11-W
" "	**28**	1	Tallahassee	4-N	7-W
" "	**19**	1	Tallahassee	5-N	10-W
" "	**10**	1	Tallahassee	6-N	11-W
" "	**13**	1	Tallahassee	6-N	8-W
" "	**5**	1	Tallahassee	7-N	9-W
SNEAD	**28**	2	Tallahassee	4-N	7-W
SNELL	**2**	5	Tallahassee	7-N	12-W
" "	**28**	3	Tallahassee	4-N	7-W

Surname	Map Group	Parcels of Land	Meridian/Township/Range		
SNELL (Cont'd)	**9**	2	Tallahassee	6-N	12-W
" "	**8**	2	Tallahassee	6-N	13-W
SNELLING	**10**	6	Tallahassee	6-N	11-W
SNIPES	**27**	4	Tallahassee	4-N	8-W
SNOW	**32**	3	Tallahassee	3-N	10-W
" "	**39**	2	Tallahassee	2-N	10-W
SOREY	**11**	3	Tallahassee	6-N	10-W
" "	**12**	3	Tallahassee	6-N	9-W
SOUTER	**33**	1	Tallahassee	3-N	9-W
SPEAR	**11**	2	Tallahassee	6-N	10-W
" "	**18**	1	Tallahassee	5-N	11-W
SPEARS	**24**	10	Tallahassee	4-N	11-W
" "	**11**	2	Tallahassee	6-N	10-W
" "	**18**	1	Tallahassee	5-N	11-W
SPEIGHT	**17**	2	Tallahassee	5-N	12-W
SPEIGHTS	**4**	1	Tallahassee	7-N	10-W
SPEIR	**11**	3	Tallahassee	6-N	10-W
SPIER	**11**	1	Tallahassee	6-N	10-W
SPIERS	**11**	2	Tallahassee	6-N	10-W
" "	**10**	2	Tallahassee	6-N	11-W
SPIVEY	**17**	2	Tallahassee	5-N	12-W
SPOONER	**28**	6	Tallahassee	4-N	7-W
" "	**27**	3	Tallahassee	4-N	8-W
" "	**24**	1	Tallahassee	4-N	11-W
STALEY	**25**	4	Tallahassee	4-N	10-W
" "	**33**	3	Tallahassee	3-N	9-W
" "	**19**	2	Tallahassee	5-N	10-W
STAPLETON	**39**	2	Tallahassee	2-N	10-W
" "	**1**	2	Tallahassee	7-N	13-W
STELL	**40**	2	Tallahassee	2-N	9-W
STEPHENS	**5**	10	Tallahassee	7-N	9-W
" "	**25**	8	Tallahassee	4-N	10-W
" "	**27**	7	Tallahassee	4-N	8-W
" "	**26**	5	Tallahassee	4-N	9-W
" "	**28**	4	Tallahassee	4-N	7-W
" "	**39**	3	Tallahassee	2-N	10-W
" "	**33**	3	Tallahassee	3-N	9-W
" "	**32**	2	Tallahassee	3-N	10-W
" "	**6**	2	Tallahassee	7-N	8-W
" "	**38**	1	Tallahassee	2-N	11-W
" "	**31**	1	Tallahassee	3-N	11-W
" "	**30**	1	Tallahassee	3-N	12-W
" "	**34**	1	Tallahassee	3-N	8-W
" "	**19**	1	Tallahassee	5-N	10-W
STEWART	**25**	3	Tallahassee	4-N	10-W
" "	**13**	2	Tallahassee	6-N	8-W
" "	**34**	1	Tallahassee	3-N	8-W
" "	**26**	1	Tallahassee	4-N	9-W
" "	**2**	1	Tallahassee	7-N	12-W
STILL	**17**	4	Tallahassee	5-N	12-W
STINSON	**35**	1	Tallahassee	3-N	7-W
STOCKTON	**24**	1	Tallahassee	4-N	11-W
" "	**26**	1	Tallahassee	4-N	9-W
STONE	**35**	5	Tallahassee	3-N	7-W
" "	**18**	5	Tallahassee	5-N	11-W
" "	**34**	1	Tallahassee	3-N	8-W
" "	**19**	1	Tallahassee	5-N	10-W
" "	**17**	1	Tallahassee	5-N	12-W
" "	**10**	1	Tallahassee	6-N	11-W
STOWERS	**25**	2	Tallahassee	4-N	10-W

Surname	Map Group	Parcels of Land	Meridian/Township/Range		
STREETMAN	**26**	1	Tallahassee	4-N	9-W
STRICKLAND	**27**	3	Tallahassee	4-N	8-W
" "	**12**	2	Tallahassee	6-N	9-W
" "	**4**	2	Tallahassee	7-N	10-W
" "	**5**	2	Tallahassee	7-N	9-W
SUGGS	**8**	3	Tallahassee	6-N	13-W
SULIVAN	**33**	4	Tallahassee	3-N	9-W
SULLIVAN	**33**	8	Tallahassee	3-N	9-W
" "	**30**	6	Tallahassee	3-N	12-W
" "	**32**	1	Tallahassee	3-N	10-W
SUMMERLIN	**38**	7	Tallahassee	2-N	11-W
SUMMERS	**21**	1	Tallahassee	5-N	8-W
SUTTON	**10**	6	Tallahassee	6-N	11-W
" "	**11**	1	Tallahassee	6-N	10-W
" "	**1**	1	Tallahassee	7-N	13-W
SWAILS	**32**	2	Tallahassee	3-N	10-W
" "	**30**	1	Tallahassee	3-N	12-W
" "	**25**	1	Tallahassee	4-N	10-W
" "	**23**	1	Tallahassee	4-N	12-W
SWANSON	**33**	1	Tallahassee	3-N	9-W
SWEARINGEN	**38**	1	Tallahassee	2-N	11-W
SWEARINGIN	**24**	1	Tallahassee	4-N	11-W
SWEET	**21**	3	Tallahassee	5-N	8-W
" "	**8**	3	Tallahassee	6-N	13-W
SYFRETT	**1**	6	Tallahassee	7-N	13-W
" "	**20**	2	Tallahassee	5-N	9-W
" "	**8**	2	Tallahassee	6-N	13-W
" "	**12**	1	Tallahassee	6-N	9-W
SYPETT	**12**	1	Tallahassee	6-N	9-W
SYPHRETT	**20**	2	Tallahassee	5-N	9-W
TANNER	**24**	2	Tallahassee	4-N	11-W
TATUM	**39**	3	Tallahassee	2-N	10-W
" "	**20**	1	Tallahassee	5-N	9-W
TAWN	**1**	1	Tallahassee	7-N	13-W
TAYLOR	**11**	10	Tallahassee	6-N	10-W
" "	**8**	8	Tallahassee	6-N	13-W
" "	**23**	2	Tallahassee	4-N	12-W
" "	**10**	2	Tallahassee	6-N	11-W
" "	**17**	1	Tallahassee	5-N	12-W
" "	**16**	1	Tallahassee	5-N	13-W
" "	**9**	1	Tallahassee	6-N	12-W
TEMPLE	**24**	1	Tallahassee	4-N	11-W
THARP	**23**	6	Tallahassee	4-N	12-W
" "	**17**	3	Tallahassee	5-N	12-W
" "	**30**	2	Tallahassee	3-N	12-W
" "	**21**	1	Tallahassee	5-N	8-W
THIGPEN	**3**	1	Tallahassee	7-N	11-W
THIRBY	**24**	1	Tallahassee	4-N	11-W
THOMAS	**28**	10	Tallahassee	4-N	7-W
" "	**37**	3	Tallahassee	2-N	12-W
" "	**33**	3	Tallahassee	3-N	9-W
" "	**30**	2	Tallahassee	3-N	12-W
" "	**35**	2	Tallahassee	3-N	7-W
" "	**19**	2	Tallahassee	5-N	10-W
" "	**25**	1	Tallahassee	4-N	10-W
" "	**26**	1	Tallahassee	4-N	9-W
" "	**18**	1	Tallahassee	5-N	11-W
THOMPSON	**35**	5	Tallahassee	3-N	7-W
" "	**38**	2	Tallahassee	2-N	11-W
" "	**31**	2	Tallahassee	3-N	11-W

Surname	Map Group	Parcels of Land	Meridian/Township/Range		
THOMPSON (Cont'd)	**24**	2	Tallahassee	4-N	11-W
" "	**2**	1	Tallahassee	7-N	12-W
THORNTON	**38**	1	Tallahassee	2-N	11-W
TIDWELL	**5**	3	Tallahassee	7-N	9-W
" "	**12**	1	Tallahassee	6-N	9-W
TILLINGHAST	**40**	3	Tallahassee	2-N	9-W
" "	**33**	1	Tallahassee	3-N	9-W
TIPTON	**30**	1	Tallahassee	3-N	12-W
TONEY	**35**	8	Tallahassee	3-N	7-W
TOOLE	**9**	8	Tallahassee	6-N	12-W
" "	**17**	4	Tallahassee	5-N	12-W
" "	**30**	2	Tallahassee	3-N	12-W
" "	**21**	2	Tallahassee	5-N	8-W
TOUCHSTONE	**9**	1	Tallahassee	6-N	12-W
TOWERS	**19**	1	Tallahassee	5-N	10-W
TOWLE	**28**	1	Tallahassee	4-N	7-W
TRAMMEL	**19**	4	Tallahassee	5-N	10-W
" "	**20**	3	Tallahassee	5-N	9-W
TRAMMELL	**19**	4	Tallahassee	5-N	10-W
" "	**20**	2	Tallahassee	5-N	9-W
TRAYLOR	**34**	4	Tallahassee	3-N	8-W
" "	**27**	1	Tallahassee	4-N	8-W
TREVATHON	**12**	1	Tallahassee	6-N	9-W
TRIPP	**26**	1	Tallahassee	4-N	9-W
TRIPPE	**10**	3	Tallahassee	6-N	11-W
" "	**26**	2	Tallahassee	4-N	9-W
TRUSSELL	**6**	1	Tallahassee	7-N	8-W
TUCKER	**3**	2	Tallahassee	7-N	11-W
TURNER	**21**	6	Tallahassee	5-N	8-W
" "	**8**	4	Tallahassee	6-N	13-W
TYUS	**27**	1	Tallahassee	4-N	8-W
UNDERWOOD	**8**	5	Tallahassee	6-N	13-W
" "	**26**	2	Tallahassee	4-N	9-W
" "	**17**	2	Tallahassee	5-N	12-W
VAN PELT	**33**	1	Tallahassee	3-N	9-W
VANCE	**25**	1	Tallahassee	4-N	10-W
VAUGHN	**30**	4	Tallahassee	3-N	12-W
VICK	**19**	1	Tallahassee	5-N	10-W
VICKERS	**8**	3	Tallahassee	6-N	13-W
" "	**16**	2	Tallahassee	5-N	13-W
VICKERY	**31**	4	Tallahassee	3-N	11-W
" "	**32**	2	Tallahassee	3-N	10-W
" "	**26**	1	Tallahassee	4-N	9-W
WACASER	**26**	4	Tallahassee	4-N	9-W
WACHOB	**17**	2	Tallahassee	5-N	12-W
" "	**25**	1	Tallahassee	4-N	10-W
WADDELL	**24**	1	Tallahassee	4-N	11-W
WADKINS	**31**	3	Tallahassee	3-N	11-W
WALKER	**26**	2	Tallahassee	4-N	9-W
" "	**31**	1	Tallahassee	3-N	11-W
WALSH	**17**	2	Tallahassee	5-N	12-W
WARD	**2**	3	Tallahassee	7-N	12-W
" "	**10**	1	Tallahassee	6-N	11-W
" "	**8**	1	Tallahassee	6-N	13-W
WARDLOW	**21**	1	Tallahassee	5-N	8-W
WATERS	**30**	1	Tallahassee	3-N	12-W
WATFORD	**8**	6	Tallahassee	6-N	13-W
" "	**12**	5	Tallahassee	6-N	9-W
" "	**5**	5	Tallahassee	7-N	9-W
" "	**4**	3	Tallahassee	7-N	10-W

Surname	Map Group	Parcels of Land	Meridian/Township/Range		
WATFORD (Cont'd)	**1**	3	Tallahassee	7-N	13-W
WATSON	**9**	6	Tallahassee	6-N	12-W
" "	**25**	1	Tallahassee	4-N	10-W
" "	**24**	1	Tallahassee	4-N	11-W
" "	**10**	1	Tallahassee	6-N	11-W
WATTS	**20**	3	Tallahassee	5-N	9-W
" "	**13**	1	Tallahassee	6-N	8-W
" "	**5**	1	Tallahassee	7-N	9-W
WEBB	**18**	2	Tallahassee	5-N	11-W
" "	**33**	1	Tallahassee	3-N	9-W
" "	**9**	1	Tallahassee	6-N	12-W
" "	**2**	1	Tallahassee	7-N	12-W
WEEKS	**4**	6	Tallahassee	7-N	10-W
" "	**27**	1	Tallahassee	4-N	8-W
WELCH	**24**	1	Tallahassee	4-N	11-W
" "	**17**	1	Tallahassee	5-N	12-W
WEST	**4**	1	Tallahassee	7-N	10-W
WESTER	**27**	8	Tallahassee	4-N	8-W
" "	**24**	2	Tallahassee	4-N	11-W
" "	**34**	1	Tallahassee	3-N	8-W
WESTON	**27**	2	Tallahassee	4-N	8-W
" "	**26**	2	Tallahassee	4-N	9-W
WETHINGTON	**32**	3	Tallahassee	3-N	10-W
WHICHARD	**4**	2	Tallahassee	7-N	10-W
WHIDDON	**34**	1	Tallahassee	3-N	8-W
" "	**13**	1	Tallahassee	6-N	8-W
WHITAKER	**4**	2	Tallahassee	7-N	10-W
" "	**11**	1	Tallahassee	6-N	10-W
" "	**9**	1	Tallahassee	6-N	12-W
WHITE	**8**	6	Tallahassee	6-N	13-W
" "	**19**	3	Tallahassee	5-N	10-W
" "	**24**	2	Tallahassee	4-N	11-W
" "	**9**	2	Tallahassee	6-N	12-W
" "	**25**	1	Tallahassee	4-N	10-W
" "	**27**	1	Tallahassee	4-N	8-W
WHITEFIELD	**2**	2	Tallahassee	7-N	12-W
" "	**3**	1	Tallahassee	7-N	11-W
WHITEHEAD	**24**	3	Tallahassee	4-N	11-W
" "	**10**	3	Tallahassee	6-N	11-W
" "	**13**	1	Tallahassee	6-N	8-W
WHITEHURST	**3**	4	Tallahassee	7-N	11-W
" "	**9**	3	Tallahassee	6-N	12-W
" "	**12**	3	Tallahassee	6-N	9-W
" "	**13**	2	Tallahassee	6-N	8-W
" "	**38**	1	Tallahassee	2-N	11-W
" "	**24**	1	Tallahassee	4-N	11-W
" "	**10**	1	Tallahassee	6-N	11-W
WHITFIELD	**17**	4	Tallahassee	5-N	12-W
" "	**5**	1	Tallahassee	7-N	9-W
WHITTINGTON	**40**	1	Tallahassee	2-N	9-W
WILCOX	**35**	3	Tallahassee	3-N	7-W
" "	**21**	3	Tallahassee	5-N	8-W
" "	**24**	1	Tallahassee	4-N	11-W
WILEY	**21**	2	Tallahassee	5-N	8-W
WILLEFORD	**11**	6	Tallahassee	6-N	10-W
WILLIAMS	**8**	20	Tallahassee	6-N	13-W
" "	**1**	10	Tallahassee	7-N	13-W
" "	**2**	6	Tallahassee	7-N	12-W
" "	**16**	5	Tallahassee	5-N	13-W
" "	**7**	5	Tallahassee	6-N	14-W

Surname	Map Group	Parcels of Land	Meridian/Township/Range		
WILLIAMS (Cont'd)	**39**	4	Tallahassee	2-N	10-W
" "	**9**	4	Tallahassee	6-N	12-W
" "	**31**	3	Tallahassee	3-N	11-W
" "	**34**	3	Tallahassee	3-N	8-W
" "	**26**	2	Tallahassee	4-N	9-W
" "	**15**	2	Tallahassee	5-N	14-W
" "	**13**	2	Tallahassee	6-N	8-W
" "	**33**	1	Tallahassee	3-N	9-W
" "	**18**	1	Tallahassee	5-N	11-W
" "	**10**	1	Tallahassee	6-N	11-W
" "	**14**	1	Tallahassee	6-N	7-W
" "	**12**	1	Tallahassee	6-N	9-W
" "	**3**	1	Tallahassee	7-N	11-W
WILLIAMSON	**10**	34	Tallahassee	6-N	11-W
" "	**6**	13	Tallahassee	7-N	8-W
" "	**19**	12	Tallahassee	5-N	10-W
" "	**32**	11	Tallahassee	3-N	10-W
" "	**33**	10	Tallahassee	3-N	9-W
" "	**24**	10	Tallahassee	4-N	11-W
" "	**17**	8	Tallahassee	5-N	12-W
" "	**11**	8	Tallahassee	6-N	10-W
" "	**9**	7	Tallahassee	6-N	12-W
" "	**2**	7	Tallahassee	7-N	12-W
" "	**25**	6	Tallahassee	4-N	10-W
" "	**20**	5	Tallahassee	5-N	9-W
" "	**26**	2	Tallahassee	4-N	9-W
" "	**18**	1	Tallahassee	5-N	11-W
WILLIFORD	**3**	1	Tallahassee	7-N	11-W
WILLIS	**19**	1	Tallahassee	5-N	10-W
" "	**11**	1	Tallahassee	6-N	10-W
WILLSON	**35**	3	Tallahassee	3-N	7-W
WILSON	**4**	11	Tallahassee	7-N	10-W
" "	**11**	7	Tallahassee	6-N	10-W
" "	**10**	5	Tallahassee	6-N	11-W
" "	**31**	2	Tallahassee	3-N	11-W
" "	**35**	2	Tallahassee	3-N	7-W
" "	**28**	1	Tallahassee	4-N	7-W
WILTON	**26**	1	Tallahassee	4-N	9-W
WIMBERLEY	**20**	2	Tallahassee	5-N	9-W
WIMBERLY	**20**	2	Tallahassee	5-N	9-W
" "	**33**	1	Tallahassee	3-N	9-W
" "	**26**	1	Tallahassee	4-N	9-W
" "	**19**	1	Tallahassee	5-N	10-W
WIRT	**20**	3	Tallahassee	5-N	9-W
WITCHARD	**10**	1	Tallahassee	6-N	11-W
WITHERINGTON	**19**	1	Tallahassee	5-N	10-W
WOMBLE	**8**	1	Tallahassee	6-N	13-W
" "	**7**	1	Tallahassee	6-N	14-W
WOOD	**40**	2	Tallahassee	2-N	9-W
" "	**21**	2	Tallahassee	5-N	8-W
" "	**35**	1	Tallahassee	3-N	7-W
" "	**22**	1	Tallahassee	5-N	7-W
WOODALL	**20**	1	Tallahassee	5-N	9-W
WOODARD	**24**	2	Tallahassee	4-N	11-W
WOOLDRIDGE	**28**	3	Tallahassee	4-N	7-W
WOOTEN	**14**	1	Tallahassee	6-N	7-W
WORLEY	**7**	3	Tallahassee	6-N	14-W
WRIGHT	**30**	2	Tallahassee	3-N	12-W
WYATT	**35**	1	Tallahassee	3-N	7-W
WYNN	**25**	1	Tallahassee	4-N	10-W

Surname	Map Group	Parcels of Land	Meridian/Township/Range
WYNN (Cont'd)	**24**	1	Tallahassee 4-N 11-W
" "	**19**	1	Tallahassee 5-N 10-W
WYNNS	**25**	1	Tallahassee 4-N 10-W
" "	**19**	1	Tallahassee 5-N 10-W
YARBOROUGH	**6**	8	Tallahassee 7-N 8-W
" "	**12**	3	Tallahassee 6-N 9-W
" "	**5**	1	Tallahassee 7-N 9-W
YARBROUGH	**22**	4	Tallahassee 5-N 7-W
YAWN	**8**	1	Tallahassee 6-N 13-W
YON	**35**	2	Tallahassee 3-N 7-W
" "	**33**	2	Tallahassee 3-N 9-W
" "	**28**	1	Tallahassee 4-N 7-W
YONGE	**12**	1	Tallahassee 6-N 9-W
YORK	**8**	5	Tallahassee 6-N 13-W
YOUNG	**9**	9	Tallahassee 6-N 12-W
" "	**17**	5	Tallahassee 5-N 12-W
" "	**12**	4	Tallahassee 6-N 9-W
" "	**1**	4	Tallahassee 7-N 13-W
" "	**24**	2	Tallahassee 4-N 11-W
" "	**21**	2	Tallahassee 5-N 8-W
" "	**11**	2	Tallahassee 6-N 10-W
" "	**3**	1	Tallahassee 7-N 11-W

– Part II –

Township Map Groups

Map Group 1: Index to Land Patents

Township 7-North Range 13-West (Tallahassee)

After you locate an individual in this Index, take note of the Section and Section Part then proceed to the Land Patent map on the pages immediately following. You should have no difficulty locating the corresponding parcel of land.

The "For More Info" Column will lead you to more information about the underlying Patents. See the *Legend* at right, and the "How to Use this Book" chapter, for more information.

```
                    LEGEND
              "For More Info . . . " column
A = Authority (Legislative Act, See Appendix "A")
B = Block or Lot (location in Section unknown)
C = Cancelled Patent
F = Fractional Section
G = Group  (Multi-Patentee Patent, see Appendix "C")
V = Overlaps another Parcel
R = Re-Issued (Parcel patented more than once)

(A & G items require you to look in the Appendixes referred
to above. All other Letter-designations followed by a number
require you to locate line-items in this index that possess
the ID number found after the letter).
```

ID	Individual in Patent	Sec.	Sec. Part	Date Issued	Other Counties	For More Info . . .
13	ANDERSON, Dougald	23	E½4	1857-12-01	Holmes	A1
14	" "	24	W½2	1857-12-01		A1
15	" "	24	W½3	1857-12-01		A1
16	" "	25	NWNW	1857-12-01		A1
17	" "	26	NENE	1857-12-01	Holmes	A1
18	" "	26	SENW	1857-12-01	Holmes	A1
19	" "	26	W½NE	1857-12-01	Holmes	A1
53	BALL, Joseph L	36	N½SW	1883-08-01		A2
54	" "	36	S½NW	1883-08-01		A2
65	BAXLEY, Solomon	27	E½NW	1899-05-12	Holmes	A2
66	" "	27	E½SW	1899-05-12	Holmes	A2
5	BROWN, Benjamin A	24	E½3	1857-12-01		A1
6	" "	25	N½NE	1857-12-01		A1
7	" "	25	NENW	1857-12-01		A1
9	BROXTON, Charles	36	SESW	1897-09-20		A2
58	CHRISMAS, Moses	24	NESE	1855-05-01		A1
28	DAVIS, Hugh C	23	1	1861-04-09	Holmes	A1
29	" "	23	E½2	1861-04-09	Holmes	A1
30	" "	23	W½4	1861-04-09	Holmes	A1
47	DELOACH, John	24	E½2	1899-05-22		A2
70	DOUGHTERY, Wesley	35	SW	1860-04-02		A1
60	EVERITT, Priar L	27	NWSW	1902-10-11	Holmes	A2
61	" "	27	W½NW	1902-10-11	Holmes	A2
63	FOUNTAIN, Rebecca S	35	NESE	1903-05-25		A2
11	GAINER, David	36	E½SE	1895-02-14		A2
12	" "	36	SENE	1895-02-14		A2
64	GODWIN, Reddick	26	S½	1861-04-09	Holmes	A1
24	GRACE, Henry B	25	SWNW	1883-08-01		A2
25	" "	25	W½SW	1883-08-01		A2
26	" "	26	SENE	1883-08-01	Holmes	A2
27	" "	36	NWNW	1884-03-31		A1
36	JACKSON, James C	35	W½NW	1900-09-07		A2
37	JACKSON, James R	34	E½NW	1896-04-27	Holmes	A2
38	" "	34	W½NE	1896-04-27	Holmes	A2
56	KIRKLAND, Martha	33	W½NW	1892-05-04	Holmes	A2
57	" "	33	W½SW	1892-05-04	Holmes	A2
3	MCLENDON, Alfred	36	W½NE	1897-09-22		A2
4	" "	36	W½SE	1897-09-22		A2
55	MILLER, Lloyd J	27	SWSW	1920-09-10	Holmes	A1
52	REGISTER, Joseph A	27	E½	1860-04-02	Holmes	A1
62	REGISTER, Prior E	23	W½2	1910-05-05	Holmes	A2
51	SIKES, John	24	SENE	1843-03-10		A1
1	SMITH, Adam	25	SESE	1892-04-01		A2
2	" "	36	NENE	1892-04-01		A2
67	SMITH, Stephen H	35	NWSE	1891-07-14		A2
68	" "	35	S½NE	1891-07-14		A2

ID	Individual in Patent	Sec.	Sec. Part	Date Issued	Other Counties	For More Info . . .
69	SMITH, Stephen H (Cont'd)	35	SENW	1891-07-14		A2
73	STAPLETON, William	33	E½SE	1827-11-01	Holmes	A1
74	" "	34	W½SW	1828-02-22	Holmes	A1
59	SUTTON, Nathaniel G	35	N½NE	1890-12-11		A2
20	SYFRETT, Francis M	35	SESE	1883-08-13		A2
21	" "	36	SWSW	1883-08-13		A2
22	SYFRETT, Frederick M	35	SWSE	1888-11-22		A2
48	SYFRETT, John E	25	SESW	1906-10-24		A2
49	" "	25	SWSE	1906-10-24		A2
50	" "	36	NENW	1906-10-24		A2
23	TAWN, Henry A	35	NENW	1860-07-02		A1
8	WATFORD, Calvin	26	SWNW	1920-11-23	Holmes	A2
71	WATFORD, William J	23	S½SW	1861-04-09	Holmes	A1
72	" "	26	N½NW	1861-04-09	Holmes	A1
10	WILLIAMS, Daniel	13	S½3	1843-03-10		A1
31	WILLIAMS, Isaiah	34	E½SW	1860-04-02	Holmes	A1
32	" "	34	N½SE	1860-04-02	Holmes	A1
34	" "	34	S½SE	1860-04-02	Holmes	A1
35	" "	34	SENE	1860-10-01	Holmes	A1
33	" "	34	NENE	1861-12-05	Holmes	A1
43	WILLIAMS, Jasper N	25	N½SE	1886-11-04		A2
45	" "	25	S½NE	1886-11-04		A2
46	" "	25	SENW	1888-07-03		A1
44	" "	25	NESW	1888-07-21		A1
39	YOUNG, James T	33	E½NW	1856-06-16	Holmes	A1
40	" "	33	E½SW	1856-06-16	Holmes	A1
41	" "	33	W½NE	1856-06-16	Holmes	A1
42	" "	33	W½SE	1856-06-16	Holmes	A1

Patent Map

T7-N R13-W
Tallahassee Meridian

Map Group 1

N

Township Statistics

Parcels Mapped	:	74
Number of Patents	:	43
Number of Individuals	:	36
Patentees Identified	:	36
Number of Surnames	:	28
Multi-Patentee Parcels	:	0
Oldest Patent Date	:	11/1/1827
Most Recent Patent	:	11/23/1920
Block/Lot Parcels	:	10
Parcels Re - Issued	:	0
Parcels that Overlap	:	0
Cities and Towns	:	1
Cemeteries	:	0

Note: the area contained in this map amounts to far less than a full Township. Therefore, its contents are completely on this single page (instead of a "normal" 2-page spread).

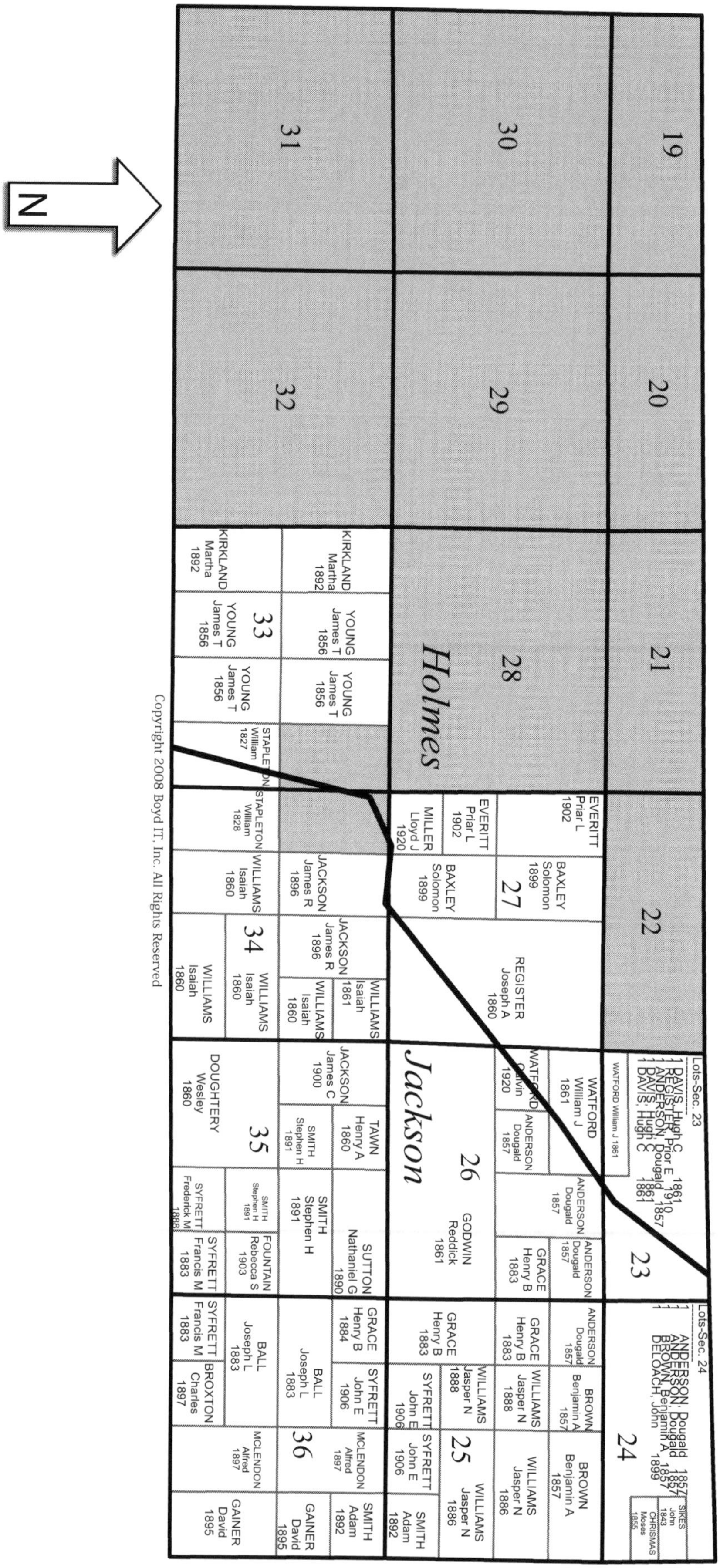

Legend

——————— Patent Boundary

━━━━━━━ Section Boundary

▨ No Patents Found
(or Outside County)

1., 2., 3., ... Lot Numbers
(when beside a name)

[ ] Group Number
(see Appendix "C")

Scale: Section = 1 mile X 1 mile
(generally, with some exceptions)

56

Map section (township grid)

31

30

19

32

29

20

Holmes

28

21

22

KIRKLAND Martha 1892

KIRKLAND Martha 1892

YOUNG James T 1856

33

YOUNG James T 1856

YOUNG James T 1856

YOUNG James T 1856

STAPLETON William 1827

EVERITT Priar L 1902

EVERITT Priar L 1902

BAXLEY Solomon 1899

27

MILLER Lloyd J 1920

BAXLEY Solomon 1899

STAPLETON William 1828

WILLIAMS Isaiah 1860

JACKSON James R 1896

REGISTER Joseph A 1860

WILLIAMS Isaiah 1860

34

JACKSON James R 1896

JACKSON James R 1861

WILLIAMS Isaiah 1860

WILLIAMS Isaiah 1861

WATFORD Calvin 1920

WATFORD William J 1861

EVERITT Priar L 1861

BAXLEY Solomon 1899

Jackson

DOUGHERTY Wesley 1860

35

JACKSON James C 1900

SMITH Stephen H 1891

TAWN Henry A 1860

26

ANDERSON Dougald 1857

WATFORD William J 1861

GRACE Henry B 1883

ANDERSON Dougald 1857

23

SMITH Stephen H 1891

SMITH Stephen H 1891

SUTTON Nathaniel G 1890

GODWIN Reddick 1861

SYFRETT Frederick M 1888

FOUNTAIN Rebecca S 1903

SMITH Stephen H 1891

GRACE Henry B 1884

GRACE Henry B 1883

GRACE Henry B 1883

ANDERSON Dougald 1857

SYFRETT Francis M 1883

SYFRETT Francis M 1883

BALL Joseph L 1883

BALL Joseph L 1883

GRACE John E 1906

SYFRETT John E 1906

WILLIAMS Jasper N 1888

WILLIAMS Jasper N 1888

BROWN Benjamin A 1857

BROWN Benjamin A 1857

BROXTON Charles 1897

36

MCLENDON Alfred 1897

MCLENDON Alfred 1897

SYFRETT John E 1906

25

WILLIAMS Jasper N 1886

WILLIAMS Jasper N 1886

24

GAINER David 1895

GAINER David 1895

SMITH Adam 1892

SMITH Adam 1892

Lots-Sec. 23
1 REXIST, Hugh C 1861
1 PRIOR, Prior E 1910
1 ANDERSON, Dougald 1857
1 BROWN, Benjamin A 1861
1 DAVIS, Hugh C 1861

Lots-Sec. 24
1 ANDERSON, Dougald 1857
1 ANDERSON, Benjamin A 1899
1 BROWN, Benjamin A 1899
1 DELOACH, John 1857

SYKES John 1843
CHRISMAS Moses 1855

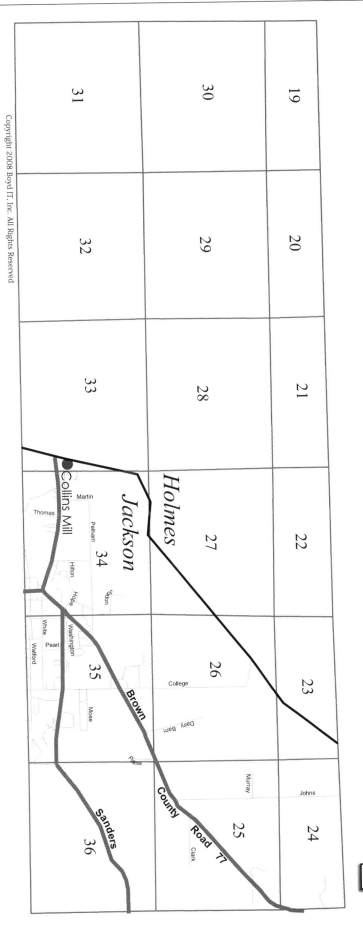

Road Map
T7-N R13-W
Tallahassee Meridian
Map Group 1

Note: the area contained in this map amounts to far less than a full Township. Therefore, its contents are completely on this single page (instead of a "normal" 2-page spread).

Cities & Towns
Collins Mill

Cemeteries
None

Legend

— Section Lines

══ Interstates

▬ Highways

— Other Roads

● Cities/Towns

✝ Cemeteries

Scale: Section = 1 mile X 1 mile
(generally, with some exceptions)

Historical Map

T7-N R13-W
Tallahassee Meridian

Map Group 1

Note: the area contained in this map amounts to far less than a full Township. Therefore, its contents are completely on this single page (instead of a "normal" 2-page spread).

Cities & Towns
Collins Mill

Cemeteries
None

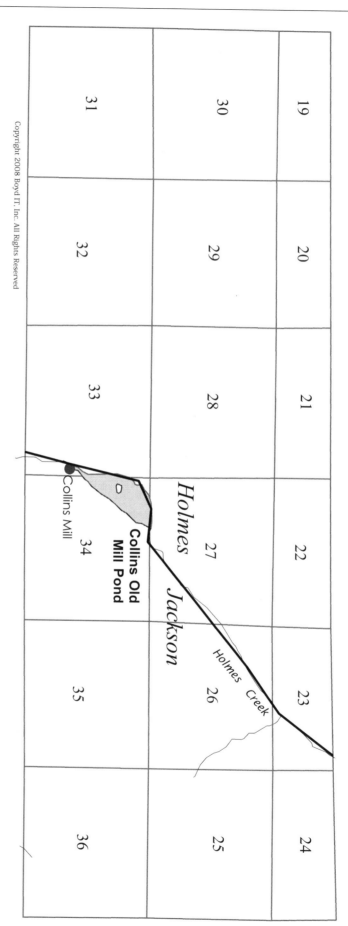

31	30	19
32	29	20
33	28	21
34	27	22
35	26	23
36	25	24

Collins Mill

Collins Old Mill Pond

Holmes

Jackson

Holmes Creek

N

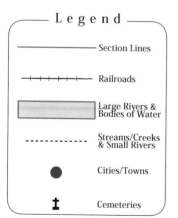

Legend

— Section Lines

++++++ Railroads

▭ Large Rivers & Bodies of Water

------- Streams/Creeks & Small Rivers

● Cities/Towns

✝ Cemeteries

Scale: Section = 1 mile X 1 mile
(there are some exceptions)

Map Group 2: Index to Land Patents

Township 7-North Range 12-West (Tallahassee)

After you locate an individual in this Index, take note of the Section and Section Part then proceed to the Land Patent map on the pages immediately following. You should have no difficulty locating the corresponding parcel of land.

The "For More Info" Column will lead you to more information about the underlying Patents. See the *Legend* at right, and the "How to Use this Book" chapter, for more information.

ID	Individual in Patent	Sec.	Sec. Part	Date Issued	Other Counties	For More Info . . .
101	ANDERSON, Duncan	20	E½NW	1831-06-25		A1
102	"	20	W½NW	1831-06-25		A1
146	BAKER, Nicholas	27	E½SW	1827-09-01		A1
147	"	27	W½SW	1847-04-26		A1
103	BEAUCHAMP, Erastus W	36	SENE	1860-04-02		A1
104	"	36	W½NE	1860-04-02		A1
153	BRADSHAW, Robert B	27	SE	1828-02-01		A1 G21
154	"	34	NE	1828-02-01		A1 G20
154	BRANTLY, Sarah	34	NE	1828-02-01		A1 G20
132	BRETT, Joseph D	19	E½SW	1844-07-10		A1
81	BROWN, Benjamin A	19	SWSW	1857-12-01		A1
82	"	30	NWNW	1857-12-01		A1
123	BROWN, John B	30	E½NW	1843-03-10		A1
125	"	30	NESW	1843-03-10		A1
122	"	20	NE	1850-08-10		A1
124	"	30	NESE	1852-09-01		A1
126	"	30	SWSE	1855-05-01		A1
169	BROWN, William	30	NWSW	1890-03-03		A2
170	"	30	SWNW	1890-03-03		A2
165	BUSH, Thomas M	29	SW	1843-03-10		A1
166	"	36	E½NW	1843-03-10		A1
167	"	36	S½	1843-03-10		A1
163	"	19	E½NE	1846-09-01		A1
164	"	24	NE	1898-04-27		A1
109	CADWELL, George	29	E½SE	1827-06-15		A1
107	CARTER, Farish	27	NE	1827-09-01		A1 G30
108	"	33	SW	1827-09-01		A1 G34
106	"	22	SE	1828-02-01		A1 G35
105	"	21	NW	1831-06-25		A1
107	CARTER, Porter	27	NE	1827-09-01		A1 G30
83	CLEMENTS, Benjamin	19	E½SE	1827-11-01		A1
84	"	19	W½SE	1827-11-01		A1
85	"	30	E½NE	1827-11-01		A1
86	"	30	W½NE	1827-11-01		A1
151	COMERFORD, Philip	19	E½NW	1843-03-10		A1
159	DANIEL, Stephen	26	SW	1827-04-02		A1
171	DONALD, William	34	E½NW	1827-04-02		A1
172	"	34	SW	1828-11-14		A1 G61 R90
127	FORT, John	24	W½SE	1828-02-01		A1
155	FOWLER, Samuel	28	NE	1827-04-02		A1 C R156
156	"	28	NE	1827-04-02		A1 C R155
99	GAINER, David	31	SWNW	1895-02-14		A2
87	HAMILTON, Benjamin	28	W½NW	1849-06-26		A1
88	"	29	E½NE	1849-06-26		A1
89	HAYS, Benjamin	33	W½SE	1828-02-01		A1
90	"	34	SW	1828-02-01		A1 C R172

ID	Individual in Patent	Sec.	Sec. Part	Date Issued	Other Counties	For More Info ...
172	HAYS, Benjamin (Cont'd)	34	SW	1828-11-14		A1 G61 R90
137	HEARIN, Joshua	31	SENE	1855-05-01		A1
138	" "	31	W½NE	1855-05-01		A1
134	HERRING, Joseph	30	SESW	1902-05-12		A1
135	" "	31	E½NW	1902-05-12		A1
136	" "	31	NESW	1902-05-12		A1
80	HINSON, Bartlett A	31	W½SW	1898-02-24		A2
111	HINSON, Harrison	31	NENE	1850-08-10		A1
117	HOOTEN, James H	19	1	1920-04-28		A1
91	HOWARD, Charles	24	W½SW	1828-02-01		A1
79	HUDSON, Asbury	20	SW	1827-04-02		A1
116	JONES, Isaiah	23	W½SE	1828-02-01		A1
119	JONES, Jessee	21	NE	1831-06-25		A1
100	KEITH, David H	24	NW	1844-07-10		A1
141	MARSHAL, Matthew	17	E½SW	1827-09-01		A1 G99
140	" "	35	W½NE	1827-09-01		A1
142	MARSHALL, Matthew	35	E½NE	1827-04-02		A1
108	MARTIN, Richard T	33	SW	1827-09-01		A1 G34
144	MCBAIN, Newnan	25	S½NE	1860-10-01		A1
145	" "	25	SE	1860-10-01		A1
153	MOORE, Guthrie	27	SE	1828-02-01		A1 G21
120	MOSES, Jessee	26	NE	1828-02-01		A1 G105
121	"	26	NW	1828-02-01		A1 G105
112	NEAL, Henry O	23	NE	1843-03-10		A1
120	ONEAL, Henry	26	NE	1828-02-01		A1 G105
121	" "	26	NW	1828-02-01		A1 G105
113	" "	23	E½NW	1839-09-20		A1
114	" "	23	W½NW	1843-03-10		A1
133	PARROT, Joseph G	32	W½NW	1828-02-01		A1
143	PHILLIPS, Nancy	20	E½SE	1827-06-15		A1
157	PINKHAM, Samuel	35	NW	1828-02-01		A1 G119
128	PORTER, John	27	NW	1847-04-26		A1
106	PORTER, Milley	22	SE	1828-02-01		A1 G35
120	ROACH, Alloway	26	NE	1828-02-01		A1 G105
121	"	26	NW	1828-02-01		A1 G105
75	SMITH, Adam	30	SWSW	1892-04-01		A2
76	" "	31	NWNW	1892-04-01		A2
129	SMITH, John	22	W½NW	1828-02-01		A1
120	" "	26	NE	1828-02-01		A1 G105
121	" "	26	NW	1828-02-01		A1 G105
152	SMITH, Powel	22	SW	1827-04-02		A1
160	SMITH, Stephen	22	1	1882-08-25		A2
161	" "	22	2	1882-08-25		A2
162	" "	22	3	1882-08-25		A2
77	SNELL, Amos	30	NWSE	1855-05-01		A1
78	" "	30	SESE	1855-05-01		A1
139	SNELL, Littleton G	31	NWSE	1852-09-01		A1
173	SNELL, William M	31	SESW	1857-07-01		A1
174	" "	31	SWSE	1857-07-01		A1
118	STEWART, James	18	4	1828-02-01		A1
172	THOMPSON, Robert	34	SW	1828-11-14		A1 G61 R90
110	WARD, George	36	NENE	1905-10-10		A2
141	WARD, James	17	E½SW	1827-09-01		A1 G99
130	WARD, John	17	SE	1827-09-01		A1
157	WEBB, James	35	NW	1828-02-01		A1 G119
158	WHITEFIELD, Seabourn B	36	W½NW	1839-09-20		A1
168	WHITEFIELD, William A	25	N½NE	1856-06-16		A1
115	WILLIAMS, Ira S	19	W½NE	1843-03-10		A1
131	WILLIAMS, John	20	W½SE	1827-06-15		A1
172	WILLIAMS, Mark	34	SW	1828-11-14		A1 G61 R90
148	WILLIAMS, Owen	28	SW	1827-09-01		A1
150	" "	33	NW	1828-02-01		A1
149	" "	32	E½NW	1843-03-10		A1
92	WILLIAMSON, Charles	31	E½SE	1827-10-01		A1
93	" "	32	E½SW	1827-10-01		A1
94	" "	32	W½SW	1827-10-01		A1
95	" "	35	E½SE	1827-10-01		A1
96	" "	35	E½SW	1827-10-01		A1
97	" "	35	W½SE	1827-10-01		A1
98	" "	35	W½SW	1827-10-01		A1

Patent Map

T7-N   R12-W
Tallahassee Meridian

Map Group 2

N

Township Statistics

Parcels Mapped	:	100
Number of Patents	:	88
Number of Individuals	:	66
Patentees Identified	:	62
Number of Surnames	:	49
Multi-Patentee Parcels	:	10
Oldest Patent Date	:	4/2/1827
Most Recent Patent	:	4/28/1920
Block/Lot Parcels	:	5
Parcels Re - Issued	:	2
Parcels that Overlap	:	0
Cities and Towns	:	2
Cemeteries	:	1

Note: the area contained in this map amounts to far less than a full Township. Therefore, its contents are completely on this single page (instead of a "normal" 2-page spread).

Legend

—————— Patent Boundary

—————— Section Boundary

No Patents Found
(or Outside County)

1., 2., 3., ...   Lot Numbers
(when beside a name)

[ ]   Group Number
(see Appendix "C")

Scale: Section = 1 mile X 1 mile
(generally, with some exceptions)

Section 19 (Lots-Sec. 19)
HINSON Bartlett A 1898 / GAINER David 1895 / SMITH Adam 1892 / SMITH Adam 1892 / BROWN William 1890 / BROWN William 1890 / BROWN Benjamin A 1857 / BROWN Benjamin A 1857 / HOOTEN James H 1920 / COMERFORD Ira S 1843 / WILLIAMS Philip 1843

Section 31
HINSON Bartlett A 1898 / HERRING Joseph 1902 / HERRING Joseph 1902 / BROWN John B 1843 / BROWN John B 1843 / BRETT Joseph D 1844 / CLEMENTS Benjamin 1827 / BUSH Thomas M 1846

Section 30
SNELL William M 1857 / SNELL William M 1857 / HERRING Joseph 1902 / HEARIN Joshua 1855 / SNELL Amos 1855 / BROWN John B 1843 / CLEMENTS Benjamin 1827 / CLEMENTS Benjamin 1827

Section 20
SNELL Littleton G 1852 / HEARIN Joshua 1855 / HINSON Harrison 1850 / SNELL Amos 1855 / BROWN John B 1852 / BROWN 1827 / CLEMENTS Benjamin 1827 / ANDERSON Duncan 1831 / ANDERSON Duncan 1831 / HUDSON Asbury 1827 / BROWN John B 1850 / WILLIAMS John 1827 / PHILLIPS Nancy 1827

WILLIAMSON Charles 1827 / WILLIAMSON Charles 1827 / HEARIN Joshua 1855 / SNELL Joshua 1855

Section 32 / 29
WILLIAMSON Charles 1827 / WILLIAMSON Charles 1827 / PARROT Joseph G 1828 / WILLIAMS Owen 1843 / BUSH Thomas M 1843 / 29

Section 21
CADWELL George 1827 / HAMILTON Benjamin 1849 / HAMILTON Benjamin 1849 / CARTER Farish 1831 / 21 / JONES Jessee 1831

Section 33 / 28
CARTER Farish 1827 / WILLIAMS Owen 1828 / CARTER [34] 1827 / 33 / WILLIAMS Owen 1827 / 28 / FOWLER Samuel 1827 / HAYS Benjamin 1828

Section 34 / 27
DONALD [61] William 1828 / HAYS Benjamin 1828 / 34 / DONALD William 1828 / BRADSHAW Robert B 1828 / BAKER Nicholas 1847 / BAKER Nicholas 1827 / BRADSHAW Robert B 1828 / PORTER John 1847 / 27 / CARTER [30] Farish 1827 / SMITH Powel 1827 / SMITH John 1828 / 22 / CARTER [35] Farish 1828

Lots-Sec. 22: 1 SMITH, Stephen 1882 / 2 SMITH, Stephen 1882 / 3 SMITH, Stephen 1882

Section 35 / 26
WILLIAMSON Charles 1827 / WILLIAMSON Charles 1827 / WILLIAMSON Charles 1827 / WILLIAMSON Charles 1827 / HAYS Benjamin 1828 / PINKHAM [119] Samuel 1828 / 35 / DANIEL Stephen 1827 / MARSHALL Matthew 1827 / MARSHALL Matthew 1827 / MOSES [105] Jessee 1828 / 26 / MOSES [105] Jessee 1828 / 23 / ONEAL Henry 1843 / ONEAL Henry 1839 / NEAL Henry O 1843 / JONES Isaiah 1828

Section 36 / 25 / 24
BUSH Thomas M 1843 / 36 / WHITEFIELD Seaborn B 1839 / BUSH Thomas M 1843 / BUSH Thomas M 1843 / BEAUCHAMP Erastus W 1860 / BEAUCHAMP Erastus W 1860 / WARD George 1905 / MCBAIN Newman 1860 / MCBAIN Newman 1860 / 25 / HOWARD Charles 1828 / 24 / KEITH David H 1844 / WHITEFIELD William A 1856 / FORT John 1828 / BUSH Thomas M 1898

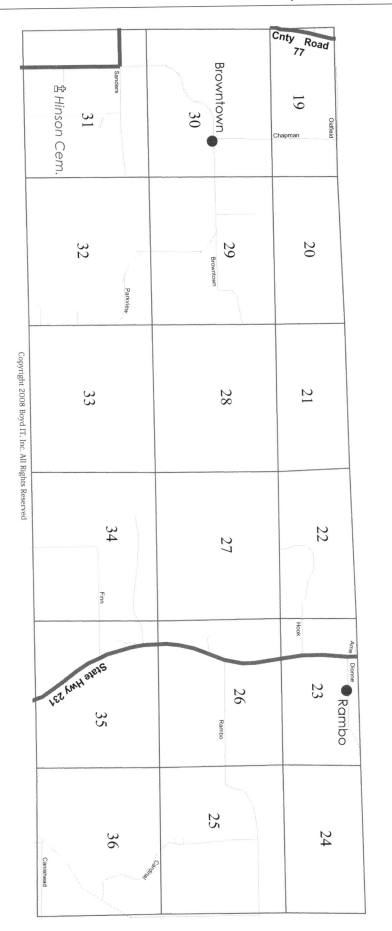

Road Map

T7-N R12-W
Tallahassee Meridian

Map Group 2

Note: the area contained in this map amounts to far less than a full Township. Therefore, its contents are completely on this single page (instead of a "normal" 2-page spread).

Cities & Towns
Browntown
Rambo

Cemeteries
Hinson Cemetery

Legend

———————	Section Lines
═══════	Interstates
━━━━━━━	Highways
———————	Other Roads
●	Cities/Towns
✝	Cemeteries

Scale: Section = 1 mile X 1 mile
(generally, with some exceptions)

Historical Map

T7-N R12-W
Tallahassee Meridian

Map Group 2

Note: the area contained in this map amounts to far less than a full Township. Therefore, its contents are completely on this single page (instead of a "normal" 2-page spread).

Cities & Towns
Browntown
Rambo

Cemeteries
Hinson Cemetery

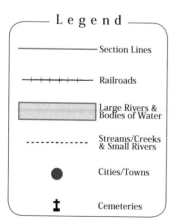

Legend

Section Lines

Railroads

Large Rivers & Bodies of Water

Streams/Creeks & Small Rivers

● Cities/Towns

✝ Cemeteries

Scale: Section = 1 mile X 1 mile
(there are some exceptions)

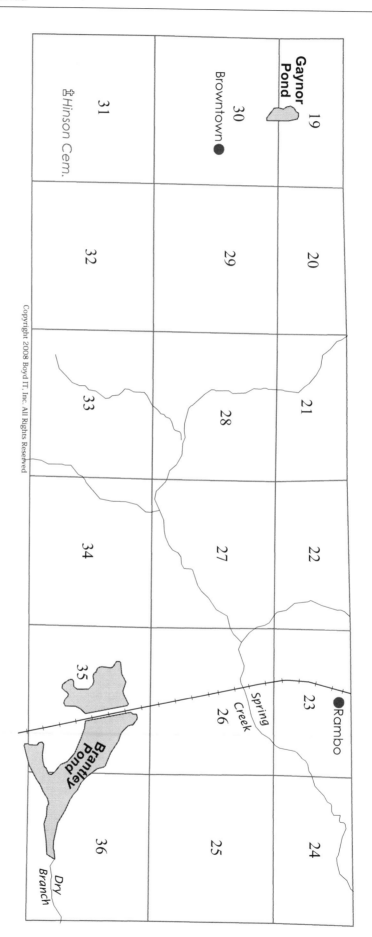

Map Group 3: Index to Land Patents

Township 7-North Range 11-West (Tallahassee)

After you locate an individual in this Index, take note of the Section and Section Part then proceed to the Land Patent map on the pages immediately following. You should have no difficulty locating the corresponding parcel of land.

The "For More Info" Column will lead you to more information about the underlying Patents. See the *Legend* at right, and the "How to Use this Book" chapter, for more information.

ID	Individual in Patent	Sec.	Sec. Part	Date Issued	Other Counties	For More Info . . .
261	ABERCROMBIE, William A	19	SESW	1860-04-02		A1
228	ARMSTRONG, Joseph A	27	W½SW	1839-09-20		A1
229	" "	28	NE	1839-09-20		A1
230	" "	33	E½NE	1839-09-20		A1
231	" "	33	SW	1839-09-20		A1
232	" "	33	W½SE	1839-09-20		A1
233	" "	34	SW	1839-09-20		A1
216	BEASLY, John	27	W½SE	1827-09-01		A1
208	BEAUCHAMP, Erastus W	31	SWNW	1860-04-02		A1
218	BEESLEY, John	27	E½NW	1828-08-22		A1
217	" "	21	W½SE	1828-09-10		A1
219	" "	27	W½NW	1829-05-01		A1
187	BLACKWELL, Amelia B	28	SW	1841-01-09		A1
202	BOZEMAN, Chapman	19	E½NW	1827-09-01		A1 G19
210	BRADBERY, James	23	E½SE	1856-06-16		A1
211	" "	23	NWSE	1856-06-16		A1
213	" "	26	NWNE	1856-06-16		A1
214	" "	26	NWNW	1856-06-16		A1
212	" "	26	N½SW	1860-04-02		A1
215	" "	26	SWNW	1860-04-02		A1
220	BRETT, John	19	NESW	1850-12-24		A1
221	" "	19	W½NE	1850-12-24		A1
193	BRUNER, Archibald	28	NESE	1856-06-16		A1
194	" "	36	S½SE	1861-12-10		A1
203	BRUNER, Daniel	33	W½NW	1856-06-16		A1
263	BRUNER, William J	30	E½NW	1857-12-01		A1
250	BUSH, Thomas M	22	E½NE	1843-03-10		A1
251	" "	23	NW	1843-03-10		A1
252	" "	31	S½	1843-03-10		A1
253	" "	32	SW	1843-03-10		A1
205	CALLOWAY, Elijah H	23	SW	1829-05-01		A1
206	" "	23	SWSE	1835-10-20		A1
244	CHRISTMAS, Nathaniel A	30	SWSW	1903-10-01		A2
195	CLEMENTS, Benjamin	19	E½NE	1827-11-01		A1
196	" "	20	E½NE	1831-06-25		A1
197	" "	20	E½NW	1831-06-25		A1
198	" "	20	W½NE	1831-06-25		A1
199	" "	20	W½NW	1831-06-25		A1
222	DANIEL, John H	19	W½SW	1857-12-01		A1
235	DANIEL, Josiah	34	SWSE	1839-09-20		A1
254	GRANGER, Thomas V	24	E½1	1896-06-23		A2
255	" "	24	E½SE	1896-06-23		A2
223	HARPER, John W	25	S½SW	1857-12-01		A1
224	" "	25	SWSE	1857-12-01		A1
225	" "	26	E½SE	1857-12-01		A1
226	" "	26	SENE	1857-12-01		A1

ID	Individual in Patent	Sec.	Sec. Part	Date Issued	Other Counties	For More Info . . .
188	HOWARD, Andrew J	30	E½SW	1860-04-02		A1
189	" "	30	NWSW	1860-04-02		A1
190	" "	30	W½SE	1860-04-02		A1
191	" "	31	N½NW	1860-04-02		A1
192	" "	31	NWNE	1860-04-02		A1
248	INGRAM, Robbard R	31	S½NE	1860-04-02		A1
242	JENKINS, Moses	21	E½SW	1838-07-28		A1
245	JENKINS, Nathaniel	21	E½SE	1856-06-16		A1
182	JONES, Allen	23	1	1860-04-02		A1
183	" "	24	2	1860-04-02		A1
184	" "	24	N½SW	1860-04-02		A1
185	" "	24	NWSE	1860-04-02		A1
186	" "	24	W½1	1860-04-02		A1
175	JONES, Allen H	24	SESW	1860-04-02		A1
176	" "	24	SWSE	1860-04-02		A1
177	" "	25	E½NW	1860-04-02		A1
178	" "	25	W½NE	1860-04-02		A1
200	JONES, Buckner	34	NW	1828-03-15		A1
207	MADDOX, Elijah L	22	W½SW	1857-12-01		A1
204	PEACOCK, Eli	33	E½SE	1828-08-22		A1
258	PEACOCK, Timothy	34	W½NE	1827-09-01		A1
256	" "	25	NWSE	1860-04-02		A1
257	" "	25	SESE	1860-04-02		A1
264	PEACOCK, William	36	E½NE	1902-07-03		A2
265	" "	36	NESE	1902-07-03		A2
179	PITTMAN, Allen J	25	NESW	1896-07-27		A2
180	" "	25	NWSW	1896-07-27		A2
181	" "	25	W½NW	1896-07-27		A2
209	PITTMAN, Ernest	24	SWSW	1908-10-26		A1
227	PITTMAN, Jones M	36	NW	1860-04-02		A1
259	PITTMAN, Wiley J	25	E½NE	1905-06-30		A2
260	" "	25	NESE	1905-06-30		A2
243	RAMSAY, Nathan	27	E½SW	1828-03-15		A1
234	SCOTT, Joseph	19	W½NW	1838-07-28		A1
202	SCOTT, Raney	19	E½NW	1827-09-01		A1 G19
246	THIGPEN, Reden G	30	SWNW	1859-06-01		A1
240	TUCKER, Lewis	14	2	1838-07-28		A1 F
241	" "	15	2	1838-07-28		A1
262	WHITEFIELD, William A	30	NWNW	1861-04-09		A1
236	WHITEHURST, Levi	26	NENE	1835-10-20		A1
237	" "	26	SWNE	1835-10-20		A1
238	WHITEHURST, Levy	26	E½NW	1828-07-22		A1
239	" "	26	W½SE	1828-07-22		A1
201	WILLIAMS, Caroline	31	SENW	1901-08-29		A2 G142
201	WILLIAMS, John	31	SENW	1901-08-29		A2 G142
249	WILLIFORD, Samuel B	36	NWSE	1856-06-16		A1
247	YOUNG, Richmond	34	E½SE	1902-12-30		A2

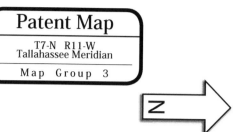

Patent Map

T7-N R11-W
Tallahassee Meridian

Map Group 3

N

Township Statistics

Parcels Mapped	:	91
Number of Patents	:	66
Number of Individuals	:	47
Patentees Identified	:	45
Number of Surnames	:	33
Multi-Patentee Parcels	:	2
Oldest Patent Date	:	9/1/1827
Most Recent Patent	:	10/26/1908
Block/Lot Parcels	:	6
Parcels Re - Issued	:	0
Parcels that Overlap	:	0
Cities and Towns	:	1
Cemeteries	:	0

Note: the area contained in this map amounts to far less than a full Township. Therefore, its contents are completely on this single page (instead of a "normal" 2-page spread).

Legend

— Patent Boundary

— Section Boundary

No Patents Found (or Outside County)

1., 2., 3., . . . Lot Numbers (when beside a name)

[ ] Group Number (see Appendix "C")

Scale: Section = 1 mile X 1 mile (generally, with some exceptions)

Map grid

Section 31

BUSH Thomas M 1843

Section 30

BEAUCHAMP Erastus W 1860
WILLIAMS [142] Caroline 1901
HOWARD Andrew J 1860
HOWARD Andrew J 1860
HOWARD Andrew J 1860
INGRAM Robbard R 1860
HOWARD Andrew J 1860

Section 19

CHRISTMAS Nathaniel A 1903
HOWARD Andrew J 1860
THIGPEN Reden G 1859
WHITEFIELD William A 1861
ABERCROMBIE William A 1860
BRUNER William J 1857
DANIEL John H 1857
BRETT John 1850
BOZEMAN [19] Chapman 1827
SCOTT Joseph 1838
BRETT John 1850
CLEMENTS Benjamin 1827

Section 32

BUSH Thomas M 1843

Section 29

CLEMENTS Benjamin 1831
CLEMENTS Benjamin 1831
CLEMENTS Benjamin 1831

Section 20

CLEMENTS Benjamin 1831
CLEMENTS Benjamin 1831

Section 33

ARMSTRONG Joseph A 1839
BRUNER Daniel 1856
ARMSTRONG Joseph A 1839
ARMSTRONG Joseph A 1839
PEACOCK Eli 1828

Section 28

BLACKWELL Amelia B 1841
ARMSTRONG Joseph A 1839
BRUNER Archibald 1856

Section 21

JENKINS Moses 1838
JENKINS Nathaniel 1856
BEESLEY John 1828

Section 34

ARMSTRONG Joseph A 1839
JONES Buckner 1828
ARMSTRONG Joseph A 1839
DANIEL Josiah 1839
YOUNG Richmond 1902
PEACOCK Timothy 1827

Section 27

RAMSAY Nathan 1828
BEASLY John 1827
BEESLEY John 1829
BEESLEY John 1828

Section 22

MADDOX Elijah L 1857
BUSH Thomas M 1843

Section 35

Section 26

BRADBERY James 1860
BRADBERY James 1856
BRADBERY James 1856
WHITEHURST Levi 1828
WHITEHURST Levi 1828
WHITEHURST Levi 1835
WHITEHURST Levi 1835
HARPER John W 1857
HARPER John W 1857

Section 23

CALLOWAY Elijah H 1829
CALLOWAY Elijah H 1835
BRADBERY James 1856
BRADBERY James 1856
CALLOWAY Elijah H 1835

BUSH Thomas M 1843
Lots-Sec. 23
JONES, Allen 1860

Section 36

PITTMAN Jones M 1860
WILLFORD Samuel B 1856
BRUNER Archibald 1861
PITTMAN Jones M 1860
PEACOCK William 1902
PEACOCK William 1902

Section 25

HARPER John W 1857
HARPER John W 1857
PITTMAN Allen H 1896
PITTMAN Allen J 1896
PITTMAN Allen J 1896
PITTMAN Allen J 1896
JONES Allen H 1860
JONES Allen H 1860
PEACOCK Timothy 1860
HARPER John W 1857
PITTMAN Timothy 1860
PITTMAN Wiley J 1905

Section 24

JONES Ernest 1908
JONES Allen 1860
JONES Allen H 1860
JONES Allen H 1860
PITTMAN Wiley J 1896
Lots-Sec. 24
2 JONES, Allen 1860
2 GRANGER, Thomas V 1896
2 JONES, Allen 1860
GRANGER Thomas V 1896

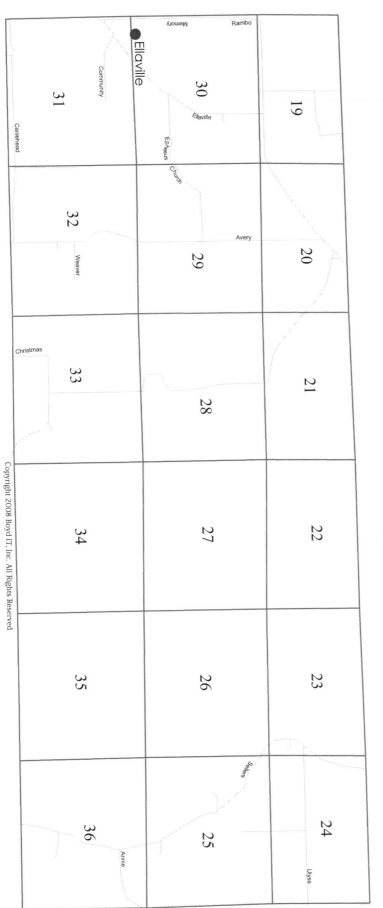

Road Map

T7-N R11-W
Tallahassee Meridian

Map Group 3

Note: the area contained in this map amounts to far less than a full Township. Therefore, its contents are completely on this single page (instead of a "normal" 2-page spread).

Cities & Towns
Ellaville

Cemeteries
None

N

Legend

———— Section Lines

══════ Interstates

▬▬▬▬ Highways

———— Other Roads

● Cities/Towns

✝ Cemeteries

Scale: Section = 1 mile X 1 mile
(generally, with some exceptions)

Historical Map

T7-N R11-W
Tallahassee Meridian

Map Group 3

Note: the area contained in this map amounts to far less than a full Township. Therefore, its contents are completely on this single page (instead of a "normal" 2-page spread).

Cities & Towns
Ellaville

Cemeteries
None

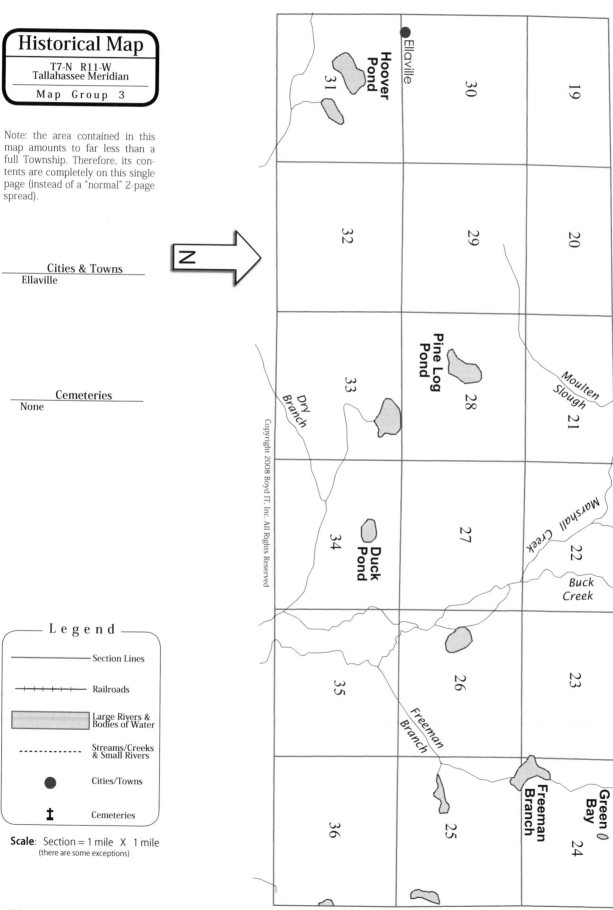

Legend

———————— Section Lines

+++++++ Railroads

▬▬▬▬ Large Rivers & Bodies of Water

- - - - - - - Streams/Creeks & Small Rivers

● Cities/Towns

✝ Cemeteries

Scale: Section = 1 mile X 1 mile
(there are some exceptions)

Map Group 4: Index to Land Patents

Township 7-North Range 10-West (Tallahassee)

After you locate an individual in this Index, take note of the Section and Section Part then proceed to the Land Patent map on the pages immediately following. You should have no difficulty locating the corresponding parcel of land.

The "For More Info" Column will lead you to more information about the underlying Patents. See the *Legend* at right, and the "How to Use this Book" chapter, for more information.

```
                    LEGEND
          "For More Info . . . " column
A = Authority (Legislative Act, See Appendix "A")
B = Block or Lot (location in Section unknown)
C = Cancelled Patent
F = Fractional Section
G = Group  (Multi-Patentee Patent, see Appendix "C")
V = Overlaps another Parcel
R = Re-Issued (Parcel patented more than once)

(A & G items require you to look in the Appendixes referred
to above. All other Letter-designations followed by a number
require you to locate line-items in this index that possess
the ID number found after the letter).
```

ID	Individual in Patent	Sec.	Sec. Part	Date Issued	Other Counties	For More Info . . .
267	ACOCK, Amos	32	E½NE	1838-07-28		A1
268	" "	32	SWNE	1838-07-28		A1
357	ANDERSON, Lucy	23	NE	1857-12-01		A1
356	" "	23	E½2NW	1860-04-02		A1
372	ANDERSON, Thomas	23	SWSE	1856-06-16		A1
371	" "	23	SW	1857-12-01		A1
301	AUSTIN, Ira J	32	W½SW	1925-11-05		A1
307	BAXTER, James D	36	E½NW	1860-04-02		A1
308	" "	36	SW	1860-04-02		A1
309	" "	36	W½NE	1860-04-02		A1
366	BAXTER, Theophilus	24	1NE	1860-04-02		A1
367	" "	24	1NW	1860-04-02		A1
368	" "	24	2NW	1860-04-02		A1
369	" "	24	NWSW	1860-04-02		A1
370	" "	24	W½2NE	1860-04-02		A1
334	BELL, John R	19	S½SW	1860-04-02		A1
335	" "	19	SWSE	1860-04-02		A1
336	" "	30	E½NW	1860-04-02		A1
337	" "	30	NWNW	1860-04-02		A1
338	" "	30	W½NE	1860-04-02		A1
362	BELL, Richard	34	NE	1856-06-16		A1
363	" "	35	NW	1856-06-16		A1
304	BROWN, James	29	NESE	1838-07-28		A1
361	BROWN, Rebecca	22	2NE	1860-07-02		A1
374	BUSH, Thomas M	31	E½SE	1843-03-10		A1
278	COLLINS, David	25	SESE	1855-05-01		A1
277	" "	25	NESE	1856-06-16		A1
375	COLLINS, Thomas R	25	NE	1857-12-01		A1
354	DEKLE, Littleton	32	E½SW	1860-04-02		A1
355	" "	33	SWNE	1860-04-02		A1
388	FOREST, William B	28	E½NE	1857-12-01		A1
385	GRAINGER, Voltaire	22	E½1NE	1860-04-02		A1
386	" "	22	NESE	1860-04-02		A1
387	" "	23	1NW	1860-04-02		A1
266	GRANGER, Alexander T	19	NWSW	1904-08-26		A2
373	GRANGER, Thomas L	22	W½1NE	1902-05-01		A2
379	GRANGER, Thomas V	19	3	1896-06-23		A2
276	HALL, Daniel	36	W½NW	1860-04-02		A1
310	HALL, James	22	S½SE	1860-04-02		A1
305	HALL, James C	23	E½SE	1860-04-02		A1
306	" "	23	NWSE	1860-04-02		A1
358	HALL, Malcolm	26	E½SW	1860-04-02		A1
359	" "	26	SE	1860-04-02		A1
360	" "	26	SWSW	1860-04-02		A1
389	HALL, William H	22	W½NW	1861-04-09		A1
391	HARPER, William	21	SENW	1840-10-10		A1

ID	Individual in Patent	Sec.	Sec. Part	Date Issued	Other Counties	For More Info . . .
392	HARPER, William (Cont'd)	21	SESW	1840-10-10		A1
296	HART, Hardy	36	SESE	1855-05-01		A1
295	" "	36	N½SE	1856-06-16		A1
352	HART, Joshua	24	NENE	1860-04-02		A1
273	KINGRY, Bryant C	19	1NE	1860-04-02		A1
332	LOCKART, John H	23	NWNW	1900-08-09		A2 R333
333	LOCKHART, John H	23	NWNW	1900-08-09		A2 C R332
311	LOWRY, James	19	E½NE	1844-07-10		A1
312	" "	19	E½SE	1844-07-10		A1 V351
313	" "	20	W½NW	1844-07-10		A1
314	" "	21	W½NE	1844-07-10		A1
315	" "	21	W½SE	1844-07-10		A1
316	" "	27	W½NW	1844-07-10		A1
317	" "	27	W½SW	1844-07-10		A1
318	" "	28	E½NW	1844-07-10		A1
319	" "	28	W½NE	1844-07-10		A1
320	" "	28	W½SE	1844-07-10		A1
321	" "	28	W½SW	1844-07-10		A1
322	" "	29	W½NW	1844-07-10		A1
323	" "	30	E½NE	1844-07-10		A1
324	" "	30	SE	1844-07-10		A1
325	" "	31	W½NE	1844-07-10		A1
326	" "	32	E½SE	1844-07-10		A1
327	" "	33	E½NE	1844-07-10		A1
328	" "	33	E½SE	1844-07-10		A1
329	" "	33	E½SW	1844-07-10		A1
330	" "	33	NW	1844-07-10		A1
331	" "	34	W½SW	1844-07-10		A1
393	MATHEWS, William	24	E½SW	1857-12-01		A1
394	" "	24	SE	1857-12-01		A1
395	" "	24	SWSW	1857-12-01		A1
396	" "	25	NWNW	1857-12-01		A1
285	MCDANIEL, Emma	28	SESE	1856-06-16		A1 G102
286	"	34	NW	1856-06-16		A1 G102
285	MCDANIEL, John	28	SESE	1856-06-16		A1 G102
286	" "	34	NW	1856-06-16		A1 G102
280	MCMILLAN, Dougald A	22	E½NW	1857-12-01		A1
281	" "	22	NESW	1857-12-01		A1
284	" "	22	W½SW	1857-12-01		A1
279	" "	21	NESE	1860-04-02		A1
282	" "	22	NWSE	1860-04-02		A1
283	" "	22	SESW	1860-04-02		A1
297	MCMILLAN, Henry C	21	NESW	1899-08-30		A2
274	MOSS, Charles D	31	NESW	1912-06-27		A1
390	PAULK, William H	30	NESW	1905-05-26		A2
383	PEACOCK, Timothy	31	E½NE	1852-09-01		A1
384	" "	31	E½NW	1857-12-01		A1
382	" "	30	S½SW	1860-04-02		A1
397	PEACOCK, William	31	NWSW	1902-07-03		A2
303	PITTMAN, James B	19	SENW	1896-07-27		A2
302	" "	19	NESW	1901-08-24		A2
351	PITTMAN, Jones M	19	NESE	1879-07-21		A2 V312
350	POLK, Jonathan	26	NENE	1857-12-01		A1
275	PURSER, Charles	32	W½SE	1838-07-28		A1
271	REDDING, Augustus B	33	W½SE	1855-05-01		A1
272	" "	33	W½SW	1855-05-01		A1
353	RIVERS, Lewis	31	NWSE	1861-12-10		A1
376	SCOTT, Thomas R	33	NWNE	1855-05-01		A1
364	SHINHOLSTER, Sebron	29	SWSE	1860-04-02		A1
365	" "	32	NWNE	1860-04-02		A1
294	SPEIGHTS, Green	36	E½NE	1860-04-02		A1
380	STRICKLAND, Thomas W	25	E½SW	1857-12-01		A1
381	" "	25	W½SE	1857-12-01		A1
298	WATFORD, Hillery	25	E½NW	1860-04-02		A1
299	" "	25	SWNW	1860-04-02		A1
300	" "	25	W½SW	1860-04-02		A1
288	WEEKS, Ferdinand J	26	NENW	1857-12-01		A1
289	" "	26	NWNE	1857-12-01		A1
293	" "	26	W½NW	1857-12-01		A1
290	" "	26	NWSW	1860-04-02		A1
291	" "	26	S½NE	1860-04-02		A1
292	" "	26	SENW	1860-04-02		A1
287	WEST, Famey	35	NE	1860-04-02		A1

ID	Individual in Patent	Sec.	Sec. Part	Date Issued	Other Counties	For More Info . . .
269	WHICHARD, Aproditus	21	1NE	1860-04-02		A1
270	" "	21	2NE	1860-04-02		A1
377	WHITAKER, Thomas R	31	S½SW	1857-12-01		A1
378	" "	31	SWSE	1857-12-01		A1
341	WILSON, John T	20	W½SW	1840-10-10		A1
348	" "	29	W½SW	1840-10-10		A1
339	" "	20	E½NW	1841-01-09		A1
340	" "	20	W½NE	1841-01-09		A1
343	" "	21	W½SW	1841-01-09		A1
344	" "	28	E½SW	1841-01-09		A1
345	" "	28	W½NW	1841-01-09		A1
347	" "	29	SESE	1841-01-09		A1
349	" "	32	W½NW	1841-01-09		A1
342	" "	21	NENW	1843-03-10		A1
346	" "	29	E½NW	1843-03-10		A1

Patent Map

T7-N R10-W
Tallahassee Meridian

Map Group 4

Township Statistics

Parcels Mapped	:	132
Number of Patents	:	88
Number of Individuals	:	56
Patentees Identified	:	55
Number of Surnames	:	40
Multi-Patentee Parcels	:	2
Oldest Patent Date	:	7/28/1838
Most Recent Patent	:	11/5/1925
Block/Lot Parcels	:	13
Parcels Re - Issued	:	1
Parcels that Overlap	:	2
Cities and Towns	:	1
Cemeteries	:	0

Note: the area contained in this map amounts to far less than a full Township. Therefore, its contents are completely on this single page (instead of a "normal" 2-page spread).

Legend

— Patent Boundary

— Section Boundary

No Patents Found (or Outside County)

1., 2., 3., ... Lot Numbers (when beside a name)

[ ] Group Number (see Appendix "C")

Scale: Section = 1 mile X 1 mile (generally, with some exceptions)

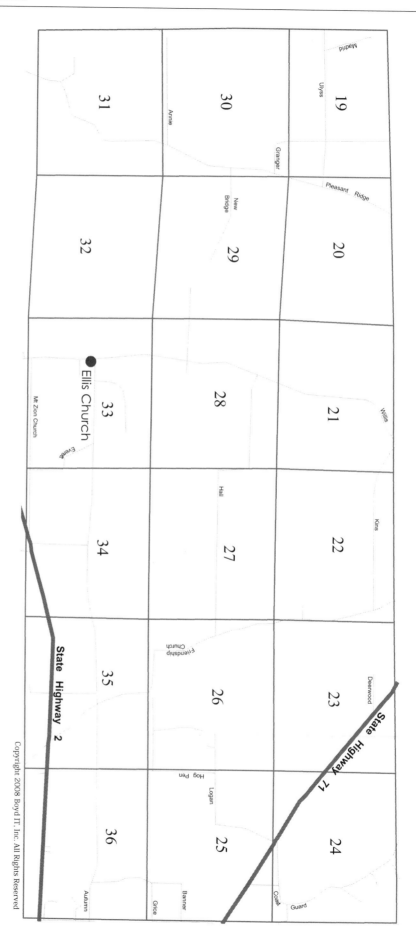

Road Map

T7-N R10-W
Tallahassee Meridian

Map Group 4

Note: the area contained in this map amounts to far less than a full Township. Therefore, its contents are completely on this single page (instead of a "normal" 2-page spread).

Cities & Towns
Ellis Church

Cemeteries
None

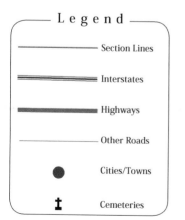

Legend

	Section Lines
	Interstates
	Highways
	Other Roads
●	Cities/Towns
✝	Cemeteries

Scale: Section = 1 mile X 1 mile
(generally, with some exceptions)

76

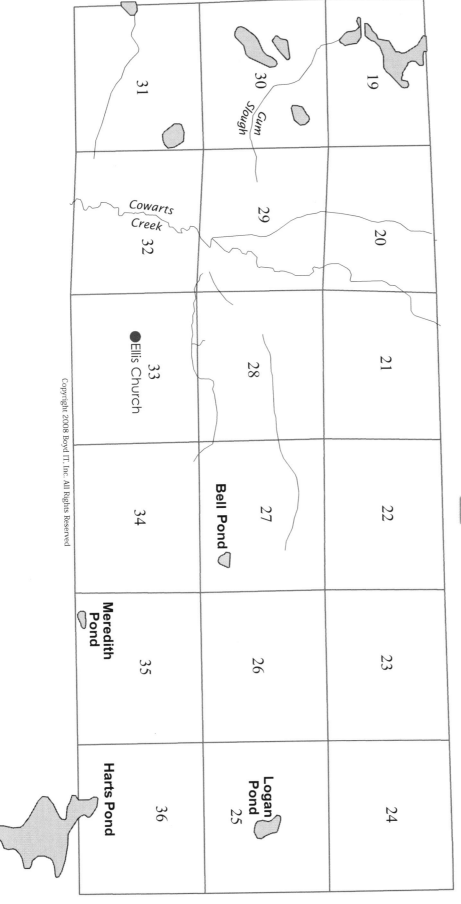

Historical Map

T7-N R10-W
Tallahassee Meridian

Map Group 4

Note: the area contained in this map amounts to far less than a full Township. Therefore, its contents are completely on this single page (instead of a "normal" 2-page spread).

Cities & Towns
Ellis Church

Cemeteries
None

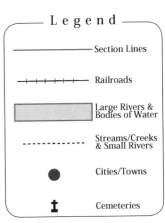

Legend

Section Lines

Railroads

Large Rivers &
Bodies of Water

Streams/Creeks
& Small Rivers

Cities/Towns

Cemeteries

Scale: Section = 1 mile X 1 mile
(there are some exceptions)

Map Group 5: Index to Land Patents

Township 7-North Range 9-West (Tallahassee)

After you locate an individual in this Index, take note of the Section and Section Part then proceed to the Land Patent map on the pages immediately following. You should have no difficulty locating the corresponding parcel of land.

The "For More Info" Column will lead you to more information about the underlying Patents. See the *Legend* at right, and the "How to Use this Book" chapter, for more information.

```
                    LEGEND
              "For More Info . . . " column
A = Authority (Legislative Act, See Appendix "A")
B = Block or Lot (location in Section unknown)
C = Cancelled Patent
F = Fractional Section
G = Group  (Multi-Patentee Patent, see Appendix "C")
V = Overlaps another Parcel
R = Re-Issued (Parcel patented more than once)

(A & G items require you to look in the Appendixes referred
to above. All other Letter-designations followed by a number
require you to locate line-items in this index that possess
the ID number found after the letter).
```

ID	Individual in Patent	Sec.	Sec. Part	Date Issued	Other Counties	For More Info . . .
513	CARLISLE, Wilson	25	SENE	1850-08-10		A1
514	" "	25	W½NE	1850-08-10		A1
512	CARLISLE, Wilson C	24	W½NE	1857-12-01		A1
403	COLLINS, Albert D	30	E½SW	1857-12-01		A1
404	" "	30	NESE	1857-12-01		A1
405	" "	30	W½SE	1857-12-01		A1
409	COLLINS, David	30	NWSW	1855-05-01		A1
410	" "	30	SESE	1855-05-01		A1
413	" "	31	NENW	1855-05-01		A1
414	" "	31	NWNE	1855-05-01		A1
411	" "	30	SWSW	1856-06-16		A1
412	" "	31	E½NE	1856-06-16		A1
415	" "	31	SENW	1856-06-16		A1
416	" "	31	SWNE	1856-06-16		A1
417	" "	31	W½NW	1856-06-16		A1
503	CONRAD, William	21	S½SW	1860-04-02		A1
504	" "	21	SENE	1860-04-02		A1
505	CONROD, William	21	SE	1857-12-01		A1
506	" "	22	SWSW	1857-12-01		A1
428	COONROD, Hester	21	SWNE	1860-04-02		A1
456	COONROD, Joseph M	21	N½SW	1860-04-02		A1
462	COONROD, Lorenzo D	21	NENE	1860-04-02		A1
463	" "	22	E½NW	1860-04-02		A1
464	" "	22	N½SW	1860-04-02		A1
465	" "	22	NWNW	1860-04-02		A1
466	" "	22	SWNW	1860-04-02		A1
498	COONROD, Thomas F	22	N½SE	1856-06-16		A1
499	" "	22	NE	1856-06-16		A1
500	" "	23	N½SW	1856-06-16		A1
493	DORSON, Samuel M	32	E½NW	1856-06-16		A1
495	" "	32	W½NE	1856-06-16		A1
494	" "	32	SW	1857-07-01		A1
507	FERGUSON, William G	36	NENW	1860-04-02		A1
508	" "	36	W½NE	1860-04-02		A1
509	" "	36	W½SE	1860-04-02		A1
450	GLADDEN, John W	33	NWSE	1861-12-10		A1
451	" "	33	SWNE	1861-12-10		A1
496	GLADDEN, Silas	33	S½NW	1857-12-01		A1
497	" "	33	SW	1857-12-01		A1
436	GRANTHAM, Joel	20	E½NE	1860-04-02		A1
427	GRICE, Hansel	21	NW	1860-04-02		A1
438	HAND, John	35	NENE	1860-04-02		A1
439	" "	36	NWNW	1860-04-02		A1
440	" "	36	S½NW	1861-12-05		A1
482	HARDEN, Permelia A	27	E½SE	1856-06-16		A1
483	" "	34	NENE	1856-06-16		A1

ID	Individual in Patent	Sec.	Sec. Part	Date Issued	Other Counties	For More Info . . .
484	HARDEN, Permelia A (Cont'd)	34	NW	1856-06-16		A1
485	" "	34	SWNE	1856-06-16		A1
467	HARDIN, Mary	27	W½SW	1857-12-01		A1
468	" "	28	SESE	1857-12-01		A1
469	" "	33	E½NE	1857-12-01		A1
470	" "	33	NESE	1857-12-01		A1
471	" "	34	N½SW	1857-12-01		A1
486	HARDIN, Permelia A	34	NWNE	1856-06-16		A1
457	HART, Joshua	19	E½NE	1860-04-02		A1
458	" "	19	NW	1860-04-02		A1
459	" "	19	NWNE	1860-04-02		A1
408	HOWARD, Catharine	20	NW	1861-02-01		A1
425	IRWIN, Freeman B	24	SWSW	1846-10-01		A1
424	" "	24	NWSW	1852-09-01		A1
455	IRWIN, Joseph	24	NENE	1855-05-01		A1
432	JOHNSON, Jasper P	19	NWSE	1860-04-02		A1
433	" "	19	SW	1860-04-02		A1
434	" "	19	SWNE	1860-04-02		A1
435	" "	30	W½NW	1860-04-02		A1
398	MARTIN, Aaron D	35	E½NW	1857-12-01		A1
400	" "	35	NWNE	1857-12-01		A1
401	" "	35	NWNW	1857-12-01		A1
399	" "	35	E½SE	1860-04-02		A1
402	" "	35	S½NE	1860-04-02		A1
448	MARTIN, John P	24	E½SW	1856-06-16		A1
449	" "	24	SE	1860-04-02		A1
423	MCANULTY, Francis A	27	E½SW	1861-04-09		A1
452	MCANULTY, John W	28	N½NE	1856-06-16		A1
453	" "	28	N½SW	1856-06-16		A1
454	" "	28	NW	1856-06-16		A1
475	MCANULTY, Nathan R	28	NESE	1857-12-01		A1
476	" "	28	S½NE	1857-12-01		A1
477	" "	28	SESW	1857-12-01		A1
478	" "	28	W½SE	1857-12-01		A1
479	" "	33	NENW	1857-12-01		A1
480	" "	33	NWNE	1857-12-01		A1
442	MCKAY, John	19	E½SE	1855-05-01		A1
443	" "	20	SE	1855-05-01		A1
444	" "	20	SW	1855-05-01		A1
445	" "	29	NE	1855-05-01		A1
446	" "	29	NW	1855-05-01		A1
447	" "	30	E½NE	1856-06-16		A1
418	MINCHIN, Edward	19	SWSE	1855-05-01		A1
492	OSWALD, Samuel H	24	SENE	1901-06-28		A2
460	PATRICK, Kingston K	36	E½SE	1860-10-01		A1
437	ROSS, John A	25	NENE	1911-11-27		A2
426	SCAMMELL, George	23	SESW	1891-02-13		A2
407	SMITH, Burrell	29	S½	1857-12-01		A1
419	STEPHENS, Edward	35	NESW	1856-06-16		A1
420	" "	35	NWSE	1856-06-16		A1
421	" "	35	SESW	1857-12-01		A1
472	STEPHENS, Middleton	28	SWSW	1860-04-02		A1
473	" "	32	E½NE	1860-04-02		A1
474	" "	32	W½NW	1860-04-02		A1
488	STEPHENS, Richard L	34	SE	1857-12-01		A1
489	" "	34	SENE	1857-12-01		A1
490	" "	35	SWNW	1857-12-01		A1
491	" "	35	W½SW	1857-12-01		A1
501	STRICKLAND, Thomas W	30	E½NW	1856-06-16		A1
502	" "	30	W½NE	1856-06-16		A1
406	TIDWELL, Archie H	33	NWNW	1902-07-03		A2
510	TIDWELL, William J	33	S½SE	1857-12-01		A1
511	" "	34	S½SW	1857-12-01		A1
430	WATFORD, James	31	E½SW	1860-04-02		A1
431	" "	31	W½SE	1860-04-02		A1
429	" "	20	W½NE	1860-07-02		A1
481	WATFORD, Nathan	31	E½SE	1857-12-01		A1
487	WATFORD, Reddin	32	SE	1857-12-01		A1
422	WATTS, Eleazer	7	2	1843-03-10		A1 F
461	WHITFIELD, Laura	22	SWSE	1860-04-02		A1
441	YARBOROUGH, John M	35	SWSE	1860-04-02		A1

Patent Map

T7-N R9-W
Tallahassee Meridian

Map Group 5

Township Statistics

Parcels Mapped	:	117
Number of Patents	:	64
Number of Individuals	:	49
Patentees Identified	:	49
Number of Surnames	:	33
Multi-Patentee Parcels	:	0
Oldest Patent Date	:	3/10/1843
Most Recent Patent	:	11/27/1911
Block/Lot Parcels	:	1
Parcels Re - Issued	:	0
Parcels that Overlap	:	0
Cities and Towns	:	1
Cemeteries	:	1

Note: the area contained in this map amounts to far less than a full Township. Therefore, its contents are completely on this single page (instead of a "normal" 2-page spread).

Legend

— Patent Boundary

— Section Boundary

No Patents Found
(or Outside County)

1., 2., 3., ... Lot Numbers
(when beside a name)

[ ] Group Number
(see Appendix "C")

Scale: Section = 1 mile X 1 mile
(generally, with some exceptions)

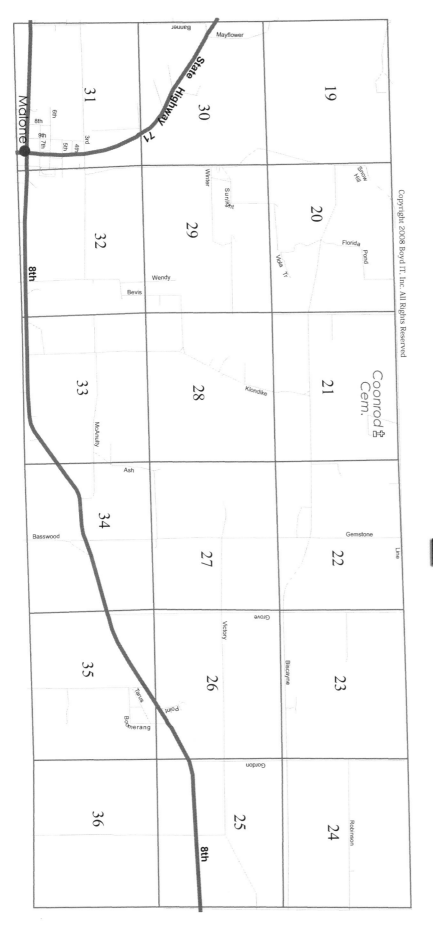

Road Map

T7-N R9-W
Tallahassee Meridian

Map Group 5

Note: the area contained in this map amounts to far less than a full Township. Therefore, its contents are completely on this single page (instead of a "normal" 2-page spread).

Cities & Towns
Malone

Cemeteries
Coonrod Cemetery

Legend

─────── Section Lines

━━━━━━━ Interstates

━━━━━━━ Highways

─────── Other Roads

● Cities/Towns

✝ Cemeteries

Scale: Section = 1 mile X 1 mile
(generally, with some exceptions)

Historical Map

T7-N R9-W
Tallahassee Meridian

Map Group 5

Note: the area contained in this map amounts to far less than a full Township. Therefore, its contents are completely on this single page (instead of a "normal" 2-page spread).

Cities & Towns
Malone

Cemeteries
Coonrod Cemetery

19	20	21 Hall Pond	22	23	24
30 Boggy Pond	29	28 Cypress Pond / Williams Pond	27	26	25
31 Malone ●	32	33	34	35	36

Florida Pond

Coonrod Cem.

N

Legend

———————— Section Lines

+++++++ Railroads

▭ Large Rivers & Bodies of Water

- - - - - - Streams/Creeks & Small Rivers

● Cities/Towns

✝ Cemeteries

Scale: Section = 1 mile X 1 mile
(there are some exceptions)

Map Group 6: Index to Land Patents

Township 7-North Range 8-West (Tallahassee)

After you locate an individual in this Index, take note of the Section and Section Part then proceed to the Land Patent map on the pages immediately following. You should have no difficulty locating the corresponding parcel of land.

The "For More Info" Column will lead you to more information about the underlying Patents. See the *Legend* at right, and the "How to Use this Book" chapter, for more information.

```
                      LEGEND
            "For More Info . . . " column
A = Authority (Legislative Act, See Appendix "A")
B = Block or Lot (location in Section unknown)
C = Cancelled Patent
F = Fractional Section
G = Group  (Multi-Patentee Patent, see Appendix "C")
V = Overlaps another Parcel
R = Re-Issued (Parcel patented more than once)

(A & G items require you to look in the Appendixes referred
to above. All other Letter-designations followed by a number
require you to locate line-items in this index that possess
the ID number found after the letter).
```

ID	Individual in Patent	Sec.	Sec. Part	Date Issued	Other Counties	For More Info . . .
605	ALMAROAD, William H	34	NESW	1856-06-16		A1
606	" "	34	SWNE	1856-06-16		A1
607	" "	34	SWNW	1856-06-16		A1
608	" "	34	W½SW	1856-06-16		A1
599	BOON, William A	27	E½SW	1856-06-16		A1
600	" "	27	NWSE	1856-06-16		A1
601	" "	27	NWSW	1856-06-16		A1
602	" "	27	W½NE	1856-06-16		A1
603	" "	28	SESE	1856-06-16		A1
604	" "	34	NENW	1856-06-16		A1
525	BROOKS, Charles F	32	S½SW	1911-09-18		A2
572	BROOKS, Joseph	14	2	1831-06-25		A1 G24
593	CALL, Richard K	35	4	1829-05-01		A1
538	CARTER, Farish	22	NE	1827-09-01		A1 G32
540	" "	23	1	1827-09-01		A1 G33
539	" "	14	1	1831-06-25		A1 G33
537	COLEMAN, Elisha	31	SESW	1906-06-04		A2
562	DAVIS, John	28	SWSE	1855-05-01		A1
563	" "	32		1855-05-01		A1 F
564	" "	32	N½SE	1855-05-01		A1 F
565	" "	33	N½NW	1855-05-01		A1
566	" "	33	NENE	1856-06-16		A1
567	" "	33	S½NW	1856-06-16		A1
568	" "	33	SW	1856-06-16		A1
569	" "	33	SWNE	1856-06-16		A1
584	GILCHRIST, Malcolm	27	E½SE	1827-10-01		A1 G72
585	" "	35	1	1827-10-01		A1 G72
586	" "	36	4	1827-10-01		A1 G72
596	GRANTLAND, Seaton	22	W½NW	1846-10-01		A1
541	GRIFFIN, General W	36	S½2	1852-09-01		A1
542	" "	36	S½3	1852-09-01		A1
536	HELMES, Edward	31	NWSW	1910-06-13		A2
573	IRVIN, Joseph	21	NWNE	1837-04-20		A1
519	IRWIN, Allen	29	S½SW	1861-12-05		A1
520	" "	30	SE	1861-12-05		A1
551	IRWIN, Henry	19	SE	1856-06-16		A1
552	" "	30	NE	1856-06-16		A1
538	IRWIN, Joseph	22	NE	1827-09-01		A1 G32
574	" "	17	E½SE	1831-06-25		A1
581	" "	22	E½NW	1838-07-28		A1
576	" "	20	E½NE	1846-10-01		A1
575	" "	19	NWNW	1855-05-01		A1
578	" "	21	NENE	1855-05-01		A1
577	" "	20	W½NE	1856-06-16		A1
579	" "	21	NW	1856-06-16		A1
580	" "	21	S½NE	1856-06-16		A1

ID	Individual in Patent	Sec.	Sec. Part	Date Issued	Other Counties	For More Info . . .
516	JOHNSON, Alexander	21	SESE	1857-12-01		A1
517	"	22	SWSW	1857-12-01		A1
518	"	28	NENE	1857-12-01		A1
540	KILBEE, William T	23	1	1827-09-01		A1 G33
539	"	14	1	1831-06-25		A1 G33
591	LOCKART, Perry J	20	SE	1857-12-01		A1
557	LOCKHART, James R	19	NENW	1861-12-05		A1
558	"	19	NWNE	1861-12-05		A1
582	LOCKHART, Joseph M	19	E½SW	1861-12-05		A1
592	LOCKHART, Perry J	20	SESW	1861-04-09		A1
598	LOCKHART, Valentine	20	NW	1861-04-09		A1
524	MCDONALD, Britton	33	W½SE	1857-12-01		A1
590	MCGEE, Moses	31	S½SE	1860-04-02		A1
553	NEEL, James A	34	NESE	1857-12-01		A1
554	"	34	SENE	1857-12-01		A1
616	NEEL, William M	36	N½2	1844-07-10		A1
611	"	33	SENE	1852-09-01		A1
609	"	27	SWSE	1856-06-16		A1
610	"	33	NESE	1856-06-16		A1
612	"	34	NWSE	1856-06-16		A1
613	"	34	S½SE	1856-06-16		A1
614	"	34	SESW	1856-06-16		A1
615	"	35	N½5	1856-06-16		A1
587	OSWALD, Marion	27	SWNW	1860-04-02		A1
588	"	28	NWSE	1860-04-02		A1
589	"	28	SWNE	1860-04-02		A1
594	OSWALD, Samuel	28	NESE	1857-12-01		A1
595	"	28	SENE	1857-12-01		A1
617	OWENS, William	10	1	1838-07-28		A1 F
583	PATRICK, Kingston K	31	SWSW	1860-07-02		A1
556	PATTERSON, James	35	NW	1828-02-01		A1
555	"	27	E½NW	1838-07-28		A1
618	PATTERSON, William	27	E½NE	1827-09-01		A1
619	"	35	7	1827-11-01		A1
620	"	35	W½SE	1828-02-01		A1 G112
522	POLLOCK, Arthur	35	SESW	1914-06-23		A2
521	PREVATT, Alto L	17	W½	1929-11-18		A2 F
571	ROACH, Jonathan	34	SENW	1852-09-01		A1
561	ROBERTS, John B	22	SE	1827-04-02		A1
572	"	14	2	1831-06-25		A1 G24
559	RODGERS, James W	31	N½SE	1897-10-28		A2
560	"	32	N½SW	1897-10-28		A2
621	ROYAL, Wilson	34	NENE	1837-04-20		A1
597	ROYALS, Shepard	33	SESE	1908-09-03		A2
515	SKIPPER, Abraham	20	NESW	1906-08-10		A2
523	STEPHENS, Benjamin H	19	SENE	1891-06-17		A2
570	STEPHENS, John I	19	NENE	1861-12-05		A1
620	TRUSSELL, John	35	W½SE	1828-02-01		A1 G112
533	WILLIAMSON, Charles	23	2	1827-10-01		A1
534	"	26	1	1827-10-01		A1
584	"	27	E½SE	1827-10-01		A1 G72
585	"	35	1	1827-10-01		A1 G72
535	"	36	1	1827-10-01		A1
586	"	36	4	1827-10-01		A1 G72
530	"	15	W½SE	1828-09-10		A1
526	"	11	1	1831-06-25		A1
527	"	15	E½NE	1831-06-25		A1
528	"	15	E½SE	1831-06-25		A1
529	"	15	W½NE	1831-06-25		A1
531	"	17	W½NE	1831-06-25		A1
532	"	17	W½SE	1831-06-25		A1
544	YARBOROUGH, Green B	22	NWSW	1852-09-01		A1
543	"	20	SWSW	1861-12-05		A1
547	YARBOROUGH, Greenberry	21	SWSE	1855-05-01		A1
549	"	28	NWNE	1855-05-01		A1
545	"	21	N½SE	1856-06-16		A1
546	"	21	SW	1856-06-16		A1
548	"	22	NESW	1856-06-16		A1
550	"	29	NW	1856-06-16		A1

Patent Map

T7-N R8-W
Tallahassee Meridian

Map Group 6

Township Statistics

Parcels Mapped	:	107
Number of Patents	:	80
Number of Individuals	:	47
Patentees Identified	:	47
Number of Surnames	:	36
Multi-Patentee Parcels	:	8
Oldest Patent Date	:	4/2/1827
Most Recent Patent	:	11/18/1929
Block/Lot Parcels	:	16
Parcels Re - Issued	:	0
Parcels that Overlap	:	0
Cities and Towns	:	0
Cemeteries	:	0

Note: the area contained in this map amounts to far less than a full Township. Therefore, its contents are completely on this single page (instead of a "normal" 2-page spread).

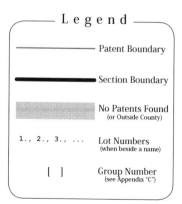

Legend

— Patent Boundary

— Section Boundary

No Patents Found (or Outside County)

1., 2., 3., ... Lot Numbers (when beside a name)

[ ] Group Number (see Appendix "C")

Scale: Section = 1 mile X 1 mile (generally, with some exceptions)

Map Parcels

Section 31

HELMES Edward 1910
PATRICK Kingston K 1860
COLEMAN Elisha 1906
MCGEE Moses 1860
RODGERS James W 1897

Section 30
IRWIN Allen 1861
IRWIN Henry 1856

Section 19
IRWIN Joseph 1855
LOCKHART James R 1861
LOCKHART James R 1861
STEPHENS John I 1861
STEPHENS Benjamin H 1891
LOCKHART Joseph M 1861
IRWIN Henry 1856

Section 32
BROOKS Charles F 1911
RODGERS James W 1897
DAVIS John 1855
DAVIS John 1855

Section 29
IRWIN Allen 1861
YARBOROUGH Greenberry 1856

Section 20
YARBOROUGH Green B 1861
LOCKHART Perry J 1861
SKIPPER Abraham 1906
LOCKHART Valentine 1861
LOCKHART Perry J 1857
IRWIN Joseph 1856

Section 21
IRWIN Joseph 1846
IRWIN Joseph 1856
YARBOROUGH Greenberry 1856
IRWIN Joseph 1856
IRWIN Joseph 1837
IRWIN Joseph 1855

Section 33
DAVIS John 1856
DAVIS John 1855
MCDONALD Britton 1857
ROYALS Shepard 1908
DAVIS John 1856
NEEL William M 1856

Section 28
DAVIS John 1855
DAVIS John 1855
OSWALD Marion 1860
OSWALD Samuel 1857
BOON William A 1856
OSWALD Samuel 1857
OSWALD Samuel 1857
YARBOROUGH Greenberry 1856
JOHNSON Alexander 1857

Section 22
JOHNSON Alexander 1857
YARBOROUGH Green B 1852
YARBOROUGH Greenberry 1856
GRANTLAND Seaton 1846
IRWIN Joseph 1838
IRWIN Joseph 1838
CARTER Farish [32] 1827
ROBERTS John B 1827

Section 27
BOON William A 1856
OSWALD Marion 1860
PATTERSON James 1838
BOON William A 1856
PATTERSON William 1827

Section 34
ALMAROAD William H 1856
NEEL William M 1856
ALMAROAD William H 1856
ROACH Jonathan 1852
ALMAROAD William H 1856
NEEL William M 1856
NEEL James A 1857
NEEL William M 1856

Section 26
BOON William A 1856
ROYAL Wilson 1837
NEEL William M 1856
GILCHRIST [72] Malcolm 1827

Lots-Sec. 26
1 WILLIAMSON, Charles 1827

Lots-Sec. 35
1 GILCHRIST, Malco[72]1827
4 CALL, Richard K 1829
7 NEEL, William M 1856
7 PATTERSON, William 1827

Lots-Sec. 23
1 ---
1 CARTER, Farish [33]1827
2 WILLIAMSON, Charles 1827

Section 35
PATTERSON James 1828
POLLOCK Arthur 1914
PATTERSON [112] William 1828
PATTERSON, William 1827

Section 36
Lots-Sec. 36
1 WILLIAMSON, Charles 1827
4 GRIFFIN, General W 1852
4 GRIFFIN, General W 1852
4 NEEL, William M 1844
4 GILCHRIST, Malco[72]1827

N

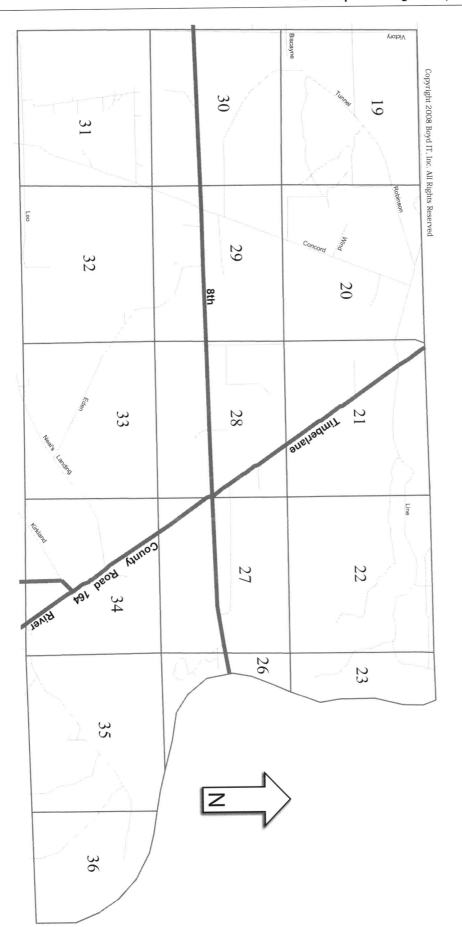

Road Map

T7-N R8-W
Tallahassee Meridian

Map Group 6

Note: the area contained in this map amounts to far less than a full Township. Therefore, its contents are completely on this single page (instead of a "normal" 2-page spread).

Cities & Towns
None

Cemeteries
None

L e g e n d

————	Section Lines
━━━━	Interstates
▬▬▬▬	Highways
————	Other Roads
●	Cities/Towns
⚰	Cemeteries

Scale: Section = 1 mile X 1 mile
(generally, with some exceptions)

Historical Map

T7-N R8-W
Tallahassee Meridian

Map Group 6

Note: the area contained in this map amounts to far less than a full Township. Therefore, its contents are completely on this single page (instead of a "normal" 2-page spread).

Cities & Towns
None

Cemeteries
None

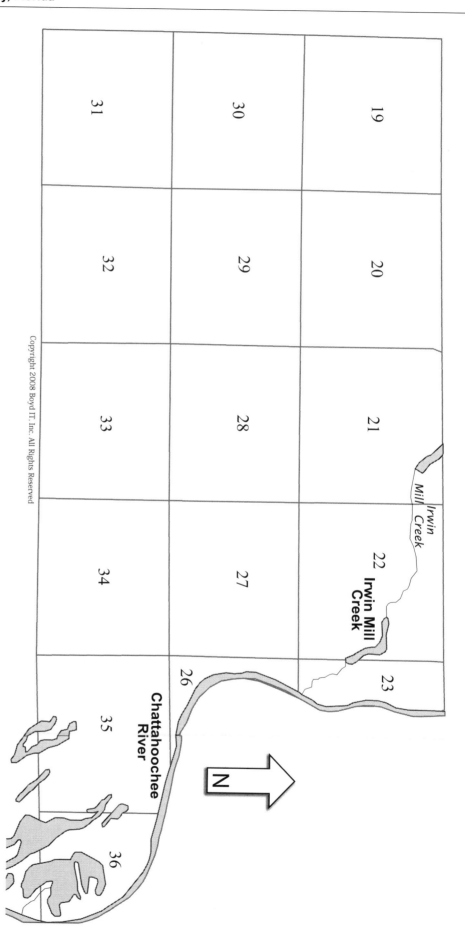

Irwin Mill Creek

Irwin Mill Creek

Chattahoochee River

N

31	30	19
32	29	20
33	28	21
34	27	22
35	26	23
36		

Legend

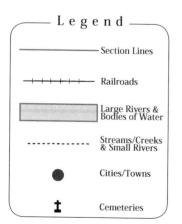

——————— Section Lines

+++++++ Railroads

Large Rivers & Bodies of Water

- - - - - Streams/Creeks & Small Rivers

● Cities/Towns

✝ Cemeteries

Scale: Section = 1 mile X 1 mile
(there are some exceptions)

Map Group 7: Index to Land Patents

Township 6-North Range 14-West (Tallahassee)

After you locate an individual in this Index, take note of the Section and Section Part then proceed to the Land Patent map on the pages immediately following. You should have no difficulty locating the corresponding parcel of land.

The "For More Info" Column will lead you to more information about the underlying Patents. See the *Legend* at right, and the "How to Use this Book" chapter, for more information.

```
                        LEGEND
              "For More Info . . . " column
A = Authority (Legislative Act, See Appendix "A")
B = Block or Lot (location in Section unknown)
C = Cancelled Patent
F = Fractional Section
G = Group  (Multi-Patentee Patent, see Appendix "C")
V = Overlaps another Parcel
R = Re-Issued (Parcel patented more than once)

(A & G items require you to look in the Appendixes referred
to above. All other Letter-designations followed by a number
require you to locate line-items in this index that possess
the ID number found after the letter).
```

ID	Individual in Patent	Sec.	Sec. Part	Date Issued	Other Counties	For More Info . . .
622	MENDHEIM, Albert A	36	NWNW	1898-02-03	Holmes	A2
630	RHODES, Jonathan B	36	NWNE	1860-04-02	Holmes	A1
629	"	"	36	NENE	1860-10-01	Holmes	A1
626	WILLIAMS, Henry A	36	E½SW	1895-01-02	Holmes	A2
627	"	"	36	NWSE	1895-01-02	Holmes	A2
628	"	"	36	SWNE	1895-01-02	Holmes	A2
632	WILLIAMS, Joseph	36	NESE	1861-04-09	Holmes	A1
633	"	"	36	SENE	1861-04-09	Holmes	A1
623	WOMBLE, Alonzo B	36	NENW	1904-12-16	Holmes	A1
624	WORLEY, Gray S	36	S½NW	1903-06-01	Holmes	A2
625	"	"	36	W½SW	1903-06-01	Holmes	A2
631	WORLEY, Joseph W	36	S½SE	1911-01-09	Holmes	A2

2

1

11

12

14

13

23

24

26

25

Jackson

Holmes

35

MENDHEIM Albert A 1898	WOMBLE Alonzo B 1904	RHODES Jonathan B 1860	RHODES Jonathan B 1860
WORLEY Gray S 1903		WILLIAMS Henry A 1895	WILLIAMS Joseph 1861
WORLEY Gray S 1903	**36** WILLIAMS Henry A 1895	WILLIAMS Henry A 1895	WILLIAMS Joseph 1861
		WORLEY Joseph W 1911	

Patent Map

T6-N R14-W
Tallahassee Meridian

Map Group 7

Township Statistics

Parcels Mapped	:	12
Number of Patents	:	8
Number of Individuals	:	7
Patentees Identified	:	7
Number of Surnames	:	5
Multi-Patentee Parcels	:	0
Oldest Patent Date	:	4/2/1860
Most Recent Patent	:	1/9/1911
Block/Lot Parcels	:	0
Parcels Re - Issued	:	0
Parcels that Overlap	:	0
Cities and Towns	:	0
Cemeteries	:	0

Note: the area contained in this map amounts to far less than a full Township. Therefore, its contents are completely on this single page (instead of a "normal" 2-page spread).

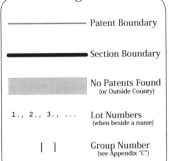

Legend

———— Patent Boundary

━━━━ Section Boundary

▨▨▨▨ No Patents Found
(or Outside County)

1., 2., 3., ...   Lot Numbers
(when beside a name)

[ ]   Group Number
(see Appendix "C")

Scale: Section = 1 mile X 1 mile
(generally, with some exceptions)

Road Map

T6-N R14-W
Tallahassee Meridian

Map Group 7

Note: the area contained in this map amounts to far less than a full Township. Therefore, its contents are completely on this single page (instead of a "normal" 2-page spread).

Cities & Towns
None

Cemeteries
None

2	1
11	12
14	13
23	24
26	25
35	36

Holmes

Jackson

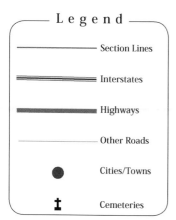

Legend

Section Lines

Interstates

Highways

Other Roads

● Cities/Towns

✝ Cemeteries

Scale: Section = 1 mile X 1 mile
(generally, with some exceptions)

2	1
11	12
14	13
23	24
26	25
35	36

Holmes

Jackson

Historical Map

T6-N R14-W
Tallahassee Meridian

Map Group 7

Note: the area contained in this map amounts to far less than a full Township. Therefore, its contents are completely on this single page (instead of a "normal" 2-page spread).

Cities & Towns
None

Cemeteries
None

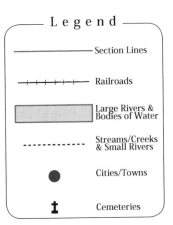

Legend

Section Lines

Railroads

Large Rivers & Bodies of Water

Streams/Creeks & Small Rivers

Cities/Towns

Cemeteries

Scale: Section = 1 mile X 1 mile
(there are some exceptions)

Map Group 8: Index to Land Patents

Township 6-North Range 13-West (Tallahassee)

After you locate an individual in this Index, take note of the Section and Section Part then proceed to the Land Patent map on the pages immediately following. You should have no difficulty locating the corresponding parcel of land.

The "For More Info" Column will lead you to more information about the underlying Patents. See the *Legend* at right, and the "How to Use this Book" chapter, for more information.

ID	Individual in Patent	Sec.	Sec. Part	Date Issued	Other Counties	For More Info . . .
715	ADAMS, James J	28	NW	1894-05-23		A2
789	ALLEN, Noah	17	N½NW	1901-08-12	Holmes	A2
790	" "	17	NWNE	1901-08-12	Holmes	A2
791	" "	17	SENW	1901-08-12	Holmes	A2
730	BAGGETT, Jefferson D	36	NE	1895-05-03		A2
676	BALL, George E	34	E½SE	1900-08-09		A2
776	BALL, Louis A	26	SW	1900-08-09		A2
792	BAREFOOT, Noah	34	NE	1890-12-11		A2
800	BEST, Sarah	19	NENW	1897-10-20	Holmes	A2 G16
801	" "	19	NWNE	1897-10-20	Holmes	A2 G16
802	" "	19	S½NW	1897-10-20	Holmes	A2 G16
761	BROOM, Joseph O	29	NESE	1894-06-20		A2
762	" "	29	W½SE	1894-06-20		A2
763	" "	32	NWNE	1894-06-20		A2
691	BROWN, Hiram	14	N½SE	1903-06-01		A2
692	" "	14	NESW	1903-06-01		A2
843	BROWN, William W	2	NWNW	1890-12-11		A2
844	" "	3	N½NE	1890-12-11		A2
845	" "	3	SWNE	1890-12-11		A2
643	CAIN, Bryant P	19	NWNW	1896-09-16	Holmes	A2
706	CARMICHAEL, James D	10	NWSW	1915-01-05		A2
717	CARTER, James O	9	NWSE	1901-08-12	Holmes	A2 V809
738	CHRISTIE, John H	20	NE	1902-12-30	Holmes	A2
774	COLLINS, Lorenzo J	32	S½SE	1897-07-03		A2
775	" "	32	S½SW	1897-07-03		A2
707	COURTNEY, James D	23	NWNW	1901-12-12		A1
640	CRUTCHFIELD, Andrew J	17	E½SE	1901-04-09	Holmes	A2
641	" "	17	SENE	1901-04-09	Holmes	A2
678	CRUTCHFIELD, George W	11	NE	1894-01-27		A2
710	CRUTCHFIELD, James H	1	SW	1891-07-14		A2
740	CRUTCHFIELD, John L	21	E½NE	1894-05-23		A2
741	" "	21	NESE	1894-05-23		A2
742	" "	22	NWSW	1894-05-23		A2
837	CRUTCHFIELD, William R	21	SESE	1892-07-11		A2
838	" "	22	SWSW	1892-07-11		A2
839	" "	28	E½NE	1892-07-11		A2
660	CUSHING, Elisha J	1	SE	1896-07-27		A2
697	DANFORD, Isaac J	22	SESE	1896-08-06		A2
698	" "	23	SWNW	1896-08-06		A2
699	" "	23	W½SW	1896-08-06		A2
657	DAVIS, David	17	W½SE	1834-08-20	Holmes	A1
716	DUNCAN, James L	11	SW	1891-11-09		A2
780	DUNCAN, Martha J	21	SENW	1899-05-22		A2
781	"	21	SWNE	1899-05-22		A2
798	ELMORE, Randal A	32	N½SW	1889-07-03		A2
833	ELMORE, William J	17	SESW	1907-04-17	Holmes	A2

ID	Individual in Patent	Sec.	Sec. Part	Date Issued	Other Counties	For More Info . . .
796	FOREHAND, Philip C	20	SWSE	1903-06-26	Holmes	A2
797	FOREHAND, Phillip	30	SE	1893-02-21	Holmes	A2
822	FOREHAND, William	20	NESW	1890-12-11	Holmes	A2
823	" "	20	NWSE	1890-12-11	Holmes	A2
824	" "	20	S½SW	1890-12-11	Holmes	A2
825	FOREHAND, William G	29	NESW	1898-05-02		A2
826	" "	29	SENW	1898-05-02		A2
827	" "	29	W½SW	1898-05-02		A2
735	FRANKLIN, John	10	NENE	1896-04-27		A2
736	" "	3	S½SE	1896-04-27		A2
737	" "	3	SESW	1896-04-27		A2
760	GOLDEN, Joseph	12	NW	1891-11-09		A2
793	GOLDEN, Noah	12	SESE	1889-07-02		A2
794	" "	13	N½NE	1889-07-02		A2
795	" "	13	NENW	1889-07-02		A2
840	GOLDEN, William R	29	NENW	1898-05-02		A2
841	" "	29	W½NW	1898-05-02		A2
842	" "	30	SENE	1898-05-02	Holmes	A2
810	GOLDING, Thomas	22	NW	1891-11-09		A2
648	GRANT, Charles G	15	N½NE	1901-11-20		A2 V851, 653
649	" "	15	S½SE	1901-11-20		A2
727	GRANT, Jefferson C	15	E½SW	1891-07-14		A2
728	" "	15	NWSE	1891-07-14		A2
729	" "	15	SENW	1891-07-14		A2
670	HARDEN, Felix	19	S½SE	1860-04-02	Holmes	A1
671	" "	30	NENE	1860-04-02	Holmes	A1
672	" "	30	NENW	1860-04-02	Holmes	A1
673	" "	30	W½NE	1860-04-02	Holmes	A1
664	HARPER, Ephraim A	3	N½SE	1890-12-11		A2
665	" "	3	NESW	1890-12-11		A2
666	" "	3	SENE	1890-12-11		A2
778	HARRELL, Margaret A	29	SESW	1899-08-14		A2
807	HARRELL, Stephen E	9	NESW	1860-07-02	Holmes	A1
808	" "	9	S½NW	1860-07-02	Holmes	A1
809	" "	9	W½SE	1860-07-02	Holmes	A1 V717
806	" "	9	NESE	1861-12-05	Holmes	A1
722	HEISLER, James S	10	N½SE	1891-11-09		A2
723	" "	10	SENE	1891-11-09		A2
711	HICKS, James H	32	N½NW	1893-08-14		A2
712	" "	32	S½NW	1893-08-14		A2
854	HILL, Woodruff F	21	E½SW	1896-01-03		A2
855	" "	21	W½SE	1896-01-03		A2
800	HOLDEN, Sarah	19	NENW	1897-10-20	Holmes	A2 G16
801	" "	19	NWNE	1897-10-20	Holmes	A2 G16
802	" "	19	S½NW	1897-10-20	Holmes	A2 G16
739	HUGHES, John	22	SWSE	1901-04-09		A2
680	JACKSON, Gillis	19	SW	1891-12-21	Holmes	A2
816	JACKSON, Thomas P	30	NWNW	1891-12-21	Holmes	A2
751	JOHNSON, John W	2	S½SE	1884-06-30		A2
752	" "	2	S½SW	1884-06-30		A2
785	JORDAN, Mary J	17	SWNE	1908-10-01	Holmes	A1
654	KIRKLAND, David A	4	NENW	1894-06-20	Holmes	A2
655	" "	4	NWSW	1894-06-20	Holmes	A2
656	" "	4	W½NW	1894-06-20	Holmes	A2
644	MATHEWS, Burrell F	22	E½SW	1899-05-22		A2
746	MCCREARY, John R	36	SE	1891-07-14		A2
819	MCINTOSH, Virginia	10	S½SE	1890-09-24		A2
834	MCKINNE, William	1	E½NE	1893-10-13		A2
835	" "	1	SWNE	1893-10-13		A2
767	MILES, Leonard R	24	SWSE	1904-07-27		A2
650	MILLER, Charles H	28	NESW	1902-10-11		A2
686	MILLER, Henry J	22	N½SE	1891-06-17		A2
687	" "	22	S½NE	1891-06-17		A2
726	MILLER, Jarid	14	NE	1891-02-13		A2
731	MILLER, John F	24	NESW	1892-04-01		A2
732	" "	24	NWSE	1892-04-01		A2
733	" "	24	SENW	1892-04-01		A2
734	" "	24	SWNE	1892-04-01		A2
805	MILLER, Solomon	10	SWNE	1898-02-24		A2
820	MILLER, William A	24	E½NE	1896-09-25		A2
821	" "	24	E½SE	1896-09-25		A2
724	MURDOCK, James W	26	NE	1895-02-14		A2
700	PARKER, J J	21	NENW	1892-06-30		A2

ID	Individual in Patent	Sec.	Sec. Part	Date Issued	Other Counties	For More Info . . .
701	PARKER, J J (Cont'd)	21	NWNE	1892-06-30		A2
702	" "	21	W½NW	1892-06-30		A2
811	PARKER, Thomas J	13	SWSW	1895-08-01		A2
812	" "	14	SESE	1895-08-01		A2
813	" "	23	NENE	1895-08-01		A2
814	" "	24	NWNW	1895-08-01		A2
846	PARKER, William W	11	NW	1891-11-09		A2
667	PHILIPS, Ezekiel A	11	SE	1892-06-06		A2
679	PHILIPS, George W	12	SW	1892-06-30		A2
828	PHILIPS, William H	3	S½NW	1905-05-17		A2
829	" "	3	W½SW	1905-05-17		A2
634	PHILLIPS, Alexander	4	SWSW	1902-10-11	Holmes	A2
635	" "	9	NWNW	1902-10-11	Holmes	A2
642	POWELL, Benjamin F	29	NE	1898-07-18		A2
708	POWELL, James F	20	E½SE	1893-12-06	Holmes	A2
709	" "	21	W½SW	1893-12-06		A2
755	REDDICK, Joseph C	30	S½NW	1900-01-27	Holmes	A2
756	" "	30	SWSW	1900-01-27	Holmes	A2
636	REGISTER, Allen N	12	SWSE	1898-04-27		A2
669	REGISTER, Ezekiel	12	N½SE	1889-10-21		A1
668	REGISTER, Ezekiel I	12	NE	1883-08-01		A2
768	REGISTER, Lewis A	26	NW	1898-07-18		A2
754	RHODES, Jonathan B	30	NWSW	1860-04-02	Holmes	A1
688	RICKS, Henry	32	E½NE	1894-01-27		A2
689	" "	32	NWSE	1894-01-27		A2
690	" "	32	SWNE	1894-01-27		A2
817	RODGERS, Union C	19	NWSE	1904-08-16	Holmes	A1
818	" "	19	S½NE	1904-08-16	Holmes	A1
782	SHARON, Martin S	23	E½SE	1896-04-27		A2
783	" "	23	SENE	1896-04-27		A2
784	" "	23	SWSE	1896-04-27		A2
743	SHIPES, John L	28	SESW	1892-06-30		A2
744	" "	28	W½SW	1892-06-30		A2
745	" "	29	SESE	1892-06-30		A2
659	SLOAN, Elijah	23	SESW	1901-10-23		A2
777	SLOANE, Major	23	NWNE	1901-10-01		A2
773	SNELL, Littleton G	1	NWNE	1856-06-16		A1
772	" "	1	NW	1857-12-01		A1
769	SUGGS, Lewis M	13	E½SW	1895-05-03		A2
770	" "	24	NENW	1895-05-03		A2
771	" "	24	NWNE	1895-05-03		A2
637	SWEET, Allen T	14	S½SW	1888-11-20		A2
638	" "	14	SWSE	1888-11-20		A2
639	" "	23	NENW	1888-11-20		A2
674	SYFRETT, Francis M	2	N½NE	1883-08-13		A2
675	SYFRETT, Frederick M	2	NENW	1888-11-22		A2
713	TAYLOR, James H	13	NESE	1895-05-03		A2
714	" "	13	SENE	1895-05-03		A2
757	TAYLOR, Joseph G	13	NWSW	1899-05-22		A2
758	" "	13	SENW	1899-05-22		A2
759	" "	13	W½NW	1899-05-22		A2
830	TAYLOR, William H	13	SESE	1893-03-27		A2
831	" "	13	SWNE	1893-03-27		A2
832	" "	13	W½SE	1893-03-27		A2
718	TURNER, James P	2	N½SE	1860-04-02		A1
719	" "	2	N½SW	1860-04-02		A1
720	" "	2	S½NE	1860-04-02		A1
721	" "	2	S½NW	1860-04-02		A1
747	UNDERWOOD, John	4	NESW	1896-11-16	Holmes	A2
748	" "	4	NWSE	1896-11-16	Holmes	A2
749	" "	4	SENW	1896-11-16	Holmes	A2
750	" "	4	SWNE	1896-11-16	Holmes	A2
815	UNDERWOOD, Thomas J	4	NWNE	1908-07-06	Holmes	A2
651	VICKERS, Charles	14	N½NW	1891-11-09		A2
652	" "	14	SENW	1891-11-09		A2
653	" "	15	NENE	1891-11-09		A2 V648
753	WARD, John W	30	E½SW	1861-04-09	Holmes	A1
658	WATFORD, Dempsey	28	SE	1890-06-05		A2
764	WATFORD, Katie	34	W½SW	1905-03-08		A2
788	WATFORD, Nelson	34	NW	1890-06-05		A2
803	WATFORD, Simpson	34	E½SW	1891-04-06		A2
804	" "	34	W½SE	1891-04-06		A2
836	WATFORD, William N	28	W½NE	1901-02-27		A1

ID	Individual in Patent	Sec.	Sec. Part	Date Issued	Other Counties	For More Info . . .
693	WHITE, Isaac H	14	NWSW	1894-05-23		A2
694	" "	14	SWNW	1894-05-23		A2
695	" "	15	NESE	1894-05-23		A2
696	" "	15	SENE	1894-05-23		A2
765	WHITE, King	10	NENW	1860-04-02		A1
766	" "	10	NWNE	1860-04-02		A1
661	WILLIAMS, Elizabeth A	24	SESW	1893-03-27		A2
662	" "	24	SWNW	1893-03-27		A2
663	" "	24	W½SW	1893-03-27		A2
677	WILLIAMS, George F	26	SE	1891-11-09		A2
681	WILLIAMS, Henry C	23	NESW	1896-06-23		A2
682	" "	23	NWSE	1896-06-23		A2
683	" "	23	SENW	1896-06-23		A2
684	" "	23	SWNE	1896-06-23		A2
703	WILLIAMS, James B	17	NESW	1891-02-13	Holmes	A2
704	" "	17	SWNW	1891-02-13	Holmes	A2
705	" "	17	W½SW	1891-02-13	Holmes	A2
725	WILLIAMS, Jane	36	SW	1893-03-27		A2 G143
725	WILLIAMS, John M	36	SW	1893-03-27		A2 G143
779	WILLIAMS, Marion W	36	NW	1898-05-02		A2
847	WILLIAMS, William	10	E½SW	1861-12-10		A1
848	" "	10	SENW	1861-12-10		A1
849	" "	10	SWSW	1861-12-10		A1
850	" "	15	NENW	1861-12-10		A1
851	" "	15	W½NE	1861-12-10		A1 V648
853	" "	9	SESE	1861-12-10	Holmes	A1
852	" "	19	NENE	1884-10-15	Holmes	A2
799	WOMBLE, Rufus E	20	NWNW	1904-09-08	Holmes	A1
685	YAWN, Henry G	3	N½NW	1897-05-25		A2
645	YORK, Calvin	19	NESE	1861-04-09	Holmes	A1
646	" "	20	NWSW	1861-04-09	Holmes	A1
647	" "	20	S½NW	1861-04-09	Holmes	A1
786	YORK, Miles H	15	W½NW	1888-11-20		A2
787	" "	15	W½SW	1888-11-20		A2

Patent Map

T6-N R13-W
Tallahassee Meridian

Map Group 8

Township Statistics

Parcels Mapped	:	222
Number of Patents	:	119
Number of Individuals	:	118
Patentees Identified	:	116
Number of Surnames	:	72
Multi-Patentee Parcels	:	4
Oldest Patent Date	:	8/20/1834
Most Recent Patent	:	1/5/1915
Block/Lot Parcels	:	0
Parcels Re-Issued	:	0
Parcels that Overlap	:	5
Cities and Towns	:	1
Cemeteries	:	1

Copyright 2008 Boyd IT. Inc. All Rights Reserved

98

Helpful Hints

1. This Map's INDEX can be found on the preceding pages.

2. Refer to Map "C" to see where this Township lies within Jackson County, Florida.

3. Numbers within square brackets [ ] denote a multi-patentee land parcel (multi-owner). Refer to Appendix "C" for a full list of members in this group.

4. Areas that look to be crowded with Patentees usually indicate multiple sales of the same parcel (Re-issues) or Overlapping parcels. See this Township's Index for an explanation of these and other circumstances that might explain "odd" groupings of Patentees on this map.

Map (Township 6-N Range 13-W) — land parcels:

YAWN Henry G 1897; BROWN William W 1890; BROWN William W 1890; SYFRETT Frederick M 1888; SYFRETT Francis M 1883; SNELL Littleton G 1857; SNELL Littleton G 1856; MCKINNE William 1893

PHILIPS William H 1905; BROWN William W 1890; HARPER Ephraim A 1890; TURNER James P 1860; TURNER James P 1860; MCKINNE William 1893

PHILIPS William H 1905; HARPER Ephraim A 1890; **3** HARPER Ephraim A 1890; TURNER James P 1860 **2**; TURNER James P 1860; **1**; CUSHING Elisha J 1896

PHILIPS William H 1905; FRANKLIN John 1896; FRANKLIN John 1896; JOHNSON John W 1884; JOHNSON John W 1884; CRUTCHFIELD James H 1891

WHITE King 1860; WHITE King 1860; FRANKLIN John 1896; PARKER William W 1891 **11**; CRUTCHFIELD George W 1894; GOLDEN Joseph 1891; REGISTER Ezekiel I 1883 **12**

WILLIAMS William 1861; MILLER Solomon 1898; HEISLER James S 1891

CARMICHAEL James D 1915; WILLIAMS William 1861 **10**; HEISLER James S 1891; DUNCAN James L 1891; PHILIPS Ezekiel A 1892; PHILIPS George W 1892; REGISTER Ezekiel 1889; REGISTER Allen N 1898; GOLDEN Noah 1889

WILLIAMS William 1861; MCINTOSH Virginia 1890

YORK Miles H 1888; WILLIAMS William 1861; GRANT Charles G 1901; VICKERS Charles 1891; VICKERS Charles 1891; GOLDEN Noah 1889; GOLDEN Noah 1889

GRANT Jefferson C 1891; WILLIAMS William 1861; WHITE Isaac H 1894; WHITE Isaac H 1894; VICKERS Charles 1891 **14**; MILLER Jarid 1891; TAYLOR Joseph G 1899; TAYLOR Joseph G 1899; TAYLOR William H 1893; TAYLOR James H 1895

15; GRANT Jefferson C 1891; WHITE Isaac H 1894; WHITE Isaac H 1894; BROWN Hiram 1903; BROWN Hiram 1903; TAYLOR Joseph G 1899 **13**; TAYLOR William H 1893; TAYLOR James H 1895

YORK Miles H 1888; GRANT Jefferson C 1891; GRANT Charles G 1901; SWEET Allen T 1888; SWEET Allen T 1888; PARKER Thomas J 1895; PARKER Thomas J 1895; SUGGS Lewis M 1895; TAYLOR William H 1893

GOLDING Thomas 1891 **22**; MILLER Henry J 1891; COURTNEY James D 1901; SWEET Allen T 1888; SLOANE Major 1901; PARKER Thomas J 1895; PARKER Thomas J 1895; SUGGS Lewis M 1895; SUGGS Lewis M 1895; MILLER William A 1896

DANFORD Isaac J 1896; WILLIAMS Henry C 1896 **23**; WILLIAMS Henry C 1896; SHARON Martin S 1896; WILLIAMS Elizabeth A 1893; MILLER John F 1892 **24**; MILLER John F 1892

CRUTCHFIELD John L 1894; MILLER Henry J 1891; WILLIAMS Henry C 1896; WILLIAMS Henry C 1896; WILLIAMS Elizabeth A 1893; MILLER John F 1892; MILLER John F 1892

MATHEWS Burrell F 1899; DANFORD Isaac J 1896; SHARON Martin S 1896; MILLER William A 1896

CRUTCHFIELD William R 1892; HUGHES John 1901; DANFORD Isaac J 1896; SLOAN Elijah 1901; SHARON Martin S 1896; WILLIAMS Elizabeth A 1893; MILES Leonard R 1904

27; REGISTER Lewis A 1898 **26**; MURDOCK James W 1895; **25**

BALL Louis A 1900; WILLIAMS George F 1891

WATFORD Nelson 1890; BAREFOOT Noah 1890 **34**; **35**; WILLIAMS Marion W 1898; BAGGETT Jefferson D 1895 **36**

WATFORD Katie 1905; WATFORD Simpson 1891; WATFORD Simpson 1891; BALL George E 1900; MCCREARY John R 1891; WILLIAMS [143] Jane 1893

Legend

— Patent Boundary

— Section Boundary

No Patents Found (or Outside County)

1., 2., 3., ... Lot Numbers (when beside a name)

[ ] Group Number (see Appendix "C")

Scale: Section = 1 mile X 1 mile (generally, with some exceptions)

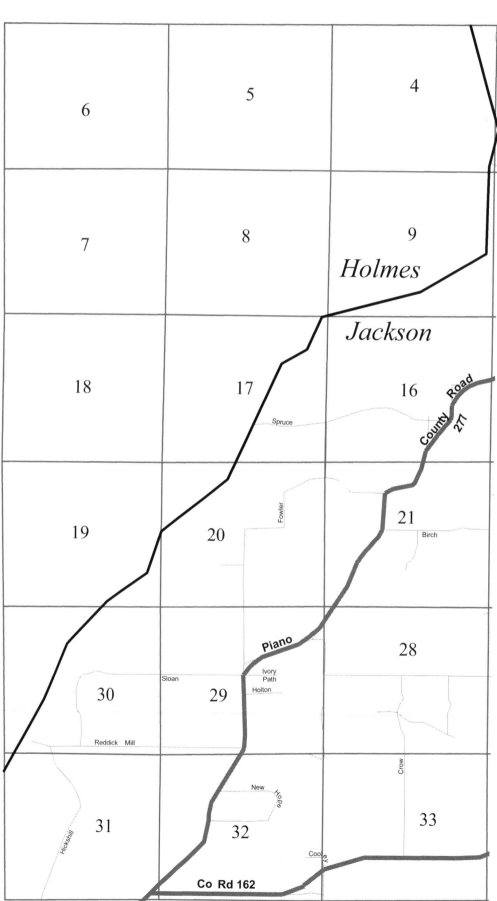

Road Map

T6-N R13-W
Tallahassee Meridian

Map Group 8

Cities & Towns
Graceville

Cemeteries
Damascus Cemetery

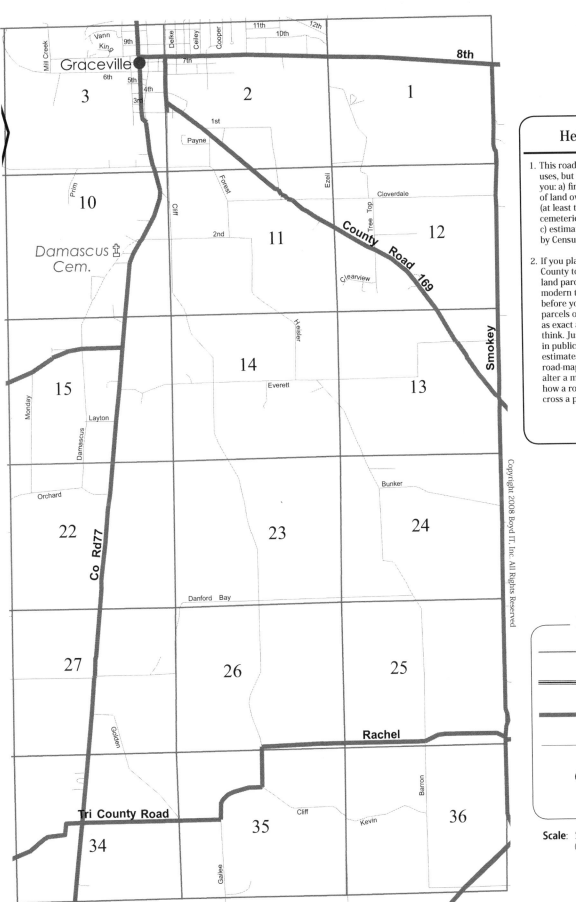

Helpful Hints

1. This road map has a number of uses, but primarily it is to help you: a) find the present location of land owned by your ancestors (at least the general area), b) find cemeteries and city-centers, and c) estimate the route/roads used by Census-takers & tax-assessors.

2. If you plan to travel to Jackson County to locate cemeteries or land parcels, please pick up a modern travel map for the area before you do. Mapping old land parcels on modern maps is not as exact a science as you might think. Just the slightest variations in public land survey coordinates, estimates of parcel boundaries, or road-map deviations can greatly alter a map's representation of how a road either does or doesn't cross a particular parcel of land.

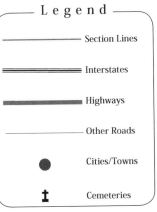

Legend

————	Section Lines
════	Interstates
━━━━	Highways
————	Other Roads
●	Cities/Towns
✝	Cemeteries

Scale: Section = 1 mile X 1 mile
(generally, with some exceptions)

Historical Map

T6-N R13-W
Tallahassee Meridian

Map Group 8

Cities & Towns
Graceville

Cemeteries
Damascus Cemetery

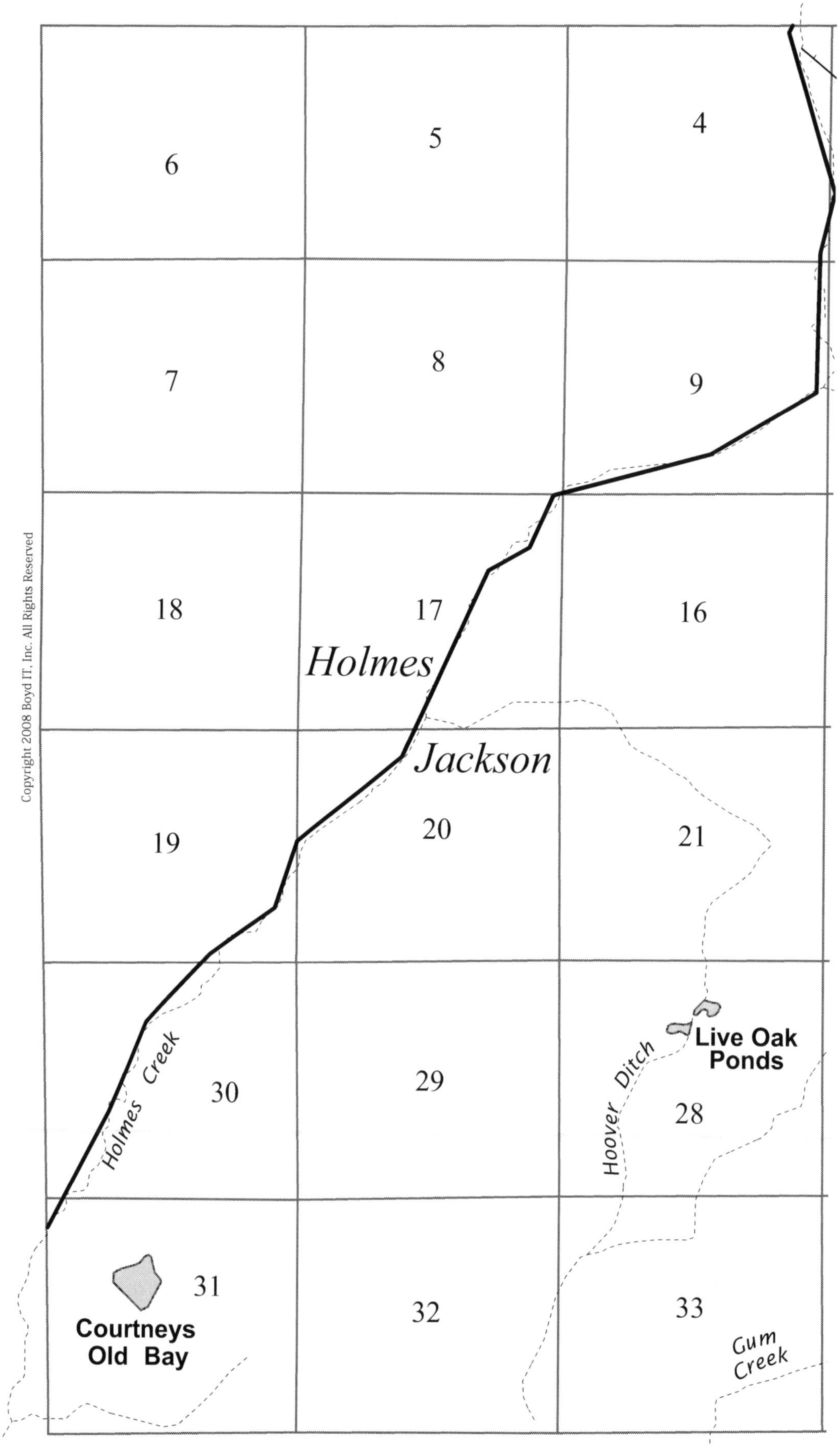

6

5

4

7

8

9

18

17

16

Holmes

19

Jackson

20

21

30

Holmes Creek

29

Hoover Ditch

Live Oak Ponds

28

31

Courtneys Old Bay

32

33

Gum Creek

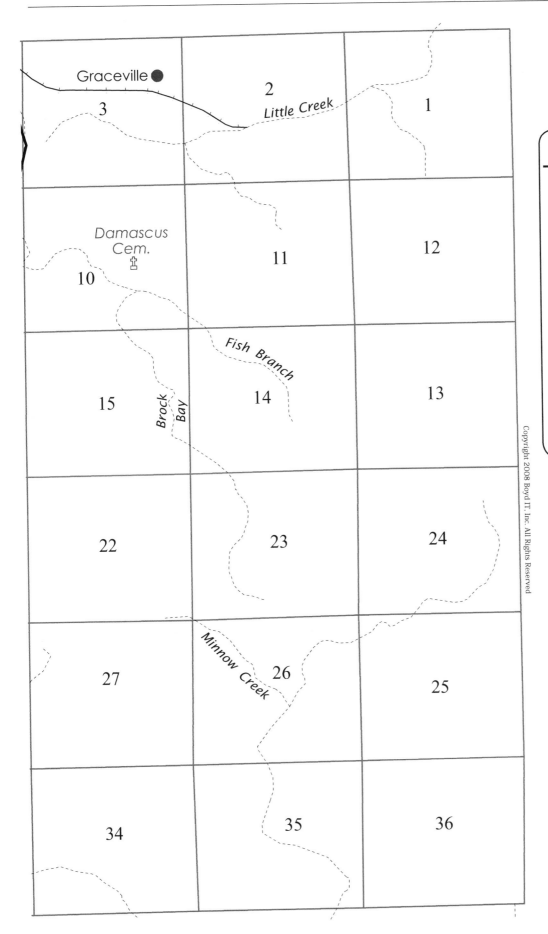

Graceville●

3

2
Little Creek

1

Damascus
Cem.
✝

10

11

12

15

Brock Bay

Fish Branch

14

13

22

23

24

27

Minnow Creek

26

25

34

35

36

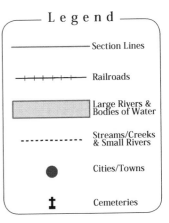

L e g e n d

———— Section Lines

+++++++ Railroads

Large Rivers &
Bodies of Water

- - - - - - Streams/Creeks
& Small Rivers

● Cities/Towns

✝ Cemeteries

Scale: Section = 1 mile X 1 mile
(there are some exceptions)

Map Group 9: Index to Land Patents

Township 6-North Range 12-West (Tallahassee)

After you locate an individual in this Index, take note of the Section and Section Part then proceed to the Land Patent map on the pages immediately following. You should have no difficulty locating the corresponding parcel of land.

The "For More Info" Column will lead you to more information about the underlying Patents. See the *Legend* at right, and the "How to Use this Book" chapter, for more information.

ID	Individual in Patent	Sec.	Sec. Part	Date Issued	Other Counties	For More Info . . .
984	ADAMS, Madison	4	SWSW	1856-06-16		A1
985	" "	8	S½SE	1857-07-01		A1
1017	ASKINS, Samuel G	3	W½SW	1827-04-02		A1
1016	" "	3	E½SW	1827-09-01		A1
1037	BAGGETT, William J	18	NESW	1897-07-03		A2
1038	" "	18	S½SW	1897-07-03		A2
1039	" "	18	SWSE	1897-07-03		A2
1021	BAKER, Simmons J	14	NESW	1850-08-10		A1
1022	" "	14	S½NW	1855-05-01		A1
996	BALL, Mary	17	NENE	1852-09-01		A1
1010	BEVERIDGE, Robert	10	E½SW	1828-09-10		A1
908	BLOUNT, Florence	26	E½SE	1902-05-01		A2
918	BLOUNT, Hugh A	13	E½NW	1856-06-16		A1
919	" "	13	W½NE	1856-06-16		A1
952	BRADLEY, John	34	E½NE	1829-04-15		A1
951	BROWN, John B	1	W½NW	1841-01-09		A1
1013	BURKETT, Sallie J	28	N½SE	1898-09-19		A2 G25
1014	" "	28	SESW	1898-09-19		A2 G25
1015	" "	28	SWSE	1898-09-19		A2 G25
1026	BUSH, Thomas M	22	SE	1843-03-10		A1
1025	CARTER, Thomas J	32	SW	1894-05-26		A2
906	CHAMBLISS, Ephraim	3	E½NE	1827-04-02		A1
930	CHASON, James	2	SW	1828-02-01		A1 G41
875	CLEMENTS, Benjamin	23	W½SE	1827-10-01		A1 G47
879	CO, Benjamin Hays And	2	W½SE	1829-05-15		A1
976	CONNER, Joseph W	7	N½SE	1900-09-07		A2
1027	CORNISH, William	13	SE	1827-04-02		A1
857	CRAWFORD, Adams	11	E½SW	1829-06-01		A1
912	DENHAM, George R	32	W½NE	1900-08-09		A2
913	" "	32	W½SE	1900-08-09		A2
1029	DONALD, William	3	NW	1827-04-02		A1
1031	" "	4	E½SE	1827-06-15		A1 G62
1032	" "	4	W½SE	1828-02-01		A1 G62
1030	" "	3	W½SE	1828-08-22		A1
1028	" "	10	NE	1829-05-15		A1
978	DUNCAN, Leven	17	S½NW	1856-06-16		A1
979	" "	17	SENE	1856-06-16		A1
980	" "	17	W½NE	1856-06-16		A1
958	ELMORE, John J	7	E½NE	1892-07-11		A2
959	" "	8	S½NW	1892-07-11		A2
878	FOSCUE, Benjamin	10	NW	1828-07-22		A1
871	FOSTER, Arthur	24	E½SW	1827-10-01		A1
872	" "	24	W½SW	1827-10-01		A1
1033	FOSTER, William	25	NE	1827-04-02		A1
875	GILCHRIST, Malcolm	23	W½SE	1827-10-01		A1 G47
981	GILLSTROP, Levin	8	NWSE	1857-12-01		A1

ID	Individual in Patent	Sec.	Sec. Part	Date Issued	Other Counties	For More Info . . .
982	GILSTRAP, Levin	4	NWSW	1839-09-20		A1
876	GLASS, Benjamin F	32	E½NE	1891-11-09		A2
877	" "	32	E½SE	1891-11-09		A2
935	GOODWIN, James	8	NESW	1860-10-01		A1
953	GREEN, John H	17	N½SE	1893-12-14		A2
954	" "	17	N½SW	1893-12-14		A2
917	HALEY, Holiday	23	SW	1827-09-01		A1 G76
916	" "	26	W½NW	1828-02-22		A1
1034	HALL, William	2	E½NW	1860-04-02		A1
930	HAYS, Benjamin	2	SW	1828-02-01		A1 G41
955	HAYS, John	4	NW	1828-02-01		A1
909	HAYWOOD, Francis P	35	NE	1850-08-10		A1
901	HENDRIX, Edward H	7	SESE	1892-07-11		A2
902	" "	8	NWSW	1892-07-11		A2
903	" "	8	S½SW	1892-07-11		A2
956	HOGG, John	23	E½NE	1827-04-02		A1
957	" "	23	W½NE	1828-02-01		A1
1036	HOGG, William	24	W½NW	1827-04-02		A1
1035	" "	24	E½NW	1828-02-01		A1
1002	HOLMES, Richard	13	E½NE	1829-05-15		A1
856	HUTSON, Aaron	3	E½SE	1828-06-20		A1
858	JOHNSON, Alford	26	E½NW	1860-04-02		A1
977	JOHNSON, King	4	NE	1828-02-01		A1
934	JOHNSTON, James G	28	E½NE	1857-07-01		A1
1011	JONES, Robert	23	E½SE	1827-04-02		A1
1012	" "	26	E½NE	1827-10-01		A1
1013	JUSTICE, Sallie J	28	N½SE	1898-09-19		A2 G25
1014	" "	28	SESW	1898-09-19		A2 G25
1015	" "	28	SWSE	1898-09-19		A2 G25
1020	LEE, Simeon A	30	NW	1896-01-03		A2
1040	LEWIS, William	13	W½SW	1827-04-02		A1
962	LONG, John M	20	SESW	1900-08-09		A2
960	LYNCH, John	11	NW	1827-04-02		A1
961	" "	4	E½SW	1828-08-22		A1
1003	MARTIN, Richard T	5	NESW	1837-04-15		A1
1043	MATHEWS, William N	10	E½SE	1857-07-01		A1
1044	" "	11	SWSW	1857-07-01		A1
931	MCCRARY, James F	20	NESW	1895-11-13		A2
932	" "	20	S½NE	1895-11-13		A2
933	" "	20	SENW	1895-11-13		A2
880	MCDANIEL, Bryant	27	SWSW	1857-07-01		A1
881	" "	28	SESE	1857-07-01		A1
882	" "	34	NWNW	1857-07-01		A1
969	MCDANIEL, John	36	W½	1850-08-10		A1
966	" "	34	E½NW	1859-06-01		A1
967	" "	34	NWNE	1859-06-01		A1
968	" "	34	NWSE	1859-06-01		A1
983	MCDANIEL, Lumpkin	26	SW	1860-04-02		A1
997	MCDANIEL, Mary S	34	NESW	1860-04-02		A1
998	" "	34	NWSW	1860-04-02		A1
999	" "	34	SWNW	1860-04-02		A1
1005	MCDANIEL, Risdon	15	NENW	1857-07-01		A1
1006	" "	15	W½NW	1857-07-01		A1
1007	" "	34	NESE	1902-04-18		A1
1008	" "	34	S½SE	1902-04-18		A1
1031	MCKAY, Charles	4	E½SE	1827-06-15		A1 G62
1032	" "	4	W½SE	1828-02-01		A1 G62
990	MERRITT, Margaret J	18	E½NW	1893-12-28		A2
991	" "	18	NWNE	1893-12-28		A2
992	" "	7	SWSE	1893-12-28		A2
950	MILES, Jarrett L	18	NENE	1906-10-24		A2
971	MILES, John W	30	SE	1894-04-10		A2
989	MILES, Manuel B	30	SW	1896-01-03		A2
1045	MILES, Willoughby	30	NE	1884-06-30		A2
1046	MILES, Wright J	17	NENW	1897-07-03		A2
1000	MILLAR, Nicholas W	22	SENW	1852-09-01		A1
911	NEELY, George P	15	SENW	1855-05-01		A1
993	PARKER, Martha	17	NWNW	1860-04-02		A1
986	PARRISH, Maggie	28	NESW	1899-08-30		A2 G110
987	" "	28	SENW	1899-08-30		A2 G110
988	" "	28	W½NE	1899-08-30		A2 G110
986	PARRISH, Richard J	28	NESW	1899-08-30		A2 G110
987	" "	28	SENW	1899-08-30		A2 G110

ID	Individual in Patent	Sec.	Sec. Part	Date Issued	Other Counties	For More Info . . .
988	PARRISH, Richard J (Cont'd)	28	W½NE	1899-08-30		A2 G110
870	PELT, Anthony V	27	SESE	1843-03-10		A1
869	" "	27	NESE	1844-07-10		A1
972	PENNINGTON, Joseph A	17	SWSW	1899-05-12		A2
973	" "	18	E½SE	1899-05-12		A2
974	" "	18	SENE	1899-05-12		A2
1023	PENNINGTON, Stephen P	20	W½NW	1892-08-01		A2
1024	" "	20	W½SW	1892-08-01		A2
925	PITTMAN, Jacob P	34	S½SW	1901-11-20		A2
994	PITTMAN, Mary A	1	E½NE	1860-04-02		A1
995	" "	1	NESE	1860-04-02		A1
939	RATHIEL, James M	32	NW	1896-01-14		A2
907	REGISTER, Ezekiel J	7	W½NW	1888-07-03		A1
920	REGISTER, Ira D	7	SW	1897-03-22		A2
926	REGISTER, James B	7	E½NW	1883-08-01		A2
927	" "	7	W½NE	1883-08-01		A2
1018	RIVES, Samuel H	12	SENE	1846-10-01		A1
1001	ROSE, Philip	27	E½SW	1828-08-22		A1
1009	SANDERS, Robert A	35	E½SW	1852-09-01		A1
1019	SCURLOCK, Sarah	35	SE	1846-09-01		A1
874	SHIVER, Asa	18	NWSW	1861-04-09		A1
873	SHIVER, Asa I	26	W½SE	1909-09-20		A2
964	SHIVER, John M	18	SWNE	1860-04-02		A1
963	" "	18	NWSE	1861-04-09		A1 F
917	SINGHTON, Joseph	23	SW	1827-09-01		A1 G76
889	SLATER, Charles	15	E½SW	1855-05-01		A1
890	" "	15	NESE	1855-05-01		A1
892	" "	15	W½SE	1855-05-01		A1
887	" "	14	SESW	1856-06-16		A1
888	" "	14	SWSW	1859-06-01		A1
891	" "	15	SESE	1859-06-01		A1
893	" "	15	W½SW	1859-06-01		A1
914	SLATON, Henry H	12	E½SW	1856-06-16		A1
915	" "	12	W½SE	1856-06-16		A1
904	SMITH, Elizabeth A	22	NWSW	1893-01-21		A2
905	" "	22	S½SW	1893-01-21		A2
970	SMITH, John	12	NENE	1846-10-01		A1
975	SMITH, Joseph M	14	NENW	1905-05-17		A2
1041	SNELL, William M	6	E½NW	1857-07-01		A1
1042	" "	6	W½NE	1857-07-01		A1
936	TAYLOR, James H	18	W½NW	1895-05-03		A2
921	TOOLE, Isaac M	17	SESW	1892-07-11		A2
922	" "	17	SWSE	1892-07-11		A2
923	" "	20	NENW	1892-07-11		A2
924	" "	20	NWNE	1892-07-11		A2
928	TOOLE, James B	28	NENW	1903-03-17		A2
940	TOOLE, James W	17	SESE	1900-09-07		A2
941	" "	20	NENE	1900-09-07		A2
965	TOOLE, John M	20	SE	1899-05-12		A2
1004	TOUCHSTONE, Richard	5	NE	1827-09-01		A1
942	WATSON, James	12	NW	1839-09-20		A1
943	" "	12	W½SW	1839-09-20		A1
944	" "	13	W½NW	1839-09-20		A1
945	" "	22	E½NE	1839-09-20		A1
946	" "	23	E½NW	1839-09-20		A1
947	" "	23	W½NW	1839-09-20		A1
929	WEBB, James B	1	W½SW	1829-05-15		A1
886	WHITAKER, Cary	36	E½	1850-08-10		A1
937	WHITE, James J	28	W½NW	1891-07-14		A2
938	" "	28	W½SW	1891-07-14		A2
883	WHITEHURST, Calvin J	5	NWSW	1852-09-01		A1
884	" "	5	SESW	1852-09-01		A1
885	" "	5	SWSW	1860-04-02		A1
859	WILLIAMS, Andrew	27	NWSW	1843-03-10		A1
910	WILLIAMS, Frederick	8	N½NW	1857-07-01		A1
948	WILLIAMS, James	27	NENW	1857-07-01		A1
949	" "	27	W½NW	1857-07-01		A1
894	WILLIAMSON, Charles	14	E½NE	1827-10-01		A1
895	" "	14	W½NE	1827-10-01		A1
896	" "	2	E½NE	1827-10-01		A1
897	" "	2	W½NE	1827-10-01		A1
898	" "	5	E½NW	1827-10-01		A1
899	" "	5	W½NW	1827-10-01		A1

ID	Individual in Patent	Sec.	Sec. Part	Date Issued	Other Counties	For More Info . . .
900	WILLIAMSON, Charles (Cont'd)	6	E½NE	1827-10-01		A1
865	YOUNG, Andrew	9	NENE	1837-04-20		A1
866	" "	9	NWNE	1837-04-20		A1
862	" "	2	W½NW	1838-07-28		A1
863	" "	26	W½NE	1838-07-28		A1
867	" "	9	SENE	1838-07-28		A1
861	" "	10	W½SW	1839-09-20		A1
864	" "	9	E½SE	1840-10-10		A1
868	" "	9	SWNE	1840-10-10		A1
860	" "	10	W½SE	1841-01-09		A1

Patent Map

T6-N R12-W
Tallahassee Meridian

Map Group 9

Township Statistics

Parcels Mapped	:	191
Number of Patents	:	144
Number of Individuals	:	111
Patentees Identified	:	107
Number of Surnames	:	84
Multi-Patentee Parcels	:	11
Oldest Patent Date	:	4/2/1827
Most Recent Patent	:	9/20/1909
Block/Lot Parcels	:	0
Parcels Re-Issued	:	0
Parcels that Overlap	:	0
Cities and Towns	:	2
Cemeteries	:	0

Copyright 2008 Boyd IT, Inc. All Rights Reserved

Section 6: SNELL William M 1857; WILLIAMSON Charles 1827

Section 5: WILLIAMSON Charles 1827; WILLIAMSON Charles 1827; TOUCHSTONE Richard 1827; WHITEHURST Calvin J 1852; MARTIN Richard T 1837; WHITEHURST Calvin J 1860; WHITEHURST Calvin J 1852

Section 4: HAYS John 1828; JOHNSON King 1828; GILSTRAP Levin 1839; LYNCH John 1828; ADAMS Madison 1856; DONALD [62] William 1828; DONALD [62] William 1827

Section 7: REGISTER Ezekiel J 1888; REGISTER James B 1883; REGISTER James B 1883; ELMORE John J 1892; CONNER Joseph W 1900; REGISTER Ira D 1897; MERRITT Margaret J 1893; HENDRIX Edward H 1892

Section 8: WILLIAMS Frederick 1857; ELMORE John J 1892; HENDRIX Edward H 1892; GOODWIN James 1860; GILLSTROP Levin 1857; HENDRIX Edward H 1892; ADAMS Madison 1857

Section 9: YOUNG Andrew 1837; YOUNG Andrew 1837; YOUNG Andrew 1840; YOUNG Andrew 1838; YOUNG Andrew 1840

Section 18: MERRITT Margaret J 1893; TAYLOR James H 1895; SHIVER John M 1860; PENNINGTON Joseph A 1899; SHIVER Asa 1861; BAGGETT William J 1897; SHIVER John M 1861; BAGGETT William J 1897; BAGGETT William J 1897; PENNINGTON Joseph A 1899

Section 17: MERRITT Margaret J 1893; MILES Jarrett L 1906; PARKER Martha 1860; MILES Wright J 1897; DUNCAN Leven 1856; BALL Mary 1852; DUNCAN Leven 1856; DUNCAN Leven 1856; GREEN John H 1893; GREEN John H 1893; PENNINGTON Joseph A 1899; TOOLE Isaac M 1892; TOOLE Isaac M 1892; TOOLE James W 1900

Section 16

Section 19

Section 20: PENNINGTON Stephen P 1892; TOOLE Isaac M 1892; TOOLE Isaac M 1892; TOOLE James W 1900; MCCRARY James F 1895; MCCRARY James F 1895; MCCRARY James F 1895; PENNINGTON Stephen P 1892; LONG John M 1900; TOOLE John M 1899

Section 21

Section 30: LEE Simeon A 1896; MILES Willoughby 1884; MILES Manuel B 1896; MILES John W 1894

Section 29

Section 28: WHITE James J 1891; TOOLE James B 1903; PARRISH [110] Maggie 1899; PARRISH [110] Maggie 1899; JOHNSTON James G 1857; WHITE James J 1891; PARRISH [110] Maggie 1899; BURKETT [25] Sallie J 1898; BURKETT [25] Sallie J 1898; BURKETT [25] Sallie J 1898; MCDANIEL Bryant 1857

Section 31

Section 32: RATHIEL James M 1896; DENHAM George R 1900; GLASS Benjamin F 1891; CARTER Thomas J 1894; DENHAM George R 1900; GLASS Benjamin F 1891

Section 33

108

DONALD
William
1827

3

CHAMBLISS
Ephraim
1827

YOUNG
Andrew
1838

HALL
William
1860

WILLIAMSON
Charles
1827

WILLIAMSON
Charles
1827

BROWN
John B
1841

1

PITTMAN
Mary A
1860

ASKINS
Samuel G
1827

ASKINS
Samuel G
1827

DONALD
William
1828

HUTSON
Aaron
1828

2

CHASON [41]
James
1828

CO
Benjamin Hays And
1829

WEBB
James B
1829

PITTMAN
Mary A
1860

FOSCUE
Benjamin
1828

10

DONALD
William
1829

LYNCH
John
1827

11

WATSON
James
1839

12

SMITH
John
1846

RIVES
Samuel H
1846

YOUNG
Andrew
1839

BEVERIDGE
Robert
1828

YOUNG
Andrew
1841

MATHEWS
William N
1857

MATHEWS
William N
1857

CRAWFORD
Adams
1829

WATSON
James
1839

SLATON
Henry H
1856

SLATON
Henry H
1856

MCDANIEL
Risdon
1857

MCDANIEL
Risdon
1857

NEELY
George P
1855

15

SMITH
Joseph M
1905

BAKER
Simmons J
1855

WILLIAMSON
Charles
1827

WILLIAMSON
Charles
1827

14

WATSON
James
1839

BLOUNT
Hugh A
1856

BLOUNT
Hugh A
1856

13

HOLMES
Richard
1829

SLATER
Charles
1859

SLATER
Charles
1855

SLATER
Charles
1855

SLATER
Charles
1855

SLATER
Charles
1859

BAKER
Simmons J
1850

SLATER
Charles
1859

SLATER
Charles
1856

LEWIS
William
1827

CORNISH
William
1827

MILLAR
Nicholas W
1852

22

WATSON
James
1839

WATSON
James
1839

WATSON
James
1839

HOGG
John
1828

HOGG
John
1827

HOGG
William
1827

HOGG
William
1828

24

SMITH
Elizabeth A
1893

BUSH
Thomas M
1843

23

HALEY [76]
Holiday
1827

CLEMENTS [47]
Benjamin
1827

JONES
Robert
1827

FOSTER
Arthur
1827

FOSTER
Arthur
1827

SMITH
Elizabeth A
1893

WILLIAMS
James
1857

WILLIAMS
James
1857

27

HALEY
Holiday
1828

JOHNSON
Alford
1860

YOUNG
Andrew
1838

26

JONES
Robert
1827

25

FOSTER
William
1827

WILLIAMS
Andrew
1843

ROSE
Philip
1828

PELT
Anthony V
1844

PELT
Anthony V
1843

MCDANIEL
Lumpkin
1860

SHIVER
Asa I
1909

BLOUNT
Florence
1902

MCDANIEL
Bryant
1857

MCDANIEL
Bryant
1857

MCDANIEL
John
1859

MCDANIEL
John
1859

BRADLEY
John
1829

34

35

HAYWOOD
Francis P
1850

WHITAKER
Cary
1850

36

MCDANIEL
Mary S
1860

MCDANIEL
Mary S
1860

MCDANIEL
Mary S
1860

MCDANIEL
John
1859

MCDANIEL
Risdon
1902

SCURLOCK
Sarah
1846

MCDANIEL
John
1850

PITTMAN
Jacob P
1901

MCDANIEL
Risdon
1902

SANDERS
Robert A
1852

Copyright 2008 Boyd IT, Inc. All Rights Reserved

Helpful Hints

1. This Map's INDEX can be found on the preceding pages.

2. Refer to Map "C" to see where this Township lies within Jackson County, Florida.

3. Numbers within square brackets [ ] denote a multi-patentee land parcel (multi-owner). Refer to Appendix "C" for a full list of members in this group.

4. Areas that look to be crowded with Patentees usually indicate multiple sales of the same parcel (Re-issues) or Overlapping parcels. See this Township's Index for an explanation of these and other circumstances that might explain "odd" groupings of Patentees on this map.

Legend

——— Patent Boundary

▬▬▬ Section Boundary

No Patents Found
(or Outside County)

1., 2., 3., ... Lot Numbers
(when beside a name)

[ ] Group Number
(see Appendix "C")

Scale: Section = 1 mile X 1 mile
(generally, with some exceptions)

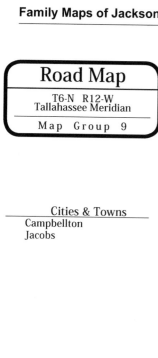

Road Map

T6-N R12-W
Tallahassee Meridian

Map Group 9

Cities & Towns
Campbellton
Jacobs

Cemeteries
None

8th

5

State Highway 2

6

Shiloh Church

4

Elmore

Carter

7

8

9

Piney Wood

Galloway

Max

18

17

16

Sharon

Springhill

County Road 169

Canary

Smokey

Parrot

20

21

19

Woodcrest

Welsh

30

29

Mimosa

28

Rachel

State Highway 273

Justic

Co Rd 169

31

32

33

Smoky

Bentley

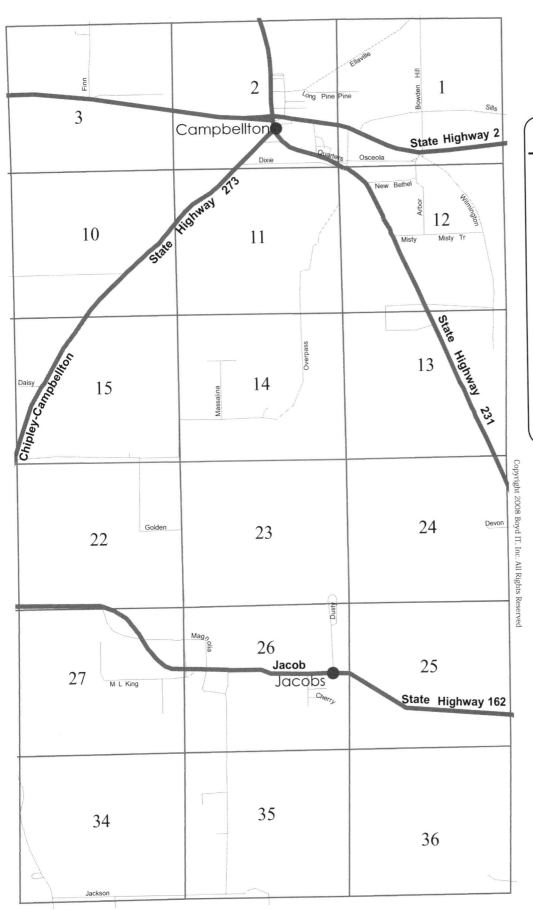

Finn

Ellaville

2

Long Pine Pine

1

Bowden Hill

Sills

3

State Highway 2

Campbellton

Dixie

Quarters

Osceola

New Bethel

Arbor

Winnington

12

Misty Misty Tr

State Highway 273

10

11

Chipley-Campbellton

Daisy

15

Massalina

14

Overpass

13

State Highway 231

Golden

22

23

24

Devon

Copyright 2008 Boyd IT, Inc. All Rights Reserved

Dusty

Magnolia

26

Jacob

Jacobs

27

M L King

Cherry

State Highway 162

25

34

35

36

Jackson

Helpful Hints

1. This road map has a number of uses, but primarily it is to help you: a) find the present location of land owned by your ancestors (at least the general area), b) find cemeteries and city-centers, and c) estimate the route/roads used by Census-takers & tax-assessors.

2. If you plan to travel to Jackson County to locate cemeteries or land parcels, please pick up a modern travel map for the area before you do. Mapping old land parcels on modern maps is not as exact a science as you might think. Just the slightest variations in public land survey coordinates, estimates of parcel boundaries, or road-map deviations can greatly alter a map's representation of how a road either does or doesn't cross a particular parcel of land.

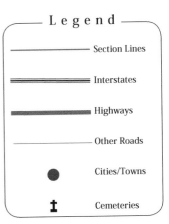

L e g e n d

———— Section Lines

▬▬▬▬ Interstates

▬▬▬▬ Highways

———— Other Roads

● Cities/Towns

† Cemeteries

Scale: Section = 1 mile X 1 mile
(generally, with some exceptions)

Historical Map

T6-N   R12-W
Tallahassee Meridian

Map Group 9

Cities & Towns
Campbellton
Jacobs

Cemeteries
None

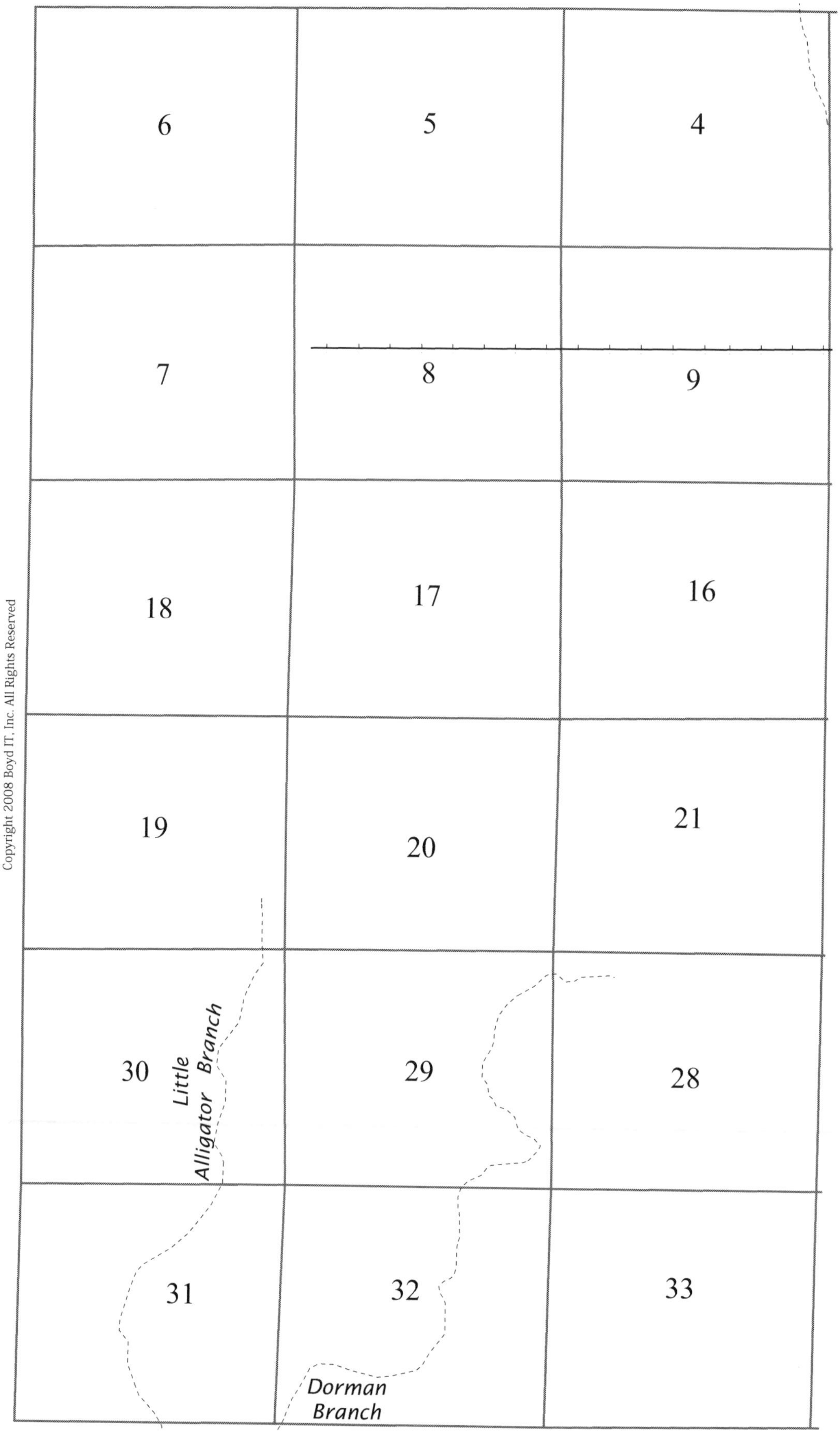

6	5	4
7	8	9
18	17	16
19	20	21
30	29	28
31	32	33

Little Alligator Branch

Dorman Branch

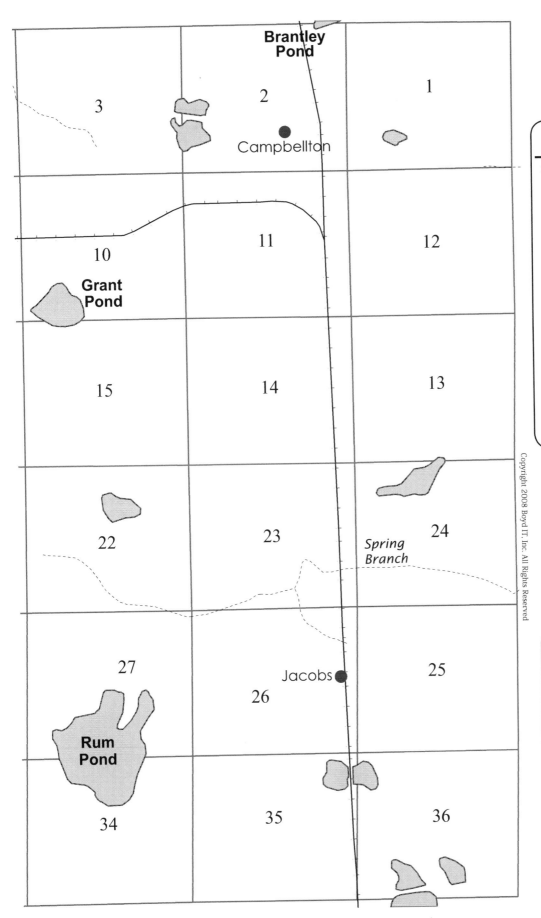

3

Brantley Pond

2

1

Campbellton

10

Grant Pond

11

12

15

14

13

22

23

24

Spring Branch

27

26

Jacobs

25

Rum Pond

34

35

36

Helpful Hints

1. This Map takes a different look at the same Congressional Township displayed in the preceding two maps. It presents features that can help you better envision the historical development of the area: a) Water-bodies (lakes & ponds), b) Water-courses (rivers, streams, etc.), c) Railroads, d) City/town center-points (where they were oftentimes located when first settled), and e) Cemeteries.

2. Using this "Historical" map in tandem with this Township's Patent Map and Road Map, may lead you to some interesting discoveries. You will often find roads, towns, cemeteries, and waterways are named after nearby landowners: sometimes those names will be the ones you are researching. See how many of these research gems you can find here in Jackson County.

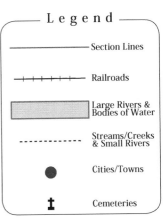

L e g e n d

—————— Section Lines

+–+–+–+–+–+ Railroads

▭ Large Rivers & Bodies of Water

- - - - - - - Streams/Creeks & Small Rivers

● Cities/Towns

⚱ Cemeteries

Scale: Section = 1 mile X 1 mile
(there are some exceptions)

Map Group 10: Index to Land Patents

Township 6-North Range 11-West (Tallahassee)

After you locate an individual in this Index, take note of the Section and Section Part then proceed to the Land Patent map on the pages immediately following. You should have no difficulty locating the corresponding parcel of land.

The "For More Info" Column will lead you to more information about the underlying Patents. See the *Legend* at right, and the "How to Use this Book" chapter, for more information.

```
                          LEGEND
                "For More Info . . . " column
A = Authority (Legislative Act, See Appendix "A")
B = Block or Lot (location in Section unknown)
C = Cancelled Patent
F = Fractional Section
G = Group  (Multi-Patentee Patent, see Appendix "C")
V = Overlaps another Parcel
R = Re-Issued (Parcel patented more than once)

(A & G items require you to look in the Appendixes referred
to above. All other Letter-designations followed by a number
require you to locate line-items in this index that possess
the ID number found after the letter).
```

ID	Individual in Patent	Sec.	Sec. Part	Date Issued	Other Counties	For More Info . . .
1154	ALLEN, Matthew J	14	SW	1839-09-20		A1
1155	"	14	W½NW	1839-09-20		A1
1156	"	15	E½	1839-09-20		A1
1157	"	15	SW	1839-09-20		A1
1166	"	31	W½NW	1839-09-20		A1 G3
1167	"	31	W½SW	1839-09-20		A1 G3
1160	"	4	E½	1839-09-20		A1 G2
1158	"	11	NW	1844-11-01		A1 G5
1159	"	11	W½SE	1844-11-01		A1 G5
1163	"	12	E½SW	1844-11-01		A1 G4
1164	"	12	W½NE	1844-11-01		A1 G4
1165	"	12	W½NW	1844-11-01		A1 G4
1161	"	4	E½NW	1844-11-01		A1 G2
1162	"	4	E½SW	1844-11-01		A1 G2
1166	ANDREWS, Hercules R	31	W½NW	1839-09-20		A1 G3
1167	"	31	W½SW	1839-09-20		A1 G3
1160	"	4	E½	1839-09-20		A1 G2
1163	"	12	E½SW	1844-11-01		A1 G4
1164	"	12	W½NE	1844-11-01		A1 G4
1165	"	12	W½NW	1844-11-01		A1 G4
1161	"	4	E½NW	1844-11-01		A1 G2
1162	"	4	E½SW	1844-11-01		A1 G2
1175	BELLAMY, Samuel C	35	NE	1840-10-10		A1
1176	"	36	NW	1840-10-10		A1
1047	BLACKWELL, Amelia B	1	E½SW	1840-10-10		A1
1048	"	1	W½SE	1841-01-09		A1
1096	BRIDGEMAN, Daniel	19	SE	1827-04-02		A1 G22
1125	BRITT, John	9	SE	1827-09-01		A1
1210	BRITT, William	17	NW	1827-09-01		A1 G23
1183	BUSH, Thomas M	1	W½NW	1843-03-10		A1
1184	"	1	W½SW	1843-03-10		A1
1185	"	2	E½NE	1843-03-10		A1
1186	"	22	SESW	1843-03-10		A1
1187	"	23	E½SW	1843-03-10		A1
1188	"	23	NE	1843-03-10		A1
1189	"	23	SENW	1843-03-10		A1
1190	"	23	W½NW	1843-03-10		A1
1191	"	24	SW	1843-03-10		A1
1192	"	24	W½NW	1843-03-10		A1
1193	"	25	E½SW	1843-03-10		A1
1194	"	25	W½SW	1843-03-10		A1
1195	"	26	E½SE	1843-03-10		A1
1196	"	26	W½NE	1843-03-10		A1
1197	"	4	W½NW	1843-03-10		A1
1198	"	5	E½NE	1843-03-10		A1
1199	"	5	W½NE	1843-03-10		A1

ID	Individual in Patent	Sec.	Sec. Part	Date Issued	Other Counties	For More Info . . .
1200	BUSH, Thomas M (Cont'd)	5	W½NW	1843-03-10		A1
1201	" "	6	E½NW	1843-03-10		A1
1202	" "	6	NE	1843-03-10		A1
1203	" "	8	NE	1843-03-10		A1
1104	CALLAWAY, Elizabeth	5	SWSW	1843-03-10		A1
1109	CALLAWAY, Fair B	9	SWNW	1855-05-01		A1
1105	" "	4	W½SW	1856-06-16		A1
1106	" "	5	SE	1856-06-16		A1
1107	" "	9	NENW	1856-06-16		A1
1108	" "	9	NWNW	1856-06-16		A1
1102	CALLOWAY, Elijah H	5	E½SW	1827-09-01		A1
1101	" "	12	E½NW	1829-05-01		A1
1103	CALLOWAY, Elisha	12	E½NE	1828-07-22		A1
1110	CALLOWAY, Fair B	8	NW	1859-06-01		A1 G29
1179	CAMP, Sextus	18	SE	1827-04-02		A1
1210	CARTER, Farish	17	NW	1827-09-01		A1 G23
1051	CLEMENTS, Benjamin	28	W½NE	1827-11-01		A1
1052	" "	31	E½NW	1827-11-01		A1
1124	CLEMENTS, Jesse B	21	E½NE	1827-10-01		A1 G51
1096	CO, R C Allen And	19	SE	1827-04-02		A1 G22
1127	COWART, John E	22	SE	1828-08-22		A1
1050	DANIEL, Appellas	19	SW	1827-09-01		A1
1141	DANIEL, Jonas	3	SE	1827-04-02		A1
1145	DANIEL, Josiah	7	NENE	1841-01-09		A1
1144	" "	7	E½NW	1843-03-10		A1
1146	" "	7	W½NE	1843-03-10		A1
1110	" "	8	NW	1859-06-01		A1 G29
1097	DAWSON, David	20	SE	1829-04-02		A1
1098	DAWSON, Dread	20	SW	1827-04-02		A1 V1211
1126	DIVINE, John	19	NE	1827-04-02		A1
1209	DRAKE, William B	10	E½SE	1827-10-01		A1 G63
1056	FOSCUE, Benjamin	18	SW	1827-04-02		A1
1059	" "	17	NE	1827-09-01		A1 G68
1055	" "	18	E½NW	1829-04-02		A1
1053	" "	14	E½NW	1829-06-15		A1
1054	" "	14	W½NE	1829-06-15		A1
1057	" "	8	SE	1829-06-15		A1
1058	" "	8	SW	1829-06-15		A1
1111	GALLAWAY, Fair B	9	NWNE	1860-04-02		A1
1209	GAMBLE, John G	10	E½SE	1827-10-01		A1 G63
1128	" "	10	E½SW	1827-10-01		A1
1129	" "	10	W½SE	1827-10-01		A1
1130	" "	10	W½SW	1827-11-01		A1
1131	" "	15	E½NW	1827-11-01		A1
1132	" "	15	W½NW	1827-11-01		A1
1152	GILCHRIST, Malcolm	36	E½SW	1827-10-01		A1 G72
1207	GRAINGER, Voltier	22	NESW	1841-01-09		A1
1060	HAMILTON, Benjamin G	12	SE	1838-07-28		A1
1133	HOLLAND, John	28	SW	1827-04-02		A1
1151	HOLLAND, Lewis	33	NW	1827-04-02		A1
1142	HOWEL, Joseph	32	NE	1827-06-15		A1
1121	JARRATT, James S	13	E½NE	1915-11-26		A1
1122	" "	13	SWNE	1915-11-26		A1
1172	JEMISON, Robert	21	E½SE	1827-10-01		A1 G82
1173	" "	21	E½SW	1827-10-01		A1 G82
1135	JONES, John T	5	E½NW	1828-08-22		A1
1204	KEITH, Thomas R	10	NE	1827-11-01		A1
1205	" "	11	SW	1827-11-01		A1
1206	" "	24	E½	1827-11-01		A1
1153	KENT, Marmaduke	30	NE	1827-06-15		A1 G87
1120	LISTER, James C	32	SW	1827-06-15		A1
1208	MILLER, Warren	34	NE	1828-02-01		A1
1143	MONTFORD, Joseph	22	E½NW	1839-09-20		A1
1166	MOORING, William S	31	W½NW	1839-09-20		A1 G3
1167	" "	31	W½SW	1839-09-20		A1 G3
1217	" "	31	E½NE	1848-08-26		A1
1218	" "	31	E½SE	1848-08-26		A1
1177	OVERTON, Samuel R	36	SE	1827-04-02		A1 G109
1153	" "	30	NE	1827-06-15		A1 G87
1134	PARKER, John	27	W½SE	1827-09-01		A1
1094	PEEBLES, D	11	E½SE	1827-11-01		A1 G114
1095	" "	14	E½NE	1827-11-01		A1 G114
1094	PEEBLES, H	11	E½SE	1827-11-01		A1 G114

ID	Individual in Patent	Sec.	Sec. Part	Date Issued	Other Counties	For More Info . . .
1095	PEEBLES, H (Cont'd)	14	E½NE	1827-11-01		A1 G114
1119	PELT, Jacob J	1	NESE	1856-06-16		A1
1123	POWELL, Jasper	11	W½NE	1903-08-25		A2
1099	REYNOLDS, Edward	2	W½NW	1839-09-20		A1
1100	" "	2	W½SE	1839-09-20		A1
1158	" "	11	NW	1844-11-01		A1 G5
1159	" "	11	W½SE	1844-11-01		A1 G5
1163	" "	12	E½SW	1844-11-01		A1 G4
1164	" "	12	W½NE	1844-11-01		A1 G4
1165	" "	12	W½NW	1844-11-01		A1 G4
1171	SCURLOCK, P	32	SE	1827-06-15		A1
1174	SIMPSON, Robert	31	E½SW	1834-08-20		A1
1113	SLATON, Henry H	7	NWSW	1856-06-16		A1
1114	" "	7	SENE	1856-06-16		A1
1178	SMITH, Samuel	7	SWSW	1855-05-01		A1
1214	SNELLING, William F	26	W½NW	1838-07-28		A1
1215	" "	26	W½SW	1838-07-28		A1
1216	" "	27	E½NW	1838-07-28		A1
1212	" "	23	W½SW	1839-09-20		A1
1211	" "	20	E½SW	1843-03-10		A1 V1098
1213	" "	26	E½NW	1860-04-02		A1
1061	SPIERS, Bracney T	25	NESE	1855-05-01		A1
1062	" "	26	W½SE	1855-05-01		A1
1177	STONE, L M	36	SE	1827-04-02		A1 G109
1063	SUTTON, C	29	NW	1829-04-02		A1 G133
1168	SUTTON, Oliver	13	E½SE	1834-08-20		A1
1169	" "	25	NWSE	1839-09-20		A1
1170	" "	26	E½NE	1843-03-10		A1
1182	SUTTON, Theophilus	32	NW	1827-04-02		A1
1181	" "	25	E½NE	1829-05-15		A1
1112	TAYLOR, Harbert	33	SW	1827-04-02		A1
1118	TAYLOR, Herbert	22	NE	1839-09-20		A1
1115	TRIPPE, Henry	34	SW	1827-09-01		A1
1116	" "	33	E½SE	1828-02-01		A1 G139
1117	" "	34	E½NW	1828-02-01		A1 G140
1116	TRIPPE, Jonathan T	33	E½SE	1828-02-01		A1 G139
1117	TRIPPE, Sarah	34	E½NW	1828-02-01		A1 G140
1117	TRIPPE, Simeon	34	E½NW	1828-02-01		A1 G140
1059	WARD, John	17	NE	1827-09-01		A1 G68
1063	WATSON, W J	29	NW	1829-04-02		A1 G133
1147	WHITEHEAD, Levi	13	E½NW	1839-09-20		A1
1148	" "	13	E½SW	1839-09-20		A1
1149	" "	24	E½NW	1839-09-20		A1
1150	WHITEHURST, Levi	13	W½SE	1837-04-20		A1
1049	WILLIAMS, Andrew	17	SE	1827-09-01		A1
1064	WILLIAMSON, Charles	10	E½NW	1827-10-01		A1
1065	" "	10	W½NW	1827-10-01		A1
1066	" "	13	W½NW	1827-10-01		A1
1067	" "	13	W½SW	1827-10-01		A1
1068	" "	14	E½SE	1827-10-01		A1
1069	" "	14	W½SE	1827-10-01		A1
1124	" "	21	E½NE	1827-10-01		A1 G51
1070	" "	21	E½NW	1827-10-01		A1
1172	" "	21	E½SE	1827-10-01		A1 G82
1173	" "	21	E½SW	1827-10-01		A1 G82
1071	" "	21	W½NE	1827-10-01		A1
1072	" "	21	W½NW	1827-10-01		A1
1073	" "	21	W½SE	1827-10-01		A1
1074	" "	21	W½SW	1827-10-01		A1
1075	" "	22	W½NW	1827-10-01		A1
1076	" "	22	W½SW	1827-10-01		A1
1077	" "	27	E½SE	1827-10-01		A1
1078	" "	27	E½SW	1827-10-01		A1
1079	" "	27	W½SW	1827-10-01		A1
1080	" "	28	E½NE	1827-10-01		A1
1081	" "	28	E½SE	1827-10-01		A1
1082	" "	28	W½SE	1827-10-01		A1
1083	" "	35	E½NW	1827-10-01		A1
1084	" "	35	E½SE	1827-10-01		A1
1085	" "	35	E½SW	1827-10-01		A1
1086	" "	35	W½NW	1827-10-01		A1
1087	" "	35	W½SE	1827-10-01		A1
1088	" "	35	W½SW	1827-10-01		A1 F

ID	Individual in Patent	Sec.	Sec. Part	Date Issued	Other Counties	For More Info . . .
1152	WILLIAMSON, Charles (Cont'd)	36	E½SW	1827-10-01		A1 G72
1090	" "	36	W½SW	1827-10-01		A1
1091	" "	7	E½SE	1827-10-01		A1
1092	" "	7	E½SW	1827-10-01		A1
1093	" "	7	W½SE	1827-10-01		A1
1089	" "	36	NE	1827-11-01		A1
1136	WILSON, John T	27	NE	1839-09-20		A1
1139	" "	34	NWSE	1839-09-20		A1
1137	" "	27	W½NW	1843-03-10		A1
1140	" "	34	SWSE	1843-03-10		A1
1138	" "	34	E½SE	1856-06-16		A1
1180	WITCHARD, Solomon	23	NENW	1841-01-09		A1

Patent Map

T6-N R11-W
Tallahassee Meridian

Map Group 10

Township Statistics

Parcels Mapped	:	172
Number of Patents	:	150
Number of Individuals	:	75
Patentees Identified	:	72
Number of Surnames	:	59
Multi-Patentee Parcels	:	26
Oldest Patent Date	:	4/2/1827
Most Recent Patent	:	11/26/1915
Block/Lot Parcels	:	0
Parcels Re - Issued	:	0
Parcels that Overlap	:	2
Cities and Towns	:	1
Cemeteries	:	1

BUSH
Thomas M
1843

BUSH
Thomas M
1843

6

BUSH
Thomas M
1843

JONES
John T
1828

BUSH
Thomas M
1843

5

BUSH
Thomas M
1843

BUSH
Thomas M
1843

ALLEN [2]
Matthew J
1844

4

ALLEN [2]
Matthew J
1839

CALLOWAY
Elizabeth
1843

CALLOWAY
Elijah H
1827

CALLAWAY
Fair B
1856

CALLAWAY
Fair B
1856

ALLEN [2]
Matthew J
1844

DANIEL
Josiah
1843

DANIEL
Josiah
1841

DANIEL
Josiah
1843

SLATON
Henry H
1856

CALLOWAY [29]
Fair B
1859

BUSH
Thomas M
1843

CALLAWAY
Fair B
1856

CALLAWAY
Fair B
1856

GALLAWAY
Fair B
1860

CALLAWAY
Fair B
1855

9

SLATON
Henry H
1856

SMITH
Samuel
1855

7

WILLIAMSON
Charles
1827

WILLIAMSON
Charles
1827

WILLIAMSON
Charles
1827

8

FOSCUE
Benjamin
1829

FOSCUE
Benjamin
1829

BRITT
John
1827

FOSCUE
Benjamin
1829

18

FOSCUE
Benjamin
1827

CAMP
Sextus
1827

BRITT [23]
William
1827

17

FOSCUE [68]
Benjamin
1827

WILLIAMS
Andrew
1827

16

19

DIVINE
John
1827

DANIEL
Appellas
1827

BRIDGEMAN [22]
Daniel
1827

20

DAWSON
Dread
1827

SNELLING
William F
1843

DAWSON
David
1829

WILLIAMSON
Charles
1827

WILLIAMSON
Charles
1827

WILLIAMSON
Charles
1827

CLEMENTS [51]
Jesse B
1827

21

WILLIAMSON
Charles
1827

WILLIAMSON
Charles
1827

JEMISON [82]
Robert
1827

JEMISON [82]
Robert
1827

30

KENT [87]
Marmaduke
1827

29

SUTTON [133]
C
1829

28

CLEMENTS
Benjamin
1827

WILLIAMSON
Charles
1827

HOLLAND
John
1827

WILLIAMSON
Charles
1827

WILLIAMSON
Charles
1827

ALLEN [3]
Matthew J
1839

31

CLEMENTS
Benjamin
1827

SIMPSON
Robert
1834

ALLEN [3]
Matthew J
1839

MOORING
William S
1848

MOORING
William S
1848

32

SUTTON
Theophilus
1827

HOWEL
Joseph
1827

LISTER
James C
1827

SCURLOCK
P
1827

33

HOLLAND
Lewis
1827

TAYLOR
Harbert
1827

TRIPPE [139]
Henry
1828

Section 3
REYNOLDS Edward 1839

BUSH Thomas M 1843

BUSH Thomas M 1843

Section 2
DANIEL Jonas 1827

REYNOLDS Edward 1839

Section 1
BUSH Thomas M 1843

BLACKWELL Amelia B 1840

BLACKWELL Amelia B 1841

PELT Jacob J 1856

Section 10
WILLIAMSON Charles 1827

WILLIAMSON Charles 1827

KEITH Thomas R 1827

GAMBLE John G 1827

GAMBLE John G 1827

GAMBLE John G 1827

DRAKE [63] William B 1827

Section 11
ALLEN [5] Matthew J 1844

POWELL Jasper 1903

KEITH Thomas R 1827

ALLEN [5] Matthew J 1844

PEEBLES [114] D 1827

Section 12
ALLEN [4] Matthew J 1844

CALLOWAY Elijah H 1829

ALLEN [4] Matthew J 1844

CALLOWAY Elisha 1828

ALLEN [4] Matthew J 1844

HAMILTON Benjamin G 1838

Section 15
GAMBLE John G 1827

GAMBLE John G 1827

ALLEN Matthew J 1839

ALLEN Matthew J 1839

Section 14
ALLEN Matthew J 1839

FOSCUE Benjamin 1829

FOSCUE Benjamin 1829

PEEBLES [114] D 1827

WILLIAMSON Charles 1827

WILLIAMSON Charles 1827

ALLEN Matthew J 1839

WILLIAMSON Charles 1827

Section 13
WHITEHEAD Levi 1839

WILLIAMSON Charles 1827

JARRATT James S 1915

JARRATT James S 1915

WHITEHEAD Levi 1839

WHITEHURST Levi 1837

SUTTON Oliver 1834

Section 22
MONTFORD Joseph 1839

TAYLOR Herbert 1839

WILLIAMSON Charles 1827

GRAINGER Voltier 1841

COWART John E 1828

WILLIAMSON Charles 1827

BUSH Thomas M 1843

Section 23
BUSH Thomas M 1843

WITCHARD Solomon 1841

BUSH Thomas M 1843

BUSH Thomas M 1843

SNELLING William F 1839

BUSH Thomas M 1843

Section 24
BUSH Thomas M 1843

WHITEHEAD Levi 1839

KEITH Thomas R 1827

BUSH Thomas M 1843

Section 27
WILSON John T 1843

SNELLING William F 1838

WILSON John T 1839

WILLIAMSON Charles 1827

WILLIAMSON Charles 1827

WILLIAMSON Charles 1827

PARKER John 1827

Section 26
SNELLING William F 1838

SNELLING William F 1860

BUSH Thomas M 1843

SUTTON Oliver 1843

SNELLING William F 1838

SPIERS Bracney T 1855

BUSH Thomas M 1843

Section 25
SUTTON Theophilus 1829

BUSH Thomas M 1843

BUSH Thomas M 1843

SUTTON Oliver 1839

SPIERS Bracney T 1855

Section 34
TRIPPE [140] Henry 1828

MILLER Warren 1828

WILSON John T 1839

WILSON John T 1843

WILSON John T 1856

TRIPPE Henry 1827

Section 35
WILLIAMSON Charles 1827

WILLIAMSON Charles 1827

BELLAMY Samuel C 1840

WILLIAMSON Charles 1827

WILLIAMSON Charles 1827

Section 36
BELLAMY Samuel C 1840

WILLIAMSON Charles 1827

GILCHRIST [72] Malcolm 1827

OVERTON [109] Samuel R 1827

WILLIAMSON Charles 1827

Helpful Hints

1. This Map's INDEX can be found on the preceding pages.

2. Refer to Map "C" to see where this Township lies within Jackson County, Florida.

3. Numbers within square brackets [ ] denote a multi-patentee land parcel (multi-owner). Refer to Appendix "C" for a full list of members in this group.

4. Areas that look to be crowded with Patentees usually indicate multiple sales of the same parcel (Re-issues) or Overlapping parcels. See this Township's Index for an explanation of these and other circumstances that might explain "odd" groupings of Patentees on this map.

Legend

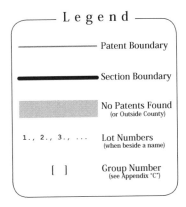

———— Patent Boundary

———— Section Boundary

No Patents Found (or Outside County)

1., 2., 3., ... Lot Numbers (when beside a name)

[ ] Group Number (see Appendix "C")

Scale: Section = 1 mile X 1 mile (generally, with some exceptions)

Road Map

T6-N R11-W
Tallahassee Meridian

Map Group 10

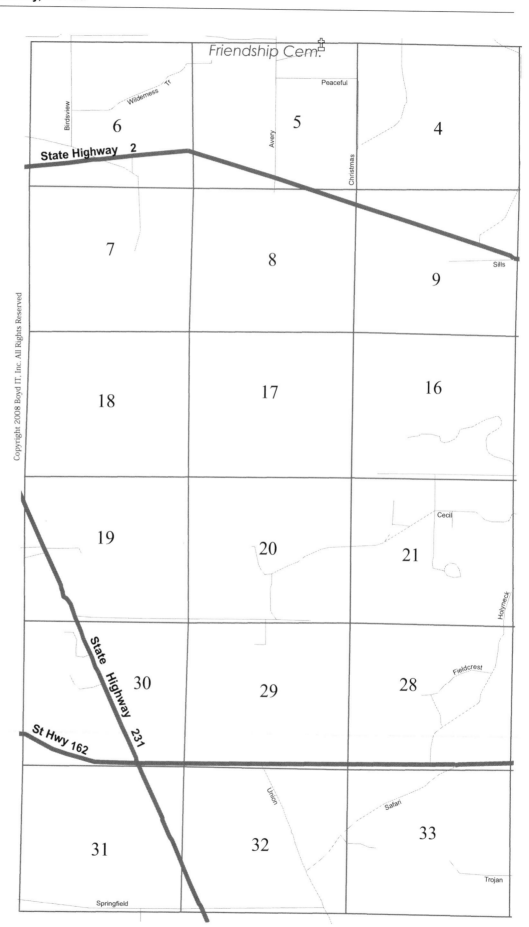

Cities & Towns
Sills

Copyright 2008 Boyd IT. Inc. All Rights Reserved

Cemeteries
Friendship Cemetery

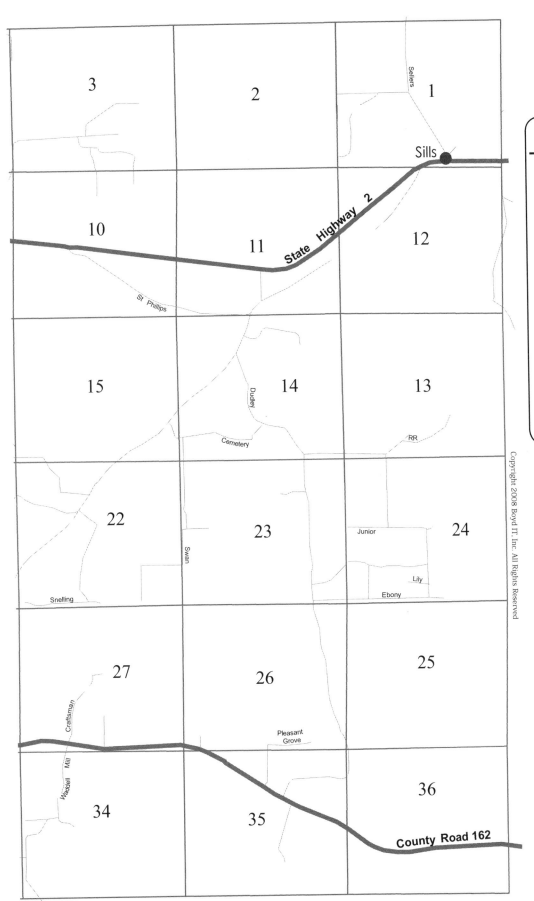

Helpful Hints

1. This road map has a number of uses, but primarily it is to help you: a) find the present location of land owned by your ancestors (at least the general area), b) find cemeteries and city-centers, and c) estimate the route/roads used by Census-takers & tax-assessors.

2. If you plan to travel to Jackson County to locate cemeteries or land parcels, please pick up a modern travel map for the area before you do. Mapping old land parcels on modern maps is not as exact a science as you might think. Just the slightest variations in public land survey coordinates, estimates of parcel boundaries, or road-map deviations can greatly alter a map's representation of how a road either does or doesn't cross a particular parcel of land.

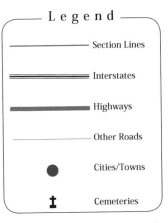

L e g e n d

———————	Section Lines
▬▬▬▬▬▬▬	Interstates
▬▬▬▬▬▬▬	Highways
———————	Other Roads
●	Cities/Towns
⚓	Cemeteries

Scale: Section = 1 mile X 1 mile
(generally, with some exceptions)

Historical Map

T6-N R11-W
Tallahassee Meridian

Map Group 10

Cities & Towns
Sills

Cemeteries
Friendship Cemetery

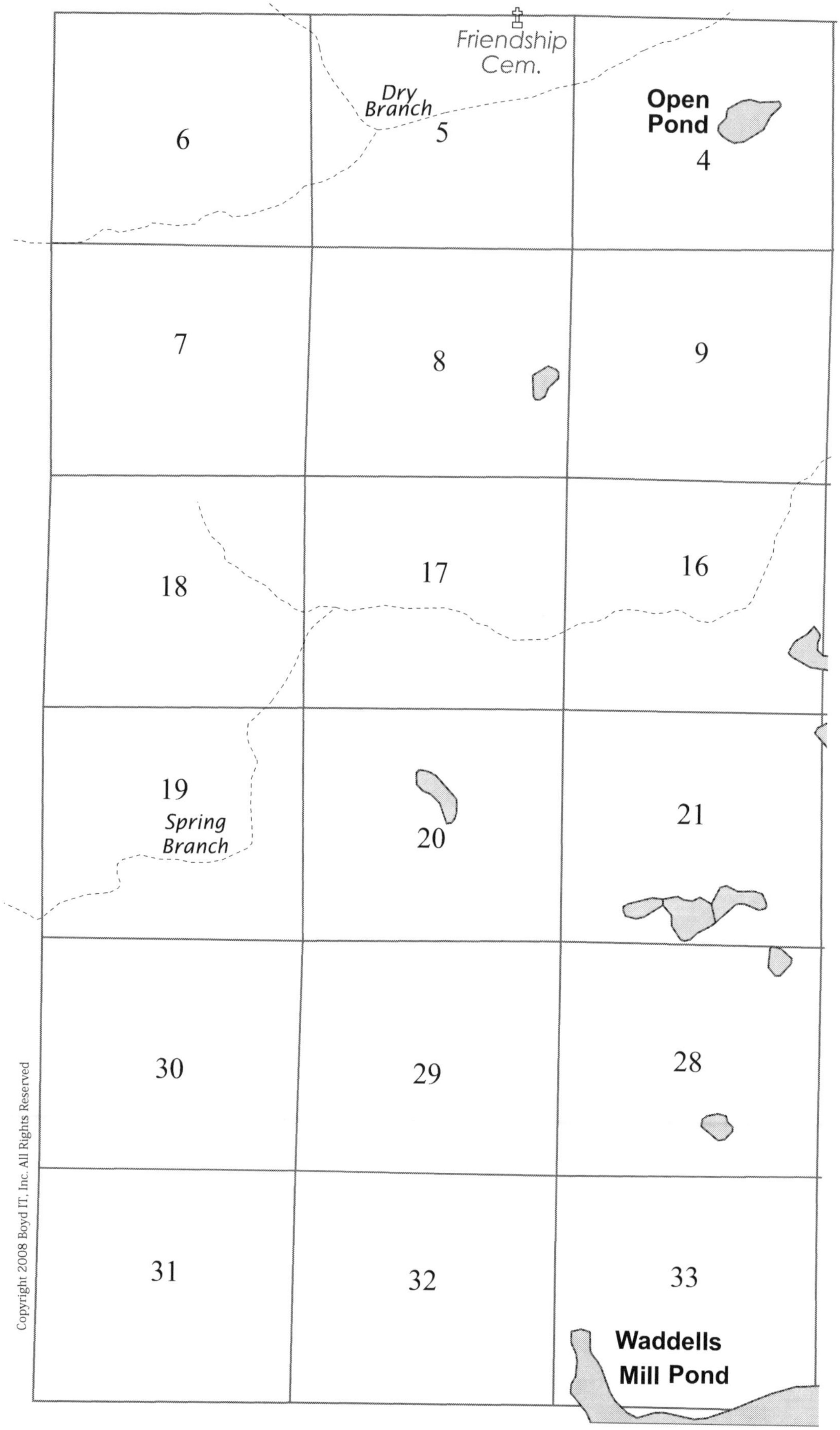

Friendship
Cem.

Dry
Branch

Open
Pond

6

5

4

7

8

9

18

17

16

19

Spring
Branch

20

21

30

29

28

31

32

33

Waddells
Mill Pond

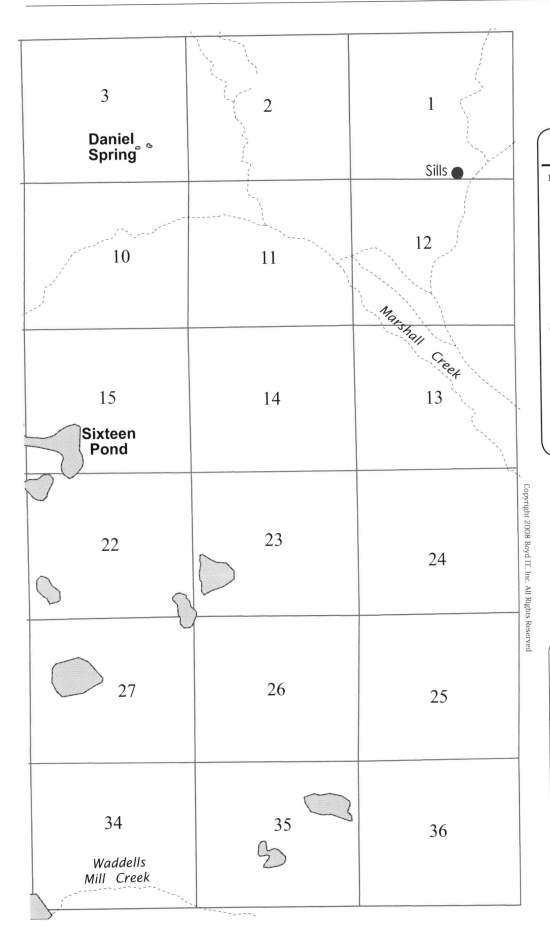

3

Daniel Spring

2

1

Sills ●

10

11

12

Marshall Creek

15

14

13

Sixteen Pond

22

23

24

27

26

25

34

35

36

Waddells Mill Creek

Helpful Hints

1. This Map takes a different look at the same Congressional Township displayed in the preceding two maps. It presents features that can help you better envision the historical development of the area: a) Water-bodies (lakes & ponds), b) Water-courses (rivers, streams, etc.), c) Railroads, d) City/town center-points (where they were oftentimes located when first settled), and e) Cemeteries.

2. Using this "Historical" map in tandem with this Township's Patent Map and Road Map, may lead you to some interesting discoveries. You will often find roads, towns, cemeteries, and waterways are named after nearby landowners: sometimes those names will be the ones you are researching. See how many of these research gems you can find here in Jackson County.

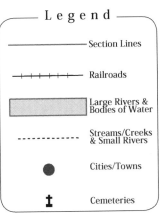

L e g e n d

——————— Section Lines

+++++++ Railroads

▨ Large Rivers & Bodies of Water

--------- Streams/Creeks & Small Rivers

● Cities/Towns

‡ Cemeteries

Scale: Section = 1 mile X 1 mile
(there are some exceptions)

Map Group 11: Index to Land Patents

Township 6-North Range 10-West (Tallahassee)

After you locate an individual in this Index, take note of the Section and Section Part then proceed to the Land Patent map on the pages immediately following. You should have no difficulty locating the corresponding parcel of land.

The "For More Info" Column will lead you to more information about the underlying Patents. See the *Legend* at right, and the "How to Use this Book" chapter, for more information.

```
                              LEGEND
                    "For More Info . . . " column
      A = Authority (Legislative Act, See Appendix "A")
      B = Block or Lot (location in Section unknown)
      C = Cancelled Patent
      F = Fractional Section
      G = Group  (Multi-Patentee Patent, see Appendix "C")
      V = Overlaps another Parcel
      R = Re-Issued (Parcel patented more than once)

      (A & G items require you to look in the Appendixes referred
      to above. All other Letter-designations followed by a number
      require you to locate line-items in this index that possess
      the ID number found after the letter).
```

ID	Individual in Patent	Sec.	Sec. Part	Date Issued	Other Counties	For More Info . . .
1229	ACOCK, Amos	36	SWSW	1837-04-15		A1
1441	ACOCK, William	26	E½SW	1838-07-28		A1
1303	BAKER, James L	7	E½SE	1860-10-01		A1
1292	BATTLE, Isaac L	28	E½NE	1843-03-10		A1 G14
1259	BAXTER, David	10	NWSW	1838-07-28		A1
1260	" "	10	S½NW	1855-05-01		A1
1257	" "	10	E½SW	1856-06-16		A1
1258	" "	10	NWNW	1856-06-16		A1
1261	" "	10	SWSW	1856-06-16		A1
1262	" "	3	SWSW	1856-06-16		A1
1263	" "	9	E½SE	1856-06-16		A1
1264	" "	9	SWSE	1856-06-16		A1
1298	BAXTER, Israel	18	E½SE	1830-11-01		A1
1300	" "	20	W½NW	1830-11-01		A1
1297	" "	17	W½NW	1843-03-10		A1
1299	" "	20	E½NW	1843-03-10		A1
1296	BAXTER, Israel A	8	SWNW	1855-05-01		A1
1293	" "	8	E½SW	1857-12-01		A1
1294	" "	8	S½NE	1857-12-01		A1
1295	" "	8	SE	1857-12-01		A1
1310	BAXTER, James O	21	E½SE	1827-11-01		A1
1312	" "	27	NW	1828-02-01		A1 G15
1309	" "	20	W½SW	1829-06-15		A1
1305	" "	20	E½SW	1833-05-16		A1
1308	" "	20	W½SE	1838-07-28		A1
1311	" "	29	NW	1838-07-28		A1
1306	" "	20	NESE	1848-11-01		A1
1307	" "	20	SENE	1855-05-01		A1
1427	BAXTER, Solomon	15	SESE	1855-05-01		A1
1428	" "	17	SWNE	1855-05-01		A1
1426	" "	15	NESE	1856-06-16		A1
1433	BAXTER, Theophilus	20	W½NE	1852-09-01		A1
1277	BELLAMY, Edward C	26	W½NE	1844-07-10		A1
1276	" "	23	W½SE	1855-05-01		A1
1273	" "	22	SENE	1856-06-16		A1
1274	" "	23	NENE	1856-06-16		A1
1275	" "	23	W½NE	1856-06-16		A1
1420	BELLAMY, Samuel C	31	W½NW	1840-10-10		A1
1419	" "	31	E½SE	1843-03-10		A1
1226	BLACKWELL, Amelia B	18	NW	1841-01-09		A1
1227	" "	6	SE	1841-01-09		A1
1228	" "	6	W½NE	1841-01-09		A1
1318	BROWN, John B	18	E½NE	1830-12-28		A1
1319	" "	19	E½NE	1830-12-28		A1
1320	" "	8	W½SW	1834-08-20		A1
1437	BUSH, Thomas M	18	W½NE	1843-03-10		A1

ID	Individual in Patent	Sec.	Sec. Part	Date Issued	Other Counties	For More Info . . .
1438	BUSH, Thomas M (Cont'd)	6	E½NE	1843-03-10		A1
1336	BUTLER, Joseph	4	SESE	1860-04-02		A1
1246	CARTER, Charles	4	SWSW	1855-05-01		A1
1247	" "	5	NENE	1855-05-01		A1
1248	" "	5	W½SE	1855-05-01		A1
1317	CHUMNEY, John A	17	SWSW	1852-09-01		A1
1240	CLEMENTS, Benjamin	34	N½NE	1827-10-01		A1 V1316
1409	COE, Sampson	5	E½NW	1861-12-05		A1
1410	" "	9	N½NE	1861-12-05		A1
1411	" "	9	NWSE	1861-12-05		A1
1412	" "	9	SWNE	1861-12-05		A1
1393	COOPER, Richard G	32	SW	1855-05-01		A1 G60
1394	" "	32	SWNE	1856-06-16		A1 G60
1316	CORLEY, Jeremiah	34	E½NE	1828-02-01		A1 V1240
1353	DABBADGE, Lydia	4	W½SE	1860-04-02		A1
1346	DEKLE, Littleton	3	E½NW	1860-04-02		A1
1431	DEKLE, Thadeous G	2	NW	1860-04-02		A1
1432	" "	3	NE	1860-04-02		A1
1331	FERGUSON, John T	17	NWSW	1852-09-01		A1
1429	FLORIDA, State Of	18	NESW	1916-04-08		A3
1430	" "	18	NWSE	1916-04-08		A3
1342	FLOYD, Lewis B	4	SWNE	1843-03-10		A1
1337	" "	3	W½NW	1856-06-16		A1
1338	" "	4	E½NE	1856-06-16		A1
1339	" "	4	E½NW	1856-06-16		A1
1340	" "	4	NESE	1856-06-16		A1
1341	" "	4	NWNE	1856-06-16		A1
1281	GARRETT, Henry K	12	NE	1855-05-01		A1
1347	GRIFFIN, Lucy	33	SE	1828-02-01		A1
1242	HAMILTON, Benjamin G	7	SW	1838-07-28		A1
1243	" "	7	W½NE	1838-07-28		A1
1244	" "	7	W½SE	1838-07-28		A1
1424	HATTON, Seaborn J	13	NW	1857-12-01		A1
1425	" "	14	NENE	1857-12-01		A1
1230	HAYS, Amos	32	NWNE	1860-04-02		A1
1231	" "	32	SENW	1860-04-02		A1
1335	HILL, Jonathan G	4	NWSW	1852-09-01		A1
1241	HURST, Benjamin F	4	SESW	1856-06-16		A1
1443	HURST, William	8	N½NE	1859-06-01		A1
1444	" "	9	N½NW	1859-06-01		A1
1396	KIDD, Robert	9	N½SW	1857-12-01		A1
1397	" "	9	S½NW	1857-12-01		A1
1467	KILBEE, William T	22	SW	1829-06-01		A1
1282	KNAPP, Henry	13	NESW	1855-05-01		A1
1284	" "	13	SESW	1855-05-01		A1
1285	" "	13	SWSW	1855-05-01		A1
1283	" "	13	NWSW	1856-06-16		A1
1292	LEWIS, John W	28	E½NE	1843-03-10		A1 G14
1328	LOGATHREE, John	34	SE	1828-02-01		A1 G97
1279	LONG, Felix H	23	S½NW	1855-05-01		A1 C R1278
1278	LONG, Felix H G	23	S½NW	1922-02-13		A1 R1279
1328	LOTT, John	34	SE	1828-02-01		A1 G97
1329	" "	34	NW	1829-05-15		A1 C R1330
1330	" "	34	NW	1922-01-30		A1 R1329
1349	LOTT, Luke	33	E½NW	1838-07-28		A1
1350	" "	33	SENE	1838-07-28		A1
1351	" "	33	W½NE	1838-07-28		A1
1348	" "	32	E½NE	1843-03-10		A1
1352	" "	33	W½NW	1843-03-10		A1
1395	LOTT, Robert A	34	SW	1827-04-02		A1
1304	LOWRY, James	4	W½NW	1844-07-10		A1
1280	MARSHALL, Henry D	7	W½NW	1828-09-10		A1
1291	MARSHALL, Isaac H	7	E½NW	1828-09-10		A1
1321	MAZLEY, John E	11	SESE	1857-12-01		A1
1286	MCDANIEL, Henry	10	SWSE	1856-06-16		A1
1288	" "	15	E½NW	1856-06-16		A1 V1289, 1450
1289	" "	15	SENW	1856-06-16		A1 V1288
1290	" "	15	W½NE	1856-06-16		A1
1287	" "	11	SWSW	1860-04-02		A1
1400	MCDANIEL, Robert	10	SENE	1850-08-10		A1
1398	" "	10	N½NE	1856-06-16		A1 C
1402	" "	10	SWNE	1856-06-16		A1 C R1403
1404	" "	11	NWSW	1856-06-16		A1 C R1405

ID	Individual in Patent	Sec.	Sec. Part	Date Issued	Other Counties	For More Info . . .
1406	MCDANIEL, Robert (Cont'd)	11	SWSE	1856-06-16		A1 C R1407
1399	" "	10	N½SE	1858-11-23		A1
1403	" "	10	SWNE	1858-11-23		A1 R1402
1405	" "	11	NWSW	1858-11-23		A1 R1404
1407	" "	11	SWSE	1858-11-23		A1 R1406
1401	" "	10	SESE	1859-06-01		A1
1408	" "	11	W½NW	1859-06-01		A1
1445	MCNEALEY, William	29	E½SW	1838-07-28		A1
1446	MCNEALLY, William	28	E½SE	1837-04-15		A1
1447	" "	28	W½SW	1848-09-15		A1
1448	" "	29	E½SE	1848-09-15		A1
1222	MCNEALY, Adam	29	W½NE	1843-03-10		A1
1219	" "	14	SE	1855-05-01		A1
1220	" "	17	NENE	1856-06-16		A1
1221	" "	17	NENW	1856-06-16		A1
1223	" "	29	W½SW	1856-06-16		A1
1224	" "	30	E½SE	1856-06-16		A1
1225	" "	30	SENE	1856-06-16		A1
1456	MCNEALY, William	28	W½NE	1829-04-01		A1
1459	" "	32	NENW	1838-07-28		A1
1457	" "	29	E½NE	1840-10-10		A1
1458	" "	29	W½SE	1843-03-10		A1
1452	" "	20	SESE	1855-05-01		A1
1453	" "	22	N½NW	1855-05-01		A1
1454	" "	22	NWNE	1855-05-01		A1
1449	" "	15	E½SW	1856-06-16		A1
1450	" "	15	NENW	1856-06-16		A1 V1288
1451	" "	15	W½NW	1856-06-16		A1
1455	" "	28	E½SW	1856-06-16		A1
1460	" "	32	NWNW	1856-06-16		A1
1462	MCNEELY, William	28	W½SE	1828-02-22		A1
1461	" "	28	SENW	1837-04-15		A1
1463	MCNEILLY, William	28	W½NW	1827-11-01		A1
1371	MORGAN, Nicholas	11	NENE	1855-05-01		A1
1372	" "	11	NESW	1855-05-01		A1
1373	" "	11	SENE	1855-05-01		A1
1374	" "	11	SENW	1855-05-01		A1
1377	" "	12	NWNW	1855-05-01		A1
1378	" "	12	SWNW	1855-05-01		A1
1370	" "	11	N½SE	1856-06-16		A1
1375	" "	11	SESW	1856-06-16		A1
1376	" "	11	SWNE	1856-06-16		A1
1369	MORGAN, Nicholas M	12	E½NW	1856-06-16		A1
1393	MYRICK, Thomas N	32	SW	1855-05-01		A1 G60
1394	" "	32	SWNE	1856-06-16		A1 G60
1315	PATTERSON, James	27	NE	1827-09-01		A1 G111
1312	" "	27	NW	1828-02-01		A1 G15
1314	" "	27	W½SE	1828-03-15		A1
1313	" "	27	E½SW	1829-04-15		A1
1301	PELT, Jacob J	6	SESW	1856-06-16		A1
1302	" "	6	W½SW	1856-06-16		A1
1235	PRATHER, Anderson T	14	SENW	1855-05-01		A1
1236	" "	17	E½SW	1855-05-01		A1
1237	" "	21	NWSW	1855-05-01		A1
1238	" "	30	NENE	1855-05-01		A1
1234	" "	14	S½NE	1856-06-16		A1
1239	" "	30	W½NE	1856-06-16		A1
1232	" "	14	NENW	1860-04-02		A1
1233	" "	14	NWNE	1860-04-02		A1
1435	PRATHER, Thomas F	18	SWSE	1859-06-01		A1
1436	" "	19	W½NE	1859-06-01		A1
1343	RIVERS, Lewis	6	NESW	1861-12-10		A1
1344	" "	6	S½NW	1861-12-10		A1
1368	ROBERSON, Morning	25	NENW	1850-08-10		A1
1359	ROBERTS, Mary	35	NESE	1837-04-20		A1
1360	" "	35	SESE	1837-04-20		A1
1363	" "	36	E½SW	1837-04-20		A1
1365	" "	36	NWSW	1837-04-20		A1
1354	" "	25	E½SE	1838-07-28		A1
1355	" "	25	SW	1838-07-28		A1
1356	" "	25	W½SE	1838-07-28		A1
1357	" "	26	SE	1838-07-28		A1
1358	" "	35	NE	1838-07-28		A1

ID	Individual in Patent	Sec.	Sec. Part	Date Issued	Other Counties	For More Info . . .
1361	ROBERTS, Mary (Cont'd)	36	E½NE	1838-07-28		A1
1362	" "	36	E½SE	1838-07-28		A1
1364	" "	36	NW	1838-07-28		A1
1366	" "	36	W½NE	1838-07-28		A1
1367	" "	36	W½SE	1838-07-28		A1
1315	ROBINSON, Hugh	27	NE	1827-09-01		A1 G111
1323	ROULHAC, John G	21	S½NE	1852-09-01		A1
1324	" "	21	W½SE	1852-09-01		A1
1325	" "	22	S½NW	1852-09-01		A1
1326	" "	22	SWNE	1852-09-01		A1
1322	" "	15	W½SW	1856-06-16		A1
1327	" "	27	W½SW	1857-07-01		A1
1382	SIMONS, Peter	35	W½SW	1829-05-01		A1
1381	" "	35	W½SE	1829-05-15		A1
1464	SOREY, William	25	NE	1846-09-01		A1
1465	" "	25	SENW	1848-04-10		A1
1466	" "	25	W½NW	1848-11-01		A1
1265	SPEAR, David	23	NENW	1838-07-28		A1
1266	" "	23	NWSW	1838-07-28		A1
1268	SPEARS, David	26	E½NW	1837-04-15		A1
1267	" "	22	SE	1838-07-28		A1
1270	SPEIR, David	26	W½NW	1827-04-02		A1
1271	" "	35	W½NW	1828-07-22		A1
1269	" "	23	SESW	1835-10-20		A1
1272	SPIER, David	23	SWSW	1837-04-20		A1
1245	SPIERS, Bracney T	30	NWSW	1855-05-01		A1
1345	SPIERS, Lidia	30	NESW	1900-08-09		A2
1434	SUTTON, Theophilus	30	W½NW	1829-05-15		A1
1392	TAYLOR, Peter	3	SWSE	1838-07-28		A1
1383	" "	10	NENE	1850-08-10		A1
1384	" "	10	NENW	1855-05-01		A1
1385	" "	10	NWNE	1855-05-01		A1
1390	" "	3	NESW	1855-05-01		A1
1391	" "	3	SESE	1855-05-01		A1
1386	" "	11	NENW	1859-06-01		A1
1387	" "	11	NWNE	1859-06-01		A1
1388	" "	2	SW	1859-06-01		A1
1389	" "	3	N½SE	1859-06-01		A1
1439	WHITAKER, Thomas R	6	N½NW	1857-12-01		A1
1415	WILLEFORD, Samuel B	23	E½SE	1850-08-10		A1
1416	" "	26	NENE	1850-08-10		A1
1417	" "	26	SENE	1850-08-10		A1
1414	" "	21	NWNW	1852-09-01		A1
1413	" "	17	SENE	1856-06-16		A1
1418	" "	9	S½SW	1856-06-16		A1
1251	WILLIAMSON, Charles	31	SW	1827-04-02		A1
1249	" "	26	W½SW	1827-10-01		A1
1250	" "	27	E½SE	1827-10-01		A1
1252	" "	31	W½SE	1827-10-01		A1
1253	" "	32	E½SE	1827-10-01		A1
1254	" "	32	W½SE	1827-10-01		A1
1255	" "	33	E½SW	1827-10-01		A1
1256	" "	33	W½SW	1827-10-01		A1
1442	WILLIS, William B	15	W½SE	1856-06-16		A1
1333	WILSON, John T	5	W½NE	1840-10-10		A1
1332	" "	5	E½SW	1841-01-09		A1
1334	" "	8	E½NW	1841-01-09		A1
1423	WILSON, Samuel W	5	SENE	1846-10-01		A1
1421	" "	4	NESW	1848-10-01		A1
1422	" "	5	NESE	1852-09-01		A1
1440	WILSON, Thomas	5	SESE	1852-09-01		A1
1379	YOUNG, Orman	35	E½NW	1829-06-01		A1
1380	" "	35	E½SW	1829-06-01		A1

Patent Map

T6-N R10-W
Tallahassee Meridian

Map Group 11

Township Statistics

Parcels Mapped	:	249
Number of Patents	:	196
Number of Individuals	:	88
Patentees Identified	:	87
Number of Surnames	:	68
Multi-Patentee Parcels	:	6
Oldest Patent Date	:	4/2/1827
Most Recent Patent	:	2/13/1922
Block/Lot Parcels	:	0
Parcels Re-Issued	:	5
Parcels that Overlap	:	5
Cities and Towns	:	2
Cemeteries	:	2

Copyright 2008 Boyd IT, Inc. All Rights Reserved

Section 3
FLOYD Lewis B 1856
DEKLE Littleton 1860
DEKLE Thadeous G 1860
3
TAYLOR Peter 1855
TAYLOR Peter 1859
BAXTER David 1856
TAYLOR Peter 1838
TAYLOR Peter 1855

Section 2
DEKLE Thadeous G 1860
2
TAYLOR Peter 1859

Section 1
1

Section 10
BAXTER David 1856
TAYLOR Peter 1855
TAYLOR Peter 1855 / MCDANIEL Robert 1856
TAYLOR Peter 1850
BAXTER David 1855
MCDANIEL Robert 1856 / MCDANIEL Robert 1858
MCDANIEL Robert 1850
BAXTER David 1838
BAXTER David 1856
10
MCDANIEL Robert 1858
BAXTER David 1856
MCDANIEL Henry 1856
MCDANIEL Robert 1859

Section 11
MCDANIEL Robert 1859
TAYLOR Peter 1859
TAYLOR Peter 1859
MORGAN Nicholas 1855
MORGAN Nicholas 1856
MORGAN Nicholas 1855
MORGAN Nicholas 1855
MORGAN Nicholas 1855
MORGAN Nicholas 1855
11
MORGAN Nicholas 1856
MCDANIEL Henry 1860
MORGAN Nicholas 1856
MCDANIEL Robert 1856
MAZLEY John E 1857

Section 12
MORGAN Nicholas 1855
MORGAN Nicholas M
1856
12
GARRETT Henry K 1855

Section 15
MCNEALY William 1856
MCDANIEL Henry 1856 / MCDANIEL Henry 1856
MCDANIEL Henry 1856
MCNEALY William 1856
15
ROULHAC John G 1856
MCNEALY William 1856
WILLIS William B 1856
BAXTER Solomon 1856
BAXTER Solomon 1855

Section 14
PRATHER Anderson T 1860
PRATHER Anderson T 1860
HATTON Seaborn J 1857
PRATHER Anderson T 1855
PRATHER Anderson T 1856
14
MCNEALY Adam 1855

Section 13
HATTON Seaborn J 1857
13
KNAPP Henry 1856
KNAPP Henry 1855
KNAPP Henry 1855
KNAPP Henry 1855

Section 22
MCNEALY William 1855
MCNEALY William 1855
ROULHAC John G 1852
ROULHAC John G 1852
BELLAMY Edward C 1856
KILBEE William T 1829
22
SPEARS David 1838

Section 23
SPEAR David 1838
LONG Felix H 1855
LONG Felix H G 1922
BELLAMY Edward C 1856
SPEAR David 1838
23
SPIER David 1837
SPEIR David 1835
BELLAMY Edward C 1855
WILLEFORD Samuel B 1850

Section 24
BELLAMY Edward C 1856
24

Section 27
BAXTER [15] James O 1828
PATTERSON [111] James 1827
27
ROULHAC John G 1857
PATTERSON James 1829
PATTERSON James 1828
WILLIAMSON Charles 1827

Section 26
SPEIR David 1827
SPEARS David 1837
BELLAMY Edward C 1844
WILLEFORD Samuel B 1850
26
WILLEFORD Samuel B 1850
WILLIAMSON Charles 1827
ACOCK William 1838

Section 25
ROBERSON Morning 1850
SOREY William 1846
SOREY William 1848
SOREY William 1848
25

Section 36
ROBERTS Mary 1838
ROBERTS Mary 1838
ROBERTS Mary 1838

Section 35
ROBERTS Mary 1838
ROBERTS Mary 1838
ROBERTS Mary 1838

Section 34
ROULHAC John G 1857
LOTT John 1829
LOTT John 1922
CLEMENTS Benjamin 1827
CORLEY Jeremiah 1828
34
LOTT Robert A 1827
LOGATHREE [97] John 1828

Section 35 (continued)
SPEIR David 1828
YOUNG Orman 1829
ROBERTS Mary 1838
35
SIMONS Peter 1829
YOUNG Orman 1829
SIMONS Peter 1829
ROBERTS Mary 1837
ROBERTS Mary 1837
ROBERTS Mary 1837

Section 36 (continued)
ROBERTS Mary 1838
ROBERTS Mary 1838
36
ACOCK Amos 1837
ROBERTS Mary 1837
ROBERTS Mary 1838
ROBERTS Mary 1838

Helpful Hints

1. This Map's INDEX can be found on the preceding pages.

2. Refer to Map "C" to see where this Township lies within Jackson County, Florida.

3. Numbers within square brackets [ ] denote a multi-patentee land parcel (multi-owner). Refer to Appendix "C" for a full list of members in this group.

4. Areas that look to be crowded with Patentees usually indicate multiple sales of the same parcel (Re-issues) or Overlapping parcels. See this Township's Index for an explanation of these and other circumstances that might explain "odd" groupings of Patentees on this map.

Legend

———— Patent Boundary

▬▬▬▬ Section Boundary

No Patents Found (or Outside County)

1., 2., 3., ... Lot Numbers (when beside a name)

[ ] Group Number (see Appendix "C")

Scale: Section = 1 mile X 1 mile (generally, with some exceptions)

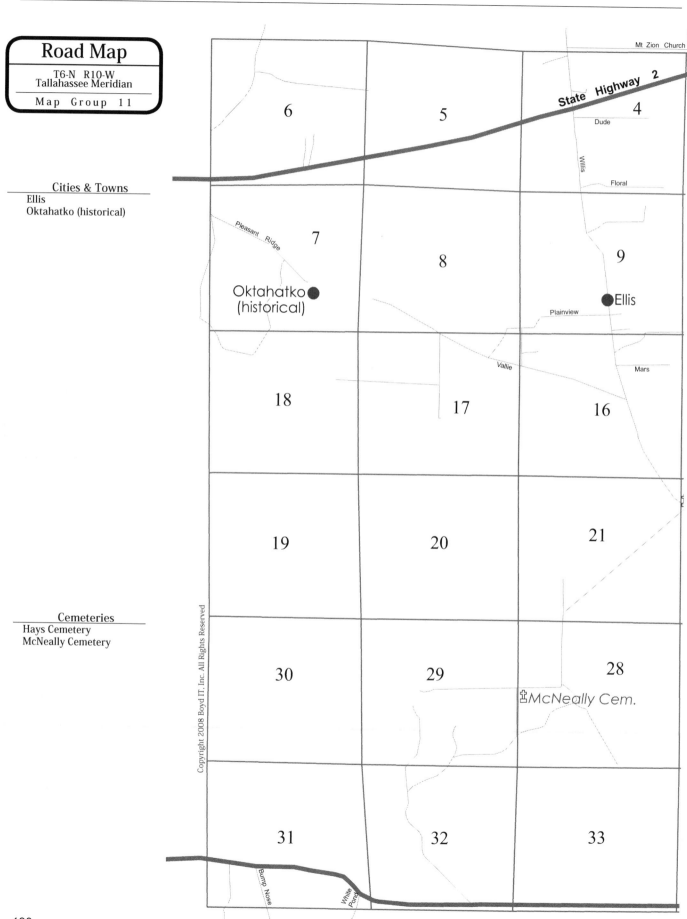

Road Map

T6-N R10-W
Tallahassee Meridian

Map Group 11

Cities & Towns

Ellis
Oktahatko (historical)

Cemeteries

Hays Cemetery
McNeally Cemetery

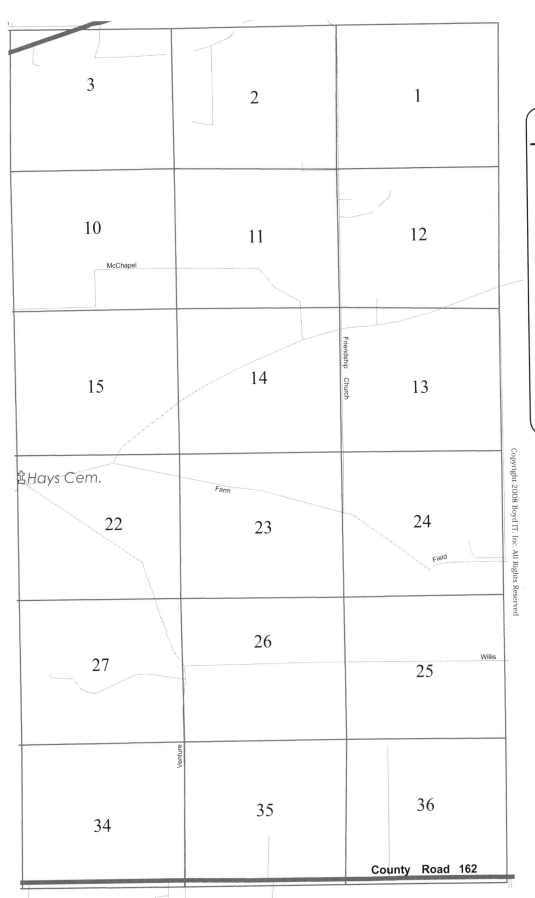

3

2

1

10

11

12

McChapel

15

14

13

Friendship Church

🕆 Hays Cem.

22

Farm

23

24

Field

26

27

Willis

25

Venture

34

35

36

County Road 162

Helpful Hints

1. This road map has a number of uses, but primarily it is to help you: a) find the present location of land owned by your ancestors (at least the general area), b) find cemeteries and city-centers, and c) estimate the route/roads used by Census-takers & tax-assessors.

2. If you plan to travel to Jackson County to locate cemeteries or land parcels, please pick up a modern travel map for the area before you do. Mapping old land parcels on modern maps is not as exact a science as you might think. Just the slightest variations in public land survey coordinates, estimates of parcel boundaries, or road-map deviations can greatly alter a map's representation of how a road either does or doesn't cross a particular parcel of land.

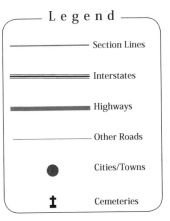

L e g e n d

————	Section Lines
▬▬▬▬	Interstates
▬▬▬▬	Highways
————	Other Roads
●	Cities/Towns
🕆	Cemeteries

Scale: Section = 1 mile X 1 mile
(generally, with some exceptions)

Historical Map

T6-N R10-W
Tallahassee Meridian

Map Group 11

Cities & Towns

Ellis
Oktahatko (historical)

Cemeteries

Hays Cemetery
McNeally Cemetery

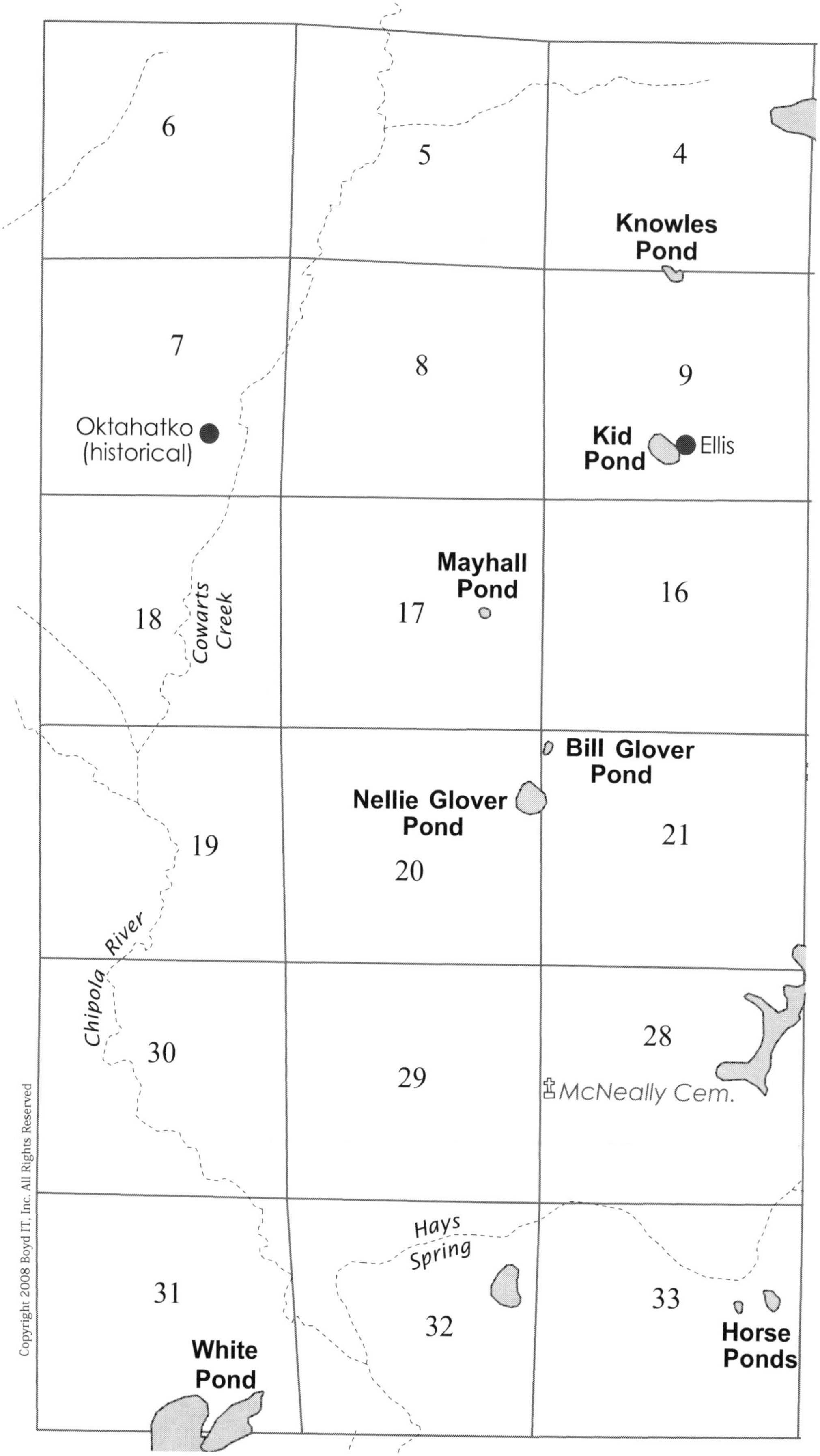

6
5
4
Knowles Pond
7
8
9
Oktahatko (historical)
Kid Pond
Ellis
18
Cowarts Creek
17
Mayhall Pond
16
Bill Glover Pond
Nellie Glover Pond
19
20
21
Chipola River
30
29
28
McNeally Cem.
31
32
33
Hays Spring
White Pond
Horse Ponds

3	Goose Pond 2	Harts Pond 1
Taylor Bay 10	11	12
15	Parker Pond 14	13
Hays Cem. 22	23	24
Hays Spring Run 27	Mill Pond Jericho Pond 26	25
Lot Run Lot Pond 34	35	36

Helpful Hints

1. This Map takes a different look at the same Congressional Township displayed in the preceding two maps. It presents features that can help you better envision the historical development of the area: a) Water-bodies (lakes & ponds), b) Water-courses (rivers, streams, etc.), c) Railroads, d) City/town center-points (where they were oftentimes located when first settled), and e) Cemeteries.

2. Using this "Historical" map in tandem with this Township's Patent Map and Road Map, may lead you to some interesting discoveries. You will often find roads, towns, cemeteries, and waterways are named after nearby landowners: sometimes those names will be the ones you are researching. See how many of these research gems you can find here in Jackson County.

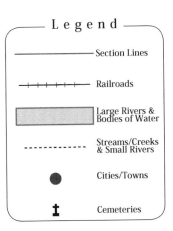

L e g e n d

— Section Lines

+++++ Railroads

Large Rivers & Bodies of Water

----- Streams/Creeks & Small Rivers

● Cities/Towns

✝ Cemeteries

Scale: Section = 1 mile X 1 mile
(there are some exceptions)

133

Map Group 12: Index to Land Patents

Township 6-North Range 9-West (Tallahassee)

After you locate an individual in this Index, take note of the Section and Section Part then proceed to the Land Patent map on the pages immediately following. You should have no difficulty locating the corresponding parcel of land.

The "For More Info" Column will lead you to more information about the underlying Patents. See the *Legend* at right, and the "How to Use this Book" chapter, for more information.

```
                    LEGEND
            "For More Info . . . " column
A = Authority (Legislative Act, See Appendix "A")
B = Block or Lot (location in Section unknown)
C = Cancelled Patent
F = Fractional Section
G = Group  (Multi-Patentee Patent, see Appendix "C")
V = Overlaps another Parcel
R = Re-Issued (Parcel patented more than once)

(A & G items require you to look in the Appendixes referred
to above. All other Letter-designations followed by a number
require you to locate line-items in this index that possess
the ID number found after the letter).
```

ID	Individual in Patent	Sec.	Sec. Part	Date Issued	Other Counties	For More Info . . .
1614	ALMAROAD, William H	24	NENE	1855-05-01		A1
1488	ALSOBROOK, Eliza	13	S½	1860-07-02		A1
1539	ALSOBROOK, Johnson	19	W½SE	1848-11-01		A1
1540	" "	30	NENE	1848-11-01		A1
1537	" "	19	NESE	1850-08-10		A1
1538	" "	19	SESE	1852-09-01		A1
1530	AVERY, John H	1	N½SE	1860-07-02		A1
1474	BARKLEY, Bolden B	20	SESE	1850-08-10		A1
1475	" "	21	SWSW	1850-08-10		A1
1476	" "	29	E½NE	1850-08-10		A1
1477	BARKLEY, Bolyn B	32	SWNW	1852-09-01		A1
1607	BARNACASCEL, Uriah	12	N½SE	1856-06-16		A1
1608	" "	12	S½NE	1856-06-16		A1
1609	BARNACASTLE, Uriah	12	NENE	1855-05-01		A1
1494	BATES, Henry	8	SENW	1844-07-10		A1
1495	" "	8	SWNE	1844-07-10		A1
1490	BAXTER, Ely J	5	SWSW	1855-05-01		A1
1489	" "	5	NWSW	1856-06-16		A1
1506	BAXTER, Israel	8	NWNW	1855-05-01		A1
1502	" "	5	E½SW	1859-06-01		A1
1503	" "	5	W½SE	1859-06-01		A1
1504	" "	8	NENW	1859-06-01		A1
1505	" "	8	NWNE	1859-06-01		A1
1507	" "	8	W½SE	1859-06-01		A1
1508	BAXTER, Jacob	7	SE	1857-12-01		A1
1518	BAXTER, James O	6	SWSE	1855-05-01		A1
1517	" "	11	W½	1856-06-16		A1
1525	BAXTER, John	2	SESW	1860-07-02		A1
1595	BAXTER, Solomon	2	W½SW	1856-06-16		A1
1593	" "	2	NESW	1857-07-01		A1
1594	" "	2	NW	1857-07-01		A1
1596	" "	3	E½NE	1857-07-01		A1
1622	BAXTER, William M	7	E½NE	1852-09-01		A1
1600	BRUNSON, Thomas	21	NW	1855-05-01		A1
1541	CLARK, Jonas H	36	SE	1857-12-01		A1
1500	COOK, Isaac N	20	N½SE	1857-07-01		A1 V1559, 1560
1501	" "	20	S½NE	1857-07-01		A1 V1548, 1557
1527	COOK, John F	36	NENE	1855-05-01		A1
1528	" "	36	NWNE	1855-05-01		A1
1526	" "	25	S½SE	1856-06-16		A1
1529	" "	36	S½NE	1856-06-16		A1
1585	COOK, Shadrack	1	SWSW	1857-12-01		A1
1586	" "	11	N½NE	1857-12-01		A1
1589	" "	2	S½SE	1857-12-01		A1
1587	" "	11	SWNE	1860-04-02		A1
1588	" "	11	W½SE	1860-04-02		A1

ID	Individual in Patent	Sec.	Sec. Part	Date Issued	Other Counties	For More Info . . .
1610	DICKSON, William B	32	E½SE	1846-10-01		A1
1611	" "	32	NWNE	1846-10-01		A1
1612	" "	32	SENW	1855-05-01		A1
1613	" "	32	SWNE	1855-05-01		A1
1582	DOZIER, Pryor	10	NE	1857-07-01		A1
1468	FULLERTON, Addison	3	S½NW	1857-12-01		A1
1469	" "	3	SW	1857-12-01		A1
1470	" "	4	E½NE	1857-12-01		A1
1583	FULLERTON, Richard	3	W½NE	1860-04-02		A1
1509	GILES, James H	4	SWSE	1860-04-02		A1
1511	GILES, James J	4	NENW	1856-06-16		A1
1512	" "	4	NWNE	1856-06-16		A1
1516	" "	4	SWNW	1856-06-16		A1
1510	" "	4	N½SW	1857-12-01		A1
1513	" "	4	NWSE	1857-12-01		A1
1514	" "	4	SENW	1857-12-01		A1
1515	" "	4	SWNE	1857-12-01		A1
1590	GLADDEN, Silas	4	NWNW	1857-12-01		A1
1591	" "	5	NENE	1857-12-01		A1
1492	GLOVER, George K	1	N½NE	1860-07-02		A1
1493	" "	1	SENE	1860-07-02		A1
1519	GODWIN, James W	1	NENW	1898-10-04		A2
1520	" "	1	SWNE	1898-10-04		A2
1598	GODWIN, Thomas A	24	E½NW	1860-07-02		A1
1599	" "	24	W½NE	1860-07-02		A1
1491	GRANBERRY, George	33	NE	1855-05-01		A1
1481	GRAY, Davis	31	NENE	1855-05-01		A1
1482	" "	32	NENE	1855-05-01		A1
1546	HEARN, Laurence H	20	E½SW	1850-08-10		A1
1547	" "	20	SWSE	1850-08-10		A1
1548	" "	20	W½NE	1850-08-10		A1 V1501
1549	HEARN, Lawrence H	34	W½SW	1846-10-01		A1
1556	HEARN, Margaret	34	E½SE	1859-06-01		A1
1554	HEARN, Margaret A	34	E½SW	1856-06-16		A1
1555	" "	34	W½SE	1856-06-16		A1
1581	HOLDER, Nazareth	33	E½SW	1859-06-01		A1
1584	HOLLINGSWORTH, Richard	34	NW	1857-12-01		A1
1553	HYATT, Lewis	3	SE	1857-12-01		A1
1626	KIMBELL, William T	11	SESE	1898-10-04		A2
1627	" "	12	SWSW	1898-10-04		A2
1628	" "	13	W½NW	1898-10-04		A2
1569	LANCASTER, Mary	19	N½SW	1850-08-10		A1
1570	" "	19	SESW	1850-08-10		A1
1534	MARTIN, John P	8	E½SW	1838-07-28		A1
1479	MATHEWS, Charles	32	SW	1846-09-01		A1
1480	" "	32	W½SE	1846-09-01		A1
1522	MERCER, Jesse W	30	E½SW	1857-12-01		A1
1542	MERCER, Joshua	29	NESW	1846-10-01		A1
1544	" "	29	SESW	1846-10-01		A1
1545	" "	29	SWSW	1846-10-01		A1
1543	" "	29	NWSW	1848-04-10		A1
1597	MERCER, Susanah I	6	SESE	1855-05-01		A1
1602	MERCER, Thomas R	4	E½SE	1857-12-01		A1
1603	" "	9	E½NW	1857-12-01		A1
1604	" "	9	NE	1857-12-01		A1
1615	MERCER, William H	32	NENW	1846-10-01		A1
1616	" "	32	NWNW	1846-10-01		A1
1485	MINCHIN, Edward	1	E½SW	1856-06-16		A1
1486	" "	1	S½SE	1856-06-16		A1
1567	PENDER, Marmaduke	20	SWNW	1850-08-10		A1
1568	" "	20	W½SW	1850-08-10		A1
1558	PENDER, Marmaduke B	20	NENW	1852-09-01		A1
1566	" "	29	NWNE	1852-09-01		A1
1557	" "	20	E½NE	1855-05-01		A1 V1501
1559	" "	20	NESE	1855-05-01		A1 V1500
1560	" "	20	NWSE	1855-05-01		A1 V1500
1561	" "	21	NWSW	1855-05-01		A1
1562	" "	21	SESW	1855-05-01		A1
1563	" "	28	NENW	1855-05-01		A1
1564	" "	28	SENW	1855-05-01		A1
1565	" "	28	W½NW	1855-05-01		A1
1498	ROBERSON, Hugh	8	E½NE	1856-06-16		A1
1499	" "	9	W½NW	1856-06-16		A1

ID	Individual in Patent	Sec.	Sec. Part	Date Issued	Other Counties	For More Info . . .
1496	ROBERSON, Hugh (Cont'd)	4	S½SW	1857-12-01		A1
1497	" "	5	E½SE	1857-12-01		A1
1578	ROBERSON, Mourning	20	SENW	1848-04-10		A1
1577	" "	20	NWNW	1855-05-01		A1
1571	ROBERTS, Mary	30	W½SW	1838-07-28		A1
1575	" "	31	W½NW	1838-07-28		A1
1576	" "	31	W½SW	1838-07-28		A1
1573	" "	31	E½SW	1846-09-01		A1
1572	" "	31	E½NW	1848-11-01		A1
1574	" "	31	W½NE	1848-11-01		A1
1535	ROGERS, John	10	NW	1857-12-01		A1
1605	ROGERS, Thomas	21	NESW	1856-06-16		A1
1601	ROGERS, Thomas L	1	S½NW	1857-12-01		A1
1471	SMITH, Alexander	12	SESW	1906-01-30		A2
1483	SMITH, Dempsy	24	W½NW	1895-05-03		A2
1536	SMITH, John	1	NWSW	1904-08-26		A2
1625	SOREY, William	30	SWNW	1850-08-10		A1
1624	" "	30	SENE	1852-09-01		A1
1623	" "	30	NWNW	1855-05-01		A1
1592	STRICKLAND, Simon J	24	SENE	1859-06-01		A1
1606	STRICKLAND, Thomas W	12	NWNE	1855-05-01		A1
1523	SYFRETT, John A	31	SE	1843-03-10		A1
1524	SYPETT, John A	31	SENE	1848-11-01		A1
1617	TIDWELL, William J	3	N½NW	1857-12-01		A1
1484	TREVATHON, Demsey	19	SWSW	1850-08-10		A1
1472	WATFORD, Aurena	5	SENE	1860-04-02		A1
1473	" "	5	W½NE	1860-04-02		A1
1521	WATFORD, James	6	W½NE	1860-04-02		A1
1579	WATFORD, Nathan	5	NW	1857-07-01		A1
1580	" "	6	E½NE	1857-12-01		A1
1550	WHITEHURST, Levi W	12	S½SE	1860-04-02		A1
1551	" "	13	E½NW	1860-04-02		A1
1552	" "	13	NE	1860-04-02		A1
1487	WILLIAMS, Edward	33	SE	1855-05-01		A1
1531	YARBOROUGH, John M	1	NWNW	1860-04-02		A1
1532	" "	2	N½SE	1860-04-02		A1
1533	" "	2	NE	1860-04-02		A1
1478	YONGE, Chandler C	24	S½	1857-07-01		A1
1618	YOUNG, William L	11	NESE	1856-06-16		A1
1619	" "	11	SENE	1856-06-16		A1
1620	" "	12	NESW	1856-06-16		A1
1621	" "	12	SENW	1856-06-16		A1

Patent Map

T6-N R9-W
Tallahassee Meridian

Map Group 12

Township Statistics

Parcels Mapped	:	161
Number of Patents	:	111
Number of Individuals	:	76
Patentees Identified	:	76
Number of Surnames	:	47
Multi-Patentee Parcels	:	0
Oldest Patent Date	:	7/28/1838
Most Recent Patent	:	1/30/1906
Block/Lot Parcels	:	0
Parcels Re - Issued	:	0
Parcels that Overlap	:	6
Cities and Towns	:	2
Cemeteries	:	1

Copyright 2008 Boyd IT. Inc. All Rights Reserved

TIDWELL William J 1857		BAXTER Solomon 1857	BAXTER Solomon 1857	YARBOROUGH John M 1860	YARBOROUGH John M 1860	GODWIN James W 1898	GLOVER George K 1860

TIDWELL
William J
1857

FULLERTON
Richard
1860

BAXTER
Solomon
1857

BAXTER
Solomon
1857

YARBOROUGH
John M
1860

2

YARBOROUGH
John M
1860

GODWIN
James W
1898

GLOVER
George K
1860

FULLERTON
Addison
1857

ROGERS
Thomas L
1857

GODWIN
James W
1898

GLOVER
George K
1860

FULLERTON
Addison
1857

3

HYATT
Lewis
1857

BAXTER
Solomon
1856

BAXTER
Solomon
1857

YARBOROUGH
John M
1860

SMITH
John
1904

1

AVERY
John H
1860

BAXTER
John
1860

COOK
Shadrack
1857

COOK
Shadrack
1857

MINCHIN
Edward
1856

MINCHIN
Edward
1856

ROGERS
John
1857

DOZIER
Pryor
1857

10

BAXTER
James O
1856

11

COOK
Shadrack
1857

COOK
Shadrack
1860

YOUNG
William L
1856

STRICKLAND
Thomas W
1855

BARNACASTLE
Uriah
1855

YOUNG
William L
1856

12

BARNACASCEL
Uriah
1856

YOUNG
William L
1856

YOUNG
William L
1856

BARNACASCEL
Uriah
1856

COOK
Shadrack
1860

KIMBELL
William T
1898

KIMBELL
William T
1898

SMITH
Alexander
1906

WHITEHURST
Levi W
1860

15

14

KIMBELL
William T
1898

WHITEHURST
Levi W
1860

WHITEHURST
Levi W
1860

13

ALSOBROOK
Eliza
1860

22

23

SMITH
Dempsy
1895

GODWIN
Thomas A
1860

GODWIN
Thomas A
1860

ALMAROAD
William H
1855

STRICKLAND
Simon J
1859

24

YONGE
Chandler C
1857

27

26

25

COOK
John F
1856

COOK
John F
1855

COOK
John F
1855

COOK
John F
1856

HOLLINGSWORTH
Richard
1857

34

35

36

CLARK
Jonas H
1857

HEARN
Margaret A
1856

HEARN
Margaret A
1856

HEARN
Lawrence H
1846

HEARN
Margaret
1859

Helpful Hints

1. This Map's INDEX can be found on the preceding pages.

2. Refer to Map "C" to see where this Township lies within Jackson County, Florida.

3. Numbers within square brackets [ ] denote a multi-patentee land parcel (multi-owner). Refer to Appendix "C" for a full list of members in this group.

4. Areas that look to be crowded with Patentees usually indicate multiple sales of the same parcel (Re-issues) or Overlapping parcels. See this Township's Index for an explanation of these and other circumstances that might explain "odd" groupings of Patentees on this map.

Legend

———— Patent Boundary

▬▬▬▬ Section Boundary

▨▨▨▨ No Patents Found (or Outside County)

1., 2., 3., ... Lot Numbers (when beside a name)

[ ] Group Number (see Appendix "C")

Scale: Section = 1 mile X 1 mile (generally, with some exceptions)

Road Map

T6-N R9-W
Tallahassee Meridian

Map Group 12

Cities & Towns

Bascom
Greenwood

Cemeteries

Nubbin Ridge Cemetery

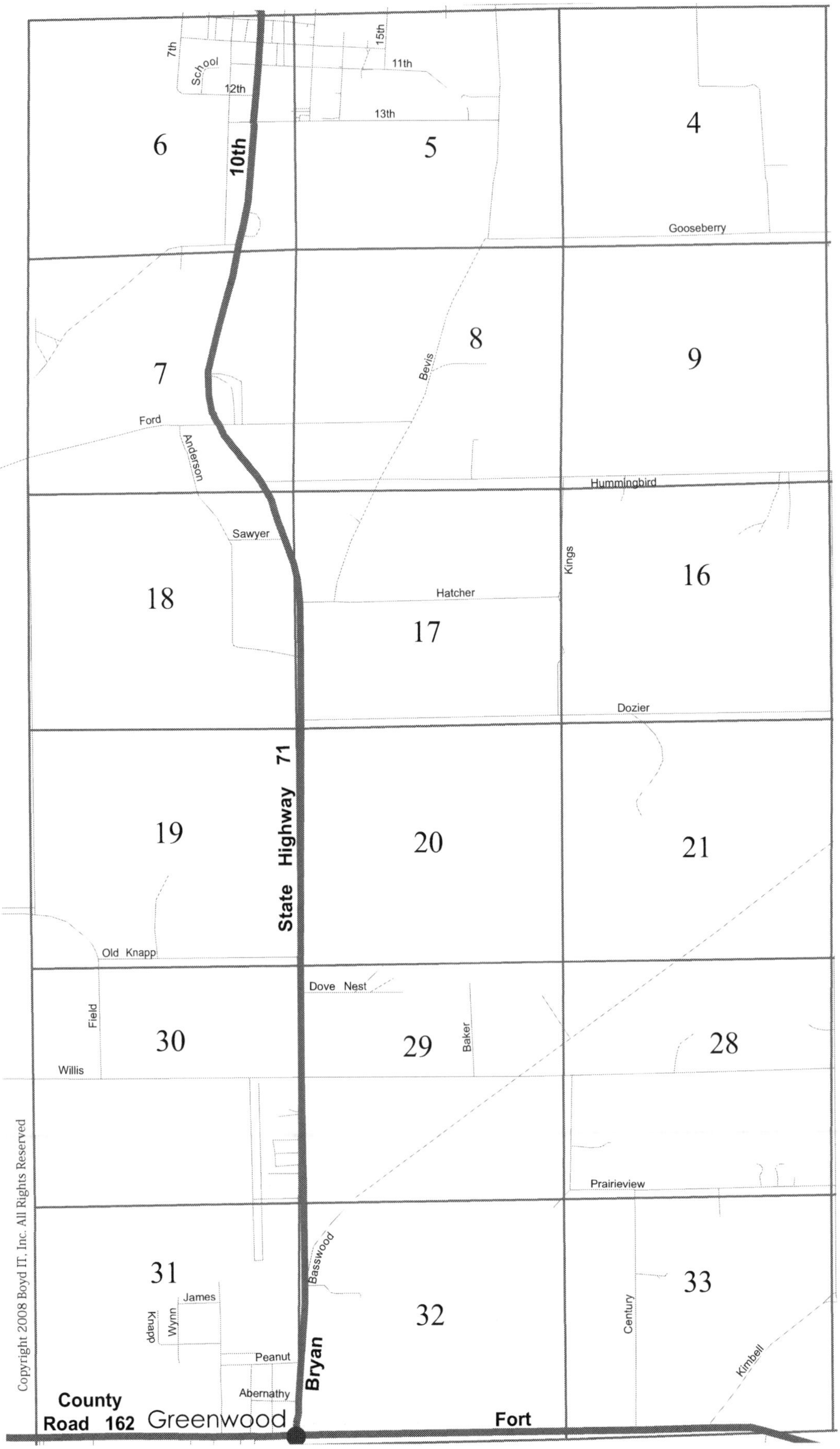

7th

School

12th

15th

11th

13th

6

10th

5

4

Gooseberry

7

8

Bevis

9

Ford

Anderson

Hummingbird

Sawyer

18

Hatcher

Kings

16

17

Dozier

State Highway 71

19

20

21

Old Knapp

Dove Nest

Field

30

29

Baker

28

Willis

Prairieview

31

James

Knapp

Wynn

Basswood

32

Century

33

Peanut

Abernathy

Bryan

Kimbell

**County
Road 162** Greenwood

Fort

140

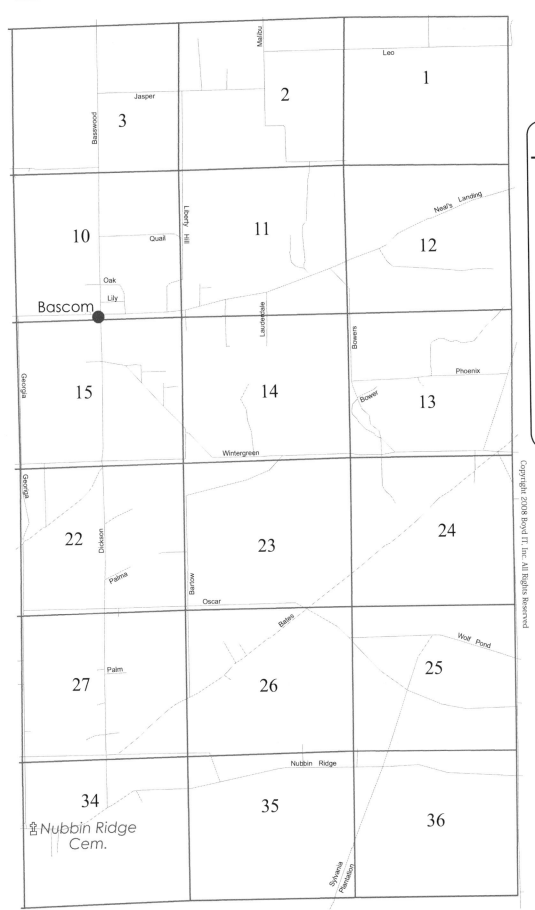

Helpful Hints

1. This road map has a number of uses, but primarily it is to help you: a) find the present location of land owned by your ancestors (at least the general area), b) find cemeteries and city-centers, and c) estimate the route/roads used by Census-takers & tax-assessors.

2. If you plan to travel to Jackson County to locate cemeteries or land parcels, please pick up a modern travel map for the area before you do. Mapping old land parcels on modern maps is not as exact a science as you might think. Just the slightest variations in public land survey coordinates, estimates of parcel boundaries, or road-map deviations can greatly alter a map's representation of how a road either does or doesn't cross a particular parcel of land.

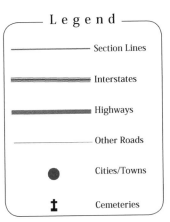

L e g e n d

Section Lines

Interstates

Highways

Other Roads

Cities/Towns

Cemeteries

Scale: Section = 1 mile X 1 mile
(generally, with some exceptions)

141

Historical Map

T6-N R9-W
Tallahassee Meridian

Map Group 12

Cities & Towns
Bascom
Greenwood

Cemeteries
Nubbin Ridge Cemetery

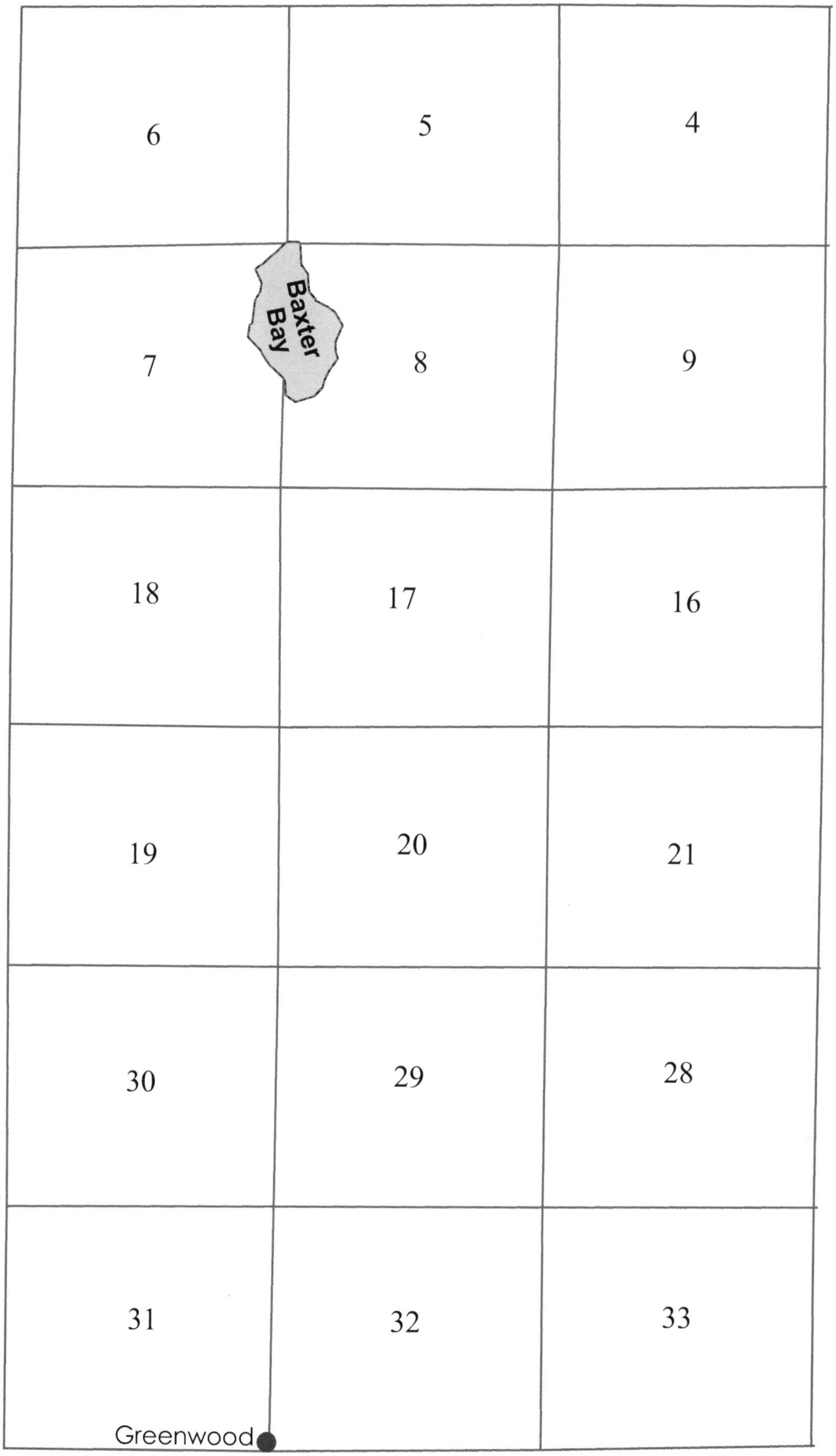

6	5	4
7	8	9
18	17	16
19	20	21
30	29	28
31	32	33

Baxter Bay

Greenwood

3	2	1 McArthur Pond
10	11	12
15 Bascom ●	14	13
22	23	24
27	26	25
34 ☨ Nubbin Ridge Cem.	35	36

Helpful Hints

1. This Map takes a different look at the same Congressional Township displayed in the preceding two maps. It presents features that can help you better envision the historical development of the area: a) Water-bodies (lakes & ponds), b) Water-courses (rivers, streams, etc.), c) Railroads, d) City/town center-points (where they were oftentimes located when first settled), and e) Cemeteries.

2. Using this "Historical" map in tandem with this Township's Patent Map and Road Map, may lead you to some interesting discoveries. You will often find roads, towns, cemeteries, and waterways are named after nearby landowners: sometimes those names will be the ones you are researching. See how many of these research gems you can find here in Jackson County.

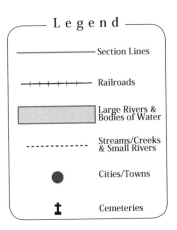

L e g e n d

——————— Section Lines

+—+—+—+—+—+ Railroads

▢ Large Rivers & Bodies of Water

- - - - - - - Streams/Creeks & Small Rivers

● Cities/Towns

☨ Cemeteries

Scale: Section = 1 mile X 1 mile
(there are some exceptions)

Map Group 13: Index to Land Patents

Township 6-North Range 8-West (Tallahassee)

After you locate an individual in this Index, take note of the Section and Section Part then proceed to the Land Patent map on the pages immediately following. You should have no difficulty locating the corresponding parcel of land.

The "For More Info" Column will lead you to more information about the underlying Patents. See the *Legend* at right, and the "How to Use this Book" chapter, for more information.

ID	Individual in Patent	Sec.	Sec. Part	Date Issued	Other Counties	For More Info . . .
1731	ALFORD, John B	22	NWNE	1857-12-01		A1
1812	ALMAROAD, William H	2	NESW	1859-06-01		A1
1636	ANDERSON, Arthur	15	SWNW	1856-06-16		A1
1635	" "	15	NWNW	1857-12-01		A1
1788	AVERY, Thomas	6	E½SW	1860-04-02		A1
1789	" "	6	W½SW	1860-04-02		A1
1790	" "	7	NENW	1860-04-02		A1
1791	" "	7	NWNE	1860-04-02		A1
1792	" "	7	NWNW	1860-04-02		A1
1718	BAKER, James L	20	E½NE	1857-07-01		A1
1719	" "	20	E½SE	1857-07-01		A1
1796	BARNACASCEL, Uriah	7	SWNW	1856-06-16		A1
1682	BARNACASTLE, Harriet H	5	S½SE	1857-12-01		A1
1683	" "	5	SESW	1857-12-01		A1
1684	" "	8	E½NW	1857-12-01		A1
1685	" "	8	W½NE	1857-12-01		A1
1703	BARNACASTLE, James C	8	N½SE	1855-05-01		A1
1704	" "	8	NENE	1856-06-16		A1
1705	" "	8	S½SE	1856-06-16		A1
1706	" "	8	SW	1856-06-16		A1
1707	" "	8	W½NW	1856-06-16		A1
1708	" "	9	NWNW	1856-06-16		A1
1637	BAZZEL, Benjamin F	27	NWSW	1859-06-01		A1
1638	" "	27	SWNW	1859-06-01		A1
1639	" "	28	E½NE	1859-06-01		A1
1640	" "	28	SWNE	1859-06-01		A1
1694	BAZZEL, Isham H	27	E½SW	1856-06-16		A1
1695	" "	34	NENW	1856-06-16		A1
1641	BAZZELL, Benjamin F	28	SESE	1861-04-09		A1
1696	BAZZELL, Isham H	33	SENE	1856-06-16		A1
1697	" "	34	NWNW	1856-06-16		A1
1736	BAZZELL, John T	33	W½SE	1859-06-01		A1
1781	BAZZELL, Samuel E	28	W½SE	1911-04-20		A2
1642	BAZZLE, Benjamin F	28	NESE	1855-05-01		A1
1737	BAZZLE, John T	33	SESE	1855-05-01		A1
1738	" "	34	SWSW	1855-05-01		A1
1755	BELSON, Madison	15	E½SE	1902-12-30		A2
1749	BOIT, Joseph H	10	NWSE	1857-07-01		A1
1634	BOLTON, Amanda	13	SWNW	1857-12-01		A1
1686	BRINSON, Henry	11	W½SW	1896-09-25		A2
1835	BROGDEN, William W	36	N½SW	1895-02-14		A2
1836	" "	36	SWSW	1895-02-14		A2
1728	BROGDON, Jesse	27	SESE	1857-12-01		A1
1729	" "	34	NENE	1857-12-01		A1
1730	" "	34	W½NE	1861-09-10		A1 F
1658	BROWN, Elizabeth	11	E½SE	1859-06-01		A1

ID	Individual in Patent	Sec.	Sec. Part	Date Issued	Other Counties	For More Info . . .
1659	BROWN, Elizabeth (Cont'd)	11	NWSE	1859-06-01		A1
1660	" "	11	SENE	1859-06-01		A1
1661	" "	12	W½SW	1859-06-01		A1
1662	" "	14	N½NE	1859-06-01		A1
1679	BROWN, Green W	3	SWSE	1905-01-30		A2
1701	BROWN, James	11	SWSE	1835-10-20		A1
1702	"	12	1	1837-04-15		A1
1673	BRYAN, Green L	18	NENE	1860-07-02		A1
1674	" "	7	E½NE	1860-07-02		A1
1675	" "	7	N½SE	1860-07-02		A1
1676	" "	7	SENW	1860-07-02		A1
1677	" "	7	SESE	1860-07-02		A1
1678	" "	7	SWNE	1860-07-02		A1
1734	CLOUD, John H	34	S½NW	1896-01-14		A2
1720	COKER, James P	30	NW	1860-07-02		A1
1721	" "	30	SE	1860-07-02		A1
1692	COOK, Isaac N	30	SW	1857-07-01		A1
1745	COX, Joseph B	34	E½SE	1860-04-02		A1
1744	" "	23	NE	1890-04-29		A2
1813	COX, William H	26	E½NE	1889-07-31		A2
1814	" "	26	NESE	1889-07-31		A2
1815	" "	26	NWNE	1889-07-31		A2
1709	CULVER, James	14	NWSW	1894-08-09		A2
1710	" "	14	SENW	1894-08-09		A2
1711	" "	14	W½NW	1894-08-09		A2
1741	DANIEL, Jordan	17	S½SE	1902-12-30		A2
1742	" "	17	S½SW	1902-12-30		A2
1650	DAY, Daniel	22	NENW	1904-05-05		A2
1651	" "	22	W½NW	1904-05-05		A2
1757	DICKINSON, Marmaduke N	19	E½SE	1855-05-01		A1
1758	" "	20	W½SW	1855-05-01		A1
1759	DICKSON, Marmaduke N	19	W½NE	1857-07-01		A1
1760	" "	19	W½SE	1857-07-01		A1
1761	" "	30	NE	1857-07-01		A1
1807	DICKSON, William B	17	N½NE	1857-07-01		A1
1808	" "	17	N½SW	1857-07-01		A1
1809	" "	17	NW	1857-07-01		A1
1787	DUDLEY, Spencer	24	E½SE	1860-07-02		A1
1782	ERWIN, Samuel J	18	N½NW	1860-07-02		A1
1783	" "	18	NWNE	1860-07-02		A1
1784	" "	7	SW	1860-07-02		A1
1785	" "	7	SWSE	1860-07-02		A1
1648	FORD, Charles W	28	NWNE	1904-12-20		A2
1668	FOULK, George W	5	E½NW	1860-04-02		A1
1672	" "	5	SWNW	1860-04-02		A1
1669	" "	5	N½SE	1861-12-05		A1
1670	" "	5	NESW	1861-12-05		A1
1671	" "	5	NWNW	1861-12-05		A1
1772	FRANKLIN, Osborn R	11	NENE	1852-09-01		A1
1773	" "	2	SESW	1852-09-01		A1
1739	GARBETT, John V	34	E½SW	1860-07-02		A1
1740	" "	34	W½SE	1860-07-02		A1
1743	GARDNER, Joseph A	6	SE	1860-04-02		A1
1746	GLISSON, Joseph	36	N½NW	1860-07-02		A1
1747	" "	36	SENW	1860-07-02		A1
1748	" "	36	SWNW	1860-10-01		A1
1763	GLISSON, Mary J	26	E½SW	1890-04-29		A2
1764	" "	26	SENW	1890-04-29		A2
1765	" "	26	SWNE	1890-04-29		A2
1771	GLISSON, Noah G	26	S½SE	1895-10-22		A2
1655	GODWIN, Edwin	29	W½SE	1857-12-01		A1
1656	" "	32	N½SE	1857-12-01		A1
1657	" "	32	NE	1857-12-01		A1
1725	GODWIN, James W	13	NWNW	1888-07-03		A1
1726	" "	14	NENW	1888-07-03		A1
1793	GODWIN, Thomas	18	E½SW	1860-04-02		A1
1794	" "	18	S½NE	1860-04-02		A1
1795	" "	18	SE	1860-04-02		A1
1712	GOFF, James	13	W½SW	1860-10-01		A1
1666	GRIFFIN, General W	2	E½SE	1852-09-01		A1
1664	" "	11	NW	1856-06-16		A1
1665	" "	11	W½NE	1856-06-16		A1
1667	" "	2	SWSE	1856-06-16		A1

ID	Individual in Patent	Sec.	Sec. Part	Date Issued	Other Counties	For More Info . . .
1663	GRIFFIN, General W (Cont'd)	11	NESW	1860-04-02		A1
1716	GRIMESLEY, James J	2	NWSE	1857-12-01		A1
1717	" "	2	SWNE	1857-12-01		A1
1767	GRIMESLEY, Matthew	8	SENE	1860-04-02		A1
1786	HAND, Samuel W	32	S½SE	1899-05-22		A2
1649	HARGROVE, Dan	15	SENW	1908-07-06		A2
1713	HARVEY, James H	10	E½SE	1855-05-01		A1
1714	" "	10	SESW	1859-06-01		A1
1715	" "	15	NE	1859-06-01		A1
1816	HARVEY, William H	3	NWSW	1859-06-01		A1
1817	" "	3	W½NW	1859-06-01		A1
1818	" "	4	W½SW	1859-06-01		A1
1629	HOLMES, Abram	15	W½SE	1898-03-21		A2
1778	JARDAN, Robert J	15	NENW	1857-12-01		A1
1691	JONES, Irvin	15	W½SW	1898-12-12		A2 G83
1750	JONES, Joseph	15	E½SW	1898-12-12		A2
1691	JONES, Mary	15	W½SW	1898-12-12		A2 G83
1820	KELLEY, William	24	S½NE	1856-06-16		A1
1821	KELLY, William	24	E½NW	1857-07-01		A1
1822	" "	24	W½NW	1860-04-02		A1
1643	KIDD, Benjamin F	34	NWSW	1901-04-09		A2
1768	LASHLEY, Moses F	22	SE	1898-02-03		A2
1777	LASHLEY, Richmond	22	SW	1894-04-10		A2
1631	LAWSON, Alexander	26	NENW	1901-08-12		A2
1632	" "	26	NWSW	1901-08-12		A2
1633	" "	26	W½NW	1901-08-12		A2
1766	LAWSON, Mary R	23	NW	1900-09-07		A2
1775	LEE, Richard	18	SWNW	1860-04-02		A1
1776	" "	18	W½SW	1860-04-02		A1
1823	LOOPER, William	23	SW	1894-05-23		A2
1811	LOVVITT, William B	10	SWNE	1857-07-01		A1
1810	" "	10	SENE	1859-06-01		A1
1769	MCGEE, Moses	6	E½NW	1860-04-02		A1
1770	" "	6	NE	1860-04-02		A1
1698	MILLS, Jackson P	22	E½NE	1900-09-07		A2
1699	" "	22	SENW	1900-09-07		A2
1700	" "	22	SWNE	1900-09-07		A2
1644	MOTT, Benjamin H	31	E½	1857-12-01		A1
1645	NEEL, Benjamin H	3	NENW	1857-12-01		A1
1652	NEEL, Daniel O	2	NWNE	1838-07-28		A1
1825	NEEL, William M	2	NWSW	1852-09-01		A1
1826	" "	2	SWNW	1852-09-01		A1
1827	" "	3	N½SE	1852-09-01		A1
1829	" "	3	SENE	1852-09-01		A1
1828	" "	3	NESW	1855-05-01		A1
1830	" "	3	SENW	1855-05-01		A1
1824	" "	2	E½NW	1856-06-16		A1
1831	" "	3	SESE	1856-06-16		A1
1832	NICKELS, William	32	W½	1859-06-01		A1
1647	NOBLES, Catharine	1	1	1834-08-20		A1
1762	NOBLES, Martin A	10	N½NE	1857-07-01		A1
1833	NOBLES, William	1	3	1837-04-20		A1
1722	NORRIS, James P	19	E½NE	1905-06-30		A2
1723	" "	20	W½NW	1905-06-30		A2
1653	ONEIL, Daniel	1	2	1837-04-20		A1
1654	" "	2	E½NE	1837-04-20		A1
1803	OWENS, Whitman H	13	E½SW	1837-04-20		A1
1804	" "	13	W½NE	1837-04-20		A1
1805	" "	13	W½SE	1837-04-20		A1
1806	" "	24	NWNE	1837-04-20		A1
1802	" "	13	E½SE	1838-07-28		A1
1687	PARRAMORE, Henry H	9	S½SE	1906-03-12		A2
1688	" "	9	S½SW	1906-03-12		A2
1751	PATRICK, Kingston K	6	NWNW	1860-07-02		A1
1693	PERKINS, Isaac	28	SW	1892-10-08		A2
1756	PLAYER, Mahalah	26	SWSW	1902-12-30		A2
1834	POPE, William S	13	E½NE	1830-11-01		A1
1819	PYKE, William H	12	3	1828-02-01		A1
1724	RAY, James	23	SE	1896-07-27		A2
1735	RICKS, John	1	4	1835-10-20		A1
1689	ROACH, Hubbard A	14	SE	1892-06-06		A2
1753	ROACH, Lewis D	14	E½SW	1898-02-24		A2
1754	" "	14	SWSW	1898-02-24		A2

ID	Individual in Patent	Sec.	Sec. Part	Date Issued	Other Counties	For More Info . . .
1780	ROBERTS, Rutledge	5	W½SW	1857-07-01		A1
1797	ROBINSON, Walter J	24	SWSE	1856-06-16		A1
1798	" "	24	SWSW	1856-06-16		A1
1799	" "	25	NESW	1856-06-16		A1
1800	" "	25	W½SE	1856-06-16		A1
1801	" "	25	W½SW	1856-06-16		A1
1690	SANBURN, Ira	12	4	1827-10-01		A1
1774	SMITH, Perry	6	SWNW	1910-05-09		A2
1680	STEWART, Harmon	20	E½SW	1894-04-10		A2
1681	" "	20	W½SE	1894-04-10		A2
1733	WATTS, John D	34	SENE	1902-07-03		A2
1630	WHIDDON, Alexander L	24	NWSE	1890-04-29		A2
1779	WHITEHEAD, Robert J	4	N½	1857-07-01		A1
1732	WHITEHURST, John B	19	W½	1857-12-01		A1
1752	WHITEHURST, Levi W	18	SENW	1859-06-01		A1
1646	WILLIAMS, Caroline	14	S½NE	1891-02-13		A2
1727	WILLIAMS, James	13	E½NW	1860-07-02		A1

Patent Map

T6-N R8-W
Tallahassee Meridian

Map Group 13

Township Statistics

Parcels Mapped	:	208
Number of Patents	:	134
Number of Individuals	:	108
Patentees Identified	:	107
Number of Surnames	:	81
Multi-Patentee Parcels	:	1
Oldest Patent Date	:	10/1/1827
Most Recent Patent	:	4/20/1911
Block/Lot Parcels	:	7
Parcels Re-Issued	:	0
Parcels that Overlap	:	0
Cities and Towns	:	4
Cemeteries	:	1

Copyright 2008 Boyd IT, Inc. All Rights Reserved

Section 1 / 2 / 3 area

HARVEY William H 1859

NEEL Benjamin H 1857

NEEL William M 1855

NEEL William M 1852

NEEL William M 1852

NEEL William M 1856

NEEL Daniel O 1838

GRIMESLEY James J 1857

2

ONEIL Daniel 1837

1

HARVEY William H 1859

NEEL William M 1855

3

NEEL William M 1852

NEEL William M 1852

ALMAROAD William H 1859

GRIMESLEY James J 1857

GRIFFIN General W 1852

BROWN Green W 1905

NEEL William M 1856

FRANKLIN Osborn R 1852

GRIFFIN General W 1856

Section 10 / 11 / 12 area

10

NOBLES Martin A 1857

LOVVITT William B 1857

LOVVITT William B 1859

BOIT Joseph H 1857

HARVEY James H 1859

GRIFFIN General W 1856

11

GRIFFIN General W 1856

GRIFFIN General W 1860

HARVEY James H 1855

BRINSON Henry 1896

FRANKLIN Osborn R 1852

BROWN Elizabeth 1859

BROWN Elizabeth 1859

BROWN James 1835

12

BROWN Elizabeth 1859

BROWN Elizabeth 1859

Section 13 / 14 / 15 area

ANDERSON Arthur 1857

JARDAN Robert J 1857

HARVEY James H 1859

GODWIN James W 1888

BROWN Elizabeth 1859

GODWIN James W 1888

WILLIAMS James 1860

OWENS Whitman H 1837

POPE William S 1830

ANDERSON Arthur 1856

HARGROVE Dan 1908

15

CULVER James 1894

CULVER James 1894

WILLIAMS Caroline 1891

BOLTON Amanda 1857

13

JONES [83] Irvin 1898

JONES Joseph 1898

HOLMES Abram 1898

BELSON Madison 1902

CULVER James 1894

ROACH Lewis D 1898

14

ROACH Hubbard A 1892

GOFF James 1860

OWENS Whitman H 1837

OWENS Whitman H 1837

OWENS Whitman H 1838

ROACH Lewis D 1898

Section 22 / 23 / 24 area

DAY Daniel 1904

DAY Daniel 1904

ALFORD John B 1857

MILLS Jackson P 1900

MILLS Jackson P 1900

MILLS Jackson P 1900

LAWSON Mary R 1900

23

COX Joseph B 1890

OWENS Whitman H 1837

KELLY William 1860

KELLY William 1857

24

KELLEY William 1856

22

LASHLEY Richmond 1894

LASHLEY Moses F 1898

LOOPER William 1894

RAY James 1896

ROBINSON Walter J 1856

WHIDDON Alexander L 1890

ROBINSON Walter J 1856

DUDLEY Spencer 1860

Section 25 / 26 / 27 area

BAZZEL Benjamin F 1859

BAZZEL Benjamin F 1859

27

BAZZEL Isham H 1856

BROGDON Jesse 1857

LAWSON Alexander 1901

LAWSON Alexander 1901

LAWSON Alexander 1901

PLAYER Mahalah 1902

LAWSON Alexander 1901

GLISSON Mary J 1890

26

GLISSON Mary J 1890

COX William H 1889

GLISSON Mary J 1890

GLISSON Noah G 1895

COX William H 1889

COX William H 1889

COX William H 1889

25

ROBINSON Walter J 1856

ROBINSON Walter J 1856

ROBINSON Walter J 1856

Section 34 / 35 / 36 area

BAZZELL Isham H 1856

BAZZEL Isham H 1856

BROGDON Jesse 1861

BROGDON Jesse 1857

CLOUD John H 1896

34

WATTS John D 1902

KIDD Benjamin F 1901

GARBETT John V 1860

GARBETT John V 1860

COX Joseph B 1860

BAZZLE John T 1855

35

GLISSON Joseph 1860

GLISSON Joseph 1860

GLISSON Joseph 1860

BROGDEN William W 1895

36

BROGDEN William W 1895

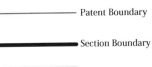

Legend

——————— Patent Boundary

━━━━━━━ Section Boundary

▨▨▨ No Patents Found (or Outside County)

1., 2., 3., ... Lot Numbers (when beside a name)

[ ] Group Number (see Appendix "C")

Scale: Section = 1 mile X 1 mile (generally, with some exceptions)

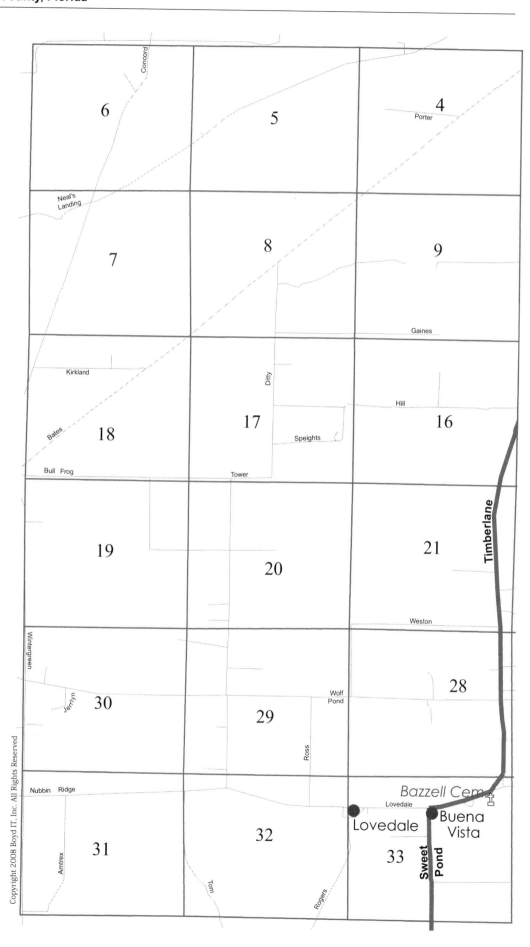

Road Map

T6-N R8-W
Tallahassee Meridian

Map Group 13

Cities & Towns
Buena Vista
Hornsville
Lovedale
Parramore

Cemeteries
Bazzell Cemetery

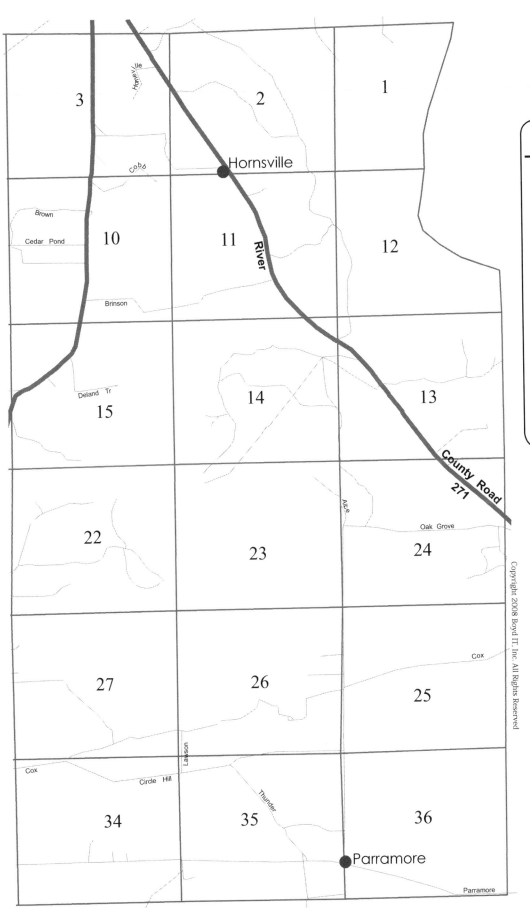

3

2

1

Honeyville

Cobb

● Hornsville

Brown

Cedar Pond

10

11

River

12

Brinson

Deland Tr

15

14

13

County Road 271

Alice

Oak Grove

22

23

24

Cox

27

26

25

Lawson

Cox

Circle Hill

Thunder

34

35

36

● Parramore

Parramore

Copyright 2008 Boyd IT, Inc. All Rights Reserved

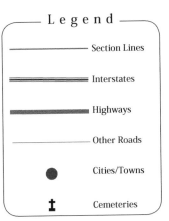

Helpful Hints

1. This road map has a number of uses, but primarily it is to help you: a) find the present location of land owned by your ancestors (at least the general area), b) find cemeteries and city-centers, and c) estimate the route/roads used by Census-takers & tax-assessors.

2. If you plan to travel to Jackson County to locate cemeteries or land parcels, please pick up a modern travel map for the area before you do. Mapping old land parcels on modern maps is not as exact a science as you might think. Just the slightest variations in public land survey coordinates, estimates of parcel boundaries, or road-map deviations can greatly alter a map's representation of how a road either does or doesn't cross a particular parcel of land.

L e g e n d

———————	Section Lines
═══════	Interstates
▓▓▓▓▓▓▓	Highways
—————	Other Roads
●	Cities/Towns
✝	Cemeteries

Scale: Section = 1 mile X 1 mile
(generally, with some exceptions)

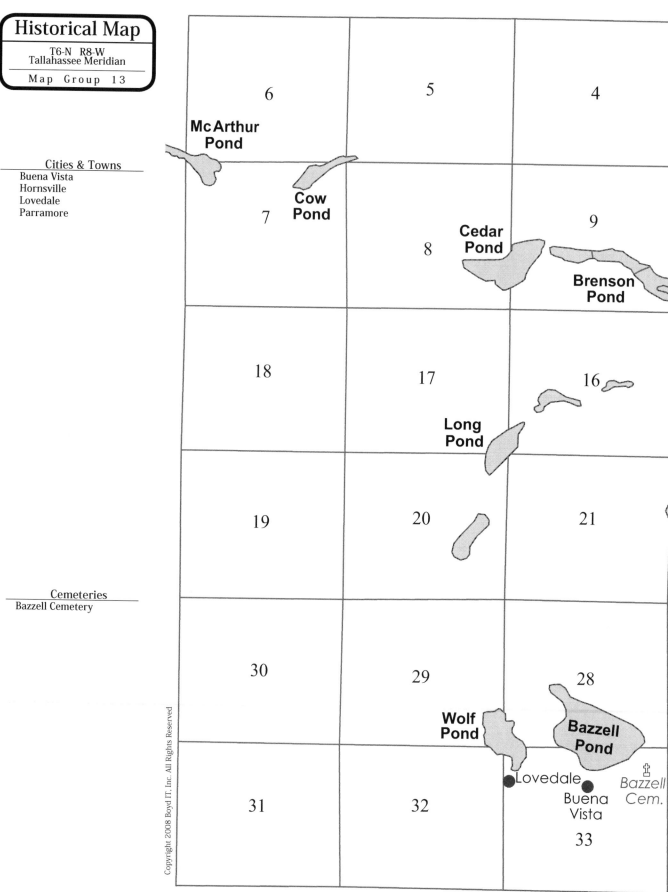

Historical Map

T6-N R8-W
Tallahassee Meridian

Map Group 13

Cities & Towns
Buena Vista
Hornsville
Lovedale
Parramore

Cemeteries
Bazzell Cemetery

6

5

4

McArthur
Pond

7

Cow
Pond

8

Cedar
Pond

9

Brenson
Pond

18

17

16

Long
Pond

19

20

21

30

29

28

Wolf
Pond

Bazzell
Pond

Lovedale

Buena
Vista

Bazzell
Cem.

31

32

33

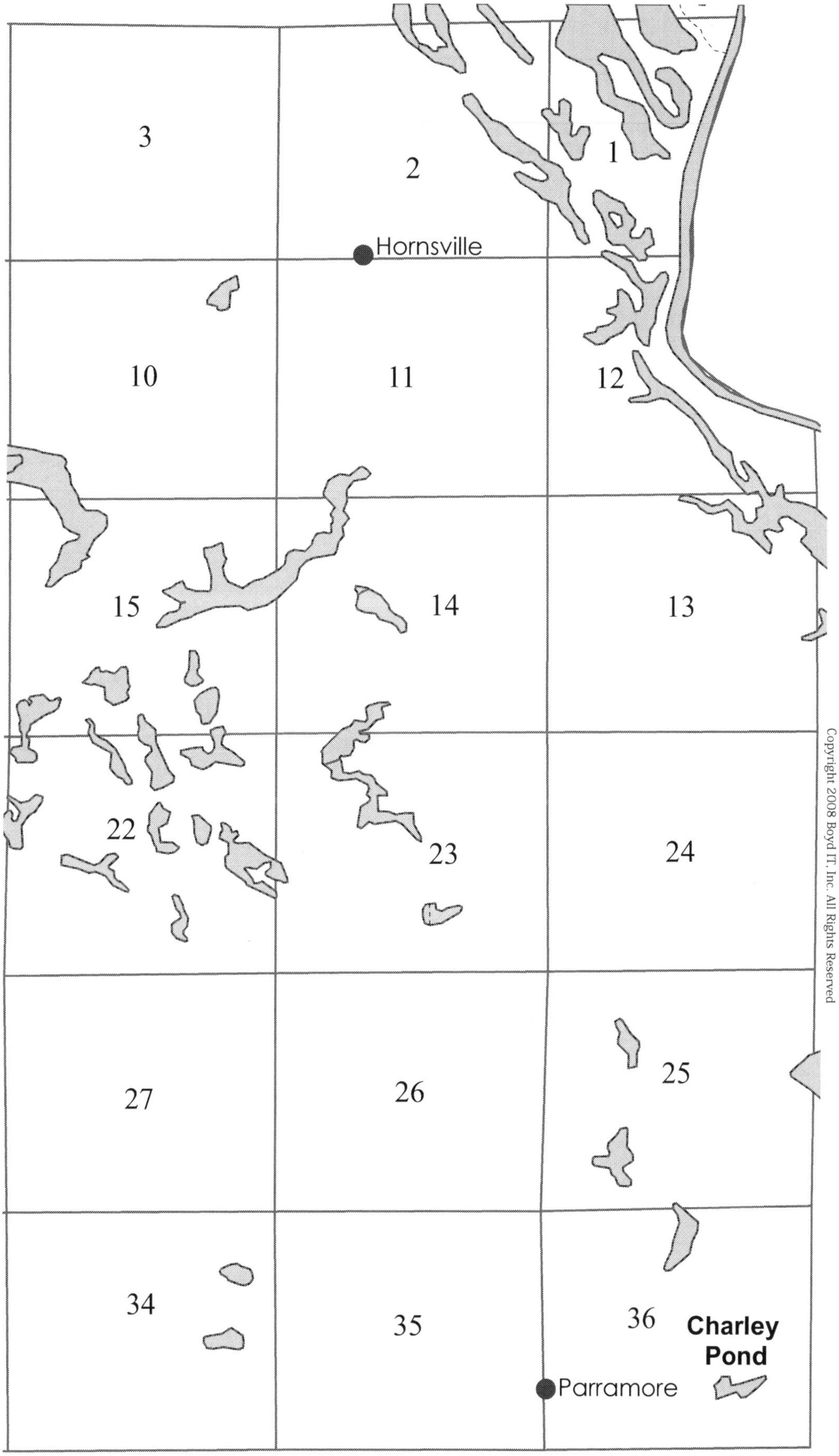
3
2
1
Hornsville
10
11
12
15
14
13
22
23
24
27
26
25
34
35
36
Charley Pond
Parramore

Helpful Hints

1. This Map takes a different look at the same Congressional Township displayed in the preceding two maps. It presents features that can help you better envision the historical development of the area: a) Water-bodies (lakes & ponds), b) Water-courses (rivers, streams, etc.), c) Railroads, d) City/town center-points (where they were oftentimes located when first settled), and e) Cemeteries.
2. Using this "Historical" map in tandem with this Township's Patent Map and Road Map, may lead you to some interesting discoveries. You will often find roads, towns, cemeteries, and waterways are named after nearby landowners: sometimes those names will be the ones you are researching. See how many of these research gems you can find here in Jackson County.

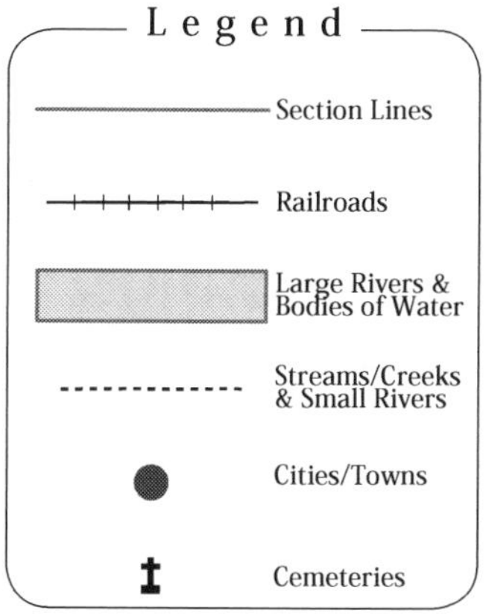
Legend
Section Lines
Railroads
Large Rivers & Bodies of Water
Streams/Creeks & Small Rivers
Cities/Towns
Cemeteries

Scale: Section = 1 mile X 1 mile
(there are some exceptions)

Map Group 14: Index to Land Patents

Township 6-North Range 7-West (Tallahassee)

After you locate an individual in this Index, take note of the Section and Section Part then proceed to the Land Patent map on the pages immediately following. You should have no difficulty locating the corresponding parcel of land.

The "For More Info" Column will lead you to more information about the underlying Patents. See the *Legend* at right, and the "How to Use this Book" chapter, for more information.

```
                          LEGEND
                "For More Info . . . " column
A = Authority (Legislative Act, See Appendix "A")
B = Block or Lot (location in Section unknown)
C = Cancelled Patent
F = Fractional Section
G = Group  (Multi-Patentee Patent, see Appendix "C")
V = Overlaps another Parcel
R = Re-Issued (Parcel patented more than once)

(A & G items require you to look in the Appendixes referred
to above. All other Letter-designations followed by a number
require you to locate line-items in this index that possess
the ID number found after the letter).
```

ID	Individual in Patent	Sec.	Sec. Part	Date Issued	Other Counties	For More Info . . .
1846	ADAMS, Robert C	29	2	1841-01-09		A1 F
1847	" "	29	4	1841-01-09		A1 F
1848	" "	31	E½NE	1841-01-09		A1
1849	" "	32	W½NE	1843-03-10		A1
1838	ALLEN, Richard C	18	3	1830-11-01		A1
1839	" "	19	1	1830-11-01		A1
1840	" "	20	1	1830-11-01		A1
1841	" "	29	1	1830-11-01		A1
1844	" "	33	1	1830-11-01		A1
1845	" "	33	2	1830-11-01		A1
1842	" "	32	E½NE	1830-12-28		A1
1843	" "	32	E½SE	1830-12-28		A1
1858	BAKER, William J	30	NWNE	1855-05-01		A1
1859	" "	30	NWNW	1855-05-01		A1
1851	BALTZELL, Thomas	32	W½SE	1843-03-10		A1
1860	BOROUM, William J	32	S½NW	1859-06-01		A1
1857	BOWER, William H	30	SESE	1852-09-01		A1
1861	CORBITT, William L	19	7	1838-07-28		A1 F
1850	DUDLEY, Spencer	19	W½SW	1860-07-02		A1
1855	LITTLETON, Thomas	28		1828-03-15		A1 G95 F
1854	" "	29	5	1829-05-15		A1
1852	" "	19	2	1841-01-09		A1 F
1853	" "	19	5	1841-01-09		A1 F
1862	LITTLETON, William	19	3	1841-01-09		A1 F
1856	OWENS, Whitman H	18	2	1837-04-20		A1
1863	POPE, William S	18	1	1830-11-01		A1
1864	" "	7	1	1830-11-01		A1
1855	WILLIAMS, G R	28		1828-03-15		A1 G95 F
1837	WOOTEN, Edward L	30	NENW	1852-09-01		A1

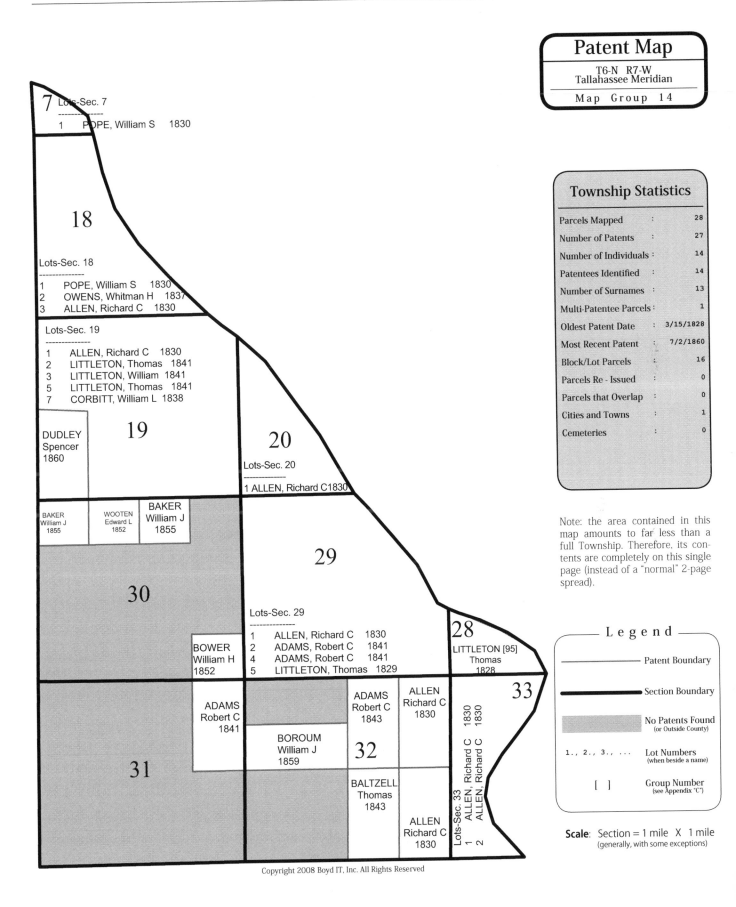

7 Lots-Sec. 7
----
1   POPE, William S   1830

18

Lots-Sec. 18
----
1   POPE, William S   1830
2   OWENS, Whitman H   1837
3   ALLEN, Richard C   1830

Lots-Sec. 19
----
1   ALLEN, Richard C   1830
2   LITTLETON, Thomas 1841
3   LITTLETON, William 1841
5   LITTLETON, Thomas 1841
7   CORBITT, William L 1838

19

DUDLEY
Spencer
1860

20

Lots-Sec. 20
----
1 ALLEN, Richard C 1830

BAKER
William J
1855

WOOTEN
Edward L
1852

BAKER
William J
1855

30

29

Lots-Sec. 29
----
1   ALLEN, Richard C   1830
2   ADAMS, Robert C   1841
4   ADAMS, Robert C   1841
5   LITTLETON, Thomas   1829

28
LITTLETON [95]
Thomas
1828

BOWER
William H
1852

ADAMS
Robert C
1841

ADAMS
Robert C
1843

ALLEN
Richard C
1830

33

BOROUM
William J
1859

32

BALTZELL
Thomas
1843

ALLEN
Richard C
1830

31

Lots-Sec. 33
1   ALLEN, Richard C   1830
2   ALLEN, Richard C   1830

Township Statistics

Parcels Mapped	:	28
Number of Patents	:	27
Number of Individuals	:	14
Patentees Identified	:	14
Number of Surnames	:	13
Multi-Patentee Parcels	:	1
Oldest Patent Date	:	3/15/1828
Most Recent Patent	:	7/2/1860
Block/Lot Parcels	:	16
Parcels Re - Issued	:	0
Parcels that Overlap	:	0
Cities and Towns	:	1
Cemeteries	:	0

Note: the area contained in this map amounts to far less than a full Township. Therefore, its contents are completely on this single page (instead of a "normal" 2-page spread).

Legend

————	Patent Boundary
▬▬▬	Section Boundary
▨	No Patents Found (or Outside County)
1., 2., 3., ...	Lot Numbers (when beside a name)
[ ]	Group Number (see Appendix "C")

Scale: Section = 1 mile X 1 mile
(generally, with some exceptions)

Road Map

T6-N R7-W
Tallahassee Meridian

Map Group 14

Note: the area contained in this map amounts to far less than a full Township. Therefore, its contents are completely on this single page (instead of a "normal" 2-page spread).

Cities & Towns
Haynes

Cemeteries
None

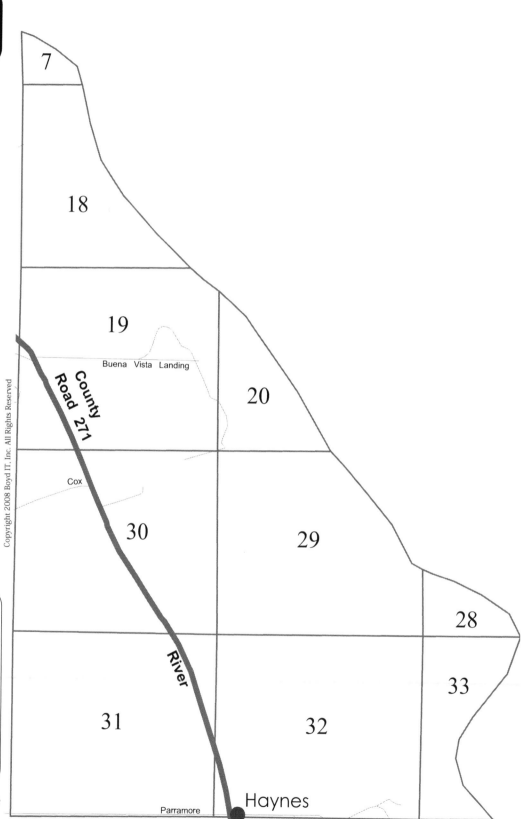

L e g e n d

——————— Section Lines

══════════ Interstates

▬▬▬▬▬ Highways

——————— Other Roads

● Cities/Towns

✝ Cemeteries

Scale: Section = 1 mile X 1 mile
(generally, with some exceptions)

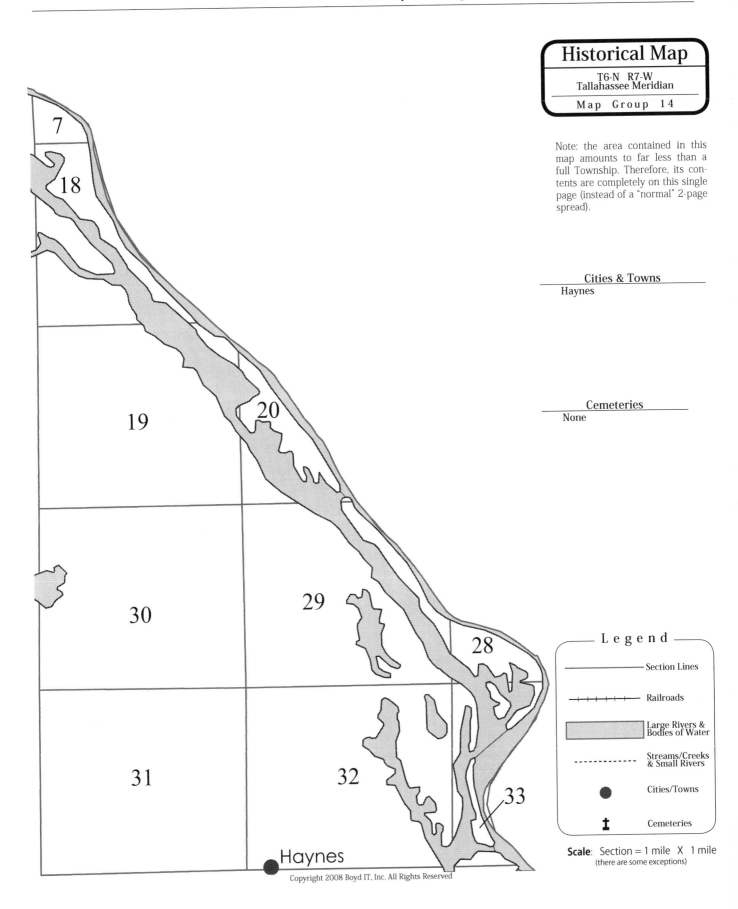

Map Group 15: Index to Land Patents

Township 5-North Range 14-West (Tallahassee)

After you locate an individual in this Index, take note of the Section and Section Part then proceed to the Land Patent map on the pages immediately following. You should have no difficulty locating the corresponding parcel of land.

The "For More Info" Column will lead you to more information about the underlying Patents. See the *Legend* at right, and the "How to Use this Book" chapter, for more information.

```
                    LEGEND
          "For More Info . . . " column
A = Authority (Legislative Act, See Appendix "A")
B = Block or Lot (location in Section unknown)
C = Cancelled Patent
F = Fractional Section
G = Group  (Multi-Patentee Patent, see Appendix "C")
V = Overlaps another Parcel
R = Re-Issued (Parcel patented more than once)

(A & G items require you to look in the Appendixes referred
to above. All other Letter-designations followed by a number
require you to locate line-items in this index that possess
the ID number found after the letter).
```

ID	Individual in Patent	Sec.	Sec. Part	Date Issued	Other Counties	For More Info . . .
1870	AUSTON, John G	12	NENW	1910-07-18	Holmes	A2
1871	COLLINS, Lorenzo J	12	NESE	1903-05-25	Holmes	A2
1872	" "	12	S½SE	1903-05-25	Holmes	A2
1873	ELMORE, Mark	12	E½SW	1860-04-02	Holmes	A1
1865	FOWLER, Abram	12	NWSE	1860-04-02	Holmes	A1
1866	" "	12	NWSW	1860-04-02	Holmes	A1
1867	" "	12	SENW	1860-04-02	Holmes	A1
1868	" "	12	SWNE	1860-04-02	Holmes	A1
1869	" "	12	SWNW	1860-04-02	Holmes	A1
1874	WILLIAMS, Owen	12	E½NE	1860-04-02	Holmes	A1
1875	" "	12	NWNE	1860-04-02	Holmes	A1

Patent Map

T5-N R14-W
Tallahassee Meridian

Map Group 15

2

1

AUSTON John G 1910	WILLIAMS Owen 1860	WILLIAMS Owen 1860
FOWLER Abram 1860	FOWLER Abram 1860	FOWLER Abram 1860

11

FOWLER Abram 1860	**12** ELMORE Mark 1860	FOWLER Abram 1860	COLLINS Lorenzo J 1903
		COLLINS Lorenzo J 1903	

14

Holmes

13

Jackson

Washington

23

24

26

25

35

36

Township Statistics

Parcels Mapped	:	11
Number of Patents	:	6
Number of Individuals	:	5
Patentees Identified	:	5
Number of Surnames	:	5
Multi-Patentee Parcels	:	0
Oldest Patent Date	:	4/2/1860
Most Recent Patent	:	7/18/1910
Block/Lot Parcels	:	0
Parcels Re - Issued	:	0
Parcels that Overlap	:	0
Cities and Towns	:	0
Cemeteries	:	0

Note: the area contained in this map amounts to far less than a full Township. Therefore, its contents are completely on this single page (instead of a "normal" 2-page spread).

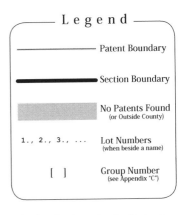

Legend

——— Patent Boundary

▬▬▬ Section Boundary

▨▨▨ No Patents Found
(or Outside County)

1., 2., 3., ... Lot Numbers
(when beside a name)

[ ] Group Number
(see Appendix "C")

Scale: Section = 1 mile X 1 mile
(generally, with some exceptions)

Road Map

T5-N R14-W
Tallahassee Meridian

Map Group 15

Note: the area contained in this map amounts to far less than a full Township. Therefore, its contents are completely on this single page (instead of a "normal" 2-page spread).

Cities & Towns
None

Cemeteries
None

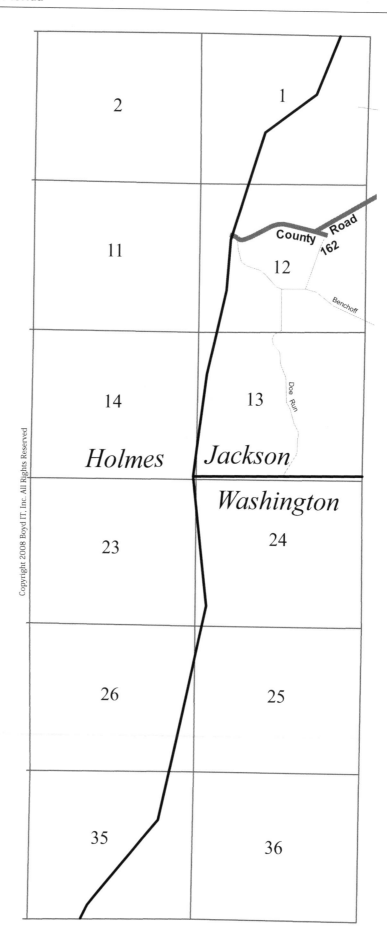

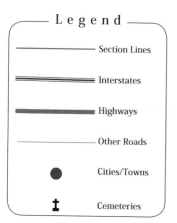

Legend

——————— Section Lines

═══════ Interstates

━━━━━━ Highways

——————— Other Roads

● Cities/Towns

✝ Cemeteries

Scale: Section = 1 mile X 1 mile
(generally, with some exceptions)

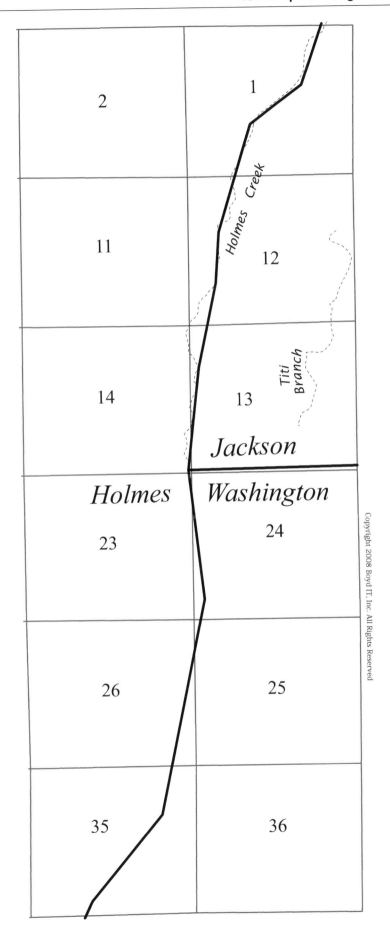

Holmes Creek

2

1

11

12

Titi Branch

14

13

Jackson

Holmes   *Washington*

23

24

26

25

35

36

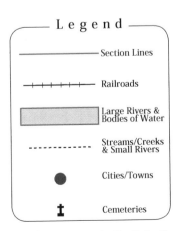

Historical Map

T5-N R14-W
Tallahassee Meridian

Map Group 15

Note: the area contained in this map amounts to far less than a full Township. Therefore, its contents are completely on this single page (instead of a "normal" 2-page spread).

Cities & Towns
None

Cemeteries
None

Legend

———— Section Lines

—+++++— Railroads

▨ Large Rivers & Bodies of Water

-------- Streams/Creeks & Small Rivers

● Cities/Towns

✝ Cemeteries

Scale: Section = 1 mile X 1 mile
(there are some exceptions)

Map Group 16: Index to Land Patents

Township 5-North Range 13-West (Tallahassee)

After you locate an individual in this Index, take note of the Section and Section Part then proceed to the Land Patent map on the pages immediately following. You should have no difficulty locating the corresponding parcel of land.

The "For More Info" Column will lead you to more information about the underlying Patents. See the *Legend* at right, and the "How to Use this Book" chapter, for more information.

```
                    LEGEND
            "For More Info . . . " column
A = Authority (Legislative Act, See Appendix "A")
B = Block or Lot (location in Section unknown)
C = Cancelled Patent
F = Fractional Section
G = Group  (Multi-Patentee Patent, see Appendix "C")
V = Overlaps another Parcel
R = Re-Issued (Parcel patented more than once)

(A & G items require you to look in the Appendixes referred
to above. All other Letter-designations followed by a number
require you to locate line-items in this index that possess
the ID number found after the letter).
```

ID	Individual in Patent	Sec.	Sec. Part	Date Issued	Other Counties	For More Info . . .
1883	ADAMS, Coalson	8	SW	1898-01-07		A2
1885	ADAMS, Franklin L	6	E½SE	1894-03-08		A2
1886	" "	6	SESW	1894-03-08		A2
1887	" "	6	SWSE	1894-03-08		A2
1896	ADAMS, James M	10	N½SW	1892-09-09		A2
1897	" "	10	S½NW	1892-09-09		A2
1898	" "	10	S½SW	1893-03-27		A2
1899	" "	10	W½SE	1893-03-27		A2
1890	BRUNER, Jackson	12	W½NE	1899-05-22		A2
1891	" "	12	W½SE	1899-05-22		A2
1894	BUIE, James A	4	SE	1895-06-17		A2
1876	COOLEY, Alfred	4	SW	1896-01-03		A2
1919	DAVIS, Ratcliff F	14	NE	1894-01-27		A2
1900	HICKS, James W	6	NESW	1892-08-01		A2
1902	" "	6	W½SW	1892-08-01		A2
1901	" "	6	NWSE	1895-06-17		A2
1877	HOUGH, Alonzo	8	SENW	1901-06-25		A2 G80
1878	" "	8	W½NW	1901-06-25		A2 G80
1889	HOUGH, Ira	8	SE	1894-06-20		A2
1877	HOUGH, Mary	8	SENW	1901-06-25		A2 G80
1878	" "	8	W½NW	1901-06-25		A2 G80
1903	HUFF, Jesse	8	NENW	1898-09-19		A2
1904	" "	8	NWNE	1898-09-19		A2
1905	" "	8	S½NE	1898-09-19		A2
1909	HUGHES, John B	10	NWNW	1901-12-12		A1
1928	LEADBETTER, William D	12	E½NE	1895-10-16		A2
1929	" "	12	E½SE	1895-10-16		A2
1880	MCCRARY, Andrew F	2	E½NW	1892-11-15		A2
1881	" "	2	N½SW	1892-11-15		A2
1934	MCCRARY, William U	2	E½SE	1895-02-14		A2
1935	" "	2	S½NE	1895-02-14		A2
1927	MOON, William B	4	NW	1900-09-07		A2
1913	OBRIEN, John J	2	W½NW	1903-06-26		A2
1914	PRIM, John J	18	N½SW	1895-10-22		A2
1915	" "	18	NWSE	1895-10-22		A2
1916	" "	18	SWNE	1895-10-22		A2
1923	PRIM, Tamer A	18	NW	1892-04-09		A2
1888	RHODES, Harrison A	2	NWSE	1903-06-26		A2
1908	RHODES, John A	2	N½NE	1902-07-03		A2
1924	RHODES, Thomas C	14	N½NW	1896-08-27		A2
1925	" "	14	NWSW	1896-08-27		A2
1926	" "	14	SWNW	1896-08-27		A2
1879	RICHTER, Amandus L	12	SW	1902-07-03		A2
1910	RICHTER, John F	14	N½SE	1897-09-20		A2
1911	" "	14	NESW	1897-09-20		A2
1912	" "	14	SENW	1897-09-20		A2

ID	Individual in Patent	Sec.	Sec. Part	Date Issued	Other Counties	For More Info . . .
1930	SHIPE, William H	18	NESE	1897-08-16		A2
1931	" "	18	S½SE	1897-08-16		A2
1932	" "	18	SENE	1897-08-16		A2
1920	SIMS, Robert H	10	NENE	1898-02-03		A2
1921	" "	10	NENW	1898-02-03		A2
1922	" "	10	W½NE	1898-02-03		A2
1906	SMITH, Jesse P	14	S½SE	1899-01-23		A2
1907	" "	14	S½SW	1899-01-23		A2
1933	TAYLOR, William L	6	NW	1892-08-01		A2
1892	VICKERS, Jacob	4	E½NE	1888-11-20		A2
1893	" "	4	W½NE	1896-09-25		A2
1882	WILLIAMS, Charles N	18	N½NE	1905-05-17		A2
1884	WILLIAMS, Dougald C	6	NE	1892-08-01		A2
1895	WILLIAMS, James A	12	NW	1895-02-14		A2
1917	WILLIAMS, Melissa C	2	S½SW	1896-04-27		A2
1918	" "	2	SWSE	1896-04-27		A2

Patent Map

T5-N R13-W
Tallahassee Meridian

Map Group 16

N ⟹

Township Statistics

Parcels Mapped	:	60
Number of Patents	:	36
Number of Individuals	:	34
Patentees Identified	:	33
Number of Surnames	:	22
Multi-Patentee Parcels	:	2
Oldest Patent Date	:	11/20/1888
Most Recent Patent	:	5/17/1905
Block/Lot Parcels	:	0
Parcels Re - Issued	:	0
Parcels that Overlap	:	0
Cities and Towns	:	1
Cemeteries	:	1

Note: the area contained in this map amounts to far less than a full Township. Therefore, its contents are completely on this single page (instead of a "normal" 2-page spread).

Legend

— Patent Boundary

━ Section Boundary

▒ No Patents Found
(or Outside County)

1., 2., 3., ... Lot Numbers
(when beside a name)

[ ] Group Number
(see Appendix "C")

Scale: Section = 1 mile X 1 mile
(generally, with some exceptions)

Copyright 2008 Boyd IT, Inc. All Rights Reserved

Section 6
TAYLOR William L 1892
HICKS James W 1892
ADAMS Franklin L 1894
HICKS James W 1892
HICKS James W 1895
ADAMS Franklin L 1894
WILLIAMS Dougald C 1892
ADAMS Franklin L 1894

Section 7

Section 18
PRIM Tamer A 1892
PRIM John J 1895
PRIM John J 1895
WILLIAMS Charles N 1905
PRIM John J 1895
PRIM John J 1895
SHIPE William H 1897
SHIPE William H 1897
SHIPE William H 1897

Section 17

Section 8
HOUGH [80] Alonzo 1901
ADAMS Coalson 1898
HOUGH [80] Alonzo 1901
HUFF Jesse 1898
HUFF Jesse 1898
HOUGH Ira 1894
HUFF Jesse 1898

Section 5

Section 16

Section 9

Section 4
COOLEY Alfred 1896
MOON William B 1900
BUIE James A 1895
VICKERS Jacob 1896
VICKERS Jacob 1888

Section 15

Section 10
ADAMS James M 1893
ADAMS James M 1892
ADAMS James M 1892
HUGHES John B 1901
SIMS Robert H 1898
ADAMS James M 1893
ADAMS James M
SIMS Robert H 1898
SIMS Robert H 1898

Section 3

Section 14
SMITH Jesse P 1899
RHODES Thomas C 1896
RHODES Thomas C 1896
RHODES Thomas C 1896
RICHTER John F 1897
RICHTER John F 1897
RHODES Thomas C 1896
SMITH Jesse P 1899
RICHTER John F 1897
DAVIS Ratcliff F 1894

Section 11

Section 2
OBRIEN John J 1903
MCCRARY Andrew F 1892
MCCRARY Andrew F
WILLIAMS Melissa C 1896
RHODES Harrison A 1903
WILLIAMS Melissa C 1896
RHODES John A 1902
MCCRARY William U 1895
MCCRARY William U

Section 13

Section 12
RICHTER Amandus L 1902
WILLIAMS James A 1895
BRUNER Jackson 1899
BRUNER Jackson 1899
LEADBETTER William D 1895
LEADBETTER William D 1895

Section 1

164

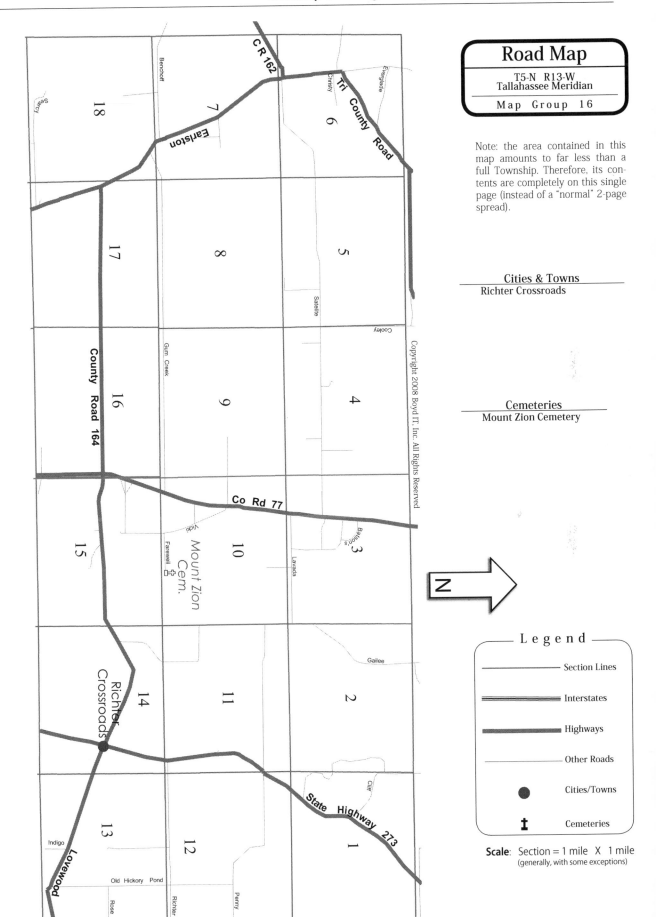

Road Map
T5-N R13-W
Tallahassee Meridian
Map Group 16

Note: the area contained in this map amounts to far less than a full Township. Therefore, its contents are completely on this single page (instead of a "normal" 2-page spread).

Cities & Towns
Richter Crossroads

Cemeteries
Mount Zion Cemetery

Legend
— Section Lines
— Interstates
— Highways
— Other Roads
● Cities/Towns
✝ Cemeteries

Scale: Section = 1 mile X 1 mile
(generally, with some exceptions)

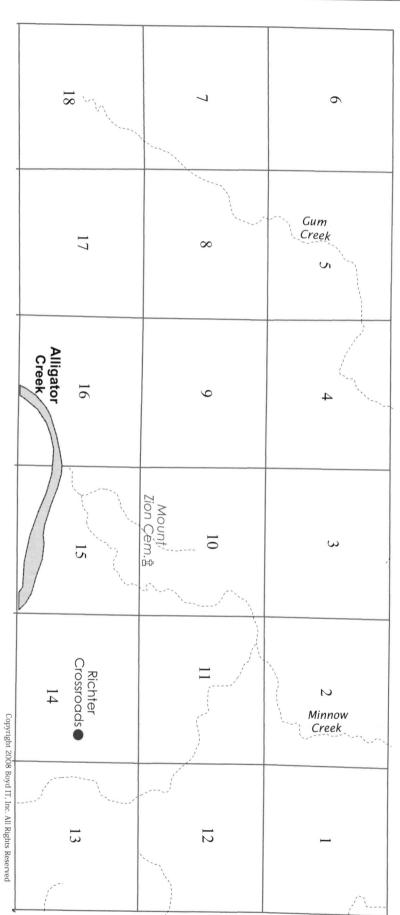

Historical Map

T5-N R13-W
Tallahassee Meridian

Map Group 16

Note: the area contained in this map amounts to far less than a full Township. Therefore, its contents are completely on this single page (instead of a "normal" 2-page spread).

Cities & Towns
Richter Crossroads

Cemeteries
Mount Zion Cemetery

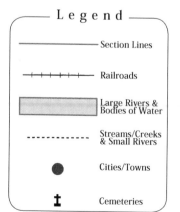

Legend

———— Section Lines

+++++ Railroads

▨ Large Rivers & Bodies of Water

- - - - - Streams/Creeks & Small Rivers

● Cities/Towns

✝ Cemeteries

Scale: Section = 1 mile X 1 mile
(there are some exceptions)

Map Group 17: Index to Land Patents

Township 5-North Range 12-West (Tallahassee)

After you locate an individual in this Index, take note of the Section and Section Part then proceed to the Land Patent map on the pages immediately following. You should have no difficulty locating the corresponding parcel of land.

The "For More Info" Column will lead you to more information about the underlying Patents. See the *Legend* at right, and the "How to Use this Book" chapter, for more information.

```
                          LEGEND
            "For More Info . . . " column
A = Authority (Legislative Act, See Appendix "A")
B = Block or Lot (location in Section unknown)
C = Cancelled Patent
F = Fractional Section
G = Group  (Multi-Patentee Patent, see Appendix "C")
V = Overlaps another Parcel
R = Re-Issued (Parcel patented more than once)

(A & G items require you to look in the Appendixes referred
to above. All other Letter-designations followed by a number
require you to locate line-items in this index that possess
the ID number found after the letter).
```

ID	Individual in Patent	Sec.	Sec. Part	Date Issued	Other Counties	For More Info . . .
2058	ADAMS, Thomas C	6	NW	1897-10-28		A2
1990	BASS, Isaac	30	W½NW	1899-05-22		A2
1991	" "	30	W½SW	1899-05-22		A2
1944	BIBB, Benajah S	1	NE	1839-09-20		A1 G17
1945	" "	1	NW	1839-09-20		A1 G17
1946	" "	1	W½SE	1839-09-20		A1 G17
1947	" "	11	E½SE	1839-09-20		A1 G17
1948	" "	11	NENW	1839-09-20		A1 G17
1949	" "	11	SESW	1839-09-20		A1 G17
1950	" "	12	E½NW	1839-09-20		A1 G17
1951	" "	12	SW	1839-09-20		A1 G17
1952	" "	24	W½NW	1839-09-20		A1 G17
2078	BLOUNT, Willie	13	SE	1827-04-02		A1
2056	BONTIUE, Stuart	4	NESW	1897-07-03		A2
2057	" "	4	S½SW	1897-07-03		A2
1981	BOWEN, Frank	36	NENE	1889-07-02		A2
2010	BRAXTON, John	22	SW	1893-03-27		A2
1996	BROXTON, James	22	E½NE	1891-06-17		A2
1997	" "	22	E½SE	1891-06-17		A2
1971	BRUNER, Daniel Z	18	N½NE	1892-07-11		A2
1972	" "	18	N½NW	1892-07-11		A2
2073	BRUNER, William R	8	S½SW	1903-06-01		A2
2074	" "	8	W½SE	1903-06-01		A2
1957	BUTLER, Bennett	22	NW	1893-03-03		A2 G27
1957	BUTLER, Catharine	22	NW	1893-03-03		A2 G27
1973	CALHOUN, Dugald	4	NENE	1860-04-02		A1
1974	" "	4	NW	1860-04-02		A1
1975	" "	4	NWSW	1860-04-02		A1
1976	" "	4	W½NE	1860-04-02		A1
1980	CARTER, Farish	24	E½SE	1848-11-01		A1
2042	CARTER, Nancy A	6	NE	1899-06-22		A2 G37
2039	CO, R C Allen And	24	E½NW	1827-10-01		A1 G70
2045	COX, R F	28	SE	1890-12-27		A2
2041	DEKLE, Mathew L	24	W½SW	1888-07-21		A1
2011	DENHAM, John D	4	SENE	1905-06-30		A2
2065	DRAKE, William B	1	E½SW	1827-10-01		A1 G65
2066	" "	1	W½SW	1827-10-01		A1 G65
2067	" "	2	E½SE	1827-10-01		A1 G65
2068	" "	2	W½SE	1827-10-01		A1 G65
1982	ELDRIDGE, George N	20	N½NW	1906-03-31		A1 F
1954	FOSCUE, Benjamin	12	NE	1829-06-15		A1
1953	" "	1	E½SE	1830-11-01		A1
2016	GILBERT, John W	32	N½NW	1896-04-27		A2
2017	" "	32	NWNE	1896-04-27		A2
2039	GILCHRIST, Malcolm	24	E½NW	1827-10-01		A1 G70
1944	GILMER, Charles L	1	NE	1839-09-20		A1 G17

ID	Individual in Patent	Sec.	Sec. Part	Date Issued	Other Counties	For More Info . . .
1945	GILMER, Charles L (Cont'd)	1	NW	1839-09-20		A1 G17
1946	" "	1	W½SE	1839-09-20		A1 G17
1947	" "	11	E½SE	1839-09-20		A1 G17
1948	" "	11	NENW	1839-09-20		A1 G17
1949	" "	11	SESW	1839-09-20		A1 G17
1950	" "	12	E½NW	1839-09-20		A1 G17
1951	" "	12	SW	1839-09-20		A1 G17
1952	" "	24	W½NW	1839-09-20		A1 G17
2069	GILMER, William B	13	SW	1839-09-20		A1
1944	GILMER, William B S	1	NE	1839-09-20		A1 G17
1945	" "	1	NW	1839-09-20		A1 G17
1946	" "	1	W½SE	1839-09-20		A1 G17
1947	" "	11	E½SE	1839-09-20		A1 G17
1948	" "	11	NENW	1839-09-20		A1 G17
1949	" "	11	SESW	1839-09-20		A1 G17
1950	" "	12	E½NW	1839-09-20		A1 G17
1951	" "	12	SW	1839-09-20		A1 G17
1952	" "	24	W½NW	1839-09-20		A1 G17
1936	GODWIN, Alexander R	36	NESE	1861-04-09		A1
1937	" "	36	SENE	1861-04-09		A1
2046	HARRELL, Ransom	18	S½SW	1892-04-23		A2
2075	HAYES, William R	18	E½SE	1893-07-06		A2
2076	" "	18	SENE	1893-07-06		A2
2077	" "	18	SWSE	1893-07-06		A2
2024	HODGES, Jonathan	24	NE	1828-02-01		A1 G78
1983	HOGG, Hatton M	13	E½NW	1829-05-01		A1
1984	" "	13	W½NE	1829-05-01		A1
2048	JEMISON, Robert	24	E½SW	1827-10-01		A1 G82
2049	" "	24	W½SE	1827-10-01		A1 G82
2053	JOHNSON, Stonewall J	20	NWSW	1897-03-22		A2
2054	" "	20	S½SW	1897-03-22		A2
2055	" "	20	SWNW	1897-03-22		A2
2018	JOHNSTON, John W	14	NESW	1860-04-02		A1
2019	" "	14	NW	1860-04-02		A1
2020	" "	14	W½SW	1860-04-02		A1
1985	JONES, Henry	26	E½SW	1894-02-24		A2
1986	" "	26	S½SE	1894-02-24		A2
2029	JOWERS, Joseph J	20	NESW	1902-09-26		A2
1989	JUSTICE, Henry W	28	NW	1896-11-16		A2
1998	KEISER, James E	20	S½SE	1891-11-09		A2
2060	KEISER, Vashti	28	S½NE	1890-12-11		A2
2000	KING, James R	6	NESW	1904-07-27		A2
2001	" "	6	NWSE	1904-07-27		A2
2002	" "	6	W½SW	1904-07-27		A2
2050	KIRKLAND, Robert	36	W½NW	1890-12-01		A2
2038	LAMBERT, Lewis Q	28	N½NE	1899-05-12		A2
1938	LAND, Allen	34	NE	1893-10-13		A2
2021	LEVY, John W	36	NWSE	1893-10-13		A2
2022	" "	36	S½SE	1893-10-13		A2
2059	MATHIS, Tony	6	NESE	1913-02-13		A2
1958	MCDANIEL, Bonie	4	N½SE	1897-07-03		A2
1992	MCDANIEL, Ivy	3	E½NW	1857-07-01		A1
1993	" "	3	SWNE	1857-07-01		A1
2023	MCDANIEL, John W	32	SW	1900-08-09		A2
2047	MCDANIEL, Risdon	3	N½NE	1902-04-18		A1
2052	MCDANIEL, Silas	4	S½SE	1857-07-01		A1
2043	MCQUAGGE, Norman D	34	W½NW	1899-08-14		A2
2044	" "	34	W½SW	1899-08-14		A2
2042	MILES, Nancy A	6	NE	1899-06-22		A2 G37
2012	PARISH, John N	10	E½SE	1894-08-09		A2
2013	" "	10	SENE	1894-08-09		A2
1999	PILCHER, James F	30	SESW	1907-05-06		A1
2063	PIPPEN, William A	26	W½NW	1900-07-12		A2
2064	" "	26	W½SW	1900-07-12		A2
2030	POWELL, Joseph	20	N½SE	1893-12-28		A2
2031	" "	20	SENW	1893-12-28		A2
2032	" "	20	SWNE	1893-12-28		A2
2036	RIDDICK, Julian F	34	E½NW	1896-04-27		A2
2037	" "	34	E½SW	1896-04-27		A2
1959	SAPP, Burris	28	SW	1903-09-05		A1
2033	SCURLOCK, Joshua	2	NW	1827-04-02		A1
2035	" "	2	W½SW	1827-10-01		A1
2034	" "	2	W½NE	1829-06-15		A1

ID	Individual in Patent	Sec.	Sec. Part	Date Issued	Other Counties	For More Info . . .
2051	SCURLOCK, Sarah	2	E½NE	1838-07-28		A1
2061	SCURLOCK, Walton L	10	N½NE	1860-04-02		A1
2062	" "	10	NENW	1860-04-02		A1
1962	SHOUPE, Caspar C	10	NWNW	1905-05-17		A2 R1963
1962	" "	10	NWNW	1905-05-17		A2 C R1963
1963	" "	10	NWNW	1905-05-17		A2 R1962
1963	" "	10	NWNW	1905-05-17		A2 C R1962
1994	SHOUPPE, J D	10	SESW	1890-12-27		A2
1995	" "	10	SWSE	1890-12-27		A2
2005	SHOUPPE, Jefferson D	10	SWSW	1901-05-08		A2
2070	SILLIVENT, William H	30	NESW	1896-04-27		A2
2071	" "	30	SESE	1896-04-27		A2
2072	" "	30	W½SE	1896-04-27		A2
1987	SPEIGHT, Henry	26	E½NW	1892-12-03		A2
1988	" "	26	W½NE	1892-12-03		A2
2025	SPIVEY, Joseph C	22	W½NE	1892-08-01		A2 G131
2026	" "	22	W½SE	1892-08-01		A2 G131
2025	SPIVEY, Sarah J	22	W½NE	1892-08-01		A2 G131
2026	" "	22	W½SE	1892-08-01		A2 G131
2006	STILL, John A	18	NESW	1892-08-01		A2
2007	" "	18	NWSE	1892-08-01		A2
2008	" "	18	SENW	1892-08-01		A2
2009	" "	18	SWNE	1892-08-01		A2
2024	STONE, L M	24	NE	1828-02-01		A1 G78
1977	TAYLOR, Elizabeth A	2	E½SW	1828-02-01		A1
1955	THARP, Benjamin R	26	E½NE	1893-02-21		A2
1956	" "	26	N½SE	1893-02-21		A2
2040	THARP, Mary E	34	SE	1897-05-25		A2 G134
2040	THARP, William A	34	SE	1897-05-25		A2 G134
1960	TOOLE, Calvin	8	E½NE	1896-09-25		A2
1961	" "	8	E½SE	1896-09-25		A2
1964	TOOLE, Charles W	8	N½NW	1900-08-09		A2
1965	" "	8	W½NE	1900-08-09		A2
2014	UNDERWOOD, John N	20	E½NE	1860-07-02		A1
2015	" "	20	NWNE	1860-07-02		A1
2027	WACHOB, Joseph F	11	NESW	1839-09-20		A1
2028	" "	11	SENW	1839-09-20		A1
2003	WALSH, James	36	E½NW	1892-04-09		A2
2004	" "	36	W½NE	1892-04-09		A2
1970	WELCH, Columbus	36	SW	1892-04-09		A2
1966	WHITFIELD, Charles	8	N½SW	1896-08-17		A2
1967	" "	8	S½NW	1896-08-17		A2
1978	WHITFIELD, Elvin	18	NWSW	1891-12-21		A2
1979	" "	18	SWNW	1891-12-21		A2
2065	WILLIAMSON, Charles	1	E½SW	1827-10-01		A1 G65
2066	" "	1	W½SW	1827-10-01		A1 G65
2067	" "	2	E½SE	1827-10-01		A1 G65
2068	" "	2	W½SE	1827-10-01		A1 G65
2048	" "	24	E½SW	1827-10-01		A1 G82
2049	" "	24	W½SE	1827-10-01		A1 G82
1968	" "	11	NE	1827-11-01		A1
1969	" "	12	W½NW	1827-11-01		A1
1943	YOUNG, Andrew	13	W½NW	1834-08-20		A1
1939	" "	11	W½SE	1838-07-28		A1
1941	" "	12	W½SE	1838-07-28		A1
1940	" "	12	E½SE	1839-09-20		A1
1942	" "	13	E½NE	1839-09-20		A1

Patent Map

T5-N R12-W
Tallahassee Meridian

Map Group 17

Township Statistics

Parcels Mapped	:	143
Number of Patents	:	97
Number of Individuals	:	85
Patentees Identified	:	77
Number of Surnames	:	67
Multi-Patentee Parcels	:	22
Oldest Patent Date	:	4/2/1827
Most Recent Patent	:	2/13/1913
Block/Lot Parcels	:	0
Parcels Re - Issued	:	1
Parcels that Overlap	:	0
Cities and Towns	:	1
Cemeteries	:	0

6
ADAMS
Thomas C
1897

CARTER [37]
Nancy A
1899

KING
James R
1904

KING
James R
1904

KING
James R
1904

MATHIS
Tony
1913

5

4
CALHOUN
Dugald
1860

CALHOUN
Dugald
1860

CALHOUN
Dugald
1860

CALHOUN
Dugald
1860

DENHAM
John D
1905

CALHOUN
Dugald
1860

BONTIUE
Stuart
1897

MCDANIEL
Bonie
1897

BONTIUE
Stuart
1897

MCDANIEL
Silas
1857

7

TOOLE
Charles W
1900

TOOLE
Charles W
1900

TOOLE
Calvin
1896

WHITFIELD
Charles
1896

8

WHITFIELD
Charles
1896

BRUNER
William R
1903

TOOLE
Calvin
1896

BRUNER
William R
1903

9

BRUNER
Daniel Z
1892

BRUNER
Daniel Z
1892

WHITFIELD
Elvin
1891

STILL
John A
1892

STILL
John A
1892

HAYES
William R
1893

18

WHITFIELD
Elvin
1891

STILL
John A
1892

STILL
John A
1892

HAYES
William R
1893

HARRELL
Ransom
1892

HAYES
William R
1893

17

16

19

ELDRIDGE
George N
1906

UNDERWOOD
John N
1860

JOHNSON
Stonewall J
1897

POWELL
Joseph
1893

POWELL
Joseph
1893

UNDERWOOD
John N
1860

JOHNSON
Stonewall J
1897

JOWERS
Joseph J
1902

20

POWELL
Joseph
1893

JOHNSON
Stonewall J
1897

KEISER
James E
1891

21

BASS
Isaac
1899

30

BASS
Isaac
1899

SILLIVENT
William H
1896

SILLIVENT
William H
1896

PILCHER
James F
1907

SILLIVENT
William H
1896

29

JUSTICE
Henry W
1896

LAMBERT
Lewis Q
1899

KEISER
Vashti
1890

28

SAPP
Burris
1903

COX
R F
1890

31

GILBERT
John W
1896

GILBERT
John W
1896

32

MCDANIEL
John W
1900

33

MCDANIEL Ivy 1857	MCDANIEL Risdon 1902 / MCDANIEL Ivy 1857	SCURLOCK Joshua 1827 / SCURLOCK Joshua 1829 / SCURLOCK Sarah 1838	BIBB [17] Benajah S 1839 / BIBB [17] Benajah S 1839 / **1**

3

SCURLOCK Joshua 1827 / TAYLOR Elizabeth A 1828 / **2** / DRAKE [65] William B 1827 / DRAKE [65] William B 1827

DRAKE [65] William B 1827 / DRAKE [65] William B 1827 / BIBB [17] Benajah S 1839 / FOSCUE Benjamin 1830

SHOUPE Caspar C 1905 / SCURLOCK Walton L 1860 / SCURLOCK Walton L 1860 / PARISH John N 1894

10

SHOUPPE Jefferson D 1901 / SHOUPPE J D 1890 / SHOUPPE J D 1890 / PARISH John N 1894

BIBB [17] Benajah S 1839 / WILLIAMSON Charles 1827 / **11** / WACHOB Joseph F 1839 / WACHOB Joseph F 1839 / YOUNG Andrew 1838 / BIBB [17] Benajah S 1839 / BIBB [17] Benajah S 1839

BIBB [17] Benajah S 1839 / WILLIAMSON Charles 1827 / FOSCUE Benjamin 1829 / **12** / BIBB [17] Benajah S 1839 / YOUNG Andrew 1838 / YOUNG Andrew 1839

15

JOHNSTON John W 1860 / **14** / JOHNSTON John W 1860 / JOHNSTON John W 1860

YOUNG Andrew 1834 / HOGG Hatton M 1829 / HOGG Hatton M 1829 / YOUNG Andrew 1839 / **13** / BLOUNT Willie 1827 / GILMER William B 1839

BUTLER [27] Bennett 1893 / **22** / SPIVEY [131] Joseph C 1892 / BROXTON James 1891 / BRAXTON John 1893 / SPIVEY [131] Joseph C 1892 / BROXTON James 1891

23

BIBB [17] Benajah S 1839 / GILCHRIST [70] Malcolm 1827 / HODGES [78] Jonathan 1828 / **24** / JEMISON [82] Robert 1827 / DEKLE Mathew L 1888 / JEMISON [82] Robert 1827 / CARTER Farish 1848

27

PIPPEN William A 1900 / SPEIGHT Henry 1892 / SPEIGHT Henry 1892 / **26** / THARP Benjamin R 1893 / PIPPEN William A 1900 / JONES Henry 1894 / THARP Benjamin R 1893 / JONES Henry 1894

25

MCQUAGGE Norman D 1899 / RIDDICK Julian F 1896 / LAND Allen 1893 / **34** / MCQUAGGE Norman D 1899 / RIDDICK Julian F 1896 / THARP [134] Mary E 1897

35

KIRKLAND Robert 1890 / WALSH James 1892 / WALSH James 1892 / BOWEN Frank 1889 / GODWIN Alexander R 1861 / LEVY John W 1893 / GODWIN Alexander R 1861 / **36** / WELCH Columbus 1892 / LEVY John W 1893

Helpful Hints

1. This Map's INDEX can be found on the preceding pages.

2. Refer to Map "C" to see where this Township lies within Jackson County, Florida.

3. Numbers within square brackets [ ] denote a multi-patentee land parcel (multi-owner). Refer to Appendix "C" for a full list of members in this group.

4. Areas that look to be crowded with Patentees usually indicate multiple sales of the same parcel (Re-issues) or Overlapping parcels. See this Township's Index for an explanation of these and other circumstances that might explain "odd" groupings of Patentees on this map.

Legend

——— Patent Boundary

━━━ Section Boundary

▒▒▒ No Patents Found (or Outside County)

1., 2., 3., ... Lot Numbers (when beside a name)

[ ] Group Number (see Appendix "C")

Scale: Section = 1 mile X 1 mile (generally, with some exceptions)

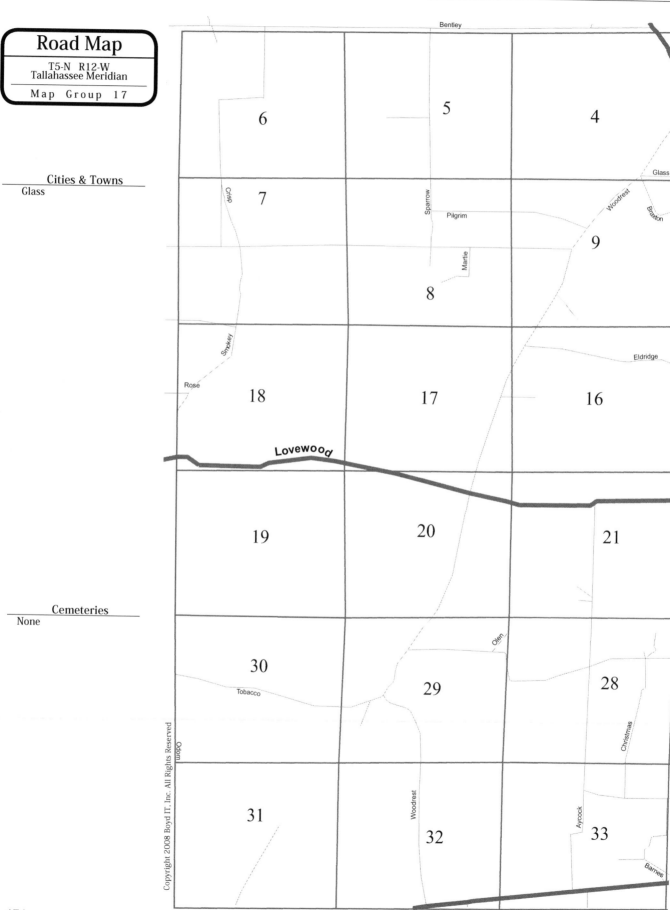

Road Map

T5-N R12-W
Tallahassee Meridian

Map Group 17

Cities & Towns
Glass

Cemeteries
None

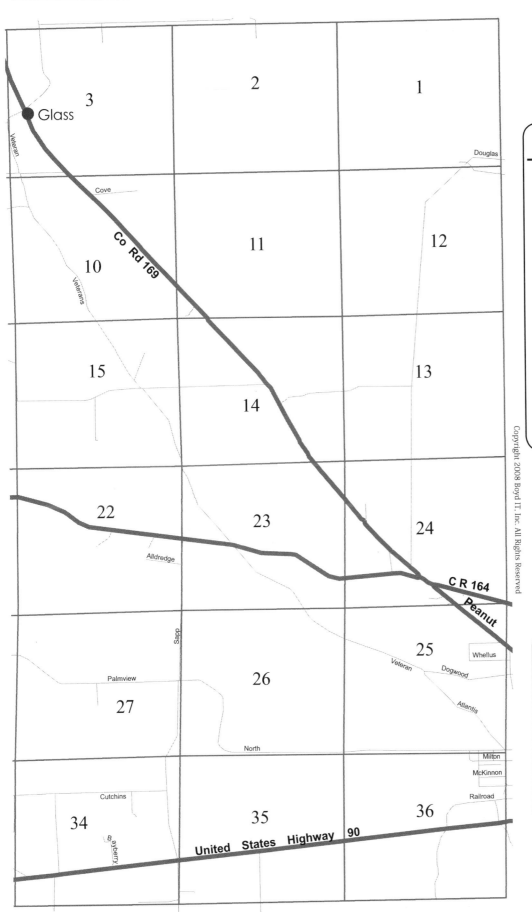

3

Glass

2

1

Veteran

Cove

Douglas

Co Rd 169

10

11

12

Veterans

15

13

14

22

24

23

Alldredge

CR 164

Peanut

Sapp

25

Whellus

Veteran

Dogwood

Palmview

26

Atlantis

27

North

Milton

McKinnon

Cutchins

Railroad

34

35

36

Bayberry

United States Highway 90

Helpful Hints

1. This road map has a number of uses, but primarily it is to help you: a) find the present location of land owned by your ancestors (at least the general area), b) find cemeteries and city-centers, and c) estimate the route/roads used by Census-takers & tax-assessors.

2. If you plan to travel to Jackson County to locate cemeteries or land parcels, please pick up a modern travel map for the area before you do. Mapping old land parcels on modern maps is not as exact a science as you might think. Just the slightest variations in public land survey coordinates, estimates of parcel boundaries, or road-map deviations can greatly alter a map's representation of how a road either does or doesn't cross a particular parcel of land.

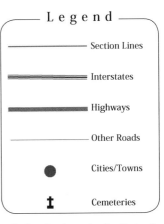

L e g e n d

———————— Section Lines

════════ Interstates

▬▬▬▬▬▬ Highways

———————— Other Roads

● Cities/Towns

✝ Cemeteries

Scale: Section = 1 mile X 1 mile
(generally, with some exceptions)

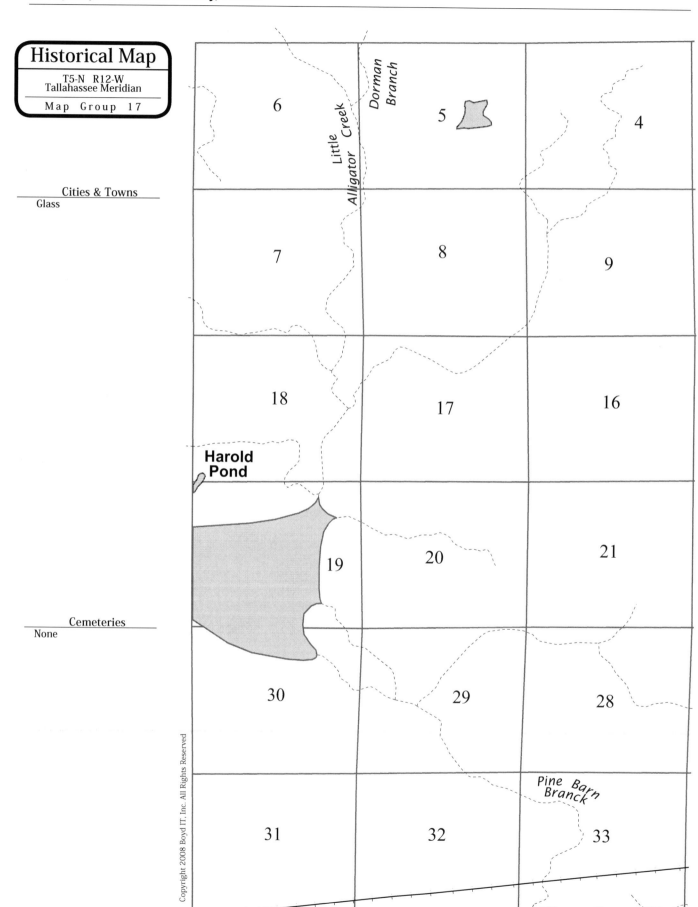

Historical Map

T5-N R12-W
Tallahassee Meridian

Map Group 17

Cities & Towns
Glass

Cemeteries
None

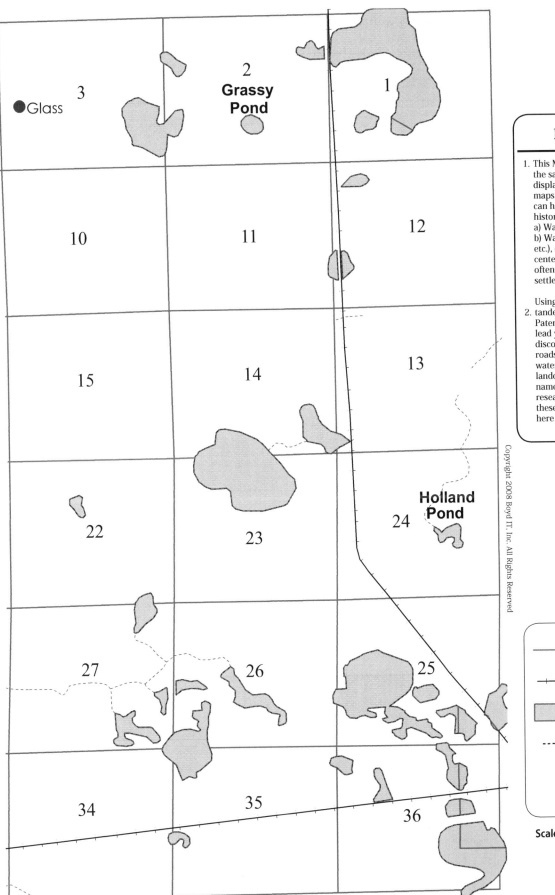

3

● Glass

2
**Grassy
Pond**

1

10

11

12

15

14

13

22

23

**Holland
Pond**

24

27

26

25

34

35

36

Helpful Hints

1. This Map takes a different look at the same Congressional Township displayed in the preceding two maps. It presents features that can help you better envision the historical development of the area: a) Water-bodies (lakes & ponds), b) Water-courses (rivers, streams, etc.), c) Railroads, d) City/town center-points (where they were oftentimes located when first settled), and e) Cemeteries.

2. Using this "Historical" map in tandem with this Township's Patent Map and Road Map, may lead you to some interesting discoveries. You will often find roads, towns, cemeteries, and waterways are named after nearby landowners: sometimes those names will be the ones you are researching. See how many of these research gems you can find here in Jackson County.

L e g e n d

———————— Section Lines

++++++++ Railroads

▭ Large Rivers & Bodies of Water

- - - - - - - Streams/Creeks & Small Rivers

● Cities/Towns

† Cemeteries

Scale: Section = 1 mile X 1 mile
(there are some exceptions)

Map Group 18: Index to Land Patents

Township 5-North Range 11-West (Tallahassee)

After you locate an individual in this Index, take note of the Section and Section Part then proceed to the Land Patent map on the pages immediately following. You should have no difficulty locating the corresponding parcel of land.

The "For More Info" Column will lead you to more information about the underlying Patents. See the *Legend* at right, and the "How to Use this Book" chapter, for more information.

```
                    LEGEND
            "For More Info . . . " column
A = Authority (Legislative Act, See Appendix "A")
B = Block or Lot (location in Section unknown)
C = Cancelled Patent
F = Fractional Section
G = Group  (Multi-Patentee Patent, see Appendix "C")
V = Overlaps another Parcel
R = Re-Issued (Parcel patented more than once)

(A & G items require you to look in the Appendixes referred
to above. All other Letter-designations followed by a number
require you to locate line-items in this index that possess
the ID number found after the letter).
```

ID	Individual in Patent	Sec.	Sec. Part	Date Issued	Other Counties	For More Info . . .
2082	BOWER, E J	9	NW	1827-04-02		A1
2083	BRANTLEY, Elbert	4	SW	1931-03-24		A1
2091	CLARK, John	11	SE	1827-04-02		A1
2096	" "	11	SW	1827-04-02		A1 G46
2092	" "	12	SW	1827-04-02		A1
2093	" "	13	NW	1827-04-02		A1
2094	" "	13	SE	1827-04-02		A1
2095	" "	14	NE	1827-04-02		A1
2099	" "	24	NE	1827-09-01		A1 G43
2098	" "	11	NE	1828-02-01		A1 G45
2097	" "	14	W½NW	1828-02-01		A1 G44
2106	CO, R C Allen And	11	NW	1827-04-02		A1 G52
2107	" "	14	SE	1827-04-02		A1 G53
2100	DAVIDSON, John	9	NE	1827-04-02		A1
2101	DICKSON, John	6	E½NE	1879-07-21		A2
2118	DUBOSE, Wade H	8	NW	1827-04-02		A1
2112	GOFF, Thomas	10	NE	1840-11-24		A1
2081	HOGG, Benjamin	15	NW	1827-06-27		A1
2110	HULL, Sarah	2	NW	1827-06-15		A1
2113	HULL, Thomas H	3	NE	1827-06-15		A1
2084	JACKSON, George	22	NW	1827-04-02		A1
2090	JACKSON, John B	21	E½NE	1827-04-02		A1
2119	JACKSON, William A	15	SW	1827-04-02		A1
2111	LANGSTON, Seth S	4	SE	1827-06-15		A1
2103	LEWIS, Joseph	14	SW	1827-04-02		A1 G92
2115	MCKINNE, Thomas	6	E½SE	1882-05-20		A2
2089	MONTFORT, Jeffrey	5	NE	1827-04-02		A1
2099	NOOGIN, Matthew	24	NE	1827-09-01		A1 G43
2097	PADGETT, Elijah	14	W½NW	1828-02-01		A1 G44
2102	POPE, John M	22	SE	1827-04-02		A1
2121	POPE, William S	22	NE	1827-04-02		A1
2080	RIVIERE, Alexander M	3	NW	1827-04-02		A1 G126
2079	" "	3	SW	1827-04-02		A1
2080	RIVIERE, Henry L	3	NW	1827-04-02		A1 G126
2086	RUSS, James B	5	SW	1827-04-02		A1
2103	RUSS, Joseph	14	SW	1827-04-02		A1 G92
2104	" "	23	NW	1827-04-02		A1
2116	RUSS, Thomas	8	E½SE	1848-09-15		A1
2117	" "	9	W½SW	1848-09-15		A1
2120	RUSS, William	8	NE	1849-06-13		A1
2109	SCURLOCK, Samuel	5	NW	1827-04-02		A1
2114	SCURLOCK, Thomas J	5	SE	1827-04-02		A1
2122	SPEAR, William	13	NE	1827-06-15		A1
2123	SPEARS, William	12	NE	1827-04-02		A1
2085	STONE, Henry D	23	NE	1827-04-02		A1
2106	STONE, James M	11	NW	1827-04-02		A1 G52

ID	Individual in Patent	Sec.	Sec. Part	Date Issued	Other Counties	For More Info . . .
2105	STONE, L M	13	SW	1827-04-02		A1 G132
2107	" "	14	SE	1827-04-02		A1 G53
2098	STONE, Louisana W	11	NE	1828-02-01		A1 G45
2105	THOMAS, David	13	SW	1827-04-02		A1 G132
2087	WEBB, James	10	SW	1827-04-02		A1
2088	" "	9	SE	1827-06-15		A1
2108	WILLIAMS, Robert W	10	SE	1827-04-02		A1
2096	WILLIAMSON, Charles	11	SW	1827-04-02		A1 G46

Patent Map

T5-N R11-W
Tallahassee Meridian

Map Group 18

Township Statistics

Parcels Mapped	:	45
Number of Patents	:	45
Number of Individuals	:	40
Patentees Identified	:	39
Number of Surnames	:	28
Multi-Patentee Parcels	:	9
Oldest Patent Date	:	4/2/1827
Most Recent Patent	:	3/24/1931
Block/Lot Parcels	:	0
Parcels Re - Issued	:	0
Parcels that Overlap	:	0
Cities and Towns	:	2
Cemeteries	:	0

6	DICKSON John 1879	SCURLOCK Samuel 1827 5	MONTFORT Jeffrey 1827	4	
	MCKINNE Thomas 1882	RUSS James B 1827	SCURLOCK Thomas J 1827	BRANTLEY Elbert 1931	LANGSTON Seth S 1827
7	DUBOSE Wade H 1827 8	RUSS William 1849	BOWER E J 1827	DAVIDSON John 1827 9	
		RUSS Thomas 1848	RUSS Thomas 1848	WEBB James 1827	
18	17		16		
19	20		21	JACKSON John B 1827	
30	29		28		
31	32		33		

RIVIERE [126] Alexander M 1827	HULL Thomas H 1827 3	HULL Sarah 1827 2		1
RIVIERE Alexander M 1827				

	GOFF Thomas 1840 10	CO [52] R C Allen And 1827	CLARK [45] John 1828 11	SPEARS William 1827
WEBB James 1827	WILLIAMS Robert W 1827	CLARK [46] John 1827	CLARK John 1827	CLARK John 1827 12

HOGG Benjamin 1827 15		CLARK [44] John 1828	14	CLARK John 1827	CLARK John 1827 13	SPEAR William 1827
JACKSON William A 1827		LEWIS [92] Joseph 1827	CO [53] R C Allen And 1827	STONE [132] L M 1827	CLARK John 1827

JACKSON George 1827	POPE William S 1827 22 POPE John M 1827	RUSS Joseph 1827 23	STONE Henry D 1827	24	CLARK [43] John 1827

27	26	25

34	35	36

Helpful Hints

1. This Map's INDEX can be found on the preceding pages.

2. Refer to Map "C" to see where this Township lies within Jackson County, Florida.

3. Numbers within square brackets [ ] denote a multi-patentee land parcel (multi-owner). Refer to Appendix "C" for a full list of members in this group.

4. Areas that look to be crowded with Patentees usually indicate multiple sales of the same parcel (Re-issues) or Overlapping parcels. See this Township's Index for an explanation of these and other circumstances that might explain "odd" groupings of Patentees on this map.

Legend

— Patent Boundary

— Section Boundary

No Patents Found
(or Outside County)

1., 2., 3., ...   Lot Numbers
(when beside a name)

[ ]   Group Number
(see Appendix "C")

Scale: Section = 1 mile X 1 mile
(generally, with some exceptions)

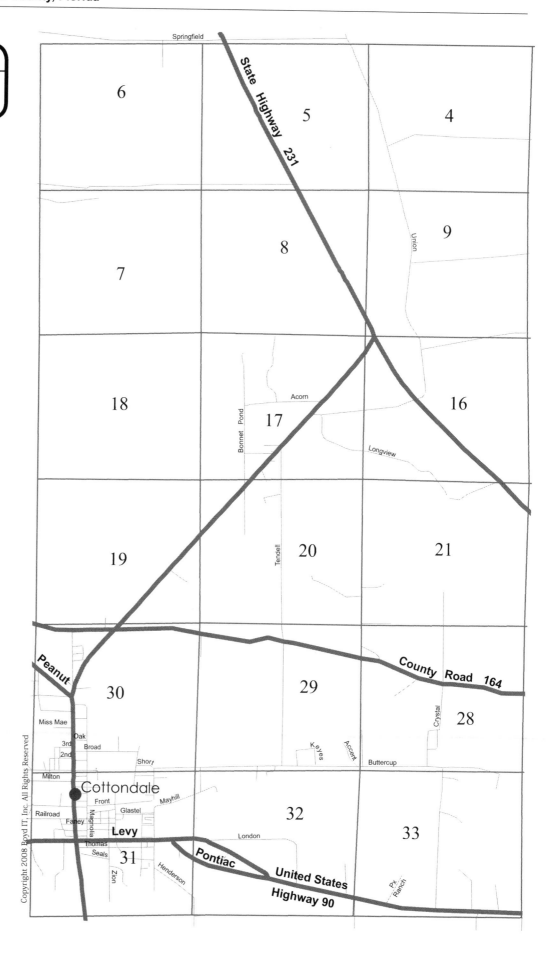

Road Map

T5-N R11-W
Tallahassee Meridian

Map Group 18

Cemeteries
None

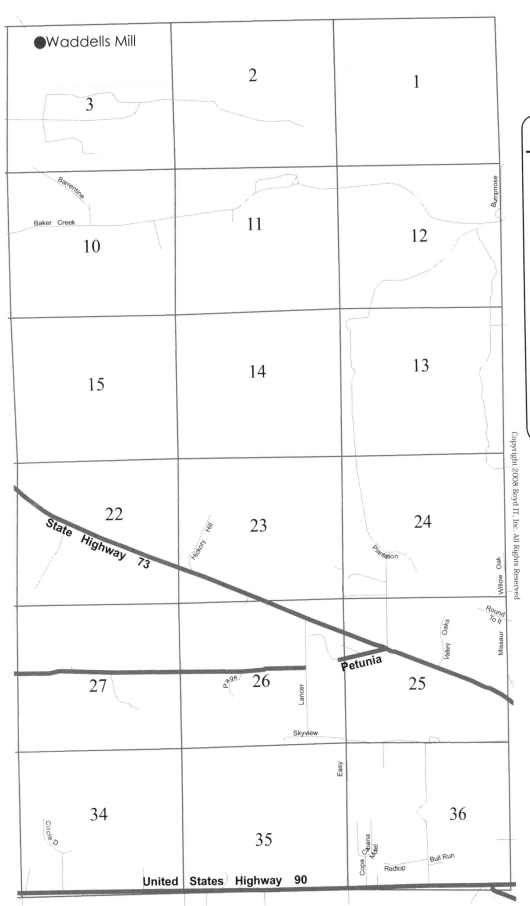

Waddells Mill

3

2

1

Barrentine

Baker Creek

10

11

12

Bumpnose

15

14

13

22

State Highway 73

Hickory Hill

23

Plantation

24

Willow Oak

Round To It

Valley Oaks

Missaur

Petunia

Page

27

26

Lancer

25

Skyview

Easy

34

Circle D

35

36

Copa Cabana Motel

Redtop

Bull Run

United States Highway 90

Copyright 2008 Boyd IT, Inc. All Rights Reserved

Helpful Hints

1. This road map has a number of uses, but primarily it is to help you: a) find the present location of land owned by your ancestors (at least the general area), b) find cemeteries and city-centers, and c) estimate the route/roads used by Census-takers & tax-assessors.

2. If you plan to travel to Jackson County to locate cemeteries or land parcels, please pick up a modern travel map for the area before you do. Mapping old land parcels on modern maps is not as exact a science as you might think. Just the slightest variations in public land survey coordinates, estimates of parcel boundaries, or road-map deviations can greatly alter a map's representation of how a road either does or doesn't cross a particular parcel of land.

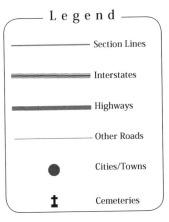

L e g e n d

——————— Section Lines

════════ Interstates

▬▬▬▬▬▬ Highways

——————— Other Roads

● Cities/Towns

✝ Cemeteries

Scale: Section = 1 mile X 1 mile
(generally, with some exceptions)

Historical Map

T5-N R11-W
Tallahassee Meridian

Map Group 18

Cities & Towns
Cottondale
Waddells Mill

Cemeteries
None

6

5

Maybet
Pond

Snelling
Pond

Waddells
Mill Pond

4

Roulhac
Pond

Russ Mill Creek

7

8

9

Jenkins
Pond

Middle
Pond

Lockey
Pond

18

17

16

Bonnet
Pond

Red
Pond

Open
Pond

Guy
Pond

19

20

21

Jackson
Pond

Gnat
Hole Pond

30

29

28

Mary
Pond

Caney
Pond

Cold
Pond

●Cottondale

Frank
Pond

31

32

McNealy
Pond

33

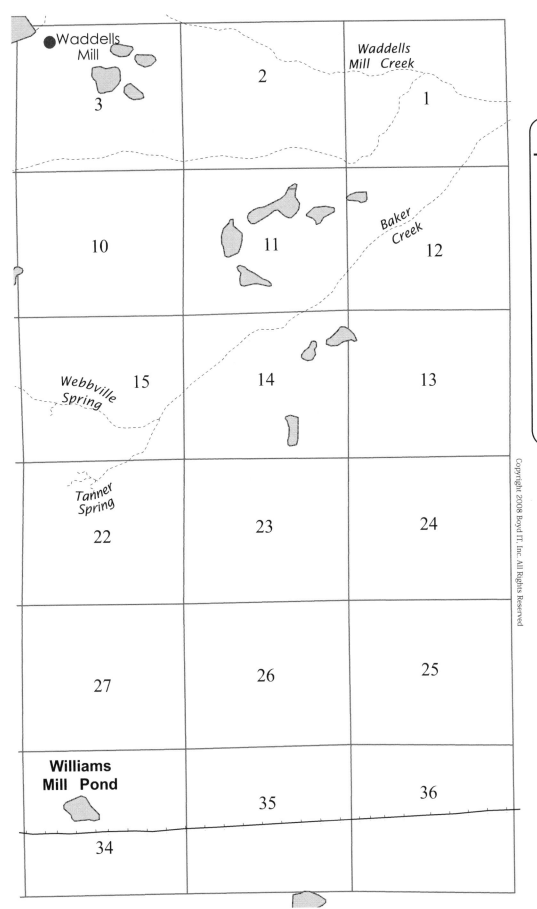

Waddells
Mill

3

2

Waddells
Mill Creek

1

10

11

Baker
Creek

12

Webbville
Spring

15

14

13

Tanner
Spring

22

23

24

27

26

25

**Williams
Mill Pond**

35

36

34

Helpful Hints

1. This Map takes a different look at the same Congressional Township displayed in the preceding two maps. It presents features that can help you better envision the historical development of the area: a) Water-bodies (lakes & ponds), b) Water-courses (rivers, streams, etc.), c) Railroads, d) City/town center-points (where they were oftentimes located when first settled), and e) Cemeteries.

2. Using this "Historical" map in tandem with this Township's Patent Map and Road Map, may lead you to some interesting discoveries. You will often find roads, towns, cemeteries, and waterways are named after nearby landowners: sometimes those names will be the ones you are researching. See how many of these research gems you can find here in Jackson County.

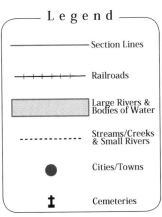

L e g e n d

——————— Section Lines

+—+—+—+—+—+ Railroads

Large Rivers &
Bodies of Water

- - - - - - - Streams/Creeks
& Small Rivers

● Cities/Towns

✝ Cemeteries

Scale: Section = 1 mile X 1 mile
(there are some exceptions)

Map Group 19: Index to Land Patents

Township 5-North Range 10-West (Tallahassee)

After you locate an individual in this Index, take note of the Section and Section Part then proceed to the Land Patent map on the pages immediately following. You should have no difficulty locating the corresponding parcel of land.

The "For More Info" Column will lead you to more information about the underlying Patents. See the *Legend* at right, and the "How to Use this Book" chapter, for more information.

```
                    LEGEND
          "For More Info . . . " column
A = Authority (Legislative Act, See Appendix "A")
B = Block or Lot (location in Section unknown)
C = Cancelled Patent
F = Fractional Section
G = Group   (Multi-Patentee Patent, see Appendix "C")
V = Overlaps another Parcel
R = Re-Issued (Parcel patented more than once)

(A & G items require you to look in the Appendixes referred
to above. All other Letter-designations followed by a number
require you to locate line-items in this index that possess
the ID number found after the letter).
```

ID	Individual in Patent	Sec.	Sec. Part	Date Issued	Other Counties	For More Info . . .
2138	ACOCK, Amos	1	E½NW	1829-06-15		A1
2233	ALLEN, Matthew J	28	NE	1846-09-01		A1 G6
2139	BAKER, Anderson	20	E½SE	1878-11-30		A2
2269	BAKER, Simmons J	32	E½NW	1844-07-10		A1
2265	BELLAMY, Samuel C	32	E½SW	1838-07-28		A1
2267	" "	32	W½SE	1838-07-28		A1
2266	" "	32	W½NW	1843-03-10		A1
2175	BRYAN, Elijah	1	NESE	1837-04-20		A1
2176	" "	12	E½NW	1837-04-20		A1
2177	" "	12	W½NW	1837-04-20		A1
2178	" "	13	SESE	1838-07-28		A1
2146	CHAIRES, Benjamin	28	E½NW	1827-10-01		A1 G38
2147	" "	28	E½SE	1827-10-01		A1 G38
2148	" "	28	W½NW	1827-10-01		A1 G38
2149	" "	28	W½SE	1827-10-01		A1 G38
2150	" "	32	E½NE	1827-10-01		A1 G39
2143	" "	33	E½NE	1827-10-01		A1
2144	" "	33	W½NE	1827-10-01		A1
2145	" "	34	W½NW	1827-10-01		A1
2142	" "	30	E½SW	1828-08-22		A1
2216	CHRISTOFF, Lewis	8	W½NW	1827-04-02		A1 G42
2152	CLEMENTS, Benjamin	3	W½SW	1827-10-01		A1 G50
2151	" "	3	W½NW	1827-11-01		A1
2292	CO, R C Allen And	18	NE	1827-04-02		A1 G89
2268	" "	18	NW	1827-04-02		A1 G59
2230	" "	7	NW	1827-04-02		A1 G67
2206	" "	7	SW	1827-04-02		A1 G86
2268	COOK, Simeon	18	NW	1827-04-02		A1 G59
2282	DRAKE, William B	26	E½NW	1827-10-01		A1 G64
2283	" "	26	W½NW	1827-10-01		A1 G64
2235	DUDLEY, Mingo C	29	W½NE	1893-01-21		A1
2280	FARR, Toliver	32	SWSW	1857-12-01		A1
2191	FINLAYSON, James A	29	SW	1889-06-03		A2
2230	FLETCHER, Mary	7	NW	1827-04-02		A1 G67
2182	FORT, Isaac	5	E½NW	1837-04-15		A1
2183	" "	5	E½SW	1837-04-15		A1
2184	" "	5	W½NE	1837-04-15		A1
2185	" "	5	W½SE	1837-04-15		A1
2135	FORTUNE, Adam	34	SW	1827-04-02		A1
2136	" "	34	W½SE	1828-02-22		A1
2134	" "	33	E½SE	1828-03-15		A1
2124	" "	23	E½SE	1829-05-15		A1
2125	" "	23	W½SE	1829-05-15		A1
2129	" "	24	W½NW	1829-06-01		A1
2126	" "	24	E½NW	1829-06-15		A1
2127	" "	24	E½SW	1829-06-15		A1

ID	Individual in Patent	Sec.	Sec. Part	Date Issued	Other Counties	For More Info . . .
2130	FORTUNE, Adam (Cont'd)	24	W½SW	1830-11-01		A1
2128	" "	24	NWNE	1835-10-20		A1
2131	" "	25	E½NE	1837-04-15		A1
2132	" "	25	NESE	1837-04-15		A1
2133	" "	25	SWNE	1837-04-15		A1
2241	GAUTIER, Peter W	19	E½SW	1829-05-01		A1
2242	" "	30	W½NW	1829-05-01		A1
2240	" "	19	E½SE	1839-09-20		A1
2243	" "	31	E½NE	1839-09-20		A1
2218	GILCHRIST, Malcolm	23	E½NE	1827-10-01		A1 G71
2219	" "	23	W½NE	1827-10-01		A1 G71
2244	GOTIER, Peter W	30	E½NW	1827-10-01		A1
2245	GUATIER, Peter W	19	NE	1854-02-15		A1
2221	HARDIN, Martin	10	NW	1827-04-02		A1
2222	" "	4	SE	1827-04-02		A1
2223	" "	4	SW	1827-04-02		A1
2224	" "	5	E½SE	1827-04-02		A1
2225	" "	9	NE	1827-04-02		A1
2226	" "	9	NW	1827-04-02		A1
2227	" "	9	SE	1827-04-02		A1
2228	" "	9	SW	1827-04-02		A1
2284	HARVEY, William H	36	NW	1843-03-10		A1
2285	" "	36	NWNE	1843-03-10		A1
2212	HOPSON, John	30	SE	1827-04-02		A1 V2258
2168	HORNE, Duke W	3	NENW	1837-04-15		A1
2169	" "	3	SENW	1837-04-20		A1
2293	HORT, William P	18	SE	1829-04-02		A1
2154	HUNTER, Burton	28	W½SW	1878-11-30		A2
2198	KEITH, James	34	E½NW	1828-09-10		A1
2199	" "	34	E½SE	1828-09-10		A1
2200	" "	34	W½NE	1828-09-10		A1
2282	KEITH, Thomas R	26	E½NW	1827-10-01		A1 G64
2283	" "	26	W½NW	1827-10-01		A1 G64
2273	" "	27	E½SE	1827-10-01		A1 G84
2274	" "	27	W½SE	1827-10-01		A1 G84
2275	" "	34	E½NE	1827-10-01		A1 G84
2276	" "	35	E½SW	1827-10-01		A1 G84
2277	" "	35	W½NW	1827-10-01		A1 G84
2279	" "	35	W½SE	1827-10-01		A1 G85
2278	" "	35	W½SW	1827-10-01		A1 G84
2271	" "	13	NE	1827-11-01		A1
2272	" "	13	W½	1827-11-01		A1
2206	KENT, Jessee	7	SW	1827-04-02		A1 G86
2220	KENT, Marmaduke	7	SE	1827-06-15		A1
2292	KENT, William	18	NE	1827-04-02		A1 G89
2217	KILBEE, Lucy	4	NW	1828-02-01		A1
2298	KILBEE, William T	23	NW	1827-04-02		A1 G90
2297	" "	35	W½NE	1827-10-01		A1
2296	" "	25	E½NW	1829-06-15		A1
2165	LEWIS, David	36	NENE	1843-03-10		A1
2166	" "	36	SWNE	1843-03-10		A1
2246	LONG, Richard H	11	E½NW	1834-08-20		A1
2247	" "	11	W½NE	1834-08-20		A1
2259	" "	32	E½SE	1834-08-20		A1
2253	" "	2	E½SW	1837-04-15		A1
2255	" "	2	W½SE	1837-04-15		A1
2256	" "	2	W½SW	1837-04-15		A1
2248	" "	11	W½NW	1837-04-20		A1
2249	" "	12	E½SW	1837-04-20		A1
2250	" "	12	NWSW	1837-04-20		A1
2252	" "	2	E½NW	1837-04-20		A1
2254	" "	2	W½NW	1837-04-20		A1
2257	" "	3	W½SE	1837-04-20		A1
2258	" "	30	E½SE	1837-04-20		A1 V2212
2262	" "	33	W½SW	1837-04-20		A1
2261	" "	32	SWNE	1838-07-28		A1
2251	" "	13	W½SE	1839-09-20		A1
2260	" "	32	NWNE	1856-06-16		A1
2205	LOTT, Jesse	24	SWNE	1838-07-28		A1
2263	LOVE, Richard	33	N½NW	1893-02-01		A2
2137	MANDELL, Addison	35	E½NE	1829-06-15		A1
2213	MARTIN, John P	13	NESE	1837-04-20		A1
2218	MATTHEWS, Charles L	23	E½NE	1827-10-01		A1 G71

ID	Individual in Patent	Sec.	Sec. Part	Date Issued	Other Counties	For More Info . . .
2219	MATTHEWS, Charles L (Cont'd)	23	W½NE	1827-10-01		A1 G71
2273	" "	27	E½SE	1827-10-01		A1 G84
2274	" "	27	W½SE	1827-10-01		A1 G84
2275	" "	34	E½NE	1827-10-01		A1 G84
2156	" "	35	E½NW	1827-10-01		A1 G100
2276	" "	35	E½SW	1827-10-01		A1 G84
2277	" "	35	W½NW	1827-10-01		A1 G84
2278	" "	35	W½SW	1827-10-01		A1 G84
2287	MAULDIN, William J	24	E½NE	1829-05-15		A1
2288	" "	24	SE	1829-05-15		A1
2289	" "	26	E½SE	1829-05-15		A1
2291	" "	26	W½SE	1829-06-15		A1
2290	" "	26	NE	1830-12-28		A1
2229	NOLL, Martin	19	NW	1827-04-02		A1
2281	NOLL, Warren	17	SW	1827-04-02		A1
2201	PATTERSON, James	3	NE	1829-05-01		A1
2170	PEYTON, Edward W	25	NWSW	1837-04-20		A1
2171	" "	25	SESE	1837-04-20		A1
2172	" "	25	SESW	1843-03-10		A1
2173	" "	25	SWSW	1843-03-10		A1
2174	" "	25	W½SE	1843-03-10		A1
2236	PORTER, Nathan	22	NE	1827-06-15		A1 G122
2237	PORTER, Nathaniel	8	SENE	1902-01-25		A1
2207	ROBERTS, John B	1	SW	1828-02-22		A1
2210	" "	2	E½NE	1828-02-22		A1
2209	" "	1	W½NW	1828-03-15		A1
2211	" "	2	E½SE	1834-08-20		A1
2208	" "	1	SWNE	1835-10-20		A1
2232	ROBERTS, Mary	2	W½NE	1837-04-15		A1
2231	" "	1	NWNE	1837-04-20		A1
2190	ROBINSON, Jacob	22	SE	1827-04-02		A1 G128
2298	" "	23	NW	1827-04-02		A1 G90
2146	" "	28	E½NW	1827-10-01		A1 G38
2147	" "	28	E½SE	1827-10-01		A1 G38
2148	" "	28	W½NW	1827-10-01		A1 G38
2149	" "	28	W½SE	1827-10-01		A1 G38
2188	" "	33	E½SW	1837-04-20		A1
2189	" "	33	W½SE	1837-04-20		A1
2233	" "	28	NE	1846-09-01		A1 G6
2150	ROBINSON, Jacob W	32	E½NE	1827-10-01		A1 G39
2203	ROBINSON, Jerry	29	NESE	1890-04-29		A2
2264	ROBINSON, Robert	29	E½NE	1890-04-29		A2
2286	ROBINSON, William H	25	W½NW	1837-04-20		A1
2140	RUSS, Anderson	28	E½SW	1882-05-20		A2
2234	SIMMS, Miles	26	SW	1828-02-01		A1 G130
2239	SIMONS, Peter	25	NWNE	1839-09-20		A1
2294	SLOAN, William	35	E½SE	1830-11-01		A1
2295	" "	36	SW	1830-11-01		A1
2186	SMITH, Isaac	29	W½SE	1888-06-13		A2
2155	STALEY, Caroline B	36	SENE	1856-06-16		A1
2238	STALEY, Nelson O	36	SWSE	1857-07-01		A1
2153	STEPHENS, Benjamin	36	E½SE	1828-02-01		A1
2216	STONE, L M	8	W½NW	1827-04-02		A1 G42
2167	THOMAS, David	11	E½NE	1827-10-01		A1 G135
2279	" "	35	W½SE	1827-10-01		A1 G85
2179	TOWERS, Frances	30	W½SW	1828-09-10		A1
2164	TRAMMEL, Daniel	12	SE	1833-05-16		A1
2192	TRAMMEL, James J	12	E½NE	1829-05-15		A1
2194	" "	6	W½SE	1837-04-20		A1 C
2193	" "	12	W½NE	1850-06-10		A1
2202	TRAMMELL, James	1	SESE	1835-10-20		A1
2196	TRAMMELL, James J	1	W½SE	1828-03-15		A1
2197	" "	12	SWSW	1837-04-15		A1
2195	" "	1	E½NE	1838-07-28		A1
2180	VICK, George C	29	SESE	1894-03-08		A2
2214	WHITE, John	18	E½SW	1882-09-25		A1
2215	WHITE, Julia	19	W½SE	1888-11-15		A2 G141
2215	WHITE, King	19	W½SE	1888-11-15		A2 G141
2270	WHITE, Thomas M	15	NW	1849-12-20		A1
2161	WILLIAMSON, Charles	15	SW	1827-04-02		A1
2167	" "	11	E½NE	1827-10-01		A1 G135
2158	" "	11	E½SW	1827-10-01		A1
2159	" "	11	W½SE	1827-10-01		A1

ID	Individual in Patent	Sec.	Sec. Part	Date Issued	Other Counties	For More Info . . .
2160	WILLIAMSON, Charles (Cont'd)	11	W½SW	1827-10-01		A1
2162	" "	3	E½SW	1827-10-01		A1
2152	" "	3	W½SW	1827-10-01		A1 G50
2156	" "	35	E½NW	1827-10-01		A1 G100
2163	" "	5	E½NE	1827-10-01		A1
2157	" "	11	E½SE	1827-11-01		A1
2190	WILLIAMSON, Nathan	22	SE	1827-04-02		A1 G128
2236	" "	22	NE	1827-06-15		A1 G122
2204	WILLIS, Jesse H	27	SW	1841-01-09		A1
2187	WIMBERLY, Isaac	25	NESW	1837-04-15		A1
2234	WITHERINGTON, Mahala	26	SW	1828-02-01		A1 G130
2181	WYNN, Hamp	32	NWSW	1899-08-30		A2
2141	WYNNS, Anson	20	W½SE	1883-08-13		A2

Patent Map

T5-N R10-W
Tallahassee Meridian

Map Group 19

Township Statistics

Parcels Mapped	:	175
Number of Patents	:	172
Number of Individuals	:	83
Patentees Identified	:	84
Number of Surnames	:	64
Multi-Patentee Parcels	:	30
Oldest Patent Date	:	4/2/1827
Most Recent Patent	:	1/25/1902
Block/Lot Parcels	:	0
Parcels Re-Issued	:	0
Parcels that Overlap	:	2
Cities and Towns	:	0
Cemeteries	:	1

6

TRAMMEL
James J
1837

FORT
Isaac
1837

FORT
Isaac
1837

5

WILLIAMSON
Charles
1827

KILBEE
Lucy
1828

4

FORT
Isaac
1837

FORT
Isaac
1837

HARDIN
Martin
1827

HARDIN
Martin
1827

HARDIN
Martin
1827

FLETCHER [67]
Mary
1827

7

CHRISTOFF [42]
Lewis
1827

8

PORTER
Nathaniel
1902

HARDIN
Martin
1827

HARDIN
Martin
1827

9

KENT [86]
Jessee
1827

KENT
Marmaduke
1827

HARDIN
Martin
1827

HARDIN
Martin
1827

COOK [59]
Simeon
1827

KENT [89]
William
1827

18

WHITE
John
1882

HORT
William P
1829

17

NOLL
Warren
1827

16

NOLL
Martin
1827

19

GUATIER
Peter W
1854

20

21

GAUTIER
Peter W
1829

WHITE [141]
Julia
1888

GAUTIER
Peter W
1839

WYNNS
Anson
1883

BAKER
Anderson
1878

GAUTIER
Peter W
1829

GOTIER
Peter W
1827

30

29

DUDLEY
Mingo C
1893

ROBINSON
Robert
1890

CHAIRES [38]
Benjamin
1827

CHAIRES [38]
Benjamin
1827

28

ALLEN [6]
Matthew J
1846

TOWERS
Frances
1828

CHAIRES
Benjamin
1828

HOPSON
John
1827

LONG
Richard H
1837

FINLAYSON
James A
1889

SMITH
Isaac
1888

ROBINSON
Jerry
1890

VICK
George C
1894

HUNTER
Burton
1878

RUSS
Anderson
1882

CHAIRES [38]
Benjamin
1827

CHAIRES [38]
Benjamin
1827

31

GAUTIER
Peter W
1839

BELLAMY
Samuel C
1843

BAKER
Simmons J
1844

32

LONG
Richard H
1856

LONG
Richard H
1838

CHAIRES [39]
Benjamin
1827

LOVE
Richard
1893

33

CHAIRES
Benjamin
1827

CHAIRES
Benjamin
1827

WYNN
Hamp
1899

BELLAMY
Samuel C
1838

BELLAMY
Samuel C
1838

LONG
Richard H
1834

LONG
Richard H
1837

ROBINSON
Jacob
1837

FARR
Toliver
1857

ROBINSON
Jacob
1837

FORTUNE
Adam
1828

Section 3
CLEMENTS Benjamin 1827
HORNE Duke W 1837
PATTERSON James 1829
HORNE Duke W 1837

Section 2
LONG Richard H 1837
LONG Richard H 1837
ROBERTS Mary 1837
ROBERTS John B 1828

Section 1
ROBERTS John B 1828
ACOCK Amos 1829
ROBERTS Mary 1837
ROBERTS John B 1835
TRAMMELL James J 1838

CLEMENTS [50] Benjamin 1827
WILLIAMSON Charles 1827
LONG Richard H 1837
LONG Richard H 1837
LONG Richard H 1837
LONG Richard H 1837
ROBERTS John B 1834
ROBERTS John B 1828
TRAMMELL James J 1828
BRYAN Elijah 1837
TRAMMELL James 1835

Section 10
HARDIN Martin 1827

Section 11
LONG Richard H 1837
LONG Richard H 1834
LONG Richard H 1834
THOMAS [135] David 1827
WILLIAMSON Charles 1827
WILLIAMSON Charles 1827
WILLIAMSON Charles 1827
WILLIAMSON Charles 1827

Section 12
BRYAN Elijah 1837
BRYAN Elijah 1837
TRAMMEL James J 1850
TRAMMEL James J 1829
LONG Richard H 1837
TRAMMELL James J 1837
LONG Richard H 1837
TRAMMEL Daniel 1833

Section 15
WHITE Thomas M 1849
WILLIAMSON Charles 1827

Section 14

Section 13
KEITH Thomas R 1827
KEITH Thomas R 1827
LONG Richard H 1839
MARTIN John P 1837
BRYAN Elijah 1838

Section 22
PORTER [122] Nathan 1827
ROBINSON [128] Jacob 1827

Section 23
KILBEE [90] William T 1827
GILCHRIST [71] Malcolm 1827
GILCHRIST [71] Malcolm 1827
FORTUNE Adam 1829
FORTUNE Adam 1829

Section 24
FORTUNE Adam 1829
FORTUNE Adam 1829
FORTUNE Adam 1830
FORTUNE Adam 1829
FORTUNE Adam 1835
LOTT Jesse 1838
MAULDIN William J 1829
MAULDIN William J 1829

Section 27

Section 26
DRAKE [64] William B 1827
DRAKE [64] William B 1827
MAULDIN William J 1830
SIMMS [130] Miles 1828
MAULDIN William J 1829
MAULDIN William J 1829
WILLIS Jesse H 1841
KEITH [84] Thomas R 1827
KEITH [84] Thomas R 1827

Section 25
ROBINSON William H 1837
KILBEE William T 1829
SIMONS Peter 1839
FORTUNE Adam 1837
FORTUNE Adam 1837
PEYTON Edward W 1837
WIMBERLY Isaac 1837
PEYTON Edward W 1843
FORTUNE Adam 1837
PEYTON Edward W 1843
PEYTON Edward W 1843
PEYTON Edward W 1837

Section 34
CHAIRES Benjamin 1827
KEITH James 1828
KEITH James 1828
FORTUNE Adam 1828
FORTUNE Adam 1827
KEITH James 1828
KEITH [84] Thomas R 1827

Section 35
KEITH [84] Thomas R 1827
MATTHEWS [100] Charles L 1827
KILBEE William T 1827
MANDELL Addison 1829
KEITH [84] Thomas R 1827
KEITH [84] Thomas R 1827
KEITH [85] Thomas R 1827
SLOAN William 1830

Section 36
HARVEY William H 1843
LEWIS David 1843
LEWIS David 1843
STALEY Caroline B 1856
HARVEY William H 1843
SLOAN William 1830
STALEY Nelson O 1857
STEPHENS Benjamin 1828

Helpful Hints

1. This Map's INDEX can be found on the preceding pages.

2. Refer to Map "C" to see where this Township lies within Jackson County, Florida.

3. Numbers within square brackets [ ] denote a multi-patentee land parcel (multi-owner). Refer to Appendix "C" for a full list of members in this group.

4. Areas that look to be crowded with Patentees usually indicate multiple sales of the same parcel (Re-issues) or Overlapping parcels. See this Township's Index for an explanation of these and other circumstances that might explain "odd" groupings of Patentees on this map.

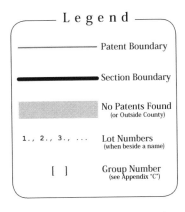

Legend

———— Patent Boundary

▬▬▬▬ Section Boundary

░░░░ No Patents Found (or Outside County)

1., 2., 3., ... Lot Numbers (when beside a name)

[ ] Group Number (see Appendix "C")

Scale: Section = 1 mile X 1 mile (generally, with some exceptions)

191

Road Map

T5-N R10-W
Tallahassee Meridian

Map Group 19

Cities & Towns
None

Cemeteries
Pinecrest Memorial Gardens

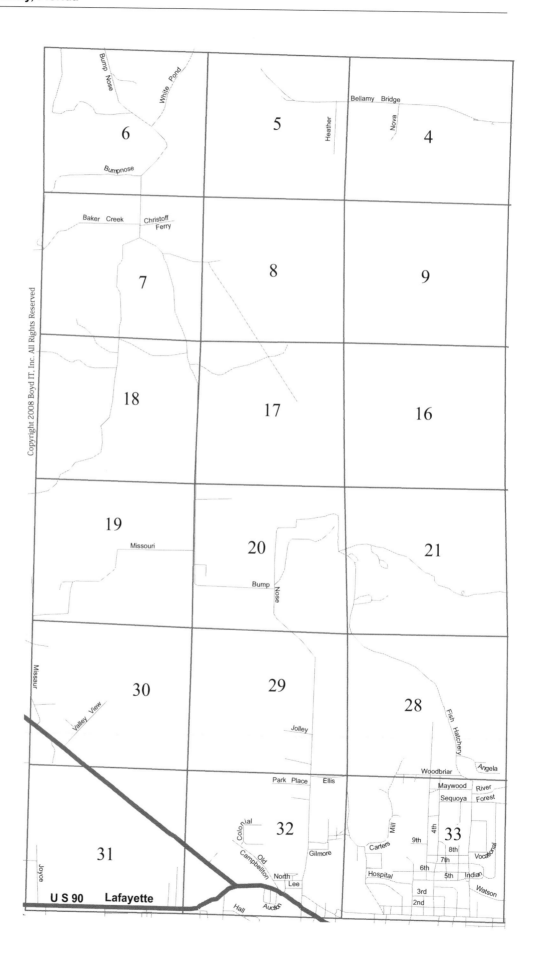

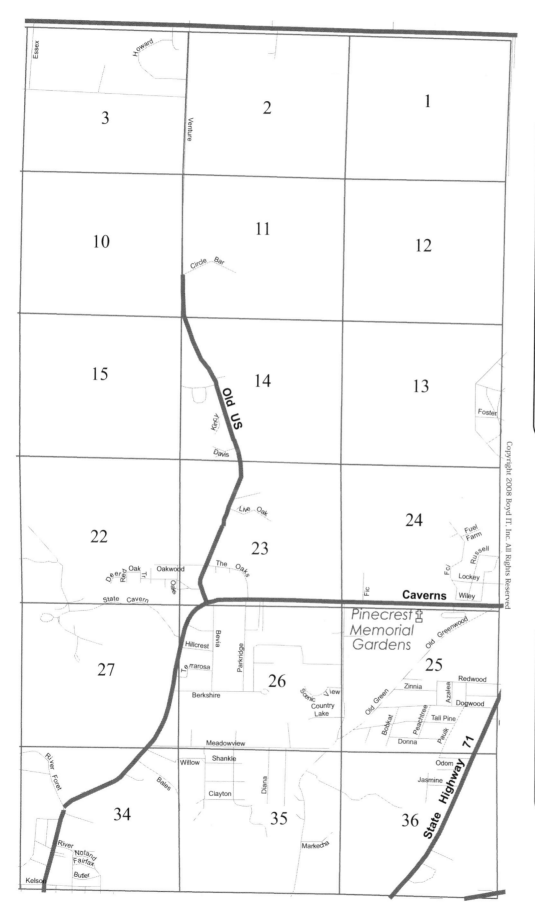

Helpful Hints

1. This road map has a number of uses, but primarily it is to help you: a) find the present location of land owned by your ancestors (at least the general area), b) find cemeteries and city-centers, and c) estimate the route/roads used by Census-takers & tax-assessors.

2. If you plan to travel to Jackson County to locate cemeteries or land parcels, please pick up a modern travel map for the area before you do. Mapping old land parcels on modern maps is not as exact a science as you might think. Just the slightest variations in public land survey coordinates, estimates of parcel boundaries, or road-map deviations can greatly alter a map's representation of how a road either does or doesn't cross a particular parcel of land.

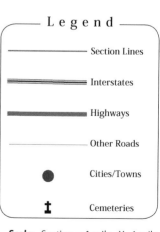

L e g e n d

————————	Section Lines
════════	Interstates
▬▬▬▬▬▬	Highways
————	Other Roads
●	Cities/Towns
✝	Cemeteries

Scale: Section = 1 mile X 1 mile
(generally, with some exceptions)

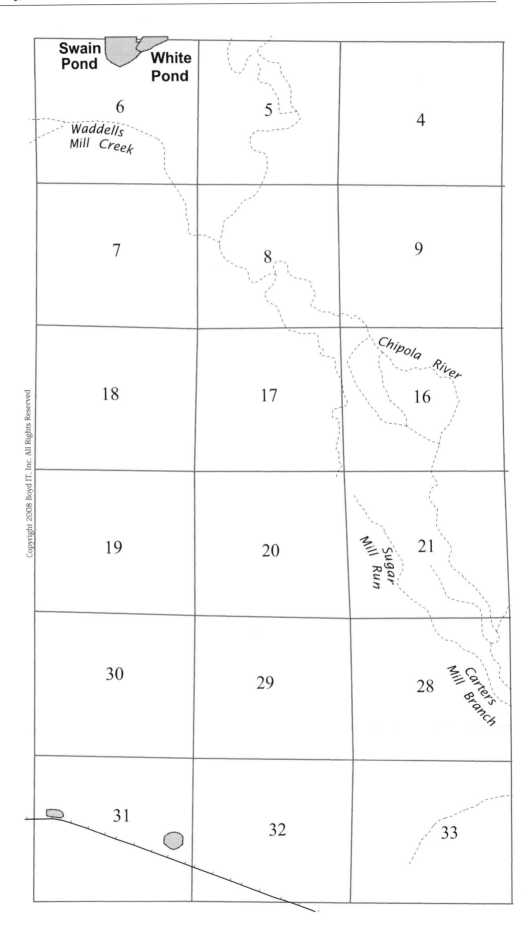

Historical Map

T5-N R10-W
Tallahassee Meridian

Map Group 19

Cities & Towns
None

Cemeteries
Pinecrest Memorial Gardens

Swain Pond

White Pond

Waddells Mill Creek

Chipola River

Sugar Mill Run

Carter's Mill Branch

6   5   4

7   8   9

18   17   16

19   20   21

30   29   28

31   32   33

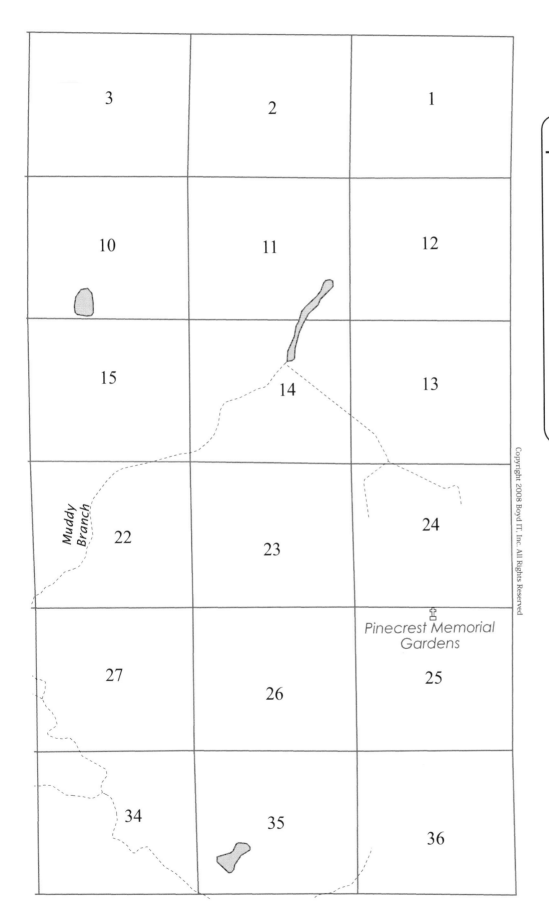

3

2

1

10

11

12

15

14

13

Muddy Branch

22

23

24

27

26

25

† Pinecrest Memorial Gardens

34

35

36

Helpful Hints

1. This Map takes a different look at the same Congressional Township displayed in the preceding two maps. It presents features that can help you better envision the historical development of the area: a) Water-bodies (lakes & ponds), b) Water-courses (rivers, streams, etc.), c) Railroads, d) City/town center-points (where they were oftentimes located when first settled), and e) Cemeteries.

2. Using this "Historical" map in tandem with this Township's Patent Map and Road Map, may lead you to some interesting discoveries. You will often find roads, towns, cemeteries, and waterways are named after nearby landowners: sometimes those names will be the ones you are researching. See how many of these research gems you can find here in Jackson County.

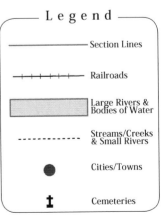

L e g e n d

———————— Section Lines

+‒+‒+‒+‒+‒ Railroads

▨ Large Rivers & Bodies of Water

- - - - - - - Streams/Creeks & Small Rivers

● Cities/Towns

† Cemeteries

Scale: Section = 1 mile X 1 mile
(there are some exceptions)

195

Map Group 20: Index to Land Patents

Township 5-North Range 9-West (Tallahassee)

After you locate an individual in this Index, take note of the Section and Section Part then proceed to the Land Patent map on the pages immediately following. You should have no difficulty locating the corresponding parcel of land.

The "For More Info" Column will lead you to more information about the underlying Patents. See the *Legend* at right, and the "How to Use this Book" chapter, for more information.

ID	Individual in Patent	Sec.	Sec. Part	Date Issued	Other Counties	For More Info . . .
2365	ACOCK, Isaac	6	SENW	1837-04-20		A1
2431	ALLEN, Matthew J	31	E½SW	1844-11-01		A1
2432	" "	31	W½NW	1844-11-01		A1
2433	" "	31	W½SE	1844-11-01		A1
2301	BARNES, Alfred	36	NE	1896-12-11		A2
2446	BELCHER, Richard H	36	SWSE	1904-08-30		A2
2426	BELL, Marmaduke H	3	NENW	1848-04-10		A1
2427	" "	3	NWNW	1848-04-10		A1
2383	BLACKMON, Jesse	13	W½NE	1857-12-01		A1
2310	BLACKSHEAR, David	10	S½SW	1848-11-01		A1
2314	" "	15	E½NW	1848-11-01		A1
2313	" "	15	E½NE	1850-08-10		A1
2316	" "	15	W½NW	1850-08-10		A1
2311	" "	10	W½SE	1852-09-01		A1
2315	" "	15	W½NE	1852-09-01		A1
2312	" "	11	W½SW	1855-05-01		A1
2320	BRYAN, Edward	19	E½NW	1837-04-20		A1
2321	" "	19	SENE	1837-04-20		A1
2322	" "	19	W½NE	1837-04-20		A1
2318	" "	17	SESE	1838-07-28		A1
2319	" "	17	SWSE	1838-07-28		A1
2317	" "	10	N½SW	1846-10-01		A1
2343	BRYAN, Elijah	7	NW	1828-03-01		A1
2342	" "	7	E½SW	1833-05-16		A1
2346	" "	7	W½SW	1833-05-16		A1
2326	" "	17	E½SW	1837-04-15		A1
2327	" "	17	SWSW	1837-04-15		A1
2330	" "	18	W½SE	1837-04-15		A1
2331	" "	19	NENE	1837-04-15		A1
2333	" "	20	NWNW	1837-04-15		A1
2341	" "	7	E½NE	1837-04-15		A1
2344	" "	7	SE	1837-04-15		A1
2345	" "	7	W½NE	1837-04-15		A1
2328	" "	18	NW	1837-04-20		A1
2329	" "	18	NWNE	1837-04-20		A1
2332	" "	19	S½	1837-04-20		A1
2334	" "	20	W½SW	1837-04-20		A1
2349	" "	8	W½NW	1837-04-20		A1
2335	" "	5	E½NW	1838-07-28		A1
2336	" "	5	E½SW	1838-07-28		A1
2337	" "	5	W½NW	1838-07-28		A1
2338	" "	5	W½SW	1838-07-28		A1
2339	" "	6	E½NE	1838-07-28		A1
2340	" "	6	E½SE	1838-07-28		A1
2347	" "	8	E½SW	1842-05-02		A1
2348	" "	8	NWSW	1842-05-02		A1

ID	Individual in Patent	Sec.	Sec. Part	Date Issued	Other Counties	For More Info . . .
2389	BRYAN, John	15	W½SW	1846-10-01		A1
2388	" "	15	E½SW	1855-05-01		A1
2462	BRYAN, William	20	E½NE	1837-04-20		A1
2463	" "	20	NWNE	1837-04-20		A1
2464	" "	20	SENW	1837-04-20		A1
2454	CALHOUN, Seaborn A	25	E½SE	1856-06-16		A1
2455	"	26	SENE	1861-04-09		A1
2440	CANELEY, Philemon	21	NWSW	1837-04-15		A1
2441	" "	21	SESW	1837-04-15		A1
2390	CARTER, John C	28	SW	1828-02-01		A1 G36
2465	CHAMBLESS, William	29	SE	1828-02-01		A1 G40
2303	CLEMENTS, Benjamin	31	E½NE	1827-10-01		A1 G49
2451	COBB, Robert B	31	W½SW	1828-08-22		A1
2442	CONELLY, Philemon	21	NESW	1838-07-28		A1
2443	" "	21	W½SE	1838-07-28		A1
2444	" "	27	W½NW	1843-03-10		A1
2445	CONELY, Philemon	21	SWSW	1837-04-15		A1
2406	DICKERSON, John P	21	SWNE	1846-10-01		A1
2407	DICKINSON, John P	21	NWNE	1846-10-01		A1
2350	DICKSON, Emily B	10	E½SE	1852-09-01		A1
2351	" "	10	NE	1852-09-01		A1
2352	" "	2	SWSW	1852-09-01		A1
2355	" "	3	SESE	1852-09-01		A1
2353	" "	2	W½NW	1855-05-01		A1
2354	" "	3	E½NE	1855-05-01		A1
2429	DICKSON, Marmaduke N	5	W½SE	1846-10-01		A1
2428	" "	5	E½SE	1852-09-01		A1
2471	DURHAM, William T	20	NENW	1837-04-15		A1
2299	EDWARDS, Abram B	20	SWNE	1837-04-15		A1
2300	" "	20	SWNW	1837-04-15		A1
2391	EDWARDS, John	20	E½SW	1837-04-20		A1
2392	" "	21	SWNW	1837-04-20		A1
2393	EDWARDS, John J	18	W½SW	1833-05-16		A1
2394	" "	20	SE	1837-04-20		A1
2395	" "	21	E½NW	1838-07-28		A1
2459	EDWARDS, Thomas W	8	E½SE	1843-03-10		A1
2458	" "	8	E½NE	1846-10-01		A1
2460	" "	9	W½NW	1846-10-01		A1
2461	" "	9	W½SW	1846-10-01		A1
2457	" "	26	NWNE	1852-09-01		A1
2430	EMBREY, Martin T	12	NESE	1855-05-01		A1
2396	GRANBERRY, John M	11	E½SW	1855-05-01		A1
2305	GRAVES, Charles M	24	SE	1859-06-01		A1
2308	HARTSFIELD, Charles N	24	NE	1856-06-16		A1
2307	" "	13	SE	1857-12-01		A1
2302	HARVEY, Alfred R	4	SWNE	1855-05-01		A1
2416	HARVEY, John S	10	E½NW	1846-10-01		A1
2417	" "	3	SWSW	1846-10-01		A1
2453	HARVEY, Sarah	10	NWNW	1846-09-01		A1
2425	HEARN, Laurence H	4	NWNE	1850-08-10		A1
2450	HODGSON, Richard W	3	SWNW	1855-05-01		A1
2438	HOLDER, Nazareth	4	E½NE	1859-06-01		A1
2439	" "	4	E½NW	1859-06-01		A1
2390	KILBEE, William T	28	SW	1828-02-01		A1 G36
2452	LEWIS, Romeo	33	W½SE	1827-09-01		A1 G93
2356	LONG, Felix H	2	NENW	1860-04-02		A1
2357	" "	2	NWSW	1860-04-02		A1
2449	LONG, Richard H	6	W½NW	1838-07-28		A1
2447	" "	6	NENW	1839-09-20		A1
2448	" "	6	NWNE	1839-09-20		A1 F
2409	MADDOX, John P	18	E½NE	1835-10-20		A1
2408	" "	17	W½NW	1837-04-15		A1
2410	" "	8	E½NW	1837-04-20		A1
2412	" "	8	SWSW	1837-04-20		A1
2411	" "	8	NWSE	1838-07-28		A1
2413	MADDUX, John P	8	SWSE	1837-04-20		A1
2414	" "	8	W½NE	1838-07-28		A1
2358	MARTIN, Gibson	18	E½SW	1837-04-15		A1
2359	" "	18	SWNE	1837-04-15		A1
2361	MARTIN, Gipson	17	NESE	1837-04-20		A1
2362	" "	17	SENE	1837-04-20		A1
2363	" "	19	W½NW	1837-04-20		A1
2360	" "	17	NENE	1838-07-28		A1

ID	Individual in Patent	Sec.	Sec. Part	Date Issued	Other Counties	For More Info . . .
2415	MARTIN, John P	17	NWSE	1837-04-20		A1
2306	MATHEWS, Charles	5	W½NE	1846-09-01		A1
2303	MATTHEWS, Charles L	31	E½NE	1827-10-01		A1 G49
2304	" "	31	W½NE	1827-10-01		A1 G100
2309	MCLEROY, Charles S	11	NW	1855-05-01		A1
2456	MCLEROY, Thomas	26	NENE	1855-05-01		A1
2423	MERCER, Joshua	3	NESE	1855-05-01		A1
2424	" "	3	NWSW	1855-05-01		A1
2419	MICHAUX, Joseph T	12	NE	1857-07-01		A1
2420	" "	12	SESE	1857-07-01		A1
2421	" "	12	W½SE	1857-07-01		A1
2422	" "	13	NENE	1857-07-01		A1
2377	MILLS, James	28	NW	1828-09-10		A1
2378	" "	28	SE	1828-09-10		A1
2397	MILTON, John	26	N½SE	1855-05-01		A1
2398	" "	26	NENW	1855-05-01		A1
2399	" "	26	SWSE	1855-05-01		A1
2400	" "	35	N½SE	1855-05-01		A1
2401	" "	35	NESW	1855-05-01		A1
2402	" "	35	SWNE	1855-05-01		A1 R2403
2403	" "	35	SWNE	1855-05-01		A1 R2402
2404	" "	36	E½SE	1856-06-16		A1
2405	" "	36	NWSE	1856-06-16		A1
2379	MURPHY, James S	31	E½SE	1827-04-02		A1
2380	" "	32	SW	1827-06-15		A1 G106
2323	PAYTON, Edward W	31	E½NW	1837-04-15		A1
2472	POWELL, William T	21	E½SE	1844-07-10		A1
2468	RAWLS, William	2	SESW	1852-09-01		A1
2366	ROBINSON, Isaac	34	W½NW	1837-04-20		A1 G127
2367	" "	34	W½SW	1837-04-20		A1 G127
2366	ROBINSON, William H	34	W½NW	1837-04-20		A1 G127
2367	" "	34	W½SW	1837-04-20		A1 G127
2466	" "	27	W½SW	1844-07-10		A1
2467	" "	28	NE	1844-07-10		A1
2469	SILLS, William	1	NE	1859-06-01		A1
2380	SIMMS, Ambrose	32	SW	1827-06-15		A1 G106
2382	SIMMS, Jeremiah	32	NW	1827-04-02		A1
2465	SIMMS, Miles	29	SE	1828-02-01		A1 G40
2470	SIMMS, William	30	SW	1827-06-15		A1
2384	SYFRETT, John A	17	NENW	1837-04-20		A1
2385	" "	17	W½NE	1837-04-20		A1
2386	SYPHRETT, John A	17	NWSW	1835-10-20		A1
2387	" "	17	SENW	1837-04-15		A1
2418	TATUM, John	21	NWNW	1839-09-20		A1
2374	TRAMMEL, James J	6	E½SW	1833-05-16		A1
2373	" "	12	W½NE	1837-04-20		A1 C
2375	" "	6	W½SE	1850-06-03		A1
2381	TRAMMELL, James	18	E½SE	1835-10-20		A1
2376	TRAMMELL, James J	6	W½SW	1828-03-15		A1
2324	WATTS, Eleasur	5	NENE	1846-10-01		A1
2325	WATTS, Eleazar	4	W½NW	1857-07-01		A1
2364	WATTS, Hale	6	SWNE	1838-07-28		A1
2304	WILLIAMSON, Charles	31	W½NE	1827-10-01		A1 G100
2434	WILLIAMSON, Nathan	32	NE	1827-04-02		A1
2435	"	32	SE	1827-04-02		A1
2436	"	33	NW	1827-04-02		A1
2437	"	33	SW	1827-04-02		A1
2369	WIMBERLEY, Isaac	22	SWSW	1846-10-01		A1
2368	" "	22	SESW	1852-09-01		A1
2371	WIMBERLY, Isaac	22	NWSW	1850-08-10		A1
2370	" "	22	NESW	1852-09-01		A1
2473	WIRT, William	33	E½SE	1827-09-01		A1
2474	" "	33	NE	1827-09-01		A1
2452	" "	33	W½SE	1827-09-01		A1 G93
2372	WOODALL, James B	29	SW	1827-04-02		A1

Patent Map

T5-N R9-W
Tallahassee Meridian

Map Group 20

Township Statistics

Parcels Mapped	:	176
Number of Patents	:	158
Number of Individuals	:	81
Patentees Identified	:	78
Number of Surnames	:	60
Multi-Patentee Parcels	:	8
Oldest Patent Date	:	4/2/1827
Most Recent Patent	:	8/30/1904
Block/Lot Parcels	:	0
Parcels Re - Issued	:	1
Parcels that Overlap	:	0
Cities and Towns	:	1
Cemeteries	:	0

Map grid:

Section 6: LONG Richard H 1838; LONG Richard H 1839; LONG Richard H 1839; BRYAN Elijah 1838; ACOCK Isaac 1837; WATTS Hale 1838; TRAMMELL James J 1828; TRAMMEL James J 1833; 6; TRAMMEL James J 1850; BRYAN Elijah 1838

Section 5: BRYAN Elijah 1838; BRYAN Elijah 1838; MATHEWS Charles 1846; WATTS Eleasur 1846; 5; BRYAN Elijah 1838; BRYAN Elijah 1838; DICKSON Marmaduke N 1846; DICKSON Marmaduke N 1852

Section 4: WATTS Eleazar 1857; HOLDER Nazareth 1859; HEARN Laurence H 1850; HARVEY Alfred R 1855; HOLDER Nazareth 1859; 4

Section 7: BRYAN Elijah 1828; BRYAN Elijah 1837; BRYAN Elijah 1837; BRYAN Elijah 1833; BRYAN Elijah 1833; 7; BRYAN Elijah 1837

Section 8: BRYAN Elijah 1837; MADDOX John P 1837; MADDUX John P 1838; 8; BRYAN Elijah 1842; MADDOX John P 1837; BRYAN Elijah 1842; MADDOX John P 1838; MADDUX John P 1837; EDWARDS Thomas W 1843

Section 9: EDWARDS Thomas W 1846; EDWARDS Thomas W 1846; EDWARDS Thomas W 1846; 9

Section 18: BRYAN Elijah 1837; BRYAN Elijah 1837; MADDOX John P 1835; 18; MARTIN Gibson 1837; EDWARDS John J 1833; MARTIN Gibson 1837; BRYAN Elijah 1837; TRAMMELL James 1835

Section 17: MADDOX John P 1837; SYFRETT John A 1837; SYFRETT John A 1837; SYPHRETT John A 1837; 17; SYPHRETT John A 1835; BRYAN Elijah 1837; MARTIN John P 1837; BRYAN Elijah 1837; BRYAN Edward 1838; BRYAN Edward 1838

Section 16: MARTIN Gipson 1838; MARTIN Gipson 1837; 16

Section 19: MARTIN Gipson 1837; BRYAN Edward 1837; BRYAN Edward 1837; BRYAN Elijah 1837; BRYAN Edward 1837; 19; BRYAN Elijah 1837

Section 20: BRYAN Elijah 1837; DURHAM William T 1837; BRYAN William 1837; EDWARDS Abram B 1837; BRYAN William 1837; EDWARDS Abram B 1837; EDWARDS John 1837; BRYAN Elijah 1837; 20; EDWARDS John J 1837; BRYAN William 1837

Section 21: TATUM John 1839; EDWARDS John J 1838; DICKINSON John P 1846; DICKERSON John P 1846; EDWARDS John 1837; CANELEY Philemon 1837; CONELLY Philemon 1838; 21; CONELY Philemon 1837; CONELLY Philemon 1838; CANELEY Philemon 1837; POWELL William T 1844

Section 28: MILLS James 1828; 28; CARTER [36] John C 1828

Section 21 area: ROBINSON William H 1844; MILLS James 1828

Section 30: 30; SIMMS William 1827

Section 29: 29; WOODALL James B 1827

Section 32 area: CHAMBLESS [40] William 1828

Section 31: PAYTON Edward W 1837; MATTHEWS [100] Charles L 1827; CLEMENTS [49] Benjamin 1827; ALLEN Matthew J 1844; 31; COBB Robert B 1828; ALLEN Matthew J 1844; ALLEN Matthew J 1844; MURPHY James S 1827

Section 32: SIMMS Jeremiah 1827; WILLIAMSON Nathan 1827; 32; MURPHY [106] James S 1827; WILLIAMSON Nathan 1827

Section 33: WILLIAMSON Nathan 1827; WIRT William 1827; 33; WILLIAMSON Nathan 1827; LEWIS [93] Romeo 1827; WIRT William 1827

BELL Marmaduke H 1848	BELL Marmaduke H 1848	DICKSON Emily B 1855		LONG Felix H 1860	
HODGSON Richard W 1855			DICKSON Emily B 1855	**2**	SILLS William 1859 **1**
MERCER Joshua 1855	**3**	MERCER Joshua 1855	LONG Felix H 1860		
HARVEY John S 1846		DICKSON Emily B 1852	DICKSON Emily B 1852	RAWLS William 1852	

HARVEY Sarah 1846	HARVEY John S 1846	DICKSON Emily B 1852	MCLEROY Charles S 1855	**11**	TRAMMEL James J 1837 MICHAUX Joseph T 1857
	10				MICHAUX Joseph T 1857 EMBREY Martin T 1855
BRYAN Edward 1846		DICKSON Emily B 1852	GRANBERRY John M 1855	**12**	MICHAUX Joseph T 1857
BLACKSHEAR David 1848	BLACKSHEAR David 1852		BLACKSHEAR David 1855		

BLACKSHEAR David 1850	BLACKSHEAR David 1848	BLACKSHEAR David 1852 BLACKSHEAR David 1850	**14**	BLACKMON Jesse 1857 MICHAUX Joseph T 1857	
	15			**13**	
BRYAN John 1846	BRYAN John 1855			HARTSFIELD Charles N 1857	

			HARTSFIELD Charles N 1856
22	**23**	**24**	
WIMBERLY Isaac 1850	WIMBERLY Isaac 1852		GRAVES Charles M 1859
WIMBERLEY Isaac 1846	WIMBERLEY Isaac 1852		

		MILTON John 1855	EDWARDS Thomas W 1852	MCLEROY Thomas 1855
CONELLY Philemon 1843	**27**		CALHOUN Seaborn A 1861	**25**
		26	MILTON John 1855	
ROBINSON William H 1844			MILTON John 1855	CALHOUN Seaborn A 1856

ROBINSON [127] Isaac 1837	**34**	MILTON John 1855 MILTON John 1855	BARNES Alfred 1896 **36**
ROBINSON [127] Isaac 1837		MILTON John 1855 **35** MILTON John 1855	MILTON John 1856 MILTON John 1856 BELCHER Richard H 1904

Helpful Hints

1. This Map's INDEX can be found on the preceding pages.

2. Refer to Map "C" to see where this Township lies within Jackson County, Florida.

3. Numbers within square brackets [ ] denote a multi-patentee land parcel (multi-owner). Refer to Appendix "C" for a full list of members in this group.

4. Areas that look to be crowded with Patentees usually indicate multiple sales of the same parcel (Re-issues) or Overlapping parcels. See this Township's Index for an explanation of these and other circumstances that might explain "odd" groupings of Patentees on this map.

L e g e n d

————————	Patent Boundary
━━━━━━━━	Section Boundary
▒▒▒▒▒▒	No Patents Found (or Outside County)
1., 2., 3., ...	Lot Numbers (when beside a name)
[ ]	Group Number (see Appendix "C")

Scale: Section = 1 mile X 1 mile
(generally, with some exceptions)

Road Map

T5-N R9-W
Tallahassee Meridian

Map Group 20

Cities & Towns
Chipola Terrace

Cemeteries
None

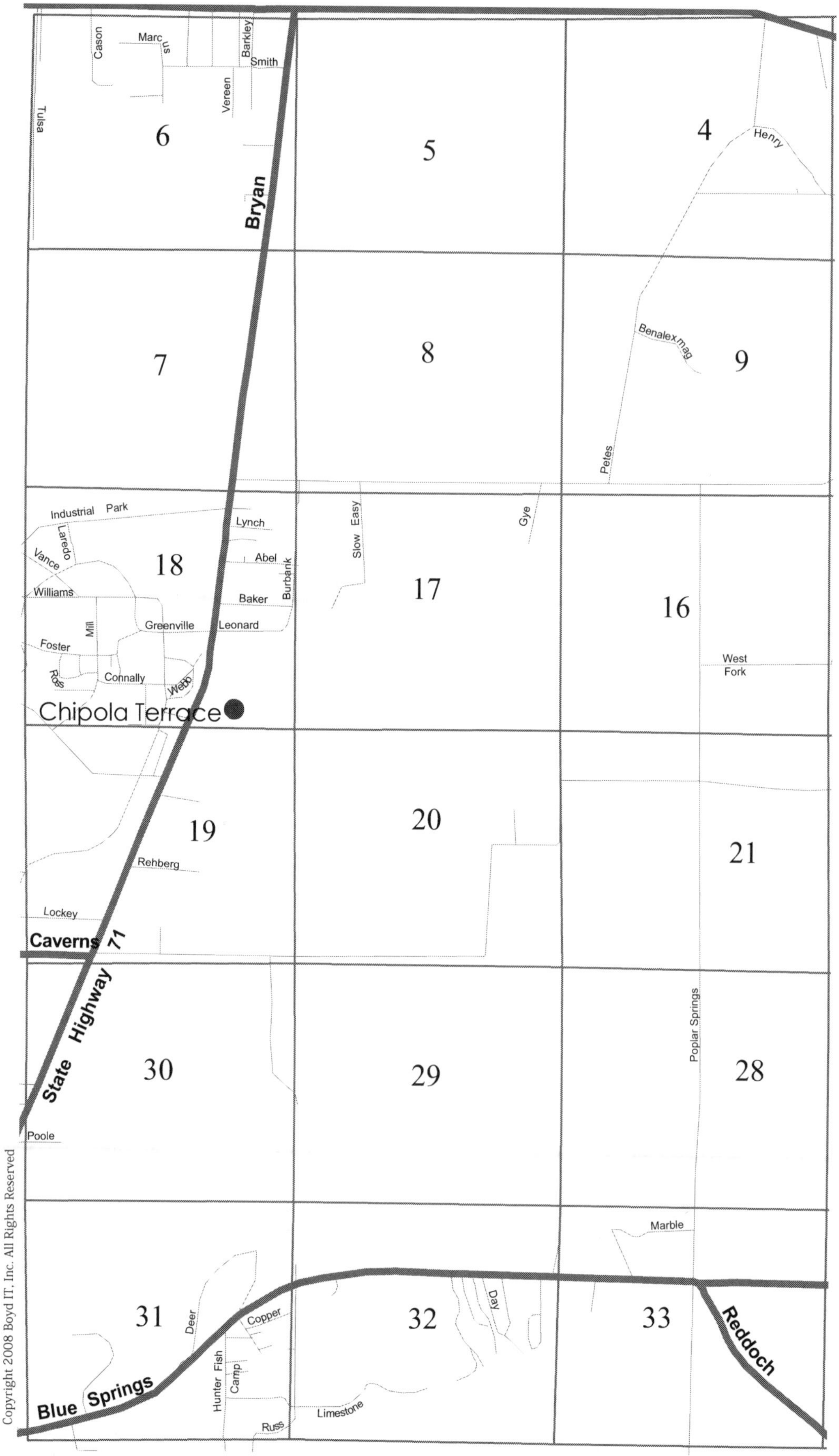

Tulsa

Cason

Marcus

Vereen

Barkley

Smith

6

Bryan

5

4

Henry

7

8

Benalex mag

9

Petes

Industrial Park

Laredo

Vance

Lynch

Abel

Burbank

Baker

Williams

Mill

Greenville

Leonard

Foster

Ross

Connally

Webb

18

Slow Easy

17

Gye

16

West Fork

Chipola Terrace●

19

Rehberg

20

21

Lockey

Caverns

State Highway 71

Poole

30

29

Poplar Springs

28

Copyright 2008 Boyd IT, Inc. All Rights Reserved

Marble

31

Deer

Copper

Hunter Fish Camp

Russ

Blue Springs

Limestone

32

Day

33

Reddoch

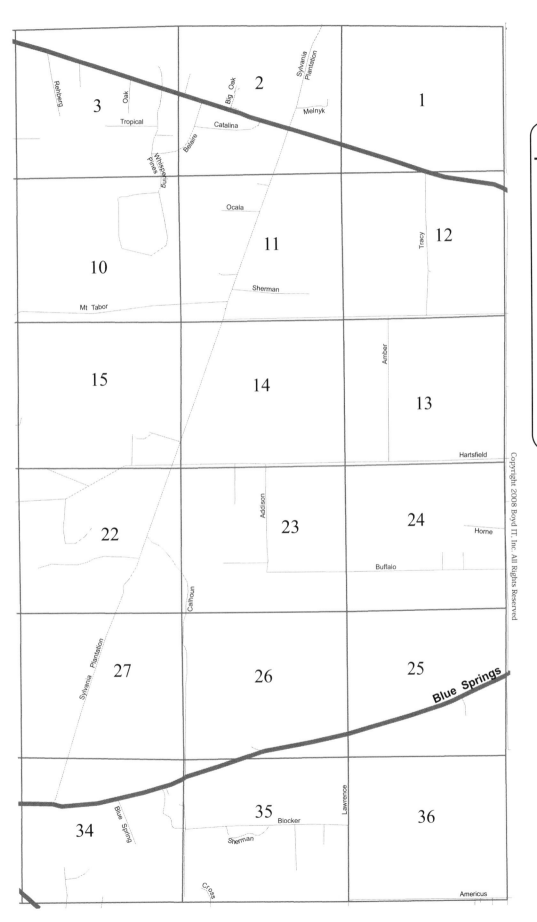

Rehberg

Oak

Big Oak

2

Sylvania Plantation

3

1

Tropical

Catalina

Melnyk

Belaire

Whispering Pines

Ocala

11

Tracy

12

10

Sherman

Mt Tabor

15

14

Amber

13

Hartsfield

Addison

22

23

24

Horne

Calhoun

Buffalo

Sylvania Plantation

27

26

25

Blue Springs

34

Blue Spring

35

Blocker

Lawrence

36

Sherman

Cross

Americus

Helpful Hints

1. This road map has a number of uses, but primarily it is to help you: a) find the present location of land owned by your ancestors (at least the general area), b) find cemeteries and city-centers, and c) estimate the route/roads used by Census-takers & tax-assessors.

2. If you plan to travel to Jackson County to locate cemeteries or land parcels, please pick up a modern travel map for the area before you do. Mapping old land parcels on modern maps is not as exact a science as you might think. Just the slightest variations in public land survey coordinates, estimates of parcel boundaries, or road-map deviations can greatly alter a map's representation of how a road either does or doesn't cross a particular parcel of land.

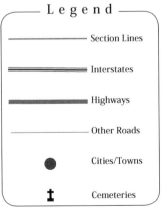

L e g e n d

———————	Section Lines
═══════════	Interstates
▨▨▨▨▨▨▨	Highways
———	Other Roads
●	Cities/Towns
✝	Cemeteries

Scale: Section = 1 mile X 1 mile
(generally, with some exceptions)

Historical Map

T5-N R9-W
Tallahassee Meridian

Map Group 20

Cities & Towns
Chipola Terrace

Cemeteries
None

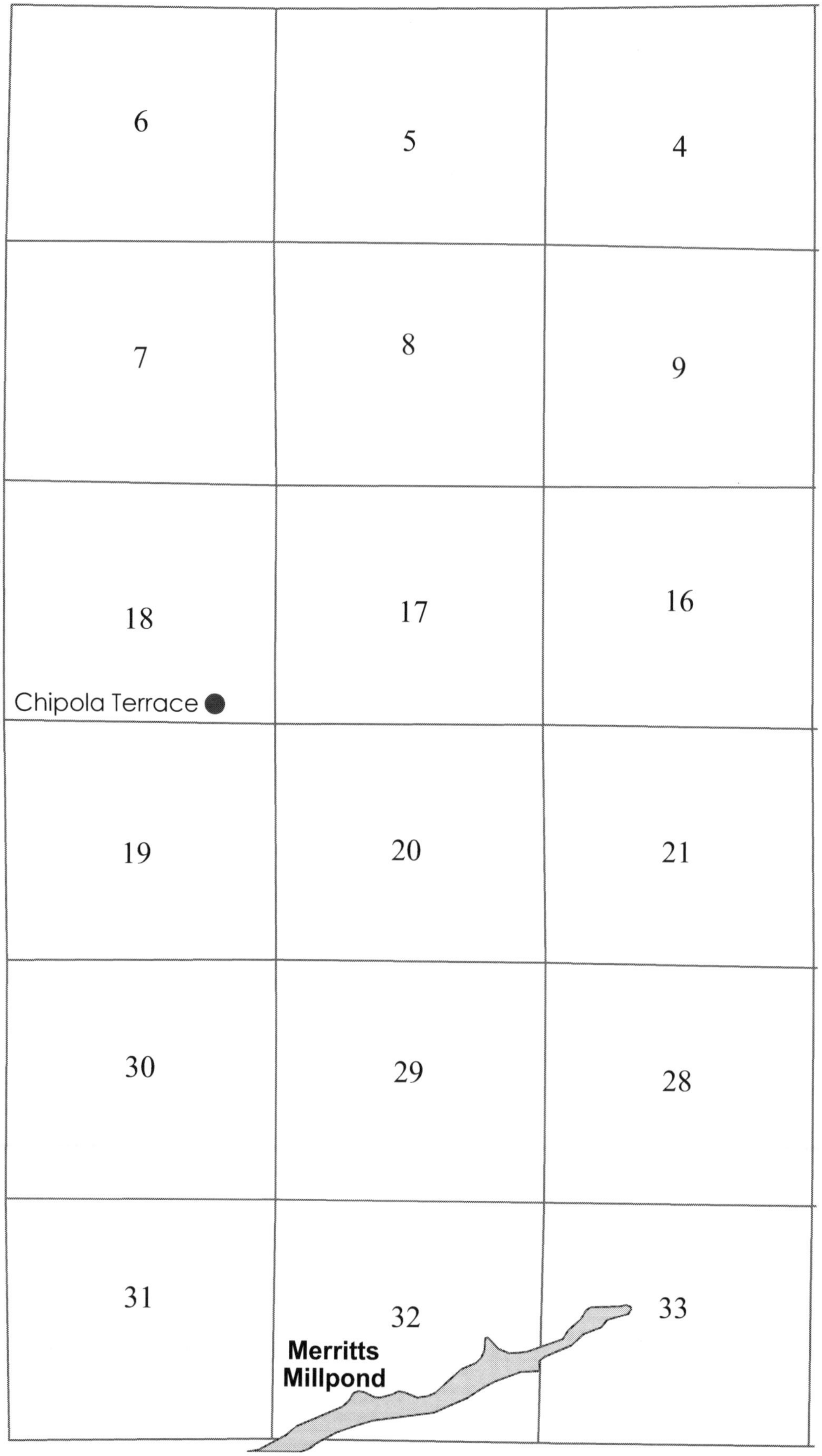

6	5	4
7	8	9
18	17	16
19	20	21
30	29	28
31	32	33

Chipola Terrace ●

Merritts Millpond

3	2	1
10	11	12
15	14	13
22	23	24
27	26	25
34	35	36

Helpful Hints

1. This Map takes a different look at the same Congressional Township displayed in the preceding two maps. It presents features that can help you better envision the historical development of the area: a) Water-bodies (lakes & ponds), b) Water-courses (rivers, streams, etc.), c) Railroads, d) City/town center-points (where they were oftentimes located when first settled), and e) Cemeteries.

   Using this "Historical" map in
2. tandem with this Township's Patent Map and Road Map, may lead you to some interesting discoveries. You will often find roads, towns, cemeteries, and waterways are named after nearby landowners: sometimes those names will be the ones you are researching. See how many of these research gems you can find here in Jackson County.

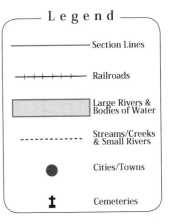

Legend

— Section Lines

+++++ Railroads

Large Rivers & Bodies of Water

- - - - - Streams/Creeks & Small Rivers

● Cities/Towns

✝ Cemeteries

Scale: Section = 1 mile X 1 mile
(there are some exceptions)

Map Group 21: Index to Land Patents

Township 5-North Range 8-West (Tallahassee)

After you locate an individual in this Index, take note of the Section and Section Part then proceed to the Land Patent map on the pages immediately following. You should have no difficulty locating the corresponding parcel of land.

The "For More Info" Column will lead you to more information about the underlying Patents. See the *Legend* at right, and the "How to Use this Book" chapter, for more information.

```
                    LEGEND
          "For More Info . . . " column
A = Authority (Legislative Act, See Appendix "A")
B = Block or Lot (location in Section unknown)
C = Cancelled Patent
F = Fractional Section
G = Group (Multi-Patentee Patent, see Appendix "C")
V = Overlaps another Parcel
R = Re-Issued (Parcel patented more than once)

(A & G items require you to look in the Appendixes referred
to above. All other Letter-designations followed by a number
require you to locate line-items in this index that possess
the ID number found after the letter).
```

ID	Individual in Patent	Sec.	Sec. Part	Date Issued	Other Counties	For More Info . . .
2523	ALLEN, Francis T	20	N½NE	1857-12-01		A1
2580	ALLEN, John W	8	NW	1891-11-09		A2
2587	ALLEN, Joseph T	8	W½NE	1896-08-06		A2
2612	ARNOLD, Sterling	29	W½NW	1852-09-01		A1
2611	" "	29	NWSW	1855-05-01		A1
2613	ARNOLD, Sturling	29	SWSW	1856-06-16		A1
2614	" "	30	N½SE	1856-06-16		A1
2615	" "	30	S½NE	1856-06-16		A1
2484	BAIRD, Benjamin C	12	SENW	1856-06-16		A1
2485	" "	12	SWNE	1856-06-16		A1
2486	" "	12	W½SE	1856-06-16		A1
2503	BASFORD, Chesterfield	28	NWSE	1899-08-14		A2
2562	BASFORD, John	28	NWSW	1857-07-01		A1
2563	" "	28	S½NW	1857-07-01		A1
2564	" "	29	NESE	1857-07-01		A1
2561	" "	28	NESW	1882-08-25		A2
2581	BASFORD, John W	26	N½NE	1903-03-17		A2
2582	" "	26	NESE	1903-03-17		A2
2583	" "	26	SENE	1903-03-17		A2
2577	BAZZELL, John T	3	NWNW	1855-05-01		A1
2578	" "	4	NENE	1859-06-01		A1
2579	" "	4	NWNW	1860-10-01		A1
2538	BLACKMAN, Jack B	30	S½SE	1903-06-26		A2
2633	BOROUM, William	11	N½NW	1856-06-16		A1
2639	" "	9	NESW	1856-06-16		A1
2640	" "	9	NW	1856-06-16		A1
2641	" "	9	SE	1856-06-16		A1
2642	" "	9	SWNE	1856-06-16		A1
2634	" "	2	E½SW	1857-12-01		A1
2635	" "	2	S½NE	1857-12-01		A1
2636	" "	2	SENW	1857-12-01		A1
2637	" "	2	SWSW	1857-12-01		A1
2638	" "	2	W½SE	1857-12-01		A1
2568	BROGDEN, John D	2	E½SE	1895-02-14		A2
2631	BRYAN, Webb	36	W½SE	1901-12-30		A2
2643	BRYAN, William	17	N½SE	1857-07-01		A1
2644	" "	17	SW	1857-07-01		A1
2645	" "	20	N½NW	1857-07-01		A1
2610	BURNES, Simeon	9	NWNE	1856-06-16		A1
2607	" "	10	NENW	1857-12-01		A1
2608	" "	10	W½NW	1857-12-01		A1
2609	" "	9	NENE	1857-12-01		A1
2497	BURNS, Benjamin M	8	E½NE	1857-07-01		A1
2498	" "	8	SE	1857-07-01		A1
2617	CAIN, Thomas J	7	E½SW	1857-07-01		A1
2618	" "	7	NW	1857-07-01		A1

ID	Individual in Patent	Sec.	Sec. Part	Date Issued	Other Counties	For More Info . . .
2540	CLOUD, James	11	NESW	1856-06-16		A1
2541	" "	11	NWSE	1856-06-16		A1
2542	" "	11	W½NE	1856-06-16		A1
2566	CLOUD, John	21	SENE	1856-06-16		A1
2565	" "	21	N½SE	1857-12-01		A1
2567	" "	22	SWNW	1860-04-02		A1
2652	CLOUD, Zachariah	2	N½NE	1891-04-22		A2
2653	" "	2	NENW	1891-04-22		A2
2504	COBB, Christopher C	13	E½SW	1857-07-01		A1
2505	" "	13	SWSE	1857-07-01		A1
2506	" "	24	N½NE	1857-07-01		A1
2507	" "	24	NENW	1857-07-01		A1
2508	" "	24	W½NW	1857-07-01		A1
2543	COOK, James	19	SESE	1857-07-01		A1
2632	COULTER, Wiley H	22	NWSW	1857-12-01		A1
2592	DAVIS, Louis A	36	NE	1905-05-26		A2
2593	EMBREY, Martin T	7	NWSW	1855-05-01		A1
2646	FULGHAM, William E	31	SESE	1857-07-01		A1
2647	" "	32	NWSW	1857-07-01		A1
2654	GRANT, Zachariah	12	E½SW	1860-04-02		A1
2655	" "	12	NWSW	1860-04-02		A1
2656	" "	12	SWNW	1860-04-02		A1 R2600
2572	GRAY, John P	32	NESW	1893-01-21		A2
2573	" "	32	W½SE	1893-01-21		A2
2601	GREEN, Rufus L	4	SWSW	1909-09-20		A2
2518	HAMILTON, Elijah	34	N½SE	1903-08-17		A2
2519	" "	34	SWNE	1903-08-17		A2
2590	HAMILTON, Levi	22	NESW	1860-04-02		A1
2589	" "	22	E½NW	1860-07-02		A1
2657	HAMILTON, Zachariah	34	N½SW	1883-08-13		A2
2658	" "	34	S½NW	1883-08-13		A2
2659	HAMILTON, Zack	34	N½NW	1897-07-03		A2
2525	HARPER, Henry	20	NWSE	1857-12-01		A1
2649	HATCHER, William G	32	NENE	1902-01-17		A2
2522	HEWETT, Esther	21	SENW	1852-09-01		A1
2536	HEWETT, Isabel	21	S½SE	1857-07-01		A1
2537	" "	28	NENE	1857-07-01		A1
2483	HINSON, Augustine W	26	SESE	1856-06-16		A1
2524	HINSON, Hadley	27	NESE	1855-05-01		A1
2594	JACKSON, Martin V	22	E½SE	1890-04-29		A2
2595	" "	22	W½SE	1907-04-17		A2
2597	JACKSON, Robert A	18	NWSE	1856-06-16		A1
2598	" "	18	SESW	1856-06-16		A1
2599	" "	18	SWNE	1856-06-16		A1
2499	JONES, Benjamin P	22	NWNW	1897-09-20		A2
2616	JUSTISS, Thomas E	20	S½NE	1896-01-03		A2
2648	KILCREASE, William E	26	SWNW	1852-09-01		A1
2480	KNOWLES, Alfred S	6	N½	1857-07-01		A1
2651	KNOWLES, William K	6	S½	1857-07-01		A1
2621	LEONARD, Thomas	18	E½NE	1856-06-16		A1
2622	" "	18	E½NW	1856-06-16		A1
2623	" "	18	NESE	1856-06-16		A1
2624	" "	18	NWNE	1856-06-16		A1
2625	" "	18	NWNW	1856-06-16		A1
2626	" "	7	SWSW	1856-06-16		A1
2500	LEWIS, Buck	36	SW	1901-04-09		A2
2520	LEWIS, Ella F	28	SESW	1895-06-17		A2
2521	" "	28	SWSE	1895-06-17		A2
2544	LEWIS, James D	28	SWSW	1898-05-12		A2
2588	LEWIS, Joshua	36	E½SE	1899-05-12		A2
2596	MCDONALD, Peter N	33	NENW	1857-12-01		A1
2571	MESSER, John	20	SWNW	1897-01-23		A2
2512	MITCHELL, David	24	E½SE	1902-07-03		A2
2513	" "	24	SENE	1902-07-03		A2
2514	" "	24	SWSE	1902-07-03		A2
2627	MITCHELL, Thomas	8	SW	1896-04-27		A2
2591	MONEYHAM, Lewis	20	E½SE	1860-07-02		A1
2487	NEEL, Benjamin H	32	E½SE	1856-06-16		A1
2488	" "	33	N½SW	1856-06-16		A1
2489	" "	33	S½NW	1856-06-16		A1
2490	" "	33	SWSW	1856-06-16		A1
2509	NEEL, Daniel B	34	S½SW	1892-05-26		A2
2510	" "	34	SWSE	1906-02-17		A1

ID	Individual in Patent	Sec.	Sec. Part	Date Issued	Other Counties	For More Info . . .
2511	NEEL, Daniel O	24	NWSE	1909-09-20		A2
2619	NEEL, Thomas J	36	NW	1900-01-27		A2
2475	NICKELS, Alfred	15	NESW	1857-12-01		A1
2476	" "	15	NWSE	1857-12-01		A1
2477	" "	15	SENE	1857-12-01		A1
2478	" "	15	W½NE	1857-12-01		A1
2479	" "	15	W½SW	1857-12-01		A1
2501	OWENS, Charles C	24	SW	1903-05-25		A2
2502	PARKER, Charley	12	NWNW	1903-05-25		A2
2534	PERKINS, Isaac	19	NENW	1859-06-01		A1
2535	" "	19	W½NW	1859-06-01		A1
2556	PURVIS, Jesse	14	NENW	1856-06-16		A1
2557	" "	14	SESW	1856-06-16		A1
2558	" "	14	W½NE	1856-06-16		A1
2559	" "	14	W½NW	1856-06-16		A1
2560	" "	14	W½SW	1856-06-16		A1
2570	RABOURN, John L	10	SENW	1859-06-01		A1
2586	RABOURN, Jordan	17	S½SE	1857-07-01		A1
2545	ROBERTS, James G	18	S½SE	1860-04-02		A1
2630	ROBINSON, Walter J	35	SESE	1855-05-01		A1
2650	ROBINSON, William H	26	W½SW	1829-05-15		A1
2529	RUSK, Hugh	26	E½NW	1857-12-01		A1
2530	" "	26	E½SW	1857-12-01		A1
2531	" "	26	NWNW	1857-12-01		A1
2532	" "	26	SWNE	1857-12-01		A1
2533	" "	26	W½SE	1857-12-01		A1
2603	SCOTT, Samuel	2	W½NW	1882-08-25		A2
2602	" "	2	NWSW	1898-04-27		A2
2481	SELLERS, Asbury	29	NWNE	1848-11-01		A1
2482	" "	29	SWNE	1852-09-01		A1
2526	SELLERS, Henry L	21	SWNE	1856-06-16		A1
2527	" "	28	NENW	1857-12-01		A1
2528	" "	28	W½NE	1857-12-01		A1
2574	SELLERS, John	21	SW	1856-06-16		A1
2575	" "	22	SENE	1859-06-01		A1
2576	" "	22	W½NE	1859-06-01		A1
2569	SELLERS, John F	27	SENE	1855-05-01		A1
2515	SHACKELFORD, Edward	13	W½SW	1857-12-01		A1
2516	" "	14	SE	1857-12-01		A1
2517	" "	23	N½NE	1857-12-01		A1
2604	SHARP, Samuel	14	NESW	1885-06-20		A2
2605	" "	14	SENW	1885-06-20		A2
2539	SIMMONS, James A	32	NW	1857-07-01		A1
2620	SUMMERS, Thomas J	22	SESW	1859-06-01		A1
2546	SWEET, James L	4	E½NW	1860-07-02		A1
2547	" "	4	E½SW	1860-07-02		A1
2548	" "	4	W½NE	1860-07-02		A1
2606	THARP, Samuel	14	E½NE	1899-08-30		A2
2628	TOOLE, Thomas	4	NWSW	1897-01-21		A2
2629	" "	4	SWNW	1897-01-21		A2
2491	TURNER, Benjamin L	27	NWSW	1856-06-16		A1
2492	" "	28	E½SE	1857-12-01		A1
2493	" "	33	E½NE	1857-12-01		A1
2494	" "	33	E½SE	1857-12-01		A1
2495	" "	33	NWSE	1857-12-01		A1
2496	" "	33	SWNE	1857-12-01		A1
2600	WARDLOW, Romulus	12	SWNW	1903-05-25		A2 R2656
2551	WILCOX, James	19	NESE	1856-06-16		A1
2552	" "	20	NWSW	1856-06-16		A1
2553	" "	30	N½NE	1860-04-02		A1
2554	WILEY, James	20	NESW	1856-06-16		A1
2555	" "	20	SENW	1856-06-16		A1
2549	WOOD, James S	7	N½SE	1857-07-01		A1
2550	" "	7	NE	1857-07-01		A1
2584	YOUNG, John	24	SENW	1896-01-03		A2
2585	" "	24	SWNE	1896-01-03		A2

Patent Map

T5-N R8-W
Tallahassee Meridian

Map Group 21

Township Statistics

Parcels Mapped	:	185
Number of Patents	:	114
Number of Individuals	:	90
Patentees Identified	:	90
Number of Surnames	:	63
Multi-Patentee Parcels	:	0
Oldest Patent Date	:	5/15/1829
Most Recent Patent	:	9/20/1909
Block/Lot Parcels	:	0
Parcels Re - Issued	:	1
Parcels that Overlap	:	0
Cities and Towns	:	2
Cemeteries	:	2

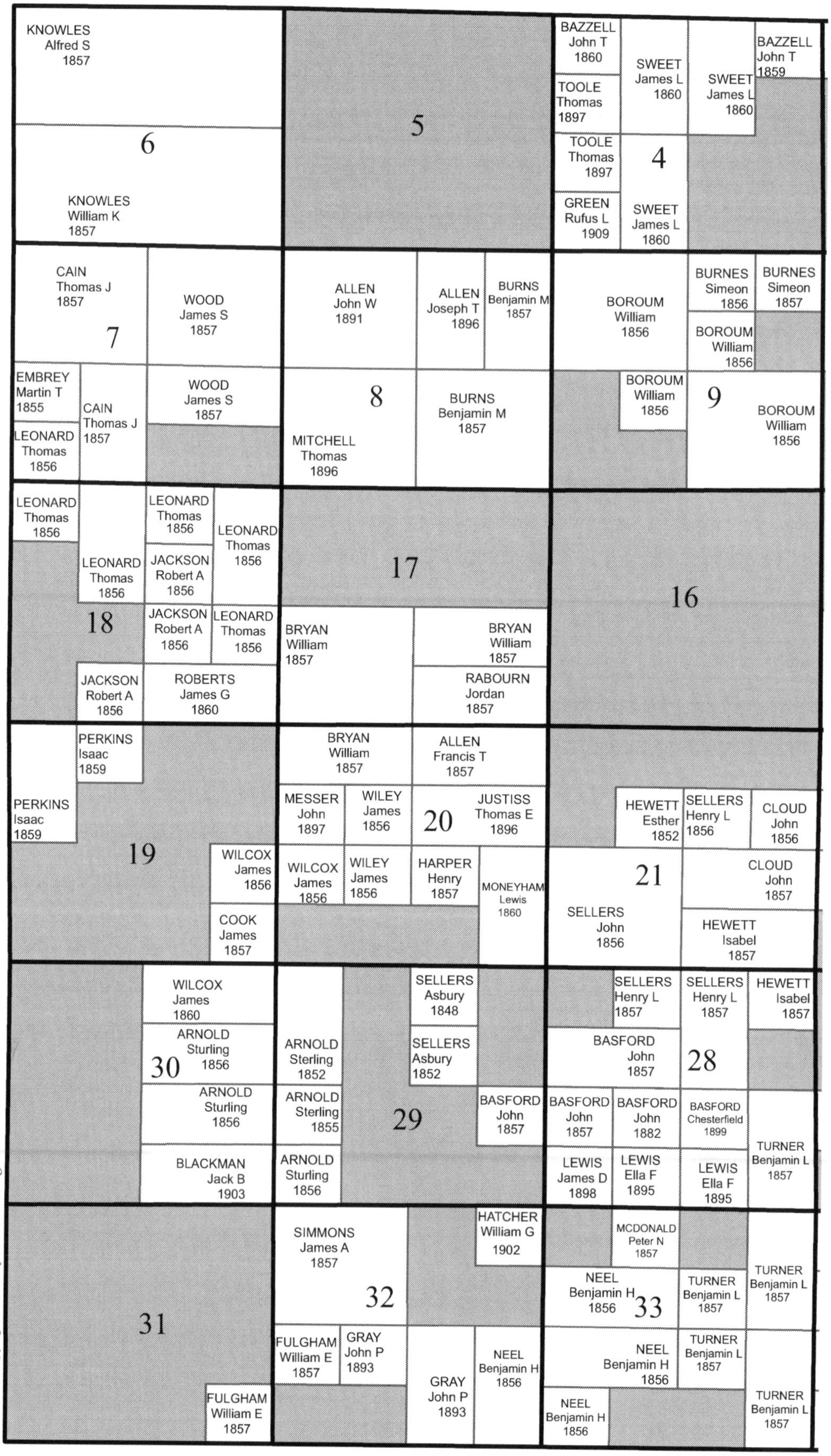

KNOWLES Alfred S 1857
6
KNOWLES William K 1857
5
BAZZELL John T 1860
TOOLE Thomas 1897
SWEET James L 1860
SWEET James L 1860
BAZZELL John T 1859
TOOLE Thomas 1897
4
GREEN Rufus L 1909
SWEET James L 1860
CAIN Thomas J 1857
WOOD James S 1857
7
EMBREY Martin T 1855
CAIN Thomas J 1857
WOOD James S 1857
LEONARD Thomas 1856
ALLEN John W 1891
ALLEN Joseph T 1896
BURNS Benjamin M 1857
8
MITCHELL Thomas 1896
BURNS Benjamin M 1857
BOROUM William 1856
BURNES Simeon 1856
BURNES Simeon 1857
BOROUM William 1856
BOROUM William 1856
9
BOROUM William 1856
LEONARD Thomas 1856
LEONARD Thomas 1856
LEONARD Thomas 1856
LEONARD Thomas 1856
JACKSON Robert A 1856
18
JACKSON Robert A 1856
LEONARD Thomas 1856
JACKSON Robert A 1856
ROBERTS James G 1860
17
BRYAN William 1857
BRYAN William 1857
RABOURN Jordan 1857
16
PERKINS Isaac 1859
PERKINS Isaac 1859
19
WILCOX James 1856
COOK James 1857
BRYAN William 1857
ALLEN Francis T 1857
MESSER John 1897
WILEY James 1856
20
JUSTISS Thomas E 1896
WILCOX James 1856
WILEY James 1856
HARPER Henry 1857
MONEYHAM Lewis 1860
HEWETT Esther 1852
SELLERS Henry L 1856
CLOUD John 1856
21
CLOUD John 1857
SELLERS John 1856
HEWETT Isabel 1857
WILCOX James 1860
ARNOLD Sturling 1856
30
ARNOLD Sturling 1856
BLACKMAN Jack B 1903
ARNOLD Sterling 1852
ARNOLD Sterling 1855
ARNOLD Sturling 1856
SELLERS Asbury 1848
SELLERS Asbury 1852
29
BASFORD John 1857
SELLERS Henry L 1857
SELLERS Henry L 1857
HEWETT Isabel 1857
BASFORD John 1857
28
BASFORD John 1857
BASFORD John 1882
BASFORD Chesterfield 1899
LEWIS James D 1898
LEWIS Ella F 1895
LEWIS Ella F 1895
TURNER Benjamin L 1857
31
FULGHAM William E 1857
SIMMONS James A 1857
32
HATCHER William G 1902
FULGHAM William E 1857
GRAY John P 1893
GRAY John P 1893
NEEL Benjamin H 1856
MCDONALD Peter N 1857
NEEL Benjamin H 1856
33
TURNER Benjamin L 1857
TURNER Benjamin L 1857
TURNER Benjamin L 1857
NEEL Benjamin H 1856
NEEL Benjamin H 1856
TURNER Benjamin L 1857

BAZZELL John T 1855	SCOTT Samuel 1882 / CLOUD Zachariah 1891 / CLOUD Zachariah 1891 / BOROUM William 1857 / BOROUM William 1857	
3	SCOTT Samuel 1898 / BOROUM William 1857 / **2** / BROGDEN John D 1895 / BOROUM William 1857	**1**
BOROUM William 1857		

BURNES Simeon 1857 / BURNES Simeon 1857 / RABOURN John L 1859 / **10**

BOROUM William 1856 / **11** / CLOUD James 1856 / CLOUD James 1856 / CLOUD James 1856

PARKER Charley 1903 / **12** / WARDLOW Romulus GRANT1903 Zachariah 1860 / BAIRD Benjamin C 1856 / BAIRD Benjamin C 1856 / GRANT Zachariah 1860 / GRANT Zachariah 1860 / BAIRD Benjamin C 1856

15 / NICKELS Alfred 1857 / NICKELS Alfred 1857 / NICKELS Alfred 1857 / NICKELS Alfred 1857 / NICKELS Alfred 1857

PURVIS Jesse 1856 / PURVIS Jesse 1856 / SHARP Samuel 1885 / PURVIS Jesse 1856 / THARP Samuel 1899 / PURVIS Jesse 1856 / SHARP Samuel 1885 / **14** / PURVIS Jesse 1856 / SHACKELFORD Edward 1857

SHACKELFORD Edward 1857 / COBB Christopher C 1857 / **13** / COBB Christopher C 1857

JONES Benjamin P 1897 / HAMILTON Levi 1860 / SELLERS John 1859 / SELLERS John 1859 / CLOUD John 1860 / COULTER Wiley H 1857 / HAMILTON Levi 1860 / **22** / SUMMERS Thomas J 1859 / JACKSON Martin V 1907 / JACKSON Martin V 1890

SHACKELFORD Edward 1857 / **23**

COBB Christopher C 1857 / COBB Christopher C 1857 / COBB Christopher C 1857 / YOUNG John 1896 / YOUNG John 1896 / MITCHELL David 1902 / **24** / NEEL Daniel O 1909 / MITCHELL David 1902 / OWENS Charles C 1903 / MITCHELL David 1902

27 / SELLERS John F 1855 / KILCREASE William E 1852 / **26** / HINSON Hadley 1855 / TURNER Benjamin L 1856 / ROBINSON William H 1829 / RUSK Hugh 1857 / RUSK Hugh 1857 / RUSK Hugh 1857 / BASFORD John W 1903 / RUSK Hugh 1857 / BASFORD John W 1903 / RUSK Hugh 1857 / BASFORD John W 1903 / HINSON Augustine W 1856

25

HAMILTON Zack 1897 / HAMILTON Zachariah 1883 / **34** / HAMILTON Elijah 1903 / HAMILTON Zachariah 1883 / HAMILTON Elijah 1903 / NEEL Daniel B 1892 / NEEL Daniel B 1906

35 / ROBINSON Walter J 1855

NEEL Thomas J 1900 / DAVIS Louis A 1905 / **36** / LEWIS Buck 1901 / BRYAN Webb 1901 / LEWIS Joshua 1899

Helpful Hints

1. This Map's INDEX can be found on the preceding pages.

2. Refer to Map "C" to see where this Township lies within Jackson County, Florida.

3. Numbers within square brackets [ ] denote a multi-patentee land parcel (multi-owner). Refer to Appendix "C" for a full list of members in this group.

4. Areas that look to be crowded with Patentees usually indicate multiple sales of the same parcel (Re-issues) or Overlapping parcels. See this Township's Index for an explanation of these and other circumstances that might explain "odd" groupings of Patentees on this map.

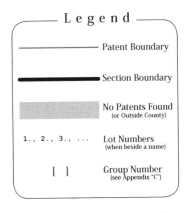

— Legend —

———— Patent Boundary

▬▬▬▬ Section Boundary

░░░░ No Patents Found (or Outside County)

1., 2., 3., ...   Lot Numbers (when beside a name)

[ ]   Group Number (see Appendix "C")

Scale: Section = 1 mile X 1 mile (generally, with some exceptions)

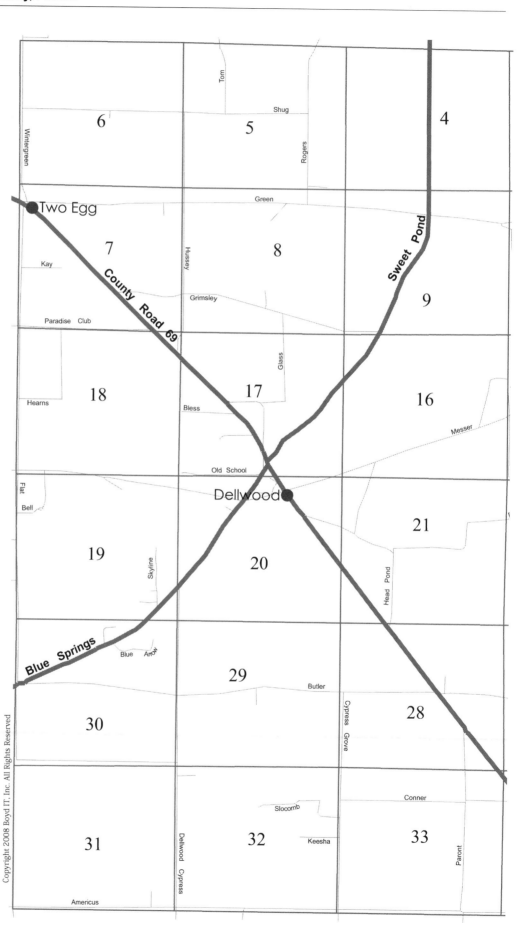

Road Map

T5-N R8-W
Tallahassee Meridian

Map Group 21

Cities & Towns
Dellwood
Two Egg

Cemeteries
Cow Pen Cemetery
Sand Ridge Cemetery

Helpful Hints

1. This road map has a number of uses, but primarily it is to help you: a) find the present location of land owned by your ancestors (at least the general area), b) find cemeteries and city-centers, and c) estimate the route/roads used by Census-takers & tax-assessors.

2. If you plan to travel to Jackson County to locate cemeteries or land parcels, please pick up a modern travel map for the area before you do. Mapping old land parcels on modern maps is not as exact a science as you might think. Just the slightest variations in public land survey coordinates, estimates of parcel boundaries, or road-map deviations can greatly alter a map's representation of how a road either does or doesn't cross a particular parcel of land.

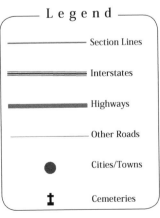

Legend

————	Section Lines
▬▬▬▬	Interstates
▬▬▬▬	Highways
————	Other Roads
●	Cities/Towns
✝	Cemeteries

Scale: Section = 1 mile X 1 mile
(generally, with some exceptions)

Historical Map

T5-N R8-W
Tallahassee Meridian

Map Group 21

Cities & Towns
Dellwood
Two Egg

Cemeteries
Cow Pen Cemetery
Sand Ridge Cemetery

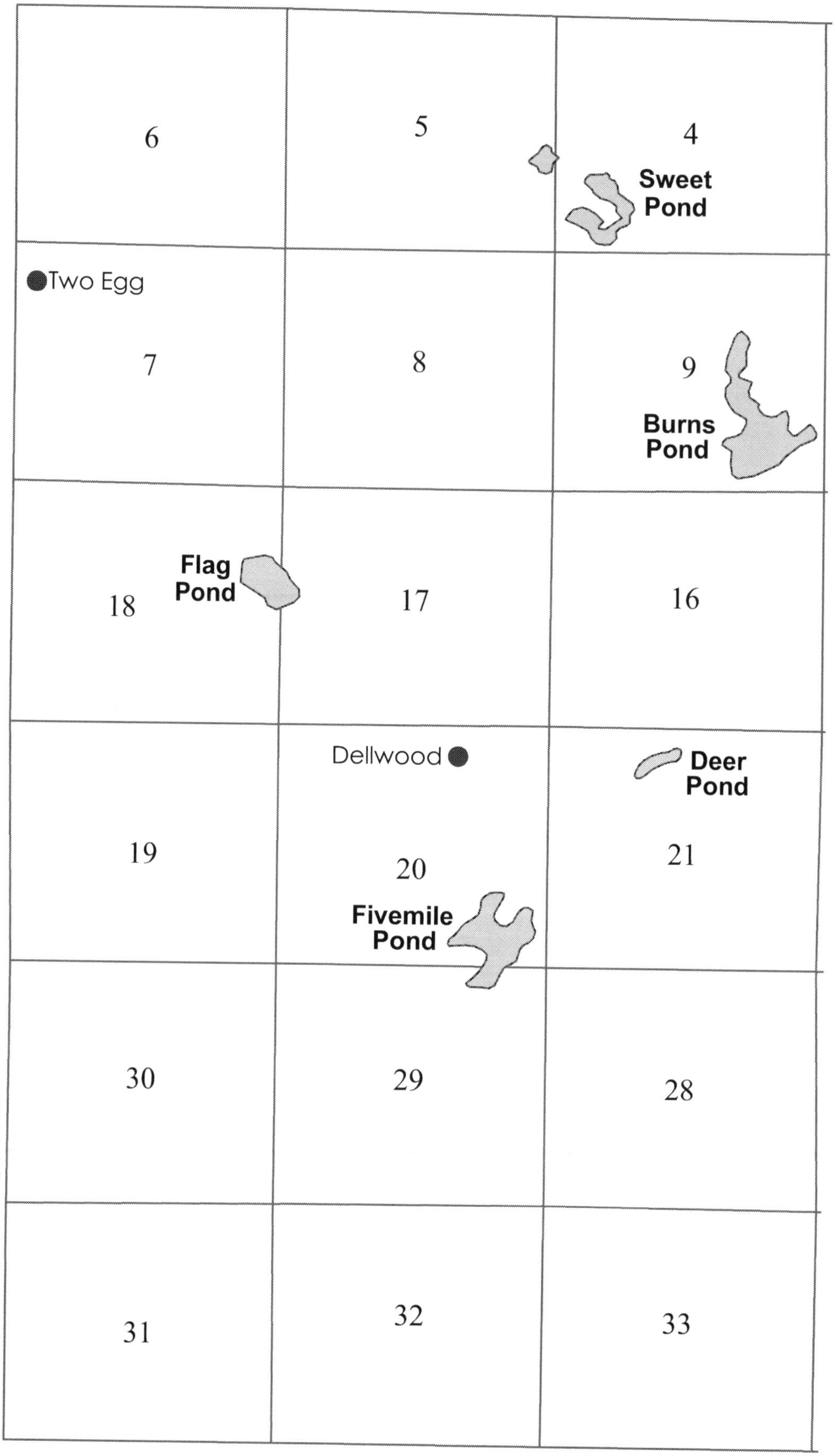

| 6 | 5 | 4 |

Sweet Pond

| ●Two Egg | | |
| 7 | 8 | 9 |

Burns Pond

Flag Pond

| 18 | 17 | 16 |

Dellwood ●

Deer Pond

| 19 | 20 | 21 |

Fivemile Pond

| 30 | 29 | 28 |

| 31 | 32 | 33 |

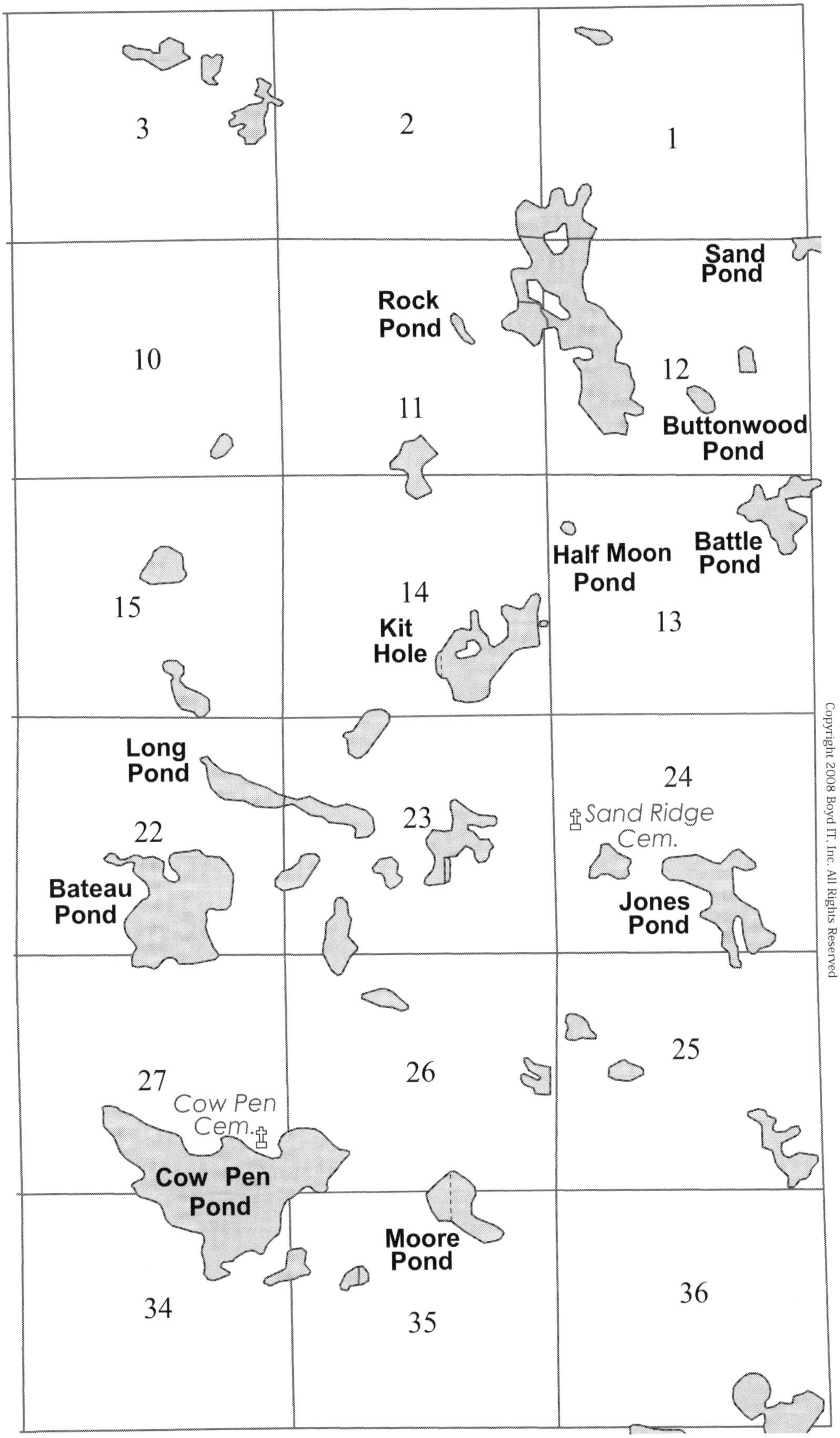
3
2
1
10
Rock Pond
11
12
Sand Pond
Buttonwood Pond
15
14
Kit Hole
Half Moon Pond
Battle Pond
13
Long Pond
22
Bateau Pond
23
24
Sand Ridge Cem.
Jones Pond
27
Cow Pen Cem.
Cow Pen Pond
26
25
34
Moore Pond
35
36

Helpful Hints

1. This Map takes a different look at the same Congressional Township displayed in the preceding two maps. It presents features that can help you better envision the historical development of the area: a) Water-bodies (lakes & ponds), b) Water-courses (rivers, streams, etc.), c) Railroads, d) City/town center-points (where they were oftentimes located when first settled), and e) Cemeteries.
2. Using this "Historical" map in tandem with this Township's Patent Map and Road Map, may lead you to some interesting discoveries. You will often find roads, towns, cemeteries, and waterways are named after nearby landowners: sometimes those names will be the ones you are researching. See how many of these research gems you can find here in Jackson County.

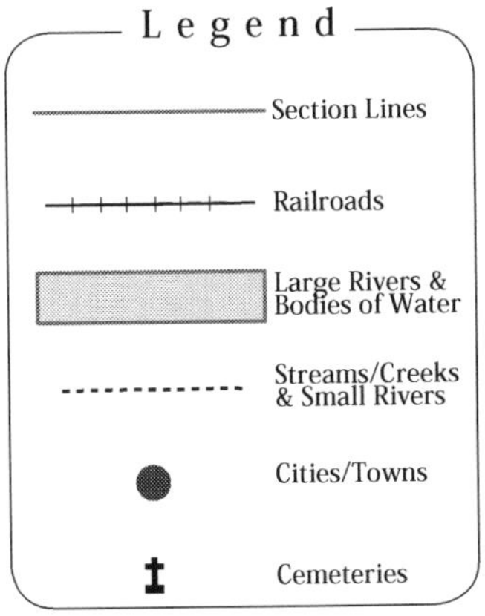
Legend
Section Lines
Railroads
Large Rivers & Bodies of Water
Streams/Creeks & Small Rivers
Cities/Towns
Cemeteries

Scale: Section = 1 mile X 1 mile
(there are some exceptions)

Map Group 22: Index to Land Patents

Township 5-North Range 7-West (Tallahassee)

After you locate an individual in this Index, take note of the Section and Section Part then proceed to the Land Patent map on the pages immediately following. You should have no difficulty locating the corresponding parcel of land.

The "For More Info" Column will lead you to more information about the underlying Patents. See the *Legend* at right, and the "How to Use this Book" chapter, for more information.

```
                          LEGEND
                "For More Info . . . " column
 A = Authority (Legislative Act, See Appendix "A")
 B = Block or Lot (location in Section unknown)
 C = Cancelled Patent
 F = Fractional Section
 G = Group  (Multi-Patentee Patent, see Appendix "C")
 V = Overlaps another Parcel
 R = Re-Issued (Parcel patented more than once)

 (A & G items require you to look in the Appendixes referred
 to above. All other Letter-designations followed by a number
 require you to locate line-items in this index that possess
 the ID number found after the letter).
```

ID	Individual in Patent	Sec.	Sec. Part	Date Issued	Other Counties	For More Info . . .
2714	ALLEN, Richard C	34	1	1830-11-01		A1
2718	BALTZELL, Thomas	5	E½NE	1837-04-20		A1
2720	" "	5	NWSW	1837-04-20		A1
2721	" "	5	SE	1837-04-20		A1
2719	" "	5	NESW	1838-07-28		A1
2722	" "	5	W½NE	1838-07-28		A1
2693	BIRD, Irwin	17	5	1856-06-16		A1
2694	" "	20	2	1856-06-16		A1
2695	" "	20	5	1856-06-16		A1
2696	" "	20	N½4	1856-06-16		A1
2697	" "	20	S½1	1856-06-16		A1
2698	" "	29	N½2	1856-06-16		A1
2699	BROWN, Isaac	17	3	1830-11-01		A1
2709	BROWN, Leavin	17	6	1838-07-28		A1 F
2708	" "	17	1	1841-01-09		A1 F
2715	BRUTON, Robert B	18	E½SW	1897-10-20		A2
2716	"	18	NWSE	1897-10-20		A2
2729	COMPTON, William W	17	4	1857-12-01		A1
2730	" "	18	E½SE	1857-12-01		A1
2731	" "	18	S½NE	1857-12-01		A1
2732	" "	18	SWSE	1857-12-01		A1
2733	" "	19	NENE	1857-12-01		A1
2717	GRACE, Samuel	8	S½4	1909-01-11		A2
2711	GRANGER, Lucretia N	18	W½SW	1905-11-24		A2
2710	HAIR, Leutisia	20	S½3	1855-05-01		A1
2661	HAMILTON, David	4	2	1830-11-01		A1
2662	" "	9	1	1830-11-01		A1
2701	HAMILTON, Joel	8	3	1833-05-16		A1
2723	HARE, Thomas	33	6	1850-08-10		A1
2724	" "	33	7	1850-08-10		A1
2663	HAYWOOD, Francis P	17	8	1852-09-01		A1
2668	" "	8	7	1852-09-01		A1
2664	" "	7	E½NE	1855-05-01		A1
2665	" "	7	E½NW	1856-06-16		A1
2666	" "	7	W½NE	1856-06-16		A1
2667	" "	8	6	1856-06-16		A1
2669	" "	8	N½4	1856-06-16		A1
2670	" "	8	S½2	1856-06-16		A1
2676	HINSON, Hadley	29	7	1852-09-01		A1
2677	" "	29	8	1852-09-01		A1
2671	" "	19	SESW	1855-05-01		A1
2672	" "	19	SWSE	1855-05-01		A1
2673	" "	20	S½4	1855-05-01		A1
2674	" "	29	5	1855-05-01		A1
2675	" "	29	6	1855-05-01		A1
2678	" "	29	S½4	1855-05-01		A1

ID	Individual in Patent	Sec.	Sec. Part	Date Issued	Other Counties	For More Info . . .
2679	HINSON, Hadley (Cont'd)	30	NE	1855-05-01		A1
2681	" "	30	NWSE	1855-05-01		A1
2682	" "	30	S½SE	1855-05-01		A1
2680	" "	30	NESE	1859-06-01		A1
2725	KING, Thomas	5	SWNW	1844-07-10		A1
2726	" "	6	SENE	1844-07-10		A1
2660	KOONCE, Collins	18	N½NE	1908-10-29		A2
2704	MALONEY, John	33	1	1830-11-01		A1
2705	" "	33	2	1830-11-01		A1
2706	" "	33	5	1830-11-01		A1
2712	NASH, Peter	30	NESW	1910-09-01		A2
2702	RAINS, John M	20	6	1856-06-16		A1
2703	" "	20	7	1856-06-16		A1
2683	RASK, Hugh	20	N½1	1850-08-10		A1
2700	ROBINSON, James H	32	NWNW	1903-12-17		A2
2727	ROBINSON, Walter J	31	SWNE	1855-05-01		A1
2738	ROYAL, Wilson	4	1	1828-02-01		A1 G129
2685	RUSK, Hugh	21	1	1848-02-07		A1
2686	" "	21	2	1848-02-07		A1
2687	" "	21	3	1848-02-07		A1
2688	" "	5	8	1848-11-01		A1
2689	" "	9	2	1850-08-10		A1
2690	" "	9	3	1850-08-10		A1
2691	" "	9	4	1850-08-10		A1
2692	" "	9	5	1850-08-10		A1
2684	" "	17	7	1852-09-01		A1
2738	SANBURN, Ira	4	1	1828-02-01		A1 G129
2707	SAXON, Joseph T	9	SW	1850-08-10		A1
2728	SHERMAN, William	30	S½SW	1900-09-07		A2
2713	WOOD, Priscilla	20	N½3	1852-09-01		A1
2734	YARBROUGH, William	19	E½SE	1857-12-01		A1
2735	" "	19	NESW	1857-12-01		A1
2736	" "	19	NWSE	1857-12-01		A1
2737	" "	19	W½SW	1857-12-01		A1

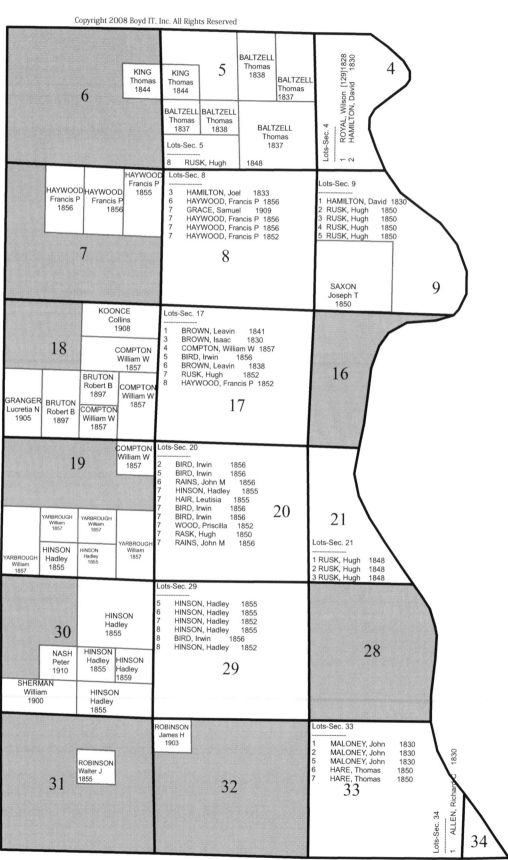

Patent Map

T5-N R7-W
Tallahassee Meridian

Map Group 22

Township Statistics

Parcels Mapped	:	79
Number of Patents	:	56
Number of Individuals	:	30
Patentees Identified	:	29
Number of Surnames	:	27
Multi-Patentee Parcels	:	1
Oldest Patent Date	:	2/1/1828
Most Recent Patent	:	9/1/1910
Block/Lot Parcels	:	46
Parcels Re - Issued	:	0
Parcels that Overlap	:	0
Cities and Towns	:	2
Cemeteries	:	2

Note: the area contained in this map amounts to far less than a full Township. Therefore, its contents are completely on this single page (instead of a "normal" 2-page spread).

Legend

—————— Patent Boundary

━━━━━━ Section Boundary

░░░░░░ No Patents Found
(or Outside County)

1., 2., 3., ... Lot Numbers
(when beside a name)

[ ] Group Number
(see Appendix "C")

Scale: Section = 1 mile X 1 mile
(generally, with some exceptions)

218

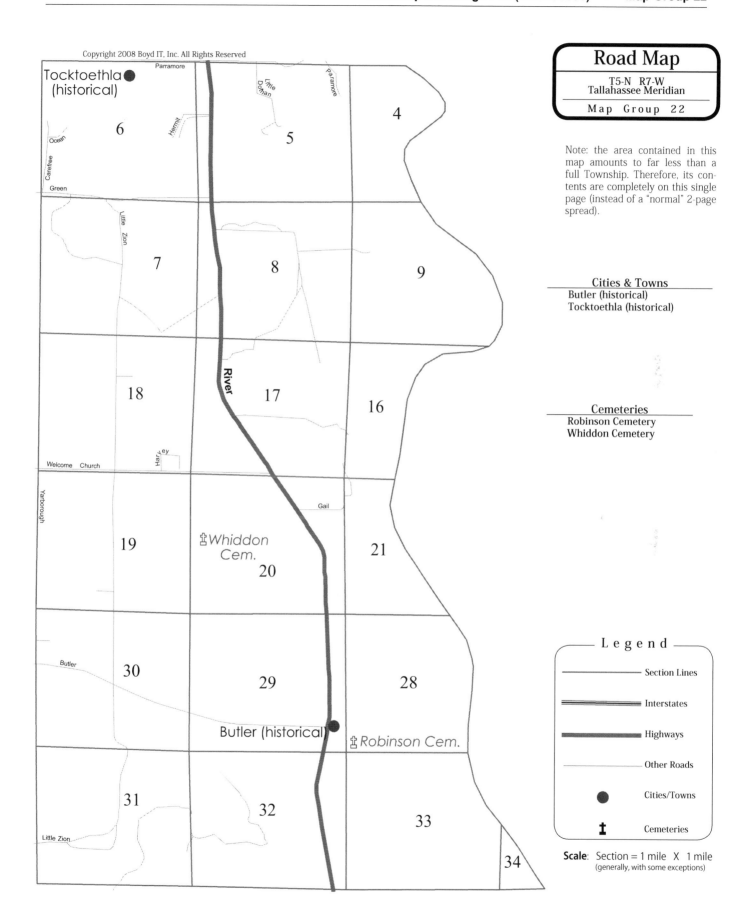

Tocktoethla ●
(historical)

Parramore

Little Doman

Paramore

Hermit

6

5

4

Ocean

Carefree

Green

Little Zion

7

8

9

River

18

17

16

Harvey

Welcome   Church

Yarborough

Gail

19

☩Whiddon
Cem.

20

21

Butler

30

29

28

Butler (historical) ●

☩Robinson Cem.

Little Zion

31

32

33

34

Road Map

T5-N R7-W
Tallahassee Meridian

Map Group 22

Note: the area contained in this map amounts to far less than a full Township. Therefore, its contents are completely on this single page (instead of a "normal" 2-page spread).

Cities & Towns
Butler (historical)
Tocktoethla (historical)

Cemeteries
Robinson Cemetery
Whiddon Cemetery

Legend
———— Section Lines
════ Interstates
▬▬▬ Highways
———— Other Roads
● Cities/Towns
☩ Cemeteries

Scale: Section = 1 mile X 1 mile
(generally, with some exceptions)

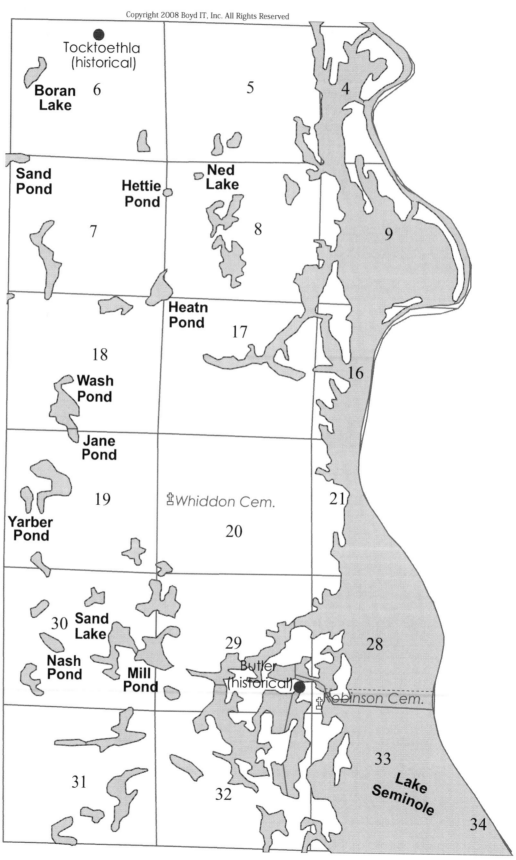

Historical Map

T5-N R7-W
Tallahassee Meridian

Map Group 22

Note: the area contained in this map amounts to far less than a full Township. Therefore, its contents are completely on this single page (instead of a "normal" 2-page spread).

Cities & Towns
Butler (historical)
Tocktoethla (historical)

Cemeteries
Robinson Cemetery
Whiddon Cemetery

Legend
——————— Section Lines

+—+—+—+— Railroads

▭ Large Rivers & Bodies of Water

- - - - - - Streams/Creeks & Small Rivers

● Cities/Towns

✝ Cemeteries

Scale: Section = 1 mile X 1 mile
(there are some exceptions)

Tocktoethla (historical)

Boran Lake   6   5   4

Sand Pond   Hettie Pond   Ned Lake

7   8   9

Heatn Pond   17

18   16

Wash Pond

Jane Pond

19   ✝ Whiddon Cem.   21

Yarber Pond   20

30   Sand Lake   29   28

Nash Pond   Mill Pond   Butler (historical)   Robinson Cem.

31   32   33   Lake Seminole   34

Map Group 23: Index to Land Patents

Township 4-North Range 12-West (Tallahassee)

After you locate an individual in this Index, take note of the Section and Section Part then proceed to the Land Patent map on the pages immediately following. You should have no difficulty locating the corresponding parcel of land.

The "For More Info" Column will lead you to more information about the underlying Patents. See the *Legend* at right, and the "How to Use this Book" chapter, for more information.

```
                    LEGEND
          "For More Info . . . " column
A = Authority (Legislative Act, See Appendix "A")
B = Block or Lot (location in Section unknown)
C = Cancelled Patent
F = Fractional Section
G = Group  (Multi-Patentee Patent, see Appendix "C")
V = Overlaps another Parcel
R = Re-Issued (Parcel patented more than once)

(A & G items require you to look in the Appendixes referred
to above. All other Letter-designations followed by a number
require you to locate line-items in this index that possess
the ID number found after the letter).
```

ID	Individual in Patent	Sec.	Sec. Part	Date Issued	Other Counties	For More Info . . .
2791	BARNES, Newton A	26	N½SW	1899-08-14		A2
2793	BARNES, Robert P	34	N½NW	1899-05-12		A2
2794	" "	34	NWNE	1899-05-12		A2
2760	BROCK, Jacob F	12	NWSW	1908-07-06		A2
2761	" "	12	SWNW	1908-07-06		A2
2792	BROCK, Richard S	36	W½NW	1901-04-09		A2
2815	BROCK, William G	22	SESE	1906-03-28		A2 R2816
2815	" "	22	SESE	1906-03-28		A2 C R2816
2816	" "	22	SESE	1906-03-28		A2 R2815
2816	" "	22	SESE	1906-03-28		A2 C R2815
2740	BUSH, Allen H	14	SW	1892-11-15		A2
2756	BUSH, Green B	24	E½NW	1898-09-19		A2
2757	" "	24	NESW	1898-09-19		A2
2758	" "	24	NWNW	1898-09-19		A2
2759	BUSH, Jackson M	24	NE	1898-02-03		A2
2780	CORBIN, John W	36	SESW	1904-08-30		A2
2781	" "	36	SWSE	1904-08-30		A2
2782	" "	36	W½SW	1904-08-30		A2
2798	CORBIN, Samuel H	22	SW	1897-03-22		A2
2812	CORTNEY, William	3	NESW	1857-12-01		A1
2813	" "	3	SENW	1857-12-01		A1
2750	CREAMER, George W	10	E½NE	1894-05-23		A2
2751	" "	10	E½SE	1894-05-23		A2
2770	CREMER, Jeremiah	22	NW	1896-11-16		A2
2765	CUTCHIN, James	2	SW	1892-08-13		A2
2766	CUTCHIN, James D	2	NE	1892-05-26		A2
2803	DAVIS, Thomas L	34	E½SE	1902-07-03		A2
2804	" "	34	SWSE	1902-07-03		A2
2762	DILLMORE, James A	14	N½NW	1896-11-16		A2
2763	" "	14	NWNE	1896-11-16		A2
2764	" "	14	SWNW	1896-11-16		A2
2818	DILLMORE, William W	14	S½SE	1900-08-09		A2
2785	ELDRIDGE, Joseph C	22	N½SE	1897-04-14		A2
2786	" "	22	SWNE	1897-04-14		A2
2787	" "	22	SWSE	1897-04-14		A2
2741	FILLMAN, Burrell T	10	S½SW	1902-12-30		A2
2799	FLORIDA, State Of	14	SENW	1908-11-19		A3
2771	GAY, John B	14	N½SE	1893-05-26		A2
2772	" "	14	S½NE	1893-05-26		A2
2739	GILBERT, Alford C	34	SW	1899-05-12		A2
2795	GILBERT, Rufus	26	E½NE	1897-12-01		A2
2796	" "	26	NWSE	1897-12-01		A2
2797	" "	26	SWNE	1897-12-01		A2
2752	HOLLEY, George W	12	SESE	1903-06-01		A2
2817	JOHNSON, William	10	N½SW	1857-12-01		A1
2773	KENT, John B	24	E½SE	1857-07-01		A1

ID	Individual in Patent	Sec.	Sec. Part	Date Issued	Other Counties	For More Info . . .
2779	MAYO, John N	36	E½NE	1902-07-03		A2
2810	MAYO, William A	36	E½NW	1897-12-07		A2
2811	" "	36	W½NE	1897-12-07		A2
2749	MELVIN, George G	10	SWSE	1899-05-22		A2
2805	MELVIN, Thomas	24	NWSW	1904-09-08		A1 R2806
2805	" "	24	NWSW	1904-09-08		A1 C R2806
2806	" "	24	NWSW	1904-09-08		A1 R2805
2806	" "	24	NWSW	1904-09-08		A1 C R2805
2807	" "	24	SWNW	1904-09-08		A1 R2808
2807	" "	24	SWNW	1904-09-08		A1 C R2808
2808	" "	24	SWNW	1904-09-08		A1 R2807
2808	" "	24	SWNW	1904-09-08		A1 C R2807
2809	MELVIN, Wesley J	26	NWNE	1903-05-25		A2
2783	MORRIS, John W	26	S½SE	1901-06-25		A2
2784	" "	26	S½SW	1901-06-25		A2
2800	NELSON, Thomas B	34	NWSE	1895-10-09		A2
2801	" "	34	S½NW	1895-10-09		A2
2802	" "	34	SWNE	1895-10-09		A2
2742	PERRITT, Elizabeth	36	E½SE	1901-07-20		A2 G115
2743	" "	36	NESW	1901-07-20		A2 G115
2744	" "	36	NWSE	1901-07-20		A2 G115
2742	PERRITT, Samuel B	36	E½SE	1901-07-20		A2 G115
2743	" "	36	NESW	1901-07-20		A2 G115
2744	" "	36	NWSE	1901-07-20		A2 G115
2753	SAPP, George W	22	N½NE	1897-12-01		A2
2767	SEAY, James W	24	S½SW	1896-04-27		A2
2768	" "	24	SWSE	1896-04-27		A2
2814	SEAY, William E	26	NW	1899-06-13		A2
2754	SHORES, George W	12	N½SE	1890-04-29		A2
2755	" "	12	S½NE	1890-04-29		A2
2774	SHORES, John B	2	NW	1898-04-06		A2
2788	SHORES, Moses R	12	E½SW	1891-11-09		A2
2789	" "	12	SENW	1891-11-09		A2
2790	" "	12	SWSE	1891-11-09		A2
2745	SWAILS, Frank L	26	NESE	1905-12-30		A1
2775	TAYLOR, John J	10	SENW	1894-07-31		A2
2776	" "	10	W½NW	1894-07-31		A2
2746	THARP, George A	10	NENW	1899-08-30		A2
2747	" "	10	NWSE	1899-08-30		A2
2748	" "	10	W½NE	1899-08-30		A2
2769	THARP, Jefferson D	2	SE	1892-04-01		A2
2777	THARP, John J	12	N½NE	1899-05-22		A2
2778	" "	12	N½NW	1899-05-22		A2

Patent Map

T4-N R12-W
Tallahassee Meridian

Map Group 23

Township Statistics

Parcels Mapped	:	80
Number of Patents	:	48
Number of Individuals	:	47
Patentees Identified	:	46
Number of Surnames	:	29
Multi-Patentee Parcels	:	3
Oldest Patent Date	:	7/1/1857
Most Recent Patent	:	11/19/1908
Block/Lot Parcels	:	0
Parcels Re-Issued	:	3
Parcels that Overlap	:	0
Cities and Towns	:	1
Cemeteries	:	0

Note: the area contained in this map amounts to far less than a full Township. Therefore, its contents are completely on this single page (instead of a "normal" 2-page spread).

Legend

— Patent Boundary

— Section Boundary

No Patents Found
(or Outside County)

1., 2., 3., ... Lot Numbers
(when beside a name)

[ ] Group Number
(see Appendix "C")

Scale: Section = 1 mile X 1 mile
(generally, with some exceptions)

Section 3
CORTNEY William 1857
CORTNEY William 1857

Section 2
SHORES John B 1898
CUTCHIN James D 1892
CUTCHIN James 1892
THARP Jefferson D 1892

Section 1

Section 10
TAYLOR John J 1894
THARP George A 1899
TAYLOR John J 1894
CREAMER George W 1894
THARP George A 1899
JOHNSON William 1857
THARP George A 1899
CREAMER George W 1894
FILLMAN Burrell T 1902
MELVIN George G 1899

Section 11

Section 12
THARP John J 1899
THARP John J 1899
BROCK Jacob F 1908
SHORES Moses R 1891
SHORES George W 1890
BROCK Jacob F 1908
SHORES George W 1890
SHORES Moses R 1891
SHORES Moses R 1891
HOLLEY George W 1903

Section 15

Section 14
DILLMORE James A 1896
DILLMORE James A 1896
DILLMORE James A 1896
FLORIDA State Of 1908
GAY John B 1893
BUSH Allen H 1892
GAY John B 1893
DILLMORE William W 1900

Section 13

Section 22
CREMER Jeremiah 1896
SAPP George W 1897
ELDRIDGE Joseph C 1897
CORBIN Samuel H 1897
ELDRIDGE Joseph C 1897
ELDRIDGE Joseph C 1897
BROCK William G 1906

Section 23

Section 24
BUSH Green B 1898
BUSH Jackson M 1898
MELVIN Thomas 1904
BUSH Green B 1898
MELVIN Thomas 1904
BUSH Green B 1898
KENT John B 1857
SEAY James W 1896
SEAY James W 1896

Section 27

Section 26
SEAY William E 1899
MELVIN Wesley J 1903
GILBERT Rufus 1897
GILBERT Rufus 1897
BARNES Newton A 1899
GILBERT Rufus 1897
SWAILS Frank L 1905
MORRIS John W 1901
MORRIS John W 1901

Section 25

Section 34
BARNES Robert P 1899
BARNES Robert P 1899
NELSON Thomas B 1895
NELSON Thomas B 1895
GILBERT Alford C 1899
NELSON Thomas B 1895
DAVIS Thomas L 1902
DAVIS Thomas L 1902

Section 35

Section 36
BROCK Richard S 1901
MAYO William A 1897
MAYO William A 1897
MAYO John N 1902
CORBIN John W 1904
PERRITT [115] Elizabeth 1901
PERRITT [115] Elizabeth 1901
PERRITT [115] Elizabeth 1901
CORBIN John W 1904
CORBIN John W 1904

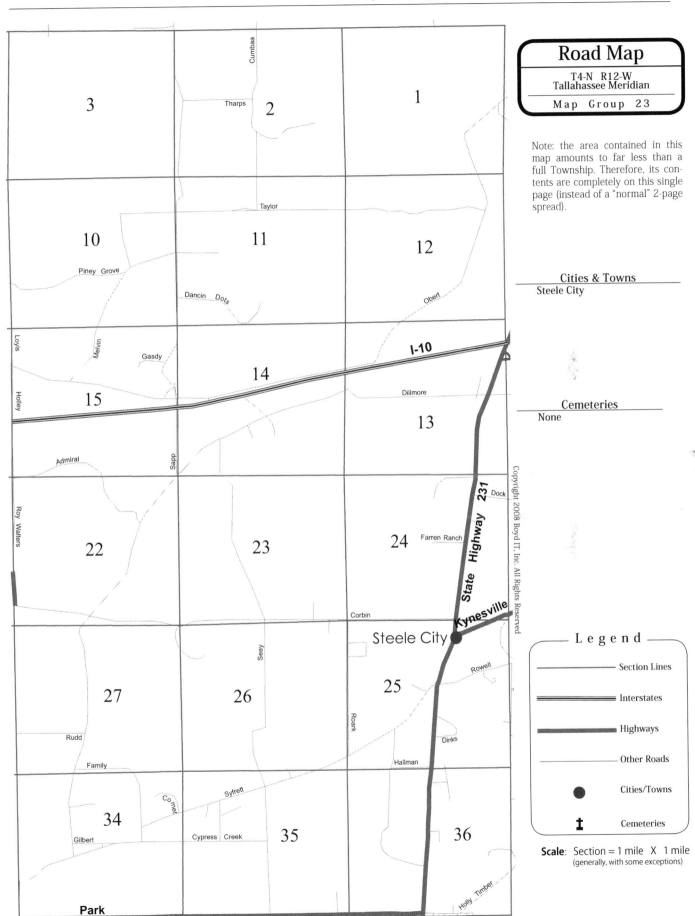

Note: the area contained in this map amounts to far less than a full Township. Therefore, its contents are completely on this single page (instead of a "normal" 2-page spread).

Cities & Towns
Steele City

Cemeteries
None

Legend
Section Lines
Interstates
Highways
Other Roads
Cities/Towns
Cemeteries

Scale: Section = 1 mile X 1 mile
(generally, with some exceptions)

Historical Map

T4-N R12-W
Tallahassee Meridian

Map Group 23

Note: the area contained in this map amounts to far less than a full Township. Therefore, its contents are completely on this single page (instead of a "normal" 2-page spread).

Cities & Towns

Steele City

Cemeteries

None

Legend

- Section Lines
- Railroads
- Large Rivers & Bodies of Water
- Streams/Creeks & Small Rivers
- Cities/Towns
- Cemeteries

Scale: Section = 1 mile X 1 mile
(there are some exceptions)

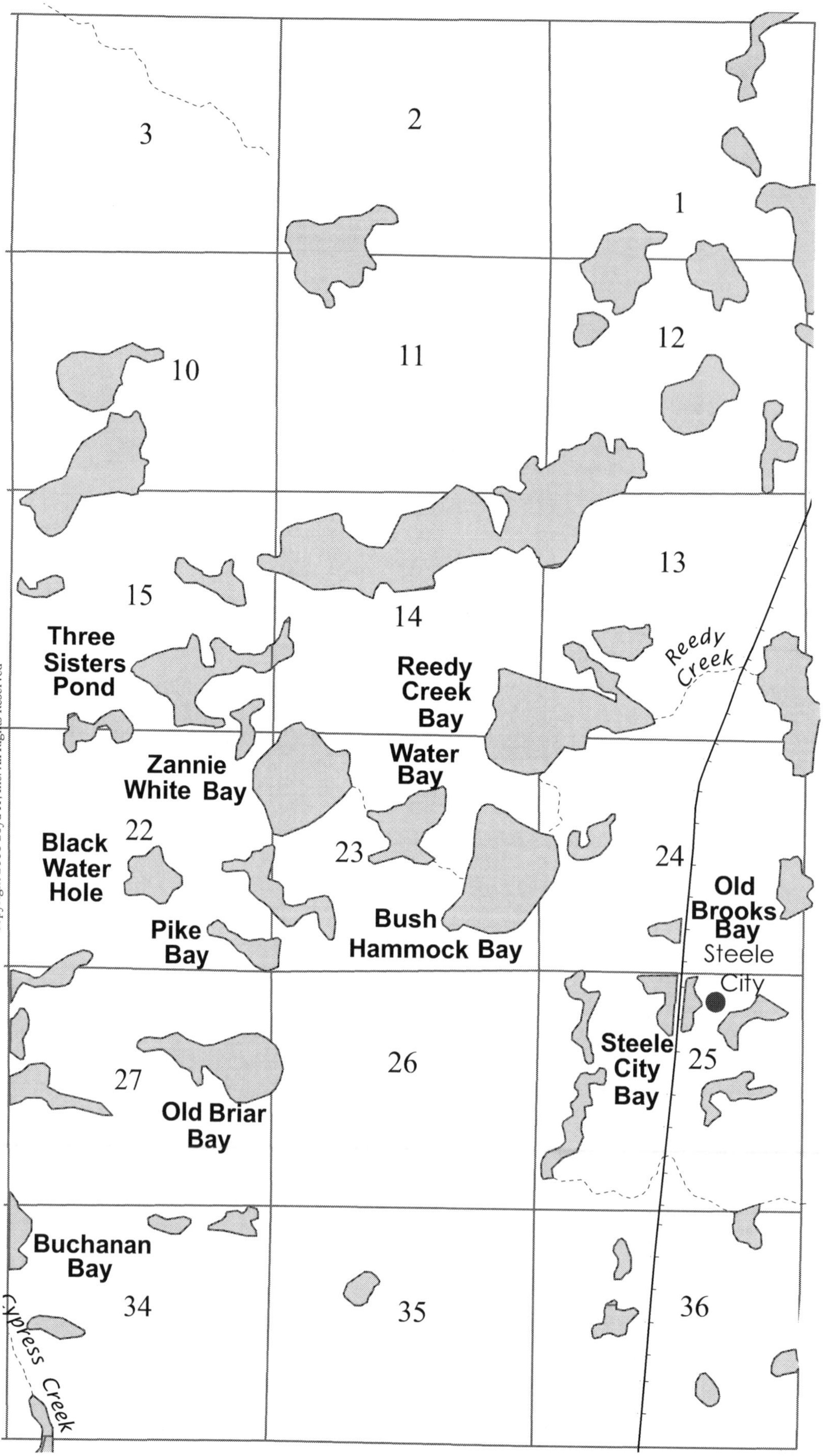

3
2
1
10
11
12
15
14
13
Three Sisters Pond
Reedy Creek Bay
Reedy Creek
Zannie White Bay
Water Bay
Black Water Hole
22
23
24
Old Brooks Bay
Pike Bay
Bush Hammock Bay
Steele City
27
26
25
Steele City Bay
Old Briar Bay
Buchanan Bay
34
35
36
Cypress Creek

Map Group 24: Index to Land Patents

Township 4-North Range 11-West (Tallahassee)

After you locate an individual in this Index, take note of the Section and Section Part then proceed to the Land Patent map on the pages immediately following. You should have no difficulty locating the corresponding parcel of land.

The "For More Info" Column will lead you to more information about the underlying Patents. See the *Legend* at right, and the "How to Use this Book" chapter, for more information.

```
┌─────────────────────────────────────────────────────────┐
│                        LEGEND                            │
│            "For More Info . . . " column                 │
│  ─────────────────────────────────────────────────       │
│  A = Authority (Legislative Act, See Appendix "A")       │
│  B = Block or Lot (location in Section unknown)          │
│  C = Cancelled Patent                                    │
│  F = Fractional Section                                  │
│  G = Group  (Multi-Patentee Patent, see Appendix "C")    │
│  V = Overlaps another Parcel                             │
│  R = Re-Issued (Parcel patented more than once)          │
│                                                          │
│  (A & G items require you to look in the Appendixes      │
│  referred to above. All other Letter-designations        │
│  followed by a number require you to locate line-items   │
│  in this index that possess the ID number found after    │
│  the letter).                                            │
└─────────────────────────────────────────────────────────┘
```

ID	Individual in Patent	Sec.	Sec. Part	Date Issued	Other Counties	For More Info . . .
2895	ALLEN, Irvin	19	W½SW	1859-06-01		A1
2927	ATTAWAY, Lawrence M	12	NESE	1857-12-01		A1
2827	BARFIELD, Archibald	21	NESW	1857-12-01		A1
2828	" "	21	NWSE	1857-12-01		A1
2829	" "	21	NWSW	1859-06-01		A1
2830	" "	21	SENW	1859-06-01		A1
2831	" "	21	SESW	1859-06-01		A1
2832	" "	21	SWNE	1859-06-01		A1
2820	BELLAMY, Aesop	10	SENW	1883-04-20		A2
2880	BELLAMY, Fuller	2	W½SW	1894-04-10		A2
2921	BISHOP, Joseph	34	SW	1894-04-10		A2
2965	BLOUNT, Thomas	18	NE	1890-04-29		A2
2897	BRANON, Jackson G	18	NESW	1897-11-10		A2
2898	" "	18	NWSE	1897-11-10		A2
2899	" "	18	W½SW	1897-11-10		A2
2942	BROCK, Pinckney D	18	E½SE	1895-10-09		A2
2943	" "	18	SESW	1895-10-09		A2
2944	" "	18	SWSE	1895-10-09		A2
2910	BROOKS, John	36	NENE	1897-05-25		A2
2847	BROWN, Charles	12	E½SW	1893-10-13		A2
2848	" "	12	W½SE	1893-10-13		A2
2886	BROWN, Henry	12	W½NE	1895-06-17		A2
2954	BROWN, Roxey A	2	NW	1896-08-06		A2
2958	BROWN, Samuel	12	E½NE	1893-10-13		A2
2905	BUCHANAN, James H	20	NW	1900-08-09		A2
2971	BUSH, Thomas M	22	SE	1843-03-10		A1
2972	" "	27	E½SE	1843-03-10		A1
2973	" "	27	W½NE	1843-03-10		A1
2867	CAMPBELL, David	6	E½SW	1890-06-05		A2
2868	" "	6	NWSW	1890-06-05		A2
2869	" "	6	SWSE	1890-06-05		A2
2841	CLEMENTS, Benjamin	15	E½NW	1827-10-01		A1 G48
2842	" "	15	W½NW	1827-10-01		A1 G48
2839	" "	35	E½NW	1827-10-01		A1 G47
2840	" "	35	W½NW	1827-10-01		A1 G47
2957	COGBURN, Samuel A	28	SE	1897-05-25		A2 G55
2957	COGBURN, Susan C	28	SE	1897-05-25		A2 G55
2933	COLBERT, Martha C	6	E½NW	1889-07-02		A2
2934	" "	6	NWNE	1889-07-02		A2
2980	COLLINS, William	36	SENE	1839-09-20		A1
2981	" "	36	W½NE	1839-09-20		A1
2834	CONNER, Augustus O	14	NESW	1891-05-04		A2
2835	" "	14	S½SW	1891-05-04		A2
2836	" "	14	SWSE	1891-05-04		A2
2997	CONNER, William O	14	NESE	1883-08-01		A2
2998	" "	14	NWSE	1889-07-03		A2

ID	Individual in Patent	Sec.	Sec. Part	Date Issued	Other Counties	For More Info . . .
2999	CONNER, William O (Cont'd)	14	SWNE	1889-07-03		A2
2875	COTTON, Emanuel	26	NWSE	1894-04-10		A2
2911	DAVIDSON, John	3	E½SW	1827-11-01		A1
2837	DICKENS, Benjamin A	35	SWNE	1855-05-01		A1
2838	" "	36	SWNW	1855-05-01		A1
2819	DOWLING, Aaron	6	NENE	1889-07-03		A2
2920	EVERITT, Joseph B	5	SESW	1846-10-01		A1
2966	GAFF, Thomas	9	W½SE	1827-10-01		A1
2902	GAKRINS, James	15	SESW	1857-12-01		A1
2903	" "	15	SWSE	1857-12-01		A1
2904	" "	22	NENW	1857-12-01		A1 V2896
2935	GAY, Martin	28	SW	1897-03-03		A2
2967	GAY, Thomas	26	NWNW	1840-10-10		A1
2968	" "	27	NENE	1840-10-10		A1
2987	GAY, William	23	SE	1857-12-01		A1
2988	" "	23	SENE	1857-12-01		A1
2989	" "	23	SESW	1857-12-01		A1
2990	" "	24	SWNW	1857-12-01		A1
3000	GAY, William W	30	SE	1898-02-24		A2
2878	GILBERT, Flora	10	SW	1888-11-15		A2
2839	GILCHRIST, Malcolm	35	E½NW	1827-10-01		A1 G47
2840	" "	35	W½NW	1827-10-01		A1 G47
2970	GOFF, Thomas	9	W½SW	1827-10-01		A1
2969	" "	9	E½SE	1829-05-15		A1
2955	GOODWIN, Roxey	26	E½SW	1889-07-03		A2
2956	" "	26	S½SE	1889-07-03		A2
2960	GRIFFIN, Shady M	8	SWNW	1889-07-02		A2
2961	" "	8	W½SW	1889-07-02		A2
2843	HALL, Bryant H	12	SESE	1897-07-03		A2
2913	HARPER, John	18	N½NW	1883-08-13		A2
2982	HARPER, William E	8	E½SW	1891-02-13		A2
2983	" "	8	W½SE	1891-02-13		A2
2953	HILL, Rod	24	NE	1895-06-17		A2
2881	HOLMES, Gatson	36	SESE	1915-08-18		A2
2883	HOWARD, George	36	NESE	1843-03-10		A1
2924	HOWARD, Joshua	36	SWSE	1859-06-01		A1
2841	JEMISON, Robert	15	E½NW	1827-10-01		A1 G48
2842	" "	15	W½NW	1827-10-01		A1 G48
2928	JENKINS, Lieurany	11	NENE	1856-06-16		A1
2929	" "	14	SENE	1856-06-16		A1
2844	JOHNSON, Burrell	2	E½SW	1898-04-06		A2
2845	" "	2	NWSE	1898-04-06		A2
2846	" "	2	SWNE	1898-04-06		A2
2849	JONES, Charles	36	NWSE	1909-11-08		A2
2884	JONES, Gilbert	36	NWNW	1896-10-16		A2
2914	KENT, John	24	SW	1889-07-02		A2
2939	KENT, Noah	34	N½NW	1906-06-04		A2
2908	KING, Jason	6	W½NW	1889-07-02		A2
2917	KNIGHT, John T	2	N½NE	1896-06-23		A2
2887	LAMB, Henry J	24	SE	1895-06-17		A2
2906	LAND, James M	20	NE	1897-12-01		A2
2963	LAND, Stephen W	20	SE	1893-11-04		A2
2946	LAWRENCE, Richard C	1	NESW	1857-12-01		A1
2947	" "	1	NWSE	1857-12-01		A1
2948	" "	1	SENW	1857-12-01		A1
2949	" "	1	W½NE	1857-12-01		A1
2901	LEONARD, James D	30	SW	1897-08-05		A2
2940	LEVEY, Patrick	22	NWNW	1838-07-28		A1 V2896
2959	LEWIS, Seth P	35	E½SW	1828-08-22		A1
2976	LEWIS, Turner	34	SE	1896-06-10		A2
2995	LONG, William	10	NWNW	1899-05-12		A2
2984	MASHBURN, William F	32	NW	1901-12-04		A2
2996	MASHBURN, William N	32	SE	1901-11-20		A2
2863	MCGUIRE, Daniel J	13	NESW	1859-06-01		A1
2864	" "	13	NWSE	1859-06-01		A1
2865	" "	13	SENW	1859-06-01		A1
2866	" "	13	SWNE	1859-06-01		A1
2941	MCLEVY, Patrick	22	SENW	1843-03-10		A1 V2896
2936	MORRIS, Miles G	30	NE	1900-08-09		A2
2861	OLIVE, Columbus	24	N½NW	1898-05-16		A2
2862	" "	24	SENW	1898-05-16		A2
2873	PADGETT, Elijah M	14	NWSW	1906-09-14		A2
2874	" "	14	W½NW	1906-09-14		A2

ID	Individual in Patent	Sec.	Sec. Part	Date Issued	Other Counties	For More Info . . .
2919	PADGETT, John W	22	NE	1890-12-27		A2
2962	PETERSON, Stephen	34	SENE	1890-04-29		A2
2950	PITTMAN, Robert	12	N½NW	1895-06-17		A2
2951	" "	12	NWSW	1895-06-17		A2
2952	" "	12	SWNW	1895-06-17		A2
2877	POPE, Emanuel	4	E½SE	1884-06-30		A2
2876	" "	4	E½NE	1892-04-09		A2
2916	POPE, John	10	E½SE	1894-01-27		A2
2922	PORTER, Joseph	26	W½NE	1895-06-17		A2
2879	POWELL, Frank	26	NENE	1897-03-22		A2 R2974
2937	RAMSEY, Nathan	10	NENW	1839-09-20		A1
2938	" "	10	SWNW	1839-09-20		A1
2907	RAWLS, James W	28	NW	1896-08-24		A2
2822	REVERE, Alexander M	5	E½NE	1828-03-15		A1
2833	RIVIRE, Armistead S	4	W½NW	1843-03-10		A1
2923	RUSS, Joseph	15	W½SW	1827-11-01		A1
2860	SCOTT, Charley	30	NW	1897-05-25		A2
2900	SKINNER, James A	12	SENW	1898-04-27		A2
2909	SKINNER, Jasper R	12	SWSW	1900-09-07		A2
2991	SKINNER, William J	2	E½SE	1897-03-22		A2
2992	" "	2	SENE	1897-03-22		A2
2993	" "	2	SWSE	1897-03-22		A2
2926	SMITH, Julia	34	S½NW	1896-01-03		A2
2823	SPEARS, Alfred B	10	E½NE	1894-01-27		A2
2890	SPEARS, Hugh	3	W½NE	1843-03-10		A1
2891	" "	3	W½SE	1843-03-10		A1
2893	" "	8	NENW	1843-03-10		A1
2894	" "	8	NWNE	1843-03-10		A1
2889	" "	3	E½NE	1856-06-16		A1
2892	" "	4	W½SW	1859-06-01		A1
2932	SPEARS, Mansfield	26	NENW	1896-01-03		A2
2977	SPEARS, Washington	10	W½NE	1895-10-09		A2
2978	" "	10	W½SE	1895-10-09		A2
2925	SPOONER, Julia A	18	S½NW	1899-08-30		A2
2915	STOCKTON, John N	26	W½SW	1838-07-28		A1 R2870
2979	SWEARINGIN, William A	20	SW	1898-02-03		A2
2896	TANNER, Jack	22	NW	1893-05-26		A2 V2940, 2941, 2904
2945	TANNER, Rachael	4	W½NE	1883-08-13		A2
2918	TEMPLE, John T	14	SESE	1906-03-31		A1 F
2964	THIRBY, Susan	13	SESE	1857-12-01		A1
2825	THOMPSON, Amos M	14	E½NW	1900-08-09		A2
2826	" "	14	N½NE	1900-08-09		A2
2824	WADDELL, Alfred	8	NWNW	1890-04-29		A2
2885	WATSON, Harry	34	N½NE	1894-01-27		A2
2994	WELCH, William J	6	S½NE	1893-05-06		A2
2985	WESTER, William F	6	N½SE	1893-07-06		A2
2986	" "	6	SESE	1893-07-06		A2
2821	WHITE, Aesop	4	NENW	1904-11-26		A2
3001	WHITE, William	3	W½SW	1827-11-01		A1
2871	WHITEHEAD, Edwin	35	E½NE	1843-03-10		A1
2872	" "	36	E½NW	1843-03-10		A1
2870	" "	26	W½SW	1846-04-01		A1 R2915
2882	WHITEHURST, George E	28	NE	1903-03-17		A2
2912	WILCOX, John H	32	NE	1898-04-06		A2
2850	WILLIAMSON, Charles	17	E½NE	1827-10-01		A1
2856	" "	9	E½NW	1827-10-01		A1
2857	" "	9	E½SW	1827-10-01		A1
2858	" "	9	W½NE	1827-10-01		A1
2859	" "	9	W½NW	1827-10-01		A1
2851	" "	4	E½SW	1827-11-01		A1
2852	" "	4	W½SE	1827-11-01		A1
2853	" "	5	W½SE	1827-11-01		A1
2854	" "	8	E½NE	1827-11-01		A1
2855	" "	8	E½SE	1827-11-01		A1
2930	WOODARD, Littleton H	8	SENW	1857-12-01		A1
2931	" "	8	SWNE	1857-12-01		A1
2888	WYNN, Henry L	34	SWNE	1903-05-25		A2
2974	YOUNG, Tony	26	NENE	1893-10-13		A2 R2879
2975	" "	26	SENE	1893-10-13		A2

Patent Map

T4-N R11-W
Tallahassee Meridian

Map Group 24

Township Statistics

Parcels Mapped	:	183
Number of Patents	:	136
Number of Individuals	:	114
Patentees Identified	:	112
Number of Surnames	:	89
Multi-Patentee Parcels	:	5
Oldest Patent Date	:	10/1/1827
Most Recent Patent	:	8/18/1915
Block/Lot Parcels	:	0
Parcels Re-Issued	:	2
Parcels that Overlap	:	4
Cities and Towns	:	1
Cemeteries	:	0

KING Jason 1889

COLBERT Martha C 1889

DOWLING Aaron 1889

WELCH William J 1893

COLBERT Martha C 1889

CAMPBELL David 1890

6

WESTER William F 1893

CAMPBELL David 1890

CAMPBELL David 1890

WESTER William F 1893

5

EVERITT Joseph B 1846

WILLIAMSON Charles 1827

REVERE Alexander M 1828

RIVIRE Armistead S 1843

WHITE Aesop 1904

TANNER Rachael 1883

POPE Emanuel 1892

SPEARS Hugh 1859

4

WILLIAMSON Charles 1827

WILLIAMSON Charles 1827

POPE Emanuel 1884

WADDELL Alfred 1890

SPEARS Hugh 1843

SPEARS Hugh 1843

WILLIAMSON Charles 1827

WILLIAMSON Charles 1827

WILLIAMSON Charles 1827

GRIFFIN Shady M 1889

WOODARD Littleton H 1857

WOODARD Littleton H 1857

WILLIAMSON Charles 1827

7

GRIFFIN Shady M 1889

HARPER William E 1891

8

HARPER William E 1891

WILLIAMSON Charles 1827

GOFF Thomas 1827

9

WILLIAMSON Charles 1827

GAFF Thomas 1827

GOFF Thomas 1829

HARPER John 1883

BLOUNT Thomas 1890

WILLIAMSON Charles 1827

SPOONER Julia A 1899

18

17

16

BRANON Jackson G 1897

BRANON Jackson G 1897

BRANON Jackson G 1897

BROCK Pinckney D 1895

BROCK Pinckney D 1895

BROCK Pinckney D 1895

19

BUCHANAN James H 1900

LAND James M 1897

20

SWEARINGIN William A 1898

LAND Stephen W 1893

BARFIELD Archibald 1859

BARFIELD Archibald 1857

21

BARFIELD Archibald 1859

BARFIELD Archibald 1857

BARFIELD Archibald 1859

ALLEN Irvin 1859

BARFIELD Archibald 1859

SCOTT Charley 1897

MORRIS Miles G 1900

30

LEONARD James D 1897

GAY William W 1898

29

RAWLS James W 1896

28

GAY Martin 1897

WHITEHURST George E 1903

COGBURN [55] Samuel A 1897

31

MASHBURN William F 1901

WILCOX John H 1898

32

MASHBURN William N 1901

33

Section 1 area:

SPEARS Hugh 1843
SPEARS Hugh 1856
BROWN Roxey A 1896
KNIGHT John T 1896
LAWRENCE Richard C 1857
LAWRENCE Richard C 1857
1
JOHNSON Burrell 1898
SKINNER William J 1897

WHITE William 1827
3
DAVIDSON John 1827
SPEARS Hugh 1843
BELLAMY Fuller 1894
2
JOHNSON Burrell 1898
JOHNSON Burrell 1898
SKINNER William J 1897
SKINNER William J 1897
LAWRENCE Richard C 1857
LAWRENCE Richard C 1857

Middle sections:

LONG William 1899
RAMSEY Nathan 1839
SPEARS Washington 1895
SPEARS Alfred B 1894
11
JENKINS Lieurany 1856
PITTMAN Robert 1895
BROWN Henry 1895
BROWN Samuel 1893
RAMSEY Nathan 1839
BELLAMY Aesop 1883
PITTMAN Robert 1895
SKINNER James A 1898
12

GILBERT Flora 1888
10
SPEARS Washington 1895
POPE John 1894
PITTMAN Robert 1895
BROWN Charles 1893
BROWN Charles 1893
ATTAWAY Lawrence M 1857
SKINNER Jasper R 1900
HALL Bryant H 1897

Sections 15, 14, 13:

CLEMENTS [48] Benjamin 1827
CLEMENTS [48] Benjamin 1827
15
THOMPSON Amos M 1900
PADGETT Elijah M 1906
14
THOMPSON Amos M 1900
CONNER William O 1889
JENKINS Lieurany 1856
MCGUIRE Daniel J 1859
13
MCGUIRE Daniel J 1859

PADGETT Elijah M 1906
CONNER Augustus O 1891
CONNER William O 1889
CONNER William O 1883
MCGUIRE Daniel J 1859
MCGUIRE Daniel J 1859

RUSS Joseph 1827
GAKRINS James 1857
GAKRINS James 1857
CONNER Augustus O 1891
CONNER Augustus O 1891
TEMPLE John T 1906
THIRBY Susan 1857

Sections 22, 23, 24:

LEVEY Patrick 1838
GAKRINS James 1857
PADGETT John W 1890
23
OLIVE Columbus 1898
GAY William 1857
OLIVE Columbus 1898
HILL Rod 1895

TANNER Jack 1893
MCLEVY Patrick 1843
GAY William 1857
GAY William 1857
OLIVE Columbus 1898
22
BUSH Thomas M 1843
GAY William 1857
KENT John 1889
24
GAY William 1857
LAMB Henry J 1895

Sections 27, 26, 25:

GAY Thomas 1840
GAY Thomas 1840
SPEARS Mansfield 1896
PORTER Joseph 1895
YOUNG Tony 1893
POWELL Frank 1897
BUSH Thomas M 1843
26
YOUNG Tony 1893
27
BUSH Thomas M 1843
WHITEHEAD Edwin 1846
STOCKTON John N 1838
GOODWIN Roxey 1889
COTTON Emanuel 1894
GOODWIN Roxey 1889
25

Sections 34, 35, 36:

KENT Noah 1906
WATSON Harry 1894
CLEMENTS [47] Benjamin 1827
WHITEHEAD Edwin 1843
JONES Gilbert 1896
WHITEHEAD Edwin 1843
COLLINS William 1839
BROOKS John 1897

SMITH Julia 1896
WYNN Henry L 1903
PETERSON Stephen 1890
CLEMENTS [47] Benjamin 1827
35
DICKENS Benjamin A 1855
DICKENS Benjamin A 1855
COLLINS William 1839

34
LEWIS Turner 1896
LEWIS Seth P 1828
36
JONES Charles 1909
HOWARD George 1843

BISHOP Joseph 1894
HOWARD Joshua 1859
HOLMES Gatson 1915

Helpful Hints

1. This Map's INDEX can be found on the preceding pages.

2. Refer to Map "C" to see where this Township lies within Jackson County, Florida.

3. Numbers within square brackets [ ] denote a multi-patentee land parcel (multi-owner). Refer to Appendix "C" for a full list of members in this group.

4. Areas that look to be crowded with Patentees usually indicate multiple sales of the same parcel (Re-issues) or Overlapping parcels. See this Township's Index for an explanation of these and other circumstances that might explain "odd" groupings of Patentees on this map.

Legend

— Patent Boundary

— Section Boundary

No Patents Found (or Outside County)

1., 2., 3., ... Lot Numbers (when beside a name)

[ ] Group Number (see Appendix "C")

Scale: Section = 1 mile X 1 mile (generally, with some exceptions)

Road Map

T4-N R11-W
Tallahassee Meridian

Map Group 24

Cities & Towns
Kynesville

6

5

4

Maple

Lotus

Moore

Henderson

Ruby

State Highway 231

7

Jr

8

9

Lawrenceville

Barber

Cartledge

I-10

18

17

16

Dillmore

Standland

Phillips

20

Rogers

19

Cycle

21

Kynesville ●

Helen

Cemeteries
None

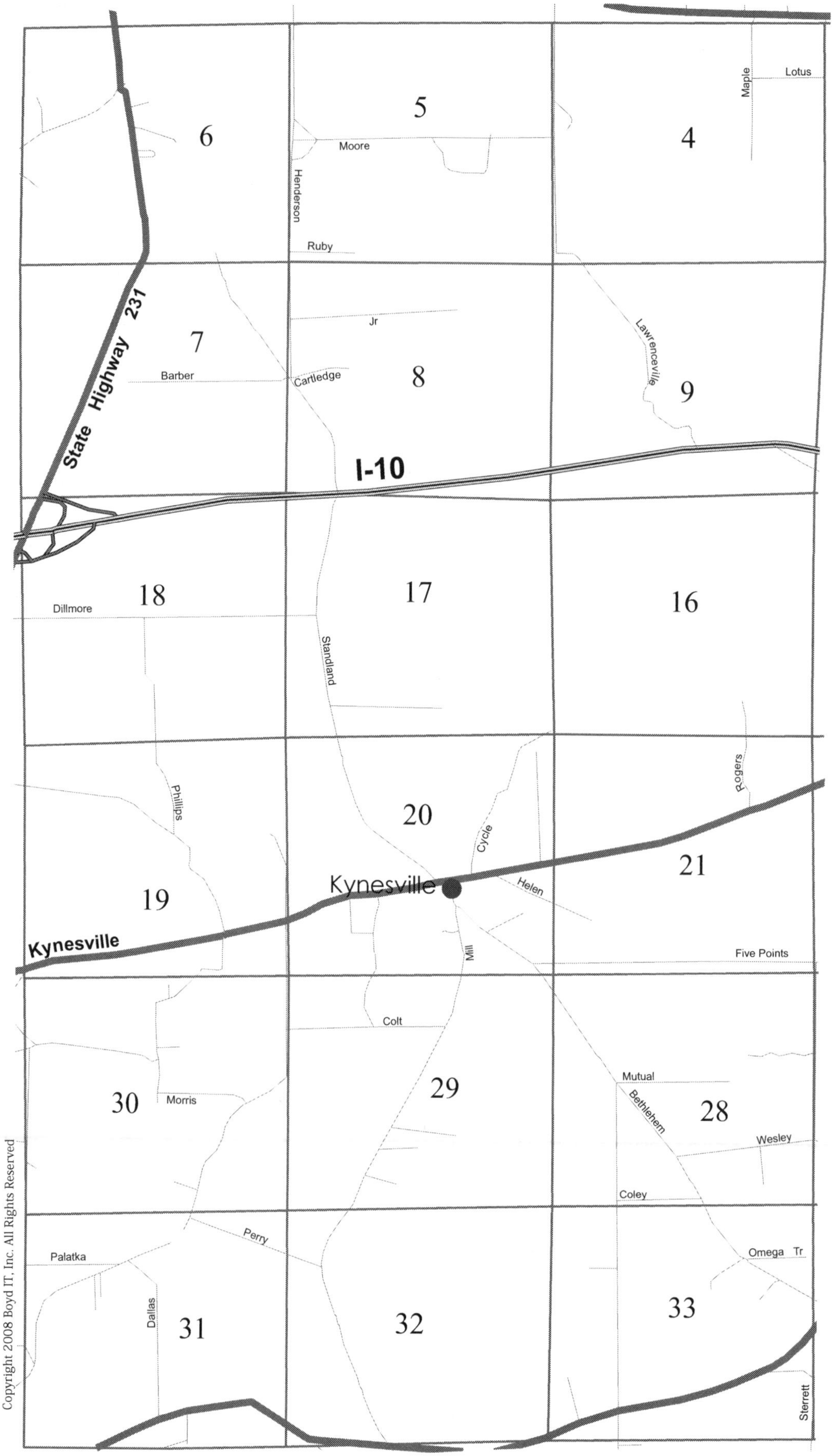

Kynesville

Mill

Five Points

Colt

Mutual

30

Morris

29

Bethlehem

28

Wesley

Coley

Palatka

Perry

Omega Tr

Dallas

31

32

33

Sterrett

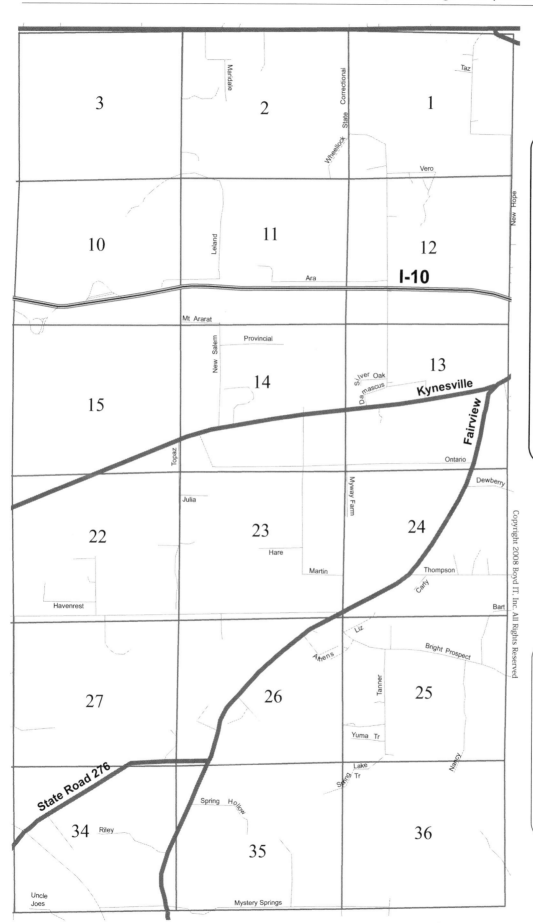

3

2

1

Maridale

Taz

Wheellock State Correctional

Vero

New Hope

10

11

12

Leland

Ara

I-10

Mt Ararat

New Salem

Provincial

15

14

13

Silver Oak

Damascus

Kynesville

Fairview

Topaz

Ontario

Dewberry

Julia

22

23

24

Hare

Martin

Thompson

Carly

Bart

Havenrest

Liz

Bright Prospect

Athens

Tanner

27

26

25

Yuma Tr

Lake

Nancy

Spring Tr

State Road 276

Spring Hollow

34

Riley

35

36

Uncle Joes

Mystery Springs

Helpful Hints

1. This road map has a number of uses, but primarily it is to help you: a) find the present location of land owned by your ancestors (at least the general area), b) find cemeteries and city-centers, and c) estimate the route/roads used by Census-takers & tax-assessors.

2. If you plan to travel to Jackson County to locate cemeteries or land parcels, please pick up a modern travel map for the area before you do. Mapping old land parcels on modern maps is not as exact a science as you might think. Just the slightest variations in public land survey coordinates, estimates of parcel boundaries, or road-map deviations can greatly alter a map's representation of how a road either does or doesn't cross a particular parcel of land.

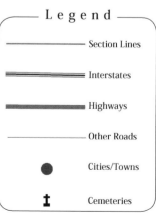

Legend

——————— Section Lines

═══════ Interstates

━━━━━━ Highways

——————— Other Roads

● Cities/Towns

⚰ Cemeteries

Scale: Section = 1 mile X 1 mile
(generally, with some exceptions)

Historical Map

T4-N R11-W
Tallahassee Meridian

Map Group 24

6

Mary Ann Pond

5

4

Cities & Towns
Kynesville

7

8

9

18

17

16

Doc Tharpe Bay

Tharp Mill Pond

19

20

21

Kynesville ●

Cemeteries
None

Little Dry Creek

30

29

28

31

32

33

3	2	Jenkins Pond 1
10	Bell Pond 11	12
15	14	13 Cave Spring
22	23	24
27	26	25
34	Springboard Spring 35	Black Hole 36 Blue Sink

Helpful Hints

1. This Map takes a different look at the same Congressional Township displayed in the preceding two maps. It presents features that can help you better envision the historical development of the area: a) Water-bodies (lakes & ponds), b) Water-courses (rivers, streams, etc.), c) Railroads, d) City/town center-points (where they were oftentimes located when first settled), and e) Cemeteries.

2. Using this "Historical" map in tandem with this Township's Patent Map and Road Map, may lead you to some interesting discoveries. You will often find roads, towns, cemeteries, and waterways are named after nearby landowners: sometimes those names will be the ones you are researching. See how many of these research gems you can find here in Jackson County.

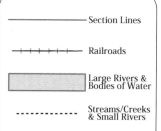

Legend

————————	Section Lines
+‑+‑+‑+‑+‑+	Railroads
▭	Large Rivers & Bodies of Water
- - - - - -	Streams/Creeks & Small Rivers
●	Cities/Towns
‡	Cemeteries

Scale: Section = 1 mile X 1 mile
(there are some exceptions)

Map Group 25: Index to Land Patents

Township 4-North Range 10-West (Tallahassee)

After you locate an individual in this Index, take note of the Section and Section Part then proceed to the Land Patent map on the pages immediately following. You should have no difficulty locating the corresponding parcel of land.

The "For More Info" Column will lead you to more information about the underlying Patents. See the *Legend* at right, and the "How to Use this Book" chapter, for more information.

ID	Individual in Patent	Sec.	Sec. Part	Date Issued	Other Counties	For More Info . . .
3097	ALLEN, John	30	S½SW	1896-04-27		A2
3146	ATTAWAY, Lawrence M	7	NWSW	1857-12-01		A1
3204	BANKS, William	2	W½SE	1827-10-01		A1
3205	"	25	W½NW	1827-10-01		A1
3206	"	26	E½SE	1827-10-01		A1
3207	"	36	W½NW	1827-10-01		A1
3168	BAREFOOT, Redding	30	N½NE	1892-12-03		A2
3169	"	30	N½NW	1892-12-03		A2
3005	BATTLE, Amos I	11	E½NE	1828-09-10		A1
3009	"	11	E½SW	1828-09-10		A1 G13
3006	"	11	NW	1828-09-10		A1
3007	"	11	SE	1828-09-10		A1
3010	"	11	W½NE	1828-09-10		A1 G13
3008	"	11	W½SW	1828-09-10		A1
3209	BELLAMY, William H	34	NESW	1892-08-27		A2
3210	"	34	NWSE	1892-08-27		A2
3211	"	34	SWSE	1892-08-27		A2
3012	BEVERIDGE, Anna M	4	E½SE	1828-02-22		A1
3013	"	4	W½SE	1828-09-10		A1
3178	BEVERIDGE, Robert	10	E½NE	1827-11-01		A1
3179	"	3	W½SW	1827-11-01		A1
3025	BLACKSHEAR, Cato	18	SE	1898-04-27		A2
3029	BLACKSHEAR, Daniel	18	SW	1893-12-28		A2
3041	BRAXTON, Eli	24	NENW	1916-05-16		A2
3064	BRYAN, Henry	27	NESE	1859-06-01		A1
3065	"	27	NWNE	1859-06-01		A1
3066	"	27	W½SE	1859-06-01		A1
3067	"	28	SENW	1859-06-01		A1
3068	"	28	SWNE	1859-06-01		A1
3069	"	28	W½SE	1859-06-01		A1
3208	BRYAN, William C	4	W½NW	1835-10-20		A1
3098	BUSH, John	9	E½NW	1844-07-10		A1
3135	BUSH, John W	9	W½NW	1839-09-20		A1
3177	CALL, Richard K	3	E½SW	1827-10-01		A1 G28
3171	"	10	W½NE	1827-11-01		A1
3172	"	23	E½SE	1830-12-28		A1
3173	"	24	SW	1830-12-28		A1
3175	"	26	E½NE	1830-12-28		A1
3176	"	4	E½NW	1830-12-28		A1
3174	"	25	E½NW	1833-05-16		A1
3147	CARAWAY, Major J	18	NE	1895-10-09		A2
3053	CARTER, Farish	2	W½NW	1834-08-20		A1 G31
3020	CHAIRES, Benjamin	10	W½SE	1827-10-01		A1
3021	"	15	W½NE	1827-10-01		A1
3018	"	10	E½NW	1827-11-01		A1
3022	"	3	E½NW	1827-11-01		A1

ID	Individual in Patent	Sec.	Sec. Part	Date Issued	Other Counties	For More Info . . .
3019	CHAIRES, Benjamin (Cont'd)	10	W½NW	1828-08-22		A1
3063	CHAIRES, Green H	3	E½NE	1828-08-22		A1
3123	CHAPMAN, John R	26	NESW	1840-10-10		A1
3124	" "	26	W½SE	1840-10-10		A1
3125	" "	35	E½SE	1840-10-10		A1
3127	" "	36	W½SW	1840-10-10		A1
3126	" "	35	W½SE	1841-01-09		A1
3119	" "	23	E½NW	1843-03-10		A1
3120	" "	23	NE	1843-03-10		A1
3121	" "	23	W½NW	1843-03-10		A1
3122	" "	24	W½NW	1843-03-10		A1
3101	CLEMMONS, John	6	NW	1894-05-23		A2
3023	COKER, Benjamin	6	W½SE	1899-09-30		A2
3170	COLEMAN, Reuben	6	NE	1899-08-30		A2
3082	CONNELL, James S	22	SENE	1885-12-10		A1
3194	COOK, Thomas	1	NWNE	1855-05-01		A1
3004	COOLEY, Alfred	22	NENE	1857-12-01		A1
3218	COWARD, Zachariah	15	W½NW	1833-05-16		A1
3096	DAVIS, Joe	24	SENE	1913-05-26		A2
3102	DAVIS, John	3	W½NE	1827-04-02		A1
3202	DAVIS, Walter	3	W½SE	1827-06-15		A1
3216	DICKENS, Willie	28	SWNW	1900-09-07		A2
3045	DICKEY, Elvira J	30	N½SW	1899-03-17		A2
3046	" "	30	S½NW	1899-03-17		A2
3180	DICKSON, Salina	8	SWSE	1897-07-03		A2
3203	DRAKE, William B	2	E½NW	1827-10-01		A1 G65
3104	DURHAM, John	34	E½SE	1841-01-09		A1
3106	" "	35	NWSW	1841-01-09		A1
3103	" "	34	E½NW	1856-06-16		A1
3105	" "	34	S½NE	1856-06-16		A1
3107	" "	35	SWSW	1856-06-16		A1
3141	DYKES, Joseph	22	N½NW	1891-07-30		A2
3142	" "	22	SENW	1891-07-30		A2
3201	FARR, Toliver	5	W½NW	1857-12-01		A1
3109	FOLSOM, John	13	NENE	1852-09-01		A1
3099	FOLSOM, John C	13	NWNE	1855-05-01		A1
3100	" "	13	SENE	1859-06-01		A1
3189	FOLSOM, Sidney S	1	SENE	1843-03-10		A1
3190	" "	12	SWNE	1843-03-10		A1
3002	FORTUNE, Adam	3	W½NW	1828-03-15		A1
3055	FOWLE, Frederick	35	E½SW	1829-05-01		A1
3196	GAUTIER, Thomas N	29	SENW	1859-06-01		A1
3197	" "	30	SESE	1859-06-01		A1
3198	" "	32	S½NW	1859-06-01		A1
3199	" "	32	SWNE	1859-06-01		A1
3195	GILBERT, Thomas L	18	W½NW	1895-10-16		A2
3148	GILCHRIST, Malcolm	35	E½NE	1827-10-01		A1 G72
3149	" "	35	W½NE	1827-10-01		A1 G72
3200	GODFREY, Thomas P	12	NWSE	1835-10-20		A1
3053	GRANTLAND, Seaton	2	W½NW	1834-08-20		A1 G31
3044	HARVEY, Elmira	28	N½SW	1900-08-09		A2 G77
3070	HAWKINS, Henry	8	E½SE	1890-06-05		A2
3160	HAYNES, Nancy M	33	SE	1857-12-01		A1
3161	" "	34	SESW	1857-12-01		A1
3162	" "	34	W½SW	1857-12-01		A1
3061	HOWARD, George	31	SENW	1843-03-10		A1
3062	" "	31	SW	1843-03-10		A1
3144	HOWELL, Joseph H	23	W½SE	1830-12-28		A1
3017	HUNTER, Asbury	20	NE	1891-05-04		A2
3212	HURST, William	22	W½NE	1857-12-01		A1
3080	JOINER, James	20	SE	1895-10-16		A2
3136	JONES, Jonathan	15	W½SE	1829-05-15		A1
3074	KILBEE, Huldah	31	SESE	1859-06-01		A1
3075	" "	31	W½SE	1859-06-01		A1
3076	" "	32	SWSW	1859-06-01		A1
3108	KING, John E	24	E½SE	1889-06-29		A2
3090	LOFTIN, Jeremiah	8	E½NE	1834-08-20		A1
3011	LOTT, Ann M	5	SESE	1855-05-01		A1
3016	MADDOX, Artimissy	32	SESW	1891-02-13		A2 G98
3016	MADDOX, George W	32	SESW	1891-02-13		A2 G98
3014	MALTSBY, Archibald	4	NWNE	1837-04-15		A1
3015	" "	4	SWNE	1837-04-15		A1
3003	MANDELL, Addison	4	E½NE	1829-05-01		A1

ID	Individual in Patent	Sec.	Sec. Part	Date Issued	Other Counties	For More Info . . .
3145	MARSHALL, Joseph	28	N½NE	1890-12-27		A2
3167	MATTHEWS, Rayford	6	SW	1895-10-22		A2
3083	MCCLELLAN, James S	8	NESW	1857-07-01		A1
3084	" "	8	NWSE	1857-07-01		A1
3085	" "	8	SENW	1857-07-01		A1
3086	" "	8	W½NE	1857-07-01		A1
3071	MCMULLEN, Henry P	4	NWSW	1884-06-30		A1
3030	MCQUAGE, Daniel	9	E½NE	1838-07-28		A1
3034	MCQUAGGE, Daniel	15	E½NW	1833-05-16		A1
3035	" "	26	W½NE	1834-03-28		A1
3032	" "	10	NWSW	1840-10-10		A1
3031	" "	10	E½SE	1843-03-10		A1
3033	" "	15	E½NE	1843-03-10		A1
3036	MCQUAIG, Daniel	4	E½SW	1838-07-28		A1 G103
3060	MERCER, George D	36	SESW	1878-06-24		A2
3050	MERRITT, Ethington J	25	NWSE	1855-05-01		A1
3051	" "	25	W½NE	1855-05-01		A1
3047	" "	13	S½SE	1902-09-02		A1
3048	" "	24	N½NE	1902-09-02		A1
3049	" "	25	E½SE	1902-09-02		A1
3052	MERRITT, Ethrington J	25	NESW	1843-03-10		A1
3056	MING, Frederick L	25	W½SW	1838-07-28		A1
3137	MORRIS, Jonathan	9	NESE	1843-03-10		A1
3131	MYRICK, John T	21	E½NE	1857-07-01		A1
3132	" "	21	SWNW	1857-07-01		A1
3133	" "	22	SW	1857-07-01		A1
3134	" "	22	SWSE	1857-07-01		A1
3043	PADGET, Elijah	35	E½NW	1834-08-20		A1
3042	" "	26	SESW	1837-04-15		A1
3112	PADGETT, John	26	SWSW	1841-01-09		A1
3113	" "	35	W½NW	1841-01-09		A1
3114	" "	8	NWNW	1846-10-01		A1
3191	PADGETT, Stephen J	30	N½SE	1900-07-12		A2
3192	" "	30	S½NE	1900-07-12		A2
3193	PADGETT, Theophilus W	30	SWSE	1900-08-09		A2
3115	PADJETT, John	5	W½SW	1856-06-16		A1
3116	" "	6	SESE	1856-06-16		A1
3117	" "	8	NENW	1856-06-16		A1
3118	" "	8	SWNW	1856-06-16		A1
3138	PELT, Jonathan	13	NENW	1850-08-10		A1
3139	" "	13	SWNE	1857-07-01		A1
3140	" "	13	W½SW	1859-06-01		A1
3187	PELT, Seaborn	24	SENW	1857-12-01		A1
3188	" "	24	SWNE	1857-12-01		A1
3040	PEYTON, Edward W	1	NENE	1843-03-10		A1
3037	PITTMAN, Edward C	36	E½NW	1843-03-10		A1
3057	PITTMAN, Frederick R	26	SENW	1855-05-01		A1
3058	" "	34	NENE	1855-05-01		A1
3059	" "	36	E½NE	1855-05-01		A1
3110	POPE, John M	12	E½NE	1828-02-22		A1
3111	" "	12	E½SE	1828-02-22		A1
3087	PORTER, James T	20	NW	1898-04-06		A2
3081	POWERS, James	22	NWSE	1891-06-17		A2
3217	ROULHAC, Writon	28	SESW	1888-11-20		A2
3054	SEXTON, Francis M	20	SW	1890-08-06		A2
3073	SHACKELFORD, Hinton E	18	E½NW	1895-10-16		A2
3151	SIMMES, Miles	2	NE	1827-06-15		A1
3072	SIMMONS, Henry	34	NWNE	1891-11-09		A2
3077	SIMMONS, J W	10	SWSW	1888-11-14		A2
3091	SIMS, Jeremiah	1	NESE	1835-10-20		A1
3095	" "	12	SWSE	1843-03-10		A1
3092	" "	1	SESE	1844-07-10		A1
3093	" "	12	E½NW	1844-07-10		A1
3094	" "	12	NWNE	1844-07-10		A1
3158	SIMS, Miles	2	E½SE	1828-02-22		A1
3009	" "	11	E½SW	1828-09-10		A1 G13
3010	" "	11	W½NE	1828-09-10		A1 G13
3153	" "	14	E½SW	1830-12-28		A1
3154	" "	14	NW	1830-12-28		A1
3156	" "	14	W½NE	1830-12-28		A1
3159	" "	36	W½SE	1830-12-28		A1
3152	" "	14	E½NE	1834-08-20		A1
3155	" "	14	SE	1834-08-20		A1

ID	Individual in Patent	Sec.	Sec. Part	Date Issued	Other Counties	For More Info . . .
3157	SIMS, Miles (Cont'd)	14	W½SW	1834-08-20		A1
3213	SIMS, William	10	E½SW	1828-03-15		A1
3215	" "	36	SESE	1843-03-10		A1
3214	" "	36	NESE	1856-06-16		A1
3163	STALEY, Nelson O	1	E½NW	1857-07-01		A1
3164	" "	1	S½SW	1857-07-01		A1
3165	" "	1	SWNE	1857-07-01		A1
3166	" "	1	W½SE	1857-07-01		A1
3038	STEPHENS, Edward	32	N½SW	1890-06-05		A2
3039	" "	32	W½SE	1890-06-05		A2
3078	STEPHENS, Jacob	24	NWSE	1859-06-01		A1
3079	" "	24	SWSE	1859-06-01		A1
3181	STEPHENS, Samuel	33	E½SW	1857-12-01		A1
3182	" "	33	S½NE	1857-12-01		A1
3183	" "	33	SENW	1857-12-01		A1
3184	" "	34	W½NW	1857-12-01		A1
3128	STEWART, John	15	NESE	1843-03-10		A1
3130	" "	15	SESW	1856-06-16		A1
3129	" "	15	SESE	1857-07-01		A1
3185	STOWERS, Samuel	12	SW	1830-12-28		A1
3186	" "	12	W½NW	1834-08-20		A1
3089	SWAILS, Jasper	8	S½SW	1856-06-16		A1
3177	THOMAS, David	3	E½SW	1827-10-01		A1 G28
3150	VANCE, Miles M	6	NESE	1846-10-01		A1
3143	WACHOB, Joseph F	9	W½NE	1828-02-22		A1
3088	WATSON, James	5	E½NE	1839-09-20		A1
3036	WHITE, Thomas M	4	E½SW	1838-07-28		A1 G103
3203	WILLIAMSON, Charles	2	E½NW	1827-10-01		A1 G65
3026	" "	2	E½SW	1827-10-01		A1
3027	" "	2	W½SW	1827-10-01		A1
3028	" "	3	E½SE	1827-10-01		A1
3148	" "	35	E½NE	1827-10-01		A1 G72
3149	" "	35	W½NE	1827-10-01		A1 G72
3044	WYNN, Elmira	28	N½SW	1900-08-09		A2 G77
3024	WYNNS, Benjamin	5	NWNE	1843-03-10		A1

Patent Map

T4-N R10-W
Tallahassee Meridian

Map Group 25

Township Statistics

Parcels Mapped	:	217
Number of Patents	:	175
Number of Individuals	:	115
Patentees Identified	:	112
Number of Surnames	:	95
Multi-Patentee Parcels	:	10
Oldest Patent Date	:	4/2/1827
Most Recent Patent	:	5/16/1916
Block/Lot Parcels	:	0
Parcels Re-Issued	:	0
Parcels that Overlap	:	0
Cities and Towns	:	3
Cemeteries	:	8

6
CLEMMONS John 1894
COLEMAN Reuben 1899
MATTHEWS Rayford 1895
COKER Benjamin 1899
VANCE Miles M 1846
PADJETT John 1856

FARR Toliver 1857
PADJETT John 1856

5
WYNNS Benjamin 1843
WATSON James 1839
LOTT Ann M 1855

BRYAN William C 1835
CALL Richard K 1830
MCMULLEN Henry P 1884
MCQUAIG [103] Daniel 1838

4
MALTSBY Archibald 1837
MALTSBY Archibald 1837
MANDELL Addison 1829
BEVERIDGE Anna M 1828
BEVERIDGE Anna M 1828

7
ATTAWAY Lawrence M 1857

PADGETT John 1846
PADGETT John 1856
PADJETT John 1856
MCCLELLAN James S 1857
MCCLELLAN James S 1857
MCCLELLAN James S 1857
SWAILS Jasper 1856

PADJETT John 1856
MCCLELLAN James S 1857
MCCLELLAN James S 1857
DICKSON Salina 1897

8
LOFTIN Jeremiah 1834
HAWKINS Henry 1890

BUSH John W 1839
BUSH John 1844

9
WACHOB Joseph F 1828
MCQUAGE Daniel 1838
MORRIS Jonathan 1843

18
GILBERT Thomas L 1895
SHACKELFORD Hinton E 1895
CARAWAY Major J 1895
BLACKSHEAR Daniel 1893
BLACKSHEAR Cato 1898

17

16

19

PORTER James T 1898
SEXTON Francis M 1890

20
HUNTER Asbury 1891
JOINER James 1895

MYRICK John T 1857

21
MYRICK John T 1857

30
BAREFOOT Redding 1892
BAREFOOT Redding 1892
DICKEY Elvira J 1899
PADGETT Stephen J 1900
DICKEY Elvira J 1899
PADGETT Stephen J 1900
ALLEN John 1896
PADGETT Theophilus W 1900
GAUTIER Thomas N 1859

29
GAUTIER Thomas N 1859

MARSHALL Joseph 1890
DICKENS Willie 1900
BRYAN Henry 1859
BRYAN Henry 1859
HARVEY [77] Elmira 1900
ROULHAC Writon 1888

28
BRYAN Henry 1859

31
HOWARD George 1843
KILBEE Huldah 1859
HOWARD George 1843

GAUTIER Thomas N 1859
STEPHENS Edward 1890
KILBEE Huldah 1859
GAUTIER Thomas N 1859

32
STEPHENS Edward 1890
KILBEE Huldah 1859
MADDOX [98] Artimissy 1891

STEPHENS Samuel 1857
STEPHENS Samuel 1857

33
STEPHENS Samuel 1857
HAYNES Nancy M 1857

FORTUNE Adam 1828

CHAIRES Benjamin 1827
3
DAVIS John 1827
CHAIRES Green H 1828
CARTER [31] Farish 1834
DRAKE [65] William B 1827
SIMMES Miles 1827
2

STALEY Nelson O 1857
COOK Thomas 1855
PEYTON Edward W 1843
STALEY Nelson O 1857
FOLSOM Sidney S 1843

BEVERIDGE Robert 1827
CALL [28] Richard K 1827
DAVIS Walter 1827
WILLIAMSON Charles 1827
WILLIAMSON Charles 1827
WILLIAMSON Charles 1827
BANKS William 1827
SIMS Miles 1828

1
STALEY Nelson O 1857
STALEY Nelson O 1857
SIMS Jeremiah 1835
SIMS Jeremiah 1844

CHAIRES Benjamin 1828
CHAIRES Benjamin 1827
10
CALL Richard K 1827
BEVERIDGE Robert 1827
BATTLE Amos I 1828
BATTLE [13] Amos I 1828
BATTLE Amos I 1828
STOWERS Samuel 1834
12
SIMS Jeremiah 1844
SIMS Jeremiah 1844
FOLSOM Sidney S 1843
POPE John M 1828

MCQUAGGE Daniel 1840
SIMMONS J W 1888
SIMS William 1828
CHAIRES Benjamin 1827
MCQUAGGE Daniel 1843
BATTLE Amos I 1828
BATTLE [13] Amos I 1828
11
BATTLE Amos I 1828
STOWERS Samuel 1830
GODFREY Thomas P 1835
SIMS Jeremiah 1843
POPE John M 1828

COWARD Zachariah 1833
15
MCQUAGGE Daniel 1833
CHAIRES Benjamin 1827
MCQUAGGE Daniel 1843
SIMS Miles 1830
14
SIMS Miles 1830
SIMS Miles 1834

PELT Jonathan 1850
FOLSOM John C 1855
FOLSOM John 1852
PELT Jonathan 1857
FOLSOM John C 1859
13

STEWART John 1856
JONES Jonathan 1829
STEWART John 1843
STEWART John 1857
SIMS Miles 1834
SIMS Miles 1830
SIMS Miles 1834
PELT Jonathan 1859
MERRITT Ethington J 1902

DYKES Joseph 1891
DYKES Joseph 1891
HURST William 1857
COOLEY Alfred 1857
CONNELL James S 1885
CHAPMAN John R 1843
CHAPMAN John R 1843
CHAPMAN John R 1843
CHAPMAN John R 1843
BRAXTON Eli 1916
PELT Seaborn 1857
MERRITT Ethington J 1902
PELT Seaborn 1857
DAVIS Joe 1913

22
MYRICK John T 1857
POWERS James 1891
MYRICK John T 1857
23
HOWELL Joseph H 1830
CALL Richard K 1830
24
CALL Richard K 1830
STEPHENS Jacob 1859
STEPHENS Jacob 1859
KING John E 1889

BRYAN Henry 1859
PITTMAN Frederick R 1855
26
MCQUAGGE Daniel 1834
CALL Richard K 1830
BANKS William 1827
CALL Richard K 1833
25
MERRITT Ethington J 1855

27
BRYAN Henry 1859
BRYAN Henry 1859
BRYAN Henry 1859
CHAPMAN John R 1840
PADGETT John 1841
PADGET Elijah 1837
CHAPMAN John R 1840
BANKS William 1827
MING Frederick L 1838
MERRITT Ethington J 1843
MERRITT Ethington J 1855
MERRITT Ethington J 1902

STEPHENS Samuel 1857
DURHAM John 1856
SIMMONS Henry 1891
PITTMAN Frederick R 1855
DURHAM John 1856
34
PADGETT John 1841
GILCHRIST [72] Malcolm 1827
GILCHRIST [72] Malcolm 1827
PADGET Elijah 1834
35
BANKS William 1827
PITTMAN Edward C 1843
36
PITTMAN Frederick R 1855

HAYNES Nancy M 1857
BELLAMY William H 1892
HAYNES Nancy M 1857
BELLAMY William H 1892
BELLAMY William H 1892
DURHAM John 1841
DURHAM John 1856
DURHAM John 1841
FOWLE Frederick 1829
CHAPMAN John R 1841
CHAPMAN John R 1840
CHAPMAN John R 1840
MERCER George D 1878
SIMS Miles 1830
SIMS William 1856
SIMS William 1843

Helpful Hints

1. This Map's INDEX can be found on the preceding pages.

2. Refer to Map "C" to see where this Township lies within Jackson County, Florida.

3. Numbers within square brackets [ ] denote a multi-patentee land parcel (multi-owner). Refer to Appendix "C" for a full list of members in this group.

4. Areas that look to be crowded with Patentees usually indicate multiple sales of the same parcel (Re-issues) or Overlapping parcels. See this Township's Index for an explanation of these and other circumstances that might explain "odd" groupings of Patentees on this map.

Legend

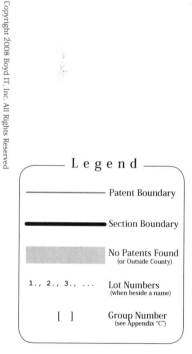

——— Patent Boundary

▬▬▬ Section Boundary

░░░ No Patents Found (or Outside County)

1., 2., 3., ... Lot Numbers (when beside a name)

[ ] Group Number (see Appendix "C")

Scale: Section = 1 mile X 1 mile (generally, with some exceptions)

243

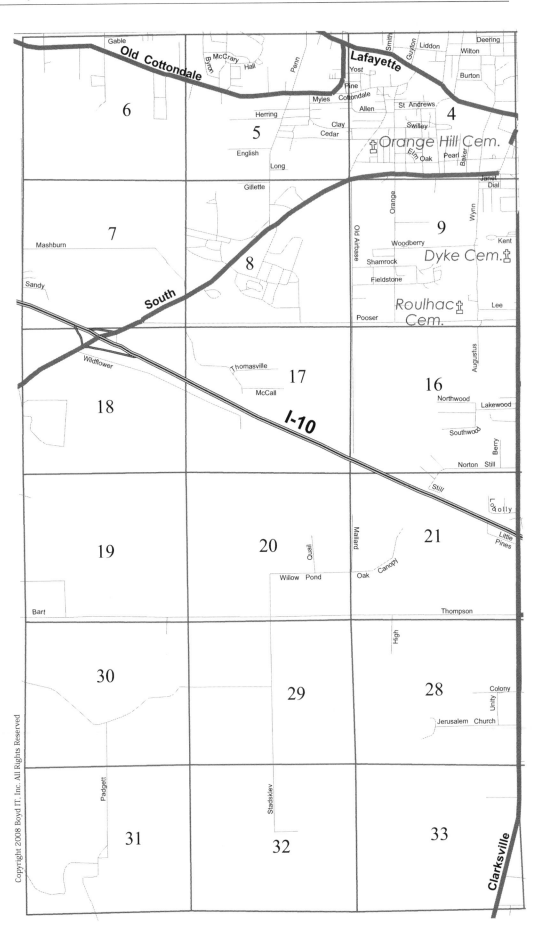

Road Map

T4-N R10-W
Tallahassee Meridian

Map Group 25

Cities & Towns
Mallory Heights
Marianna
Oakdale

Cemeteries
Braxton Cemetery
Dyke Cemetery
Grant Cemetery
Orange Hill Cemetery
Pelt Cemetery
Riverside Cemetery
Roulhac Cemetery
Sims Cemetery

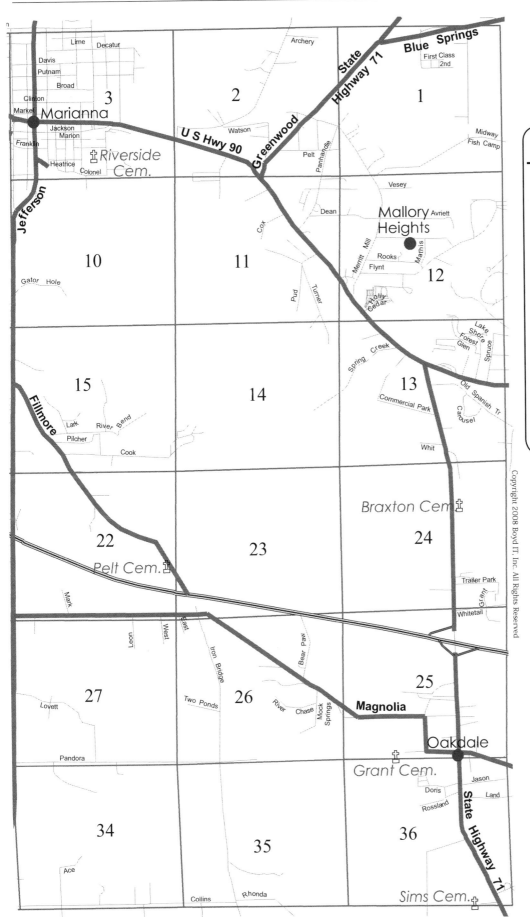

Helpful Hints

1. This road map has a number of uses, but primarily it is to help you: a) find the present location of land owned by your ancestors (at least the general area), b) find cemeteries and city-centers, and c) estimate the route/roads used by Census-takers & tax-assessors.

2. If you plan to travel to Jackson County to locate cemeteries or land parcels, please pick up a modern travel map for the area before you do. Mapping old land parcels on modern maps is not as exact a science as you might think. Just the slightest variations in public land survey coordinates, estimates of parcel boundaries, or road-map deviations can greatly alter a map's representation of how a road either does or doesn't cross a particular parcel of land.

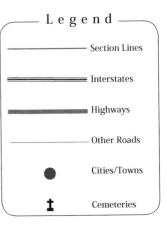

Legend

———————	Section Lines
══════════	Interstates
▬▬▬▬▬▬	Highways
———————	Other Roads
●	Cities/Towns
✝	Cemeteries

Scale: Section = 1 mile X 1 mile
(generally, with some exceptions)

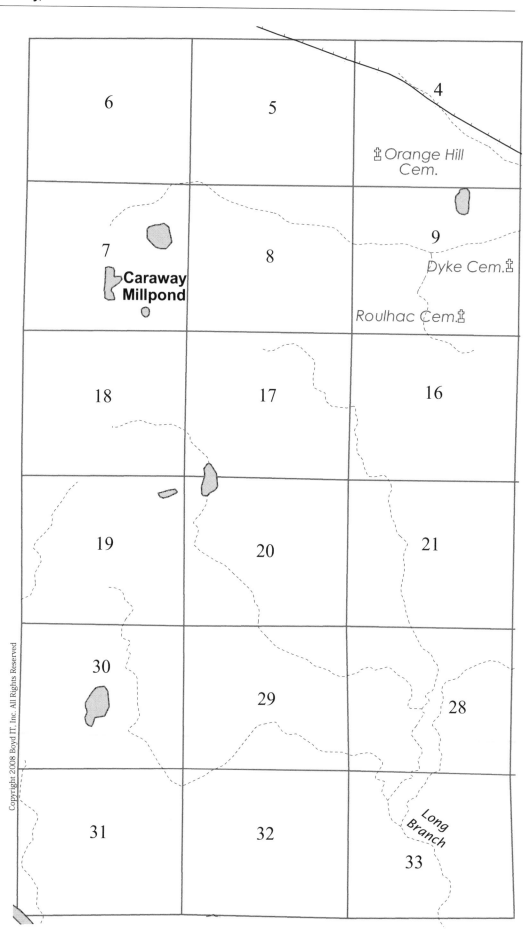

Historical Map

T4-N R10-W
Tallahassee Meridian

Map Group 25

Cities & Towns
Mallory Heights
Marianna
Oakdale

Cemeteries
Braxton Cemetery
Dyke Cemetery
Grant Cemetery
Orange Hill Cemetery
Pelt Cemetery
Riverside Cemetery
Roulhac Cemetery
Sims Cemetery

6

5

4

⚰ Orange Hill Cem.

7

8

9

Caraway Millpond

Dyke Cem. ⚰

Roulhac Cem. ⚰

18

17

16

19

20

21

30

29

28

31

32

33

Long Branch

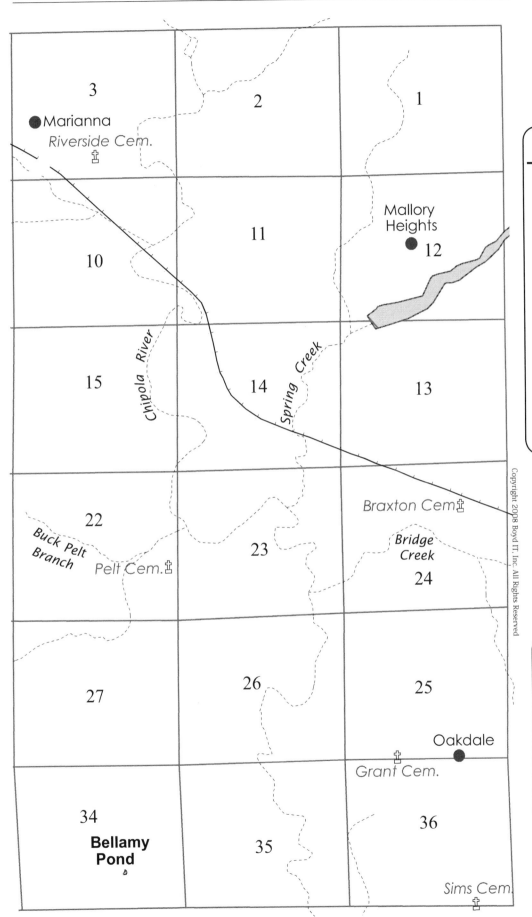

3

●Marianna

Riverside Cem.
✝

2

1

Mallory
Heights
● 12

11

10

Chipola River

Spring Creek

15

14

13

22

*Buck Pelt
Branch*

Pelt Cem. ✝

23

Braxton Cem ✝

*Bridge
Creek*

24

27

26

25

Oakdale
✝   ●

Grant Cem.

34

**Bellamy
Pond**
♭

35

36

Sims Cem.
✝

Helpful Hints

1. This Map takes a different look at the same Congressional Township displayed in the preceding two maps. It presents features that can help you better envision the historical development of the area: a) Water-bodies (lakes & ponds), b) Water-courses (rivers, streams, etc.), c) Railroads, d) City/town center-points (where they were oftentimes located when first settled), and e) Cemeteries.

2. Using this "Historical" map in tandem with this Township's Patent Map and Road Map, may lead you to some interesting discoveries. You will often find roads, towns, cemeteries, and waterways are named after nearby landowners: sometimes those names will be the ones you are researching. See how many of these research gems you can find here in Jackson County.

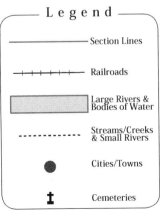

L e g e n d

——————— Section Lines

+++++++ Railroads

Large Rivers &
Bodies of Water

- - - - - Streams/Creeks
& Small Rivers

● Cities/Towns

✝ Cemeteries

Scale: Section = 1 mile X 1 mile
(there are some exceptions)

Map Group 26: Index to Land Patents

Township 4-North Range 9-West (Tallahassee)

After you locate an individual in this Index, take note of the Section and Section Part then proceed to the Land Patent map on the pages immediately following. You should have no difficulty locating the corresponding parcel of land.

The "For More Info" Column will lead you to more information about the underlying Patents. See the *Legend* at right, and the "How to Use this Book" chapter, for more information.

ID	Individual in Patent	Sec.	Sec. Part	Date Issued	Other Counties	For More Info . . .
3235	BATTLE, Bennett S	7	NENE	1855-05-01		A1
3238	" "	7	SWNE	1855-05-01		A1
3237	" "	7	SESE	1856-06-16		A1
3239	" "	8	SWNW	1856-06-16		A1
3240	" "	8	W½SW	1856-06-16		A1
3236	" "	7	NESW	1859-06-01		A1
3347	BELL, Nelson	18	SE	1897-09-20		A2
3261	BLACK, George	18	NE	1894-03-08		A2
3246	BURNHAM, Canna	30	SE	1903-12-17		A2
3221	BYRD, Archibald D	36	E½NW	1857-12-01		A1
3222	" "	36	N½SW	1857-12-01		A1
3314	BYRD, John A	24	SW	1857-12-01		A1
3315	" "	24	W½SE	1857-12-01		A1
3316	" "	25	E½NW	1857-12-01		A1
3263	CARROLL, George P	26	N½SW	1898-10-04		A2
3264	" "	26	SWNE	1898-10-04		A2
3306	CARROLL, Jesse D	26	S½SW	1903-05-25		A2
3332	CARROLL, John S	26	SE	1895-10-16		A2
3308	CLARK, Jesse M	11	NENW	1852-09-01		A1
3307	" "	10	NENE	1856-06-16		A1
3309	" "	11	NESE	1856-06-16		A1
3310	" "	11	NWNW	1856-06-16		A1
3311	" "	11	SENE	1856-06-16		A1
3312	" "	12	N½SW	1856-06-16		A1
3313	" "	3	S½SE	1856-06-16		A1
3277	CLAY, Henry	18	SWNW	1898-10-04		A2
3278	" "	18	W½SW	1898-10-04		A2
3227	CLEMENTS, Benjamin	5	W½SW	1827-10-01		A1 G48
3226	" "	6	E½NE	1827-10-01		A1 G50
3294	COMERFORD, James E	22	NENW	1911-09-21		A1
3300	COMERFORD, James R	24	SWNW	1901-04-09		A2
3318	COMERFORD, John	15	SWSW	1852-09-01		A1
3317	" "	15	NWSW	1856-06-16		A1
3319	" "	15	W½NW	1856-06-16		A1
3351	COMERFORD, Philip	10	SENW	1843-03-10		A1
3270	COOK, Green B	34	N½NW	1897-10-20		A2
3271	" "	34	SENW	1897-10-20		A2
3272	" "	34	SWNE	1897-10-20		A2
3281	CUTCHIN, Isaac G	26	W½NW	1898-04-06		A2
3219	DAVIS, Alburn E	22	SWSW	1912-04-18		A2
3335	DAVIS, John W	30	W½NW	1890-12-11		A2
3303	DAY, Jefferson	30	W½SW	1904-12-20		A2
3273	DICKENS, Harry	18	E½NW	1897-05-25		A2
3274	" "	18	NWNW	1897-05-25		A2
3249	DYKES, Daniel G	20	S½SE	1901-07-20		A2
3250	EDWARDS, Delilah	24	E½NW	1860-07-02		A1

ID	Individual in Patent	Sec.	Sec. Part	Date Issued	Other Counties	For More Info . . .
3251	EDWARDS, Delilah (Cont'd)	24	S½NE	1860-07-02		A1
3225	EMANUEL, Asa	28	NE	1898-02-24		A2
3360	GOFF, Samuel	30	E½NW	1900-08-09		A2
3275	GRANT, Hawkins	20	SENW	1894-07-31		A2
3276	" "	20	W½NE	1894-07-31		A2
3248	GRANTHAM, Cornelius	5	W½SE	1827-04-02		A1 G74
3382	GRUBBS, William	24	E½SE	1889-06-29		A2
3223	GUNDERSON, Arsena	22	NESE	1901-04-09		A2
3224	" "	22	SENE	1901-04-09		A2
3243	HATHAWAY, Bird B	23	NENW	1856-06-16		A1
3241	" "	14	E½NW	1860-04-02		A1
3242	" "	14	SW	1860-04-02		A1
3244	" "	23	NWNW	1860-04-02		A1
3252	HILL, Dempsey	34	SW	1894-01-27		A2
3302	HILL, James W	34	SWNW	1903-05-25		A2
3352	HILL, Redding H	22	E½SW	1895-10-16		A2
3353	" "	22	S½SE	1895-10-16		A2
3354	HODGES, Richard	11	N½SW	1856-06-16		A1
3355	" "	11	NWSE	1856-06-16		A1
3356	" "	11	SWNW	1856-06-16		A1
3357	" "	11	SWSE	1856-06-16		A1
3265	HORN, George W	20	SW	1893-01-21		A2
3228	INGRAM, Benjamin H	32	W½NW	1906-03-12		A2
3227	JEMISON, Robert	5	W½SW	1827-10-01		A1 G48
3341	JONES, Jonathan	12	SESW	1857-07-01		A1
3388	JONES, William S	12	E½NE	1857-07-01		A1
3389	" "	12	E½SE	1857-07-01		A1
3390	" "	13	NENE	1857-07-01		A1
3320	MCCORMICK, John	5	E½SW	1827-06-15		A1
3321	" "	7	E½NW	1828-03-01		A1
3322	" "	7	W½NW	1830-11-01		A1
3383	MCCROAN, William H	36	W½NW	1902-12-30		A2
3229	MCNEALY, Benjamin	30	SESW	1894-03-08		A2
3350	MCPARLAND, Peter	25	E½	1859-06-01		A1
3262	MERCER, George E	28	NW	1896-11-16		A2
3363	MERCER, Silas N	30	NE	1889-07-02		A2
3374	MERCER, Vann S	28	W½SW	1900-08-09		A2
3254	MERRITT, Ethington J	19	NWNW	1902-09-02		A1
3381	MILLER, William G	36	S½SW	1904-08-26		A2
3326	MILTON, John	10	NWNE	1850-08-10		A1
3327	" "	10	NWNW	1850-08-10		A1
3329	" "	3	E½SW	1850-08-10		A1
3330	" "	3	N½SE	1850-08-10		A1
3328	" "	11	N½NE	1855-05-01		A1
3323	" "	1	E½NE	1856-06-16		A1
3324	" "	1	NESE	1856-06-16		A1
3325	" "	1	W½SE	1856-06-16		A1
3257	MING, Frederick L	5	SESE	1844-07-10		A1
3364	MING, Susan A	8	E½NW	1856-06-16		A1
3365	" "	8	N½SE	1856-06-16		A1
3366	" "	8	NESW	1856-06-16		A1
3367	" "	8	NWNW	1856-06-16		A1
3368	" "	9	NWSW	1856-06-16		A1
3369	" "	9	SWNW	1856-06-16		A1
3379	MING, William A	8	S½SE	1904-01-27		A2
3380	" "	8	SESW	1904-01-27		A2
3301	MURPHY, James S	5	NW	1827-04-02		A1
3258	PITTMAN, Frederick R	31	E½SE	1855-05-01		A1
3259	" "	32	SENW	1859-06-01		A1
3260	" "	32	SW	1859-06-01		A1
3279	PITTS, Isaac B	34	N½NE	1903-05-25		A2
3280	" "	34	SENE	1903-05-25		A2
3290	POOSER, Jacob H	4	E½SW	1850-08-10		A1
3288	" "	10	SWNW	1856-06-16		A1
3289	" "	10	SWSW	1856-06-16		A1
3291	" "	9	S½NE	1856-06-16		A1
3292	" "	9	S½SE	1856-06-16		A1
3293	" "	9	S½SW	1856-06-16		A1
3336	POOSER, John W	10	E½SW	1857-07-01		A1
3337	" "	10	SESE	1857-07-01		A1
3338	" "	10	W½SE	1857-07-01		A1
3339	" "	11	SWSW	1857-07-01		A1
3340	" "	14	W½NW	1857-07-01		A1

ID	Individual in Patent	Sec.	Sec. Part	Date Issued	Other Counties	For More Info . . .
3255	ROBINSON, Francis A	8	NE	1856-06-16		A1
3266	ROBINSON, George W	10	NENW	1852-09-01		A1
3267	" "	2	SWNW	1852-09-01		A1
3282	ROBINSON, Isaac	3	NW	1838-07-28		A1 G127
3283	" "	3	W½NE	1838-07-28		A1 G127
3375	ROBINSON, Walter J	2	S½	1848-11-01		A1
3376	" "	3	E½NE	1848-11-01		A1
3385	ROBINSON, William H	4	NW	1828-08-22		A1
3384	" "	4	NE	1829-05-01		A1
3282	" "	3	NW	1838-07-28		A1 G127
3283	" "	3	W½NE	1838-07-28		A1 G127
3295	SCOTT, James F	23	S½SE	1859-06-01		A1
3296	" "	25	NWNW	1859-06-01		A1
3297	" "	26	E½NE	1859-06-01		A1
3298	" "	26	E½NW	1859-06-01		A1
3299	" "	26	NWNE	1859-06-01		A1
3333	SIMMS, John	6	NW	1828-02-01		A1
3345	SIMMS, Miles	5	NE	1827-06-15		A1
3348	SIMMS, Osborne	20	E½NE	1895-02-14		A2
3349	" "	20	N½SE	1895-02-14		A2
3220	SIMS, Ambrose	15	E½SW	1830-11-01		A1
3284	SIMS, Isaac	32	NENE	1884-06-30		A2
3285	" "	32	NESE	1884-06-30		A2
3286	" "	32	S½NE	1884-06-30		A2
3305	SIMS, Jeremiah	6	W½SW	1828-07-22		A1
3304	" "	6	E½SW	1834-08-20		A1
3334	SIMS, John	7	W½SW	1829-05-15		A1
3346	SIMS, Morris	24	N½NE	1856-06-16		A1
3372	SIMS, Thomas	34	SE	1895-06-28		A2
3391	SIMS, William	31	NWSW	1856-06-16		A1
3233	STEPHENS, Benjamin	23	SWNE	1843-03-10		A1
3230	" "	23	E½NE	1856-06-16		A1
3231	" "	23	NWNE	1856-06-16		A1
3232	" "	23	NWSE	1856-06-16		A1
3234	" "	24	NWNW	1856-06-16		A1
3256	STEWART, Frederick H	32	SESE	1893-11-04		A2
3331	STOCKTON, John N	12	W½SE	1838-07-28		A1
3253	STREETMAN, Esta T	28	E½SE	1905-11-08		A2
3248	THOMAS, David	5	W½SE	1827-04-02		A1 G74
3358	TRIPP, Richard	7	SENE	1848-04-10		A1
3245	TRIPPE, Bryan	6	SE	1827-04-02		A1 G138
3245	TRIPPE, Charles	6	SE	1827-04-02		A1 G138
3359	TRIPPE, Richard	7	NWNE	1844-07-10		A1
3377	UNDERWOOD, Walter	20	NENW	1893-12-28		A2
3378	" "	20	W½NW	1893-12-28		A2
3344	VICKERY, Joseph T	14	SE	1856-06-16		A1
3361	WACASER, Sidney S	32	NENW	1911-06-26		A2
3362	" "	32	NWNE	1911-06-26		A2
3386	WACASER, William H	28	E½SW	1896-01-14		A2
3387	" "	28	W½SE	1896-01-14		A2
3268	WALKER, George	3	W½SW	1844-07-10		A1
3269	" "	4	SE	1844-07-10		A1
3342	WESTON, Joseph L	36	E½NE	1857-12-01		A1
3343	" "	36	E½SE	1857-12-01		A1
3370	WILLIAMS, Thomas F	36	W½NE	1898-04-06		A2
3371	" "	36	W½SE	1898-04-06		A2
3226	WILLIAMSON, Charles	6	E½NE	1827-10-01		A1 G50
3247	" "	6	W½NE	1827-10-01		A1
3373	WILTON, Thomas	12	W½NE	1829-06-15		A1
3287	WIMBERLY, Isaac	22	NENE	1856-06-16		A1

Patent Map

T4-N R9-W
Tallahassee Meridian

Map Group 26

Township Statistics

Parcels Mapped	:	173
Number of Patents	:	113
Number of Individuals	:	93
Patentees Identified	:	91
Number of Surnames	:	63
Multi-Patentee Parcels	:	6
Oldest Patent Date	:	4/2/1827
Most Recent Patent	:	4/18/1912
Block/Lot Parcels	:	0
Parcels Re - Issued	:	0
Parcels that Overlap	:	0
Cities and Towns	:	1
Cemeteries	:	2

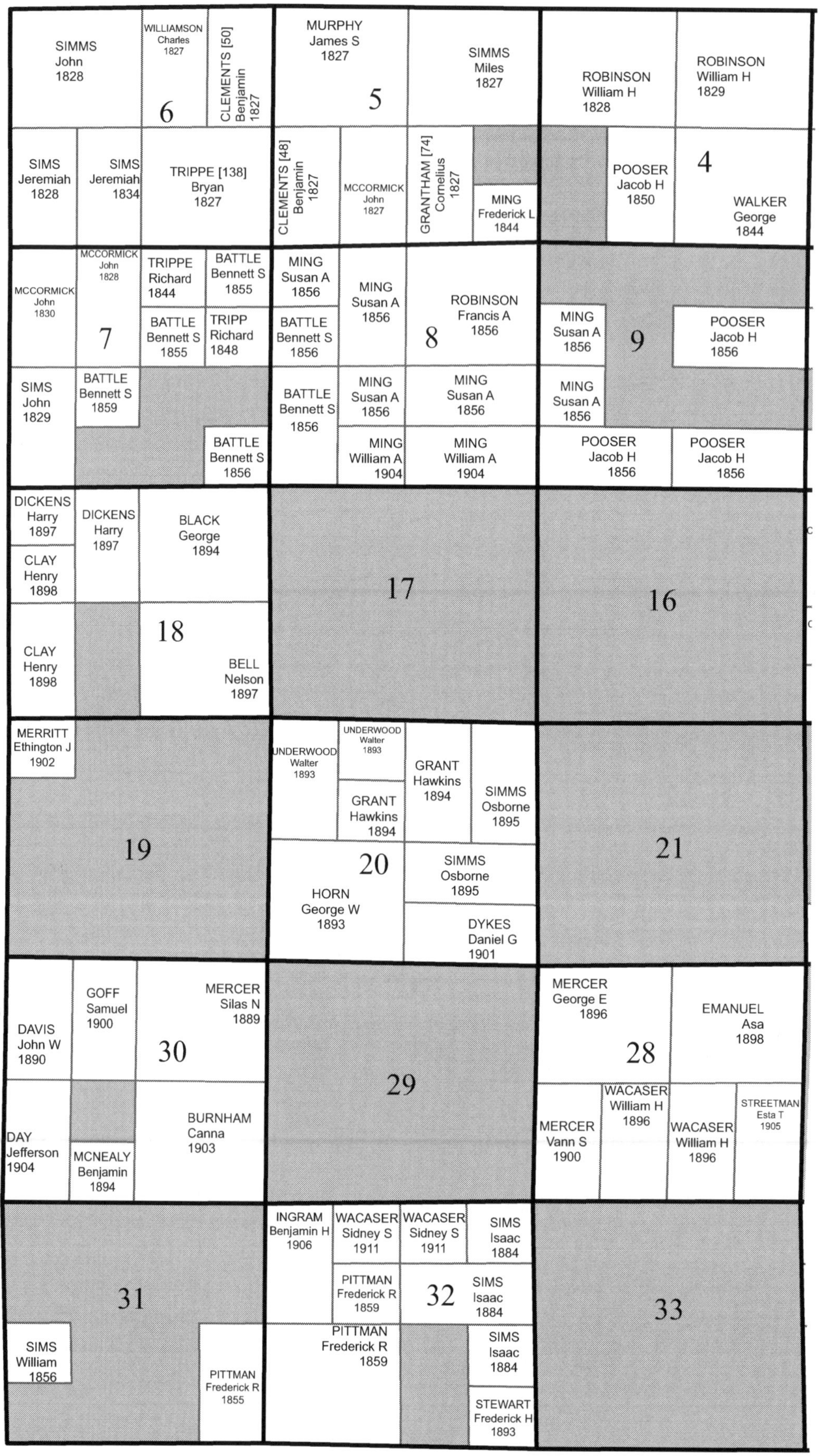

Map grid with the following labeled parcels:

Section 6: SIMMS John 1828; WILLIAMSON Charles 1827; CLEMENTS [50] Benjamin 1827; SIMS Jeremiah 1828; SIMS Jeremiah 1834; TRIPPE [138] Bryan 1827

Section 5: MURPHY James S 1827; SIMMS Miles 1827; CLEMENTS [48] Benjamin 1827; MCCORMICK John 1827; GRANTHAM [74] Cornelius 1827; MING Frederick L 1844

Section 4: ROBINSON William H 1828; ROBINSON William H 1829; POOSER Jacob H 1850; WALKER George 1844

Section 7: MCCORMICK John 1828; MCCORMICK John 1830; TRIPPE Richard 1844; BATTLE Bennett S 1855; BATTLE Bennett S 1855; TRIPP Richard 1848; SIMS John 1829; BATTLE Bennett S 1859; BATTLE Bennett S 1856

Section 8: MING Susan A 1856; MING Susan A 1856; BATTLE Bennett S 1856; ROBINSON Francis A 1856; BATTLE Bennett S 1856; MING Susan A 1856; MING Susan A 1856; MING William A 1904; MING William A 1904

Section 9: MING Susan A 1856; POOSER Jacob H 1856; MING Susan A 1856; POOSER Jacob H 1856; POOSER Jacob H 1856

Section 18: DICKENS Harry 1897; DICKENS Harry 1897; BLACK George 1894; CLAY Henry 1898; CLAY Henry 1898; BELL Nelson 1897

Section 17: (shaded)

Section 16: (shaded)

Section 19: MERRITT Ethington J 1902

Section 20: UNDERWOOD Walter 1893; UNDERWOOD Walter 1893; GRANT Hawkins 1894; GRANT Hawkins 1894; SIMMS Osborne 1895; SIMMS Osborne 1895; HORN George W 1893; DYKES Daniel G 1901

Section 21: (shaded)

Section 30: DAVIS John W 1890; GOFF Samuel 1900; MERCER Silas N 1889; DAY Jefferson 1904; MCNEALY Benjamin 1894; BURNHAM Canna 1903

Section 29: (shaded)

Section 28: MERCER George E 1896; EMANUEL Asa 1898; MERCER Vann S 1900; WACASER William H 1896; WACASER William H 1896; STREETMAN Esta T 1905

Section 31: SIMS William 1856; PITTMAN Frederick R 1855

Section 32: INGRAM Benjamin H 1906; WACASER Sidney S 1911; WACASER Sidney S 1911; SIMS Isaac 1884; PITTMAN Frederick R 1859; SIMS Isaac 1884; PITTMAN Frederick R 1859; SIMS Isaac 1884; STEWART Frederick H 1893

Section 33: (shaded)

Map

Section	Patentees
Section 3	ROBINSON [127] Isaac 1838; ROBINSON [127] Isaac 1838; ROBINSON Walter J 1848; ROBINSON George W 1852; 3; WALKER George 1844; MILTON John 1850; MILTON John 1850; CLARK Jesse M 1856
Section 2	2; ROBINSON Walter J 1848
Section 1	MILTON John 1856; MILTON John 1856; MILTON John 1856; 1

Section 10: MILTON John 1850; ROBINSON George W 1852; MILTON John 1850; CLARK Jesse M 1856; POOSER Jacob H 1856; COMERFORD Philip 1843; 10; POOSER John W 1857; POOSER John W 1857; POOSER Jacob H 1856; POOSER John W 1857

Section 11: CLARK Jesse M 1856; CLARK Jesse M 1852; MILTON John 1855; HODGES Richard 1856; 11; CLARK Jesse M 1856; HODGES Richard 1856; HODGES Richard 1856; CLARK Jesse M 1856; POOSER John W 1857; HODGES Richard 1856

Section 12: 12; WILTON Thomas 1829; JONES William S 1857; CLARK Jesse M 1856; STOCKTON John N 1838; JONES Jonathan 1857; JONES William S 1857

Section 15: COMERFORD John 1856; 15; COMERFORD John 1856; COMERFORD John 1852; SIMS Ambrose 1830

Section 14: POOSER John W 1857; HATHAWAY Bird B 1860; 14; HATHAWAY Bird B 1860; VICKERY Joseph T 1856

Section 13: 13; JONES William S 1857

Section 22: COMERFORD James E 1911; 22; HILL Redding H 1895; DAVIS Alburn E 1912

Section 23: WIMBERLY Isaac 1856; HATHAWAY Bird B 1860; HATHAWAY Bird B 1856; STEPHENS Benjamin 1856; STEPHENS Benjamin 1856; GUNDERSON Arsena 1901; STEPHENS Benjamin 1843; GUNDERSON Arsena 1901; HILL Redding H 1895; 23; STEPHENS Benjamin 1856; SCOTT James F 1859

Section 24: STEPHENS Benjamin 1856; EDWARDS Delilah 1860; SIMS Morris 1856; COMERFORD James R 1901; EDWARDS Delilah 1860; 24; BYRD John A 1857; BYRD John A 1857; GRUBBS William 1889

Section 27: 27

Section 26: CUTCHIN Isaac G 1898; SCOTT James F 1859; SCOTT James F 1859; SCOTT James F 1859; CARROLL George P 1898; CARROLL George P 1898; 26; CARROLL Jesse D 1903; CARROLL John S 1895

Section 25: SCOTT James F 1859; BYRD John A 1857; 25; MCPARLAND Peter 1859

Section 34: COOK Green B 1897; PITTS Isaac B 1903; HILL James W 1903; COOK Green B 1897; COOK Green B 1897; PITTS Isaac B 1903; HILL Dempsey 1894; 34; SIMS Thomas 1895

Section 35: 35

Section 36: MCCROAN William H 1902; WILLIAMS Thomas F 1898; WESTON Joseph L 1857; BYRD Archibald D 1857; 36; BYRD Archibald D 1857; WILLIAMS Thomas F 1898; WESTON Joseph L 1857; MILLER William G 1904

Helpful Hints

1. This Map's INDEX can be found on the preceding pages.

2. Refer to Map "C" to see where this Township lies within Jackson County, Florida.

3. Numbers within square brackets [ ] denote a multi-patentee land parcel (multi-owner). Refer to Appendix "C" for a full list of members in this group.

4. Areas that look to be crowded with Patentees usually indicate multiple sales of the same parcel (Re-issues) or Overlapping parcels. See this Township's Index for an explanation of these and other circumstances that might explain "odd" groupings of Patentees on this map.

Legend

- —— Patent Boundary
- ━━ Section Boundary
- No Patents Found (or Outside County)
- 1., 2., 3., ... Lot Numbers (when beside a name)
- [ ] Group Number (see Appendix "C")

Scale: Section = 1 mile X 1 mile (generally, with some exceptions)

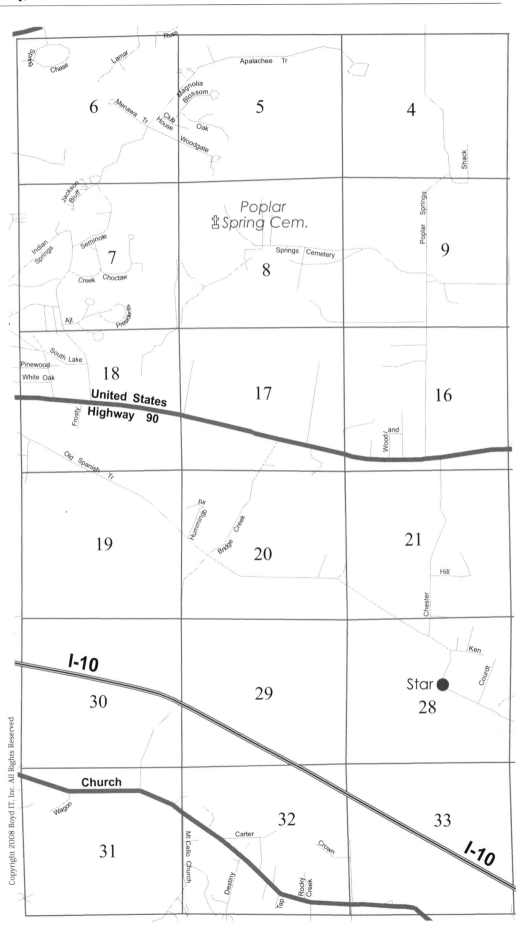

Road Map

T4-N R9-W
Tallahassee Meridian

Map Group 26

Cities & Towns

Star

Cemeteries

Hill Cemetery
Poplar Spring Cemetery

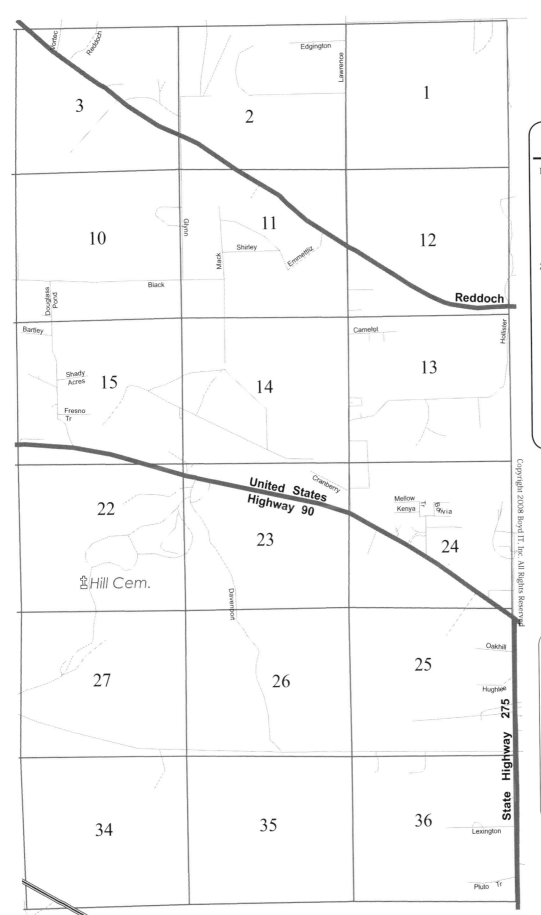

3

2

1

Vortec

Reddoch

Edgington

Lawrence

10

11

12

Glynn

Mack

Shirley

Emmettliz

Black

Reddoch

Douglass Pond

Bartley

Camelot

15

14

13

Shady Acres

Hollister

Fresno Tr

22

Cranberry

United States Highway 90

23

Mellow Kenya

Bonia

Tr

24

‡ Hill Cem.

Davenport

27

26

Oakhill

25

Hughlee

34

35

36

Lexington

Pluto Tr

Helpful Hints

1. This road map has a number of uses, but primarily it is to help you: a) find the present location of land owned by your ancestors (at least the general area), b) find cemeteries and city-centers, and c) estimate the route/roads used by Census-takers & tax-assessors.

2. If you plan to travel to Jackson County to locate cemeteries or land parcels, please pick up a modern travel map for the area before you do. Mapping old land parcels on modern maps is not as exact a science as you might think. Just the slightest variations in public land survey coordinates, estimates of parcel boundaries, or road-map deviations can greatly alter a map's representation of how a road either does or doesn't cross a particular parcel of land.

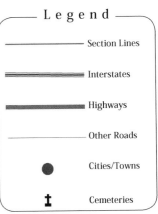

L e g e n d

—————— Section Lines

══════ Interstates

━━━━━━ Highways

————— Other Roads

● Cities/Towns

‡ Cemeteries

Scale: Section = 1 mile X 1 mile
(generally, with some exceptions)

State Highway 275

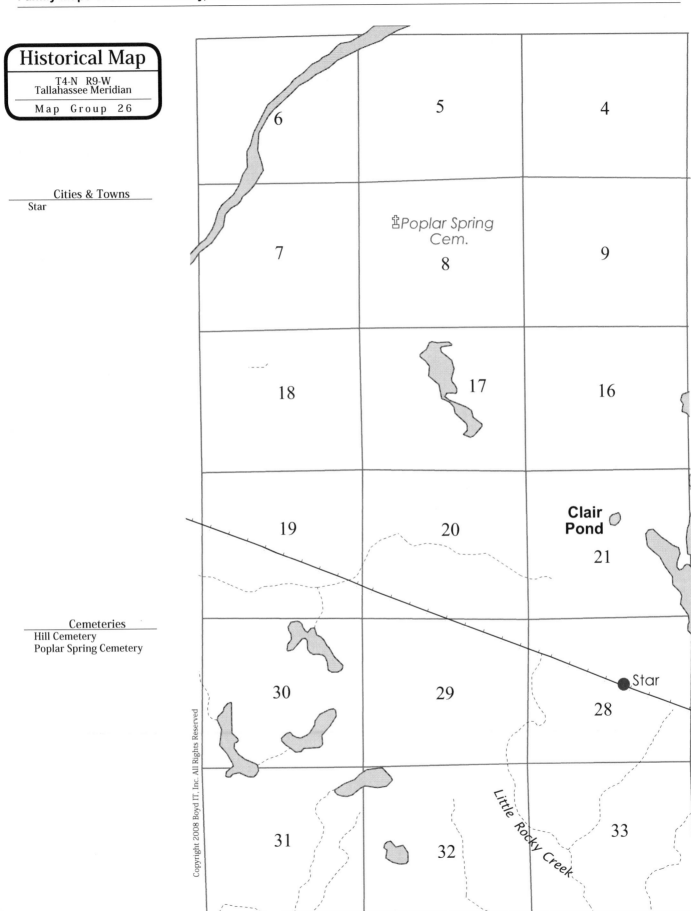

Historical Map

T4-N R9-W
Tallahassee Meridian

Map Group 26

Cities & Towns
Star

Cemeteries
Hill Cemetery
Poplar Spring Cemetery

6

5

4

⚰Poplar Spring
Cem.

7

8

9

18

17

16

19

20

Clair
Pond

21

30

29

Star

28

31

32

Little Rocky Creek

33

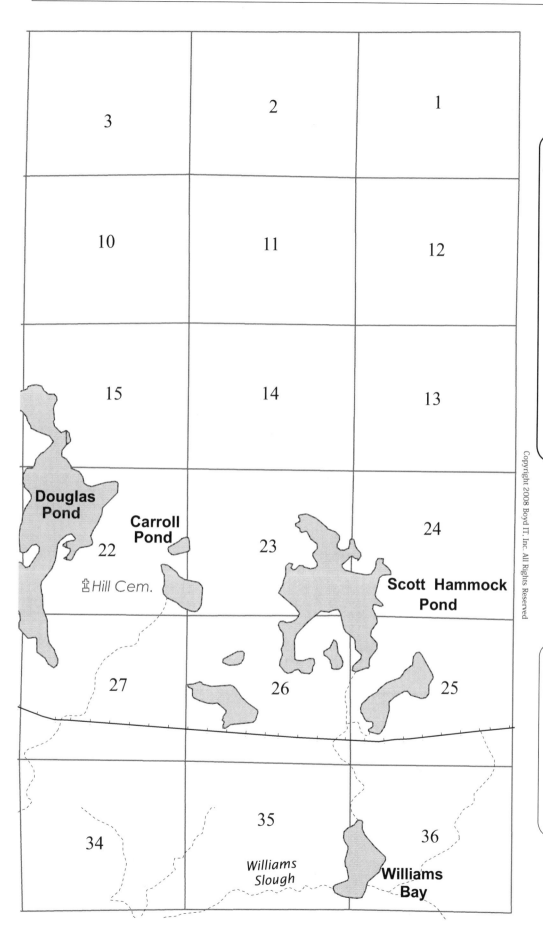

3

2

1

10

11

12

15

14

13

Douglas
Pond

Carroll
Pond

22

23

24

⚱Hill Cem.

Scott Hammock
Pond

27

26

25

34

35

36

Williams
Slough

Williams
Bay

Helpful Hints

Helpful Hints

1. This Map takes a different look at the same Congressional Township displayed in the preceding two maps. It presents features that can help you better envision the historical development of the area: a) Water-bodies (lakes & ponds), b) Water-courses (rivers, streams, etc.), c) Railroads, d) City/town center-points (where they were oftentimes located when first settled), and e) Cemeteries.

2. Using this "Historical" map in tandem with this Township's Patent Map and Road Map, may lead you to some interesting discoveries. You will often find roads, towns, cemeteries, and waterways are named after nearby landowners: sometimes those names will be the ones you are researching. See how many of these research gems you can find here in Jackson County.

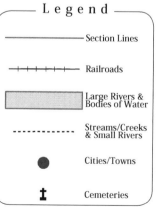

Legend

Section Lines

┼┼┼┼┼┼ Railroads

Large Rivers &
Bodies of Water

- - - - - Streams/Creeks
& Small Rivers

● Cities/Towns

✝ Cemeteries

Scale: Section = 1 mile X 1 mile
(there are some exceptions)

Map Group 27: Index to Land Patents

Township 4-North Range 8-West (Tallahassee)

After you locate an individual in this Index, take note of the Section and Section Part then proceed to the Land Patent map on the pages immediately following. You should have no difficulty locating the corresponding parcel of land.

The "For More Info" Column will lead you to more information about the underlying Patents. See the *Legend* at right, and the "How to Use this Book" chapter, for more information.

```
                    LEGEND
          "For More Info . . . " column

A = Authority (Legislative Act, See Appendix "A")
B = Block or Lot (location in Section unknown)
C = Cancelled Patent
F = Fractional Section
G = Group  (Multi-Patentee Patent, see Appendix "C")
V = Overlaps another Parcel
R = Re-Issued (Parcel patented more than once)

(A & G items require you to look in the Appendixes referred
to above. All other Letter-designations followed by a number
require you to locate line-items in this index that possess
the ID number found after the letter).
```

ID	Individual in Patent	Sec.	Sec. Part	Date Issued	Other Counties	For More Info . . .
3493	BAKER, John	17	SESE	1857-07-01		A1
3494	" "	20	NENE	1857-07-01		A1
3486	BEVIS, John A	30	SW	1885-06-03		A1
3537	BLACKMON, Sarah M	6	NWNE	1893-05-19		A2 G18
3414	BLOOD, Caleb H	13	NW	1857-12-01		A1
3415	" "	13	W½NE	1857-12-01		A1
3416	" "	14	E½NE	1857-12-01		A1
3467	BRADLEY, Iziah	28	SW	1889-06-21		A2
3411	BRYANT, Berry E	4	SESW	1900-08-09		A2
3481	BRYANT, James W	34	NESW	1891-11-09		A2
3482	" "	34	S½SW	1891-11-09		A2
3483	" "	34	SWSE	1891-11-09		A2
3521	BRYANT, Newton B	26	SE	1890-12-27		A2
3491	BYRD, John B	6	W½SE	1901-04-09		A2
3474	CARPENTER, James	20	NWNE	1890-12-11		A2
3475	" "	20	S½NE	1890-12-11		A2
3473	" "	20	NENW	1892-06-06		A2
3547	CARPENTER, William	21	SENE	1837-04-15		A1
3548	" "	21	SWNE	1855-05-01		A1
3546	" "	20	E½SE	1891-04-06		A2
3495	CARTWRIGHT, John C	36	N½NW	1891-05-04		A2
3496	" "	36	NWNE	1891-05-04		A2
3497	" "	36	SWNW	1891-05-04		A2
3460	CLOUD, Henry	8	SESW	1891-02-13		A2
3461	" "	8	SWNW	1891-02-13		A2
3462	" "	8	W½SW	1891-02-13		A2
3442	COLLINS, Francis M	11	SW	1856-06-16		A1
3443	" "	14	N½NW	1856-06-16		A1 V3429
3444	" "	14	SENW	1856-06-16		A1 V3429
3445	" "	14	SWNE	1857-12-01		A1
3485	CROWELL, Jesse	21	E½NW	1856-06-16		A1
3542	DANIEL, Thomas N	2	E½SW	1889-07-03		A2
3543	" "	2	W½SE	1889-07-03		A2
3560	DAUGHERTY, William H	21	NWNW	1855-05-01		A1
3562	DAUGHTRY, William H	28	NENW	1856-06-16		A1
3561	" "	21	E½SW	1857-12-01		A1
3412	DOLTON, Burrel	36	1	1856-06-16		A1
3413	" "	36	8	1856-06-16		A1
3520	DYKES, Moses	26	NE	1889-07-27		A2
3540	DYKES, Thomas J	34	N½NE	1891-06-17		A2
3541	" "	34	N½NW	1891-06-17		A2
3470	EDENFIELD, James A	11	E½NE	1857-12-01		A1
3471	" "	11	NENW	1857-12-01		A1
3472	" "	11	NWNE	1857-12-01		A1
3427	EDWARDS, Delilah	19	W½NW	1860-07-02		A1
3553	FULGHAM, William E	5	N½NW	1855-06-15		A1

ID	Individual in Patent	Sec.	Sec. Part	Date Issued	Other Counties	For More Info . . .
3554	FULGHAM, William E (Cont'd)	5	SWSW	1856-06-16		A1
3552	" "	5	E½SW	1857-07-01		A1
3555	" "	5	W½NE	1857-07-01		A1
3556	" "	6	NENE	1857-07-01		A1
3394	GARNER, Alexander	6	NESW	1890-12-11		A2
3395	" "	6	SWNW	1890-12-11		A2
3396	" "	6	W½SW	1890-12-11		A2
3422	GODWIN, Clarence	6	SESW	1906-06-30		A1
3559	GRISSETT, William	11	SE	1857-12-01		A1
3557	GRUBB, William F	28	SENW	1896-01-03		A2
3558	" "	28	W½NW	1896-01-03		A2
3525	GRUBBS, Rachael	30	N½NE	1897-03-03		A2 R3487
3563	HAIRE, William	1	SESW	1857-12-01		A1
3564	" "	12	NW	1857-12-01		A1
3407	HAMILTON, Archibald R	3	SWNE	1904-12-20		A2
3438	HAMILTON, Evan S	8	NENE	1855-05-01		A1
3439	" "	8	SENE	1856-06-16		A1
3437	" "	8	N½NW	1857-07-01		A1
3440	" "	8	W½NE	1857-07-01		A1
3449	HAMILTON, Frank P	8	SE	1888-11-20		A2
3510	HAMILTON, Levi	5	NESE	1856-06-16		A1
3511	" "	5	SESE	1857-07-01		A1
3509	" "	5	E½NE	1859-06-01		A1
3512	HAMILTON, Mack	8	NESW	1899-08-30		A2
3513	" "	8	SENW	1899-08-30		A2
3565	HARPER, William	13	E½NE	1857-12-01		A1
3566	" "	13	E½SE	1857-12-01		A1
3567	" "	24	N½NE	1857-12-01		A1
3436	HEWETT, Emery W	20	W½SE	1895-02-14		A2
3441	HILL, Evriett	9	NW	1857-12-01		A1
3450	HILL, George	22	E½NE	1894-08-09		A2
3451	" "	22	E½SE	1894-08-09		A2
3549	HILL, William D	18	N½SW	1890-12-11		A2
3550	" "	18	NWSE	1890-12-11		A2
3551	" "	18	SESW	1890-12-11		A2
3522	HINSON, Philip	4	E½SE	1857-12-01		A1
3523	" "	4	NE	1857-12-01		A1
3524	" "	4	NWSE	1857-12-01		A1
3531	HODGSON, Richard W	1	SE	1859-06-01		A1
3532	" "	12	W½NE	1859-06-01		A1
3433	JETER, Elijah	32	N½NW	1894-05-23		A2
3434	" "	32	NWNE	1894-05-23		A2
3435	" "	32	SWNW	1894-05-23		A2
3538	JETER, Seaborn	34	NESE	1895-06-17		A2
3539	" "	34	SENE	1895-06-17		A2
3568	JOHNSON, William	28	NE	1889-06-29		A2
3575	JONES, William S	7	NWNW	1857-07-01		A1
3576	" "	7	W½SW	1857-07-01		A1
3537	JORDAN, Thomas K	6	NWNE	1893-05-19		A2 G18
3428	KING, Edgar H	34	SWNW	1896-08-26		A1
3545	KIRKLAND, William A	15	SESE	1857-12-01		A1
3535	MATHIS, Samuel	32	E½NE	1896-04-27		A2
3536	" "	32	E½SE	1896-04-27		A2
3533	MAWHINNEY, Robert E	30	NW	1898-04-06		A2 R3534
3448	MCFARLAND, Frank	20	SW	1891-05-04		A2
3500	MCFARLAND, John	28	SE	1896-01-03		A2
3492	MCLANE, John B	10	SW	1896-08-06		A2
3487	MCLEOD, John A	30	N½NE	1898-02-03		A2 C R3525
3488	" "	30	N½SE	1898-02-03		A2
3489	" "	30	S½NE	1898-02-03		A2 R3490
3489	" "	30	S½NE	1898-02-03		A2 C R3490
3490	" "	30	S½NE	1898-02-03		A2 R3489
3490	" "	30	S½NE	1898-02-03		A2 C R3489
3484	MCMILLAN, James W	12	E½NE	1857-12-01		A1
3401	MCMULLEN, Andrew J	36	NESE	1891-02-13		A2
3402	" "	36	SWNE	1891-02-13		A2
3403	" "	36	W½SE	1891-02-13		A2
3404	MCMULLIAN, Andrew J	36	15	1912-05-20		A1
3469	MERCER, Jacob	10	E½SE	1857-07-01		A1
3498	MORGAN, John D	24	W½	1857-12-01		A1
3534	MOWHINNEY, Robert E	30	NW	1898-04-06		A2 C R3533
3420	NEEL, Charles Arthur	2	SENW	1932-09-15		A2
3452	NEEL, George W	4	E½NW	1898-02-03		A2

ID	Individual in Patent	Sec.	Sec. Part	Date Issued	Other Counties	For More Info . . .
3464	NEEL, Hugh W	4	N½SW	1892-05-04		A2 G107
3465	" "	4	W½NW	1892-05-04		A2 G107
3464	NEEL, Sarah	4	N½SW	1892-05-04		A2 G107
3465	" "	4	W½NW	1892-05-04		A2 G107
3455	OWENS, Griffin	1	SWSW	1857-12-01		A1
3456	"	2	SESE	1857-12-01		A1
3399	PEACOCK, Alonzo	10	N½NW	1895-10-16		A2
3400	" "	10	SENW	1895-10-16		A2
3477	PEACOCK, James J	2	N½NW	1857-12-01		A1
3478	" "	2	W½NE	1857-12-01		A1
3479	" "	3	N½NE	1857-12-01		A1
3480	" "	3	NENW	1857-12-01		A1
3392	PLAYER, Aaron F	15	NE	1857-12-01		A1
3572	PLAYER, William	15	NESE	1857-12-01		A1
3393	PORTER, Albert L	26	E½SW	1900-09-07		A2
3405	PRESTON, Andrew J	20	SENW	1897-06-07		A2
3406	" "	20	W½NW	1897-06-07		A2
3573	PROCTOR, William	36	SENW	1894-02-24		A2
3571	PROCTOR, William P	36	NESW	1905-05-26		A2
3424	REISSER, Cornelius	6	SESE	1859-06-01		A1
3425	" "	6	SWNE	1859-06-01		A1
3476	ROACH, James H	34	SESE	1906-03-28		A2
3574	ROBERTS, William	22	NESW	1855-05-01		A1
3466	ROBINSON, Isaac	21	W½SE	1838-07-28		A1 G127
3466	ROBINSON, William H	21	W½SE	1838-07-28		A1 G127
3397	ROULHAC, Allen	6	N½NW	1897-03-22		A2
3398	" "	6	SENW	1897-03-22		A2
3463	RUSS, Hosea	32	SW	1898-06-23		A2
3528	SADLER, Richard	24	SESE	1856-06-16		A1
3529	" "	24	W½SE	1856-06-16		A1
3530	" "	25	NENE	1856-06-16		A1
3526	" "	24	NESE	1857-07-01		A1
3527	" "	24	SENE	1857-07-01		A1
3506	SCOTT, Lawson L	32	SENW	1891-07-14		A2
3507	" "	32	SWNE	1891-07-14		A2
3508	" "	32	W½SE	1891-07-14		A2
3417	SHELFER, Calvin	22	SESW	1891-12-21		A2
3418	" "	22	SWSE	1891-12-21		A2
3419	" "	22	W½SW	1891-12-21		A2
3577	SIMPSON, William	12	SE	1856-06-16		A1
3421	SIMS, Charles	18	N½	1857-07-01		A1
3519	SIMS, Morris	18	SWSW	1856-06-16		A1
3578	SIMSON, William	12	SW	1856-06-16		A1
3468	SNIPES, Jackson	22	SWNE	1855-05-01		A1
3503	SNIPES, John	22	SENW	1855-05-01		A1
3514	SNIPES, Martin J	22	NWSE	1856-06-16		A1
3569	SNIPES, William M	34	NWSW	1857-12-01		A1
3408	SPOONER, Benjamin	3	SENW	1857-12-01		A1
3409	"	3	SW	1857-12-01		A1
3410	"	3	W½NW	1857-12-01		A1
3423	STEPHENS, Cornelious	14	SWNW	1902-07-03		A2
3446	STEPHENS, Francis M	18	E½SE	1895-10-22		A2
3447	" "	18	SWSE	1895-10-22		A2
3515	STEPHENS, Miller	10	E½NE	1856-06-16		A1
3516	" "	10	W½NE	1856-06-16		A1
3517	" "	11	W½NW	1856-06-16		A1
3518	" "	3	E½SE	1856-06-16		A1
3457	STRICKLAND, Hadley H	34	NWSE	1896-04-27		A2
3458	" "	34	SENW	1896-04-27		A2
3459	" "	34	SWNE	1896-04-27		A2
3499	TRAYLOR, John M	30	S½SE	1898-02-03		A2
3570	TYUS, William M	10	W½SE	1895-05-03		A2
3426	WEEKS, Darlin F	2	E½NE	1898-05-16		A2
3429	WESTER, Elias	14	E½NW	1856-06-16		A1 V3443, 3444
3431	" "	14	SW	1856-06-16		A1
3432	" "	23	SWNE	1856-06-16		A1
3430	" "	14	NWNE	1857-07-01		A1
3453	WESTER, George W	13	E½SW	1894-04-10		A2
3454	" "	13	W½SE	1894-04-10		A2
3501	WESTER, John R	13	W½SW	1892-12-03		A2
3502	" "	14	E½SE	1892-12-03		A2
3504	WESTON, Joseph L	31	W½NW	1857-12-01		A1
3505	" "	31	W½SW	1857-12-01		A1

ID	Individual in Patent	Sec.	Sec. Part	Date Issued	Other Counties	For More Info . . .
3544	WHITE, Wesley	26	NW	1895-02-14		A2

Patent Map

T4-N R8-W
Tallahassee Meridian

Map Group 27

Township Statistics

Parcels Mapped	:	187
Number of Patents	:	117
Number of Individuals	:	105
Patentees Identified	:	102
Number of Surnames	:	78
Multi-Patentee Parcels	:	4
Oldest Patent Date	:	4/15/1837
Most Recent Patent	:	9/15/1932
Block/Lot Parcels	:	3
Parcels Re - Issued	:	3
Parcels that Overlap	:	3
Cities and Towns	:	2
Cemeteries	:	5

ROULHAC Allen 1897

BLACKMON [18] Sarah M 1893

FULGHAM William E 1857

FULGHAM William E 1855

FULGHAM William E 1857

5

HAMILTON Levi 1859

NEEL [107] Hugh W 1892

NEEL George W 1898

HINSON Philip 1857

4

GARNER Alexander 1890

ROULHAC Allen 1897

REISSER Cornelius 1859

GARNER Alexander 1890

GARNER Alexander 1890

6

BYRD John B 1901

GODWIN Clarence 1906

REISSER Cornelius 1859

FULGHAM William E 1856

FULGHAM William E 1857

HAMILTON Levi 1856

HAMILTON Levi 1857

NEEL [107] Hugh W 1892

HINSON Philip 1857

BRYANT Berry E 1900

HINSON Philip 1857

JONES William S 1857

HAMILTON Evan S 1857

HAMILTON Evan S 1857

HAMILTON Evan S 1855

HILL Evriett 1857

CLOUD Henry 1891

HAMILTON Mack 1899

HAMILTON Evan S 1856

9

7

HAMILTON Mack 1899

8

JONES William S 1857

CLOUD Henry 1891

CLOUD Henry 1891

HAMILTON Frank P 1888

SIMS Charles 1857

18

HILL William D 1890

HILL William D 1890

17

16

SIMS Morris 1856

HILL William D 1890

STEPHENS Francis M 1895

STEPHENS Francis M 1895

BAKER John 1857

EDWARDS Delilah 1860

CARPENTER James 1892

CARPENTER James 1890

BAKER John 1857

DAUGHERTY William H 1855

CROWELL Jesse 1856

PRESTON Andrew J 1897

PRESTON Andrew J 1897

CARPENTER James 1890

CARPENTER William 1855

CARPENTER William 1837

19

21

20

DAUGHTRY William H 1857

MCFARLAND Frank 1891

HEWETT Emery W 1895

CARPENTER William 1891

ROBINSON [127] Isaac 1838

MOWHINNEY Robert E 1898

MAWHINNEY Robert E 1898

MCLEOD John A 1898

GRUBBS Rachael 1897

GRUBB William F 1896

DAUGHTRY William H 1856

JOHNSON William 1889

30

MCLEOD John A 1898

29

GRUBB William F 1896

28

BEVIS John A 1885

MCLEOD John A 1898

BRADLEY Iziah 1889

MCFARLAND John 1896

TRAYLOR John M 1898

JETER Elijah 1894

JETER Elijah 1894

MATHIS Samuel 1896

WESTON Joseph L 1857

JETER Elijah 1894

SCOTT Lawson L 1891

SCOTT Lawson L 1891

31

32

33

WESTON Joseph L 1857

RUSS Hosea 1898

SCOTT Lawson L 1891

MATHIS Samuel 1896

SPOONER Benjamin 1857	PEACOCK James J 1857	PEACOCK James J 1857	PEACOCK James J 1857	PEACOCK James J 1857	WEEKS Darlin F 1898	1
	SPOONER Benjamin 1857	HAMILTON Archibald R 1904	NEEL Charles Arthur 1932	2		
3		STEPHENS Miller 1856	DANIEL Thomas N 1889	DANIEL Thomas N 1889		HODGSON Richard W 1859
SPOONER Benjamin 1857				OWENS Griffin 1857	OWENS Griffin 1857	HAIRE William 1857

Helpful Hints

1. This Map's INDEX can be found on the preceding pages.

2. Refer to Map "C" to see where this Township lies within Jackson County, Florida.

3. Numbers within square brackets [ ] denote a multi-patentee land parcel (multi-owner). Refer to Appendix "C" for a full list of members in this group.

4. Areas that look to be crowded with Patentees usually indicate multiple sales of the same parcel (Re-issues) or Overlapping parcels. See this Township's Index for an explanation of these and other circumstances that might explain "odd" groupings of Patentees on this map.

PEACOCK Alonzo 1895	STEPHENS Miller 1856	STEPHENS Miller 1856	STEPHENS Miller 1856	EDENFIELD James A 1857	EDENFIELD James A 1857	HODGSON Richard W 1859	MCMILLAN James W 1857
PEACOCK Alonzo 1895 10					EDENFIELD James A 1857	HAIRE William 1857
MCLANE John B 1896	TYUS William M 1895	MERCER Jacob 1857	COLLINS Francis M 1856	11	GRISSETT William 1857	SIMSON William 1856 12	SIMPSON William 1856

	PLAYER Aaron F 1857	COLLINS Francis M 1856	WESTER Elias 1856	WESTER Elias 1857	BLOOD Caleb H 1857	BLOOD Caleb H 1857	BLOOD Caleb H 1857	HARPER William 1857
		STEPHENS Cornelious 1902	COLLINS Francis M 1856	COLLINS Francis M 1857		13		
15	PLAYER William 1857	WESTER Elias 1856	14	WESTER John R 1892	WESTER John R 1892	WESTER George W 1894	HARPER William 1857
	KIRKLAND William A 1857				WESTER George W 1894		

Legend

Patent Boundary

Section Boundary

No Patents Found (or Outside County)

1., 2., 3., ... Lot Numbers (when beside a name)

[ ] Group Number (see Appendix "C")

	SNIPES John 1855 22	SNIPES Jackson 1855	HILL George 1894	23	WESTER Elias 1856	MORGAN John D 1857	HARPER William 1857 24	SADLER Richard 1857
SHELFER Calvin 1891	ROBERTS William 1855	SNIPES Martin J 1856				SADLER Richard 1856	SADLER Richard 1857
	SHELFER Calvin 1891	SHELFER Calvin 1891	HILL George 1894				SADLER Richard 1856

27	WHITE Wesley 1895	26	DYKES Moses 1889	25	SADLER Richard 1856
	PORTER Albert L 1900	BRYANT Newton B 1890		

Scale: Section = 1 mile X 1 mile (generally, with some exceptions)

	DYKES Thomas J 1891	DYKES Thomas J 1891	35	CARTWRIGHT John C 1891	CARTWRIGHT John C 1891	
KING Edgar H 1896	STRICKLAND Hadley H 1896 34	STRICKLAND Hadley H 1896	JETER Seaborn 1895		CARTWRIGHT John C 1891	PROCTOR William 1894 36	MCMULLEN Andrew J 1891
SNIPES William M 1857	BRYANT James W 1891	STRICKLAND Hadley H 1896	JETER Seaborn 1895		PROCTOR William P 1905 Lots-Sec. 36	MCMULLEN Andrew J 1891	MCMULLEN Andrew J 1891
	BRYANT James W 1891	BRYANT James W 1891	ROACH James H 1906		1 DOLTON, Burrel 1856 8 DOLTON, Burrel 1856 15 MCMULLIAN, Andrew J 1912	

263

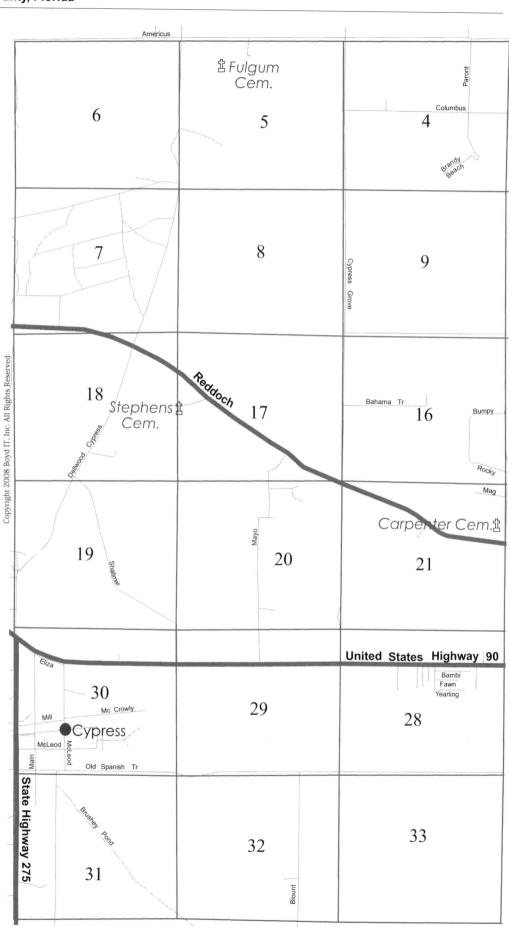

Road Map

T4-N R8-W
Tallahassee Meridian

Map Group 27

Cities & Towns
Cypress
Grand Ridge

Cemeteries
Carpenter Cemetery
Fulgum Cemetery
Simpsons Cemetery
Stephens Cemetery
Wester Cemetery

Americus

⚰ *Fulgum Cem.*

Paront

Columbus

6

5

4

Brandy Beach

7

8

Cypress Grove

9

Reddoch

18

Stephens ⚰ Cem.

17

Bahama Tr

16

Bumpy

Dellwood Cypress

Rocky

Mag

Carpenter Cem. ⚰

19

Shalimar

Mayo

20

21

United States Highway 90

Eliza

Bambi
Fawn
Yearling

30

Mc Crowly

29

28

Mill

● Cypress

McLeod

McLeod

Main

Old Spanish Tr

State Highway 275

Brushey Pond

31

32

Blount

33

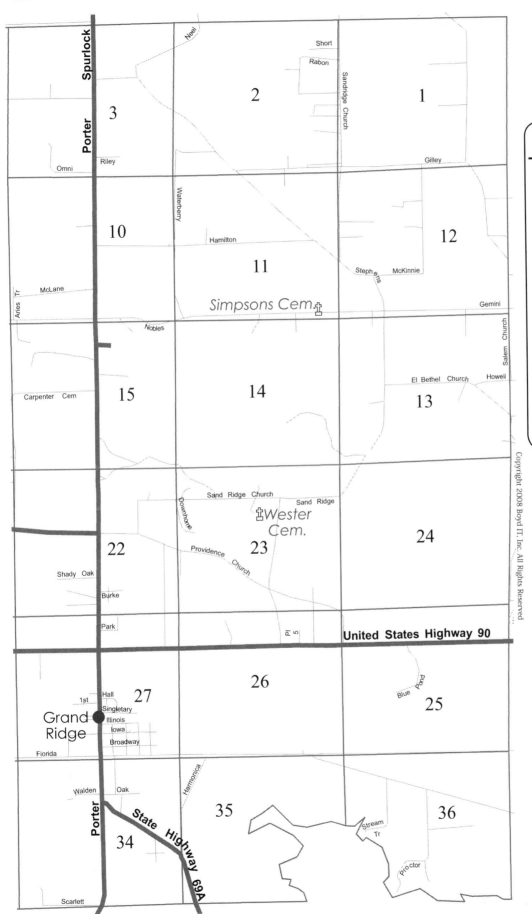

Helpful Hints

1. This road map has a number of uses, but primarily it is to help you: a) find the present location of land owned by your ancestors (at least the general area), b) find cemeteries and city-centers, and c) estimate the route/roads used by Census-takers & tax-assessors.

2. If you plan to travel to Jackson County to locate cemeteries or land parcels, please pick up a modern travel map for the area before you do. Mapping old land parcels on modern maps is not as exact a science as you might think. Just the slightest variations in public land survey coordinates, estimates of parcel boundaries, or road-map deviations can greatly alter a map's representation of how a road either does or doesn't cross a particular parcel of land.

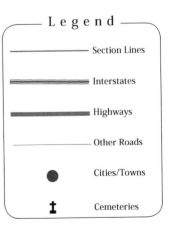

L e g e n d

———————	Section Lines
══════════	Interstates
━━━━━━━━	Highways
———————	Other Roads
●	Cities/Towns
✝	Cemeteries

Scale: Section = 1 mile X 1 mile
(generally, with some exceptions)

Historical Map

T4-N R8-W
Tallahassee Meridian

Map Group 27

Cities & Towns
Cypress
Grand Ridge

Cemeteries
Carpenter Cemetery
Fulgum Cemetery
Simpsons Cemetery
Stephens Cemetery
Wester Cemetery

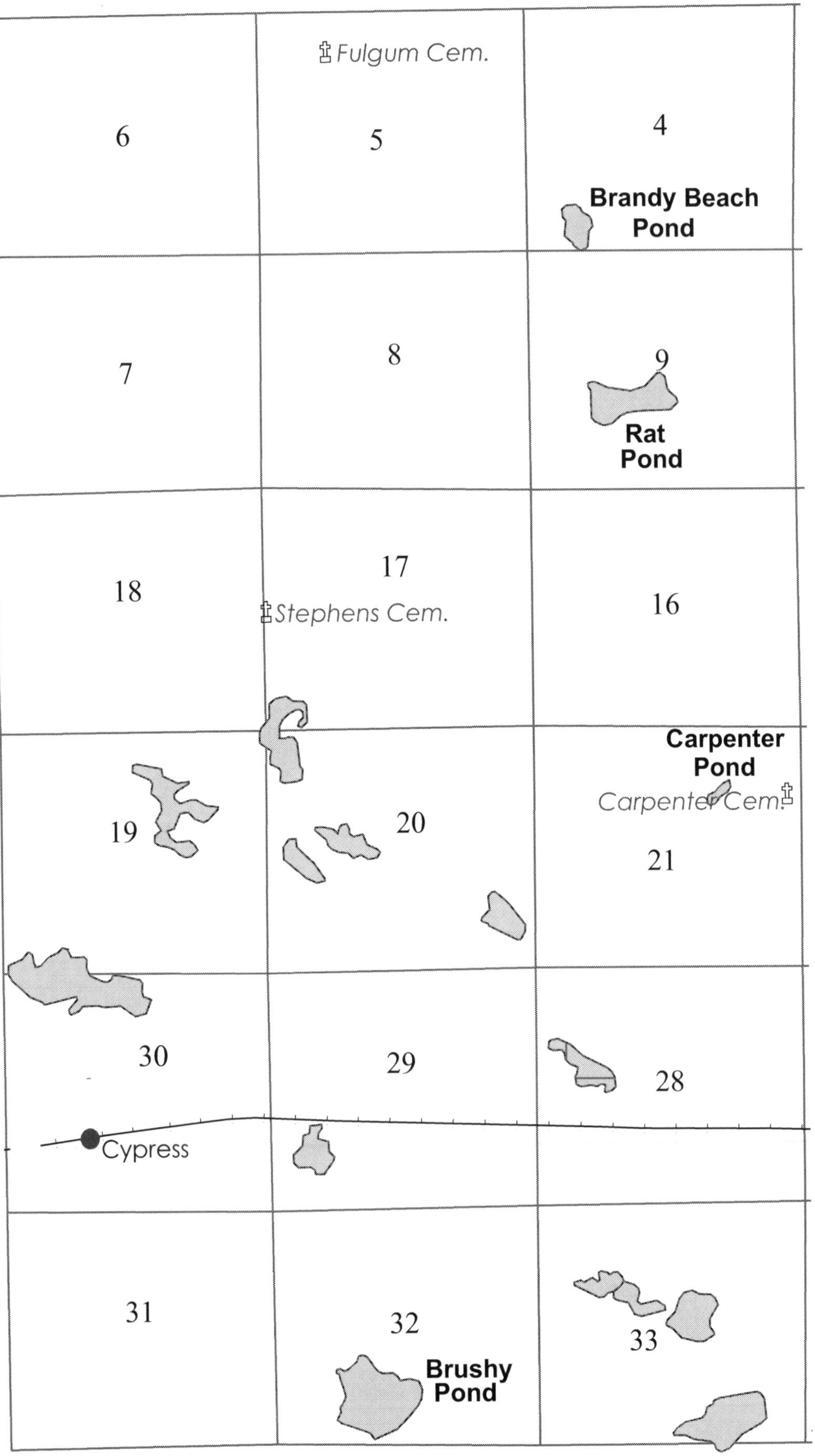

⚱ *Fulgum Cem.*

6

5

4

Brandy Beach Pond

7

8

9

Rat Pond

18

17

⚱ *Stephens Cem.*

16

19

20

Carpenter Pond

Carpenter Cem. ⚱

21

30

29

28

Cypress

31

32

Brushy Pond

33

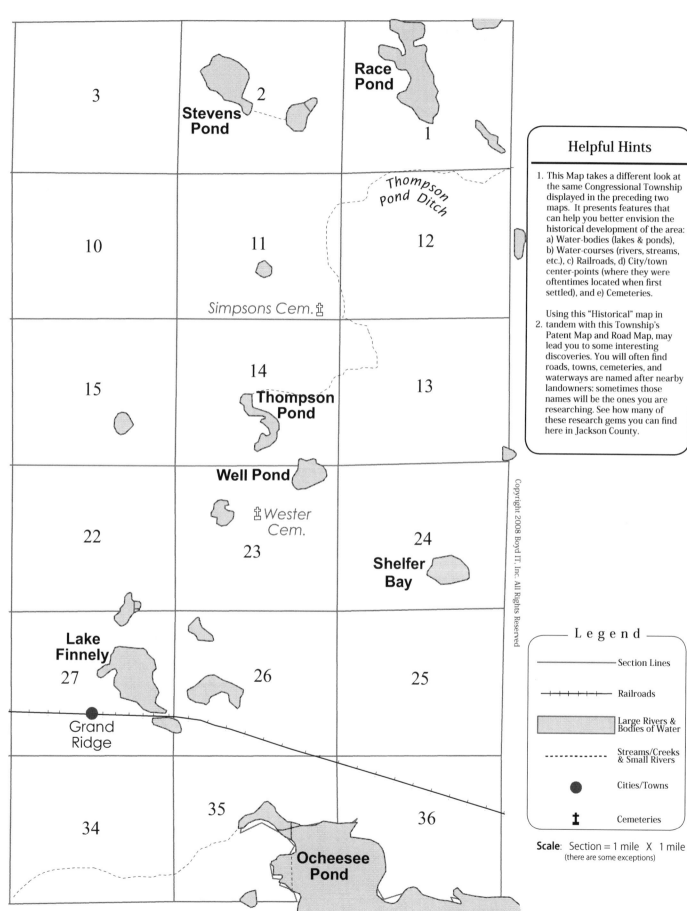

3

2

Race Pond

Stevens Pond

1

Thompson Pond Ditch

10

11

12

Simpsons Cem. ✝

14

15

Thompson Pond

13

Well Pond

✝*Wester Cem.*

22

23

24

Shelfer Bay

Lake Finnely

27

26

25

Grand Ridge

34

35

Ocheesee Pond

36

Helpful Hints

1. This Map takes a different look at the same Congressional Township displayed in the preceding two maps. It presents features that can help you better envision the historical development of the area: a) Water-bodies (lakes & ponds), b) Water-courses (rivers, streams, etc.), c) Railroads, d) City/town center-points (where they were oftentimes located when first settled), and e) Cemeteries.

2. Using this "Historical" map in tandem with this Township's Patent Map and Road Map, may lead you to some interesting discoveries. You will often find roads, towns, cemeteries, and waterways are named after nearby landowners: sometimes those names will be the ones you are researching. See how many of these research gems you can find here in Jackson County.

L e g e n d

———— Section Lines

+++++ Railroads

▨ Large Rivers & Bodies of Water

- - - - Streams/Creeks & Small Rivers

● Cities/Towns

✝ Cemeteries

Scale: Section = 1 mile X 1 mile
(there are some exceptions)

Map Group 28: Index to Land Patents

Township 4-North Range 7-West (Tallahassee)

After you locate an individual in this Index, take note of the Section and Section Part then proceed to the Land Patent map on the pages immediately following. You should have no difficulty locating the corresponding parcel of land.

The "For More Info" Column will lead you to more information about the underlying Patents. See the *Legend* at right, and the "How to Use this Book" chapter, for more information.

```
┌─────────────────────────────────────────────────────────┐
│                      LEGEND                              │
│            "For More Info . . . " column                 │
│ A = Authority (Legislative Act, See Appendix "A")        │
│ B = Block or Lot (location in Section unknown)           │
│ C = Cancelled Patent                                     │
│ F = Fractional Section                                   │
│ G = Group  (Multi-Patentee Patent, see Appendix "C")     │
│ V = Overlaps another Parcel                              │
│ R = Re-Issued (Parcel patented more than once)           │
│                                                          │
│ (A & G items require you to look in the Appendixes       │
│ referred to above. All other Letter-designations        │
│ followed by a number require you to locate line-items    │
│ in this index that possess the ID number found after     │
│ the letter).                                             │
└─────────────────────────────────────────────────────────┘
```

ID	Individual in Patent	Sec.	Sec. Part	Date Issued	Other Counties	For More Info . . .
3664	ALLEN, Richard C	25	E½SE	1830-11-01		A1
3666	" "	36	E½NE	1830-12-28		A1
3665	" "	25	SWSE	1838-07-28		A1
3667	" "	36	E½NW	1838-07-28		A1
3668	" "	36	W½NE	1838-07-28		A1
3649	ANDERSON, John B	22	NWSE	1852-09-01		A1
3647	BOYKIN, Jane C	28	SE	1889-07-03		A2
3656	BROWN, Leaven	4	NENW	1846-04-01		A1
3657	" "	4	NWNW	1846-04-01		A1
3669	CALL, Richard K	4	SENW	1838-07-28		A1
3670	" "	4	SW	1838-07-28		A1
3671	" "	4	SWNW	1838-07-28		A1
3672	" "	4	W½NE	1838-07-28		A1
3673	" "	4	W½SE	1838-07-28		A1
3674	" "	9	W½	1838-07-28		A1
3675	" "	9	W½NE	1838-07-28		A1
3676	" "	9	W½SE	1838-07-28		A1
3605	CHAIRES, Benjamin	25	SENW	1838-07-28		A1
3606	" "	25	SW	1838-07-28		A1
3607	" "	25	W½NW	1838-07-28		A1
3608	" "	26	SE	1838-07-28		A1
3609	" "	35	NE	1838-07-28		A1
3610	" "	36	S½	1838-07-28		A1
3611	" "	36	W½NW	1838-07-28		A1
3658	CHERRY, Mortimer K	6	SE	1857-12-01		A1
3720	COX, Willoughby S	32	SESE	1856-06-16		A1
3721	" "	33	SENW	1856-06-16		A1
3723	" "	33	W½SE	1856-06-16		A1
3722	" "	33	SW	1857-07-01		A1
3613	DALTON, Burrel	31	NWNE	1857-12-01		A1
3579	DICKSON, Abner J	18	NENE	1885-03-20		A1
3697	DICKSON, William	7	NESE	1857-12-01		A1
3698	" "	8	NWSW	1857-12-01		A1
3614	DOLTON, Burrel	31	N½NW	1856-06-16		A1
3684	DUNLAP, Thomas	15	3	1833-05-16		A1
3685	" "	4	E½NE	1833-05-16		A1
3686	" "	4	E½SE	1833-05-16		A1
3687	" "	9	E½NE	1833-05-16		A1
3688	" "	9	E½SE	1833-05-16		A1
3650	FAIRCLOTH, John	22	NENW	1852-09-01		A1
3648	FAIRCLOTH, John A	21	SW	1859-06-01		A1
3696	FAIRCLOTH, Wiley J	21	S½NE	1857-07-01		A1
3681	FREEMAN, Silas L	28	W½NW	1898-07-18		A2
3699	GORMAN, William	21	NENE	1855-05-01		A1
3700	" "	21	NW	1856-06-16		A1
3701	" "	21	NWNE	1856-06-16		A1

ID	Individual in Patent	Sec.	Sec. Part	Date Issued	Other Counties	For More Info . . .
3654	GRAY, Joseph P	22	NWNW	1852-09-01		A1
3659	GRIMSLEY, Moses	30	NESW	1890-06-05		A2
3660	" "	30	NWSE	1890-06-05		A2
3661	" "	30	SENW	1890-06-05		A2
3662	" "	30	SWNE	1890-06-05		A2
3632	HAIR, Frank	20	N½SE	1894-05-23		A2
3633	" "	20	S½NE	1894-05-23		A2
3702	HARPER, William	18	W½NW	1857-12-01		A1
3636	HATCHER, George H	20	S½SW	1896-08-06		A2
3663	HATCHER, Philip G	30	E½NE	1892-08-01		A2
3695	HATCHER, Warren E	20	S½SE	1892-07-11		A2
3651	HENRY, John	32	SENW	1891-07-14		A2
3583	HEWETT, Allen B	30	W½NW	1892-11-15		A2
3584	" "	30	W½SW	1892-11-15		A2
3592	HODGSON, Alonzo G	17	NENW	1855-05-01		A1 G79
3593	" "	18	NENW	1855-05-01		A1 G79
3594	" "	18	NWNE	1855-05-01		A1 G79
3589	" "	6	NE	1855-05-01		A1
3590	" "	6	NW	1855-05-01		A1
3595	" "	7	E½SW	1855-05-01		A1 G79
3596	" "	7	SWSW	1855-05-01		A1 G79
3597	" "	8	E½SW	1855-05-01		A1 G79
3585	" "	17	SENW	1856-06-16		A1
3586	" "	17	W½NW	1856-06-16		A1
3587	" "	18	S½NE	1856-06-16		A1
3588	" "	18	SENW	1856-06-16		A1
3591	" "	7	W½SE	1856-06-16		A1
3592	HODGSON, Richard W	17	NENW	1855-05-01		A1 G79
3593	" "	18	NENW	1855-05-01		A1 G79
3594	" "	18	NWNE	1855-05-01		A1 G79
3595	" "	7	E½SW	1855-05-01		A1 G79
3596	" "	7	SWSW	1855-05-01		A1 G79
3597	" "	8	E½SW	1855-05-01		A1 G79
3677	" "	7	E½NW	1859-06-01		A1
3615	HOWELL, Charles Q	8	SWSW	1897-03-03		A2
3629	HUBBARD, Elijah	22	NENE	1843-03-10		A1
3630	" "	22	NWNE	1843-03-10		A1
3652	JONES, John R	33	SESE	1852-09-01		A1
3616	KEMP, Daniel A	21	SESE	1857-07-01		A1
3617	" "	21	SWSE	1857-07-01		A1
3653	MCCRARY, John W	29	NWSW	1857-12-01		A1
3703	MCKEOWN, William J	32	E½SW	1888-11-22		A2
3704	" "	32	W½SE	1888-11-22		A2
3645	MCMILLAN, James W	7	W½NW	1857-12-01		A1
3626	MITCHELL, Edward M	30	E½SE	1891-02-13		A2
3627	" "	30	SESW	1891-02-13		A2
3628	" "	30	SWSE	1891-02-13		A2
3618	MONEYHAM, Darius M	18	SW	1890-12-27		A2
3580	MOORE, Alfred A	17	E½SE	1857-12-01		A1
3581	" "	17	N½NE	1857-12-01		A1
3582	" "	20	NW	1857-12-01		A1
3612	NEEL, Bennett F	20	N½SW	1895-10-09		A2
3682	PATTERSON, Solomon	35	NENW	1838-07-28		A1
3637	PEACOCK, Gideon B	19	NWNE	1857-07-01		A1
3655	PIOUS, Joseph	32	NENW	1894-07-31		A2
3705	PLAYER, William J	32	W½NW	1895-06-17		A2
3706	" "	32	W½SW	1895-06-17		A2
3631	POPE, Elizabeth	28	E½NE	1843-03-10		A1 G120
3642	POPE, Harriet	35	NESW	1846-09-01		A1
3641	" "	27	SW	1859-06-01		A1
3631	POPE, Henry	28	E½NE	1843-03-10		A1 G120
3631	POPE, John	28	E½NE	1843-03-10		A1 G120
3631	POPE, Margaret	28	E½NE	1843-03-10		A1 G120
3711	POPE, William S	27	W½NW	1830-11-01		A1
3707	" "	25	NE	1837-04-20		A1 C R3708
3709	" "	25	NENW	1837-04-20		A1
3710	" "	25	NWSE	1838-07-28		A1
3631	" "	28	E½NE	1843-03-10		A1 G120
3708	" "	25	NE	1950-04-04		A1 R3707
3713	SADLER, William	18	SE	1857-12-01		A1
3712	" "	17	W½SE	1859-06-01		A1
3691	SCARLOCK, Walton L	22	SWSW	1852-09-01		A1
3692	SCHURLOCK, Walton L	28	SWNE	1857-12-01		A1

ID	Individual in Patent	Sec.	Sec. Part	Date Issued	Other Counties	For More Info . . .
3680	SCURLOCK, Sarah	17	W½SW	1838-07-28		A1
3679	" "	15	4	1841-01-09		A1 F
3693	SCURLOCK, Walton L	22	E½SE	1859-06-01		A1
3694	" "	22	S½NE	1859-06-01		A1
3635	SMITH, Gabriel	34	W½NW	1887-10-15		A1
3689	SNEAD, Walter R	28	E½NW	1889-07-02		A2
3690	" "	28	NWNE	1889-07-02		A2
3638	SNELL, Hamlin V	15	5	1838-07-28		A1 F
3639	" "	15	6	1838-07-28		A1 F
3640	" "	15	7	1838-07-28		A1 F
3714	SPOONER, William	32	NENE	1857-12-01		A1
3715	" "	33	NENW	1857-12-01		A1
3716	" "	33	NESE	1857-12-01		A1
3717	" "	33	SENE	1857-12-01		A1
3718	" "	33	W½NE	1857-12-01		A1
3719	" "	33	W½NW	1857-12-01		A1
3601	STEPHENS, Benjamin B	22	SESW	1857-07-01		A1
3602	" "	22	SWSE	1857-07-01		A1
3603	" "	27	E½NW	1857-07-01		A1
3604	" "	27	W½NE	1857-07-01		A1
3619	THOMAS, David	10	1	1830-11-01		A1
3620	" "	10	2	1830-11-01		A1
3621	" "	10	3	1830-11-01		A1
3622	" "	10	4	1830-11-01		A1
3623	" "	15	2	1830-11-01		A1
3624	" "	3	1	1830-11-01		A1
3625	" "	3	2	1830-11-01		A1
3643	THOMAS, James	30	NENW	1891-02-13		A2
3644	" "	30	NWNE	1891-02-13		A2
3678	THOMAS, Robert	28	SW	1890-12-27		A2
3634	TOWLE, Fredrick	15	1	1830-11-01		A1
3683	WILSON, Stephen G	17	SESW	1846-09-01		A1
3598	WOOLDRIDGE, Andrew J	32	NESE	1895-05-03		A2
3599	" "	32	SENE	1895-05-03		A2
3600	" "	32	W½NE	1895-05-03		A2
3646	YON, James	34	E½SW	1856-06-16		A1

Patent Map

T4-N R7-W
Tallahassee Meridian

Map Group 28

Township Statistics

Parcels Mapped	:	145
Number of Patents	:	101
Number of Individuals	:	67
Patentees Identified	:	65
Number of Surnames	:	53
Multi-Patentee Parcels	:	7
Oldest Patent Date	:	11/1/1830
Most Recent Patent	:	4/4/1950
Block/Lot Parcels	:	13
Parcels Re - Issued	:	1
Parcels that Overlap	:	0
Cities and Towns	:	3
Cemeteries	:	2

Map (Patent grid)

Section 6
HODGSON Alonzo G 1855
HODGSON Alonzo G 1855
CHERRY Mortimer K 1857

Section 5

Section 4
BROWN Leaven 1846
BROWN Leaven 1846
CALL Richard K 1838
CALL Richard K 1838
CALL Richard K 1838
DUNLAP Thomas 1833
CALL Richard K 1838
CALL Richard K 1838
DUNLAP Thomas 1833

Section 7
MCMILLAN James W 1857
HODGSON Richard W 1859
HODGSON [79] Alonzo G 1855
HODGSON [79] Alonzo G 1855
HODGSON Alonzo G 1856
DICKSON William 1857

Section 8
DICKSON William 1857
HODGSON [79] Alonzo G 1855
HOWELL Charles Q 1897

Section 9
CALL Richard K 1838
CALL Richard K 1838
DUNLAP Thomas 1833
CALL Richard K 1838
DUNLAP Thomas 1833

HARPER William 1857
HODGSON [79] Alonzo G 1855
HODGSON [79] Alonzo G 1855
DICKSON Abner J 1885
HODGSON Alonzo G 1856
HODGSON [79] Alonzo G 1855
MOORE Alfred A 1857
HODGSON Alonzo G 1856
HODGSON Alonzo G 1856
HODGSON Alonzo G 1856

Section 16

MONEYHAM Darius M 1890
Section 18
SADLER William 1857
SCURLOCK Sarah 1838
Section 17
WILSON Stephen G 1846
SADLER William 1859
MOORE Alfred A 1857

PEACOCK Gideon B 1857
Section 19
MOORE Alfred A 1857
Section 20
HAIR Frank 1894
NEEL Bennett F 1895
HAIR Frank 1894
HATCHER George H 1896
HATCHER Warren E 1892
GORMAN William 1856
Section 21
GORMAN William 1856
GORMAN William 1855
FAIRCLOTH Wiley J 1857
FAIRCLOTH John A 1859
KEMP Daniel A 1857
KEMP Daniel A 1857

Section 30
HEWETT Allen B 1892
THOMAS James 1891
THOMAS James 1891
HATCHER Philip G 1892
GRIMSLEY Moses 1890
GRIMSLEY Moses 1890
HEWETT Allen B 1892
GRIMSLEY Moses 1890
GRIMSLEY Moses 1890
MITCHELL Edward M 1891
MITCHELL Edward M 1891
MITCHELL Edward M 1891

Section 29
MCCRARY John W 1857

Section 28
FREEMAN Silas L 1898
SNEAD Walter R 1889
SNEAD Walter R 1889
POPE [120] Elizabeth 1843
SCHURLOCK Walton L 1857
THOMAS Robert 1890
BOYKIN Jane C 1889

Section 31
DOLTON Burrel 1856
DALTON Burrel 1857

Section 32
PLAYER William J 1895
PIOUS Joseph 1894
HENRY John 1891
WOOLDRIDGE Andrew J 1895
SPOONER William 1857
WOOLDRIDGE Andrew J 1895
SPOONER William 1857
SPOONER William 1857
SPOONER William 1857
COX Willoughby S 1856
SPOONER William 1857
PLAYER William J 1895
MCKEOWN William J 1888
MCKEOWN William J 1888
WOOLDRIDGE Andrew J 1895
COX Willoughby S 1856
Section 33
COX Willoughby S 1857
COX Willoughby S 1856
SPOONER William 1857
JONES John R 1852

272

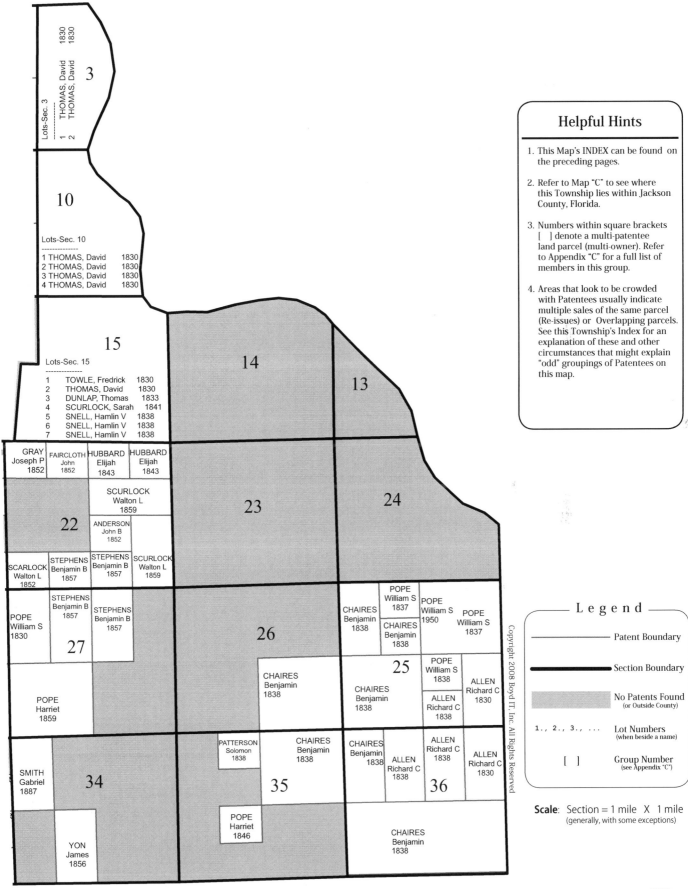

Helpful Hints

1. This Map's INDEX can be found on the preceding pages.

2. Refer to Map "C" to see where this Township lies within Jackson County, Florida.

3. Numbers within square brackets [ ] denote a multi-patentee land parcel (multi-owner). Refer to Appendix "C" for a full list of members in this group.

4. Areas that look to be crowded with Patentees usually indicate multiple sales of the same parcel (Re-issues) or Overlapping parcels. See this Township's Index for an explanation of these and other circumstances that might explain "odd" groupings of Patentees on this map.

3

1830
1830
THOMAS, David
THOMAS, David

Lots-Sec. 3

1
2

10

Lots-Sec. 10
----
1 THOMAS, David   1830
2 THOMAS, David   1830
3 THOMAS, David   1830
4 THOMAS, David   1830

15

14

13

Lots-Sec. 15
----
1   TOWLE, Fredrick   1830
2   THOMAS, David   1830
3   DUNLAP, Thomas   1833
4   SCURLOCK, Sarah   1841
5   SNELL, Hamlin V   1838
6   SNELL, Hamlin V   1838
7   SNELL, Hamlin V   1838

| GRAY Joseph P 1852 | FAIRCLOTH John 1852 | HUBBARD Elijah 1843 | HUBBARD Elijah 1843 |

SCURLOCK
Walton L
1859

22

ANDERSON
John B
1852

23

24

SCARLOCK
Walton L
1852

STEPHENS
Benjamin B
1857

STEPHENS
Benjamin B
1857

SCURLOCK
Walton L
1859

POPE
William S
1837

POPE
William S
1950

POPE
William S
1837

CHAIRES
Benjamin
1838

CHAIRES
Benjamin
1838

STEPHENS
Benjamin B
1857

POPE
William S
1830

STEPHENS
Benjamin B
1857

27

26

25

CHAIRES
Benjamin
1838

POPE
William S
1838

ALLEN
Richard C
1830

POPE
Harriet
1859

CHAIRES
Benjamin
1838

CHAIRES
Benjamin
1838

ALLEN
Richard C
1838

SMITH
Gabriel
1887

34

PATTERSON
Solomon
1838

CHAIRES
Benjamin
1838

35

CHAIRES
Benjamin
1838

ALLEN
Richard C
1838

ALLEN
Richard C
1838

ALLEN
Richard C
1830

36

YON
James
1856

POPE
Harriet
1846

CHAIRES
Benjamin
1838

Legend

Patent Boundary

Section Boundary

No Patents Found
(or Outside County)

1., 2., 3., ...   Lot Numbers
(when beside a name)

[ ]   Group Number
(see Appendix "C")

Scale: Section = 1 mile X 1 mile
(generally, with some exceptions)

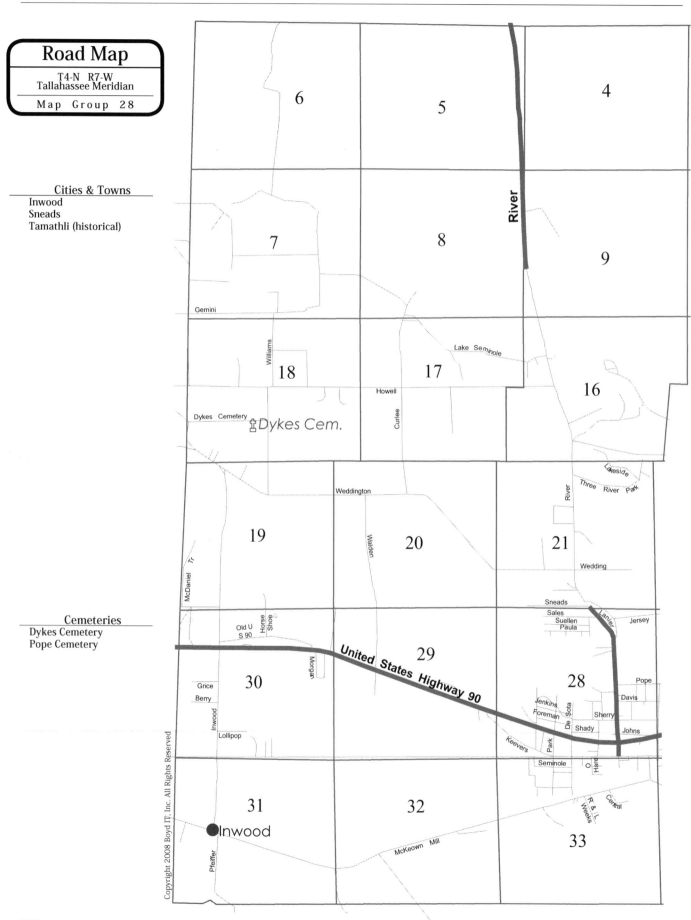

Road Map

T4-N R7-W
Tallahassee Meridian

Map Group 28

Cities & Towns

Inwood
Sneads
Tamathli (historical)

Cemeteries

Dykes Cemetery
Pope Cemetery

6

5

4

River

7

8

9

Gemini

Williams

18

17

Lake Seminole

16

Howell

Dykes Cemetery

Curlee

†Dykes Cem.

Weddington

Lakeside

Three River Park

River

19

20

21

Walden

Wedding

McDaniel Tr

Sneads

Lanier

Horse Shoe

Old U S 90

Morgan

United States Highway 90

29

Sales
Suellen
Paula

Jersey

30

Grice

Berry

Inwood

Lollipop

28

Jenkins

Foreman

De Sota

Park

Keevers

Shady

Sherry

Pope

Davis

Johns

Seminole

O
Hare

31

Inwood

32

McKeown Mill

33

R & L
Weeks

Central

Pfeiffer

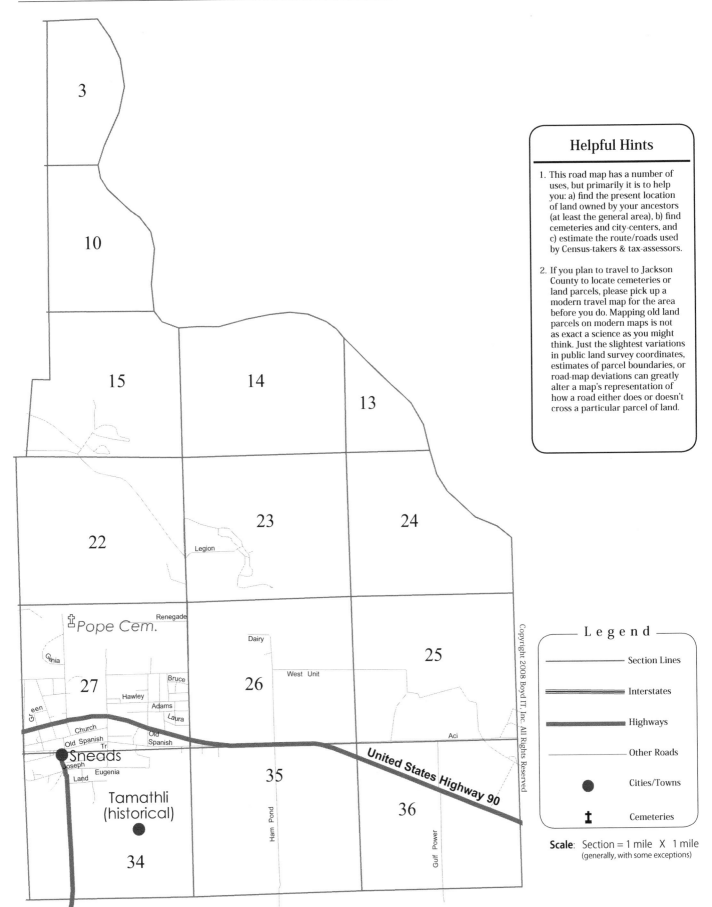

3

10

15

14

13

22

23

24

Legion

Pope Cem.

Renegade

25

Genia

Dairy

West Unit

27

Bruce

26

Hawley

Adams

Green

Laura

Church

Old Spanish
Tr

Old
Spanish

Aci

Sneads

Joseph

Eugenia

Land

United States Highway 90

Tamathli
(historical)

35

36

Ham Pond

Gulf Power

34

L e g e n d

Section Lines

Interstates

Highways

Other Roads

Cities/Towns

Cemeteries

Scale: Section = 1 mile X 1 mile
(generally, with some exceptions)

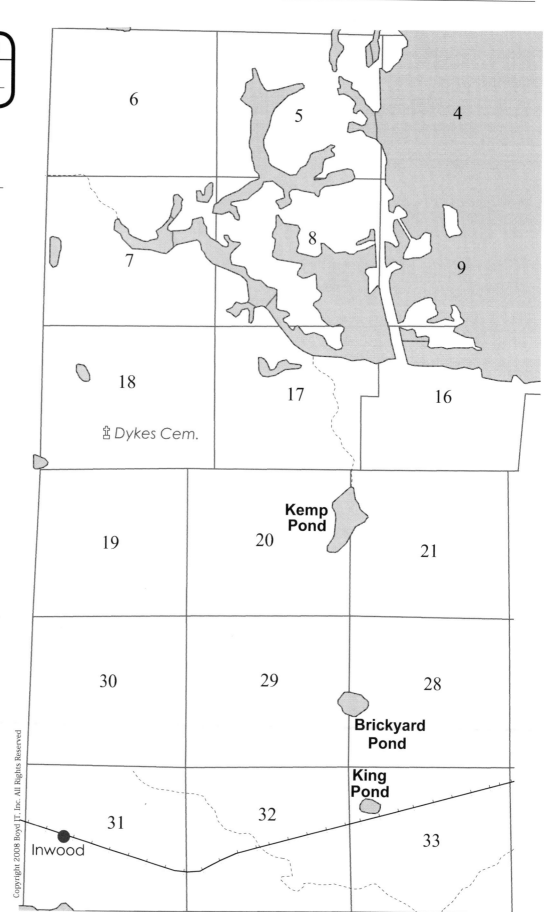

Historical Map

T4-N R7-W
Tallahassee Meridian

Map Group 28

Cities & Towns
Inwood
Sneads
Tamathli (historical)

Cemeteries
Dykes Cemetery
Pope Cemetery

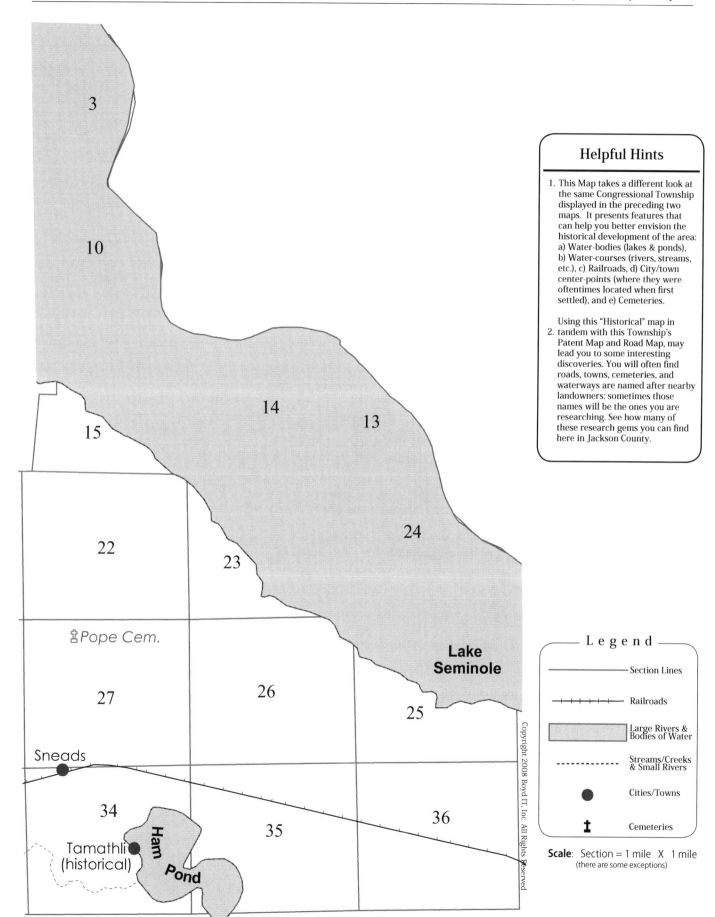

3

10

14

13

15

24

22

23

☥ *Pope Cem.*

Lake Seminole

27

26

25

Sneads

34

35

36

Ham Pond

Tamathli (historical)

Helpful Hints

1. This Map takes a different look at the same Congressional Township displayed in the preceding two maps. It presents features that can help you better envision the historical development of the area: a) Water-bodies (lakes & ponds), b) Water-courses (rivers, streams, etc.), c) Railroads, d) City/town center-points (where they were oftentimes located when first settled), and e) Cemeteries.

2. Using this "Historical" map in tandem with this Township's Patent Map and Road Map, may lead you to some interesting discoveries. You will often find roads, towns, cemeteries, and waterways are named after nearby landowners: sometimes those names will be the ones you are researching. See how many of these research gems you can find here in Jackson County.

L e g e n d

——————— Section Lines

—+—+—+—+— Railroads

▨ Large Rivers & Bodies of Water

- - - - - - Streams/Creeks & Small Rivers

● Cities/Towns

☥ Cemeteries

Scale: Section = 1 mile X 1 mile (there are some exceptions)

Map Group 29: Index to Land Patents

Township 4-North Range 6-West (Tallahassee)

After you locate an individual in this Index, take note of the Section and Section Part then proceed to the Land Patent map on the pages immediately following. You should have no difficulty locating the corresponding parcel of land.

The "For More Info" Column will lead you to more information about the underlying Patents. See the *Legend* at right, and the "How to Use this Book" chapter, for more information.

```
                         LEGEND
              "For More Info . . . " column
A = Authority (Legislative Act, See Appendix "A")
B = Block or Lot (location in Section unknown)
C = Cancelled Patent
F = Fractional Section
G = Group  (Multi-Patentee Patent, see Appendix "C")
V = Overlaps another Parcel
R = Re-Issued (Parcel patented more than once)

(A & G items require you to look in the Appendixes referred
to above. All other Letter-designations followed by a number
require you to locate line-items in this index that possess
the ID number found after the letter).
```

ID	Individual in Patent	Sec.	Sec. Part	Date Issued	Other Counties	For More Info . . .
3727	ALLEN, Richard C	31	3	1834-08-20		A1 G7
3726	" "	30	N½3	1838-07-28		A1 F
3727	CALL, Richard K	31	3	1834-08-20		A1 G7
3724	GARRETT, Lafayette	31	N½6	1852-09-01		A1
3725	" "	31	S½6	1852-09-01		A1
3728	LEWIS, Romeo	30	2	1829-05-15		A1
3729	" "	30	4	1829-05-15		A1
3731	" "	31	1	1829-05-15		A1
3732	" "	31	2	1829-05-15		A1
3733	" "	31	4	1829-05-15		A1
3730	" "	30	5	1837-04-15		A1
3734	LITTLETON, Thomas	31	8	1829-05-15		A1 G94 F
3734	LITTLETON, William	31	8	1829-05-15		A1 G94 F
3734	MCCULLOH, John	31	8	1829-05-15		A1 G94 F
3735	POPE, William S	19	1	1829-05-15		A1
3736	" "	30	1	1829-05-15		A1
3737	" "	31	5	1829-06-01		A1

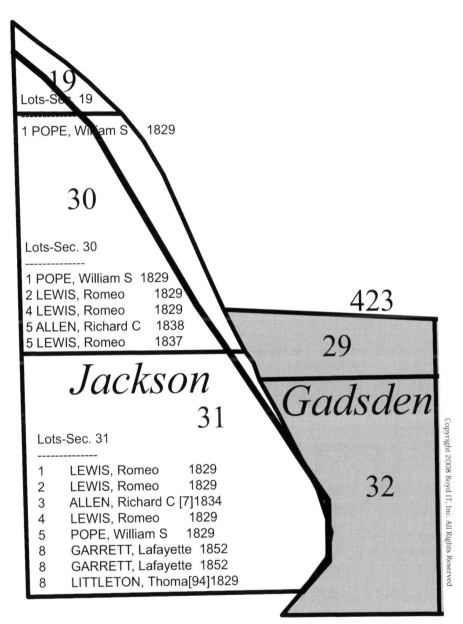

19

Lots-Sec. 19
----
1 POPE, William S 1829

30

Lots-Sec. 30
----
1 POPE, William S 1829
2 LEWIS, Romeo 1829
4 LEWIS, Romeo 1829
5 ALLEN, Richard C 1838
5 LEWIS, Romeo 1837

423

29

Jackson

31

Lots-Sec. 31
----
1   LEWIS, Romeo   1829
2   LEWIS, Romeo   1829
3   ALLEN, Richard C [7]1834
4   LEWIS, Romeo   1829
5   POPE, William S   1829
8   GARRETT, Lafayette 1852
8   GARRETT, Lafayette 1852
8   LITTLETON, Thoma[94]1829

Gadsden

32

Patent Map

T4-N R6-W
Tallahassee Meridian

Map Group 29

Township Statistics

Parcels Mapped	:	14
Number of Patents	:	14
Number of Individuals	:	8
Patentees Identified	:	6
Number of Surnames	:	7
Multi-Patentee Parcels	:	2
Oldest Patent Date	:	5/15/1829
Most Recent Patent	:	9/1/1852
Block/Lot Parcels	:	14
Parcels Re - Issued	:	0
Parcels that Overlap	:	0
Cities and Towns	:	0
Cemeteries	:	0

Note: the area contained in this map amounts to far less than a full Township. Therefore, its contents are completely on this single page (instead of a "normal" 2-page spread).

Legend

——————— Patent Boundary

━━━━━━━ Section Boundary

No Patents Found
(or Outside County)

1., 2., 3., ...   Lot Numbers
(when beside a name)

[ ]   Group Number
(see Appendix "C")

Scale: Section = 1 mile X 1 mile
(generally, with some exceptions)

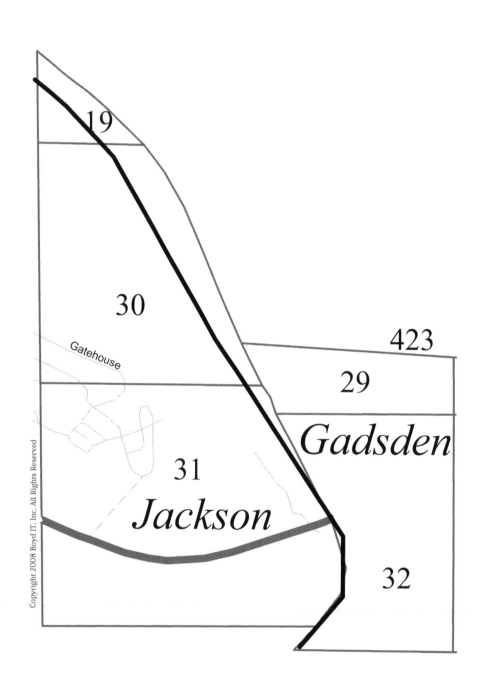

Road Map

T4-N   R6-W
Tallahassee Meridian

Map Group 29

Note: the area contained in this map amounts to far less than a full Township. Therefore, its contents are completely on this single page (instead of a "normal" 2-page spread).

Cities & Towns
None

Cemeteries
None

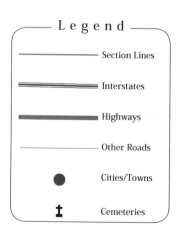

Legend

— Section Lines

— Interstates

— Highways

— Other Roads

● Cities/Towns

† Cemeteries

Scale: Section = 1 mile X 1 mile
(generally, with some exceptions)

Historical Map

T4-N R6-W
Tallahassee Meridian

Map Group 29

Note: the area contained in this map amounts to far less than a full Township. Therefore, its contents are completely on this single page (instead of a "normal" 2-page spread).

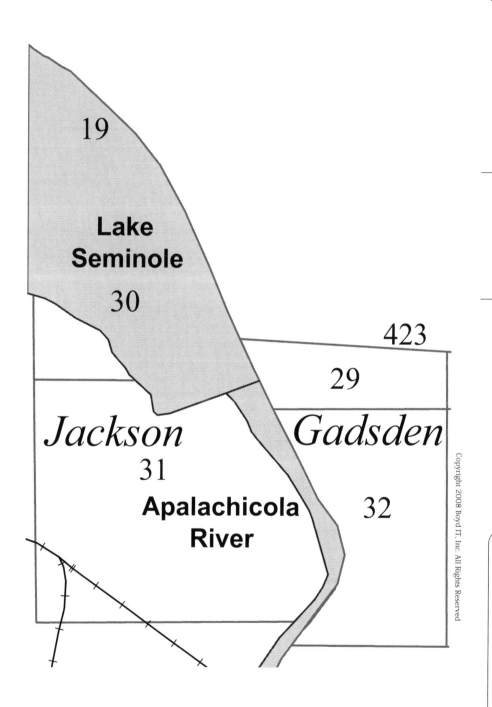

_____
Cities & Towns
None

_____
Cemeteries
None

L e g e n d

———————— Section Lines

+—+—+—+—+—+ Railroads

▓▓▓▓ Large Rivers & Bodies of Water

- - - - - - - Streams/Creeks & Small Rivers

● Cities/Towns

✝ Cemeteries

Scale: Section = 1 mile X 1 mile
(there are some exceptions)

Map Group 30: Index to Land Patents

Township 3-North Range 12-West (Tallahassee)

After you locate an individual in this Index, take note of the Section and Section Part then proceed to the Land Patent map on the pages immediately following. You should have no difficulty locating the corresponding parcel of land.

The "For More Info" Column will lead you to more information about the underlying Patents. See the *Legend* at right, and the "How to Use this Book" chapter, for more information.

```
                    LEGEND
          "For More Info . . . " column
A = Authority (Legislative Act, See Appendix "A")
B = Block or Lot (location in Section unknown)
C = Cancelled Patent
F = Fractional Section
G = Group  (Multi-Patentee Patent, see Appendix "C")
V = Overlaps another Parcel
R = Re-Issued (Parcel patented more than once)

(A & G items require you to look in the Appendixes referred
to above. All other Letter-designations followed by a number
require you to locate line-items in this index that possess
the ID number found after the letter).
```

ID	Individual in Patent	Sec.	Sec. Part	Date Issued	Other Counties	For More Info . . .
3751	ARNOLD, Dock	14	W½SE	1904-07-27		A2
3759	BARNES, George W	22	SESE	1913-06-07		A1
3765	BUTLER, James E	12	W½SE	1904-08-26		A2
3784	BUTLER, John F	12	SW	1905-02-10		A1
3787	CARROLL, John J	14	SWNE	1910-02-23		A1
3781	COGBURN, Jesse D	34	N½NE	1910-07-18		A2
3782	"	34	NWSE	1910-07-18		A2
3783	"	34	SWNE	1910-07-18		A2
3738	FENNEL, Agnes P	26	SENE	1910-01-17		A1
3761	GAY, Hinion E	22	NESE	1910-01-20		A2
3762	"	22	SENE	1910-01-20		A2
3763	"	22	W½SE	1910-01-20		A2
3766	GAY, James E	24	SW	1909-01-14		A1
3809	GLASS, William T	26	N½NE	1909-11-08		A2
3810	"	26	N½NW	1909-11-08		A2
3770	GRISSETT, James M	34	NESE	1906-06-30		A1
3771	"	34	S½SE	1906-06-30		A1
3772	"	34	SENE	1906-06-30		A1
3754	HADDOCK, Ephraim S	2	N½NW	1902-04-17		A2
3768	HOVEY, James H	2	W½NE	1902-05-01		A2
3769	"	2	W½SE	1902-05-01		A2
3739	KENT, Alexander	10	SENE	1895-11-05		A2
3740	"	10	SWNE	1895-11-05		A2
3741	"	10	W½SE	1895-11-05		A2
3747	KENT, Curby	10	NESW	1914-03-07		A2
3748	KENT, Curtis	10	E½SE	1907-04-01		A2
3795	KENT, Lewis	10	S½NW	1906-06-30		A2
3796	"	10	W½SW	1906-06-30		A2
3799	KENT, Melissa	10	N½NE	1901-06-28		A2 G88
3800	"	10	N½NW	1901-06-28		A2 G88
3792	LOVE, Lemuel C	26	NESE	1911-04-17		A2
3793	"	26	S½SE	1911-04-17		A2
3794	"	26	SESW	1911-04-17		A2
3805	MARCHANT, William J	26	NESW	1906-03-31		A1 F
3806	"	26	NWSE	1906-03-31		A1 F
3807	"	26	SENW	1906-03-31		A1 F
3808	"	26	SWNE	1906-03-31		A1 F
3757	MAYO, Francis	24	SE	1905-06-30		A2
3764	MAYO, Jacob T	24	NE	1906-03-28		A2
3773	MCLAIN, James M	14	W½SW	1904-07-27		A2
3755	MELVIN, Ephriam P	2	N½SW	1901-07-20		A2
3756	"	2	S½NW	1901-07-20		A2
3746	MICH, Charlie	36	NWNW	1918-09-27		A2
3742	MORRIS, Burris	2	E½NE	1897-12-01		A2
3743	"	2	E½SE	1897-12-01		A2
3799	MORRIS, Melissa	10	N½NE	1901-06-28		A2 G88

ID	Individual in Patent	Sec.	Sec. Part	Date Issued	Other Counties	For More Info . . .
3800	MORRIS, Melissa (Cont'd)	10	N½NW	1901-06-28		A2 G88
3802	MORRIS, Wesley C	14	N½NE	1899-05-27		A2
3803	" "	14	NESE	1899-05-27		A2
3804	" "	14	SENE	1899-05-27		A2
3811	MORRIS, Winnie E	12	W½NE	1895-10-09		A2
3791	SEWELL, John	22	SW	1906-06-04		A2
3749	SHORES, Daniel G	12	E½NE	1901-11-06		A2
3750	" "	12	E½SE	1901-11-06		A2
3758	STEPHENS, George F	2	SESW	1911-07-24		A2
3778	SULLIVAN, Jerry	14	NW	1905-12-13		A2
3785	SULLIVAN, John F	22	SENW	1906-03-28		A2
3786	" "	22	W½NW	1906-03-28		A2
3788	SULLIVAN, John O	22	N½NE	1901-06-28		A2
3789	" "	22	NENW	1901-06-28		A2
3790	" "	22	SWNE	1901-06-28		A2
3767	SWAILS, James F	12	NW	1895-10-09		A2
3744	THARP, Charles C	34	W½NW	1909-07-22		A2
3745	" "	34	W½SW	1909-07-22		A2
3797	THOMAS, Louvinia L	36	E½NW	1906-10-31		A1
3798	" "	36	N½NE	1906-10-31		A1
3801	TIPTON, Oscar L	36	S½NE	1906-06-08		A1 F
3752	TOOLE, Ellie M	26	SWNW	1911-01-16		A2
3753	" "	26	W½SW	1911-01-16		A2
3774	VAUGHN, James	3	NESW	1857-12-01		A1
3775	" "	3	NWSE	1857-12-01		A1
3776	" "	3	SENW	1857-12-01		A1
3777	" "	3	SWNE	1857-12-01		A1
3760	WATERS, Green W	24	NW	1906-03-28		A2
3779	WRIGHT, Jesse A	34	E½NW	1909-09-20		A2
3780	" "	34	E½SW	1909-09-20		A2

Patent Map

T3-N R12-W
Tallahassee Meridian

Map Group 30

Township Statistics

Parcels Mapped	:	74
Number of Patents	:	42
Number of Individuals	:	43
Patentees Identified	:	42
Number of Surnames	:	31
Multi-Patentee Parcels	:	2
Oldest Patent Date	:	12/1/1857
Most Recent Patent	:	9/27/1918
Block/Lot Parcels	:	0
Parcels Re - Issued	:	0
Parcels that Overlap	:	0
Cities and Towns	:	3
Cemeteries	:	0

Note: the area contained in this map amounts to far less than a full Township. Therefore, its contents are completely on this single page (instead of a "normal" 2-page spread).

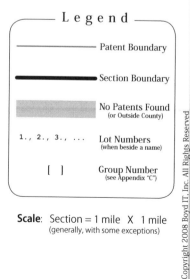

Legend

———————— Patent Boundary

———————— Section Boundary

▨ No Patents Found
(or Outside County)

1., 2., 3., ... Lot Numbers
(when beside a name)

[ ] Group Number
(see Appendix "C")

Scale: Section = 1 mile X 1 mile
(generally, with some exceptions)

3

VAUGHN James 1857

VAUGHN James 1857

VAUGHN James 1857

VAUGHN James 1857

VAUGHN James 1857

HADDOCK Ephraim S 1902

HOVEY James H 1902

MORRIS Burris 1897

MELVIN Ephriam P 1901

2

MELVIN Ephriam P 1901

HOVEY James H 1902

STEPHENS George F 1911

MORRIS Burris 1897

1

KENT [88] Melissa 1901

KENT [88] Melissa 1901

KENT Lewis 1906

10

KENT Alexander 1895

KENT Alexander 1895

KENT Lewis 1906

KENT Curby 1914

KENT Alexander 1895

KENT Curtis 1907

11

SWAILS James F 1895

MORRIS Winnie E 1895

SHORES Daniel G 1901

12

BUTLER John F 1905

BUTLER James E 1904

SHORES Daniel G 1901

15

SULLIVAN Jerry 1905

14

MORRIS Wesley C 1899

CARROLL John J 1910

MORRIS Wesley C 1899

MCLAIN James M 1904

ARNOLD Dock 1904

MORRIS Wesley C 1899

13

SULLIVAN John F 1906

SULLIVAN John O 1901

SULLIVAN John O 1901

GAY Hinion E 1910

SULLIVAN John F 1906

SULLIVAN John O 1901

SEWELL John 1906

22

GAY Hinion E 1910

GAY Hinion E 1910

BARNES George W 1913

23

WATERS Green W 1906

MAYO Jacob T 1906

24

GAY James E 1909

MAYO Francis 1905

27

GLASS William T 1909

GLASS William T 1909

TOOLE Ellie M 1911

MARCHANT William J 1906

MARCHANT William J 1906

FENNEL Agnes P 1910

26

MARCHANT William J 1906

MARCHANT William J 1906

LOVE Lemuel C 1911

TOOLE Ellie M 1911

LOVE Lemuel C 1911

LOVE Lemuel C 1911

25

THARP Charles C 1909

WRIGHT Jesse A 1909

COGBURN Jesse D 1910

COGBURN Jesse D 1910

GRISSETT James M 1906

THARP Charles C 1909

34

COGBURN Jesse D 1910

GRISSETT James M 1906

WRIGHT Jesse A 1909

GRISSETT James M 1906

35

MICH Charlie 1918

THOMAS Louvinia L 1906

THOMAS Louvinia L 1906

TIPTON Oscar L 1906

36

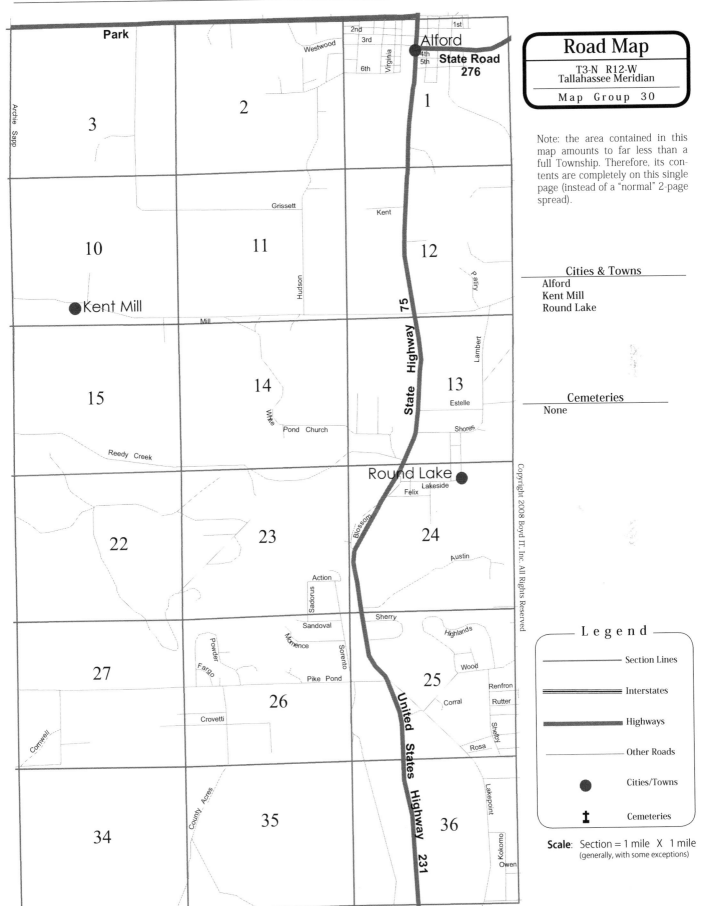

Road Map

T3-N R12-W
Tallahassee Meridian

Map Group 30

Note: the area contained in this map amounts to far less than a full Township. Therefore, its contents are completely on this single page (instead of a "normal" 2-page spread).

Cities & Towns
Alford
Kent Mill
Round Lake

Cemeteries
None

Legend

———— Section Lines

═══════ Interstates

▬▬▬▬▬ Highways

———— Other Roads

● Cities/Towns

✝ Cemeteries

Scale: Section = 1 mile X 1 mile
(generally, with some exceptions)

Historical Map

T3-N   R12-W
Tallahassee Meridian

Map Group 30

Note: the area contained in this map amounts to far less than a full Township. Therefore, its contents are completely on this single page (instead of a "normal" 2-page spread).

Cities & Towns

Alford
Kent Mill
Round Lake

Cemeteries

None

Legend

――――――― Section Lines

+++++++++ Railroads

▨▨▨▨ Large Rivers & Bodies of Water

- - - - - - Streams/Creeks & Small Rivers

● Cities/Towns

✝ Cemeteries

Scale: Section = 1 mile X 1 mile
(there are some exceptions)

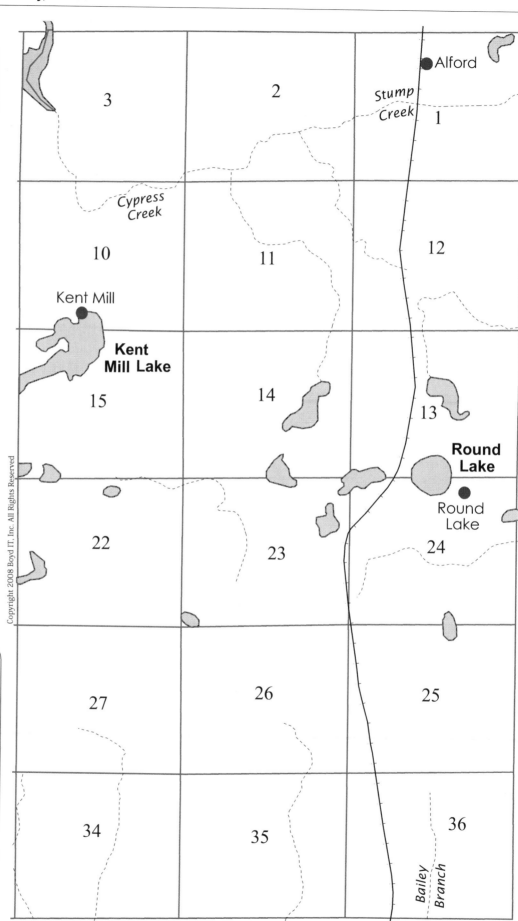

Map Group 31: Index to Land Patents

Township 3-North Range 11-West (Tallahassee)

After you locate an individual in this Index, take note of the Section and Section Part then proceed to the Land Patent map on the pages immediately following. You should have no difficulty locating the corresponding parcel of land.

The "For More Info" Column will lead you to more information about the underlying Patents. See the *Legend* at right, and the "How to Use this Book" chapter, for more information.

```
                        LEGEND
              "For More Info . . . " column
A = Authority (Legislative Act, See Appendix "A")
B = Block or Lot (location in Section unknown)
C = Cancelled Patent
F = Fractional Section
G = Group  (Multi-Patentee Patent, see Appendix "C")
V = Overlaps another Parcel
R = Re-Issued (Parcel patented more than once)

(A & G items require you to look in the Appendixes referred
to above. All other Letter-designations followed by a number
require you to locate line-items in this index that possess
the ID number found after the letter).
```

ID	Individual in Patent	Sec.	Sec. Part	Date Issued	Other Counties	For More Info . . .
3833	AARONS, Henry	32	N½NE	1910-05-09		A2
3834	" "	32	N½NW	1910-05-09		A2
3859	AARONS, John H	6	NE	1902-09-26		A2
3917	ADKINS, William B	14	SWSE	1910-05-09		A2
3872	BALDWIN, Joseph E	28	NW	1909-05-17		A2
3906	BAREFOOT, Texas Ann	30	W½NW	1910-05-05		A2
3907	" "	30	W½SW	1910-05-05		A2
3903	BOUTWELL, Sarah J	32	S½SE	1909-09-24		A1
3904	" "	32	S½SW	1909-09-24		A1
3857	BRANAN, John A	10	SE	1895-10-09		A2
3849	BRANNON, James T	10	SW	1896-06-23		A2
3814	BROOKS, Alexander	34	N½NW	1911-06-12		A2
3819	BROOKS, Cleveland B	34	N½SW	1918-02-13		A2
3820	" "	34	SWNW	1918-02-13		A2
3821	" "	34	SWSW	1918-02-13		A2
3900	BROOKS, Russell	10	NW	1898-08-15		A2
3841	BRUNER, James E	36	NENW	1938-12-02		A2
3883	CARLISLE, Mallie F	20	SENW	1914-03-12		A1
3830	CHAIRES, Green H	7	E½SE	1828-08-22		A1
3817	CURRY, Charles L	8	SE	1897-08-05		A2
3831	CURRY, Hardy	8	NW	1897-07-03		A2
3908	DANIELS, Thomas H	30	E½SW	1909-09-24		A1
3837	DARDEN, Hilliard	8	NE	1897-08-05		A2
3842	DICKERSON, James E	20	SWSW	1908-07-06		A1
3815	DUNCAN, Alexander	30	S½NE	1910-05-05		A2
3832	DUNCAN, Henrietta	6	SESE	1905-05-17		A2
3875	ELLIS, Joseph W	24	NESW	1900-08-09		A2 G66
3876	" "	24	S½NW	1900-08-09		A2 G66
3877	" "	24	SWNE	1900-08-09		A2 G66
3875	ELLIS, Louisa	24	NESW	1900-08-09		A2 G66
3876	" "	24	S½NW	1900-08-09		A2 G66
3877	" "	24	SWNE	1900-08-09		A2 G66
3816	FENNEL, Benjamin A	30	SE	1909-09-20		A2
3901	FORAN, Sarah E	32	N½SE	1909-09-20		A2
3902	" "	32	N½SW	1909-09-20		A2
3896	FOXWORTH, Ransom J	12	SW	1888-11-22		A2
3892	FREEMAN, Norman	34	NE	1908-08-17		A2
3851	GAINER, James Y	12	NW	1899-05-12		A2
3879	GOTAIR, Lizzie	34	SENW	1912-11-22		A2
3864	HILL, John	6	W½SE	1859-06-01		A1
3865	" "	7	W½NE	1859-06-01		A1
3866	HOLMES, John	4	E½NW	1898-04-06		A2
3867	" "	4	N½NE	1898-04-06		A2
3868	" "	4	S½NE	1905-10-19		A2
3826	HOWARD, George	1	NE	1852-09-01		A1
3827	" "	28	E½NE	1911-01-16		A2

ID	Individual in Patent	Sec.	Sec. Part	Date Issued	Other Counties	For More Info . . .
3828	HOWARD, George (Cont'd)	28	E½SE	1911-01-16		A2
3873	HOWELL, Joseph H	11	E½SW	1828-08-22		A1
3880	JACKSON, London K	28	W½NE	1912-11-25		A1
3881	" "	28	W½SE	1912-11-25		A1
3919	JONES, William	36	NENE	1911-12-04		A2
3913	KENT, Wiley	10	NE	1890-12-31		A1
3812	LAND, Albert L	6	N½NW	1902-07-03		A2
3813	" "	6	SWNW	1902-07-03		A2
3822	LEE, Clifford	14	NW	1896-08-06		A2
3889	LEE, Moses F	24	NWSW	1908-07-06		A1
3890	" "	24	S½SW	1908-07-06		A1
3905	LEWIS, Seth P	4	W½NW	1828-08-22		A1
3918	LIPFORD, William E	1	SESE	1859-06-01		A1
3843	LONG, James H	22	N½NW	1906-06-04		A2
3844	" "	22	SENW	1906-06-04		A2
3845	" "	22	SWNE	1906-06-04		A2
3848	LOVE, James P	11	W½SW	1835-10-20		A1
3835	MASHBURN, Henry C	28	SW	1911-04-20		A2
3823	MAYO, Elijah T	6	NESW	1904-04-08		A2
3824	" "	6	SENW	1904-04-08		A2
3825	" "	6	W½SW	1904-04-08		A2
3840	MAYO, James B	14	SW	1904-08-26		A2
3860	MAYO, John H	20	E½NE	1909-05-17		A2
3861	" "	20	E½SE	1909-05-17		A2
3869	MAYO, John M	26	NE	1912-09-19		A1
3897	MAYS, Robert J	18	E½SW	1902-07-03		A2
3898	" "	18	W½SE	1902-07-03		A2
3909	MCCORMACK, Thomas J	22	E½NE	1901-08-29		A2
3910	" "	22	E½SE	1901-08-29		A2
3878	MCLENDON, Julius C	8	SW	1897-08-05		A2
3838	MONK, Irving	30	E½NW	1908-07-06		A2
3839	" "	30	N½NE	1908-07-06		A2
3874	NEWSOME, Joseph	24	SE	1899-05-12		A2
3862	PORTER, John H	24	N½NE	1901-12-04		A2
3863	" "	24	N½NW	1901-12-04		A2
3884	RILEY, Mary	26	SW	1903-05-25		A2
3920	RILEY, William	22	NWNE	1909-12-06		A2
3870	ROBINSON, John	26	NW	1901-12-04		A2
3899	SCOTT, Rosabel	12	E½SE	1899-08-30		A2
3914	SCOTT, William A	12	S½NE	1891-11-09		A2
3915	" "	12	W½SE	1891-11-09		A2
3829	SEXTON, George L	18	W½SW	1909-05-17		A2
3850	SEXTON, James W	4	SE	1896-08-06		A2
3882	SEXTON, Lovick P	18	NW	1902-07-03		A2
3916	SHORES, William A	18	NE	1899-05-22		A2
3891	SIMS, Nancy	24	SENE	1906-09-14		A2
3885	SKETO, Matilda	22	SWNW	1906-04-26		A1 F
3886	" "	22	W½SW	1906-04-26		A1 F
3887	SKETO, Milton	14	N½NE	1901-11-16		A2
3888	" "	14	SWNE	1901-11-16		A2
3921	SKETO, William	14	E½SE	1896-04-27		A2
3922	" "	14	NWSE	1896-04-27		A2
3923	" "	14	SENE	1896-04-27		A2
3911	SMITH, Thomas	32	S½NE	1913-03-18		A2
3912	" "	32	S½NW	1913-03-18		A2
3871	STEPHENS, John S	4	SW	1893-10-13		A2
3852	THOMPSON, Jennett E	36	NWSW	1906-09-14		A2 G136
3853	" "	36	W½NW	1906-09-14		A2 G136
3852	THOMPSON, William	36	NWSW	1906-09-14		A2 G136
3853	" "	36	W½NW	1906-09-14		A2 G136
3846	VICKERY, James J	17	SESW	1859-06-01		A1
3847	" "	17	W½SE	1859-06-01		A1
3858	VICKERY, John B	18	E½SE	1905-03-20		A2
3924	VICKERY, William	20	W½NE	1857-12-01		A1
3893	WADKINS, Pitt	36	E½SE	1910-11-09		A2
3894	" "	36	SESW	1910-11-09		A2
3895	" "	36	SWSE	1910-11-09		A2
3836	WALKER, Henry	36	SWSW	1912-03-28		A2
3854	WILLIAMS, Joel C	34	E½SE	1909-05-11		A1
3855	" "	34	SESW	1909-05-11		A1
3856	" "	34	SWSE	1909-05-11		A1
3818	WILSON, Charley	34	NWSE	1911-10-09		A2
3925	WILSON, William W	36	NESW	1911-09-18		A2

Patent Map

T3-N R11-W
Tallahassee Meridian

Map Group 31

Township Statistics

Parcels Mapped	:	114
Number of Patents	:	79
Number of Individuals	:	79
Patentees Identified	:	77
Number of Surnames	:	59
Multi-Patentee Parcels	:	5
Oldest Patent Date	:	8/22/1828
Most Recent Patent	:	12/2/1938
Block/Lot Parcels	:	0
Parcels Re - Issued	:	0
Parcels that Overlap	:	0
Cities and Towns	:	0
Cemeteries	:	2

LAND
Albert L
1902

AARONS
John H
1902

6

5

LEWIS
Seth P
1828

HOLMES
John
1898

HOLMES
John
1898

HOLMES
John
1905

LAND
Albert L
1902

MAYO
Elijah T
1904

STEPHENS
John S
1893

4

SEXTON
James W
1896

MAYO
Elijah T
1904

MAYO
Elijah T
1904

HILL
John
1859

DUNCAN
Henrietta
1905

HILL
John
1859

CURRY
Hardy
1897

DARDEN
Hilliard
1897

8

9

7

CHAIRES
Green H
1828

MCLENDON
Julius C
1897

CURRY
Charles L
1897

SEXTON
Lovick P
1902

SHORES
William A
1899

18

17

16

SEXTON
George L
1909

MAYS
Robert J
1902

MAYS
Robert J
1902

VICKERY
John B
1905

VICKERY
James J
1859

VICKERY
James J
1859

CARLISLE
Mallie F
1914

VICKERY
William
1857

MAYO
John H
1909

19

20

21

DICKERSON
James E
1908

MAYO
John H
1909

BAREFOOT
Texas Ann
1910

MONK
Irving
1908

MONK
Irving
1908

BALDWIN
Joseph E
1909

JACKSON
London K
1912

HOWARD
George
1911

MONK
Irving
1908

DUNCAN
Alexander
1910

30

29

28

FENNEL
Benjamin A
1909

MASHBURN
Henry C
1911

HOWARD
George
1911

BAREFOOT
Texas Ann
1910

DANIELS
Thomas H
1909

JACKSON
London K
1912

AARONS
Henry
1910

AARONS
Henry
1910

31

SMITH
Thomas
1913

32

SMITH
Thomas
1913

33

FORAN
Sarah E
1909

FORAN
Sarah E
1909

BOUTWELL
Sarah J
1909

BOUTWELL
Sarah J
1909

Map grid

Section 3

Section 2

Section 1
HOWARD
George
1852

LIPFORD
William E
1859

Section 10
BROOKS
Russell
1898

KENT
Wiley
1890

BRANNON
James T
1896

BRANAN
John A
1895

Section 11

LOVE
James P
1835

HOWELL
Joseph H
1828

Section 12
GAINER
James Y
1899

SCOTT
William A
1891

FOXWORTH
Ransom J
1888

SCOTT
William A
1891

SCOTT
Rosabel
1899

Section 15

Section 14
LEE
Clifford
1896

SKETO
Milton
1901

SKETO
Milton
1901

SKETO
William
1896

SKETO
William
1896

MAYO
James B
1904

ADKINS
William B
1910

SKETO
William
1896

Section 13

Section 22
LONG
James H
1906

RILEY
William
1909

MCCORMACK
Thomas J
1901

SKETO
Matilda
1906

LONG
James H
1906

LONG
James H
1906

SKETO
Matilda
1906

MCCORMACK
Thomas J
1901

Section 23

Section 24
PORTER
John H
1901

PORTER
John H
1901

ELLIS [66]
Joseph W
1900

ELLIS [66]
Joseph W
1900

SIMS
Nancy
1906

LEE
Moses F
1908

ELLIS [66]
Joseph W
1900

NEWSOME
Joseph
1899

LEE
Moses F
1908

Section 27

Section 26
MAYO
John M
1912

ROBINSON
John
1901

RILEY
Mary
1903

Section 25

Section 34
BROOKS
Alexander
1911

FREEMAN
Norman
1908

BROOKS
Cleveland B
1918

GOTAIR
Lizzie
1912

BROOKS
Cleveland B
1918

WILSON
Charley
1911

WILLIAMS
Joel C
1909

BROOKS
Cleveland B
1918

WILLIAMS
Joel C
1909

WILLIAMS
Joel C
1909

Section 35

Section 36
THOMPSON [136]
Jennett E
1906

BRUNER
James E
1938

JONES
William
1911

THOMPSON [136]
Jennett E
1906

WILSON
William W
1911

WADKINS
Pitt
1910

WALKER
Henry
1912

WADKINS
Pitt
1910

WADKINS
Pitt
1910

Helpful Hints

1. This Map's INDEX can be found on the preceding pages.

2. Refer to Map "C" to see where this Township lies within Jackson County, Florida.

3. Numbers within square brackets [ ] denote a multi-patentee land parcel (multi-owner). Refer to Appendix "C" for a full list of members in this group.

4. Areas that look to be crowded with Patentees usually indicate multiple sales of the same parcel (Re-issues) or Overlapping parcels. See this Township's Index for an explanation of these and other circumstances that might explain "odd" groupings of Patentees on this map.

Legend

——— Patent Boundary

━━━ Section Boundary

No Patents Found
(or Outside County)

1., 2., 3., ... Lot Numbers
(when beside a name)

[ ] Group Number
(see Appendix "C")

Scale: Section = 1 mile X 1 mile
(generally, with some exceptions)

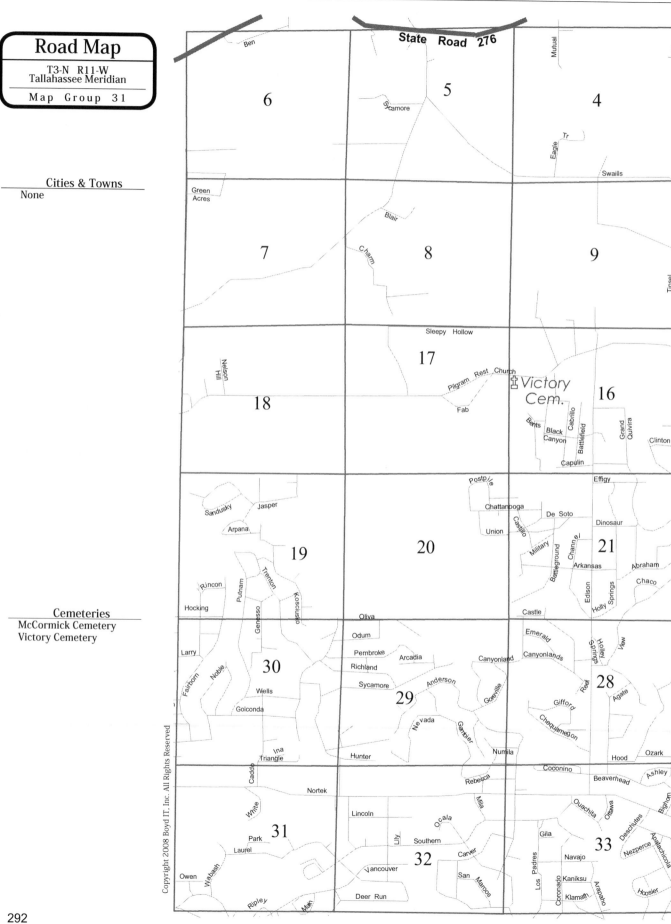

Road Map

T3-N R11-W
Tallahassee Meridian

Map Group 31

Cities & Towns
None

Cemeteries
McCormick Cemetery
Victory Cemetery

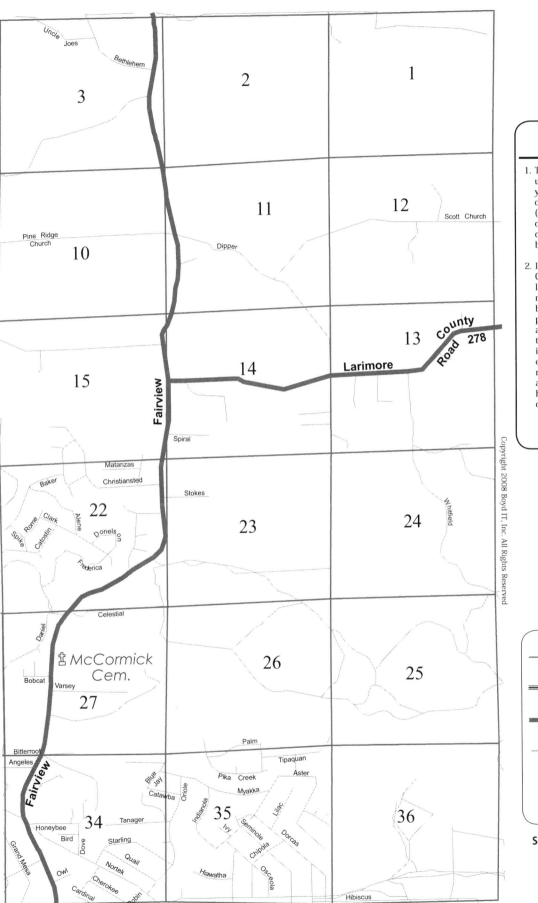

Helpful Hints

1. This road map has a number of uses, but primarily it is to help you: a) find the present location of land owned by your ancestors (at least the general area), b) find cemeteries and city-centers, and c) estimate the route/roads used by Census-takers & tax-assessors.

2. If you plan to travel to Jackson County to locate cemeteries or land parcels, please pick up a modern travel map for the area before you do. Mapping old land parcels on modern maps is not as exact a science as you might think. Just the slightest variations in public land survey coordinates, estimates of parcel boundaries, or road-map deviations can greatly alter a map's representation of how a road either does or doesn't cross a particular parcel of land.

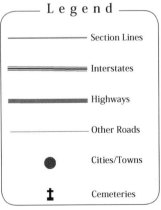

Legend

———— Section Lines

════ Interstates

▬▬▬ Highways

———— Other Roads

● Cities/Towns

✝ Cemeteries

Scale: Section = 1 mile X 1 mile
(generally, with some exceptions)

293

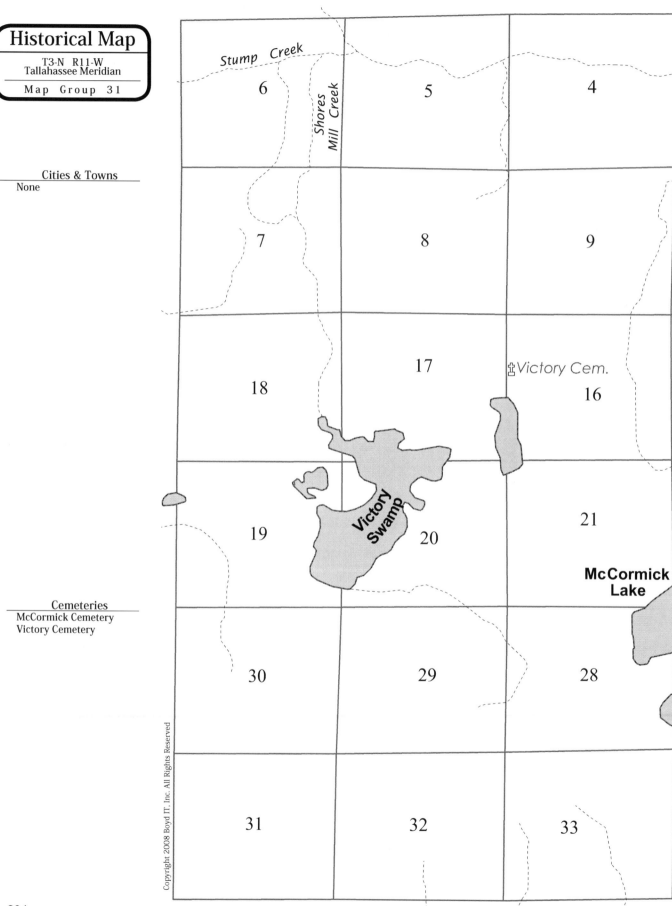

Historical Map

T3-N R11-W
Tallahassee Meridian

Map Group 31

<u>Cities & Towns</u>
None

<u>Cemeteries</u>
McCormick Cemetery
Victory Cemetery

Stump Creek

Shores Mill Creek

6

5

4

7

8

9

18

17

⚰Victory Cem.

16

19

Victory Swamp

20

21

McCormick Lake

30

29

28

31

32

33

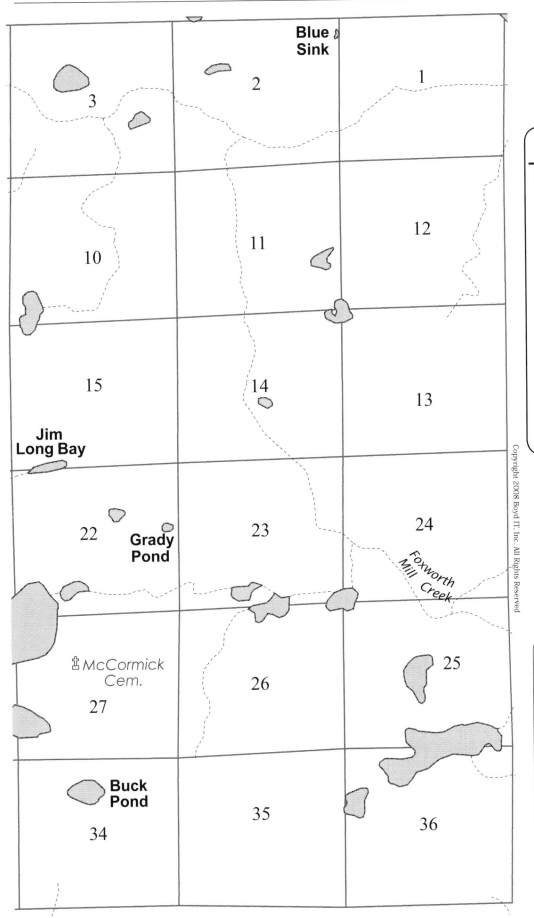

Blue Sink

3

2

1

10

11

12

15

14

13

Jim Long Bay

22

Grady Pond

23

24

Foxworth Mill Creek

⚓ McCormick Cem.

26

25

27

34

Buck Pond

35

36

Helpful Hints

1. This Map takes a different look at the same Congressional Township displayed in the preceding two maps. It presents features that can help you better envision the historical development of the area: a) Water-bodies (lakes & ponds), b) Water-courses (rivers, streams, etc.), c) Railroads, d) City/town center-points (where they were oftentimes located when first settled), and e) Cemeteries.

2. Using this "Historical" map in tandem with this Township's Patent Map and Road Map, may lead you to some interesting discoveries. You will often find roads, towns, cemeteries, and waterways are named after nearby landowners: sometimes those names will be the ones you are researching. See how many of these research gems you can find here in Jackson County.

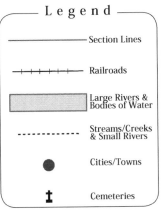

L e g e n d

——————— Section Lines

+‒+‒+‒+‒+ Railroads

▭ Large Rivers & Bodies of Water

- - - - - - - Streams/Creeks & Small Rivers

● Cities/Towns

✝ Cemeteries

Scale: Section = 1 mile X 1 mile
(there are some exceptions)

Map Group 32: Index to Land Patents

Township 3-North Range 10-West (Tallahassee)

After you locate an individual in this Index, take note of the Section and Section Part then proceed to the Land Patent map on the pages immediately following. You should have no difficulty locating the corresponding parcel of land.

The "For More Info" Column will lead you to more information about the underlying Patents. See the *Legend* at right, and the "How to Use this Book" chapter, for more information.

```
┌─────────────────────────────────────────────────────────────────┐
│                         LEGEND                                    │
│              "For More Info . . . " column                        │
│  ───────────────────────────────────────────────────             │
│  A = Authority (Legislative Act, See Appendix "A")                │
│  B = Block or Lot (location in Section unknown)                   │
│  C = Cancelled Patent                                             │
│  F = Fractional Section                                           │
│  G = Group  (Multi-Patentee Patent, see Appendix "C")             │
│  V = Overlaps another Parcel                                      │
│  R = Re-Issued (Parcel patented more than once)                   │
│                                                                   │
│  (A & G items require you to look in the Appendixes referred      │
│  to above. All other Letter-designations followed by a number     │
│  require you to locate line-items in this index that possess      │
│  the ID number found after the letter).                          │
└─────────────────────────────────────────────────────────────────┘
```

ID	Individual in Patent	Sec.	Sec. Part	Date Issued	Other Counties	For More Info . . .
3956	ADKINS, Daniel M	30	SW	1905-05-05		A1 F
4007	ADKINS, Jane C	30	SE	1905-05-05		A1 F
4064	ADKINS, Richmond L	28	NE	1899-05-12		A2
4074	BANKS, William	11	E½SE	1827-10-01		A1
4075	"	14	E½NE	1827-10-01		A1
3926	BATIE, Alex	6	N½SE	1918-08-22		A2
3927	"	6	NESW	1918-08-22		A2
4070	BELL, Silas	4	SESE	1894-01-08		A2
3932	BUSH, Asbury F	4	SWNE	1843-03-10		A1
4012	BUSH, John	4	NWNE	1843-03-10		A1
4014	"	4	W½SE	1843-03-10		A1 G26
4011	"	4	NESE	1844-07-10		A1
4013	"	4	SENE	1844-07-10		A1
4048	BUTLER, Mary E	8	NESW	1905-10-19		A2
4015	CAMPBELL, John	28	SWSW	1913-10-23		A2
3933	CHAIRES, Benjamin	12	SE	1839-09-20		A1
3934	"	13	E½SE	1839-09-20		A1
3935	"	13	NWSE	1839-09-20		A1
3936	"	13	W½NW	1839-09-20		A1
3941	CHAPMAN, Charles	2	W½SW	1882-05-20		A2
4030	CHAPMAN, John R	1	SESE	1840-10-10		A1
4031	"	1	W½SE	1840-10-10		A1
4032	"	11	NE	1840-10-10		A1
4033	"	11	W½SE	1840-10-10		A1
4034	"	14	W½NE	1840-10-10		A1
4035	"	2	E½SE	1840-10-10		A1
4029	"	1	NESE	1841-01-09		A1
4036	"	2	NE	1841-01-09		A1
4037	"	2	W½SE	1841-01-09		A1
4016	CHASON, John	10	S½NE	1859-06-01		A1
3940	CHASTINE, Cato	24	N½NW	1906-06-04		A2
4065	DUNHAM, Robert J	20	N½NW	1903-06-26		A2
3998	EAGLE, James A	34	NWSE	1912-06-27		A2
3977	FAISON, George	34	N½NW	1914-07-09		A2
4014	FINLEY, James L	4	W½SE	1843-03-10		A1 G26
4001	"	10	NWNW	1844-07-10		A1
4002	"	9	NWNE	1844-07-10		A1
4018	GAY, John	22	SWSE	1856-06-16		A1
4019	"	27	NWNE	1856-06-16		A1
4042	GILCHRIST, Malcolm	1	NW	1827-11-01		A1
4043	"	1	W½SW	1827-11-01		A1
4055	HAYNES, Nancy M	3	NWNW	1857-12-01		A1
3978	HOWARD, George	6	E½NW	1843-03-10		A1
3979	"	6	W½NE	1852-09-01		A1
4021	JONES, John	26	E½SW	1905-06-30		A2
4022	"	26	W½SE	1905-06-30		A2

ID	Individual in Patent	Sec.	Sec. Part	Date Issued	Other Counties	For More Info . . .
3959	KILBEE, Ebenezer H	3	S½SW	1859-06-01		A1
3985	KILBEE, Huldah	5	W½NW	1859-06-01		A1
3986	" "	6	E½NE	1859-06-01		A1
4060	KILBEE, Rebecca	10	SENW	1882-06-10		A2
4061	"	10	SWNW	1897-08-16		A2
4079	LARAMORE, William F	26	W½NW	1905-12-13		A2
4080	" "	26	W½SW	1905-12-13		A2
3965	LASHLEY, Eltie O	32	NESW	1910-01-20		A2 G91
3966	"	32	NWSE	1910-01-20		A2 G91
3967	"	32	W½SW	1910-01-20		A2 G91
4078	LIPFORD, William E	6	W½SW	1859-06-01		A1
3938	MADDOX, Calvin	34	E½NE	1908-10-29		A2
3939	" "	34	E½SE	1908-10-29		A2
3970	MADDOX, Francis M	20	NENE	1905-05-17		A2
3981	MADDOX, Henry C	20	SESW	1905-05-26		A2
3982	" "	20	SWNW	1905-05-26		A2
3983	" "	20	W½SW	1905-05-26		A2
4020	MADDOX, John H	32	NE	1905-05-17		A2
4040	MADDOX, Littleton	8	N½NW	1900-08-09		A2
4073	MADDOX, Wiley H	20	S½SE	1905-12-13		A2
3937	MARTIN, Cad	28	E½SE	1914-11-11		A2
4005	MAYO, James T	22	SWNW	1857-12-01		A1
4006	" "	22	W½SW	1857-12-01		A1
4025	MAYO, John P	24	NESW	1857-12-01		A1
4026	" "	24	S½NW	1857-12-01		A1
4027	" "	24	W½SW	1857-12-01		A1
4068	MCCORMICK, Sarah J	34	S½NW	1906-06-04		A2
4069	" "	34	W½NE	1906-06-04		A2
3943	MCNEALY, Charles	10	N½SW	1897-01-21		A2
4017	MEDLOACK, John D	28	NW	1901-12-04		A2
3944	MOORE, Charles	14	SENW	1905-05-26		A2
3960	PADGET, Elijah	25	SENE	1855-05-01		A1
4023	PADGETT, John M	8	E½SE	1899-08-30		A2
4024	" "	8	SENE	1899-08-30		A2
4091	PADGETT, William W	17	N½SW	1857-12-01		A1
4092	" "	17	NW	1857-12-01		A1
4093	" "	18	NENE	1857-12-01		A1
4094	" "	7	SESE	1857-12-01		A1
3961	PADJETT, Elijah	4	S½SW	1856-06-16		A1
3962	" "	5	S½SE	1856-06-16		A1
3963	" "	8	N½NE	1856-06-16		A1
3964	" "	9	N½NW	1856-06-16		A1
4003	PAGE, James	36	NE	1912-10-23		A2
4041	PATTON, Lovett	24	SESW	1912-04-18		A2
4066	PATTON, Samuel J	24	W½NE	1903-06-26		A2
3984	PEEBLES, Henry	1	E½SW	1827-10-01		A1
3974	PITTMAN, Frederick	2	W½NW	1843-03-10		A1
3975	" "	3	E½NW	1843-03-10		A1
3976	" "	3	NE	1843-03-10		A1
4056	PITTMAN, Ned	10	E½SE	1898-04-06		A2
3942	PLEDGER, Charles E	14	SW	1895-10-16		A2
3968	PLEDGER, Emmett T	36	NW	1915-03-04		A2
3969	PLEDGER, Francis A	14	SE	1901-06-28		A2
3980	PLEDGER, Harris A	26	E½SE	1908-10-26		A1
4028	PLEDGER, John P	10	S½SW	1897-08-05		A2
4038	PLEDGER, John R	22	NE	1893-02-21		A2
4058	PLEDGER, Philip M	36	N½SE	1907-04-01		A2
4059	" "	36	N½SW	1907-04-01		A2
4076	PLEDGER, William D	36	S½SE	1910-12-05		A1
4077	" "	36	S½SW	1910-12-05		A1
4081	PLEDGER, William J	22	E½NW	1897-09-20		A2
4082	" "	22	NESW	1897-09-20		A2
4083	" "	22	NWNW	1897-09-20		A2
3971	PORTER, Francis M	8	SESW	1897-03-03		A2
3972	" "	8	SWNE	1897-03-03		A2
3973	" "	8	W½SE	1897-03-03		A2
3987	PORTER, Jacob F	24	NENE	1855-05-01		A1
3994	PORTER, Jacob T	21	NWSW	1850-08-10		A1
3996	" "	24	E½SE	1852-09-01		A1
3997	" "	24	SENE	1852-09-01		A1
3988	" "	17	SWSE	1856-06-16		A1
3989	" "	20	NESW	1856-06-16		A1
3990	" "	20	NWNE	1856-06-16		A1

ID	Individual in Patent	Sec.	Sec. Part	Date Issued	Other Counties	For More Info . . .
3991	PORTER, Jacob T (Cont'd)	20	SENE	1856-06-16		A1
3992	" "	20	SENW	1856-06-16		A1
3993	" "	21	E½SW	1856-06-16		A1
3995	" "	21	SWNW	1856-06-16		A1
3999	PORTER, James B	18	S½NE	1899-05-12		A2
4000	" "	18	W½SE	1899-05-12		A2
4004	PORTER, James R	28	W½SE	1911-11-27		A2 G121
4039	PORTER, Joseph	6	W½NW	1914-01-23		A2
4004	PORTER, Louisa	28	W½SE	1911-11-27		A2 G121
4050	PORTER, Mathias	6	SWSE	1908-07-06		A2 C R4051
4052	" "	6	SWSW	1908-07-06		A2 C
4049	" "	6	SESW	1910-02-01		A2
4051	" "	6	SWSE	1910-02-01		A2 R4050
4053	PORTER, Milda A	18	E½SE	1899-09-30		A2
4085	PORTER, William T	26	E½NE	1900-09-07		A2
3928	PUMPHRAY, Alfred	18	SESW	1894-02-24		A2
3929	" "	18	SWNW	1894-02-24		A2
3930	" "	18	W½SW	1894-02-24		A2
3931	PUMPHREY, Alfred	18	NWNE	1901-06-28		A2
4071	PUMPHREY, Thomas S	22	E½SE	1903-06-01		A2
4086	PUMPHREY, William T	18	N½NW	1899-05-12		A2
4087	" "	18	NESW	1899-05-12		A2
4088	" "	18	SENW	1899-05-12		A2
4062	RANEY, Rhoda	14	NWNW	1909-01-18		A2 G124
4062	RANEY, Simon	14	NWNW	1909-01-18		A2 G124
4057	REGISTER, Olive	14	SWNW	1904-11-15		A2 G125
4057	REGISTER, Wiley	14	SWNW	1904-11-15		A2 G125
4008	RUCKER, John A	8	S½NW	1895-10-16		A2
4009	" "	8	W½SW	1895-10-16		A2
4010	SHARPE, John B	22	SESW	1901-04-09		A2
4054	SIMS, Miles	1	W½NE	1830-12-28		A1
4084	SIMS, William	1	E½NE	1856-06-16		A1
4072	SKETO, Warren	34	SWSW	1857-12-01		A1
3965	SNOW, Eltie O	32	NESE	1910-01-20		A2 G91
3966	" "	32	NWSE	1910-01-20		A2 G91
3967	" "	32	W½SW	1910-01-20		A2 G91
4063	STEPHENS, Richard	20	NESE	1843-03-10		A1
4067	STEPHENS, Samuel	4	NENW	1857-12-01		A1
4047	SULLIVAN, Martha	30	NE	1890-12-11		A2
3957	SWAILS, Dennis	26	E½NW	1896-04-27		A2
3958	" "	26	W½NE	1896-04-27		A2
4089	VICKERY, William	4	NWNW	1840-10-10		A1
4090	" "	5	NENE	1840-10-10		A1
4044	WETHINGTON, Marley A	34	E½SW	1900-08-09		A2
4045	" "	34	NWSW	1900-08-09		A2
4046	" "	34	SWSE	1900-08-09		A2
3945	WILLIAMSON, Charles	10	W½SE	1827-10-01		A1
3946	" "	12	E½NE	1827-10-01		A1
3947	" "	12	E½NW	1827-10-01		A1
3948	" "	12	E½SW	1827-10-01		A1
3949	" "	12	W½NE	1827-10-01		A1
3950	" "	12	W½NW	1827-10-01		A1
3951	" "	12	W½SW	1827-10-01		A1
3952	" "	13	E½NE	1827-10-01		A1
3953	" "	13	E½NW	1827-10-01		A1
3954	" "	13	W½NE	1827-10-01		A1
3955	" "	13	W½SW	1827-10-01		A1

Patent Map

T3-N R10-W
Tallahassee Meridian

Map Group 32

Township Statistics

Parcels Mapped	:	169
Number of Patents	:	120
Number of Individuals	:	93
Patentees Identified	:	90
Number of Surnames	:	55
Multi-Patentee Parcels	:	7
Oldest Patent Date	:	10/1/1827
Most Recent Patent	:	8/22/1918
Block/Lot Parcels	:	0
Parcels Re - Issued	:	1
Parcels that Overlap	:	0
Cities and Towns	:	0
Cemeteries	:	5

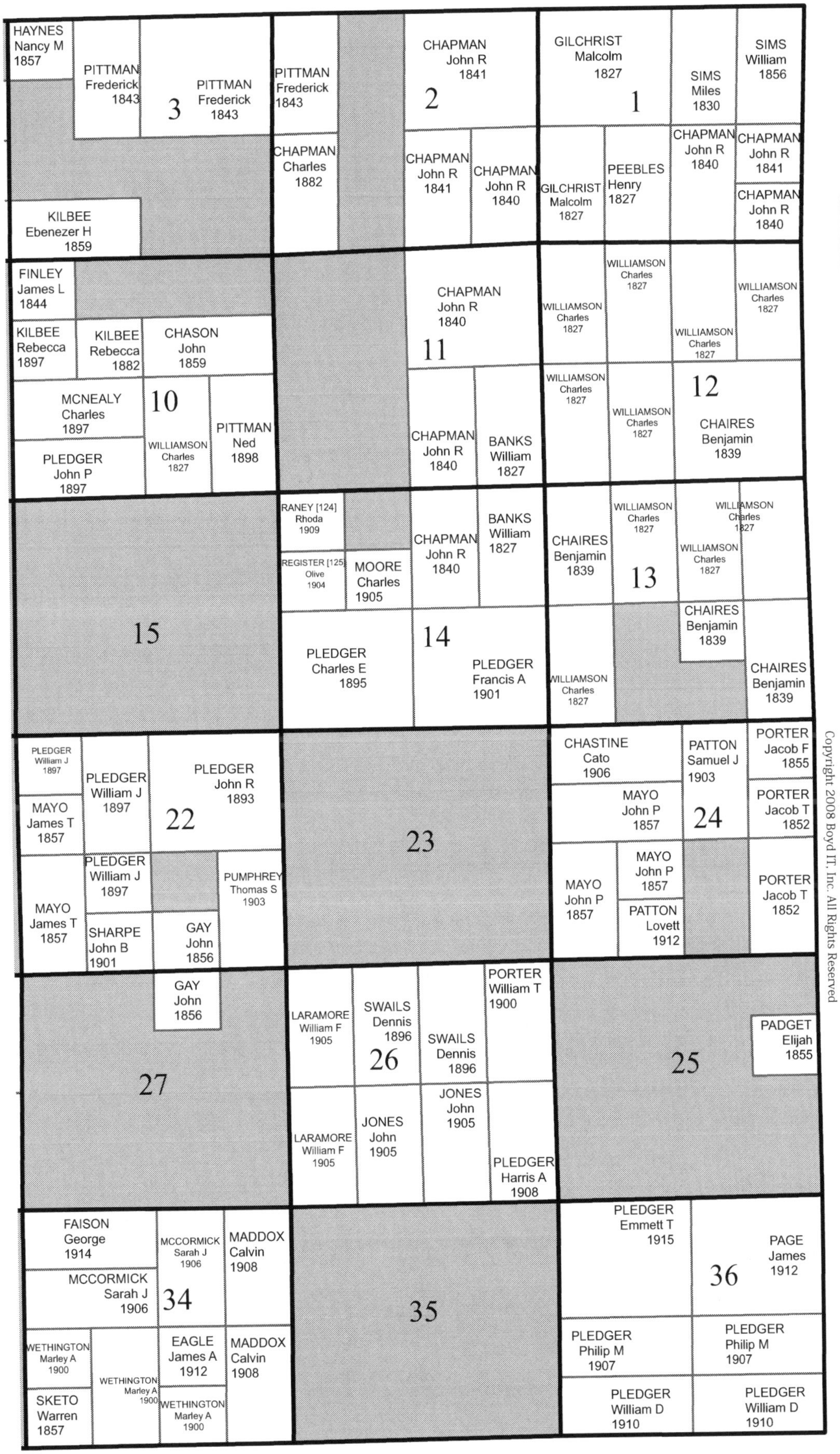
HAYNES Nancy M 1857
PITTMAN Frederick 1843
3
PITTMAN Frederick 1843
KILBEE Ebenezer H 1859
PITTMAN Frederick 1843
CHAPMAN Charles 1882
CHAPMAN John R 1841
2
CHAPMAN John R 1841
CHAPMAN John R 1840
GILCHRIST Malcolm 1827
1
SIMS Miles 1830
SIMS William 1856
GILCHRIST Malcolm 1827
PEEBLES Henry 1827
CHAPMAN John R 1840
CHAPMAN John R 1841
CHAPMAN John R 1840
FINLEY James L 1844
KILBEE Rebecca 1897
KILBEE Rebecca 1882
CHASON John 1859
MCNEALY Charles 1897
10
WILLIAMSON Charles 1827
PITTMAN Ned 1898
PLEDGER John P 1897
CHAPMAN John R 1840
11
CHAPMAN John R 1840
BANKS William 1827
WILLIAMSON Charles 1827
WILLIAMSON Charles 1827
WILLIAMSON Charles 1827
WILLIAMSON Charles 1827
WILLIAMSON Charles 1827
WILLIAMSON Charles 1827
12
CHAIRES Benjamin 1839
15
RANEY [124] Rhoda 1909
REGISTER [125] Olive 1904
MOORE Charles 1905
CHAPMAN John R 1840
BANKS William 1827
PLEDGER Charles E 1895
14
PLEDGER Francis A 1901
CHAIRES Benjamin 1839
WILLIAMSON Charles 1827
13
WILLIAMSON Charles 1827
WILLIAMSON Charles 1827
CHAIRES Benjamin 1839
WILLIAMSON Charles 1827
CHAIRES Benjamin 1839
PLEDGER William J 1897
PLEDGER William J 1897
PLEDGER John R 1893
22
MAYO James T 1857
PLEDGER William J 1897
PUMPHREY Thomas S 1903
MAYO James T 1857
SHARPE John B 1901
GAY John 1856
23
CHASTINE Cato 1906
PATTON Samuel J 1903
PORTER Jacob F 1855
MAYO John P 1857
24
PORTER Jacob T 1852
MAYO John P 1857
MAYO John P 1857
PATTON Lovett 1912
PORTER Jacob T 1852
GAY John 1856
27
LARAMORE William F 1905
SWAILS Dennis 1896
26
SWAILS Dennis 1896
PORTER William T 1900
JONES John 1905
JONES John 1905
LARAMORE William F 1905
PLEDGER Harris A 1908
25
PADGET Elijah 1855
FAISON George 1914
MCCORMICK Sarah J 1906
MADDOX Calvin 1908
MCCORMICK Sarah J 1906
34
WETHINGTON Marley A 1900
EAGLE James A 1912
MADDOX Calvin 1908
WETHINGTON Marley A 1900
SKETO Warren 1857
WETHINGTON Marley A 1900
35
PLEDGER Emmett T 1915
PAGE James 1912
36
PLEDGER Philip M 1907
PLEDGER Philip M 1907
PLEDGER William D 1910
PLEDGER William D 1910

Helpful Hints

1. This Map's INDEX can be found on the preceding pages.
2. Refer to Map "C" to see where this Township lies within Jackson County, Florida.
3. Numbers within square brackets [ ] denote a multi-patentee land parcel (multi-owner). Refer to Appendix "C" for a full list of members in this group.
4. Areas that look to be crowded with Patentees usually indicate multiple sales of the same parcel (Re-issues) or Overlapping parcels. See this Township's Index for an explanation of these and other circumstances that might explain "odd" groupings of Patentees on this map.

Legend

Patent Boundary

Section Boundary

No Patents Found (or Outside County)

1., 2., 3., ... Lot Numbers (when beside a name)

[ ] Group Number (see Appendix "C")

Scale: Section = 1 mile X 1 mile (generally, with some exceptions)

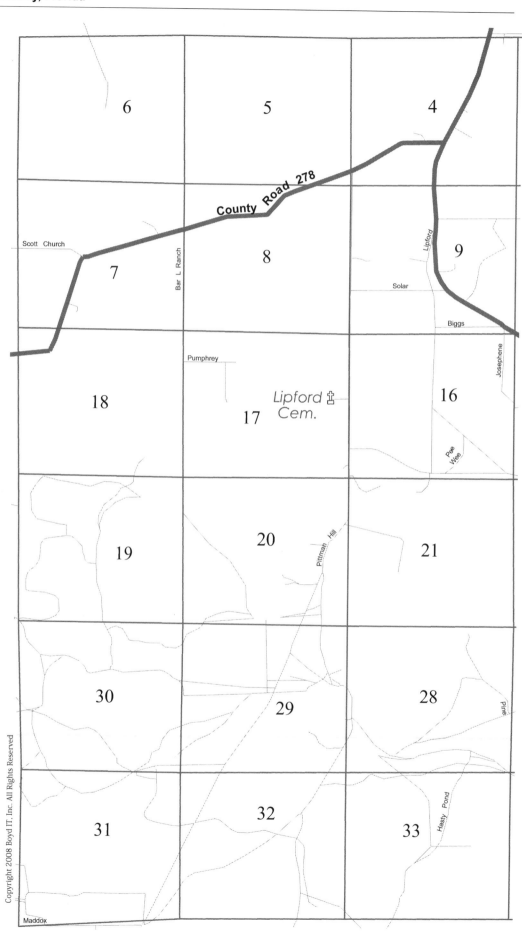

Road Map

T3-N R10-W
Tallahassee Meridian

Map Group 32

Cities & Towns
None

Cemeteries
Elder Cemetery
Jerusalem Cemetery
Lipford Cemetery
Maddox Cemetery
Pledger Cemetery

6

5

4

County Road 278

Scott Church

7

Bar L Ranch

8

Lipford

Solar

9

Biggs

Pumphrey

18

Lipford ♱
Cem.

17

Josephene

16

Pee Wee

19

20

Pittman Hill

21

30

29

28

Pine

31

32

Hasty Pond

33

Maddox

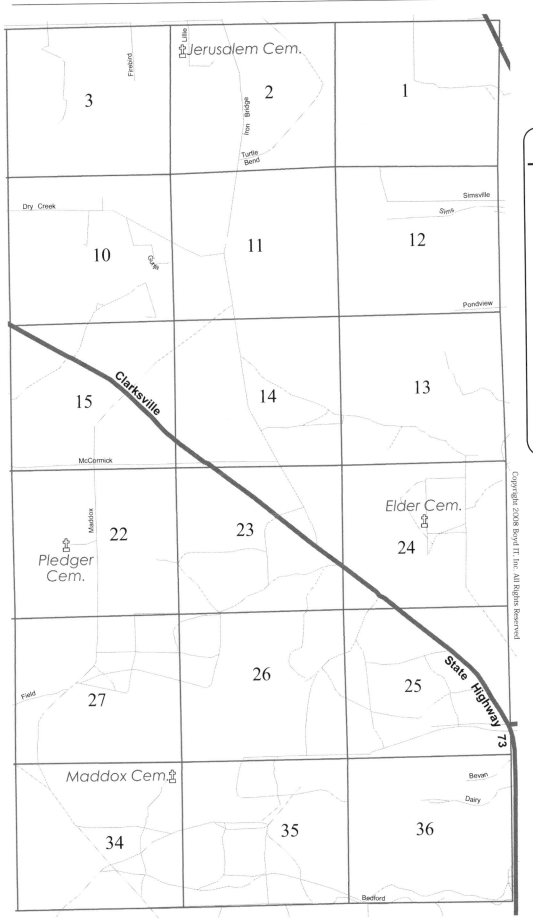

Jerusalem Cem.

Firebird

Lillie

3

2

Iron Bridge

1

Turtle Bend

Dry Creek

Simsville

Sims

10

11

12

Gunja

Pondview

Clarksville

15

14

13

McCormick

Maddox

Elder Cem.

22

23

24

Pledger Cem.

26

25

State Highway 73

Field

27

Maddox Cem.

Bevan

Dairy

34

35

36

Bedford

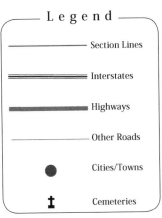

Helpful Hints

1. This road map has a number of uses, but primarily it is to help you: a) find the present location of land owned by your ancestors (at least the general area), b) find cemeteries and city-centers, and c) estimate the route/roads used by Census-takers & tax-assessors.

2. If you plan to travel to Jackson County to locate cemeteries or land parcels, please pick up a modern travel map for the area before you do. Mapping old land parcels on modern maps is not as exact a science as you might think. Just the slightest variations in public land survey coordinates, estimates of parcel boundaries, or road-map deviations can greatly alter a map's representation of how a road either does or doesn't cross a particular parcel of land.

Legend

———— Section Lines

════ Interstates

━━━━ Highways

———— Other Roads

● Cities/Towns

✝ Cemeteries

Scale: Section = 1 mile X 1 mile
(generally, with some exceptions)

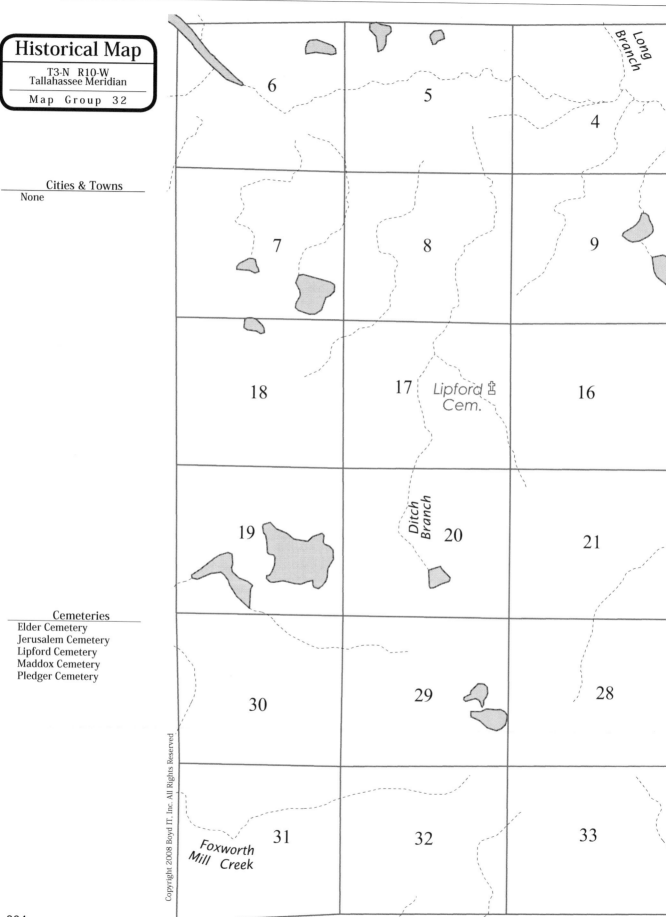

Historical Map

T3-N R10-W
Tallahassee Meridian

Map Group 32

<u>Cities & Towns</u>
None

<u>Cemeteries</u>
Elder Cemetery
Jerusalem Cemetery
Lipford Cemetery
Maddox Cemetery
Pledger Cemetery

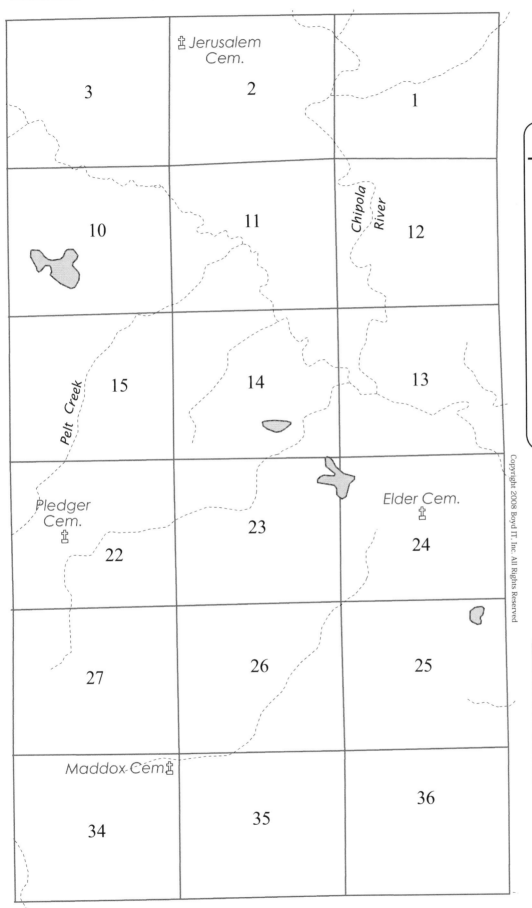

3

‡ *Jerusalem Cem.*

2

1

Chipola River

10

11

12

Pelt Creek

15

14

13

Pledger Cem. ‡

22

23

Elder Cem. ‡

24

27

26

25

Maddox Cem ‡

34

35

36

Helpful Hints

1. This Map takes a different look at the same Congressional Township displayed in the preceding two maps. It presents features that can help you better envision the historical development of the area: a) Water-bodies (lakes & ponds), b) Water-courses (rivers, streams, etc.), c) Railroads, d) City/town center-points (where they were oftentimes located when first settled), and e) Cemeteries.

2. Using this "Historical" map in tandem with this Township's Patent Map and Road Map, may lead you to some interesting discoveries. You will often find roads, towns, cemeteries, and waterways are named after nearby landowner: sometimes those names will be the ones you are researching. See how many of these research gems you can find here in Jackson County.

Legend

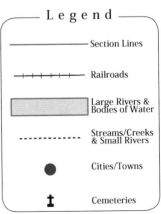

————	Section Lines
+++++++	Railroads
▨	Large Rivers & Bodies of Water
- - - - -	Streams/Creeks & Small Rivers
●	Cities/Towns
‡	Cemeteries

Scale: Section = 1 mile X 1 mile
(there are some exceptions)

Map Group 33: Index to Land Patents

Township 3-North Range 9-West (Tallahassee)

After you locate an individual in this Index, take note of the Section and Section Part then proceed to the Land Patent map on the pages immediately following. You should have no difficulty locating the corresponding parcel of land.

The "For More Info" Column will lead you to more information about the underlying Patents. See the *Legend* at right, and the "How to Use this Book" chapter, for more information.

```
                    LEGEND
            "For More Info . . . " column
A = Authority (Legislative Act, See Appendix "A")
B = Block or Lot (location in Section unknown)
C = Cancelled Patent
F = Fractional Section
G = Group  (Multi-Patentee Patent, see Appendix "C")
V = Overlaps another Parcel
R = Re-Issued (Parcel patented more than once)

(A & G items require you to look in the Appendixes referred
to above. All other Letter-designations followed by a number
require you to locate line-items in this index that possess
the ID number found after the letter).
```

ID	Individual in Patent	Sec.	Sec. Part	Date Issued	Other Counties	For More Info . . .
4242	BAGGETT, William K	36	SENW	1898-07-18		A2
4243	" "	36	W½NW	1898-07-18		A2
4232	BANKS, William	19	W½SE	1827-10-01		A1
4105	BARKLEY, Bolyn B	10	W½NW	1855-05-01		A1
4107	" "	8	N½SE	1855-05-01		A1
4109	" "	8	SENE	1855-05-01		A1
4112	" "	9	NWSE	1855-05-01		A1
4114	" "	9	SESE	1855-05-01		A1
4106	" "	17	E½NE	1859-06-01		A1
4108	" "	8	NENE	1859-06-01		A1
4110	" "	8	SESE	1859-06-01		A1
4111	" "	9	NWNW	1859-06-01		A1
4113	" "	9	S½SW	1859-06-01		A1
4115	" "	9	SWSE	1859-06-01		A1
4233	BARNETT, William	4	NW	1904-11-15		A2
4199	BEAUCHAMP, Martha E	14	SE	1899-05-12		A2
4227	BEAUCHAMP, Thomas J	24	SWNE	1907-04-01		A2
4234	BEAUCHAMP, William H	34	SE	1896-01-14		A2
4102	BLOUNT, Benjamin T	24	SESW	1900-01-27		A2
4103	" "	24	SWSE	1900-01-27		A2
4104	" "	24	W½SW	1900-01-27		A2
4216	BRYAN, Seaborne O	36	SW	1891-04-06		A2
4142	BULLOCK, George	10	NWSW	1855-05-01		A1
4143	" "	9	NESE	1855-05-01		A1
4145	BULLOCK, George K	10	NE	1857-12-01		A1
4099	CHAIRES, Benjamin	19	E½SE	1839-09-20		A1
4100	" "	30	E½NE	1839-09-20		A1
4101	" "	30	NWNE	1839-09-20		A1
4184	CHAPMAN, John R	8	E½SW	1843-03-10		A1
4185	" "	8	W½SW	1843-03-10		A1
4095	COOK, Adolphus	22	NE	1903-06-01		A2
4119	COOK, Charles F	30	SWNW	1906-03-12		A2
4120	" "	30	W½SW	1906-03-12		A2
4152	COOK, Hardy	2	NW	1896-04-27		A2
4223	COOK, Thomas	11	NW	1857-12-01		A1
4224	" "	2	SW	1857-12-01		A1
4165	COULLIETTE, James S	4	N½SE	1896-01-03		A2
4166	" "	4	N½SW	1896-01-03		A2
4172	DAVIS, Jefferson	6	S½SE	1891-07-14		A2
4144	DAWSON, George D	24	W½NW	1903-12-17		A2
4212	DICKSON, Robert S	7	E½SE	1857-12-01		A1
4214	" "	7	NWSE	1857-12-01		A1
4213	" "	7	NE	1859-06-01		A1
4151	DURDEN, Green	26	W½NW	1903-05-25		A2
4176	DURHAM, John B	26	E½NW	1901-06-25		A2
4177	" "	26	N½NE	1901-06-25		A2

ID	Individual in Patent	Sec.	Sec. Part	Date Issued	Other Counties	For More Info . . .
4201	DURHAM, Martha K	26	NWSE	1893-01-21		A2
4202	" "	26	S½SE	1893-01-21		A2
4203	" "	26	SWNE	1893-01-21		A2
4131	FOLSOM, Chesley	4	SESE	1837-04-20		A1
4132	" "	4	SESW	1837-04-20		A1
4167	FOLSOM, James Y	6	NESW	1882-12-15		A2
4168	" "	6	NWSE	1882-12-15		A2
4217	FOLSOM, Sidney S	4	SWSE	1835-10-20		A1
4225	FOLSOM, Thomas	9	NWNE	1835-10-20		A1
4226	FOLSOME, Thomas	9	NENE	1835-10-20		A1
4098	GABLE, Andrew J	12	SW	1900-08-09		A2
4160	GABLE, James H	22	SWSW	1857-12-01		A1
4161	" "	27	NWNW	1857-12-01		A1
4162	" "	28	NENE	1857-12-01		A1
4169	GAY, Jasper	28	NWSW	1859-06-01		A1
4170	" "	29	N½SE	1859-06-01		A1
4171	" "	29	S½NE	1859-06-01		A1
4194	GILCHRIST, Malcolm	17	W½SW	1827-10-01		A1 G72
4195	" "	8	E½NW	1827-10-01		A1 G72
4196	" "	8	W½NE	1827-10-01		A1 G72
4153	HAGAN, Henry C	28	NENW	1903-06-01		A2
4154	" "	28	SENE	1903-06-01		A2
4155	" "	28	W½NE	1903-06-01		A2
4123	HANSFORD, Charles M	26	SW	1892-08-01		A2
4096	HERRING, Alfred C	34	SW	1895-05-03		A2
4206	HOWARD, Mary	34	SENW	1898-04-06		A2 G81
4207	" "	34	W½NW	1898-04-06		A2 G81
4206	HOWARD, William H	34	SENW	1898-04-06		A2 G81
4207	" "	34	W½NW	1898-04-06		A2 G81
4191	HUGHES, Malachi T	36	NENW	1897-09-20		A2
4192	" "	36	SENE	1897-09-20		A2
4193	" "	36	W½NE	1897-09-20		A2
4241	JACKSON, William	14	SW	1898-04-27		A2
4182	KEEL, John G	35	NWNE	1857-12-01		A1
4249	KINGSLEY, Zephaniah A	12	SE	1902-05-01		A2
4204	LEE, Martin V	6	N½NW	1904-12-20		A2
4236	LOGAN, William H	10	NWSE	1891-05-04		A2
4237	" "	10	S½SE	1891-05-04		A2
4238	" "	10	SESW	1891-05-04		A2
4235	" "	10	NESE	1901-12-12		A1
4239	MAY, William H	32	NWSE	1903-03-17		A2
4240	" "	32	S½SE	1903-03-17		A2
4118	MAYO, Bray	19	W½SW	1850-08-10		A1
4245	MCCLELAN, William R	36	SE	1895-02-14		A2
4215	MCLELLAN, Samantha J	32	NESE	1889-10-21		A1
4146	MEARS, George M	24	NESW	1902-09-02		A1
4158	MEARS, James E	24	E½NW	1897-07-03		A2
4159	" "	24	N½NE	1897-07-03		A2
4228	MEARS, Thomas L	24	E½SE	1894-04-10		A2
4229	" "	24	NWSE	1894-04-10		A2
4230	" "	24	SENE	1894-04-10		A2
4244	MEARS, William L	36	NENE	1904-05-05		A2
4231	MERRETT, Wiley	22	E½SE	1901-08-12		A2
4156	MULKEY, Homer V	2	E½	1857-12-01		A1
4190	MUSGROVE, Larkin C	32	W½NE	1859-06-01		A1
4247	MUSGROVE, Willis S	28	S½NW	1857-12-01		A1
4205	NELSON, Mary E	12	NE	1896-04-27		A2 G108
4133	PADGETT, Elijah	30	NENW	1841-01-09		A1
4134	" "	30	NWNW	1852-09-01		A1
4121	PEACOCK, Charles K	28	E½SW	1901-06-28		A2 G113
4122	" "	28	SWSW	1901-06-28		A2 G113
4164	PEACOCK, James P	32	E½NE	1903-03-17		A2
4200	PEACOCK, Martha F	28	SE	1891-05-04		A2
4121	PEACOCK, Martha J	28	E½SW	1901-06-28		A2 G113
4122	" "	28	SWSW	1901-06-28		A2 G113
4183	PIGG, John	19	E½SW	1827-06-15		A1
4136	PITTMAN, Frederick R	5	NWSE	1855-05-01		A1
4135	" "	5	N½NW	1859-06-01		A1
4178	POOSER, John C	12	NW	1896-04-27		A2
4205	ROBERTS, Mary E	12	NE	1896-04-27		A2 G108
4163	SIMS, James J	4	NE	1898-07-18		A2
4187	SIMS, Joseph	22	E½SW	1902-07-03		A2
4188	" "	22	W½SE	1902-07-03		A2

ID	Individual in Patent	Sec.	Sec. Part	Date Issued	Other Counties	For More Info . . .
4197	SIMS, Mariah	6	SENW	1889-06-29		A2
4198	" "	6	SWNE	1889-06-29		A2
4208	SIMS, Miles	19	E½NE	1830-12-28		A1
4246	SIMS, William	6	SWNW	1856-06-16		A1
4157	SOUTER, Isham	14	NE	1899-05-12		A2
4173	STALEY, Jesse	6	N½NE	1895-11-05		A2
4174	" "	6	NESE	1895-11-05		A2
4175	" "	6	SENE	1895-11-05		A2
4209	STEPHENS, Richard W	4	SWSW	1856-06-16		A1
4210	" "	5	E½SE	1856-06-16		A1
4211	" "	9	NENW	1856-06-16		A1
4218	SULIVAN, Solomon	20	E½NE	1857-07-01		A1
4219	" "	20	NESW	1857-07-01		A1
4220	" "	20	SE	1857-07-01		A1
4221	" "	20	SWNE	1857-07-01		A1
4137	SULLIVAN, General J	17	E½NW	1856-06-16		A1
4138	" "	17	SESE	1856-06-16		A1
4139	" "	17	W½NE	1856-06-16		A1
4140	" "	17	W½SE	1856-06-16		A1
4141	" "	20	NWNE	1856-06-16		A1
4147	SULLIVAN, George W	20	SESW	1856-06-16		A1
4148	" "	28	NWNW	1856-06-16		A1
4149	" "	29	N½NE	1856-06-16		A1
4189	SWANSON, Joseph	1	W½	1857-12-01		A1
4179	THOMAS, John F O	22	NENW	1911-09-18		A2
4180	" "	22	SENW	1911-09-18		A2
4181	" "	22	W½NW	1911-09-18		A2
4150	TILLINGHAST, George W	10	E½NW	1844-07-10		A1
4186	VAN PELT, JOHN	5	SESW	1837-04-15		A1
4097	WEBB, Alfred	14	NW	1896-01-03		A2
4248	WILLIAMS, Wyatt G	22	NWSW	1921-08-10		A2
4124	WILLIAMSON, Charles	17	W½NW	1827-10-01		A1
4194	" "	17	W½SW	1827-10-01		A1 G72
4125	" "	19	E½NW	1827-10-01		A1
4126	" "	19	W½NE	1827-10-01		A1
4127	" "	19	W½NW	1827-10-01		A1
4128	" "	7	E½SW	1827-10-01		A1
4129	" "	7	W½SW	1827-10-01		A1
4195	" "	8	E½NW	1827-10-01		A1 G72
4196	" "	8	W½NE	1827-10-01		A1 G72
4130	" "	8	W½NW	1827-10-01		A1
4222	WIMBERLY, Terrence	34	NE	1894-01-27		A2
4116	YON, Braxton	26	NESE	1902-12-30		A2
4117	" "	26	SENE	1902-12-30		A2

Patent Map

T3-N R9-W
Tallahassee Meridian

Map Group 33

Township Statistics

Parcels Mapped	:	155
Number of Patents	:	103
Number of Individuals	:	86
Patentees Identified	:	83
Number of Surnames	:	62
Multi-Patentee Parcels	:	8
Oldest Patent Date	:	6/15/1827
Most Recent Patent	:	8/10/1921
Block/Lot Parcels	:	0
Parcels Re - Issued	:	0
Parcels that Overlap	:	0
Cities and Towns	:	4
Cemeteries	:	3

Section 6
LEE Martin V 1904
STALEY Jesse 1895
SIMS William 1856
SIMS Mariah 1889
SIMS Mariah 1889
STALEY Jesse 1895
FOLSOM James Y 1882
FOLSOM James Y 1882
STALEY Jesse 1895
DAVIS Jefferson 1891

Section 5
PITTMAN Frederick R 1859
PITTMAN Frederick R 1855
PELT John Van 1837
STEPHENS Richard W 1856

Section 4
BARNETT William 1904
SIMS James J 1898
COULLIETTE James S 1896
COULLIETTE James S 1896

Section 7
DICKSON Robert S 1859
WILLIAMSON Charles 1827
DICKSON Robert S 1857
WILLIAMSON Charles 1827
WILLIAMSON Charles 1827
DICKSON Robert S 1857

Section 8
WILLIAMSON Charles 1827
GILCHRIST [72] Malcolm 1827
GILCHRIST [72] Malcolm 1827
BARKLEY Bolyn B 1859
BARKLEY Bolyn B 1855
CHAPMAN John R 1843
CHAPMAN John R 1843
BARKLEY Bolyn B 1855
BARKLEY Bolyn B 1859

Section 9
BARKLEY Bolyn B 1859
STEPHENS Richard W 1856
FOLSOM Thomas 1835
FOLSOME Thomas 1835
FOLSOM Sidney S 1835
FOLSOM Chesley 1837
BARKLEY Bolyn B 1855
BULLOCK George 1855
BARKLEY Bolyn B 1859
BARKLEY Bolyn B 1859
BARKLEY Bolyn B 1855

Section 18
(blank)

Section 17
WILLIAMSON Charles 1827
SULLIVAN General J 1856
SULLIVAN General J 1856
BARKLEY Bolyn B 1859
GILCHRIST [72] Malcolm 1827
SULLIVAN General J 1856
SULLIVAN General J 1856

Section 16
(blank)

Section 19
WILLIAMSON Charles 1827
WILLIAMSON Charles 1827
WILLIAMSON Charles 1827
SIMS Miles 1830
MAYO Bray 1850
PIGG John 1827
BANKS William 1827
CHAIRES Benjamin 1839

Section 20
SULLIVAN General J 1856
SULIVAN Solomon 1857
SULIVAN Solomon 1857
SULIVAN Solomon 1857
SULIVAN Solomon 1857
SULLIVAN George W 1856

Section 21
(blank)

Section 30
PADGETT Elijah 1852
PADGETT Elijah 1841
CHAIRES Benjamin 1839
CHAIRES Benjamin 1839
COOK Charles F 1906
COOK Charles F 1906

Section 29
SULLIVAN George W 1856
GAY Jasper 1859
GAY Jasper 1859

Section 28
SULLIVAN George W 1856
HAGAN Henry C 1903
HAGAN Henry C 1903
GABLE James H 1857
MUSGROVE Willis S 1857
HAGAN Henry C 1903
GAY Jasper 1859
PEACOCK Charles K 1901 [113]
PEACOCK Martha F 1891
PEACOCK Charles K 1901 [113]

Section 31
(blank)

Section 32
MUSGROVE Larkin C 1859
PEACOCK James P 1903
MAY William H 1903
MCLELLAN Samantha J 1889
MAY William H 1903

Section 33
(blank)

3	**2** COOK Hardy 1896 / COOK Thomas 1857 / MULKEY Homer V 1857	**1** SWANSON Joseph 1857

10
BARKLEY Bolyn B 1855 — TILLINGHAST George W 1844 — BULLOCK George K 1857
BULLOCK George 1855 — LOGAN William H 1891 — LOGAN William H 1901
LOGAN William H 1891 — LOGAN William H 1891

11
COOK Thomas 1857

12
POOSER John C 1896 — NELSON [108] Mary E 1896
GABLE Andrew J 1900 — KINGSLEY Zephaniah A 1902

15

14
WEBB Alfred 1896 — SOUTER Isham 1899
JACKSON William 1898 — BEAUCHAMP Martha E 1899

13

22
THOMAS John F O 1911 — COOK Adolphus 1903
THOMAS John F O 1911 — THOMAS John F O 1911
WILLIAMS Wyatt G 1921 / GABLE James H 1857 — SIMS Joseph 1902 — SIMS Joseph 1902 — MERRETT Wiley 1901

23

24
MEARS James E 1897 — MEARS James E 1897
DAWSON George D 1903 — BEAUCHAMP Thomas J 1907 — MEARS Thomas L 1894
MEARS George M 1902 — MEARS Thomas L 1894
BLOUNT Benjamin T 1900 — BLOUNT Benjamin T 1900 — BLOUNT Benjamin T 1900 — MEARS Thomas L 1894

27
GABLE James H 1857

26
DURDEN Green 1903 — DURHAM John B 1901 — DURHAM John B 1901
DURHAM Martha K 1893 — YON Braxton 1902
DURHAM Martha K 1893 — YON Braxton 1902
HANSFORD Charles M 1892 — DURHAM Martha K 1893

25

34
HOWARD [81] Mary 1898 — WIMBERLY Terrence 1894
HOWARD [81] Mary 1898
HERRING Alfred C 1895 — BEAUCHAMP William H 1896

35
KEEL John G 1857

36
BAGGETT William K 1898 — HUGHES Malachi T 1897 — MEARS William L 1904
HUGHES Malachi T 1897
BAGGETT William K 1898 — HUGHES Malachi T 1897
MCCLELAN William R 1895
BRYAN Seaborne O 1891

Copyright 2008 Boyd IT, Inc. All Rights Reserved

Helpful Hints

1. This Map's INDEX can be found on the preceding pages.

2. Refer to Map "C" to see where this Township lies within Jackson County, Florida.

3. Numbers within square brackets [ ] denote a multi-patentee land parcel (multi-owner). Refer to Appendix "C" for a full list of members in this group.

4. Areas that look to be crowded with Patentees usually indicate multiple sales of the same parcel (Re-issues) or Overlapping parcels. See this Township's Index for an explanation of these and other circumstances that might explain "odd" groupings of Patentees on this map.

Legend

————	Patent Boundary
▬▬▬▬	Section Boundary
▒▒▒▒	No Patents Found (or Outside County)
1., 2., 3., . . .	Lot Numbers (when beside a name)
[ ]	Group Number (see Appendix "C")

Scale: Section = 1 mile X 1 mile (generally, with some exceptions)

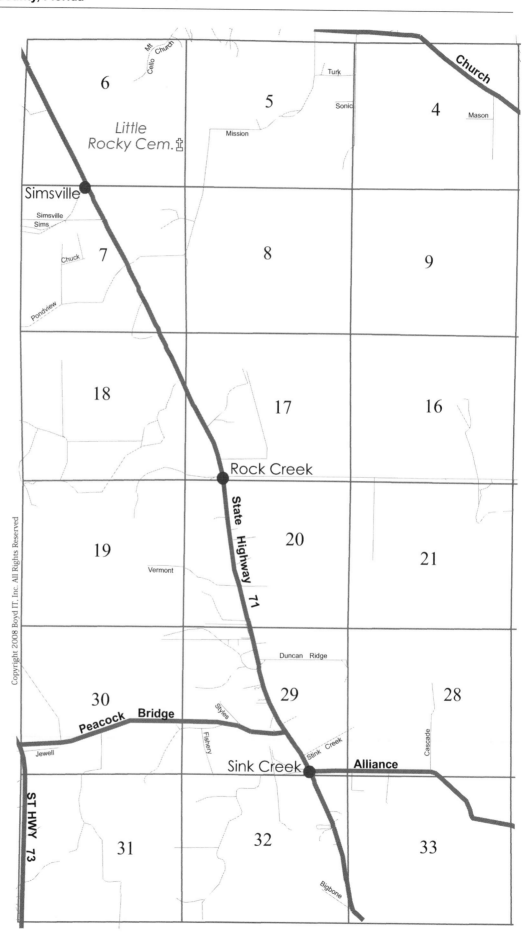

Road Map

T3-N R9-W
Tallahassee Meridian

Map Group 33

Cities & Towns
Alliance
Rock Creek
Simsville
Sink Creek

Cemeteries
Evergreen Cemetery
Little Rocky Cemetery
Logan Cemetery

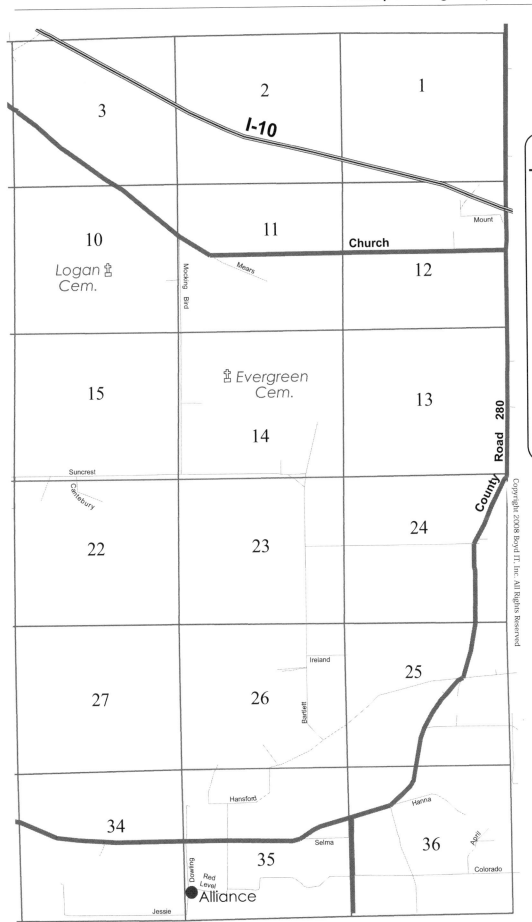

3

2

1

I-10

Mount

10

11

Church

Logan ⚱
Cem.

Mears

12

Mocking Bird

⚱ *Evergreen*
Cem.

15

13

14

County Road 280

Suncrest

Cantebury

22

23

24

Ireland

25

27

26

Bartlett

Hansford

Hanna

34

April

Selma

36

Dowling

35

Colorado

Red
Level

Jessie

● **Alliance**

Helpful Hints

1. This road map has a number of uses, but primarily it is to help you: a) find the present location of land owned by your ancestors (at least the general area), b) find cemeteries and city-centers, and c) estimate the route/roads used by Census-takers & tax-assessors.

2. If you plan to travel to Jackson County to locate cemeteries or land parcels, please pick up a modern travel map for the area before you do. Mapping old land parcels on modern maps is not as exact a science as you might think. Just the slightest variations in public land survey coordinates, estimates of parcel boundaries, or road-map deviations can greatly alter a map's representation of how a road either does or doesn't cross a particular parcel of land.

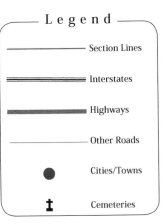

L e g e n d

———————— Section Lines

═══════ Interstates

▬▬▬▬▬ Highways

———————— Other Roads

● Cities/Towns

⚱ Cemeteries

Scale: Section = 1 mile X 1 mile
(generally, with some exceptions)

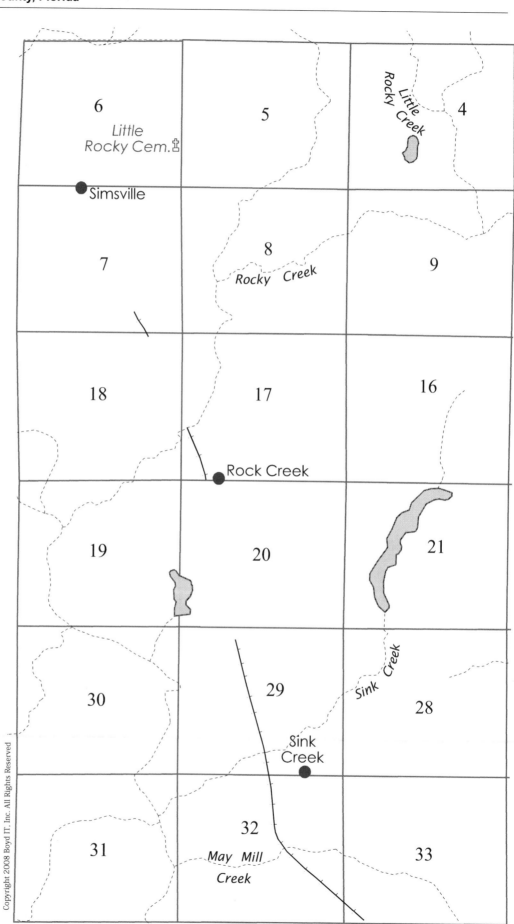

Historical Map

T3-N R9-W
Tallahassee Meridian

Map Group 33

Cities & Towns
Alliance
Rock Creek
Simsville
Sink Creek

Cemeteries
Evergreen Cemetery
Little Rocky Cemetery
Logan Cemetery

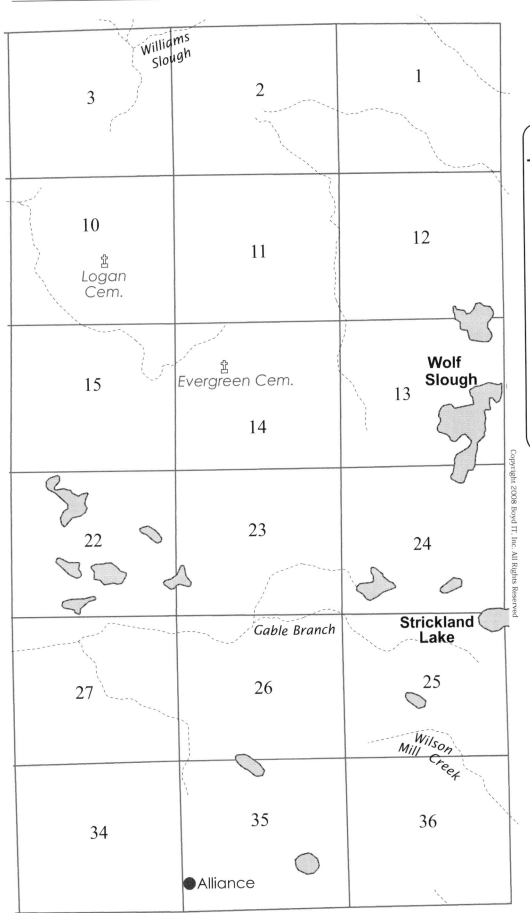

3

2

1

Williams Slough

10

11

12

⚰
Logan Cem.

15

⚰
Evergreen Cem.

14

13

Wolf Slough

22

23

24

27

26

Gable Branch

Strickland Lake

25

34

35

36

Wilson Mill Creek

● Alliance

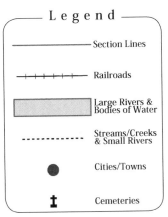

L e g e n d

————	Section Lines
+++++	Railroads
▭	Large Rivers & Bodies of Water
- - - - -	Streams/Creeks & Small Rivers
●	Cities/Towns
⚰	Cemeteries

Scale: Section = 1 mile X 1 mile
(there are some exceptions)

Map Group 34: Index to Land Patents

Township 3-North Range 8-West (Tallahassee)

After you locate an individual in this Index, take note of the Section and Section Part then proceed to the Land Patent map on the pages immediately following. You should have no difficulty locating the corresponding parcel of land.

The "For More Info" Column will lead you to more information about the underlying Patents. See the *Legend* at right, and the "How to Use this Book" chapter, for more information.

ID	Individual in Patent	Sec.	Sec. Part	Date Issued	Other Counties	For More Info . . .
4263	ALFORD, Bynum	26	N½SW	1891-07-14		A2
4264	" "	26	S½NW	1891-07-14		A2
4265	BAMBURG, Catharine	34	SWSW	1911-01-16		A2
4282	BIRGESS, Cupit	34	E½NE	1899-05-12		A2
4283	" "	34	E½SE	1899-05-12		A2
4392	BOONE, William H	14	W½NW	1898-06-01		A2
4260	BRADLEY, Berry	8	E½SW	1894-01-27		A2
4261	" "	8	NWSW	1894-01-27		A2
4262	" "	8	SENW	1894-01-27		A2
4327	BRADLEY, Jesse J	6	W½NW	1898-02-24		A2
4373	CARAWAY, Taylor	22	NE	1856-06-16		A1
4314	CARPENTER, Henry L	28	S½SW	1903-03-17		A2
4250	CARROLL, Alfred L	10	SWNW	1923-05-15		A2
4330	CHESTER, John A	8	N½NW	1903-05-25		A2
4331	" "	8	SWNW	1903-05-25		A2
4252	COMERFORD, Ann E	34	N½NW	1897-03-03		A2 G56
4253	" "	34	NWSW	1897-03-03		A2 G56
4254	" "	34	SWNW	1897-03-03		A2 G56
4266	COOK, Catharine J	18	E½SW	1903-02-28		A2 G57 R4377
4267	" "	18	W½SE	1903-02-28		A2 G57 R4378
4309	COOK, Henry G	18	E½SE	1903-05-25		A2
4310	" "	20	W½NW	1911-04-05		A2
4335	COOK, John	30	SESE	1901-08-29		A2
4377	COOK, Thomas T	18	E½SW	1896-06-26		A2 C R4266
4378	" "	18	W½SE	1896-06-26		A2 C R4267
4266	" "	18	E½SW	1903-02-28		A2 G57 R4377
4267	" "	18	W½SE	1903-02-28		A2 G57 R4378
4296	COXWELL, Enoch G	10	N½NE	1897-05-25		A2
4287	CROUCH, Ebenezer C	28	N½NW	1901-08-24		A2
4321	CUNNINGAME, James	24	SESE	1906-06-04		A2
4278	DAVIDSON, Columbus H	24	E½NE	1890-06-05		A2
4279	" "	24	N½SE	1890-06-05		A2
4291	DAVIS, Elsie	34	E½SW	1900-08-09		A2
4292	" "	34	SENW	1900-08-09		A2
4293	" "	34	SWNE	1900-08-09		A2
4315	DICKSON, Henry M	22	SENW	1942-01-23		A1
4251	DUDLEY, Allen R	4	SW	1893-04-08		A2
4318	DUDLEY, Isaac	36	E½NW	1899-08-30		A2
4387	DUDLEY, William D	4	N½NE	1895-02-14		A2
4388	" "	4	N½NW	1895-02-14		A2
4328	DURDEN, Jesse J	26	SE	1894-04-10		A2
4336	DURDEN, John	4	N½SE	1893-05-05		A2
4337	" "	4	S½NE	1893-05-05		A2
4338	" "	4	S½SE	1895-06-17		A2
4272	DYKES, Charles J	2	NENW	1897-01-21		A2
4273	" "	2	NWSE	1897-01-21		A2

ID	Individual in Patent	Sec.	Sec. Part	Date Issued	Other Counties	For More Info . . .
4274	DYKES, Charles J (Cont'd)	2	W½NE	1897-01-21		A2
4320	DYKES, Jacob H	13	SWNE	1856-06-16		A1
4393	DYKES, William H	13	E½NE	1859-06-01		A1
4271	EDENFIELD, Charles G	20	SESE	1910-09-01		A2
4270	" "	10	SWSE	1926-03-23		A2
4280	EDENFIELD, Cullen W	14	E½NW	1892-11-15		A2
4281	" "	14	S½NE	1892-11-15		A2
4339	EDENFIELD, John F	20	E½NE	1895-06-17		A2
4340	" "	20	N½SE	1895-06-17		A2
4324	FLOYD, James J	8	SE	1903-06-26		A2
4258	FOSCUE, Benjamin	13	NW	1828-07-22		A1
4259	" "	13	NWNE	1838-07-28		A1
4288	FRANCIS, Ebenezer J	24	NESW	1906-06-04		A2 G69
4288	FRANCIS, Sarah	24	NESW	1906-06-04		A2 G69
4346	FREEMAN, John M	10	SESW	1856-06-16		A1
4347	" "	15	E½NW	1856-06-16		A1
4348	" "	15	NWNE	1856-06-16		A1
4313	GABLE, Henry J	32	SE	1895-06-17		A2
4322	GABLE, James H	30	S½SW	1897-10-20		A2
4323	" "	30	SWSE	1897-10-20		A2
4295	GORDY, Emmett J	24	NW	1901-04-09		A2
4367	HAIR, Reuben V	22	NWSW	1899-06-13		A2
4368	" "	22	W½NW	1899-06-13		A2
4394	HALL, William	14	NENE	1838-07-28		A1
4395	" "	14	NWNE	1838-07-28		A1
4349	HANSFORD, John M	27	SWNE	1856-06-16		A1
4350	" "	34	NWNE	1857-12-01		A1
4379	HANSFORD, Tyns L	35	S½NW	1860-07-02		A1
4380	" "	35	SESW	1860-07-02		A1
4381	" "	35	W½SW	1860-07-02		A1
4360	HEATH, Madison	6	NE	1895-10-09		A2
4304	HERNDON, George M	20	SW	1899-11-04		A2
4396	HICKMAN, William	25	W½NW	1828-09-10		A1
4370	HOLMES, Samuel H	36	NWSW	1898-07-18		A2
4371	" "	36	W½NW	1898-07-18		A2
4311	IRWIN, Henry	35	NWSE	1857-12-01		A1
4312	" "	35	SWNE	1857-12-01		A1
4372	JACKSON, Shadrack T	36	NE	1901-11-06		A2
4300	JOHNSON, Gazaway	32	N½NW	1896-08-06		A2
4301	" "	32	NESW	1896-08-06		A2
4302	" "	32	SENW	1896-08-06		A2
4308	JOHNSON, Henrietta	8	NE	1893-04-03		A2
4341	JOHNSON, John G	36	E½SW	1896-07-27		A2
4342	" "	36	W½SE	1896-07-27		A2
4374	JOHNSON, Thomas	32	NE	1896-09-25		A2
4382	JOHNSON, Uriah S	32	SESW	1896-10-16		A2
4383	" "	32	SWNW	1896-10-16		A2
4384	" "	32	W½SW	1896-10-16		A2
4397	JOHNSON, William J	28	N½SW	1895-10-09		A2
4398	" "	28	S½NW	1895-10-09		A2
4361	KENT, Matilda F	14	N½SE	1895-11-05		A2
4362	" "	14	NESW	1895-11-05		A2
4363	" "	14	SWSE	1895-11-05		A2
4399	KENT, William	14	SESE	1902-07-03		A2
4343	KETTLEBAND, John	30	N½NE	1901-11-06		A2
4344	" "	30	NENW	1901-11-06		A2
4345	" "	30	SWNE	1901-11-06		A2
4375	LANE, Thomas N	20	E½NW	1901-04-09		A2
4376	" "	20	W½NE	1901-04-09		A2
4400	LYNN, William L	18	S½NW	1902-05-01		A2
4401	" "	18	W½SW	1902-05-01		A2
4402	LYNN, William N	18	N½NW	1899-05-22		A2
4403	" "	18	W½NE	1899-05-22		A2
4289	MCCARTY, Elijah R	10	N½NW	1892-09-27		A2
4290	" "	10	SENW	1892-09-27		A2
4316	MCCOY, Henry	34	W½SE	1906-06-04		A2
4334	MCMILLAN, John C	2	SESW	1892-05-26		A2
4284	MEARS, David L	23	SWSE	1856-06-16		A1
4285	" "	26	N½NE	1856-06-16		A1
4286	" "	26	SWNE	1856-06-16		A1
4332	MEARS, John B	30	N½SE	1898-07-18		A2
4333	" "	30	SENE	1898-07-18		A2
4303	MERCER, George F	13	SESE	1857-12-01		A1

ID	Individual in Patent	Sec.	Sec. Part	Date Issued	Other Counties	For More Info . . .
4252	MONEY, Ann E	34	N½NW	1897-03-03		A2 G56
4253	" "	34	NWSW	1897-03-03		A2 G56
4254	" "	34	SWNW	1897-03-03		A2 G56
4385	NALL, Weldon B	22	N½SE	1895-02-14		A2
4386	" "	22	SESE	1897-10-28		A2
4305	PATTERSON, Green B	15	NENE	1838-07-28		A1
4306	" "	15	SWNE	1838-07-28		A1
4356	PATTERSON, Joseph J	22	SWSE	1857-12-01		A1
4357	PATTERSON, Littleton	22	SWSW	1856-06-16		A1
4358	" "	25	E½SW	1856-06-16		A1
4359	" "	27	NWNW	1857-12-01		A1
4352	PEACOCK, John	20	SWSE	1857-12-01		A1
4317	PEEBLES, Henry	23	E½SE	1827-10-01		A1
4325	PETERS, James R	18	NENE	1904-12-20		A2
4326	" "	8	SWSW	1906-11-19		A1
4307	ROBBIRDS, Green	6	SW	1896-12-11		A2
4269	SCOTT, Charles E	30	SENW	1904-12-20		A2
4364	SCOTT, Oscar	30	N½SW	1895-05-03		A2
4365	" "	30	W½NW	1895-05-03		A2
4351	SELLERS, John M	26	S½SW	1893-05-26		A2
4366	SIMPSON, Philip A	2	W½SW	1896-06-23		A2
4389	SIMPSON, William D	14	NWSW	1896-06-23		A2
4390	" "	14	S½SW	1896-06-23		A2
4255	SIMS, Benjamin F	10	NESW	1893-04-03		A2
4256	" "	10	NWSE	1893-04-03		A2
4257	" "	10	S½NE	1893-04-03		A2
4297	SIMS, Frederick M	2	NESW	1891-06-17		A2
4298	" "	2	SENW	1891-06-17		A2
4299	" "	2	W½NW	1891-06-17		A2
4329	STEPHENS, Jesse	21	SWSW	1857-12-01		A1
4353	STEWART, John	28	SE	1900-09-07		A2
4319	STONE, Isaac H	26	N½NW	1891-07-14		A2
4268	TRAYLOR, Champion T	28	NE	1893-10-13		A2
4275	TRAYLOR, Charles M	24	NWSW	1899-05-12		A2
4276	" "	24	S½SW	1899-05-12		A2
4277	" "	24	SWSE	1899-05-12		A2
4369	WESTER, Rufus T	36	E½SE	1901-06-25		A2
4294	WHIDDON, Ely	6	SE	1896-07-27		A2
4355	WILLIAMS, John	6	E½NW	1897-03-22		A2
4354	WILLIAMS, John T	4	S½NW	1906-06-04		A2
4391	WILLIAMS, William D	24	W½NE	1890-06-05		A2

Patent Map

T3-N R8-W
Tallahassee Meridian

Map Group 34

Township Statistics

Parcels Mapped	:	154
Number of Patents	:	101
Number of Individuals	:	94
Patentees Identified	:	92
Number of Surnames	:	64
Multi-Patentee Parcels	:	6
Oldest Patent Date	:	10/1/1827
Most Recent Patent	:	1/23/1942
Block/Lot Parcels	:	0
Parcels Re - Issued	:	2
Parcels that Overlap	:	0
Cities and Towns	:	2
Cemeteries	:	1

6
BRADLEY Jesse J 1898
WILLIAMS John 1897
HEATH Madison 1895
ROBBIRDS Green 1896
WHIDDON Ely 1896

5

4
DUDLEY William D 1895
DUDLEY William D 1895
WILLIAMS John T 1906
DURDEN John 1893
DUDLEY Allen R 1893
DURDEN John 1893
DURDEN John 1895

7

8
CHESTER John A 1903
CHESTER John A 1903
BRADLEY Berry 1894
JOHNSON Henrietta 1893
BRADLEY Berry 1894
BRADLEY Berry 1894
FLOYD James J 1903
PETERS James R 1906

9

18
LYNN William N 1899
LYNN William N 1899
PETERS James R 1904
LYNN William L 1902
COOK [57] Catharine J 1903
COOK Thomas T 1896
LYNN William L 1902
COOK Thomas T 1896
COOK [57] Catharine J 1903
COOK Henry G 1903

17

16

19

20
COOK Henry G 1911
LANE Thomas N 1901
LANE Thomas N 1901
EDENFIELD John F 1895
HERNDON George M 1899
EDENFIELD John F 1895
PEACOCK John 1857
EDENFIELD Charles G 1910
STEPHENS Jesse 1857

21

30
SCOTT Oscar 1895
KETTLEBAND John 1901
KETTLEBAND John 1901
SCOTT Charles E 1904
KETTLEBAND John 1901
MEARS John B 1898
SCOTT Oscar 1895
MEARS John B 1898
GABLE James H 1897
GABLE James H 1897
COOK John 1901

29

28
CROUCH Ebenezer C 1901
TRAYLOR Champion T 1893
JOHNSON William J 1895
JOHNSON William J 1895
STEWART John 1900
CARPENTER Henry L 1903

31

32
JOHNSON Gazaway 1896
JOHNSON Thomas 1896
JOHNSON Uriah S 1896
JOHNSON Gazaway 1896
JOHNSON Gazaway 1896
JOHNSON Uriah S 1896
GABLE Henry J 1895
JOHNSON Uriah S 1896

33

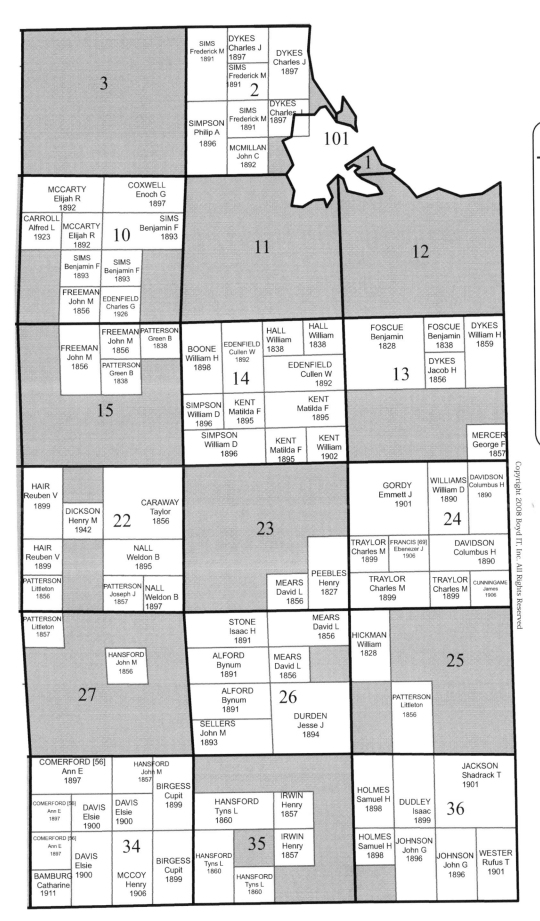

Helpful Hints

1. This Map's INDEX can be found on the preceding pages.

2. Refer to Map "C" to see where this Township lies within Jackson County, Florida.

3. Numbers within square brackets [ ] denote a multi-patentee land parcel (multi-owner). Refer to Appendix "C" for a full list of members in this group.

4. Areas that look to be crowded with Patentees usually indicate multiple sales of the same parcel (Re-issues) or Overlapping parcels. See this Township's Index for an explanation of these and other circumstances that might explain "odd" groupings of Patentees on this map.

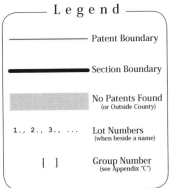

Legend

————	Patent Boundary
▬▬▬	Section Boundary
▒▒▒▒	No Patents Found (or Outside County)
1., 2., 3., . . .	Lot Numbers (when beside a name)
[ ]	Group Number (see Appendix "C")

Scale: Section = 1 mile X 1 mile (generally, with some exceptions)

321

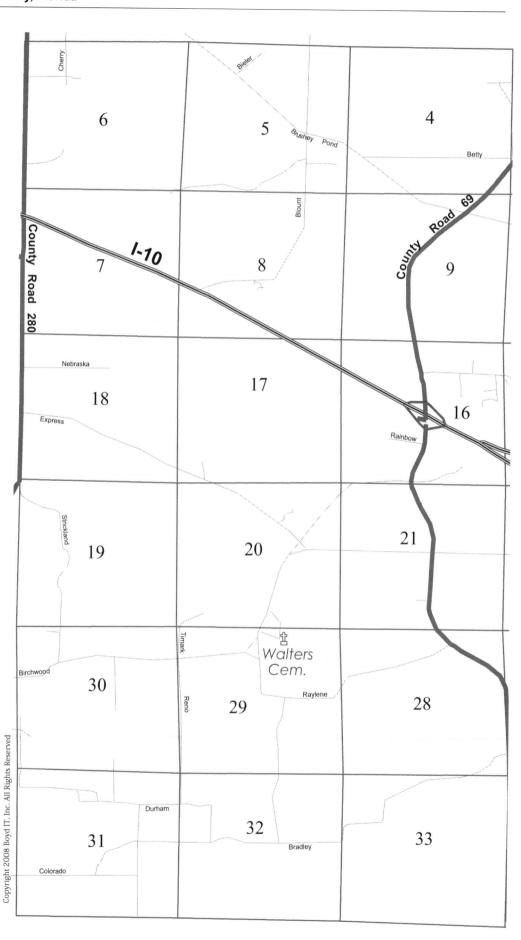

Road Map

T3-N R8-W
Tallahassee Meridian

Map Group 34

Cities & Towns
Hyhappo (historical)
Shady Grove

Cemeteries
Walters Cemetery

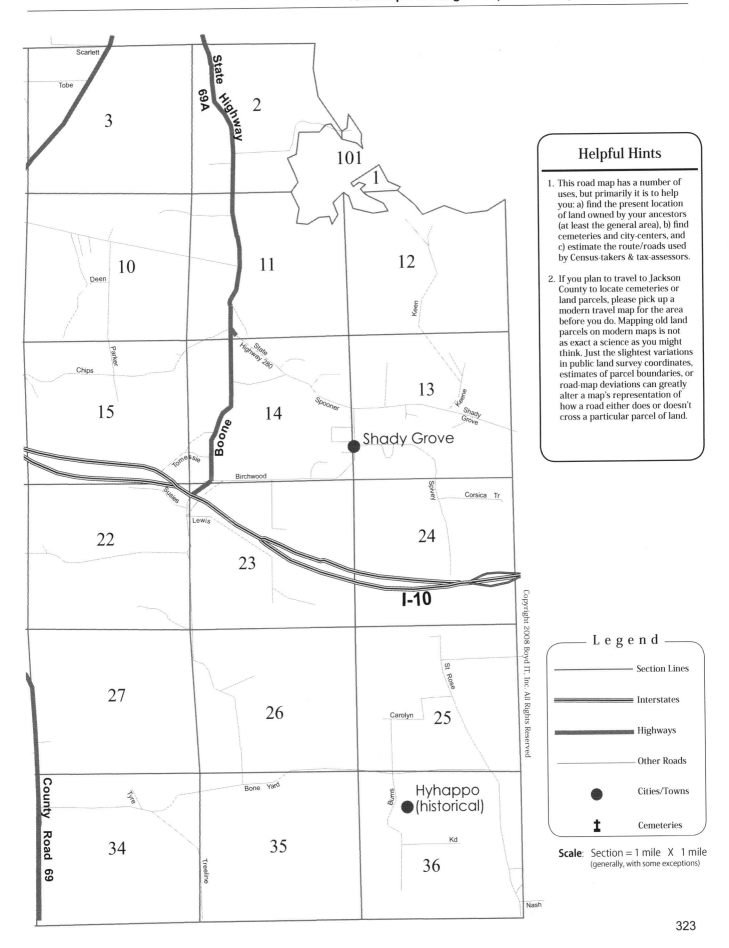

Scarlett

Tobe

3

2

101

1

10

Deen

11

12

Keen

Parker

Chips

State Highway 280

Spooner

13

Keene

15

14

Shady Grove

Boone

Shady Grove

Tomessie

Birchwood

Susies

Lewis

Corsica   Tr

Spivey

22

23

24

I-10

27

26

St. Rose

Carolyn

25

Bone   Yard

Hyhappo
(historical)

Burns

34

Tyre

35

Kd

Treeline

36

County Road 69

Nash

Helpful Hints

1. This road map has a number of uses, but primarily it is to help you: a) find the present location of land owned by your ancestors (at least the general area), b) find cemeteries and city-centers, and c) estimate the route/roads used by Census-takers & tax-assessors.

2. If you plan to travel to Jackson County to locate cemeteries or land parcels, please pick up a modern travel map for the area before you do. Mapping old land parcels on modern maps is not as exact a science as you might think. Just the slightest variations in public land survey coordinates, estimates of parcel boundaries, or road-map deviations can greatly alter a map's representation of how a road either does or doesn't cross a particular parcel of land.

Legend

~~	Section Lines
▬▬▬	Interstates
▬▬▬	Highways
———	Other Roads
●	Cities/Towns
✝	Cemeteries

Scale: Section = 1 mile X 1 mile
(generally, with some exceptions)

Historical Map

T3-N R8-W
Tallahassee Meridian

Map Group 34

6

5

**Whidden
Pond**

4

**Honey
Hill Bay**

7

8

9

**Edenfield
Bay**

18

17

16

**Long
Pond**

19

20

21

Walters
Cem.

**Strickland
Lake**

30

29

28

31

32

33

*Carpenter
Sink Creek*

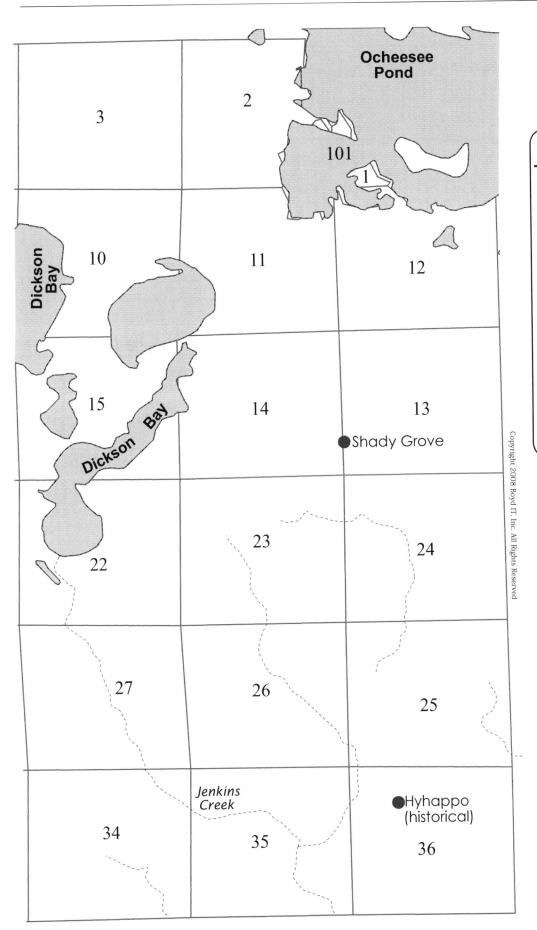

Ocheesee
Pond

3

2

101

1

Dickson Bay

10

11

12

15

14

13

Dickson Bay

●Shady Grove

22

23

24

27

26

25

Jenkins
Creek

●Hyhappo
(historical)

34

35

36

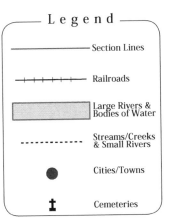

Helpful Hints

1. This Map takes a different look at
the same Congressional Township
displayed in the preceding two
maps. It presents features that
can help you better envision the
historical development of the area:
a) Water-bodies (lakes & ponds),
b) Water-courses (rivers, streams,
etc.), c) Railroads, d) City/town
center-points (where they were
oftentimes located when first
settled), and e) Cemeteries.

2. Using this "Historical" map in
tandem with this Township's
Patent Map and Road Map, may
lead you to some interesting
discoveries. You will often find
roads, towns, cemeteries, and
waterways are named after nearby
landowners: sometimes those
names will be the ones you are
researching. See how many of
these research gems you can find
here in Jackson County.

L e g e n d

——————— Section Lines

+++++++ Railroads

▭ Large Rivers &
Bodies of Water

------------ Streams/Creeks
& Small Rivers

● Cities/Towns

⚱ Cemeteries

Scale: Section = 1 mile X 1 mile
(there are some exceptions)

Map Group 35: Index to Land Patents

Township 3-North Range 7-West (Tallahassee)

After you locate an individual in this Index, take note of the Section and Section Part then proceed to the Land Patent map on the pages immediately following. You should have no difficulty locating the corresponding parcel of land.

The "For More Info" Column will lead you to more information about the underlying Patents. See the *Legend* at right, and the "How to Use this Book" chapter, for more information.

ID	Individual in Patent	Sec.	Sec. Part	Date Issued	Other Counties	For More Info . . .
4506	ADKINS, Philip	32	NE	1895-11-05		A2
4479	ARMISTEAD, L	35	1	1828-03-01	Gadsden	A1 G9
4476	" "	34	4	1830-11-01	Gadsden	A1
4477	" "	35	2	1830-11-01	Gadsden	A1 G8
4478	" "	35	3	1830-11-01	Gadsden	A1 G8
4480	ARMISTEAD, Latinus	26	5	1828-03-15	Gadsden	A1 G12 F
4482	" "	35	4	1830-12-28	Gadsden	A1 G11 C R4483
4483	" "	35	4	1833-12-24	Gadsden	A1 G11 R4482
4481	" "	35	5	1834-08-20	Gadsden	A1 G10
4484	ARMISTEAD, Latinus C	35	6	1857-12-01	Gadsden	A1
4485	" "	35	7	1857-12-01	Gadsden	A1
4479	ARMISTEAD, M A	35	1	1828-03-01	Gadsden	A1 G9
4477	" "	35	2	1830-11-01	Gadsden	A1 G8
4478	" "	35	3	1830-11-01	Gadsden	A1 G8
4481	ARMISTEAD, Marcus A	35	5	1834-08-20	Gadsden	A1 G10
4482	ARMISTEAD, Marcus Aurelius	35	4	1830-12-28	Gadsden	A1 G11 C R4483
4483	" "	35	4	1833-12-24	Gadsden	A1 G11 R4482
4411	BAYLES, Burrel	28	NWSW	1857-12-01		A1
4412	" "	28	W½NW	1857-12-01		A1
4426	BEVILL, Elizabeth A	30	E½NE	1856-06-16		A1
4427	" "	30	NWSE	1856-06-16		A1
4428	" "	30	SWNE	1856-06-16		A1
4417	BIRD, David	10	NWNE	1856-06-16		A1
4418	" "	3	E½SW	1856-06-16		A1
4419	" "	3	SWSE	1856-06-16		A1
4416	" "	10	E½NW	1857-12-01		A1
4461	BIRD, John	10	E½NE	1838-07-28		A1
4462	" "	10	NWNW	1838-07-28		A1
4465	" "	9	NESE	1838-07-28		A1 V4414
4464	" "	3	E½SE	1841-01-09		A1
4463	" "	10	W½SE	1843-03-10		A1
4479	BROWN, Isaac	35	1	1828-03-01	Gadsden	A1 G9
4480	BROWN, Levin	26	5	1828-03-15	Gadsden	A1 G12 F
4429	CARTER, Farish	28	E½SE	1834-08-20		A1 G31
4459	COE, Jesse	23	8SE	1838-07-28	Gadsden	A1 G54 F
4493	COE, Lewis	14	NESW	1887-03-10		A2
4494	" "	14	SENW	1887-03-10		A2
4413	COWAN, Charity	14	S½SW	1905-03-20		A2
4439	COX, Ira H	4	NWSW	1856-06-16		A1
4440	" "	4	SWNE	1856-06-16		A1
4438	" "	4	NW	1857-07-01		A1
4531	COX, William G	4	E½SW	1861-09-10		A1
4532	" "	4	SWSW	1861-09-10		A1
4533	" "	9	E½NW	1861-09-10		A1
4534	" "	9	NESW	1861-09-10		A1
4535	" "	9	W½SE	1861-09-10		A1 V4414

ID	Individual in Patent	Sec.	Sec. Part	Date Issued	Other Counties	For More Info . . .
4414	CULPEPPER, Charley	9	SE	1901-08-24		A2 V4465, 4535
4468	DEMONT, John N	30	NESW	1905-06-30		A2
4469	" "	30	SENW	1905-06-30		A2
4527	DOUGHTRY, Wesley	6	N½1	1857-12-01		A1
4528	" "	6	S½1	1859-06-01		A1
4432	DUKES, Henry	14	NWSW	1884-10-15		A2
4433	" "	14	SWNW	1884-10-15		A2
4421	DYKES, Dixson	31	SESW	1857-12-01		A1
4542	ELLIS, William W	20	N½NE	1902-07-03		A2
4507	FRANCIS, Randall	30	SWSW	1896-08-24		A2
4511	GRANTLAND, Seaton	13	1	1830-11-01	Gadsden	A1
4512	" "	13	2	1830-11-01	Gadsden	A1
4514	" "	20	E½SW	1830-11-01		A1 G75
4515	" "	20	W½SW	1830-11-01		A1 G75
4516	" "	29	E½NW	1830-11-01		A1 G75
4510	" "	10	E½SE	1830-12-28		A1
4513	" "	34	3	1830-12-28	Gadsden	A1
4429	" "	28	E½SE	1834-08-20		A1 G31
4487	GRIFFIN, Lenn	19	NENW	1860-07-02		A1
4488	" "	19	NWSE	1860-07-02		A1
4489	" "	19	SENW	1860-07-02		A1
4490	" "	19	SW	1860-07-02		A1
4486	HAM, Len	28	E½NW	1903-05-25		A2
4536	HAM, William H	8	SESE	1899-05-12		A2
4434	HEWETT, Henry	30	NWSW	1895-10-16		A2
4435	" "	30	SWNW	1895-10-16		A2
4497	HOLMES, Mariah	22	SENW	1890-08-05		A2
4502	JOHNSON, Neil A	14	N½NW	1884-06-30		A2
4470	JONES, John R	4	NENE	1852-09-01		A1
4471	" "	4	NWNE	1852-09-01		A1
4503	JONES, Obediance	4	SENE	1859-06-01		A1
4491	KENT, Levi	32	E½SW	1902-07-03		A2
4492	" "	32	S½NW	1902-07-03		A2
4529	KILCREASE, William E	17	NESW	1852-09-01		A1
4530	" "	17	NWSE	1852-09-01		A1
4467	LANIER, John	19	S½SE	1859-06-01		A1
4430	LEADBETTER, Green	22	SW	1889-07-02		A2
4454	LOFTIN, Jeremiah	20	W½SE	1830-11-01		A1
4457	" "	26	2	1830-11-01	Gadsden	A1 G96 F
4458	" "	26	3	1830-11-01	Gadsden	A1 G96 F
4455	" "	29	E½NE	1830-11-01		A1
4456	" "	29	W½NE	1830-11-01		A1
4521	MACK, Taylor	32	N½NW	1891-11-09		A2
4436	MATHEWS, Henry	22	N½NW	1891-06-17		A2
4437	" "	22	SWNW	1891-06-17		A2
4431	MATHIS, Green	28	NWSE	1904-12-20		A2
4504	MCCORMICK, Paul	4	SE	1838-07-28		A1
4505	" "	9	NE	1838-07-28		A1
4495	MCCORQUODALE, Malcom W	20	E½NW	1901-06-28		A2
4496	" "	20	S½NE	1901-06-28		A2
4522	MCDONALD, Thomas P	10	SESW	1894-08-09		A2
4523	" "	10	SWNW	1894-08-09		A2
4524	" "	10	W½SW	1894-08-09		A2
4445	MILLS, James	21	E½NE	1833-12-24		A1 G104 R4498
4441	MONIN, Isaac	30	E½SE	1897-05-25		A2
4473	PATTERSON, Joseph	5	E½SW	1830-11-01		A1
4474	" "	5	W½SW	1830-11-01		A1
4475	" "	8	W½NW	1830-11-01		A1
4499	PERRY, Benjamin F	26	4	1830-11-01	Gadsden	A1 G117 F
4408	" "	33	1	1830-11-01	Gadsden	A1 G116
4409	" "	33	2	1830-11-01	Gadsden	A1 G116 F
4407	" "	34	2	1830-11-01	Gadsden	A1
4445	" "	21	E½NE	1833-12-24		A1 G104 R4498
4442	PERRY, Ivory B	19	E½NE	1830-11-01		A1
4443	" "	19	W½NE	1830-11-01		A1
4444	" "	20	W½NW	1830-11-01		A1
4457	PERRY, Mills And	26	2	1830-11-01	Gadsden	A1 G96 F
4458	" "	26	3	1830-11-01	Gadsden	A1 G96 F
4499	" "	26	4	1830-11-01	Gadsden	A1 G117 F
4500	" "	34	1	1830-11-01	Gadsden	A1 G118
4498	" "	21	E½NE	1830-12-28		A1 C R4445
4415	PLAYER, Daniel H	18	E½SE	1889-07-02		A2 V4449
4460	PLAYER, Jesse	18	E½NE	1889-07-02		A2

ID	Individual in Patent	Sec.	Sec. Part	Date Issued	Other Counties	For More Info . . .
4518	ROWE, Stephen	8	N½NE	1856-06-16		A1
4519	" "	8	SENE	1856-06-16		A1
4520	" "	9	NWSW	1856-06-16		A1
4472	SCOTT, Joseph B	5	E½SE	1834-08-20		A1
4508	SCOTT, Reuben	12	1	1830-11-01	Gadsden	A1
4459	SEARCY, Isham G	23	8SE	1838-07-28	Gadsden	A1 G54 F
4525	SKRINE, V V	3	NENW	1848-11-01		A1
4446	SMITH, James N	5	SWSE	1838-07-28		A1
4447	" "	5	W½NW	1838-07-28		A1
4466	SMITH, John L	28	NE	1896-01-03		A2
4509	STINSON, Sarah	8	W½SW	1838-07-28		A1
4410	STONE, Benoni H	20	E½SE	1834-08-20		A1
4514	STONE, Henry D	20	E½SW	1830-11-01		A1 G75
4515	" "	20	W½SW	1830-11-01		A1 G75
4516	" "	29	E½NW	1830-11-01		A1 G75
4517	STONE, Shade S	10	SWNE	1895-11-05		A2
4420	THOMAS, David	26	1	1830-11-01	Gadsden	A1
4500	" "	34	1	1830-11-01	Gadsden	A1 G118
4404	THOMPSON, Adam J	28	NESW	1896-04-27		A2
4405	" "	28	S½SW	1896-04-27		A2
4406	" "	28	SWSE	1896-04-27		A2
4424	THOMPSON, Elias	30	N½NW	1896-06-26		A2
4425	" "	30	NWNE	1906-06-04		A2
4501	TONEY, Mills	33	7	1830-11-01	Gadsden	A1 G137 F
4501	TONEY, Perry	33	7	1830-11-01	Gadsden	A1 G137 F
4408	TONEY, William	33	1	1830-11-01	Gadsden	A1 G116
4409	" "	33	2	1830-11-01	Gadsden	A1 G116 F
4538	" "	33	5	1830-11-01	Gadsden	A1
4539	" "	33	6	1830-11-01	Gadsden	A1
4501	" "	33	7	1830-11-01	Gadsden	A1 G137 F
4537	" "	32	SE	1833-05-16		A1
4540	" "	33	8	1834-08-20	Gadsden	A1
4541	" "	33	9	1834-08-20	Gadsden	A1
4422	WILCOX, Edward	17	NWSW	1856-06-16		A1
4423	" "	17	SWNW	1856-06-16		A1
4448	WILCOX, James	22	SE	1855-05-01		A1
4449	WILLSON, James	18	NESE	1889-06-29		A2 V4415
4450	" "	18	SWNE	1889-06-29		A2
4451	" "	18	W½SE	1889-06-29		A2
4544	WILSON, Young T	30	SESW	1857-12-01		A1
4545	" "	30	SWSE	1857-12-01		A1
4526	WOOD, Warren L	10	NESW	1857-12-01		A1
4543	WYATT, William	2		1843-03-10		A1
4452	YON, James	3	NWNW	1852-09-01		A1
4453	" "	3	S½4	1856-06-16		A1

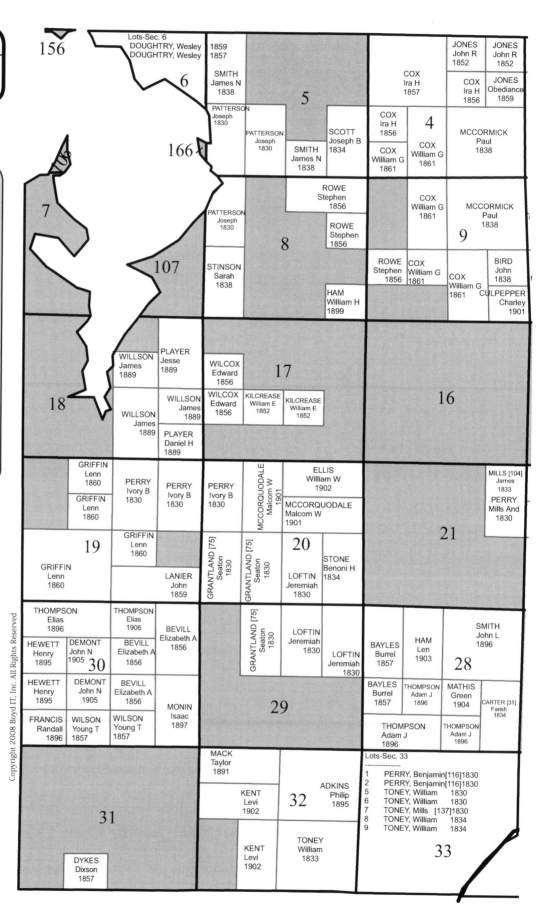

Patent Map

T3-N R7-W
Tallahassee Meridian

Map Group 35

Township Statistics

Parcels Mapped	:	142
Number of Patents	:	111
Number of Individuals	:	78
Patentees Identified	:	79
Number of Surnames	:	56
Multi-Patentee Parcels	:	20
Oldest Patent Date	:	3/1/1828
Most Recent Patent	:	6/4/1906
Block/Lot Parcels	:	31
Parcels Re - Issued	:	2
Parcels that Overlap	:	5
Cities and Towns	:	4
Cemeteries	:	2

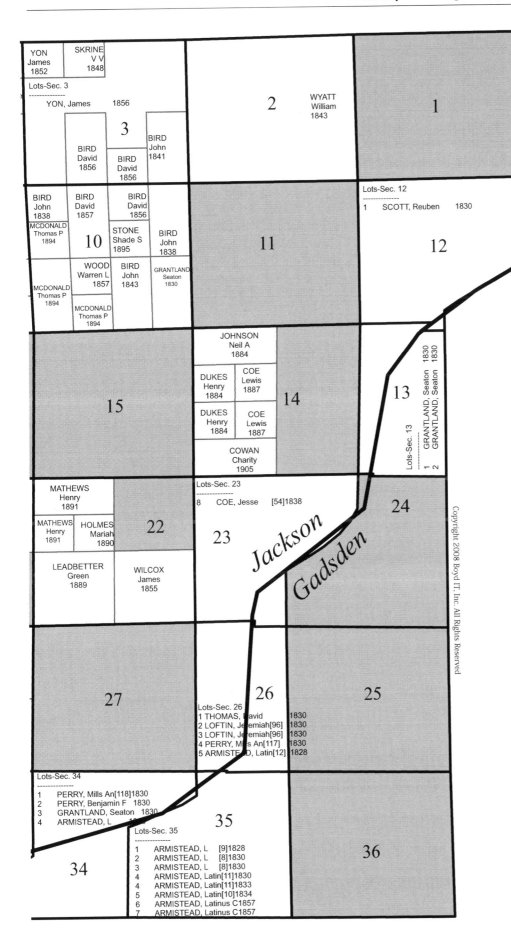

YON
James
1852

SKRINE
V V
1848

Lots-Sec. 3

YON, James   1856

3

BIRD
David
1856

BIRD
David
1856

BIRD
John
1841

2

WYATT
William
1843

1

BIRD
John
1838

BIRD
David
1857

BIRD
David
1856

MCDONALD
Thomas P
1894

10

STONE
Shade S
1895

BIRD
John
1838

WOOD
Warren L
1857

BIRD
John
1843

GRANTLAND
Seaton
1830

MCDONALD
Thomas P
1894

MCDONALD
Thomas P
1894

11

Lots-Sec. 12
----
1   SCOTT, Reuben   1830

12

JOHNSON
Neil A
1884

DUKES
Henry
1884

COE
Lewis
1887

14

DUKES
Henry
1884

COE
Lewis
1887

COWAN
Charity
1905

15

13

GRANTLAND, Seaton 1830
GRANTLAND, Seaton 1830

Lots-Sec. 13
----
1   GRANTLAND, Seaton 1830
2   GRANTLAND, Seaton 1830

MATHEWS
Henry
1891

MATHEWS
Henry
1891

HOLMES
Mariah
1890

22

LEADBETTER
Green
1889

WILCOX
James
1855

Lots-Sec. 23
----
8   COE, Jesse   [54]1838

23

Jackson

Gadsden

24

27

26

Lots-Sec. 26
1 THOMAS, David   1830
2 LOFTIN, Jeremiah[96] 1830
3 LOFTIN, Jeremiah[96] 1830
4 PERRY, Mills An[117] 1830
5 ARMISTEAD, Latin[12] 1828

25

Lots-Sec. 34
----
1   PERRY, Mills An[118]1830
2   PERRY, Benjamin F   1830
3   GRANTLAND, Seaton   1830
4   ARMISTEAD, L

34

35

Lots-Sec. 35
----
1   ARMISTEAD, L   [9]1828
2   ARMISTEAD, L   [8]1830
3   ARMISTEAD, L   [8]1830
4   ARMISTEAD, Latin[11]1830
4   ARMISTEAD, Latin[11]1833
5   ARMISTEAD, Latin[10]1834
6   ARMISTEAD, Latinus C1857
7   ARMISTEAD, Latinus C1857

36

Helpful Hints

1. This Map's INDEX can be found on the preceding pages.

2. Refer to Map "C" to see where this Township lies within Jackson County, Florida.

3. Numbers within square brackets [ ] denote a multi-patentee land parcel (multi-owner). Refer to Appendix "C" for a full list of members in this group.

4. Areas that look to be crowded with Patentees usually indicate multiple sales of the same parcel (Re-issues) or Overlapping parcels. See this Township's Index for an explanation of these and other circumstances that might explain "odd" groupings of Patentees on this map.

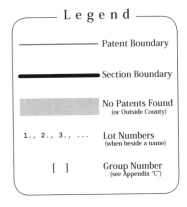

L e g e n d

—————— Patent Boundary

━━━━━━ Section Boundary

No Patents Found
(or Outside County)

1., 2., 3., ...   Lot Numbers
(when beside a name)

[ ]   Group Number
(see Appendix "C")

Scale: Section = 1 mile X 1 mile
(generally, with some exceptions)

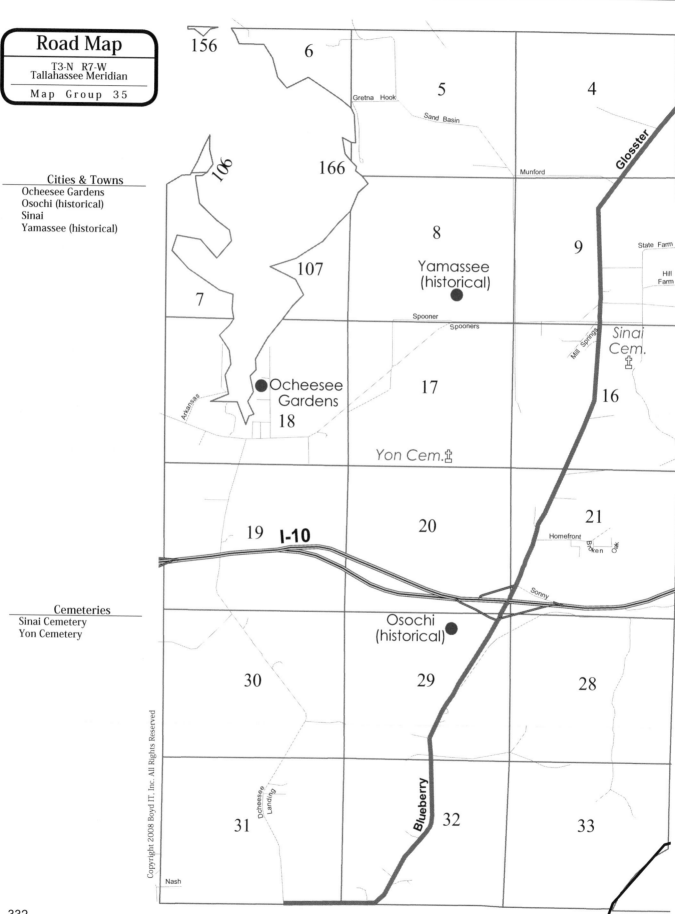

Road Map

T3-N R7-W
Tallahassee Meridian

Map Group 35

Cities & Towns
Ocheesee Gardens
Osochi (historical)
Sinai
Yamassee (historical)

Cemeteries
Sinai Cemetery
Yon Cemetery

156

6

5

4

Gretna Hook

Sand Basin

Glosster

106

166

Munford

107

8

Yamassee
(historical)

9

State Farm

Hill
Farm

7

Spooner

Spooners

Mill Springs

Sinai
Cem.

Ocheesee
Gardens

17

16

18

Arkansas

Yon Cem.

19 **I-10**

20

21

Homefront

Broken Oak

Sonny

Osochi
(historical)

30

29

28

Blueberry

31

Ocheesee Landing

32

33

Nash

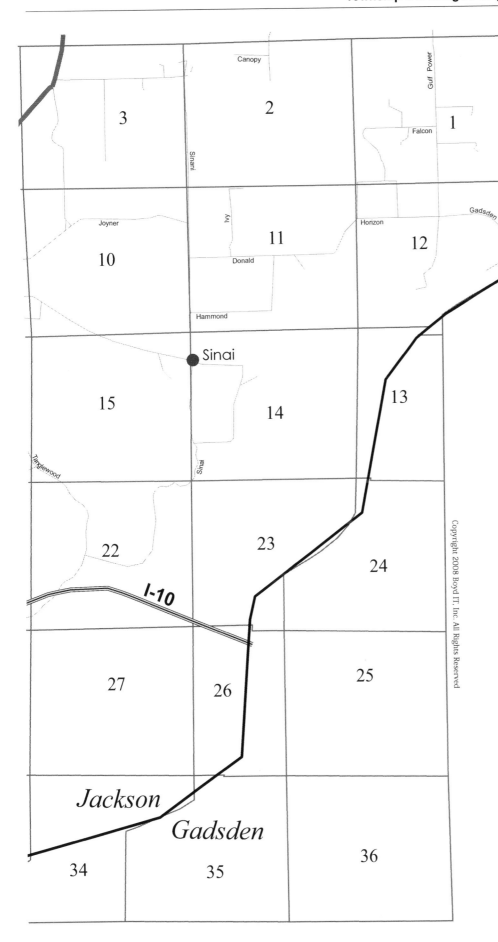

Canopy

3

2

Gulf Power

1

Falcon

Sinai

Joyner

Ivy

Gadsden Tr

11

Horizon

12

10

Donald

Hammond

● Sinai

15

14

Sinai

13

Tanglewood

22

23

24

I-10

27

26

25

Jackson

Gadsden

34

35

36

Helpful Hints

1. This road map has a number of uses, but primarily it is to help you: a) find the present location of land owned by your ancestors (at least the general area), b) find cemeteries and city-centers, and c) estimate the route/roads used by Census-takers & tax-assessors.

2. If you plan to travel to Jackson County to locate cemeteries or land parcels, please pick up a modern travel map for the area before you do. Mapping old land parcels on modern maps is not as exact a science as you might think. Just the slightest variations in public land survey coordinates, estimates of parcel boundaries, or road-map deviations can greatly alter a map's representation of how a road either does or doesn't cross a particular parcel of land.

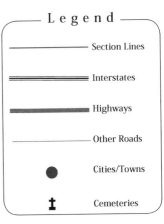

― L e g e n d ―

―――――― Section Lines

▬▬▬▬▬▬ Interstates

▬▬▬▬▬▬ Highways

―――――― Other Roads

● Cities/Towns

✝ Cemeteries

Scale: Section = 1 mile X 1 mile
(generally, with some exceptions)

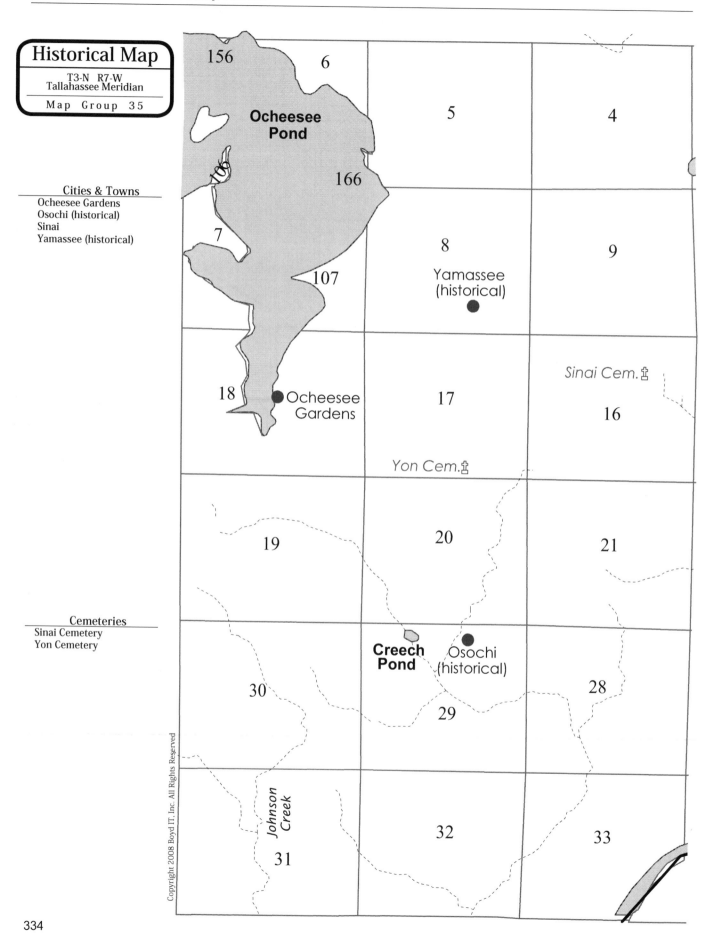

Historical Map

T3-N R7-W
Tallahassee Meridian

Map Group 35

Cities & Towns
Ocheesee Gardens
Osochi (historical)
Sinai
Yamassee (historical)

Cemeteries
Sinai Cemetery
Yon Cemetery

156

6

Ocheesee
Pond

5

4

106

166

7

8

9

107

Yamassee
(historical)

Sinai Cem.

18

17

16

Ocheesee
Gardens

Yon Cem.

19

20

21

Creech
Pond

Osochi
(historical)

30

28

29

Johnson
Creek

32

33

31

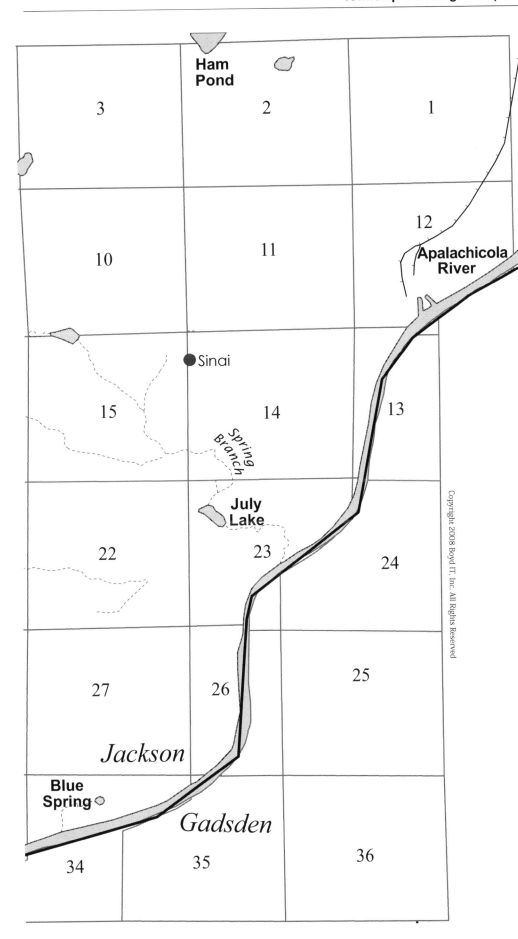

Ham
Pond

3

2

1

12

**Apalachicola
River**

10

11

● Sinai

15

14

13

*Spring
Branch*

**July
Lake**

22

23

24

27

26

25

Jackson

**Blue
Spring** ○

Gadsden

34

35

36

Copyright 2008 Boyd IT, Inc. All Rights Reserved

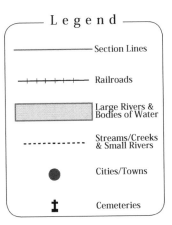

Helpful Hints

1. This Map takes a different look at the same Congressional Township displayed in the preceding two maps. It presents features that can help you better envision the historical development of the area: a) Water-bodies (lakes & ponds), b) Water-courses (rivers, streams, etc.), c) Railroads, d) City/town center-points (where they were oftentimes located when first settled), and e) Cemeteries.

2. Using this "Historical" map in tandem with this Township's Patent Map and Road Map, may lead you to some interesting discoveries. You will often find roads, towns, cemeteries, and waterways are named after nearby landowners: sometimes those names will be the ones you are researching. See how many of these research gems you can find here in Jackson County.

L e g e n d

———————	Section Lines
+++++++	Railroads
▓▓▓▓▓	Large Rivers & Bodies of Water
- - - - - - -	Streams/Creeks & Small Rivers
●	Cities/Towns
✝	Cemeteries

Scale: Section = 1 mile X 1 mile
(there are some exceptions)

Map Group 36: Index to Land Patents

Township 3-North Range 6-West (Tallahassee)

After you locate an individual in this Index, take note of the Section and Section Part then proceed to the Land Patent map on the pages immediately following. You should have no difficulty locating the corresponding parcel of land.

The "For More Info" Column will lead you to more information about the underlying Patents. See the *Legend* at right, and the "How to Use this Book" chapter, for more information.

```
┌─────────────────────────────────────────────────────────┐
│                       LEGEND                            │
│            "For More Info . . . " column                │
│  ─────────────────────────────────────────────────────  │
│  A = Authority (Legislative Act, See Appendix "A")      │
│  B = Block or Lot (location in Section unknown)         │
│  C = Cancelled Patent                                   │
│  F = Fractional Section                                 │
│  G = Group  (Multi-Patentee Patent, see Appendix "C")   │
│  V = Overlaps another Parcel                            │
│  R = Re-Issued (Parcel patented more than once)         │
│                                                         │
│  (A & G items require you to look in the Appendixes referred │
│  to above. All other Letter-designations followed by a number │
│  require you to locate line-items in this index that possess │
│  the ID number found after the letter).                 │
└─────────────────────────────────────────────────────────┘
```

ID	Individual in Patent	Sec.	Sec. Part	Date Issued	Other Counties	For More Info . . .
4550	COE, Jesse	6		1838-07-28	Gadsden	A1 G54 F
4551	FAUST, Philip	6	9	1855-05-01	Gadsden	A1
4546	GEE, Henry	7	1	1834-08-20	Gadsden	A1
4547	" "	7	2	1834-08-20	Gadsden	A1
4548	" "	7	5	1834-08-20	Gadsden	A1
4549	" "	7	6	1834-08-20	Gadsden	A1
4550	SEARCY, Isham G	6		1838-07-28	Gadsden	A1 G54 F

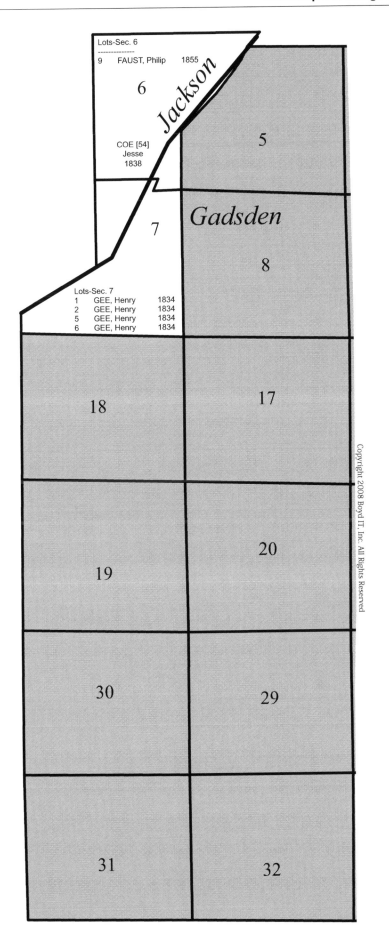

Lots-Sec. 6
----
9   FAUST, Philip   1855

6

Jackson

COE [54]
Jesse
1838

Gadsden

7

5

8

Lots-Sec. 7
1   GEE, Henry   1834
2   GEE, Henry   1834
5   GEE, Henry   1834
6   GEE, Henry   1834

18   17

19   20

30   29

31   32

Patent Map

T3-N R6-W
Tallahassee Meridian

M a p   G r o u p   3 6

Township Statistics

Parcels Mapped	:	6
Number of Patents	:	6
Number of Individuals	:	4
Patentees Identified	:	3
Number of Surnames	:	4
Multi-Patentee Parcels	:	1
Oldest Patent Date	:	8/20/1834
Most Recent Patent	:	5/1/1855
Block/Lot Parcels	:	5
Parcels Re - Issued	:	0
Parcels that Overlap	:	0
Cities and Towns	:	0
Cemeteries	:	0

Note: the area contained in this map amounts to far less than a full Township. Therefore, its contents are completely on this single page (instead of a "normal" 2-page spread).

L e g e n d

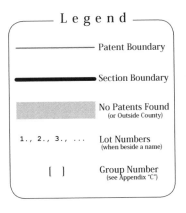

———————— Patent Boundary

———————— Section Boundary

No Patents Found
(or Outside County)

1., 2., 3., ...   Lot Numbers
(when beside a name)

[ ]   Group Number
(see Appendix "C")

Scale: Section = 1 mile X 1 mile
(generally, with some exceptions)

337

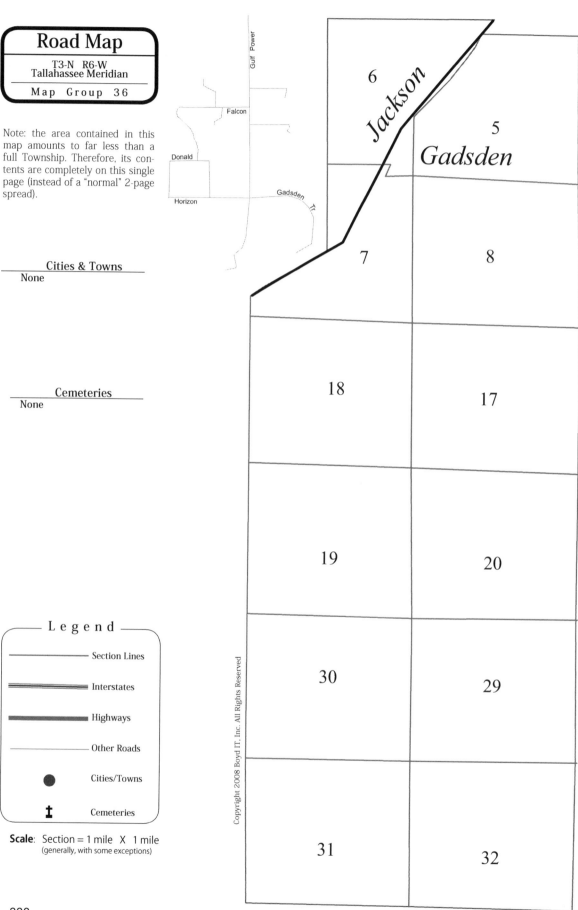

Road Map

T3-N R6-W
Tallahassee Meridian

Map Group 36

Note: the area contained in this map amounts to far less than a full Township. Therefore, its contents are completely on this single page (instead of a "normal" 2-page spread).

Cities & Towns
None

Cemeteries
None

Legend

—————— Section Lines

══════ Interstates

▬▬▬▬▬ Highways

—————— Other Roads

● Cities/Towns

† Cemeteries

Scale: Section = 1 mile X 1 mile
(generally, with some exceptions)

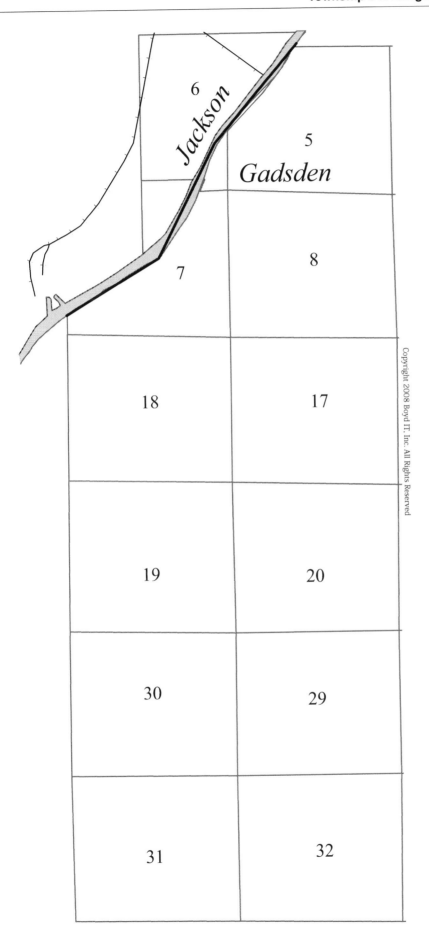

Historical Map

T3-N R6-W
Tallahassee Meridian

Map Group 36

Note: the area contained in this map amounts to far less than a full Township. Therefore, its contents are completely on this single page (instead of a "normal" 2-page spread).

Cities & Towns
None

Cemeteries
None

Legend

————	Section Lines
┼┼┼┼┼	Railroads
▭	Large Rivers & Bodies of Water
-------	Streams/Creeks & Small Rivers
●	Cities/Towns
✝	Cemeteries

Scale: Section = 1 mile X 1 mile
(there are some exceptions)

Map Group 37: Index to Land Patents

Township 2-North Range 12-West (Tallahassee)

After you locate an individual in this Index, take note of the Section and Section Part then proceed to the Land Patent map on the pages immediately following. You should have no difficulty locating the corresponding parcel of land.

The "For More Info" Column will lead you to more information about the underlying Patents. See the *Legend* at right, and the "How to Use this Book" chapter, for more information.

```
                        LEGEND
                "For More Info . . . " column
A = Authority (Legislative Act, See Appendix "A")
B = Block or Lot (location in Section unknown)
C = Cancelled Patent
F = Fractional Section
G = Group   (Multi-Patentee Patent, see Appendix "C")
V = Overlaps another Parcel
R = Re-Issued (Parcel patented more than once)

(A & G items require you to look in the Appendixes referred
to above. All other Letter-designations followed by a number
require you to locate line-items in this index that possess
the ID number found after the letter).
```

ID	Individual in Patent	Sec.	Sec. Part	Date Issued	Other Counties	For More Info . . .
4555	ALDERMAN, Benjamin	12	E½NW	1888-06-16		A1 G1
4556	" "	12	E½SE	1888-06-16		A1 G1
4557	" "	12	NWSE	1888-06-16		A1 G1
4558	" "	12	W½NE	1888-06-16		A1 G1
4559	AUSTIN, Charlie F	14	NW	1908-07-06		A1
4569	BENEFIELD, Robert A	10	E½SE	1910-02-23		A1
4570	" "	10	SESW	1910-02-23		A1
4571	" "	10	SWSE	1910-02-23		A1
4574	DANIEL, Tallie L	12	W½NW	1910-07-18		A2
4555	DANIEL, William	12	E½NW	1888-06-16		A1 G1
4556	" "	12	E½SE	1888-06-16		A1 G1
4557	" "	12	NWSE	1888-06-16		A1 G1
4558	" "	12	W½NE	1888-06-16		A1 G1
4555	DEKLE, Matheu	12	E½NW	1888-06-16		A1 G1
4556	" "	12	E½SE	1888-06-16		A1 G1
4557	" "	12	NWSE	1888-06-16		A1 G1
4558	" "	12	W½NE	1888-06-16		A1 G1
4560	FINCH, Daniel P	2	E½NW	1906-06-08		A1 F
4573	FLORIDA, State Of	12	E½NE	1908-11-19		A3
4562	KENT, Elijah B	14	SE	1907-03-08		A2
4554	MARSHALL, Annie L	14	NE	1912-02-15		A2
4572	MAYO, Robert D	2	NE	1910-07-18		A2
4555	MCKINNE, John H	12	E½NW	1888-06-16		A1 G1
4556	" "	12	E½SE	1888-06-16		A1 G1
4557	" "	12	NWSE	1888-06-16		A1 G1
4558	" "	12	W½NE	1888-06-16		A1 G1
4568	NELSON, Rambling W	12	SWSE	1905-12-30		A1
4561	SEWELL, Easter E	10	N½NW	1911-09-18		A2
4567	SEWELL, Mary M	10	W½SW	1911-09-18		A2
4564	SHORES, Ira	10	NE	1909-09-20		A2
4565	SHORES, Isaac	2	E½SW	1909-09-20		A2
4566	" "	2	W½SE	1909-09-20		A2
4552	THOMAS, Allen C	2	W½NW	1906-05-01		A1 F
4553	" "	2	W½SW	1906-05-01		A1 F
4563	THOMAS, Gideon M	12	SW	1910-09-15		A2

Patent Map

T2-N R12-W
Tallahassee Meridian

Map Group 37

Section 3	THOMAS Allen C 1906	FINCH Daniel P 1906	MAYO Robert D 1910	Section 1
	THOMAS Allen C 1906	SHORES Isaac 1909	SHORES Isaac 1909	

Section 2

SEWELL Easter E 1911	SHORES Ira 1909		DANIEL Tallie L 1910	ALDERMAN [1] Benjamin 1888	FLORIDA State Of 1908
			ALDERMAN [1] Benjamin 1888		

Section 10: SEWELL Mary M 1911, BENEFIELD Robert A 1910, BENEFIELD Robert A 1910, BENEFIELD Robert A 1910

Section 11

Section 12: ALDERMAN [1] Benjamin 1888, THOMAS Gideon M 1910, NELSON Rambling W 1905, ALDERMAN [1] Benjamin 1888

Section 15

Section 14: AUSTIN Charlie F 1908, MARSHALL Annie L 1912, KENT Elijah B 1907

Section 13

Jackson

Bay

Section 22, Section 23, Section 24

Section 27, Section 26, Section 25

Section 34, Section 35, Section 36

Township Statistics

Parcels Mapped	:	23
Number of Patents	:	16
Number of Individuals	:	19
Patentees Identified	:	16
Number of Surnames	:	15
Multi-Patentee Parcels	:	4
Oldest Patent Date	:	6/16/1888
Most Recent Patent	:	2/15/1912
Block/Lot Parcels	:	0
Parcels Re - Issued	:	0
Parcels that Overlap	:	0
Cities and Towns	:	1
Cemeteries	:	0

Note: the area contained in this map amounts to far less than a full Township. Therefore, its contents are completely on this single page (instead of a "normal" 2-page spread).

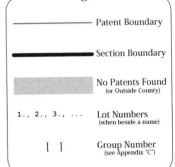

Legend

— Patent Boundary

— Section Boundary

▨ No Patents Found (or Outside County)

1., 2., 3., ... Lot Numbers (when beside a name)

[ ] Group Number (see Appendix "C")

Scale: Section = 1 mile X 1 mile (generally, with some exceptions)

Road Map

T2-N R12-W
Tallahassee Meridian

Map Group 37

Note: the area contained in this map amounts to far less than a full Township. Therefore, its contents are completely on this single page (instead of a "normal" 2-page spread).

Cities & Towns
Compass Lake

Cemeteries
None

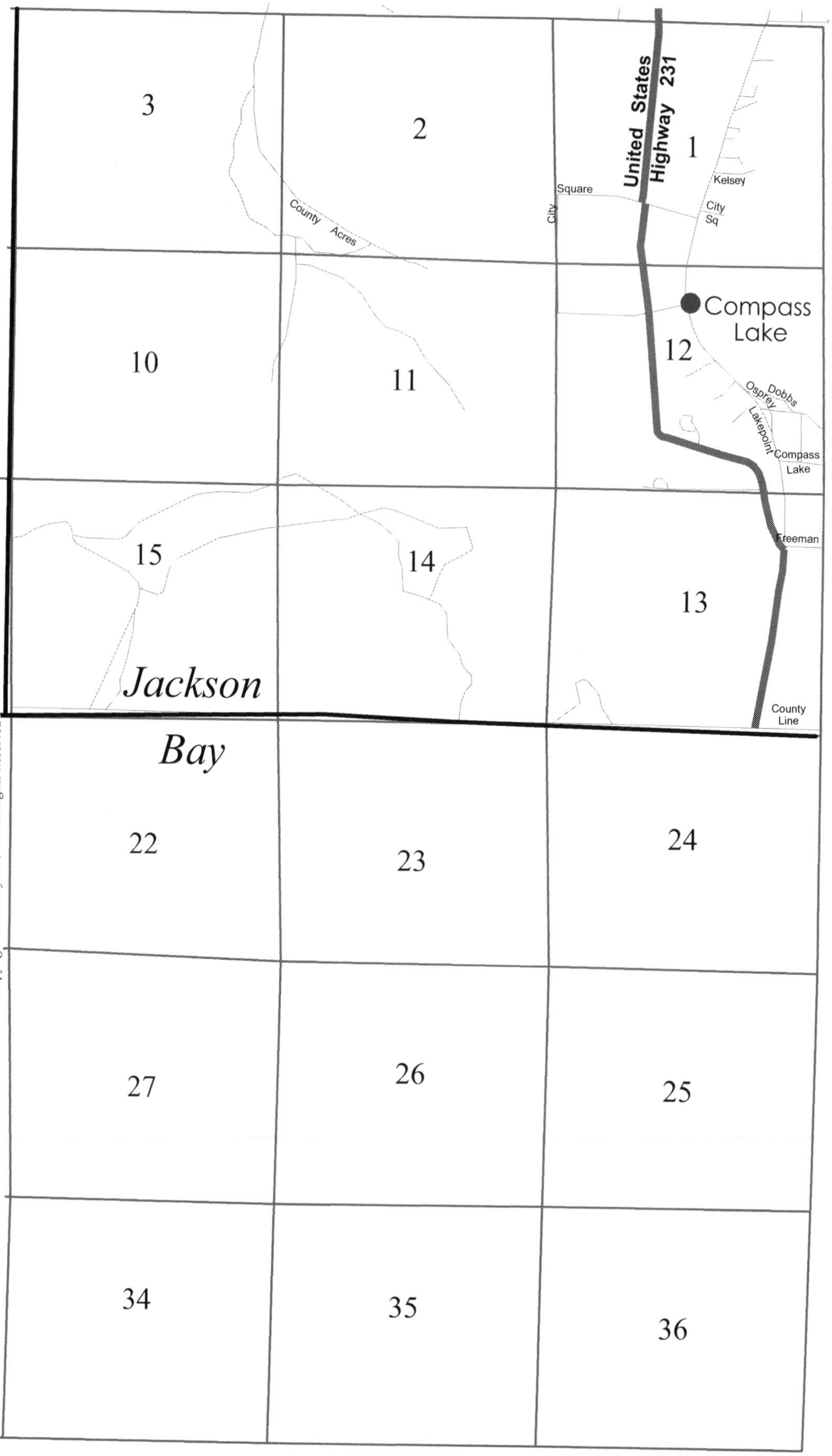

Legend

—————— Section Lines

══════ Interstates

━━━━━━ Highways

—————— Other Roads

● Cities/Towns

✝ Cemeteries

Scale: Section = 1 mile X 1 mile
(generally, with some exceptions)

3

2

1

County Acres

Square

City

United States Highway 231

Kelsey

City Sq

● Compass Lake

10

11

12

Dobbs

Osprey

Lakepoint

Compass Lake

15

14

13

Freeman

Jackson

Bay

County Line

22

23

24

27

26

25

34

35

36

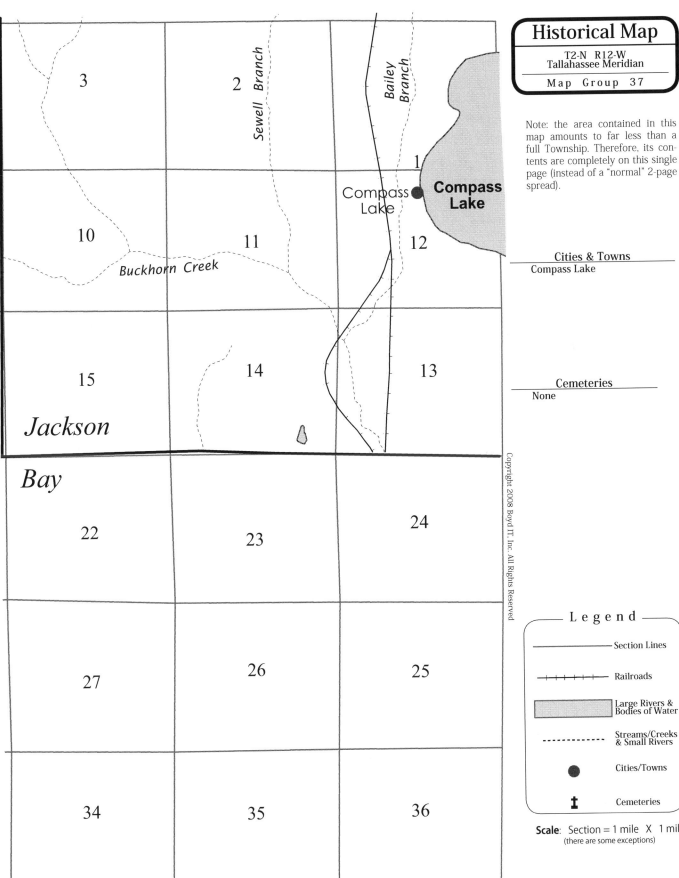

Historical Map

T2-N R12-W
Tallahassee Meridian

Map Group 37

Note: the area contained in this map amounts to far less than a full Township. Therefore, its contents are completely on this single page (instead of a "normal" 2-page spread).

Cities & Towns
Compass Lake

Cemeteries
None

Legend

———————	Section Lines
—+—+—+—	Railroads
▨	Large Rivers & Bodies of Water
- - - - - - -	Streams/Creeks & Small Rivers
●	Cities/Towns
♰	Cemeteries

Scale: Section = 1 mile X 1 mile
(there are some exceptions)

Map Group 38: Index to Land Patents

Township 2-North Range 11-West (Tallahassee)

After you locate an individual in this Index, take note of the Section and Section Part then proceed to the Land Patent map on the pages immediately following. You should have no difficulty locating the corresponding parcel of land.

The "For More Info" Column will lead you to more information about the underlying Patents. See the *Legend* at right, and the "How to Use this Book" chapter, for more information.

```
┌─────────────────────────────────────────────────────────────┐
│                        LEGEND                                │
│            "For More Info . . . " column                     │
│  A = Authority (Legislative Act, See Appendix "A")           │
│  B = Block or Lot (location in Section unknown)              │
│  C = Cancelled Patent                                        │
│  F = Fractional Section                                      │
│  G = Group  (Multi-Patentee Patent, see Appendix "C")       │
│  V = Overlaps another Parcel                                 │
│  R = Re-Issued (Parcel patented more than once)             │
│                                                              │
│  (A & G items require you to look in the Appendixes referred │
│  to above. All other Letter-designations followed by a number│
│  require you to locate line-items in this index that possess │
│  the ID number found after the letter).                      │
└─────────────────────────────────────────────────────────────┘
```

ID	Individual in Patent	Sec.	Sec. Part	Date Issued	Other Counties	For More Info . . .
4579	ALDERMAN, Benjamin	6	NESW	1888-06-16		A1 G1
4580	" "	6	SENW	1888-06-16		A1 G1
4581	" "	6	W½SE	1888-06-16		A1 G1
4579	DANIEL, William	6	NESW	1888-06-16		A1 G1
4580	" "	6	SENW	1888-06-16		A1 G1
4581	" "	6	W½SE	1888-06-16		A1 G1
4579	DEKLE, Matheu	6	NESW	1888-06-16		A1 G1
4580	" "	6	SENW	1888-06-16		A1 G1
4581	" "	6	W½SE	1888-06-16		A1 G1
4582	FARMER, Byrd G	14	NESE	1923-12-12		A1
4586	FREEMAN, Charley	8	S½NW	1909-09-20		A2
4587	" "	8	W½SW	1909-09-20		A2
4607	FREEMAN, James O	18	SE	1906-06-30		A2
4588	GRANTHAM, Chlora N	18	SW	1905-11-03		A1 G73
4628	HOLLIDAY, Theodore R	6	SESW	1904-05-24		A1
4583	LONG, Charles I	4	S½SE	1913-06-06		A1
4584	" "	4	S½SW	1913-06-06		A1
4589	MATTHEWS, Edgar I	6	N½NE	1909-11-11		A2 G101
4590	" "	6	N½NW	1909-11-11		A2 G101
4579	MCKINNE, John H	6	NESW	1888-06-16		A1 G1
4580	" "	6	SENW	1888-06-16		A1 G1
4581	" "	6	W½SE	1888-06-16		A1 G1
4575	MCQUEEN, Abe	6	E½SE	1918-08-22		A2
4629	MCRAE, William A	8	E½NE	1906-06-30		A1
4630	" "	8	E½SE	1906-06-30		A1
4618	MEDLOCK, Meredith M	2	N½NW	1913-02-14		A2
4619	" "	2	NWSW	1913-02-14		A2
4620	" "	2	SWNW	1913-02-14		A2
4623	NELSON, Rambling W	18	SENW	1911-05-25		A2
4624	" "	18	W½NW	1911-05-25		A2
4576	OWENS, Andrew P	14	SESW	1909-12-01		A1
4577	" "	14	SWSE	1909-12-01		A1
4578	" "	14	W½SW	1909-12-01		A1
4608	OWENS, James R	10	N½SE	1905-04-17		A1
4609	" "	10	S½NE	1905-04-17		A1
4596	PORTER, George W	2	N½SE	1911-09-21		A1
4597	" "	2	SENE	1911-09-21		A1
4598	" "	2	SESE	1911-09-21		A1
4594	" "	10	N½NE	1911-12-07		A1
4595	" "	10	N½NW	1911-12-07		A1
4625	PORTER, Robert J	2	N½NE	1916-06-29		A2
4626	" "	2	SENW	1916-06-29		A2
4627	" "	2	SWNE	1916-06-29		A2
4606	PUMPHREY, James H	12	SE	1913-05-26		A2
4621	REYNOLDS, Nannie E	10	E½SW	1909-05-17		A2
4622	" "	10	S½SE	1909-05-17		A2

ID	Individual in Patent	Sec.	Sec. Part	Date Issued	Other Counties	For More Info . . .
4589	RICHARDSON, Frank A	6	N½NE	1909-11-11		A2 G101
4590	"	6	N½NW	1909-11-11		A2 G101
4610	SEXTON, John F	4	N½SE	1913-06-06		A1
4611	"	4	N½SW	1913-06-06		A1
4599	SHUTES, Gordon L	10	S½NW	1906-06-30		A1
4600	"	10	W½SW	1906-06-30		A1
4585	SKINNER, Charles M	4	NW	1905-06-26		A1
4603	SKINNER, James A	4	SENE	1906-06-30		A1
4604	"	4	W½NE	1906-06-30		A1
4612	STEPHENS, John G	6	S½NE	1911-12-07		A1
4591	SUMMERLIN, Elizabeth	12	NESW	1905-05-26		A2
4592	"	12	SENW	1905-05-26		A2
4593	"	12	W½NW	1905-05-26		A2
4613	SUMMERLIN, John J	12	NE	1906-09-25		A1
4615	SUMMERLIN, Luke	2	E½SW	1902-12-30		A2
4616	"	2	SWSE	1902-12-30		A2
4617	"	2	SWSW	1902-12-30		A2
4605	SWEARINGEN, James F G	18	NE	1908-07-06		A1
4601	THOMPSON, Horton H	8	N½NW	1908-07-06		A1
4602	"	8	W½NE	1908-07-06		A1
4588	THORNTON, Chlora N	18	SW	1905-11-03		A1 G73
4614	WHITEHURST, Joseph W	18	NENW	1910-01-17		A1

Patent Map

T2-N R11-W
Tallahassee Meridian

Map Group 38

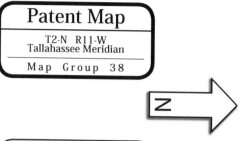

N

Township Statistics

Parcels Mapped	:	56
Number of Patents	:	30
Number of Individuals	:	34
Patentees Identified	:	29
Number of Surnames	:	28
Multi-Patentee Parcels	:	6
Oldest Patent Date	:	6/16/1888
Most Recent Patent	:	12/12/1923
Block/Lot Parcels	:	0
Parcels Re - Issued	:	0
Parcels that Overlap	:	0
Cities and Towns	:	0
Cemeteries	:	0

Note: the area contained in this map amounts to far less than a full Township. Therefore, its contents are completely on this single page (instead of a "normal" 2-page spread).

Legend

———— Patent Boundary

━━━━ Section Boundary

▓▓▓▓ No Patents Found
(or Outside County)

1., 2., 3., ... Lot Numbers
(when beside a name)

[ ] Group Number
(see Appendix "C")

Scale: Section = 1 mile X 1 mile
(generally, with some exceptions)

MATTHEWS [101]
Edgar I
1909

NELSON
Rambling W
1911

GRANTHAM [73]
Chlora N
1905

HOLLIDAY
Theodore R
1904

ALDERMAN [1]
Benjamin
1888

ALDERMAN [1]
Benjamin
1888

6

MATTHEWS [101]
Edgar I
1909

WHITEHURST
Joseph W
1910

NELSON
Rambling W
1911

18

FREEMAN
James O
1906

SWEARINGEN
James F G
1908

ALDERMAN [1]
Benjamin
1888

STEPHENS
John G
1911

MCQUEEN
Abe
1918

7

FREEMAN
Charley
1909

FREEMAN
Charley
1909

THOMPSON
Horton H
1908

THOMPSON
Horton H
1908

8

MCRAE
William A
1906

MCRAE
William A
1906

17

5

SKINNER
Charles M
1905

SEXTON
John F
1913

LONG
Charles I
1913

4

SKINNER
James A
1906

LONG
Charles I
1913

SEXTON
John F
1913

SKINNER
James A
1906

16

9

SHUTES
Gordon L
1906

SHUTES
Gordon L
1906

REYNOLDS
Nannie E
1909

PORTER
George W
1911

OWENS
James R
1905

10

PORTER
George W
1911

REYNOLDS
Nannie E
1909

3

15

OWENS
Andrew P
1909

OWENS
Andrew P
1909

OWENS
Andrew P
1909

14

FARMER
Byrd G
1923

11

SUMMERLIN
Luke
1902

MEDLOCK
Meredith M
1913

MEDLOCK
Meredith M
1913

MEDLOCK
Meredith M
1913

SUMMERLIN
Luke
1902

SUMMERLIN
Luke
1902

SUMMERLIN
Luke
1902

2

PORTER
Robert J
1916

PORTER
Robert J
1916

PORTER
George W
1911

PORTER
Robert J
1916

PORTER
Robert J
1916

PORTER
George W
1911

13

SUMMERLIN
Elizabeth
1905

SUMMERLIN
Elizabeth
1905

SUMMERLIN
Elizabeth
1905

SUMMERLIN
Elizabeth
1905

12

SUMMERLIN
John J
1906

PUMPHREY
James H
1913

1

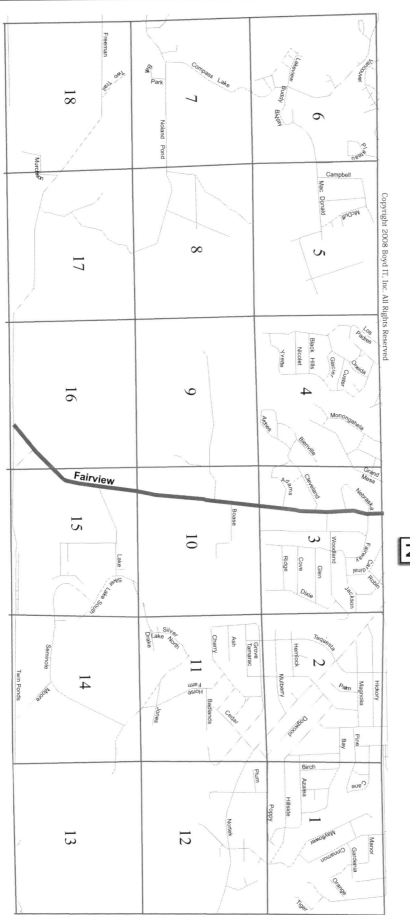

Road Map

T2-N R11-W
Tallahassee Meridian

M a p   G r o u p   38

Note: the area contained in this map amounts to far less than a full Township. Therefore, its contents are completely on this single page (instead of a "normal" 2-page spread).

Cities & Towns
None

Cemeteries
None

Legend

——————— Section Lines

═══════ Interstates

━━━━━━━ Highways

——————— Other Roads

● Cities/Towns

✝ Cemeteries

Scale: Section = 1 mile X 1 mile
(generally, with some exceptions)

Historical Map

T2-N R11-W
Tallahassee Meridian

Map Group 38

Note: the area contained in this map amounts to far less than a full Township. Therefore, its contents are completely on this single page (instead of a "normal" 2-page spread).

N

Cities & Towns
None

Cemeteries
None

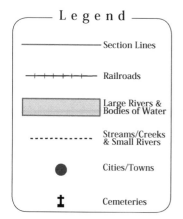

Legend

——————	Section Lines
+++++++	Railroads
�	Large Rivers & Bodies of Water
- - - - -	Streams/Creeks & Small Rivers
●	Cities/Towns
✝	Cemeteries

Scale: Section = 1 mile X 1 mile
(there are some exceptions)

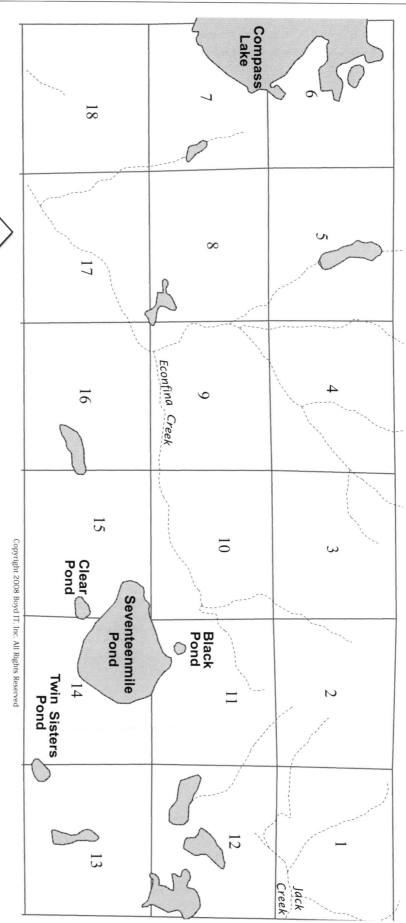

Map Group 39: Index to Land Patents

Township 2-North Range 10-West (Tallahassee)

After you locate an individual in this Index, take note of the Section and Section Part then proceed to the Land Patent map on the pages immediately following. You should have no difficulty locating the corresponding parcel of land.

The "For More Info" Column will lead you to more information about the underlying Patents. See the *Legend* at right, and the "How to Use this Book" chapter, for more information.

```
┌─────────────────────────────────────────────────────┐
│                                    LEGEND             │
│              "For More Info . . . " column            │
│ ───────────────────────────────────────────────────── │
│ A = Authority (Legislative Act, See Appendix "A")     │
│ B = Block or Lot (location in Section unknown)        │
│ C = Cancelled Patent                                  │
│ F = Fractional Section                                │
│ G = Group  (Multi-Patentee Patent, see Appendix "C")  │
│ V = Overlaps another Parcel                           │
│ R = Re-Issued (Parcel patented more than once)        │
│                                                       │
│ (A & G items require you to look in the Appendixes referred │
│ to above. All other Letter-designations followed by a number │
│ require you to locate line-items in this index that possess │
│ the ID number found after the letter).                │
└─────────────────────────────────────────────────────┘
```

ID	Individual in Patent	Sec.	Sec. Part	Date Issued	Other Counties	For More Info . . .
4648	ADKINS, Enoch W	18	W½SW	1920-06-05		A1
4651	ADKINS, Francis N	4	NESW	1905-05-26		A2
4652	" "	4	S½SW	1905-05-26		A2
4681	ADKINS, Robert R	6	SENE	1911-05-18		A1
4703	ADKINS, William M	6	SWSW	1923-11-12		A2
4641	BOGGS, Charles R	10	W½SW	1918-11-07		A2
4664	BOGGS, James W	8	NE	1905-05-17		A2
4667	BOGGS, John C	8	SE	1906-06-04		A2
4636	CHANCE, Arthur R	10	SESE	1907-06-03		A1
4637	" "	14	N½NE	1913-06-23		A2
4644	CHASON, Edward	14	E½NW	1905-05-17		A2
4645	" "	14	NESW	1905-05-17		A2
4646	" "	14	NWSE	1905-05-17		A2
4643	" "	10	SWNE	1909-01-21		A1
4675	CHASON, Mason	4	E½SE	1901-08-12		A2
4676	" "	4	SENE	1901-08-12		A2
4677	" "	4	SWSE	1901-08-12		A2
4678	" "	6	N½NE	1908-07-06		A1
4679	" "	6	N½NW	1908-07-06		A1
4691	CHASON, Susan	14	E½SE	1899-05-12		A2
4692	" "	14	SENE	1899-05-12		A2
4693	" "	14	SWSE	1899-05-12		A2
4671	COOK, Josiah C	12	E½NE	1889-11-25		A2 G58
4672	" "	12	E½SE	1889-11-25		A2 G58
4671	COOK, Mary F	12	E½NE	1889-11-25		A2 G58
4672	" "	12	E½SE	1889-11-25		A2 G58
4654	GAY, Henry E	10	E½NE	1911-05-03		A1
4655	" "	10	NESE	1911-05-03		A1
4656	" "	10	NWNE	1911-05-03		A1
4632	GILLIS, Angus M	14	SESW	1908-07-06		A1
4680	HAND, Rachel	2	S½SE	1911-06-12		A2
4631	HOLLIMAN, Aley A	2	SWNE	1911-01-16		A2
4665	JOHNSON, James W	4	E½NW	1909-01-11		A2
4666	" "	4	N½NE	1909-01-11		A2
4700	JOHNSON, William F	2	E½NE	1904-11-26		A2
4701	" "	2	NENW	1904-11-26		A2
4702	" "	2	NWNE	1904-11-26		A2
4647	KNIGHT, Ellis T	2	NWNW	1911-05-03		A2
4653	LASHLEY, George R	6	E½SE	1907-05-10		A1
4699	LASHLEY, William B	8	NW	1903-05-25		A2
4689	LIPFORD, Stephen J	10	E½SW	1905-05-17		A2
4690	" "	10	W½SE	1905-05-17		A2
4649	MADDOX, Francis M	4	NWSE	1911-04-27		A2
4650	" "	4	SWNE	1911-04-27		A2
4686	MADDOX, Samuel	2	NWSW	1911-02-23		A2
4687	" "	2	S½SW	1911-02-23		A2

ID	Individual in Patent	Sec.	Sec. Part	Date Issued	Other Counties	For More Info . . .
4688	MADDOX, Samuel (Cont'd)	2	SWNW	1911-02-23		A2
4694	MADDOX, Thomas J	18	N½NE	1905-06-26		A1
4695	" "	18	NENW	1905-06-26		A1
4696	" "	18	SENE	1905-06-26		A1
4642	MAYO, Edward C	10	NW	1905-05-17		A2
4634	MORRISON, Archibald M	14	W½NW	1906-06-30		A1
4635	" "	14	W½SW	1906-06-30		A1
4673	NIX, King D	6	E½SW	1905-05-05		A1 F
4674	" "	6	W½SE	1905-05-05		A1 F
4638	POWELL, Celia A	12	NESW	1909-09-20		A2
4639	" "	12	SENW	1909-09-20		A2
4640	" "	12	W½SW	1909-09-20		A2
4633	PUMPHREY, Ann Mary	8	SW	1909-05-17		A2 G123
4633	PUMPHREY, John W	8	SW	1909-05-17		A2 G123
4697	SKETO, Warren	3	E½NW	1856-06-16		A1
4698	" "	3	SWNW	1856-06-16		A1
4659	SNOW, James H	4	NWSW	1909-09-20		A2
4660	" "	4	W½NW	1909-09-20		A2
4657	STAPLETON, Henry J	18	E½SW	1911-04-17		A2
4658	" "	18	S½NW	1911-04-17		A2
4661	STEPHENS, James O	12	N½NW	1910-06-13		A2
4662	" "	12	NWNE	1910-06-13		A2
4663	" "	12	SWNW	1910-06-13		A2
4668	TATUM, John E	12	SESW	1914-06-11		A2
4669	" "	12	SWNE	1914-06-11		A2
4670	" "	12	W½SE	1914-06-11		A2
4683	WILLIAMS, Rudolphus L	18	SESE	1906-06-30		A1
4682	" "	18	NESE	1911-01-26		A2
4684	" "	18	SWNE	1911-01-26		A2
4685	" "	18	W½SE	1911-01-26		A2

Patent Map

T2-N R10-W
Tallahassee Meridian

Map Group 39

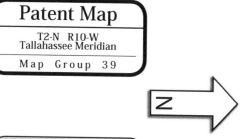

N

Township Statistics

Parcels Mapped	:	73
Number of Patents	:	41
Number of Individuals	:	38
Patentees Identified	:	36
Number of Surnames	:	25
Multi-Patentee Parcels	:	3
Oldest Patent Date	:	6/16/1856
Most Recent Patent	:	11/12/1923
Block/Lot Parcels	:	0
Parcels Re - Issued	:	0
Parcels that Overlap	:	0
Cities and Towns	:	0
Cemeteries	:	0

Note: the area contained in this map amounts to far less than a full Township. Therefore, its contents are completely on this single page (instead of a "normal" 2-page spread).

Legend

— Patent Boundary

— Section Boundary

▨ No Patents Found (or Outside County)

1., 2., 3., ... Lot Numbers (when beside a name)

[ ] Group Number (see Appendix "C")

Scale: Section = 1 mile X 1 mile (generally, with some exceptions)

Map section (patent parcels):

Section 18: ADKINS Enoch W 1920; STAPLETON Henry J 1911; STAPLETON Henry J 1911; WILLIAMS Rudolphus L 1911; 18; WILLIAMS Rudolphus L 1906

Section 6: MADDOX Thomas J 1905; STAPLETON Henry J 1911; WILLIAMS Thomas J 1911; MADDOX Thomas J 1905; MADDOX Thomas J 1905; WILLIAMS Rudolphus L 1911; ADKINS William M 1923; NIX King D 1905; NIX King D 1905; LASHLEY George R 1907; 6; ADKINS Robert R 1911

Section 7: 7

Section 5: 5; CHASON Mason 1908; CHASON Mason 1908

Section 17: 17

Section 8: PUMPHREY Ann Mary 1909 [123]; LASHLEY William B 1903; BOGGS John C 1906; 8; BOGGS James W 1905

Section 16: 16

Section 9: 9

Section 4: SNOW James H 1909; SNOW James H 1909; ADKINS Francis N 1905; ADKINS Francis N 1905; 4; MADDOX Francis M 1911; CHASON Mason 1901; MADDOX Francis M 1911; CHASON Mason 1901; JOHNSON James W 1909; JOHNSON James W 1909

Section 15: 15

Section 10: BOGGS Charles R 1918; LIPFORD Stephen J 1905; LIPFORD Stephen J 1905; MAYO Edward C 1905; 10; CHASON Edward 1909; CHANCE Arthur R 1907; GAY Henry E 1911; GAY Henry E 1911; GAY Henry E 1911

Section 3: 3; SKETO Warren 1856; SKETO Warren 1856

Section 14: MORRISON Archibald M 1906; MORRISON Archibald M 1906; CHASON Edward 1905; GILLIS Angus M 1908; CHASON Susan 1899; CHASON Edward 1905; CHASON Edward 1905; 14; CHASON Susan 1899; CHASON Susan 1899; CHASON Edward 1905; CHANCE Arthur R 1913

Section 11: 11; MADDOX Samuel 1911; MADDOX Samuel 1911; MADDOX Samuel 1911

Section 2: 2; KNIGHT Ellis T 1911; JOHNSON William F 1904; HAND Rachel 1911; HOLLIMAN Aley A 1911; JOHNSON William F 1904; JOHNSON William F 1904

Section 13: 13

Section 12: POWELL Celia A 1909; STEPHENS James O 1910; STEPHENS James O 1910; POWELL Celia A 1909; POWELL Celia A 1909; TATUM John E 1914; TATUM John E 1914; 12; TATUM John E 1914; STEPHENS James O 1910; STEPHENS James O 1910; COOK Josiah C 1889 [58]; COOK Josiah C 1889

Section 1: 1

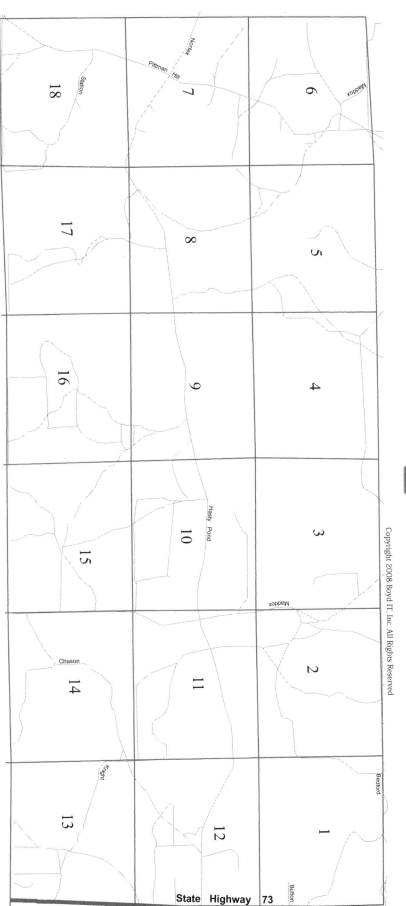

Road Map

T2-N R10-W
Tallahassee Meridian

Map Group 39

Note: the area contained in this map amounts to far less than a full Township. Therefore, its contents are completely on this single page (instead of a "normal" 2-page spread).

Cities & Towns
None

Cemeteries
None

Legend

——————	Section Lines
═══════	Interstates
——————	Highways
——————	Other Roads
●	Cities/Towns
✝	Cemeteries

Scale: Section = 1 mile X 1 mile
(generally, with some exceptions)

Historical Map

T2-N   R10-W
Tallahassee Meridian

Map Group 39

Note: the area contained in this map amounts to far less than a full Township. Therefore, its contents are completely on this single page (instead of a "normal" 2-page spread).

Cities & Towns
None

Cemeteries
None

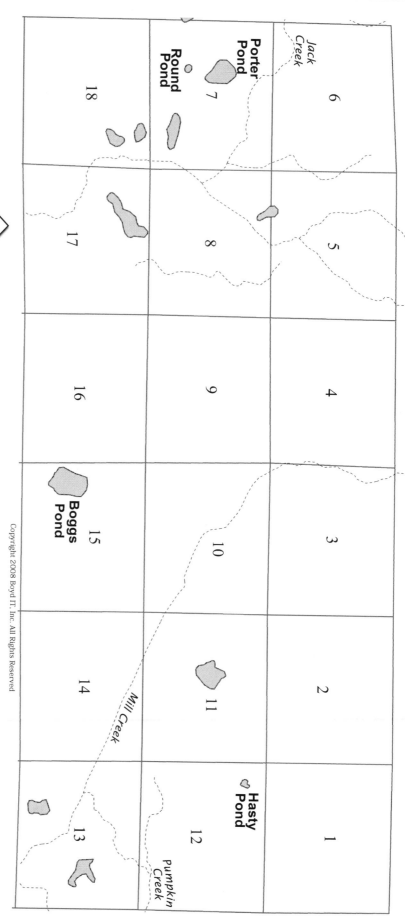

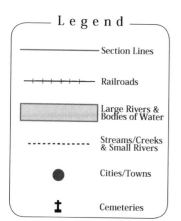

Legend

—————— Section Lines

+++++++ Railroads

▭ Large Rivers & Bodies of Water

- - - - - Streams/Creeks & Small Rivers

● Cities/Towns

☦ Cemeteries

Scale: Section = 1 mile X 1 mile
(there are some exceptions)

Map Group 40: Index to Land Patents

Township 2-North Range 9-West (Tallahassee)

After you locate an individual in this Index, take note of the Section and Section Part then proceed to the Land Patent map on the pages immediately following. You should have no difficulty locating the corresponding parcel of land.

The "For More Info" Column will lead you to more information about the underlying Patents. See the *Legend* at right, and the "How to Use this Book" chapter, for more information.

ID	Individual in Patent	Sec.	Sec. Part	Date Issued	Other Counties	For More Info . . .
4713	BROWN, John M	18	SWNE	1914-03-13	Calhoun	A2
4718	BYRD, William	18	W½SW	1852-09-01	Calhoun	A1
4717	" "	18	SWNW	1855-05-01	Calhoun	A1
4716	" "	18	SESE	1861-04-09	Calhoun	A1
4719	CARPENTER, William	18	NESE	1852-09-01	Calhoun	A1
4706	CHAPMAN, Barbara A	7	W½NE	1847-11-01	Calhoun	A1
4707	" "	7	W½SE	1847-11-01	Calhoun	A1
4714	MILTON, John	6	E½SE	1850-08-10	Calhoun	A1
4712	STELL, John H	7	E½SW	1848-04-10	Calhoun	A1
4715	STELL, Thomas J	18	NWNW	1848-11-01	Calhoun	A1
4708	TILLINGHAST, George W	18	N½NE	1846-10-01	Calhoun	A1
4709	" "	7	E½NE	1846-10-01	Calhoun	A1
4710	" "	7	E½SE	1846-10-01	Calhoun	A1
4711	WHITTINGTON, James	18	SENE	1905-03-20	Calhoun	A2
4704	WOOD, Andrew J	18	E½NW	1846-09-01	Calhoun	A1
4705	" "	6	E½NE	1846-09-01	Calhoun	A1

Map

- 6
- *Jackson*
- WOOD Andrew J 1846
- MILTON John 1850
- 5
- 7
- CHAPMAN Barbara A 1847
- TILLINGHAST George W 1846
- *Calhoun*
- TILLINGHAST George W 1846
- 8
- STELL John H 1848
- CHAPMAN Barbara A 1847
- STELL Thomas J 1848
- WOOD Andrew J 1846
- TILLINGHAST George W 1846
- BYRD William 1855
- 18
- BROWN John M 1914
- WHITTINGTON James 1905
- CARPENTER William 1852
- 17
- BYRD William 1852
- BYRD William 1861
- 19
- 20
- 30
- 29
- 31
- 32

Patent Map

T2-N R9-W
Tallahassee Meridian

Map Group 40

Township Statistics

Parcels Mapped	:	16
Number of Patents	:	15
Number of Individuals	:	10
Patentees Identified	:	10
Number of Surnames	:	9
Multi-Patentee Parcels	:	0
Oldest Patent Date	:	9/1/1846
Most Recent Patent	:	3/13/1914
Block/Lot Parcels	:	0
Parcels Re - Issued	:	0
Parcels that Overlap	:	0
Cities and Towns	:	0
Cemeteries	:	0

Note: the area contained in this map amounts to far less than a full Township. Therefore, its contents are completely on this single page (instead of a "normal" 2-page spread).

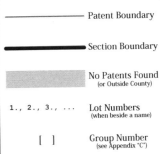

L e g e n d

Patent Boundary

Section Boundary

No Patents Found
(or Outside County)

1., 2., 3., ... Lot Numbers
(when beside a name)

[ ] Group Number
(see Appendix "C")

Scale: Section = 1 mile X 1 mile
(generally, with some exceptions)

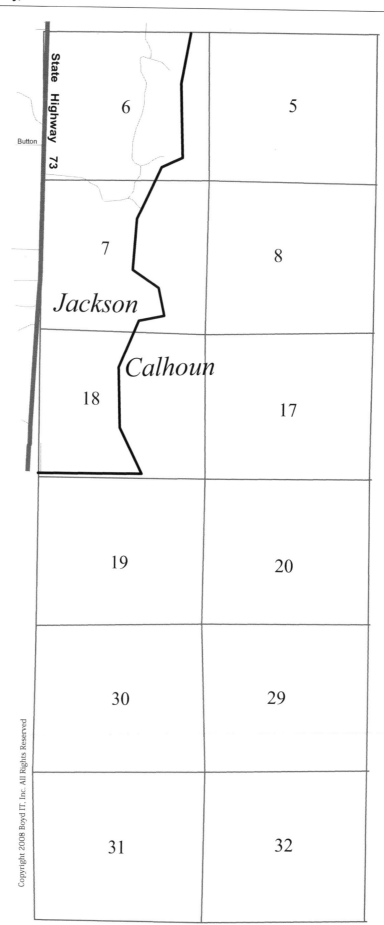

Road Map

T2-N R9-W
Tallahassee Meridian

Map Group 40

Note: the area contained in this map amounts to far less than a full Township. Therefore, its contents are completely on this single page (instead of a "normal" 2-page spread).

Cities & Towns
None

Cemeteries
None

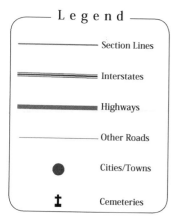

L e g e n d

——————— Section Lines

══════ Interstates

━━━━━ Highways

——————— Other Roads

● Cities/Towns

✝ Cemeteries

Scale: Section = 1 mile X 1 mile
(generally, with some exceptions)

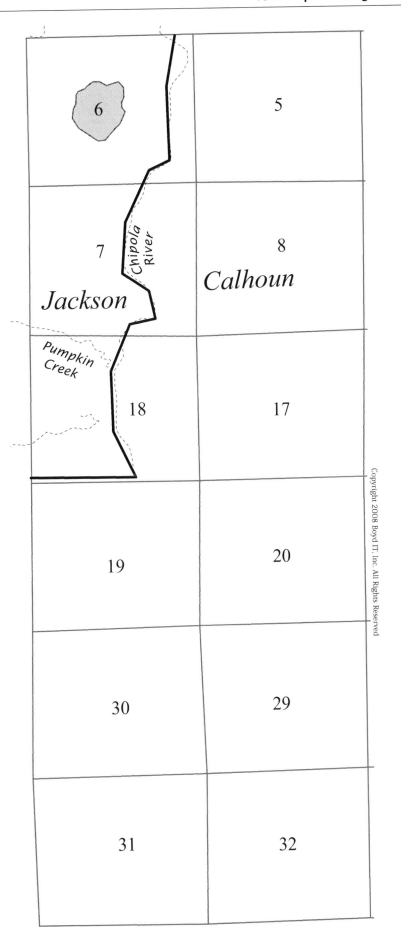

Historical Map

T2-N R9-W
Tallahassee Meridian

Map Group 40

Note: the area contained in this map amounts to far less than a full Township. Therefore, its contents are completely on this single page (instead of a "normal" 2-page spread).

Cities & Towns
None

Cemeteries
None

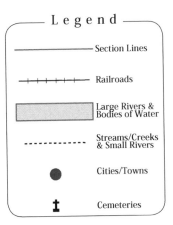

Legend

Section Lines

Railroads

Large Rivers & Bodies of Water

Streams/Creeks & Small Rivers

Cities/Towns

Cemeteries

Scale: Section = 1 mile X 1 mile
(there are some exceptions)

Appendices

Appendix A - Acts of Congress Authorizing the Patents Contained in this Book

The following Acts of Congress are referred to throughout the Indexes in this book. The text of the Federal Statutes referred to below can usually be found on the web. For more information on such laws, check out the publishers's web-site at *www.arphax.com*, go to the "Research" page, and click on the "Land-Law" link.

Ref. No.	Date and Act of Congress	Number of Parcels of Land
1	April 24, 1820: Sale-Cash Entry (3 Stat. 566)	3136
2	May 20, 1862: Homestead EntryOriginal (12 Stat. 392)	1579
3	September 28, 1850: Swamp Land Grant-Patent (9 Stat. 519)	4

Appendix B - Section Parts (Aliquot Parts)

The following represent the various abbreviations we have found thus far in describing the parts of a Public Land Section. Some of these are very obscure and rarely used, but we wanted to list them for just that reason. A full section is 1 square mile or 640 acres.

Section Part	Description	Acres
<none>	Full Acre (if no Section Part is listed, presumed a full Section)	640
<1-??>	A number represents a Lot Number and can be of various sizes	?
E½	East Half-Section	320
E½E½	East Half of East Half-Section	160
E½E½SE	East Half of East Half of Southeast Quarter-Section	40
E½N½	East Half of North Half-Section	160
E½NE	East Half of Northeast Quarter-Section	80
E½NENE	East Half of Northeast Quarter of Northeast Quarter-Section	20
E½NENW	East Half of Northeast Quarter of Northwest Quarter-Section	20
E½NESE	East Half of Northeast Quarter of Southeast Quarter-Section	20
E½NESW	East Half of Northeast Quarter of Southwest Quarter-Section	20
E½NW	East Half of Northwest Quarter-Section	80
E½NWNE	East Half of Northwest Quarter of Northeast Quarter-Section	20
E½NWNW	East Half of Northwest Quarter of Northwest Quarter-Section	20
E½NWSE	East Half of Northwest Quarter of Southeast Quarter-Section	20
E½NWSW	East Half of Northwest Quarter of Southwest Quarter-Section	20
E½S½	East Half of South Half-Section	160
E½SE	East Half of Southeast Quarter-Section	80
E½SENE	East Half of Southeast Quarter of Northeast Quarter-Section	20
E½SENW	East Half of Southeast Quarter of Northwest Quarter-Section	20
E½SESE	East Half of Southeast Quarter of Southeast Quarter-Section	20
E½SESW	East Half of Southeast Quarter of Southwest Quarter-Section	20
E½SW	East Half of Southwest Quarter-Section	80
E½SWNE	East Half of Southwest Quarter of Northeast Quarter-Section	20
E½SWNW	East Half of Southwest Quarter of Northwest Quarter-Section	20
E½SWSE	East Half of Southwest Quarter of Southeast Quarter-Section	20
E½SWSW	East Half of Southwest Quarter of Southwest Quarter-Section	20
E½W½	East Half of West Half-Section	160
N½	North Half-Section	320
N½E½NE	North Half of East Half of Northeast Quarter-Section	40
N½E½NW	North Half of East Half of Northwest Quarter-Section	40
N½E½SE	North Half of East Half of Southeast Quarter-Section	40
N½E½SW	North Half of East Half of Southwest Quarter-Section	40
N½N½	North Half of North Half-Section	160
N½NE	North Half of Northeast Quarter-Section	80
N½NENE	North Half of Northeast Quarter of Northeast Quarter-Section	20
N½NENW	North Half of Northeast Quarter of Northwest Quarter-Section	20
N½NESE	North Half of Northeast Quarter of Southeast Quarter-Section	20
N½NESW	North Half of Northeast Quarter of Southwest Quarter-Section	20
N½NW	North Half of Northwest Quarter-Section	80
N½NWNE	North Half of Northwest Quarter of Northeast Quarter-Section	20
N½NWNW	North Half of Northwest Quarter of Northwest Quarter-Section	20
N½NWSE	North Half of Northwest Quarter of Southeast Quarter-Section	20
N½NWSW	North Half of Northwest Quarter of Southwest Quarter-Section	20
N½S½	North Half of South Half-Section	160
N½SE	North Half of Southeast Quarter-Section	80
N½SENE	North Half of Southeast Quarter of Northeast Quarter-Section	20
N½SENW	North Half of Southeast Quarter of Northwest Quarter-Section	20
N½SESE	North Half of Southeast Quarter of Southeast Quarter-Section	20

Section Part	Description	Acres
N½SESW	North Half of Southeast Quarter of Southwest Quarter-Section	20
N½SESW	North Half of Southeast Quarter of Southwest Quarter-Section	20
N½SW	North Half of Southwest Quarter-Section	80
N½SWNE	North Half of Southwest Quarter of Northeast Quarter-Section	20
N½SWNW	North Half of Southwest Quarter of Northwest Quarter-Section	20
N½SWSE	North Half of Southwest Quarter of Southeast Quarter-Section	20
N½SWSE	North Half of Southwest Quarter of Southeast Quarter-Section	20
N½SWSW	North Half of Southwest Quarter of Southwest Quarter-Section	20
N½W½NW	North Half of West Half of Northwest Quarter-Section	40
N½W½SE	North Half of West Half of Southeast Quarter-Section	40
N½W½SW	North Half of West Half of Southwest Quarter-Section	40
NE	Northeast Quarter-Section	160
NEN½	Northeast Quarter of North Half-Section	80
NENE	Northeast Quarter of Northeast Quarter-Section	40
NENENE	Northeast Quarter of Northeast Quarter of Northeast Quarter	10
NENENW	Northeast Quarter of Northeast Quarter of Northwest Quarter	10
NENESE	Northeast Quarter of Northeast Quarter of Southeast Quarter	10
NENESW	Northeast Quarter of Northeast Quarter of Southwest Quarter	10
NENW	Northeast Quarter of Northwest Quarter-Section	40
NENWNE	Northeast Quarter of Northwest Quarter of Northeast Quarter	10
NENWNW	Northeast Quarter of Northwest Quarter of Northwest Quarter	10
NENWSE	Northeast Quarter of Northwest Quarter of Southeast Quarter	10
NENWSW	Northeast Quarter of Northwest Quarter of Southwest Quarter	10
NESE	Northeast Quarter of Southeast Quarter-Section	40
NESENE	Northeast Quarter of Southeast Quarter of Northeast Quarter	10
NESENW	Northeast Quarter of Southeast Quarter of Northwest Quarter	10
NESESE	Northeast Quarter of Southeast Quarter of Southeast Quarter	10
NESESW	Northeast Quarter of Southeast Quarter of Southwest Quarter	10
NESW	Northeast Quarter of Southwest Quarter-Section	40
NESWNE	Northeast Quarter of Southwest Quarter of Northeast Quarter	10
NESWNW	Northeast Quarter of Southwest Quarter of Northwest Quarter	10
NESWSE	Northeast Quarter of Southwest Quarter of Southeast Quarter	10
NESWSW	Northeast Quarter of Southwest Quarter of Southwest Quarter	10
NW	Northwest Quarter-Section	160
NWE½	Northwest Quarter of Eastern Half-Section	80
NWN½	Northwest Quarter of North Half-Section	80
NWNE	Northwest Quarter of Northeast Quarter-Section	40
NWNENE	Northwest Quarter of Northeast Quarter of Northeast Quarter	10
NWNENW	Northwest Quarter of Northeast Quarter of Northwest Quarter	10
NWNESE	Northwest Quarter of Northeast Quarter of Southeast Quarter	10
NWNESW	Northwest Quarter of Northeast Quarter of Southwest Quarter	10
NWNW	Northwest Quarter of Northwest Quarter-Section	40
NWNWNE	Northwest Quarter of Northwest Quarter of Northeast Quarter	10
NWNWNW	Northwest Quarter of Northwest Quarter of Northwest Quarter	10
NWNWSE	Northwest Quarter of Northwest Quarter of Southeast Quarter	10
NWNWSW	Northwest Quarter of Northwest Quarter of Southwest Quarter	10
NWSE	Northwest Quarter of Southeast Quarter-Section	40
NWSENE	Northwest Quarter of Southeast Quarter of Northeast Quarter	10
NWSENW	Northwest Quarter of Southeast Quarter of Northwest Quarter	10
NWSESE	Northwest Quarter of Southeast Quarter of Southeast Quarter	10
NWSESW	Northwest Quarter of Southeast Quarter of Southwest Quarter	10
NWSW	Northwest Quarter of Southwest Quarter-Section	40
NWSWNE	Northwest Quarter of Southwest Quarter of Northeast Quarter	10
NWSWNW	Northwest Quarter of Southwest Quarter of Northwest Quarter	10
NWSWSE	Northwest Quarter of Southwest Quarter of Southeast Quarter	10
NWSWSW	Northwest Quarter of Southwest Quarter of Southwest Quarter	10
S½	South Half-Section	320
S½E½NE	South Half of East Half of Northeast Quarter-Section	40
S½E½NW	South Half of East Half of Northwest Quarter-Section	40
S½E½SE	South Half of East Half of Southeast Quarter-Section	40

Section Part	Description	Acres
S½E½SW	South Half of East Half of Southwest Quarter-Section	40
S½N½	South Half of North Half-Section	160
S½NE	South Half of Northeast Quarter-Section	80
S½NENE	South Half of Northeast Quarter of Northeast Quarter-Section	20
S½NENW	South Half of Northeast Quarter of Northwest Quarter-Section	20
S½NESE	South Half of Northeast Quarter of Southeast Quarter-Section	20
S½NESW	South Half of Northeast Quarter of Southwest Quarter-Section	20
S½NW	South Half of Northwest Quarter-Section	80
S½NWNE	South Half of Northwest Quarter of Northeast Quarter-Section	20
S½NWNW	South Half of Northwest Quarter of Northwest Quarter-Section	20
S½NWSE	South Half of Northwest Quarter of Southeast Quarter-Section	20
S½NWSW	South Half of Northwest Quarter of Southwest Quarter-Section	20
S½S½	South Half of South Half-Section	160
S½SE	South Half of Southeast Quarter-Section	80
S½SENE	South Half of Southeast Quarter of Northeast Quarter-Section	20
S½SENW	South Half of Southeast Quarter of Northwest Quarter-Section	20
S½SESE	South Half of Southeast Quarter of Southeast Quarter-Section	20
S½SESW	South Half of Southeast Quarter of Southwest Quarter-Section	20
S½SESW	South Half of Southeast Quarter of Southwest Quarter-Section	20
S½SW	South Half of Southwest Quarter-Section	80
S½SWNE	South Half of Southwest Quarter of Northeast Quarter-Section	20
S½SWNW	South Half of Southwest Quarter of Northwest Quarter-Section	20
S½SWSE	South Half of Southwest Quarter of Southeast Quarter-Section	20
S½SWSE	South Half of Southwest Quarter of Southeast Quarter-Section	20
S½SWSW	South Half of Southwest Quarter of Southwest Quarter-Section	20
S½W½NE	South Half of West Half of Northeast Quarter-Section	40
S½W½NW	South Half of West Half of Northwest Quarter-Section	40
S½W½SE	South Half of West Half of Southeast Quarter-Section	40
S½W½SW	South Half of West Half of Southwest Quarter-Section	40
SE	Southeast Quarter Section	160
SEN½	Southeast Quarter of North Half-Section	80
SENE	Southeast Quarter of Northeast Quarter-Section	40
SENENE	Southeast Quarter of Northeast Quarter of Northeast Quarter	10
SENENW	Southeast Quarter of Northeast Quarter of Northwest Quarter	10
SENESE	Southeast Quarter of Northeast Quarter of Southeast Quarter	10
SENESW	Southeast Quarter of Northeast Quarter of Southwest Quarter	10
SENW	Southeast Quarter of Northwest Quarter-Section	40
SENWNE	Southeast Quarter of Northwest Quarter of Northeast Quarter	10
SENWNW	Southeast Quarter of Northwest Quarter of Northwest Quarter	10
SENWSE	Souteast Quarter of Northwest Quarter of Southeast Quarter	10
SENWSW	Southeast Quarter of Northwest Quarter of Southwest Quarter	10
SESE	Southeast Quarter of Southeast Quarter-Section	40
SESENE	SoutheastQuarter of Southeast Quarter of Northeast Quarter	10
SESENW	Southeast Quarter of Southeast Quarter of Northwest Quarter	10
SESESE	Southeast Quarter of Southeast Quarter of Southeast Quarter	10
SESESW	Southeast Quarter of Southeast Quarter of Southwest Quarter	10
SESW	Southeast Quarter of Southwest Quarter-Section	40
SESWNE	Southeast Quarter of Southwest Quarter of Northeast Quarter	10
SESWNW	Southeast Quarter of Southwest Quarter of Northwest Quarter	10
SESWSE	Southeast Quarter of Southwest Quarter of Southeast Quarter	10
SESWSW	Southeast Quarter of Southwest Quarter of Southwest Quarter	10
SW	Southwest Quarter-Section	160
SWNE	Southwest Quarter of Northeast Quarter-Section	40
SWNENE	Southwest Quarter of Northeast Quarter of Northeast Quarter	10
SWNENW	Southwest Quarter of Northeast Quarter of Northwest Quarter	10
SWNESE	Southwest Quarter of Northeast Quarter of Southeast Quarter	10
SWNESW	Southwest Quarter of Northeast Quarter of Southwest Quarter	10
SWNW	Southwest Quarter of Northwest Quarter-Section	40
SWNWNE	Southwest Quarter of Northwest Quarter of Northeast Quarter	10
SWNWNW	Southwest Quarter of Northwest Quarter of Northwest Quarter	10

Section Part	Description	Acres
SWNWSE	Southwest Quarter of Northwest Quarter of Southeast Quarter	10
SWNWSW	Southwest Quarter of Northwest Quarter of Southwest Quarter	10
SWSE	Southwest Quarter of Southeast Quarter-Section	40
SWSENE	Southwest Quarter of Southeast Quarter of Northeast Quarter	10
SWSENW	Southwest Quarter of Southeast Quarter of Northwest Quarter	10
SWSESE	Southwest Quarter of Southeast Quarter of Southeast Quarter	10
SWSESW	Southwest Quarter of Southeast Quarter of Southwest Quarter	10
SWSW	Southwest Quarter of Southwest Quarter-Section	40
SWSWNE	Southwest Quarter of Southwest Quarter of Northeast Quarter	10
SWSWNW	Southwest Quarter of Southwest Quarter of Northwest Quarter	10
SWSWSE	Southwest Quarter of Southwest Quarter of Southeast Quarter	10
SWSWSW	Southwest Quarter of Southwest Quarter of Southwest Quarter	10
W½	West Half-Section	320
W½E½	West Half of East Half-Section	160
W½N½	West Half of North Half-Section (same as NW)	160
W½NE	West Half of Northeast Quarter	80
W½NENE	West Half of Northeast Quarter of Northeast Quarter-Section	20
W½NENW	West Half of Northeast Quarter of Northwest Quarter-Section	20
W½NESE	West Half of Northeast Quarter of Southeast Quarter-Section	20
W½NESW	West Half of Northeast Quarter of Southwest Quarter-Section	20
W½NW	West Half of Northwest Quarter-Section	80
W½NWNE	West Half of Northwest Quarter of Northeast Quarter-Section	20
W½NWNW	West Half of Northwest Quarter of Northwest Quarter-Section	20
W½NWSE	West Half of Northwest Quarter of Southeast Quarter-Section	20
W½NWSW	West Half of Northwest Quarter of Southwest Quarter-Section	20
W½S½	West Half of South Half-Section	160
W½SE	West Half of Southeast Quarter-Section	80
W½SENE	West Half of Southeast Quarter of Northeast Quarter-Section	20
W½SENW	West Half of Southeast Quarter of Northwest Quarter-Section	20
W½SESE	West Half of Southeast Quarter of Southeast Quarter-Section	20
W½SESW	West Half of Southeast Quarter of Southwest Quarter-Section	20
W½SW	West Half of Southwest Quarter-Section	80
W½SWNE	West Half of Southwest Quarter of Northeast Quarter-Section	20
W½SWNW	West Half of Southwest Quarter of Northwest Quarter-Section	20
W½SWSE	West Half of Southwest Quarter of Southeast Quarter-Section	20
W½SWSW	West Half of Southwest Quarter of Southwest Quarter-Section	20
W½W½	West Half of West Half-Section	160

Appendix C - Multi-Patentee Groups

The following index presents groups of people who jointly received patents in Jackson County, Florida. The Group Numbers are used in the Patent Maps and their Indexes so that you may then turn to this Appendix in order to identify all the members of the each buying group.

Group Number 1
ALDERMAN, Benjamin; DANIEL, William; DEKLE, Matheu; MCKINNE, John H

Group Number 2
ALLEN, Matthew J; ANDREWS, Hercules R

Group Number 3
ALLEN, Matthew J; ANDREWS, Hercules R; MOORING, William S

Group Number 4
ALLEN, Matthew J; ANDREWS, Hercules R; REYNOLDS, Edward

Group Number 5
ALLEN, Matthew J; REYNOLDS, Edward

Group Number 6
ALLEN, Matthew J; ROBINSON, Jacob

Group Number 7
ALLEN, Richard C; CALL, Richard K

Group Number 8
ARMISTEAD, L; ARMISTEAD, M A

Group Number 9
ARMISTEAD, L; ARMISTEAD, M A; BROWN, Isaac

Group Number 10
ARMISTEAD, Latinus; ARMISTEAD, Marcus A

Group Number 11
ARMISTEAD, Latinus; ARMISTEAD, Marcus Aurelius

Group Number 12
ARMISTEAD, Latinus; BROWN, Levin

Group Number 13
BATTLE, Amos I; SIMS, Miles

Group Number 14
BATTLE, Isaac L; LEWIS, John W

Group Number 15
BAXTER, James O; PATTERSON, James

Group Number 16
BEST, Sarah; HOLDEN, Sarah

Group Number 17
BIBB, Benajah S; GILMER, Charles L; GILMER, William B S

Group Number 18
BLACKMON, Sarah M; JORDAN, Thomas K

Group Number 19
BOZEMAN, Chapman; SCOTT, Raney

Group Number 20
BRADSHAW, Robert B; BRANTLY, Sarah

Group Number 21
BRADSHAW, Robert B; MOORE, Guthrie

Group Number 22
BRIDGEMAN, Daniel; CO, R C Allen And

Group Number 23
BRITT, William; CARTER, Farish

Group Number 24
BROOKS, Joseph; ROBERTS, John B

Group Number 25
BURKETT, Sallie J; JUSTICE, Sallie J

Group Number 26
BUSH, John; FINLEY, James L

Group Number 27
BUTLER, Bennett; BUTLER, Catharine

Group Number 28
CALL, Richard K; THOMAS, David

Group Number 29
CALLOWAY, Fair B; DANIEL, Josiah

Group Number 30
CARTER, Farish; CARTER, Porter

Group Number 31
CARTER, Farish; GRANTLAND, Seaton

Group Number 32
CARTER, Farish; IRWIN, Joseph

Group Number 33
CARTER, Farish; KILBEE, William T

Group Number 34
CARTER, Farish; MARTIN, Richard T

Group Number 35
CARTER, Farish; PORTER, Milley

Group Number 36
CARTER, John C; KILBEE, William T

Group Number 37
CARTER, Nancy A; MILES, Nancy A

Group Number 38
CHAIRES, Benjamin; ROBINSON, Jacob

Group Number 39
CHAIRES, Benjamin; ROBINSON, Jacob W

Group Number 40
CHAMBLESS, William; SIMMS, Miles

Group Number 41
CHASON, James; HAYS, Benjamin

Group Number 42
CHRISTOFF, Lewis; STONE, L M

Group Number 43
CLARK, John; NOOGIN, Matthew

Group Number 44
CLARK, John; PADGETT, Elijah

Group Number 45
CLARK, John; STONE, Louisana W

Group Number 46
CLARK, John; WILLIAMSON, Charles

Group Number 47
CLEMENTS, Benjamin; GILCHRIST, Malcolm

Group Number 48
CLEMENTS, Benjamin; JEMISON, Robert

Group Number 49
CLEMENTS, Benjamin; MATTHEWS, Charles L

Group Number 50
CLEMENTS, Benjamin; WILLIAMSON, Charles

Group Number 51
CLEMENTS, Jesse B; WILLIAMSON, Charles

Group Number 52
CO, R C Allen And; STONE, James M

Group Number 53
CO, R C Allen And; STONE, L M

Group Number 54
COE, Jesse; SEARCY, Isham G

Group Number 55
COGBURN, Samuel A; COGBURN, Susan C

Group Number 56
COMERFORD, Ann E; MONEY, Ann E

Group Number 57
COOK, Catharine J; COOK, Thomas T

Group Number 58
COOK, Josiah C; COOK, Mary F

Group Number 59
COOK, Simeon; CO, R C Allen And

Group Number 60
COOPER, Richard G; MYRICK, Thomas N

Group Number 61
DONALD, William; HAYS, Benjamin; THOMPSON, Robert; WILLIAMS, Mark

Group Number 62
DONALD, William; MCKAY, Charles

Group Number 63
DRAKE, William B; GAMBLE, John G

Group Number 64
DRAKE, William B; KEITH, Thomas R

Group Number 65
DRAKE, William B; WILLIAMSON, Charles

Group Number 66
ELLIS, Joseph W; ELLIS, Louisa

Group Number 67
FLETCHER, Mary; CO, R C Allen And

Group Number 68
FOSCUE, Benjamin; WARD, John

Group Number 69
FRANCIS, Ebenezer J; FRANCIS, Sarah

Group Number 70
GILCHRIST, Malcolm; CO, R C Allen And

Group Number 71
GILCHRIST, Malcolm; MATTHEWS, Charles L

Group Number 72
GILCHRIST, Malcolm; WILLIAMSON, Charles

Group Number 73
GRANTHAM, Chlora N; THORNTON, Chlora N

Group Number 74
GRANTHAM, Cornelius; THOMAS, David

Group Number 75
GRANTLAND, Seaton; STONE, Henry D

Group Number 76
HALEY, Holiday; SINGHTON, Joseph

Group Number 77
HARVEY, Elmira; WYNN, Elmira

Group Number 78
HODGES, Jonathan; STONE, L M

Group Number 79
HODGSON, Alonzo G; HODGSON, Richard W

Group Number 80
HOUGH, Alonzo; HOUGH, Mary

Group Number 81
HOWARD, Mary; HOWARD, William H

Group Number 82
JEMISON, Robert; WILLIAMSON, Charles

Group Number 83
JONES, Irvin; JONES, Mary

Group Number 84
KEITH, Thomas R; MATTHEWS, Charles L

Group Number 85
KEITH, Thomas R; THOMAS, David

Group Number 86
KENT, Jessee; CO, R C Allen And

Group Number 87
KENT, Marmaduke; OVERTON, Samuel R

Group Number 88
KENT, Melissa; MORRIS, Melissa

Group Number 89
KENT, William; CO, R C Allen And

Group Number 90
KILBEE, William T; ROBINSON, Jacob

Group Number 91
LASHLEY, Eltie O; SNOW, Eltie O

Group Number 92
LEWIS, Joseph; RUSS, Joseph

Group Number 93
LEWIS, Romeo; WIRT, William

Group Number 94
LITTLETON, Thomas; LITTLETON, William;
MCCULLOH, John

Group Number 95
LITTLETON, Thomas; WILLIAMS, G R

Group Number 96
LOFTIN, Jeremiah; PERRY, Mills And

Group Number 97
LOGATHREE, John; LOTT, John

Group Number 98
MADDOX, Artimissy; MADDOX, George W

Group Number 99
MARSHAL, Matthew; WARD, James

Group Number 100
MATTHEWS, Charles L; WILLIAMSON, Charles

Group Number 101
MATTHEWS, Edgar I; RICHARDSON, Frank A

Group Number 102
MCDANIEL, Emma; MCDANIEL, John

Group Number 103
MCQUAIG, Daniel; WHITE, Thomas M

Group Number 104
MILLS, James; PERRY, Benjamin F

Group Number 105
MOSES, Jessee; ONEAL, Henry; ROACH, Alloway;
SMITH, John

Group Number 106
MURPHY, James S; SIMMS, Ambrose

Group Number 107
NEEL, Hugh W; NEEL, Sarah

Group Number 108
NELSON, Mary E; ROBERTS, Mary E

Group Number 109
OVERTON, Samuel R; STONE, L M

Group Number 110
PARRISH, Maggie; PARRISH, Richard J

Group Number 111
PATTERSON, James; ROBINSON, Hugh

Group Number 112
PATTERSON, William; TRUSSELL, John

Group Number 113
PEACOCK, Charles K; PEACOCK, Martha J

Group Number 114
PEEBLES, D; PEEBLES, H

Group Number 115
PERRITT, Elizabeth; PERRITT, Samuel B

Group Number 116
PERRY, Benjamin F; TONEY, William

Group Number 117
PERRY, Mills And; PERRY, Benjamin F

Group Number 118
PERRY, Mills And; THOMAS, David

Group Number 119
PINKHAM, Samuel; WEBB, James

Group Number 120
POPE, Elizabeth; POPE, Henry; POPE, John; POPE, Margaret; POPE, William S

Group Number 121
PORTER, James R; PORTER, Louisa

Group Number 122
PORTER, Nathan; WILLIAMSON, Nathan

Group Number 123
PUMPHREY, Ann Mary; PUMPHREY, John W

Group Number 124
RANEY, Rhoda; RANEY, Simon

Group Number 125
REGISTER, Olive; REGISTER, Wiley

Group Number 126
RIVIERE, Alexander M; RIVIERE, Henry L

Group Number 127
ROBINSON, Isaac; ROBINSON, William H

Group Number 128
ROBINSON, Jacob; WILLIAMSON, Nathan

Group Number 129
ROYAL, Wilson; SANBURN, Ira

Group Number 130
SIMMS, Miles; WITHERINGTON, Mahala

Group Number 131
SPIVEY, Joseph C; SPIVEY, Sarah J

Group Number 132
STONE, L M; THOMAS, David

Group Number 133
SUTTON, C; WATSON, W J

Group Number 134
THARP, Mary E; THARP, William A

Group Number 135
THOMAS, David; WILLIAMSON, Charles

Group Number 136
THOMPSON, Jennett E; THOMPSON, William

Group Number 137
TONEY, Mills; TONEY, Perry; TONEY, William

Group Number 138
TRIPPE, Bryan; TRIPPE, Charles

Group Number 139
TRIPPE, Henry; TRIPPE, Jonathan T

Group Number 140
TRIPPE, Henry; TRIPPE, Sarah; TRIPPE, Simeon

Group Number 141
WHITE, Julia; WHITE, King

Group Number 142
WILLIAMS, Caroline; WILLIAMS, John

Group Number 143
WILLIAMS, Jane; WILLIAMS, John M

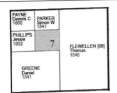

Extra! Extra! (about our Indexes)

We purposefully do not have an all-name index in the back of this volume so that our readers do not miss one of the best uses of this book: finding misspelled names among more specialized indexes.

Without repeating the text of our "How-to" chapter, we have nonetheless tried to assist our more anxious researchers by delivering a short-cut to the two county-wide Surname Indexes, the second of which will lead you to all-name indexes for each Congressional Township mapped in this volume :

For your convenience, the "How To Use this Book" Chart on page 2 is repeated on the reverse of this page.

We should be releasing new titles every week for the foreseeable future. We urge you to write, fax, call, or email us any time for a current list of titles. Of course, our web-page will always have the most current information about current and upcoming books.

Arphax Publishing Co.
2210 Research Park Blvd.
Norman, Oklahoma 73069
(800) 681-5298 toll-free
(405) 366-6181 local
(405) 366-8184 fax
info@arphax.com

www.arphax.com

How to Use This Book - A Graphical Summary

Part I
"The Big Picture"

Map A ▸ *Counties in the State*
Map B ▸ *Surrounding Counties*
Map C ▸ *Congressional Townships (Map Groups) in the County*
Map D ▸ *Cities & Towns in the County*
Map E ▸ *Cemeteries in the County*
Surnames in the County ▸ *Number of Land-Parcels for Each Surname*
Surname/Township Index ▸ *Directs you to Township Map Groups in Part II*

The <u>*Surname/Township Index*</u> *can direct you to any number of* **Township Map Groups**

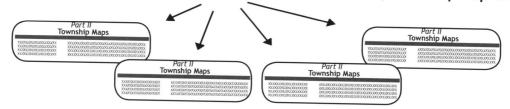

Part II
Township Map Groups
(1 for each Township in the County)

Each Township Map Group contains all four of of the following tools . . .

Land Patent Index ▸ *Every-name Index of Patents Mapped in this Township*
Land Patent Map ▸ *Map of Patents as listed in above Index*
Road Map ▸ *Map of Roads, City-centers, and Cemeteries in the Township*
Historical Map ▸ *Map of Railroads, Lakes, Rivers, Creeks, City-Centers, and Cemeteries*

Appendices

Appendix A ▸ *Congressional Authority enabling Patents within our Maps*
Appendix B ▸ *Section-Parts / Aliquot Parts (a comprehensive list)*
Appendix C ▸ *Multi-patentee Groups (Individuals within Buying Groups)*

Made in the USA
Columbia, SC
13 August 2021